Journalizing and Posting

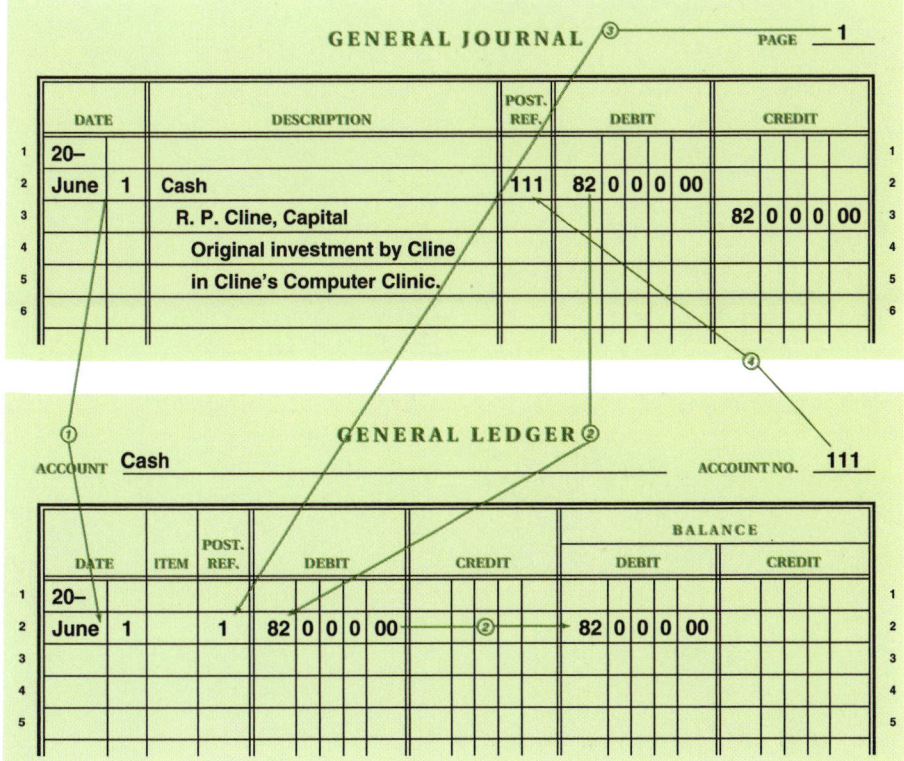

① Date of transaction
② Amount of transaction
③ Page number of the journal
④ Ledger account number

The Work Sheet

Account Name	Trial Balance		Adjustments		Adjusted Trial Balance		Income Statement		Balance Sheet	
	Debit	Credit	Debit	Credit	Debit	Credit	Debit	Credit	Debit	Credit
	Assets				Assets				Assets	
		Liabilities				Liabilities				Liabilities
		Capital				Capital				Capital
	Drawing				Drawing				Drawing	
		Revenue				Revenue		Revenue		
	Expenses				Expenses		Expenses			

Steps in the Closing Process

R Close the Revenue accounts into Income Summary.
E Close the Expenses accounts into Income Summary.
I Close the Income Summary Account into the Capital Account, transferring the net income or net loss to the Capital Account.
D Close the Drawing account into the Capital Account.

COLLEGE ACCOUNTING

1–13

COLLEGE ACCOUNTING

NINTH EDITION　　1–13

Douglas J. McQuaig
Wenatchee Valley College, Emeritus

Patricia A. Bille
Highline Community College

HOUGHTON MIFFLIN COMPANY　　BOSTON　NEW YORK

This text is sincerely dedicated to the students who will use it.

Every possible effort has been made to produce an understandable, up-to-date, and accurate presentation of the fundamentals of accounting.

This text is intended to be an important element in your course, as well as an invaluable future reference for you in the preparation of your career in business.

Best wishes for your success.

Douglas J. McQuaig

Patricia A. Bille

Executive Publisher: George Hoffman
Senior Sponsoring Editor: Ann West
Senior Marketing Manager: Mike Schenk
Marketing Coordinator: Erin Lane
Senior Development Editor: Chere Bemelmans
Editorial Assistant: Diane Akerman
Project Editor: Paula Kmetz
Art and Design Manager: Gary Crespo
Cover Design Manager: Anne S. Katzeff
Senior Photo Editor: Jennifer Meyer Dare
Composition Buyer: Chuck Dutton
New Title Project Manager: James Lonergan

Cover Photo © Y. Takahashi/Getty Images

This book is written to provide accurate and authoritative information concerning the covered topics. It is not meant to take the place of professional advice. The companies and financial information in this book have been created for instructional purposes. No reference to any specific company or person is intended or should be inferred. Any similarity with an existing company or person is coincidental.

Printed in the U.S.A.

Library of Congress Control Number: 2006938443

Instructor's examination copy
ISBN-10: 0-618-91703-9
ISBN-13: 978-0-618-91703-7

For orders, use student text ISBNs
ISBN-10: 0-618-82418-9
ISBN-13: 978-0-618-82418-2

23456789-DOW-11 10 09 08 07

Contents

PART TWO

ACCOUNTING FOR CASH AND PAYROLL

PART THREE

THE ACCOUNTING CYCLE FOR A MERCHANDISING BUSINESS: USING SPECIAL JOURNALS

The study of accounting enables college students to achieve three important objectives: (1) to train for jobs in accounting; (2) to train for other careers such as technical, managerial, and executive positions; or (3) to prepare for advanced studies in accounting and business. We designed *College Accounting* to help students reach these goals by developing their practical accounting skills in an understandable basic accounting text. But today's students need more than just basic accounting skills; students need to feel comfortable with rapidly changing technology, understand how to make sound ethical and business decisions, and become successful problem solvers and communicators. In the ninth edition, we have revised *College Accounting* to increase its relevance in today's world and to provide additional technology to help students learn basic accounting skills and think and solve problems in the current business world.

EMPHASIS ON BUILDING STUDY SKILLS AND CAREER PATHS

The ninth edition of *College Accounting* continues to emphasize the importance of college accounting as a gateway to a variety of jobs and career paths, and the program provides numerous tools aimed at enabling students to build the skills, habits, and outlook that will help them succeed in school and beyond. The text itself contains a number of features that will help students see their studies in a real-world context. Ethics, problem solving, and communications are central to today's accounting needs, and we have focused on covering these issues in a variety of ways. Three text features in particular strengthen this outlook:

Internet Links to Accounting   These chapter openers provide a hands-on look at many of today's well-known businesses that are active on the Internet. Each opener first introduces students to the company and then asks a series of questions about the company that relates directly to the chapter topics. We provide web addresses for further investigation of the company. These questions and addresses are designed to prompt discussion, written responses, or additional questions that focus on the chapter. The related end-of-chapter feature follows through to provide students with meaningful web activities. Students are exposed not only to web exploration but also to critical thinking, problem solving, and communication activities.

Careers in Your Future   Prominent business people whose professional lives began with accounting are featured throughout the text. Our hope is that their words and stories will encourage and inspire students and provide good role models as they advance in their careers.

End-of-Chapter Cases   We have provided a series of brief cases at the end of each chapter to help students keep the business perspective in mind. *Consider and Communicate, Critical Thinking, What's Wrong with This Picture?*, and

A Question of Ethics foster problem-solving and communication skills that students will need in today's business world. With each case, students have an opportunity to develop their problem-solving skills and employ their knowledge of accounting to complete a task. The cases may be appropriate for individual or team responses—discussion of these cases in class, particularly questions involving ethical issues, can be particularly useful.

The support materials and supplements for *College Accounting*, Ninth Edition, also reinforce the theme of study skills and career success. Described more fully below, the resources available in "Your Guide to an A" on the McQuaig/Bille Study Center website provide students with a wealth of opportunities to review and test their understanding of the text content. Videos outline important skills, such as organizational and writing skills, needed to succeed in school and work, and handy MP3 downloads give students the opportunity to integrate their learning into everyday life. A print supplement, *Guide to Success in College Accounting*, gives students some additional study support, such as math review, learning style assessment, and career planning.

THOROUGHLY REVISED AND RELEVANT TEXT

In addition to the new features described above, we have completely revised and updated the ninth edition to increase its relevance for today's complex and challenging world.

Major Content Changes

A complete list of content changes from the eighth to the ninth editions is available in the Transition Guide (located on the Online Learning Center website or in the *Instructor's Resource Manual with Solutions*), but a brief listing of the most important content changes follows:

- **Chapter 4: Adjusting Entries and the Work Sheet** The use of electronic spreadsheets for preparing work sheets is introduced in this chapter, and the work sheet is shown prepared manually and using Microsoft Excel. The tools used to prepare the Excel work sheet are also illustrated.
- **Chapter 5: Closing Entries and the Post-Closing Trial Balance** We describe in more detail the differences in accounting methods.
- **Chapter 7: Bank Accounts and Cash Funds** We have added a discussion of internal controls as a part of cash management as well as a discussion of electronic funds transfers.
- **Chapter 8: Employee Earnings and Deductions** We have updated the tax percentages and tax forms while including a section describing laws that affect payroll activities.
- **Appendixes C and D for Chapters 10 and 11: An Alternative to Special Journals** These new appendixes discuss and illustrate the basic general journal entries for a merchandising business. The appendixes are designed to be used in place of the coverage of special journals in Chapters 10 and 11 if a detailed discussion of special journals is not desired.

Special Text Features and Enhancements

Along with a complete revision of text and end-of-chapter assignment material, several new pedagogical features have been added to the ninth edition:

Extended Text Examples   Cline's Computer Clinic is integrated throughout Chapters 1 through 5 to illustrate the completion of the accounting cycle for a sole proprietorship service business using a general journal. Rainier Plumbing Supply is featured throughout Chapters 10 through 13 to illustrate the completion of the accounting cycle for a sole proprietorship merchandising business using special journals.

The Computer Clinic   Designed to give students experience using computers to manage accounting transactions, this continuous general ledger problem featuring *All About You Spa,* a sole proprietorship service business, begins in Chapter 3 by asking students to open the accounting books for the business. Students are required to enter into general ledger software (Peachtree, QuickBooks, or Houghton Mifflin's Windows General Ledger) the company name, company type, and chart of accounts before journalizing and posting the first month's transactions and printing a trial balance. After Chapter 4, "Adjusting Entries and the Work Sheet," students continue with *All About You Spa* by completing the end-of-the-month adjustments and printing the financial statements. After Chapter 5, "Closing Entries and the Post-Closing Trial Balance," students again work with *All About You Spa* to close the books for the month and print a post-closing trial balance.

All About You Spa returns in Chapters 10 through 13, when the owner adds two lines of merchandise to the business. Special journals for sales, purchases, cash receipts, and cash payments are introduced, and procedures are completed to end the accounting period.

ACCESSIBLE AND USER-FRIENDLY CONTENT

Although the ninth edition of *College Accounting* has been updated and revised, some things have not changed. Drawing from more than sixty-seven years of combined teaching experience, we continue to provide students with a strong basic knowledge of accounting terms, concepts, and procedures. The text is logically organized, liberally illustrated, and paced in a manner that is easy for students to read and understand. Generous use of white space provides an uncluttered reading environment with ample area for student or instructor notes.

Proven Pedagogy

The ninth edition of this text is built on a solid pedagogical foundation appreciated by instructors and students through many editions. The careful pacing of new topics, consistent review, and thorough and meaningful assignment material all create a well-balanced presentation that helps guarantee student success.

Throughout each chapter:

- **Performance objectives** appear at the beginning of each chapter to help students focus on key learning outcomes. They are then highlighted in the margin alongside the related text discussion. A performance objective number serves as a reference to the objectives in the chapter summary, exercises, and problems.

- **Key terms** appear in red and are defined in the text and repeated in a glossary at the end of the chapter.

- **Remembers,** also in the margin, provide learning hints or summaries, often alerting students to common procedural pitfalls to help them complete their work successfully.
- **FYIs,** similarly, provide practical tips or information about accounting and business.

Each chapter ends with a Review of Performance Objectives and a Glossary that lists terms with definitions. Questions, exercises, cases, and problems follow and include:

- **Discussion Questions** Questions based on the main points in the text and appropriate for either class discussion or for homework are included at the end of each chapter.
- **Exercises** For practice in applying concepts, exercises are provided with each chapter. Each exercise is described briefly in the margin with a reference to the appropriate performance objective.
- **Cases** End-of-chapter cases develop problem-solving and communication skills that will help students succeed in today's business world.
- **Problems** Each chapter contains four A and four B problems. The A and B problems are parallel in content and level of difficulty. They are arranged in order of difficulty, with Problems 1A and 1B in each chapter being the simplest and the last problem in each series being the most comprehensive. Check Figures appear alongside every A and B problem's instructions in the text.

Problems that can be solved using the Houghton Mifflin Windows General Ledger program are designated by the first icon on the left.

Problems that can be worked using Spreadsheet Applications for College Accounting are identified by the second icon on the left.

- **Before a Test Check** This feature provides questions (true/false, multiple choice, matching, and completion) and brief application problems after every two to four chapters. These pretest activities let students check their understanding of what they have read and practiced in the preceding chapters prior to taking a test.
- **Accounting Cycle Review and Comprehensive Review Problem** These features give students the opportunity to apply accounting procedures to help them understand the process they have just studied in a series of chapters (1–5) and (7–13). Accounting Cycle Review Problems A and B involve the full accounting cycle, one for Splashdown and the other for Wind Riders, both sole proprietorship service businesses. The Comprehensive Review Problem following Chapter 13 involves the full accounting cycle for Fine Fabrics, a sole proprietorship merchandising business.

Focus on the Fundamentals

College Accounting, Ninth Edition, presents the basics of accounting in a practical, easy-to-comprehend manner. Great emphasis is placed on developing a firm foundation of fundamental procedures. Appropriate repetition and extensive use of examples enable students to develop self-confidence and to make progress in gradual stages. Color photographs round out the text—and provide additional real-world insights.

Recording business transactions is directly related to the fundamental accounting equation. Each newly introduced transaction is fully illustrated and is supported with T account examples. Comprehensive reviews of T accounts, organized in relation to the fundamental accounting equation, appear in the *Working Papers with Study Guide*, student website, and *College Accounting Resources for Students* CD-ROM to assist as students review material and complete assignments.

College Accounting, Ninth Edition, is also a very readable text. We write in short sentences and use many illustrations to help students relate the words to the procedures. Each chapter of *College Accounting* has been reviewed by business instructors who teach courses in English as a Second Language and English for Special Purposes, as well as by students enrolled in these classes. With their assistance and advice, we have taken steps to ensure that the text is accessible to all readers.

Each chapter is limited to the presentation of one major concept, which is amply illustrated with business documents and report forms. As terms are introduced, they are defined thoroughly and are used in subsequent examples. Comprehension is also enhanced through the use of "Remember" and "FYI" statements, which offer a learning hint or a practical tip about a topic.

Emphasis on Accounting Terminology

We firmly believe that accounting is the language of business and that learning new terminology is an essential part of a first course. Each key term is printed in red and is explained when it is first introduced. The end-of-chapter glossary repeats the definitions of the terms presented in the chapter. In addition, page numbers are included for each glossary term, making it easy for students to refer to a term in the chapter. The glossary terms are included on electronic flash cards on the student website, providing yet another interactive opportunity for learning.

Proven Color-Coded Pedagogy

The ninth edition of *College Accounting* continues to implement a color-coded pedagogy that helps students recognize and remember key points. The pedagogical use of color also helps students understand the flow of accounting data and identify different types of documents and reports used in accounting. Finally, the use of color helps students identify the performance objectives for each chapter, recognize the performance objectives called for in each exercise, and review material efficiently and effectively.

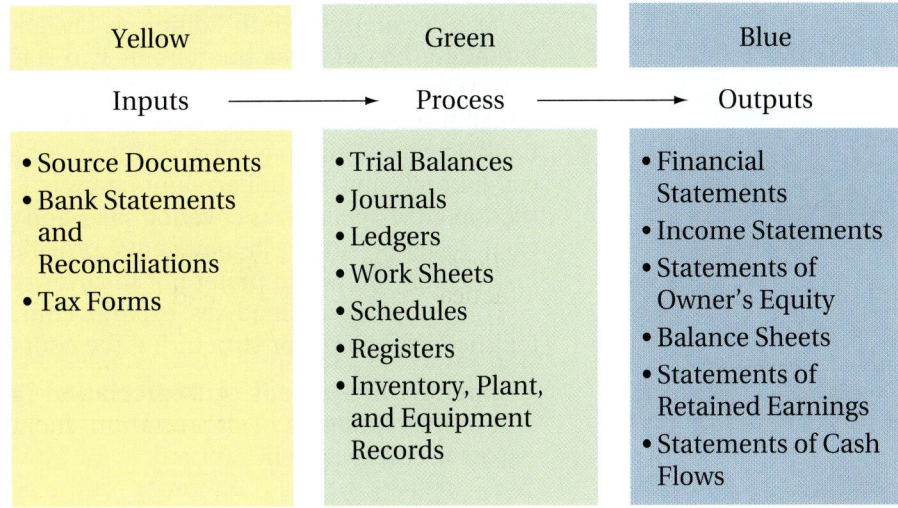

Yellow	Green	Blue
Inputs →	Process →	Outputs
• Source Documents • Bank Statements and Reconciliations • Tax Forms	• Trial Balances • Journals • Ledgers • Work Sheets • Schedules • Registers • Inventory, Plant, and Equipment Records	• Financial Statements • Income Statements • Statements of Owner's Equity • Balance Sheets • Statements of Retained Earnings • Statements of Cash Flows

The ninth edition's consistent use of color extends to the treatment of accounting forms, financial statements, and documents in the text and end-of-chapter assignments.

- **Source documents,** such as invoices, bank statements, facsimiles, and other material that originates with outside sources, are shown in yellow.
- **Working papers, journals, ledgers, trial balances, and other forms and schedules** used as part of the internal accounting process are shown in green.
- **Financial statements,** including balances sheets, income statements, statements of owners' equity, and statements of cash flows, are shown in blue.

This distinctive treatment differentiates these elements and helps students see where each element belongs in the accounting cycle. Seeing these relationships helps students understand how accountants transform data into useful information.

GUARANTEE OF QUALITY MATERIAL

Successful use of an accounting text depends on more than the interesting and memorable presentation of material by the instructor and the text. The overall quality of the chapter-opening features, examples, illustrations, color photographs, end-of-chapter questions, exercises, cases, and problems, as well as ancillary materials, are critical to learning and retaining the facts and concepts that are covered in the course. Instructors and students must be assured that these materials are complete, consistent, and accurate.

Together with our publisher, we have taken a multistep approach to ensure quality materials for classroom use. The quality-control system begins with in-depth reviews of the original manuscript and concludes with accuracy reviews of page proof by instructors who are actively teaching the course.

FLEXIBLE CHAPTER COVERAGE

College Accounting, Ninth Edition, is designed primarily for use in a course extending two or three quarters or two semesters. The text is divided into parts: Chapters 1 through 5 cover the full accounting cycle for a sole proprietorship service business. Chapters 6 through 9 cover the combined journal, bank accounts, and payroll accounting. Chapters 10 through 13 cover special journals and the full accounting cycle for a merchandising firm. In this section, new appendixes covering sales and purchases on account as well as cash receipts and cash payments provide an alternative treatment for instructors who would prefer not to cover special journals in their course.

The following appendixes expand content coverage and increase the instructor's options for structuring the course:

- **Appendix A: Methods of Depreciation (after Chapter 4)** This appendix describes methods of depreciation, including the Modified Accelerated Cost Recovery System.

- **Appendix B: Bad Debts (after Chapter 7)** This appendix covers the allowance and specific charge-off methods.
- **NEW!** **Appendix C: Sales and Purchases on Account: An Alternative to Special Journals (after Chapter 10)** This new appendix illustrates the basic general journal entries related to sales and purchases for a merchandising business. It is designed to be used in place of the coverage of special journals in Chapter 10 if a detailed discussion of special journals is not desired.
- **NEW!** **Appendix D: Cash Receipts and Cash Payments: An Alternative to Special Journals (after Chapter 11)** This new appendix illustrates the basic general journal entries related to cash receipts and cash payments for a merchandising business. It is designed to be used in place of the coverage of special journals in Chapter 11 if a detailed discussion of special journals is not desired.
- **Appendix E: Inventory Methods (after Chapter 13)** This appendix discusses methods used to determine the amount of the ending inventory for a merchandising business.
- **Appendix F: Financial Statement Analysis (after Chapter 13)** This appendix describes percentages and ratios used to interpret information in financial statements.
- **Appendix G: The Statement of Cash Flows (after Chapter 13)** This appendix discusses the indirect method of determining cash flows.

SUPPLEMENTARY LEARNING AIDS FOR STUDENTS AND SUPPORT MATERIALS FOR INSTRUCTORS

For the ninth edition, we have assembled the most comprehensive package of student and instructor aids—both print and electronic—to complement a wide variety of teaching styles and course emphases. The complete *College Accounting* teaching and learning package is listed below. Detailed descriptions of each element of the support package are available in the *Instructor's Resource Manual with Solutions* and on the instructor website.

For Students

Working Papers with Study Guide (available in print and on CD-ROM) The *Working Papers with Study Guide* contains forms for students to use in completing all of the exercises and problems in the textbook along with study materials for every chapter. It also provides an introduction to working with spreadsheets and guidelines for working a practice set. It is available in the following volumes:

- *Working Papers with Study Guide 1–13*
- *Working Papers with Study Guide 14–26*
- *Electronic Working Papers with Study Guide 1–26*

General Ledger Software CD-ROM This CD-ROM includes the thoroughly updated and enhanced Houghton Mifflin General Ledger Software, which can be used to solve selected problems (identified with the GLS icon) at the end of each text chapter. Houghton Mifflin Windows General Ledger Software offers complete coverage of accounting concepts and procedures in an extremely simple and user-friendly, computerized environment. The General Ledger Software CD-ROM is packaged with every *College Accounting* textbook.

Smarthinking Tutoring   In partnership with SMARTHINKING, we offer personalized, online tutoring during typical homework hours. Students can interact live online with an experienced SMARTHINKING "e-structor" (online tutor), submit questions and spreadsheets anytime for response by an e-structor within twenty-four hours, and review independent study resources—including interactive websites and Frequently Asked Questions posed to SMARTHINKING e-structors—around the clock.

Online Learning Center (college.hmco.com/PIC/mcquaig9)   The Online Learning Center, updated for the ninth edition, provides students with text-specific resources that reinforce key concepts in the *College Accounting* program. The Online Learning Center links students to ACE practice tests for self-quizzing, Flashcards and Crossword Puzzles to reinforce vocabulary, and suggested Internet research activities, business readings, and websites for companies featured in the text to provide real-world context. In addition, Excel spreadsheet files let students solve end-of-chapter problems using Excel spreadsheet software.

Your Guide to an A   In addition to the resources found in the Online Learning Center, every new text comes with a passkey that provides access to "Your Guide to an A," an additional set of online resources developed to reinforce chapter concepts for a variety of learning styles. These premium online study tools include MP3 downloads for audio chapter review and self-testing, an additional set of ACE practice quizzes (ACE+), online chapter study guides, and a series of skillbuilding video modules to help students develop and improve their study skills. Students who do not buy a new text will be able to purchase access to "Your Guide to an A" materials from the McQuaig/Bille website.

Peachtree Educator's Edition   This popular accounting software tool is now available to students. The educational version is the same as the professional version used by most businesses. At the option of the instructor, students can use this commercial package or the Houghton Mifflin Windows General Ledger Software to work selected problems in the text and accompanying practice sets. Instructors who prefer to use QuickBooks, another popular commercial software package, can do so by obtaining a site license or offering the option of QuickBooks on the web; all text problems can be worked using the current version of either Peachtree or QuickBooks.

Practice Sets   A wealth of manual and computerized practice sets is available for use with *College Accounting,* Ninth Edition, with new sets being developed regularly. A complete listing and description of each practice set and its support package can be found in the *Instructor's Resource Manual with Solutions,* with new sets introduced and described on the Online Teaching Center. New to the ninth edition is the *Digi-Tec* practice case, a small merchandising corporation using either a periodic or perpetual inventory system. This practice case covers a one-month accounting period, enabling the student to acquire experience in dealing with the entire accounting cycle, and can be worked manually or electronically. The CD-ROM version gives the student the option of completing the practice case using Microsoft Excel, QuickBooks (2003 or newer), Peachtree Accounting (Educational version 8), or Houghton Mifflin General Ledger Software (version 3.3, provided).

Other available practice sets include:

- *Divesports* is a unique source document simulation that requires students to work through seven months of continuous business activity for a sole proprietorship service business; *Divesports* adds merchandising in Chapter 10. *Divesports* can be assigned between Chapters 3 and 13.
- *Sounds Abound,* Second Edition, is a computerized practice set that covers a month in the life of a sole proprietorship. Assigned after Chapter 5, *Sounds Abound* can be used with Houghton Mifflin's General Ledger Software program.
- *Balloon Adventures* is a source document simulation. *Balloon Adventures* is a sole proprietorship service business using a general journal and can be assigned after Chapter 9.
- *Oak Creek Canyon Jewelers* gives students experience in recording fourth-quarter payroll and preparing end-of-quarter and end-of-year reports for a sole proprietorship. Assigned after Chapter 9, *Oak Creek Canyon* can be worked using Peachtree.
- *Rug Bug* gives students experience with a wholesale business. Assigned after Chapter 13, *Rug Bug* can be worked using Peachtree.
- *Spa Magic* is a source document simulation. It is a sole proprietorship merchandising business featuring special journals and payroll, and can be assigned after Chapter 13; it can be worked using Peachtree, QuickBooks, or Houghton Mifflin's General Ledger Software program.
- *The Wax Works: A Cumulative Shoebox Practice Set with Business Papers* is a realistic exercise in which the student/bookkeeper is "hired" by a sole proprietorship retail candle shop. It can be assigned after Chapter 13.

For Instructors

Course Management Systems Because homework and practice are integral parts of accounting courses, and because grading homework and tests can present a challenge to instructors, we offer auto-graded homework in our Course Management Systems. The Eduspace® online learning tool pairs the widely recognized resources of Blackboard with quality, text-specific content from Houghton Mifflin, including automatically graded exercises based on the exercises at the end of each text chapter. SMARTHINKING online tutoring, MP3 files of chapter summaries, Skillbuilders videos, and other resources come ready to use. Premium Blackboard course cartridges and WebCT ePacks are also available.

Instructor's Resource Manual with Solutions The *Instructor's Resource Manual with Solutions* contains valuable resources to assist instructors in teaching accounting. The IRM contains Teaching Objectives, Key Points, and Lecture Outlines for every chapter, as well as Solutions for all questions, exercises, cases, and problems in the text. In addition it includes:

- Review of T Account Placement and Representative Transactions
- Suggested Homework Check Questions with Solutions, keyed to end-of-chapter assignments, provide students with the opportunity to practice the interpretive portion of the accounting process (with suggested answers)
- Difficulty and Time Chart for Practice Sets

The *Instructor's Resource Manual with Solutions* is available in the following volumes:

- *Instructor's Resource Manual with Solutions 1–13*
- *Instructor's Resource Manual with Solutions 14–26*

Online Teaching Center (college.hmco.com/PIC/mcquaig9) The Online Teaching Center provides instructors with text-specific resources that reinforce key concepts in the *College Accounting* program. The Online Teaching Center includes password-protected course materials, such as completely revised Premium PowerPoint slides with video and original content; Classroom Response System content; sample syllabi; and Electronic Solutions, which are fully functioning Excel spreadsheets for all exercises and problems in the text.

Printed Test Bank with Achievement Tests (A and B) and HMTesting Instructor CD-ROM HMTesting—now powered by *Diploma*®—contains the computerized version of the Test Bank. HMTesting provides instructors with all the tools they need to create, customize, and deliver multiple types of tests. Instructors can add their own questions or edit existing algorithmic questions within *Diploma*'s powerful electronic platform. Instructors can select, edit, and add questions, or generate randomly selected questions to produce a test master for easy duplication. Online Testing and Gradebook functions allow instructors to administer tests via their local area network or the Internet, set up classes, record grades from tests or assignments, analyze grades, and compile class and individual statistics. HMTesting can be used on both PCs and Macintosh computers.

PowerPoint Slides—Basic and Premium Basic slides include demonstration problems, examples, accounting forms, tables, and art from the textbook. Premium slides include additional original content, supplementary teaching examples, video, photographs, and discussion questions. Both sets of slides are available at the Online Teaching Center.

Teaching and Solutions Transparencies (downloadable from the Online Teaching Center website)

ACKNOWLEDGMENTS

We sincerely thank the editorial staff of Houghton Mifflin for their continuous support. Leslie Kauffman deserves special recognition for her tireless work on our manuscript. Also, we thank our many students at Highline Community College for their observations and evaluations. During the writing of the ninth edition, we consulted many users of the text throughout the country. Their constructive suggestions are reflected in the changes that we have made. Unfortunately, space does not permit mention of all those who have contributed to this volume. Those reviewers and advisors who have contributed to *College Accounting* through their reviews, class testing, market feedback, and accuracy checking are as follows:

Joe Adamo, *Cazenovia College;* Marjorie Ashton, *Truckee Meadows Community College;* Teresa Anderson, *Eastern New Mexico University;* Gregory D. Barnes, *Clarion University;* Charles M. Betts, *Delaware Technical and Com-*

munity College; Michelle Berube, *Corinthian Colleges,* Florida; Lee Cannell, *El Paso Community College;* Steven Christian, *Jackson Community College;* Jean Condon, *Mid-Plains Community College Area (Nebraska);* Mark Dawson, *Duquesne University;* Roger Dimick, *Lamar Institute of Technology;* Patricia A. Doherty, *Boston University School of Management;* Richard Dugger, *Kilgore College;* Donna Eakman, *Montana State University, Great Falls;* Talaat Elshazly, *College of Charleston;* Nancy Fallon, *Albertus Magnus College;* Michael J. Farina, *Cerritos College;* Mark Fronke, *Cerritos College;* Allen Ford, *Institute for the Deaf, Rochester Institute of Technology;* Michael Girvin, *Highline Community College;* David Groom, *University of Hawaii—Maui Community College;* Christine Uber Grosse, *Thunderbird, The American Graduate School of International Management;* Dennis A. Gutting, *Orange County Community College;* David Hall; Scott Hays, *Central Oregon Community College;* Thea Hosselrode, *Allegany College of Maryland;* Peggy Hughes, *Allegany College of Maryland;* Ray Ingram, *Southwest Georgia Technical College;* Lori Jacobson, *North Idaho College;* Ernie Keller, *Montana State University, Great Falls;* Cathy Xanthaky Larson, *Middlesex Community College;* Susan D. Looney, *Mohave Community College;* Nelson Martin, *Wenatchee Valley College;* George J. McGowan; Gail A. Mestas; Wanda Metzgar, *Selland College of Applied Technology;* Michael Monahan; Howard Mount, *Highline Community College;* Paul Muller, *Western Nevada Community College;* Jenine Muscove, *Bradford Hall Career Institute;* Kenneth Newton, *Cleveland State Community College;* Jon Nitschke, *Montana State University, Great Falls;* Therese H. Palacios, *San Antonio College;* Janet Pasterkamp, *Montana State University, Great Falls;* Cathy Pekarek; Joel Peralto, *University of Hawaii—Hawaii Community College;* Betty Pilchard, *Heartland Community College;* Bob Sanner, *Central Community College;* Robin Shurtz; Alice Sineath, *Forsyth Technical Community College;* Marion Taube, *University of Pittsburgh;* Josephine Vondras, *Orange County Community College;* Kay Westerfield, *University of Oregon;* Jack Wiehler, *San Joaquin Delta College;* and Sara Wilson.

As always, we would like to thank our families for their understanding and cooperation. Without their support, this text would never have been written. Heartfelt appreciation is extended to my wife, Beverlie McQuaig, for her detailed proofreading and good humor. Pertinent suggestions for updating the material were given by my children: Judy McQuaig Courshon, C.P.A., M.T., of Wellspring Group PS, CPAs; John McQuaig, C.P.A., C.M.C., of McQuaig and Welk PLLC; and Laurie McQuaig, D.C. We also express continued gratitude to Bruce Bille, Tracy Bille-Newkirk, and James Newkirk, C.P.A., for their encouragement and assistance, and to the memory of Ryan Bille and Wesley and Adeline Harris for their courage and inspiration.

Douglas J. McQuaig
Patricia A. Bille

Introduction to Accounting

Performance Objectives

After you have completed this introduction to accounting, you will be able to do the following:

1. Define *accounting*.

2. Explain the importance of accounting information.

3. Describe the various career opportunities in accounting.

4. Define *ethics*.

Accounting is often called the language of business because, when confronted with events of a business nature, all people in society—owners, managers, creditors, employees, attorneys, engineers, and so forth—must use accounting terms and concepts to describe these events. Examples of accounting terms are *net, gross, yield, valuation, accrued, deferred*—the list could go on and on. So it is logical that anyone entering the business world should know enough of its "language" to communicate with others and to understand their communications.

As you acquire knowledge of accounting, you will gain an understanding of the way businesses operate and the reasoning involved in making business decisions. Even if you are not involved directly in accounting activities, you will certainly need to be sufficiently acquainted with the "language" to be able to understand the meaning of accounting information, how it is compiled, how it can be used, and its limitations.

You may be surprised to find that you are already familiar with many accounting terms. Recalling your personal business activities and relating them to your study of accounting will be very helpful to you. For example, when you purchased this textbook, you exchanged cash or a promise to pay cash for the book. As you will see, this exchange is an accounting event. You are going to recognize many activities and terms as you begin your study of accounting.

DEFINITION OF ACCOUNTING

OBJECTIVE 1
Define *accounting*.

Accounting is the process of analyzing, classifying, recording, summarizing, and interpreting business transactions in financial or monetary terms. A business **transaction** is an event that has a direct effect on the operation of an economic unit, is expressed in terms of money, and is recorded. Examples of business transactions are buying or selling goods, renting a building, paying employees, and buying insurance.

Accounting is an important part of all types of businesses. These cruise ships require the same extensive recordkeeping as any large destination resort. The ship is a large floating hotel with guests, employees, management, recreational activities, restaurants, and shops.

The primary purpose of accounting is to provide the financial information needed for the efficient operation of an economic unit. The term **economic unit** includes not only business enterprises but also not-for-profit entities, such as government bodies, churches and synagogues, clubs, and public charities. Business enterprises or organizations may be called firms or companies. All of these entities require some type of accounting records. An **accountant** is a person who keeps the financial history of the transactions of an economic unit in written form.

Because it is important that all those who receive accounting reports be able to interpret them, a set of rules or guidelines for the accounting process has been developed. These guidelines or rules are known as **generally accepted accounting principles (GAAP)**.

Bookkeeping and Accounting

There are distinctions between bookkeeping and accounting. The two processes are closely related, but there is no universally accepted line of separation. Generally, bookkeeping involves the systematic recording of business transactions in financial terms. Accounting functions at a higher level. An accountant sets up the system that a bookkeeper uses to record business transactions. An accountant may supervise the work of the bookkeeper and prepare financial statements and tax reports. Although the bookkeeper's work is more routine, it is hard to draw a line where the bookkeeper's work ends and the accountant's begins.

IMPORTANCE OF ACCOUNTING INFORMATION

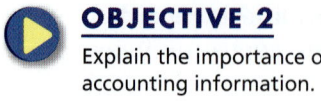

OBJECTIVE 2
Explain the importance of accounting information.

Anyone who aspires to a position of leadership in business or government needs knowledge of accounting. A study of accounting gives a person the necessary background and also gives him or her an understanding of the scope, functions, and policies of an organization. A person may not be doing the accounting work, but he or she will be continually dealing with accounting forms, language, and reports.

Users of Accounting Information

Owners Owners have invested their money or goods in a business organization. They desire information regarding the company's earnings, its prospects for future earnings, and its ability to pay its debts.

Managers Managers and supervisors have to prepare financial reports, understand accounting data contained in reports and budgets, and express future plans in financial terms. People who have management jobs must know how accounting information is developed in order to evaluate performance in meeting goals.

Creditors Creditors lend money or extend credit to the company for the purchase of goods and services. The company's creditors include suppliers, banks, and other lending institutions, such as loan companies. Creditors are interested in the firm's ability to pay its debts.

Government agencies Taxing authorities verify information submitted by companies concerning a variety of taxes, such as income taxes, sales taxes, and employment taxes. Public utilities, such as electric and gas companies, must provide financial information to regulatory agencies.

Accounting and Technology

Before the invention of calculators and computers, all business transactions were recorded by hand. Now computers perform routine recordkeeping operations and prepare financial reports. Computers are used today in all types of businesses, both large and small. One question often arises: "Is the computer taking over accountants' jobs?" Actually, with the introduction of computers, more jobs have been created to fulfill management's need for more information.

Regardless of whether a business uses a computer, the nature of accounting is the same. The computer is a powerful tool of the accountant. However, as a tool, the computer is only as useful as the ability of the operator. The operator must be skilled to key the correct information into the computer program. Otherwise, as the saying goes, "garbage in, garbage out."

CAREER OPPORTUNITIES IN ACCOUNTING

OBJECTIVE 3

Describe the various career opportunities in accounting.

To find job opportunities in accounting, all you need to do is read the newspapers' classified advertisements or browse the Internet. Although the jobs listed in these ads require varying amounts of education and experience, most of them are for positions as accounting clerks, general bookkeepers, or accountants. Let's take a look at the requirements and duties of these positions.

Accounting Clerk/Technician

An accounting clerk/technician does routine recording of financial information. The duties of accounting clerks vary with the size of the company. In small businesses, accounting clerks handle most of the recordkeeping functions. In large companies, clerks specialize in one part of the accounting system, such as payroll, accounts receivable, accounts payable, cash, inventory, or purchases. The minimum requirement for most accounting clerk positions is one term or semester of an accounting course.

General Bookkeeper

Many small- and medium-sized companies employ one person to oversee their bookkeeping operations. This person is called a general or full-charge bookkeeper. The general bookkeeper supervises the work of accounting clerks. Requirements for this job vary with the size of the company and the complexity of the accounting system. The minimum requirement for most general bookkeeper jobs is one or two years of accounting as well as experience as an accounting clerk.

Paraprofessional Accountant

To bridge a gap between the general bookkeeper and the professional accountant many firms are hiring **paraprofessional accountants**. They are able to manage the duties of the general bookkeeper as well as many of the duties of a professional accountant under that accountant's supervision. Qualifications generally include a two-year degree or certificate in accounting as well as appropriate prior experience.

Accountant

The term *accountant* describes a fairly broad range of jobs. The accountant may design and manage the entire accounting system for a business. The accountant may also prepare the financial statements and tax returns and perform audits. Many accountants enter the field with a four-year college degree in accounting; however, it is not unusual for accountants to start at entry-level positions and work their way up to management positions. Although accountants are employed in every kind of economic unit, they are classified into one of three categories: public accounting, managerial or private accounting, and not-for-profit accounting. We'll briefly look at these categories.

Accountants are employed in every kind of economic unit. Many start in entry-level positions and work their way up to management.

Public Accounting   Certified public accountants (CPAs) are independent professionals who provide services to clients for a fee. To become a CPA, a person must have a college degree, pass a rigorous examination, and generally complete a work-experience requirement. Public accountants design accounting systems, prepare tax returns, provide financial advice about business operations, and audit financial statements.

Managerial or Private Accounting   Most people who are accountants are employed by private business organizations. These accountants (not necessarily CPAs) manage the accounting system, prepare budgets, determine

Charitable organizations must be closely attuned to their cash situation as funds are donated and in turn shared with those in need. Those who manage charities must be able to report to the public and various government agencies where the money comes from, where it has gone, and how much was kept to run the charity.

costs of products, and provide financial information for managers and owners. Accountants have many opportunities to advance into top management positions. The Certified Management Accountant (CMA) exam has become an important partner to the CPA credentials.

Not-for-Profit Accounting   Not-for-profit accounting is used for government agencies, hospitals, churches and synagogues, and schools. Accountants for these organizations prepare budgets and maintain records of revenues and expenses. It should be noted that some not-for-profit organizations do in fact make a profit; however, the profit is kept in the organization and not distributed. For example, a hospital makes a profit and then reinvests the profit in modern equipment. Local, state, and federal government bodies employ vast numbers of people in accounting positions.

ETHICS

OBJECTIVE 4

Define *ethics*.

Ethics is a philosophy or code or system of morality—that is, how we conduct ourselves from day to day in a variety of situations requiring a decision, usually of a right or wrong nature. Ethics, as it relates to accounting, would be the way accountants and other keepers of financial information conduct the business of accounting according to laws of the state and their own personal code or system of morality.

There are books and textbooks available on ethics, as well as classes on the subject. With mounting evidence of questionable ethics in business reported in print and portrayed through the visual media, it is apparent that some individuals are in need of additional schooling in and practice of ethical behavior at all levels.

CHAPTER REVIEW

Online Study Center
ACE the test!

Review of Performance Objectives

1. Define *accounting*.

   Accounting is the process of analyzing, classifying, recording, summarizing, and interpreting business transactions in financial or monetary terms. It is also an information system and the language of business.

2. Explain the importance of accounting information.

   A study of accounting gives a person the necessary background to understand the scope, functions, and policies of an organization.

3. Describe the various career opportunities in accounting.

   Accountants, paraprofessional accountants, bookkeepers, and accounting clerks will find employment opportunities in several areas—in the public sector, the private sector, or not-for-profit organizations.

4. Define *ethics*.

   Ethics is a philosophy or code or system of morality—that is, how we conduct ourselves from day to day in a variety of situations requiring a decision, usually of a right or wrong nature. Ethics, as it relates to accounting, would be the way accountants and other keepers of financial information conduct themselves according to laws of the state and their own personal code or system of morality.

Glossary

Accountant A person who keeps the financial history of the transactions of an economic unit in written form; sometimes mistakenly called a bookkeeper. (2)

Accounting The process of analyzing, classifying, recording, summarizing, and interpreting business transactions in financial or monetary terms; sometimes mistakenly called bookkeeping. (1)

Economic unit Includes both business enterprises and not-for-profit entities, such as government bodies, churches and synagogues, clubs, and public charities. (2)

Ethics A philosophy or code or system of morality—that is, how we conduct ourselves from day to day in a variety of situations requiring a decision, usually of a right or wrong nature. (5)

Generally accepted accounting principles (GAAP) The rules or guidelines used for carrying out the accounting process. (2)

Paraprofessional accountant A person who is qualified in accounting to assume the duties of a general bookkeeper as well as some of those of a professional accountant under that accountant's supervision. (4)

Transaction An event directly affecting an economic entity that can be expressed in terms of money and that must be recorded in the accounting records. (1)

internet
LINKS TO ACCOUNTING

Have you ever bought clothes from Gap? How about from Banana Republic or Old Navy? All three brands belong to Gap Inc., an international specialty retailer that sells clothing, accessories, and personal care items. When you buy a pair of jeans from Gap and pay cash, it's an expense to you and revenue to the store. You can also buy those jeans using your credit card, in which case it's a liability to you because you promise to pay the credit card company for your purchase at a later date. After completing this chapter, you will understand what accounting is and why it is important. Every business transaction that takes place in each of the stores mentioned above is recorded and then reported to the parent company, Gap Inc. You can go to Gap Inc.'s website to see its annual reports: **http://www.gapinc.com/ public/Investors/inv_fin_annual_reports_and_proxy.htm**. As you view the financial statements, which begin on page 37 of the 2005 Annual Report, think about the fundamental accounting equation, which you will learn about in this chapter. At the end of the chapter is further discussion with exercises about the accounting equation as it applies to Gap Inc.

Performance Objectives

After you have completed this chapter, you will be able to do the following:

1. Define and identify *asset*, *liability*, and *owner's equity* accounts.

2. Record a group of business transactions, in column form, involving changes in assets, liabilities, and owner's equity.

3. Define and identify *revenue* and *expense* accounts.

4. Record a group of business transactions, in column form, involving all five elements of the fundamental accounting equation.

As we stated in the Introduction, accounting is the process of analyzing, classifying, recording, and summarizing business transactions. We now introduce the analyzing, classifying, and recording steps in the accounting process.

ASSETS, LIABILITIES, AND OWNER'S EQUITY

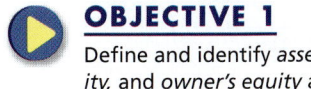

OBJECTIVE 1
Define and identify *asset, liability,* and *owner's equity* accounts.

The Fundamental Accounting Equation

Assets are properties or things of value, such as cash, equipment, copyrights, buildings, and land, owned and controlled by an economic unit or

business entity. By the term **business entity**, we mean that the business is an economic unit in itself, and the assets or properties of the business are completely separate from the owner's personal assets. However, the owner has a claim on the assets of the business and generally has a responsibility for its debts. **The owner's right, claim, or financial interest is expressed by the word equity in the business.** Another term that could be used is **capital**. Whenever you see the term **owner's equity**, it means the owner's right to or investment in the business.

Assets	=	Owner's Equity
Properties or things of value owned by the business		Owner's *right* to or investment in the business

Suppose the total value of the assets is $60,000 and the business entity does not owe any amount against the assets. Then,

Assets	=	Owner's Equity
$60,000 =		$60,000

Or suppose the assets consist of a truck that costs $32,000. The owner has invested $11,000 for the truck, and the business entity has borrowed the remainder from the bank, which is a **creditor** (one to whom money is owed). This business transaction or event can be shown as follows:

Assets	=	Liabilities	+	Owner's Equity
Items owned		Amounts owed to creditors		Owner's investment
$32,000	=	$21,000	+	$11,000

We have now introduced a new classification, **liabilities**, which represent debts. They are the amounts that the business entity owes its creditors. The debts may originate because the business bought goods or services on credit,

When a company's liabilities are greater than its assets, it may be forced into bankruptcy. The money earned from a going-out-of-business sale is used to pay creditors. Accurate accounting practices, especially tracking cash, can help a company avoid bankruptcy.

borrowed money, or otherwise created an obligation to pay. The creditors' claims to the assets have priority over the claims of the owner.

An equation expressing the relationship of assets, liabilities, and owner's equity is called the **fundamental accounting equation (Assets = Liabilities + Owner's Equity).** We'll deal with this equation constantly from now on. If we know two parts of this equation, we can determine the third. Let's look at some examples.

Determine Assets   Ms. Acosta has $16,000 invested in her travel agency, and the agency owes creditors $4,000; that is, the agency has liabilities of $4,000. Then,

Assets = Liabilities + Owner's Equity

    ?   = $4,000   + $16,000

We can find the amount of the business's assets by adding the liabilities and the owner's equity:

$ 4,000 Liabilities
+ 16,000 Owner's Equity
 $20,000 Assets

The completed equation now reads

Assets = Liabilities + Owner's Equity

$20,000 = $4,000   + $16,000

Determine Owner's Equity   Mr. Ruiz owns an auto repair shop. His business has assets of $38,000, and it owes creditors $5,000; that is, it has liabilities of $5,000. Then,

Assets = Liabilities + Owner's Equity

$38,000 = $5,000   +   ?

We find the owner's equity by subtracting the liabilities from the assets:

$38,000 Assets
−   5,000 Liabilities
 $33,000 Owner's Equity

The completed equation now reads

Assets = Liabilities + Owner's Equity

$38,000 = $5,000   + $33,000

Determine Liabilities   Mr. Vogel's insurance agency has assets of $68,000; his investment (his equity) amounts to $22,000. Then,

Assets = Liabilities + Owner's Equity

$68,000 =   ?   + $22,000

Like a balancing scale, the equation stays in balance by making equal or offsetting increases and decreases to one side or both sides.

Assets owned by a business may be as small as a calculator or as large as a delivery truck or building.

To find the firm's total liabilities, we subtract the equity from the assets:

$68,000 Assets
−   22,000 Owner's Equity
$46,000 Liabilities

The completed equation reads

Assets = Liabilities + Owner's Equity

$68,000 = $46,000   + $22,000

Recording Business Transactions

OBJECTIVE 2

Record a group of business transactions, in column form, involving changes in assets, liabilities, and owner's equity.

As you know, business transactions are events that have a direct effect on the operations of an economic unit or enterprise and are expressed in terms of money. Each business transaction must be recorded in the accounting records. As business transactions are recorded, the amounts listed under the headings Assets, Liabilities, and Owner's Equity change. However, **the total of one side of the fundamental accounting equation must always equal the total of the other side.** The categories under these three main headings are called **accounts.**

Let's look at a group of business transactions. These transactions are typical of those seen in a service or professional type of business. In these transactions, let's assume that R. P. Cline establishes her own business and calls it Cline's Computer Clinic. Cline's Computer Clinic is a **sole proprietorship**, or a one-owner business.

Transaction (a)   **Cline deposited $82,000 in a bank account in the name of the business.** Cline deposits $82,000 cash in a separate bank account in the name of Cline's Computer Clinic. This separate bank account will help Cline keep her business investment separate from her personal funds. This is an example of the **separate entity concept**, according to which a business is treated as a separate economic or accounting entity. The business is independent or stands by itself; it is separate from its owners, creditors, and customers.

The Cash account consists of bank deposits and money on hand. The business now has $82,000 more in cash than before, and Cline's investment has also increased by $82,000. The account denoted by the owner's name followed by the word *Capital* records the amount of the owner's investment, or equity, in the business. The effect of this transaction on the fundamental accounting equation is as follows:

Assets	=	**Liabilities**	+	**Owner's Equity**
Items owned		Amounts owed to creditors		Owner's investment
Cash	=			R. P. Cline, Capital
(a) **+82,000**	=			**+82,000**

Besides cash, an investment may be in the form of goods, such as equipment. The word *Capital* used under Owner's Equity therefore does not always mean that cash was invested.

Transaction (b) **Company bought equipment, paying cash, $64,000.** Cline's first task is to get her company ready for business; to do that, she needs the proper equipment. Accordingly, Cline's Computer Clinic buys equipment costing $64,000 and pays cash. **It is important to note at this point that Cline does not invest any new money. She simply exchanges part of the business's cash for equipment.** Because equipment is a new type of property for the firm, a new account, Equipment, is created. Equipment is included under Assets. As a result of this transaction, the accounting equation changes:

	Assets		=	**Liabilities**	+	**Owner's Equity**
	Items owned			Amounts owed to creditors		Owner's investment
	Cash	+ Equipment =				R. P. Cline, Capital
Initial Investment	82,000		=			82,000
(b)	−64,000	+64,000				
New balances	18,000+	64,000	=			82,000
	82,000				82,000	

Transaction (c) **Company bought equipment on account from Surgo Products, $10,000.** Cline's Computer Clinic buys equipment costing $10,000 on credit from Surgo Products.

The Equipment account shows an increase because the business owns $10,000 more in equipment. There is also an increase in liabilities because the business now owes $10,000. The liability account **Accounts Payable** is used for short-term liabilities or charge accounts, usually due within thirty days. (The company to which money is owed is called a creditor.) There is now a total of $92,000 on each side of the equals sign. Because Cline's Computer Clinic owes money to Surgo Products, Surgo Products is called a creditor of Cline's Computer Clinic.

	Assets		=	**Liabilities**	+	**Owner's Equity**
	Items owned			Amounts owed to creditors		Owner's investment
	Cash	+ Equipment =		Accounts Payable	+	R. P. Cline, Capital
Previous balances	18,000 +	64,000	=			82,000
(c)		+10,000		+10,000		
New balances	18,000 +	74,000	=	10,000	+	82,000
	92,000			92,000		

Observe that the recording of each transaction must yield an equation that is in balance. For example, transaction (b) resulted in a minus $64,000 and a plus $64,000 *on the same side,* with nothing recorded on the other side, and transaction (c) resulted in a $10,000 increase to both sides of the equation. It does not matter whether you change one side or both sides. **The important point is that whenever a transaction is properly recorded, the accounting equation remains in balance.**

Transaction (d)   Company paid Surgo Products, a creditor, on account, $6,000. Cline's Computer Clinic pays $6,000 to Surgo Products, to be applied against the firm's liability of $10,000.

With this payment, cash is being reduced. At the same time, the firm *owes* less than before, so the transaction should be recorded as a reduction in liabilities.

	Assets		=	Liabilities	+	Owner's Equity
	Items owned			Amounts owed to creditors		Owner's investment
	Cash +	Equipment =		Accounts Payable +		R. P. Cline, Capital
Previous balances	18,000 +	74,000 =		10,000	+	82,000
(d)	−6,000			−6,000		
New balances	12,000 +	74,000 =		4,000	+	82,000
	86,000				86,000	

Transaction (e)   Owner invested equipment in the business. Cline invested her own computer equipment in Cline's Computer Clinic having a **fair market value** of $6,200. **Fair market value is the present worth of an asset.** It is the amount that would be received if the asset were sold on the open market. Additional investments may be in the form of equipment, cash, tools, or real estate.

	Assets		=	Liabilities	+	Owner's Equity
	Items owned			Amounts owed to creditors		Owner's investment
	Cash +	Equipment =		Accounts Payable +		R. P. Cline, Capital
Previous balances	12,000 +	74,000 =		4,000	+	82,000
(e)		+6,200				+6,200
New balances	12,000 +	80,200 =		4,000	+	88,200
	92,200				92,200	

Accounting, as we said before, is the process of analyzing, classifying, recording, summarizing, and interpreting business transactions in terms of money. Look at the transactions thus far for Cline's Computer Clinic and see if you understand that we have gone through certain steps (in the form of questions). Let's illustrate these steps using transaction (e), owner invests equipment in the business.

1. **What accounts are involved?** Equipment and R. P. Cline, Capital are involved.
2. **What are the classifications of the accounts involved?** Equipment is an asset and R. P. Cline, Capital is an owner's equity account.

3. **Are the accounts increased or decreased?** Equipment is increased because Cline's Computer Clinic has more equipment than before. R. P. Cline, Capital is increased because Cline has a greater investment than before.
4. **Is the equation in balance after the transaction has been recorded?** Yes.

Next, we record the transaction. We will stress this step-by-step process throughout the text. This example serves as an introduction to **double-entry accounting**. The "double" element is demonstrated by the fact that each transaction must be recorded in at least two accounts, keeping the accounting equation in balance.

Summary of Transactions

Let's summarize the business transactions of Cline's Computer Clinic in column form, identifying each transaction by a letter of the alphabet. To test your understanding of the recording procedure, describe the nature of the transactions that have taken place.

	Assets		**= Liabilities +**	**Owner's Equity**
	Cash +	Equip. =	Accounts + Payable	R. P. Cline, Capital
Transaction (a)	+82,000			+82,000
Transaction (b)	−64,000	+64,000		
Balance	18,000 +	64,000 =		82,000
Transaction (c)		+10,000	+10,000	
Balance	18,000 +	74,000 =	10,000 +	82,000
Transaction (d)	−6,000		−6,000	
Balance	12,000 +	74,000 =	4,000 +	82,000
Transaction (e)		+6,200		+6,200
Balance	12,000 +	80,200 =	4,000 +	88,200
	92,200		92,200	

The following observations apply to all types of business transactions:

1. Every transaction is recorded as an increase and/or decrease in two or more accounts.
2. One side of the equation is always equal to the other side of the equation.

In this chapter we are using a column arrangement as a practical device to show how transactions are recorded. This arrangement is useful for showing increases and decreases in various accounts as a result of the transactions. We also show new balances after recording each transaction.

REVENUE AND EXPENSE ACCOUNTS

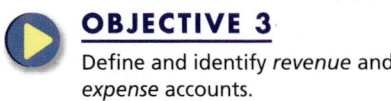

OBJECTIVE 3

Define and identify *revenue* and *expense* accounts.

Revenues are the amounts earned by a business. Examples of revenues are fees earned for performing services, income from selling merchandise, rent income for the use of property, and interest income for lending money. Revenues may be in the form of cash or credit card receipts. Revenues may also result from credit sales to charge customers, in which case cash will be received at a later time.

Expenses are the costs that relate to earning revenue (or the costs of doing business). Examples of expenses are wages expense for labor performed, rent expense for the use of property, interest expense for the use of money, and advertising expense for the use of various media (for example, newspapers, radio, and direct mail). Another example is supplies expense to include supplies used in the completion of a task performed by a service business, such as cleaning fluids used by a carpet cleaner company. Expenses may be paid in cash when incurred (that is, immediately) or at a later time. Expenses to be paid at a later time involve Accounts Payable.

Revenues and expenses directly affect owner's equity. **If a business earns revenue, an increase in owner's equity occurs. When a business incurs or pays expenses, owner's equity decreases.** For the present, think of it this way: If the company makes money, the owner's equity is increased. If the company has to pay out money for the costs of doing business, then the owner's equity is decreased. Revenues and expenses fall under the umbrella of owner's equity: Revenue increases owner's equity; expenses decrease owner's equity.

Chart of Accounts

The **chart of accounts** is the official list of accounts *tailor-made* for the business. All the company's transactions must be recorded using the official account titles.

We now present the chart of accounts for Cline's Computer Clinic. Some of the accounts are new to you, but they will be explained as we move along. When numbering account titles, the 100s are used for assets, the 200s are used for liabilities, the 300s are used for owner's equity accounts, the 400s are used for revenue accounts, and the 500s are used for expense accounts. You will encounter longer account numbers, but the first digit will usually be the same for any service business. In any case, use the exact account titles listed in the company's chart of accounts. Any changes must be approved by management.

Chart of Accounts

Assets

111 Cash
113 Accounts Receivable
117 Prepaid Insurance
124 Equipment

Liabilities

221 Accounts Payable

Owner's Equity

311 R. P. Cline, Capital
312 R. P. Cline, Drawing

Revenue (increase in Owner's Equity)

411 Income from Services

Expenses (decrease in Owner's Equity)

511 Wages Expense
512 Rent Expense
513 Supplies Expense
514 Advertising Expense
515 Utilities Expense

OBJECTIVE 4

Record a group of business transactions, in column form, involving all five elements of the fundamental accounting equation.

Recording Business Transactions

Soon after the opening of Cline's Computer Clinic, the first customers arrive, beginning a flow of revenue for the business. Let's examine more transactions of Cline's Computer Clinic for the first month of operations.

Transaction (f)   **Company sold computer repair services for cash, $3,520.**
Cline's Computer Clinic receives cash revenue of $3,520 in return for computer repair services performed for customers over two weeks. In other words, the company earns $3,520 for services performed for cash customers. Revenue has the effect of increasing owner's equity, but because the company wants to know how much revenue is earned, we set up a special column for revenue. The revenue account for Cline's Computer Clinic is called Income from Services. The accounting equation is affected as follows (PB stands for previous balance, and NB stands for new balance).

	Assets		= Liabilities +		Owner's Equity	
	Cash	+ Equipment	Accounts Payable		R. P. Cline, Capital	+ Revenue
PB	12,000 +	80,200	= 4,000	+	88,200	
(f)	+3,520					+3,520 (Income from Services)
NB	15,520 +	80,200	= 4,000	+	88,200	+ 3,520
		95,720			95,720	

Transaction (g)   **Company paid rent for the month, $900.** Shortly after opening the business, Cline's Computer Clinic pays the month's rent of $900. Rent is payment for the privilege of occupying a building.

It seems logical that, if revenue is added to owner's equity, then expenses (the opposite of revenue) must be subtracted from owner's equity. To be consistent, a separate column is set up for expenses.

We want to have a running total of the amount of expenses to be subtracted from owner's equity. To keep up this running total, as each new expense is incurred (or comes into being), it must be added to the previous total.

	Assets		= Liabilities +		Owner's Equity		
	Cash	+ Equip.	Accounts Payable		R. P. Cline, Capital	+ Revenue	− Expenses
PB	15,520 +	80,200 =	4,000	+	88,200	+ 3,520	
(g)	−900						+900 (Rent Expense)
NB	14,620 +	80,200 =	4,000	+	88,200	+ 3,520	− 900
	94,820				94,820		

Because the time period represented by the rent payment is one month or less, we record the $900 as an expense. If the payment covered a period longer than one month, we would record the amount under an asset called Prepaid Rent.

Let's review the mental process for formulating the entry by asking:

1. **What are the accounts involved?** In this transaction, they are Cash and Rent Expense.
2. **What are the classifications of the accounts involved?** Cash is an asset, and Rent Expense is an expense.
3. **Are the accounts increased or decreased?** Cash is decreased because after the payment we have less cash than we had before. Rent Expense is increased. Thus there is a $900 reduction in total owner's equity.
4. **Is the equation in balance after the transaction has been recorded?** Yes.

Banks and other financial institutions sell their services to other businesses as well as to individuals.

Transaction (h) **Company bought supplies on credit.** Cline's Computer Clinic buys CD-R recordable compact discs and holders, manuals, and invoice forms costing $870 on credit from Freeman Company. Compact discs and holders for storing troubleshooting programs and customer files during installations and repairs, as well as manuals and invoice forms, are considered to be supplies to be used up by Cline's Computer Clinic in the performance of computer repair work for clients and are recorded as an expense. For a service business, for tax purposes (IRS Notice 2001-76), supplies may now be originally recorded as an expense rather than being added to an inventory account.

	Assets	= Liabilities +	Owner's Equity		
	Cash + Equip.	Accounts Payable	R. P. Cline, Capital	+ Revenue	− Expenses
PB	14,620 + 80,200 =	4,000	+ 88,200	+ 3,520	− 900
(h)		**+870**			**+870**
					(Supplies Expense)
NB	14,620 + 80,200 =	4,870	+ 88,200	+ 3,520	− 1,770
	94,820		94,820		

Transaction (i) **Company paid for insurance.** Cline's Computer Clinic paid $480 for a one-year liability insurance policy. At the time of payment, the company has not used up the insurance; thus, it is not yet an expense. As the insurance expires (is used), it will become an expense. **However, because it is paid in advance for a period longer than one month, it has value and is therefore recorded as an asset.**

	Assets	= Liabilities +	Owner's Equity		
	Cash + Equip. + Ppd. Ins.	Accounts Payable	R. P. Cline, Capital	+ Revenue	− Expenses
PB	14,620 + 80,200	= 4,870	+ 88,200	+ 3,520	− 1,770
(i)	−480　　　　　+480				
NB	14,140 + 80,200 + 480 =	4,870	+ 88,200	+ 3,520	− 1,770
	94,820		94,820		

At the end of the year or accounting period, an adjustment will have to be made to take out the expired portion (that is, coverage for the months that have been used up) and record it as an expense. We discuss this adjustment in a later chapter.

Observe that each time a transaction is recorded, the total amount on one side of the equation **remains equal** to the total amount on the other side. As proof of this equality, look at the following computation:

Cash	$14,140	**Accounts Payable**	$ 4,870
Equipment	80,200	**R. P. Cline, Capital**	88,200
Prepaid Insurance	480	**Revenue**	3,520
		Subtotal	$96,590
		Expenses	−1,770
	$94,820		$94,820

Steps in Analyzing Transactions

Now that we have recorded transactions in all five classifications of accounts, let's pause to go through the steps we have followed:

Step 1. Read the transaction to understand what is happening and how it affects the business. For example, the business has more revenue, or has more expenses, or has more cash, or owes less to creditors.

Step 2. Identify the accounts involved and decide whether the accounts are increased or decreased. Look for Cash first; you will quickly recognize if cash is coming in or going out.

Step 3. Decide on the classifications of the accounts involved. For example, Equipment is something the business owns, and it's an asset; Accounts Payable is an amount the business owes, and it's a liability; Rent is an expense.

Step 4. After recording the transaction, make sure the accounting equation is in balance.

Transaction (j) **Company received a bill for an expense.** Cline's Computer Clinic receives a bill from the *Daily* for newspaper advertising, $340. Cline's Computer Clinic has simply received the bill for advertising; it has not paid any cash. Previously, we described an expense as money to be paid for the cost of doing business. An expense of $340 has now been incurred (or has taken place), and it should be recorded as an increase in expenses (Advertising Expense). Also, since the company owes $340 more than before and intends to pay at a later time, this amount should be recorded as an increase in Accounts Payable.

	Assets			= Liabilities +		Owner's Equity		
	Cash +	Equip. +	Ppd. Ins.	Accounts Payable	R. P. Cline, + Capital	Revenue −	Expenses	
PB	14,140 +	80,200 +	480 =	4,870	+ 88,200	+ 3,520	− 1,770	
(j)				**+340**			**+340** (Advertising Expense)	
NB	14,140 +	80,200 +	480 =	5,210	+ 88,200	+ 3,520	− 2,110	
		94,820				94,820		

Transaction (k) **Company sold services on account.** Cline's Computer Clinic signs a contract with Computer Makeovers to refurbish some of the computers it receives on a credit basis. Cline's Computer Clinic completes a refurbishing job and bills Computer Makeovers $1,470 for services performed.

A company uses the **Accounts Receivable** account to record the amounts due from (legal claims against) charge customers. Since Cline's Computer Clinic's claim against Computer Makeovers is $1,470 more than before the transaction took place, it seems logical to add $1,470 to Accounts Receivable. Revenue is earned or recognized when the service is performed, even though the $1,470 has not been received in cash. We count the $1,470 as an increase in revenue and an increase in Accounts Receivable. Keep in mind that Accounts Receivable is an asset, or something that is owned. Cline's Computer Clinic owns a claim of $1,470 against Computer Makeovers.

	Assets				=	Liabilities +		Owner's Equity		
	Cash	+ Equip.	+ Ppd. Ins.	+ Accts. Rec.	=	Accounts Payable	+	R. P. Cline, Capital	+ Revenue	− Expenses
PB	14,140	+ 80,200	+ 480		=	5,210	+	88,200	+ 3,520	− 2,110
(k)				+1,470					+1,470	
									(Income from Services)	
NB	14,140	+ 80,200	+ 480	+ 1,470	=	5,210	+	88,200	+ 4,990	− 2,110
		96,290						96,290		

When Computer Makeovers pays the $1,470 bill in cash, Cline's Computer Clinic will record this transaction as an increase in Cash and a decrease in Accounts Receivable. At that time, Cline's Computer Clinic will not have to make an entry for the revenue account, because the revenue was earned and recorded when the service was performed.

Transaction (l) **Company paid creditor on account.** Cline's Computer Clinic pays $1,800 to Surgo Products, its creditor (the party to whom it owes money), as part payment on account.

	Assets				=	Liabilities +		Owner's Equity		
	Cash	+ Equip.	+ Ppd. Ins.	+ Accts. Rec.	=	Accounts Payable	+	R. P. Cline, Capital	+ Revenue	− Expenses
PB	14,140	+ 80,200	+ 480	+ 1,470	=	5,210	+	88,200	+ 4,990	− 2,110
(l)	−1,800					−1,800				
NB	12,340	+ 80,200	+ 480	+ 1,470	=	3,410	+	88,200	+ 4,990	− 2,110
		94,490						94,490		

Transaction (m) **Company paid an expense in cash.** Cline's Computer Clinic receives a bill from Regional Power, Inc. for $320. Because the bill was not previously recorded as a liability and is to be paid immediately, we record the amount directly as an expense.

	Assets				=	Liabilities +		Owner's Equity		
	Cash	+ Equip.	+ Ppd. Ins.	+ Accts. Rec.	=	Accounts Payable	+	R. P. Cline, Capital	+ Revenue	− Expenses
PB	12,340	+ 80,200	+ 480	+ 1,470	=	3,410	+	88,200	+ 4,990	− 2,110
(m)	−320									+320
										(Utilities Expense)
NB	12,020	+ 80,200	+ 480	+ 1,470	=	3,410	+	88,200	+ 4,990	− 2,430
		94,170						94,170		

Transaction (n) **Company paid creditor on account.** Cline's Computer Clinic pays $340 to the *Daily* for advertising. Recall that this bill had previously been recorded as a liability in transaction (j).

	Assets				= Liabilities +	Owner's Equity		
	Cash	+ Equip.	+ Ppd. Ins.	+ Accts. Rec.	Accounts Payable	R. P. Cline, Capital	+ Revenue	− Expenses
PB	12,020	+ 80,200	+ 480	+ 1,470 =	3,410	+ 88,200	+ 4,990	− 2,430
(n)	−340				−340			
NB	11,680	+ 80,200	+ 480	+ 1,470 =	3,070	+ 88,200	+ 4,990	− 2,430
	93,830					93,830		

Transaction (o) **Company paid an expense in cash.** Cline's Computer Clinic pays wages of a part-time employee, $2,980.

	Assets				= Liabilities +	Owner's Equity		
	Cash	+ Equip.	+ Ppd. Ins.	+ Accts. Rec.	Accounts Payable	R. P. Cline, Capital	+ Revenue	− Expenses
PB	11,680	+ 80,200	+ 480	+ 1,470 =	3,070	+ 88,200	+ 4,990	− 2,430
(o)	−2,980							+2,980
								(Wages Expense)
NB	8,700	+ 80,200	+ 480	+ 1,470 =	3,070	+ 88,200	+ 4,990	− 5,410
	90,850					90,850		

Transaction (p) **Company buys equipment on account and makes a cash down payment.** Cline's Computer Clinic buys additional equipment from Surgo Products for $3,520, paying $620 down, with the remaining $2,900 on account. Because buying an item *on account* is the same as buying it *on credit*, both terms are used to describe such transactions.

	Assets				= Liabilities +	Owner's Equity		
	Cash	+ Equip.	+ Ppd. Ins.	+ Accts. Rec.	Accounts Payable	R. P. Cline, Capital	+ Revenue	− Expenses
PB	8,700	+ 80,200	+ 480	+ 1,470 =	3,070	+ 88,200	+ 4,990	− 5,410
(p)	−620	+3,520			+2,900			
NB	8,080	+ 83,720	+ 480	+ 1,470 =	5,970	+ 88,200	+ 4,990	− 5,410
	93,750					93,750		

Again, because the equipment is expected to last for years, Cline's Computer Clinic lists this $3,520 as an increase in the assets. Note that three accounts are involved in this transaction: Cash, because cash was paid out; Equipment, because the company has more equipment than before; and Accounts Payable, because the company owes more than before.

Transaction (q) **Company receives cash on account from credit customer.** Cline's Computer Clinic receives $850 from Computer Makeovers to apply against the amount billed in transaction (k). Computer Makeovers now owes Cline's Computer Clinic less than it did, and so Cline's Computer Clinic deducts the $850 from Accounts Receivable. An exchange of assets has no effect on the total of the equation.

	Assets			= Liabilities +		Owner's Equity		
Cash	+ Equip.	+ Ppd. Ins.	+ Accts. Rec.	Accounts Payable	R. P. Cline, Capital	+ Revenue	− Expenses	
PB 8,080	+ 83,720	+ 480	+ 1,470 =	5,970	+ 88,200	+ 4,990	− 5,410	
(q) +850			−850					
NB 8,930	+ 83,720	+ 480	+ 620 =	5,970	+ 88,200	+ 4,990	− 5,410	
93,750					93,750			

Cline's Computer Clinic previously listed the amount as revenue, so it should definitely not be recorded as revenue again. Think of paying income tax twice on the $850—once is enough.

Transaction (r)   Company sells services for cash. Cline's Computer Clinic receives revenue from cash customers for the rest of the month, $6,020.

	Assets			= Liabilities +		Owner's Equity		
Cash	+ Equip.	+ Ppd. Ins.	+ Accts. Rec.	Accounts Payable	R. P. Cline, Capital	+ Revenue	− Expenses	
PB 8,930	+ 83,720	+ 480	+ 620 =	5,970	+ 88,200	+ 4,990	− 5,410	
(r) +6,020						+6,020		
						(Income from Services)		
NB 14,950	+ 83,720	+ 480	+ 620 =	5,970	+ 88,200	+ 11,010	− 5,410	
99,770					99,770			

Transaction (s)   Owner makes a cash withdrawal. At the end of the month, Cline withdraws $3,000 in cash from the business for her personal living costs. A **withdrawal** may be considered the opposite of an investment in cash by the owner and is treated as a temporary decrease in owner's equity because it is made in anticipation of profits. Withdrawals are different from expenses. Expenses are paid to someone else for the cost of goods or services used in the business, whereas withdrawals are paid directly to the owner. A withdrawal may consist of cash or other assets.

Because the owner takes cash out of the business, there is a decrease of $3,000 in Cash. This also decreases Capital, because Cline has reduced her equity. We record $3,000 as a minus under Capital and label it as Drawing.

	Assets			= Liabilities +		Owner's Equity		
Cash	+ Equip.	+ Ppd. Ins.	+ Accts. Rec.	Accounts Payable	R. P. Cline, Capital	+ Revenue	− Expenses	
PB 14,950	+ 83,720	+ 480	+ 620 =	5,970	+ 88,200	+ 11,010	− 5,410	
(s) −3,000					−3,000			
					(Drawing)			
NB 11,950	+ 83,720	+ 480	+ 620 =	5,970	+ 85,200	+ 11,010	− 5,410	
96,770					96,770			

Summary of Transactions f Through s

Figure 1 summarizes business transactions (f) through (s) of Cline's Computer Clinic with the transactions identified by letter. To test your understanding of the recording procedure, describe the nature of the transactions.

	Assets				= Liabilities +		Owner's Equity		
	Cash	+ Equip.	+ Ppd. Ins.	+ Accts. Rec.	Accounts Payable	+	R. P. Cline, Capital	+ Revenue	− Expenses
Bal.	12,000	+ 80,200			= 4,000	+	88,200		
(f)	+3,520							+3,520 (Income from Services)	
Bal.	15,520	+ 80,200			= 4,000	+	88,200	+ 3,520	
(g)	−900								+900 (Rent Expense)
Bal.	14,620	+ 80,200			= 4,000	+	88,200	+ 3,520	− 900
(h)					+870				+870 (Supplies Expense)
Bal.	14,620	+ 80,200			= 4,870	+	88,200	+ 3,520	− 1,770
(i)	−480		+480						
Bal.	14,140	+ 80,200	+ 480		= 4,870	+	88,200	+ 3,520	− 1,770
(j)					+340				+340 (Advertising Expense)
Bal.	14,140	+ 80,200	+ 480		= 5,210	+	88,200	+ 3,520	− 2,110
(k)				+1,470				+1,470 (Income from Services)	
Bal.	14,140	+ 80,200	+ 480	+ 1,470	= 5,210	+	88,200	+ 4,990	− 2,110
(l)	−1,800				−1,800				
Bal.	12,340	+ 80,200	+ 480	+ 1,470	= 3,410	+	88,200	+ 4,990	− 2,110
(m)	−320								+320 (Utilities Expense)
Bal.	12,020	+ 80,200	+ 480	+ 1,470	= 3,410	+	88,200	+ 4,990	− 2,430
(n)	−340				−340				
Bal.	11,680	+ 80,200	+ 480	+ 1,470	= 3,070	+	88,200	+ 4,990	− 2,430
(o)	−2,980								+2,980 (Wages Expense)
Bal.	8,700	+ 80,200	+ 480	+ 1,470	= 3,070	+	88,200	+ 4,990	− 5,410
(p)	−620	+3,520			+2,900				
Bal.	8,080	+ 83,720	+ 480	+ 1,470	= 5,970	+	88,200	+ 4,990	− 5,410
(q)	+850			−850					
Bal.	8,930	+ 83,720	+ 480	+ 620	= 5,970	+	88,200	+ 4,990	− 5,410
(r)	+6,020							+6,020 (Income from Services)	
Bal.	14,950	+ 83,720	+ 480	+ 620	= 5,970	+	88,200	+ 11,010	− 5,410
(s)	−3,000						−3,000 (Drawing)		
	11,950	+ 83,720	+ 480	+ 620	= 5,970	+	85,200	+ 11,010	− 5,410

Left Side of Equals Sign		Right Side of Equals Sign	
Cash	$11,950	**Accounts Payable**	$ 5,970
Equipment	83,720	**R. P. Cline, Capital**	85,200
Prepaid Insurance	480	**Revenue**	11,010
Accounts Receivable	620	**Subtotal**	$102,180
		Expenses	−5,410
	$96,770		$ 96,770

FIGURE 1

CHAPTER REVIEW

Online Study Center
ACE the test!

Review of Performance Objectives

1. Define and identify *asset, liability*, and *owner's equity* accounts.

   Assets are cash, properties, or things of value owned by the business. *Liabilities* are amounts the business owes to creditors. *Owner's equity* is the owner's investment or net worth.

2. Record a group of business transactions, in column form, involving changes in assets, liabilities, and owner's equity.

   The accounting equation is stated as assets equals liabilities plus owner's equity. Under the appropriate classification, a separate column is set up for each account. Transactions are recorded by listing amounts as either additions to or deductions from the various accounts. The equation must always remain in balance.

3. Define and identify *revenue* and *expense* accounts.

   Revenue consists of amounts earned by a business, such as fees earned for performing services, income from selling merchandise, rent income for the use of property, or interest earned for lending money. *Expenses* are the costs of earning revenue—that is, of doing business—such as wages expense, rent expense, interest expense, and advertising expense.

4. Record a group of business transactions, in column form, involving all five elements of the fundamental accounting equation.

   The accounting equation has been expanded and appears as follows:

   Assets = Liabilities + Owner's Equity (Capital) + Revenue − Expenses

   Accounts are classified and listed under each heading. Transactions are recorded by listing amounts as either additions to or deductions from the various accounts. The equation must always remain in balance.

Glossary

Accounts The categories under the Assets, Liabilities, and Owner's Equity headings. (10)

Accounts Payable A liability account used for short-term liabilities or charge accounts, usually due within thirty days. (11)

Accounts Receivable An account used to record the amounts owed by (legal claims against) charge customers. (18)

Assets Cash, properties, and other things of value owned by an economic unit or business entity. (7)

Business entity A business enterprise, separate and distinct from the persons who supply the assets it uses. Property acquired by a business is an asset of the business. The owner is separate from the business and in fact has claims on it and a responsibility for its debts. (8)

Capital The owner's investment, or equity, in an enterprise. (8)

Chart of accounts The official list of account titles to be used to record the transactions of a business. (14)

Creditor One to whom money is owed. (8)

Double-entry accounting The system by which each business transaction is recorded in at least two accounts and the accounting equation is kept in balance. (13)

Equity The value of a right or claim to or financial interest in an asset or group of assets. (8)

Expenses The costs that relate to earning revenue (the costs of doing business); examples are wages, rent, interest, and advertising. They may be paid in cash immediately or at a future time (accounts payable). (14)

Fair market value The present worth of an asset or the amount that would be received if the asset were sold to an outsider on the open market. (12)

Fundamental accounting equation (Assets = Liabilities + Owner's Equity) An equation expressing the relationship of assets, liabilities, and owner's equity. (9)

Liabilities Debts or amounts owed to creditors. (8)

Owner's equity The owner's right to or investment in the business. (8)

Revenues The amounts a business earns; examples are fees earned for performing services, sales of merchandise, rent income, and interest income. They may be in the form of cash, credit card receipts, or accounts receivable (charge accounts). (13)

Separate entity concept The concept by which a business is treated as a separate economic or accounting entity. The business stands by itself, separate from its owners, creditors, and customers. (10)

Sole proprietorship A one-owner business. (10)

Withdrawal The taking of cash or other assets out of a business by the owner for his or her own use. (This is also referred to as *drawing*.) A withdrawal is treated as a temporary decrease in owner's equity. (20)

QUESTIONS, EXERCISES, AND CASES

Discussion Questions

1. Define assets, liabilities, owner's equity, revenues, and expenses.
2. Explain the separate entity concept.
3. How do Accounts Payable and Accounts Receivable differ?
4. Describe two ways to increase owner's equity and two ways to decrease owner's equity.
5. How will the fundamental accounting equation change if supplies are purchased on account? Explain how this purchase will or will not change the owner's equity.
6. When an owner withdraws cash or goods from the business, why is this considered an increase to the Drawing account and not an increase to the wages account?
7. Define *chart of accounts,* and identify the categories of accounts.
8. What account titles would you suggest for the chart of accounts for a jeep touring company owned by W. Sands? List the accounts by account category and include an appropriate account number for each.

Exercises

P.O. 1

Calculate missing amounts in the accounting equation.

Exercise 1-1 Complete the following equations:

a. Assets of $21,000 = Liabilities of $7,300 + Owner's Equity of $_____
b. Assets of $_____ − Liabilities of $15,000 = Owner's Equity of $25,000
c. Assets of $23,000 − Owner's Equity of $12,000 = Liabilities of $_____

P.O. 1

Calculate missing amounts in the accounting equation.

Exercise 1-2 Determine the following amounts:

a. The amount of the liabilities of a business that has $60,300 in assets and in which the owner has $35,000 equity.
b. The equity of the owner of a tour van that cost $38,000 who owes $18,400 on an installment loan payable to the bank.
c. The amount of the assets of a business that has $10,350 in liabilities and in which the owner has $24,180 equity.

P.O. 1

Formulate the accounting equation.

Exercise 1-3 Dr. L. M. Paydaar is an ophthalmologist. As of December 31, Dr. Paydaar owned the following property that related to his professional practice, Paydaar Eye Clinic:

Cash, $2,480
Professional Equipment, $58,000
Office Equipment, $10,460

On the same date, he owed the following business creditors:

Nichols Supply Company, $4,120
Rodriquez Equipment Sales, $3,970

Compute the following amounts in the accounting equation:

Assets $_____ = Liabilities $_____ + Owner's Equity $_____

P.O. 1,3

Describe transactions affecting the accounting equation.

Exercise 1-4 Describe a business transaction that will do the following:

a. Increase an asset and increase a liability
b. Decrease an asset and decrease a liability
c. Decrease an asset and increase an expense
d. Increase an asset and increase owner's equity
e. Increase an asset and decrease an asset
f. Increase an asset and increase revenue

P.O. 2

Describe various transactions.

Exercise 1-5 Describe a transaction that resulted in the following entries:

	Assets			=	Liabilities +	Owner's Equity
	Cash +	Office Equipment	+ Professional Equipment		Accounts Payable	B. Loren, Capital
(a)	+14,300					+14,300
(b)	−1,650		+1,650			
Bal.	12,650		+ 1,650	=		14,300
(c)		+550			+550	
Bal.	12,650 +	550	+ 1,650	=	550 +	14,300
(d)	−1,200		+6,000		+4,800	
Bal.	11,450 +	550	+ 7,650	=	5,350 +	14,300
(e)	−1,000				−1,000	
Bal.	10,450 +	550	+ 7,650	=	4,350 +	14,300

P.O. 1,3

Classify accounts.

Exercise 1-6 Label the following accounts as asset (A), liability (L), owner's equity (OE), revenue (R), or expense (E):

a. Office Supplies Expense
b. Professional Fees
c. Prepaid Insurance
d. R. Baca, Drawing
e. Accounts Payable
f. Service Income
g. R. Baca, Capital
h. Rent Expense
i. Accounts Receivable
j. Wages Expense

P.O. 4

Describe various transactions.

Exercise 1-7 Describe a transaction that resulted in the following changes in accounts:

a. Rent Expense is increased by $950, and Cash is decreased by $950.
b. Advertising Expense is increased by $841, and Accounts Payable is increased by $841.
c. Accounts Receivable is increased by $285, and Service Income is increased by $285.
d. Cash is decreased by $320, and C. Taylor, Drawing, is increased by $320.
e. Equipment is increased by $850, Cash is decreased by $450, and Accounts Payable is increased by $400.
f. Cash is increased by $630, and Accounts Receivable is decreased by $630.

P.O. 2,4

Describe various transactions.

Exercise 1-8 Describe the transactions that are recorded in the following equation.

	Assets			= Liabilities +		Owner's Equity		
	Cash +	Accounts Receivable	+Equipment	Accounts Payable	J. Ohno, + Capital	Revenue	−	Expenses
(a)	+22,000		+5,000		+27,000			
(b)	−1,050							+1,050 (Rent Expense)
Bal.	20,950	+	5,000 =		27,000		−	1,050
(c)		+1,800				+1,800 (Income from Services)		
Bal.	20,950 +	1,800 +	5,000 =		27,000	1,800	−	1,050
(d)	−4,000		+15,000	+11,000				
Bal.	16,950 +	1,800 +	20,000 =	11,000 +	27,000 +	1,800	−	1,050
(e)	−2,000				−2,000 (Drawing)			
Bal.	14,950 +	1,800 +	20,000 =	11,000 +	25,000 +	1,800	−	1,050
		36,750				36,750		

internet

LINKS TO ACCOUNTING

Recall from Performance Objective 1 in the chapter that the fundamental accounting equation expresses the relationship of assets, liabilities, and owner's equity. This is what the balance sheet reports. Using information from Gap Inc.'s balance sheet, found on page 38 of the 2005 Annual Report, create a completed accounting equation (Assets = Liabilities + Stockholders' Equity). The term Stockholders' Equity is used for Gap Inc. because the company sells shares of its stock to the public. On January 28, 2006, Gap Inc.'s total assets equaled $8,821,000,000; total liabilities equaled $3,396,000,000 (current liabilities of $1,942,000,000 plus long-term liabilities of $1,454,000,000); and total stockholders' equity equaled $5,425,000,000. As you can see, when we place these amounts into the fundamental accounting equation, the total of one side of the equation equals the total of the other side of the equation.

Assets	=	Liabilities	+	Stockholders' Equity
$8,821,000,000	=	$3,396,000,000	+	$5,425,000,000

1. If you purchase a pair of jeans from Gap for $40 cash, how will the store record this transaction? (Ignore sales taxes.)
2. How would Gap record a $30,000 payment for its monthly rent for one of its stores?

CONSIDER AND COMMUNICATE

A friend of yours wants to start her own house, plant, and pet sitting business. She already has a business license that is required in her city. She has had a personal checking account for years. You have told her that she also needs to open a separate account for her business needs, but she does not understand why she needs to have two separate accounts. Explain to her why she should have a business account separate from her personal account. Use some of the language of business you have learned in your text's Introduction and in this chapter.

WHAT'S WRONG WITH THIS PICTURE?

Eddie Cabrera has just opened Cabrera's Golf Cart Service. He has calculated the following amounts and then placed them in the fundamental accounting equation as he remembers it from his accounting class five years ago. He asks that you review his figures and give your opinion because he wants to start out on a correct footing.

Money in the drawer	$2,395
What I owe people	484
What people owe me	995

Assets	=	Liabilities	+	Owner's Equity
2,395		484		
995				
Totals 3,390	=	484	+	?

Eddie's Proof: A − L = OE

2,395 − 995 = 1,400 OE

1. Do you agree with Eddie's calculations?
2. If not, show how you would explain it to Eddie using the classifications of the fundamental accounting equation.

CRITICAL THINKING

Please read the following memorandum and follow the instructions set forth.

MEMORANDUM

TO: Your Name   DATE: July 31, 20—
FROM: J. Lara,   SUBJECT: Calculations for Baxter Co.
       Supervisor

Please provide the following ASAP (as soon as possible).

1. The balance of cash in Baxter Company's checkbook shows $13,740. I need to know if this ties to or matches the Cash account balance. I do know that total assets amount to $44,670. Office Equipment amounts to $3,650. Other noncash assets are Equipment, $25,480 and Prepaid Insurance, $1,800.
2. D. Baxter, the owner, wants to know the amount of his owner's equity. I pulled the outstanding bills, which amount to $8,430.
3. Please put the information in a memo addressed to me.
4. Thank you for your prompt response.

PROBLEM SET A

For additional help, see the demonstration problem at the beginning of each chapter in your Working Papers.

P.O. 1,2,3,4

Problem 1-1A In July of this year, J. L. Walters established a business called Walters Realty. The account headings are presented on the following page. Transactions completed during the month follow.

Assets		= Liabilities +		Owner's Equity		
Cash +	Office Equipment	Accounts Payable	Capital	, + Revenue	− Expenses	

a. Walters deposited $14,000 in a bank account in the name of the business.
b. Paid the office rent for the current month, $400, Ck. No. 1000 (Rent Expense).
c. Bought office supplies, paying cash, $445, Ck. No. 1001 (Supplies Expense).
d. Bought office equipment on account from Bellos Computers, $7,200.
e. Received a bill from the *Weekly Crier* for advertising, $556 (Advertising Expense).
f. Paid on account to Bellos Computers, a creditor, $1,000, Ck. No. 1002.
g. Sold services for cash, $2,960 (Service Income).
h. Received and paid the bill for utilities, $238, Ck. No. 1003 (Utilities Expense).
i. Paid on account to the *Weekly Crier,* a creditor, $556, Ck. No. 1004.
j. Paid truck expenses, $356, Ck. No. 1005 (Truck Maintenance Expense).
k. Walters withdrew cash for personal use, $1,200, Ck. No. 1006 (J. L. Walters, Drawing).

Check Figure

Left side of equals sign total, $19,965

P.O. 1,2,3,4

Instructions

1. In the equation, write the owner's name above the term *Capital.*
2. Record the transactions and the balance after each transaction. Identify the account affected when the transaction involves revenue, expenses, or a withdrawal.
3. Write the account totals from the left side of the equals sign and add them. Write the account totals from the right side of the equals sign and add them. If the two totals are not equal, first check the addition and subtraction. If you still cannot find the error, reanalyze each transaction.

Problem 1-2A In March, T. Camus, M.D., established the Camus Sports Injury Clinic. The clinic's account headings are presented below. Transactions completed during the month of March follow.

Assets			= Liabilities +		Owner's Equity		
Cash +	Office Equipment	+ Professional Equipment	Accounts Payable	Capital	, + Revenue	− Expenses	

a. Camus deposited $25,000 in a bank account in the name of the business.
b. Paid the rent for the month, $1,100, Ck. No. 1000 (Rent Expense).
c. Bought supplies on account from Herzog Co., $1,170 (Supplies Expense).
d. Bought professional equipment on account from Norman Company, $5,800.
e. Bought office equipment on account from Masterson Co., $864.
f. Sold professional services for cash, $4,820 (Professional Fees).
g. Paid on account to Norman Company, a creditor, $1,850, Ck. No. 1001.
h. Received and paid the bill for utilities, $382, Ck. No. 1002 (Utilities Expense).
i. Paid the salary of the assistant, $1,150, Ck. No. 1003 (Salary Expense).
j. Sold professional services for cash, $3,800 (Professional Fees).
k. Camus withdrew cash for personal use, $1,600, Ck. No. 1004 (T. Camus, Drawing).

Check Figure

Cash, $27,538

Instructions

1. In the equation, write the owner's name above the term *Capital*.
2. Record the transactions and the balance after each transaction. Identify the account affected when the transaction involves revenue, expenses, or a withdrawal.
3. Write the account totals from the left side of the equals sign and add them. Write the account totals from the right side of the equals sign and add them. If the two totals are not equal, first check the addition and subtraction. If you still cannot find the error, reanalyze each transaction.

P.O. 1,2,3,4

Problem 1-3A S. Strohm, Attorney at Law, opened his office on October 1. The account headings are presented below. Transactions completed during the month follow.

Assets				= Liabilities +	Owner's Equity		
Cash +	Prepaid Insurance +	Office Equipment +	Library	Accounts Payable	Capital	, + Revenue − Expenses	

a. Strohm deposited $25,000 in a bank account in the name of the business.
b. Bought office equipment on account from Milgor Company, $11,700.
c. Strohm invested his personal law library, which cost $4,700. (Increase the account Library and increase the account S. Strohm, Capital.)
d. Paid the office rent for the month, $1,050, Ck. No. 2000 (Rent Expense).
e. Bought office supplies for cash, $475, Ck. No. 2001 (Supplies Expense).
f. Bought insurance for two years, $284, Ck. No. 2002.
g. Sold legal services for cash, $3,680 (Professional Fees).
h. Received and paid the telephone bill, $328, Ck. No. 2003 (Telephone Expense).
i. Paid the salary of the part-time receptionist, $1,060, Ck. No. 2004 (Salary Expense).
j. Received and paid the bill for utilities, $188, Ck. No. 2005 (Utilities Expense).
k. Sold legal services for cash, $3,320 (Professional Fees).
l. Paid on account to Milgor Company, a creditor, $2,500, Ck. No. 2006.
m. Strohm withdrew cash for personal use, $2,200, Ck. No. 2007 (S. Strohm, Drawing).

Check Figure

Right side of equals sign total, $40,599

Instructions

1. In the equation, write the owner's name above the term *Capital*.
2. Record the transactions and the balance after each transaction. Identify the account affected when the transaction involves revenue, expenses, or a withdrawal.
3. Write the account totals from the left side of the equals sign and add them. Write the account totals from the right side of the equals sign and add them. If the two totals are not equal, first check the addition and subtraction. If you still cannot find the error, reanalyze each transaction.

P.O. 1,2,3,4

Problem 1-4A B. G. Ellison started Ellison Plant Service on May 1 of this year. The account headings are presented below. During May, Ellison completed the transactions that follow.

Assets					= Liabilities +	Owner's Equity		
Cash +	Accounts Receivable +	Prepaid Insurance +	Truck +	Equipment	Accounts Payable	Capital	, + Revenue − Expenses	

a. Ellison deposited $15,000 in a bank account in the name of the business.
b. Bought a used truck from Delgado Motors for $18,250, paying $1,200 in cash, and placing the remainder on account.
c. Bought equipment on account from Fanning Company, $2,800.
d. Paid the rent for the month, $560, Ck. No. 3001 (Rent Expense).
e. Bought insurance for the truck for the year, $680, Ck. No. 3002, Policy No. 311D.
f. Sold services for cash for the first half of the month, $3,175 (Service Income).
g. Bought supplies for cash, $483, Ck. No. 3003 (Supplies Expense).
h. Sold services on account, $944 (Service Income).
i. Received and paid the bill for utilities, $186, Ck. No. 3004 (Utilities Expense).
j. Received a bill for gas and oil for the truck, $227 (Gas and Oil Expense).
k. Sold services for cash for the remainder of the month, $3,732 (Service Income).
l. Ellison withdrew cash for personal use, $1,250, Ck. No. 3005 (B. G. Ellison, Drawing).
m. Paid wages to the employees, $2,240, Ck. Nos. 3006–3008 (Wages Expense).

Check Figure

Cash, $15,308

Instructions

1. In the equation, write the owner's name above the term *Capital*.
2. Record the transactions and the balance after each transaction. Identify the account affected when the transaction involves revenue, expenses, or a withdrawal.
3. Write the account totals from the left side of the equals sign and add them. Write the account totals from the right side of the equals sign and add them. If the two totals are not equal, first check the addition and subtraction. If you still cannot find the error, reanalyze each transaction.

PROBLEM SET B

For additional help, see the demonstration problem at the beginning of each chapter in your Working Papers.

P.O. 1,2,3,4

Problem 1-1B On June 1 of this year, J. Vance, Optometrist, established the Vance Eye Clinic. The clinic's account names are presented below. Transactions completed during the month follow.

Assets	= Liabilities +	Owner's Equity		
Cash + Office Equipment	Accounts Payable	Capital	, + Revenue − Expenses	

a. Vance deposited $20,000 in a bank account in the name of the business.
b. Paid the office rent for the month, $840, Ck. No. 1001 (Rent Expense).
c. Bought supplies for cash, $775, Ck. No. 1002 (Supplies Expense).
d. Bought office equipment on account from Espino Equipment, $9,180.
e. Bought a computer from Wesley Office Outfitters, $1,840, paying $600 in cash and placing the balance on account, Ck. No. 1003.
f. Sold professional services for cash, $2,421 (Professional Fees).

g. Paid on account to Wesley Office Outfitters, a creditor, $900, Ck. No. 1004.
h. Received and paid the bill for utilities, $243, Ck. No. 1005 (Utilities Expense).
i. Paid the salary of the assistant, $990, Ck. No. 1006 (Salary Expense).
j. Sold professional services for cash, $2,515 (Professional Fees).
k. Vance withdrew cash for personal use, $1,250, Ck. No. 1007 (J. Vance, Drawing).

Check Figure

Left side of equals sign total, $30,358

Instructions

1. In the equation, write the owner's name above the term *Capital*.
2. Record the transactions and the balance after each transaction. Identify the account affected when the transaction involves revenue, expenses, or a withdrawal.
3. Write the account totals from the left side of the equals sign and add them. Write the account totals from the right side of the equals sign and add them. If the two totals are not equal, first check the addition and subtraction. If you still cannot find the error, reanalyze each transaction.

P.O. 1,2,3,4

Problem 1-2B On July 1 of this year, R. Green established the Green Rehab Clinic. The organization's account headings are presented below. Transactions completed during the month of July follow.

Assets			= Liabilities +		Owner's Equity	
Cash +	Office Equipment	+ Professional Equipment	Accounts Payable	Capital	, + Revenue − Expenses	

a. Green deposited $15,000 in a bank account in the name of the business.
b. Paid the office rent for the month, $1,100, Ck. No. 2001 (Rent Expense).
c. Bought supplies for cash, $275, Ck. No. 2002 (Supplies Expense).
d. Bought professional equipment on account from Rehab Equipment Company, $14,200 (Professional Equipment).
e. Bought office equipment from Hi-Tech Computers, $1,870, paying $870 in cash and placing the balance on account, Ck. No. 2003.
f. Sold professional services for cash, $3,280 (Professional Fees).
g. Paid on account to Hi-Tech Computers, a creditor, $500, Ck. No. 2004.
h. Received and paid the bill for utilities, $283, Ck. No. 2005 (Utilities Expense).
i. Paid the salary of the assistant, $1,000, Ck. No. 2006 (Salary Expense).
j. Sold professional services for cash, $3,725 (Professional Fees).
k. Green withdrew cash for personal use, $1,600, Ck. No. 2007 (R. Green, Drawing).

Check Figure

Cash, $16,377

Instructions

1. In the equation, write the owner's name above the term *Capital*.
2. Record the transactions and the balance after each transaction. Identify the account affected when the transaction involves revenue, expenses, or a withdrawal.
3. Write the account totals from the left side of the equals sign and add them. Write the account totals from the right side of the equals sign and add them. If the two totals are not equal, first check the addition and subtraction. If you still cannot find the error, reanalyze each transaction.

P.O. 1,2,3,4

Problem 1-3B S. Delaney, a graphic artist, opened a studio for her professional practice on August 1. The account headings are presented below. Transactions completed during the month follow.

Assets				= Liabilities +	Owner's Equity	
Cash +	Prepaid Insurance +	Office Equipment +	Photo Equipment	Accounts Payable	Capital	, + Revenue − Expenses

a. Delaney deposited $15,500 in a bank account in the name of the business.
b. Bought office equipment on account from Stark Equipment Company, $4,120.
c. Delaney invested her personal photographic equipment, $6,260. (Increase the account Photo Equipment and increase the account S. Delaney, Capital.)
d. Paid the rent for the month, $500, Ck. No. 1000 (Rent Expense).
e. Bought supplies for cash, $345, Ck. No. 1001 (Supplies Expense).
f. Bought insurance for two years, $820, Ck. No. 1002.
g. Sold graphic services for cash, $2,985 (Professional Fees).
h. Paid the salary of the part-time assistant, $500, Ck. No. 1003 (Salary Expense).
i. Received and paid the bill for telephone service, $73, Ck. No. 1004 (Telephone Expense).
j. Paid cash for minor repairs to graphics equipment, $86, Ck. No. 1005 (Repair Expense).
k. Sold graphic services for cash, $2,936 (Professional Fees).
l. Paid on account to Stark Equipment Company, a creditor, $520, Ck. No. 1006.
m. Delaney withdrew cash for personal use, $1,000, Ck. No. 1007 (S. Delaney, Drawing).

Check Figure

Right side of equals sign total, $28,777

Instructions

1. In the equation, write the owner's name above the term *Capital.*
2. Record the transactions and the balance after each transaction. Identify the account affected when the transaction involves revenue, expenses, or a withdrawal.
3. Write the account totals from the left side of the equals sign and add them. Write the account totals from the right side of the equals sign and add them. If the two totals are not equal, first check the addition and subtraction. If you still cannot find the error, reanalyze each transaction.

P.O. 1,2,3,4

Problem 1-4B On March 1 of this year, B. Gelmond established Gelmond Catering Service. The account headings are presented below. Transactions completed during the month follow.

Assets					= Liabilities +	Owner's Equity	
Cash +	Accounts Receivable +	Prepaid Insurance +	Truck +	Equipment	Accounts Payable	Capital	, + Revenue − Expenses

a. Gelmond deposited $16,500 in a bank account in the name of the business.
b. Bought a truck from Kerry Motors for $19,490, paying $2,500 in cash and placing the balance on account, Ck. No. 500.

c. Bought catering equipment on account from Fernandez Company, $2,850.
d. Paid the rent for the month, $620, Ck. No. 501 (Rent Expense).
e. Sold catering services for cash for the first half of the month, $2,420 (Catering Income).
f. Bought supplies for cash, $180, Ck. No. 502 (Supplies Expense).
g. Bought insurance for the truck for one year, $400, Ck. No. 503.
h. Received and paid the heating bill, $104, Ck. No. 504 (Utilities Expense).
i. Received a bill from Anson Gas and Lube for gas and oil for the truck, $108 (Gas and Oil Expense).
j. Sold catering services on account, $2,824 (Catering Income).
k. Sold catering services for cash for the remainder of the month, $2,520 (Catering Income).
l. Paid the salary of the assistant, $1,120, Ck. No. 505 (Salary Expense).
m. Gelmond withdrew cash for personal use, $1,550, Ck. No. 506 (B. Gelmond, Drawing).

Check Figure

Cash, $14,966

Instructions

1. In the equation, write the owner's name above the term *Capital.*
2. Record the transactions and the balance after each transaction. Identify the account affected when the transaction involves revenue, expenses, or a withdrawal.
3. Write the account totals from the left side of the equals sign and add them. Write the account totals from the right side of the equals sign and add them. If the two totals are not equal, first check the addition and subtraction. If you still cannot find the error, reanalyze each transaction.

Citigroup, Inc. is a very large, global company consisting of many different financial services. These include banking (for example, Citibank), credit cards (for example, VISA®), and investment advising or "wealth management" (for example, the Smith Barney brokerage firm). In July 2005, Citigroup completed its sale of Travelers Life & Annuity, along with substantially all of Citigroup's international insurance businesses, to MetLife, Inc. for $10.830 billion in cash and $1.0 billion in other assets. Such large sales are governed by the Federal Securities and Exchange Commission (SEC). If you go to the SEC website, you can find a report about this sale: **http://sec.gov/Archives/edgar/data/831001/000104746906002377/ a2167745z10-k.htm#06NYC1891_1**. Page 2 tells about Citigroup's business. The Citigroup, Inc. financial statements for the year ended December 31, 2005, begin on page 103 of the report. After completing this chapter you will be able to find key information in this document—and in fact, you'll know how to record such sales for your own business. At the end of the chapter you will find further discussion and questions related to this sale.

Performance Objectives

After you have completed this chapter, you will be able to do the following:

1. Determine balances of T accounts having entries recorded on both sides of the accounts.

2. Present the fundamental accounting equation with the T account form, and label the plus and minus sides.

3. Present the fundamental accounting equation with the T account form, and label the debit and credit sides.

4. Record directly in T accounts a group of business transactions involving changes in asset, liability, owner's equity, revenue, and expense accounts for a service business.

5. Prepare a trial balance.

6. Prepare (a) an income statement, (b) a statement of owner's equity, and (c) a balance sheet.

7. Recognize the effect of transpositions and slides on account balances.

We introduced the fundamental accounting equation as *Assets = Liabilities + Owner's Equity*. We also discussed the recording of transactions involving two other classifications of accounts: *Revenue* and *Expenses*. With the addition of Revenue and Expenses, the fundamental accounting equation was brought up to its full size of five account classifications. There are only five classifications; so, as far as you go in accounting—whether you are dealing with a small, one-owner business or a large corporation—there will be these five major classifications of accounts.

In this chapter, we will record the same transactions in T account form and prove the equality of both sides of the fundamental accounting equation. We will do this using a trial balance, discussed later in this chapter.

THE T ACCOUNT FORM

So far, we have recorded business transactions in a column arrangement. For example, the Cash account column in the books of Cline's Computer Clinic is shown below.

Cash Account Column

Transaction	**(a)**	82,000
Transaction	**(b)**	−64,000
Balance		18,000
Transaction	**(d)**	−6,000
Balance		12,000
Transaction	**(f)**	+3,520
Balance		15,520
Transaction	**(g)**	−900
Balance		14,620
Transaction	**(i)**	−480
Balance		14,140
Transaction	**(l)**	−1,800
Balance		12,340
Transaction	**(m)**	−320
Balance		12,020
Transaction	**(n)**	−340
Balance		11,680
Transaction	**(o)**	−2,980
Balance		8,700
Transaction	**(p)**	−620
Balance		8,080
Transaction	**(q)**	+850
Balance		8,930
Transaction	**(r)**	+6,020
Balance		14,950
Transaction	**(s)**	−3,000
		11,950

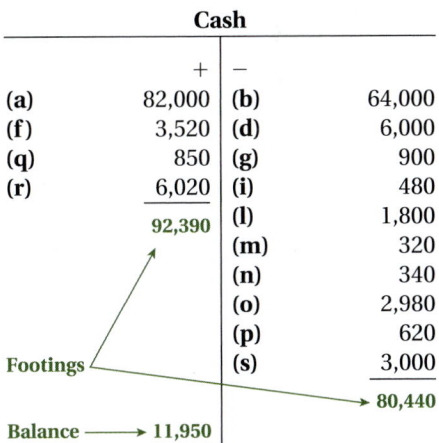

Cash

	+		−	
(a)	82,000	(b)		64,000
(f)	3,520	(d)		6,000
(q)	850	(g)		900
(r)	6,020	(i)		480
	92,390	(l)		1,800
		(m)		320
		(n)		340
		(o)		2,980
		(p)		620
		(s)		3,000
				80,440

Footings

Balance ⟶ 11,950

As an introduction to the recording of transactions, the column arrangement had the following advantages:

1. **In the process of analyzing the transaction, you**
   a. Recognized the need to determine which accounts are involved.
   b. Determined the classification of the accounts involved.
   c. Decided whether the transaction resulted in an increase or a decrease in each of these accounts.

2. **You further realized that, after each transaction had been recorded, the two sides of the fundamental accounting equation were in balance. In other words, the total of one side of the accounting equation equaled the total of the other side.**

Now, instead of recording transactions in a column for each account, we will use a **T account form** for each account. *The T account form has the advantage of providing two sides for each account; one side is used to record increases in the account, and the other side is used to record decreases.*

OBJECTIVE 1

Determine balances of T accounts having entries recorded on both sides of the accounts.

After we record a group of transactions in a T account, we add both sides and record the totals in small, pencil-written figures called **footings**. Next, we subtract one footing from the other to determine the balance of the account. For the Cash account, shown previously, the balance is $11,950 ($92,390 − $80,440).

We now record the balance on the side of the account having the larger footing, which, with a few minor exceptions, is the plus (+) side. The plus side of a T account is the side that represents the **normal balance** of that account. The normal balance may, however, fall on either the left or the right side of an account, depending on what type of account it is. To review, we presented the T account for Cash; Cash is classified as an asset, and all assets look like the following T account:

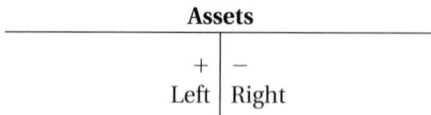

However, **not all classifications of accounts have the increase side on the left.**

Recall that we placed revenue and expenses under the umbrella of owner's equity. Revenue increases owner's equity, and expenses decrease owner's equity. The T accounts for this situation are as follows:

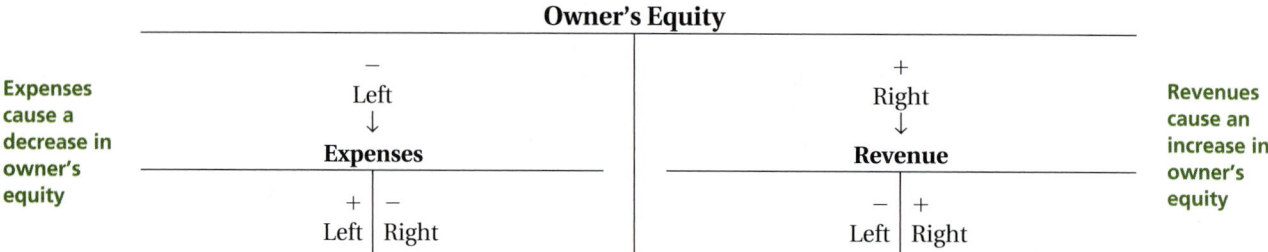

Increases in owner's equity are recorded on the right side of the account. Because revenue increases owner's equity, additions to revenue are also recorded on the right side.

Decreases in owner's equity are recorded on the left side of the account. Because expenses decrease owner's equity, additions to expenses are also recorded on the left side.

Using the five classifications of accounts, the fundamental accounting equation looks like this:

$$\text{Assets} = \text{Liabilities} + \overbrace{\underbrace{\text{Owner's Equity}}_{\text{Capital} + \text{Revenue} - \text{Expenses}}}$$

REMEMBER!

The entry for a business transaction may include any combination of pluses and minuses: pluses and pluses, pluses and minuses, or minuses and minuses.

Because revenue and expenses appear separately in the income statement, we will stretch out the equation to include them as separate headings, as shown here:

$$\text{Assets} = \text{Liabilities} + \text{Capital} + \text{Revenue} - \text{Expenses}$$

We can now restate the equation with the T account forms and plus and minus signs for each account classification:

Assets	=	**Liabilities**	+	**Owner's Equity**	+	**Revenue**	−	**Expenses**
+ | −		− | +		− | +		− | +		+ | −
Left | Right		Left | Right		Left | Right		Left | Right		Left | Right

OBJECTIVE 2

Present the fundamental accounting equation with the T account form, and label the plus and minus sides.

Before we go on, let us point out the increase, or plus, side of each account classification. You can recognize these in the accounting equation using T accounts.

Assets   The *left* side is the *increase* side.
Liabilities   The *right* side is the *increase* side.
Owner's Equity   The *right* side is the *increase* side.
Revenue   The *right* side is the *increase* side.
Expenses   The *left* side is the *increase* side.

Because revenue is an addition to owner's equity, the placement of the plus and minus signs is the same as for owner's equity. On the other hand, because expenses are treated as deductions from owner's equity, the placement of the plus and minus signs is reversed. We will use this form of the fundamental accounting equation throughout the remainder of the text.

Your accounting background up to this point has taught you to analyze business transactions to determine which accounts are involved and to recognize that each amount should be recorded as either an increase or a decrease in these accounts. Now the recording process becomes a simple matter of knowing which side of the T accounts should be used to record increases and which should be used to record decreases. **Generally, you will not be using the minus side of the revenue and expense accounts, since transactions involving revenue and expense accounts usually result in increases in these accounts.** An exception to this statement is where errors have been made and require correction. Let's now add the last element to the T account before we record the familiar Cline's Computer Clinic transactions.

THE T ACCOUNT FORM WITH DEBITS AND CREDITS

OBJECTIVE 3

Present the fundamental accounting equation with the T account form, and label the debit and credit sides.

The left side of a T account is called the **debit** side; the right side is called the **credit** side. The T accounts representing the accounting equation now contain both the signs and the words *Debit* and *Credit*. There are only five classifications of accounts. These classifications are contained in the fundamental accounting equation:

Assets	=	Liabilities	+	Owner's Equity	+	Revenue	−	Expenses
+ −		− +		− +		− +		+ −
Debit Credit		Debit Credit		Debit Credit		Debit Credit		Debit Credit

The following table summarizes debits and credits and how they are affected by increases and decreases. **The critical rule to remember is that the amount placed on the debit side of one or more accounts MUST equal the amount placed on the credit side of another account or accounts.**

Debits Signify		Credits Signify	
Increases in	Assets Drawing Expenses	Decreases in	Assets Drawing Expenses
Decreases in	Liabilities Capital Revenue	Increases in	Liabilities Capital Revenue

Debit is always the left side of the account, and credit is always the right side of the account. The + or −, however, changes with the type of account.

Before we begin recording, notice the new T account below the Capital account, Drawing. Recall that the Capital account is increased when amounts are invested and decreased when amounts are taken out.

Capital

−	+
Debit	Credit
	Amounts invested

Drawing

+	−
Debit	Credit
Amounts withdrawn	

We reserve the minus or debit side of the Capital account for permanent withdrawals, those made when the owner decides to reduce the size of the business permanently or when a net loss forces such a reduction. This concept is best illustrated by showing the Drawing T account under the umbrella of the Capital T account.

Capital

–	+
Debit	Credit

Drawing

+	–
Debit	Credit

RECORDING BUSINESS TRANSACTIONS IN T ACCOUNTS

OBJECTIVE 4

Record directly in T accounts a group of business transactions involving changes in asset, liability, owner's equity, revenue, and expense accounts for a service business.

Our task now is to learn how to record business transactions in the T account form. First, let's review the steps in analyzing a business transaction.

1. **Decide which accounts are involved.**
2. **Classify the accounts involved** (asset, liability, capital, revenue, expense).
3. **Decide if the accounts involved are increased or decreased.**
4. **Decide which accounts are debited and which accounts are credited.**
5. **Check to see if the equation is in balance after the transaction has been recorded.**

For example, let's analyze the first transaction of the Cline's Computer Clinic transactions using this five-step process. To formulate the entry, you must be able to visualize the fundamental accounting equation in the form of T accounts. With that in mind, the first transaction is as follows:

In transaction (a), Cline deposited $82,000 in a bank account in the name of the business. This transaction results in an increase to Cash with a debit and an increase in the Capital account with a credit.

1. **Decide which accounts are involved.** The two accounts involved are Cash and R. P. Cline, Capital.
2. **Classify the accounts involved (asset, liability, capital, revenue, expense).** Cash is an asset and R. P. Cline, Capital, is an owner's equity account.
3. **Decide if the accounts involved are increased or decreased.** Cash is being deposited in the bank account, an increase to Cash. The owner has invested that cash in the business and has increased R. P. Cline, Capital.
4. **Write the transaction as a debit to one account (or accounts) and a credit to another account (or accounts).** Since Cash is an asset and Cash is increased, Cash is debited. We now need an offsetting credit. R. P. Cline, Capital, is an owner's equity account and is increased. R. P. Cline, Capital, is credited. You now have a debit equal to a credit.
5. **Check:** There is at least one account debited and at least one account credited, *and* the total amount(s) debited equal the total amount(s) credited. **You now have a debit equal to a credit, an $82,000 debit to Cash and an $82,000 credit to R. P. Cline, Capital.**

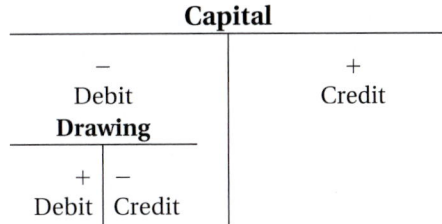

Stores such as this bike shop classify revenue accounts for each service activity—sales, repairs, and rentals. They may also classify expense accounts separately.

The resulting transaction in T account form follows:

	Cash			**R. P. Cline, Capital**	
	+	–		–	+
	Debit	Credit		Debit	Credit
(a)	82,000			**(a)**	82,000

In transaction (b), Cline's Computer Clinic bought equipment, paying cash, $64,000. This transaction results in an increase to Equipment with a debit and a decrease to Cash with a credit.

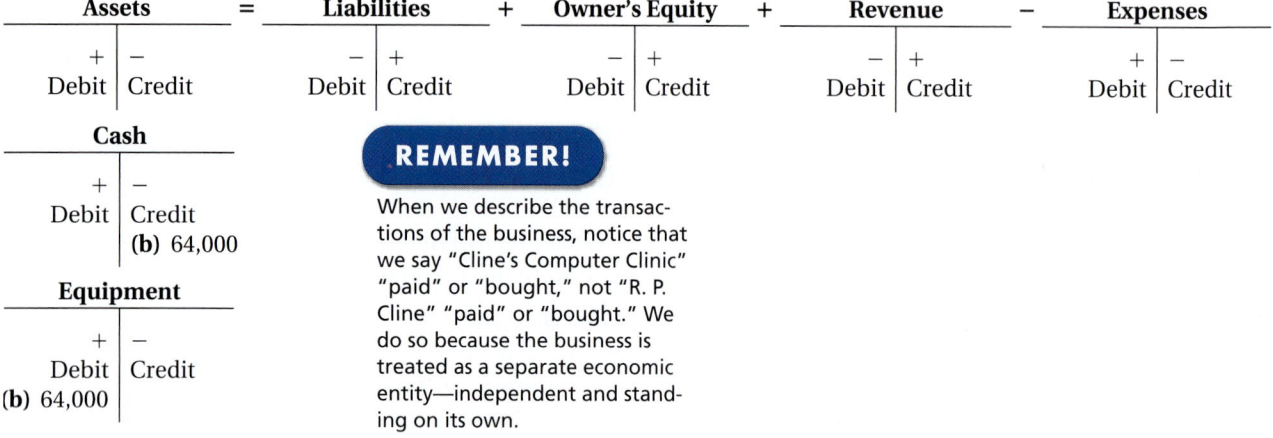

REMEMBER!

When we describe the transactions of the business, notice that we say "Cline's Computer Clinic" "paid" or "bought," not "R. P. Cline" "paid" or "bought." We do so because the business is treated as a separate economic entity—independent and standing on its own.

In transaction (c), Cline's Computer Clinic bought equipment on account from Surgo Products, $10,000. This transaction results in an increase to Equipment with a debit and an increase to Accounts Payable with a credit and is shown in T accounts as follows:

Assets	=	Liabilities	+	Owner's Equity	+	Revenue	−	Expenses
+ | −		− | +		− | +		− | +		+ | −
Debit | Credit		Debit | Credit		Debit | Credit		Debit | Credit		Debit | Credit

Equipment	Accounts Payable
+ | −	− | +
Debit | Credit	Debit | Credit
(c) 10,000 |	| (c) 10,000

In transaction (d), Cline's Computer Clinic paid Surgo Products, a creditor, $6,000. This transaction results in a decrease to Cash with a credit and a decrease to Accounts Payable with a debit.

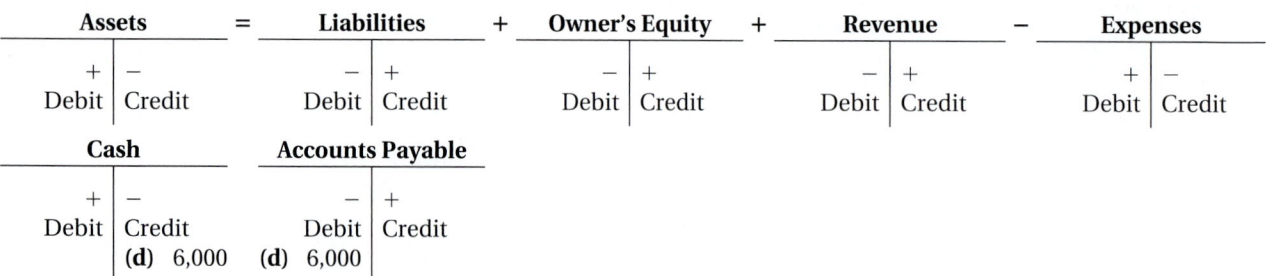

In transaction (e), R. P. Cline invests her personal computer in the business with a fair market value of $6,200.

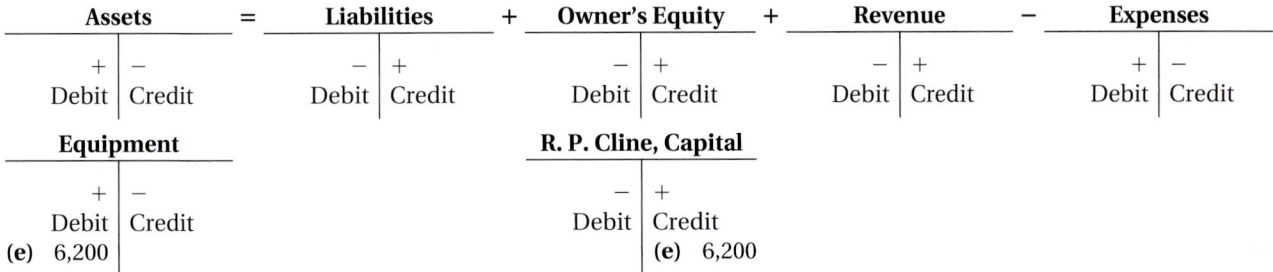

Assets	=	Liabilities	+	Owner's Equity	+	Revenue	−	Expenses
+ | −		− | +		− | +		− | +		+ | −
Debit | Credit		Debit | Credit		Debit | Credit		Debit | Credit		Debit | Credit

Equipment

+	−
Debit	Credit
(e) 6,200	

R. P. Cline, Capital

−	+
Debit	Credit
	(e) 6,200

Here is a restatement of the accounts after recording transactions (a) through (e). To test your understanding of the process, trace through the recording of each transaction and describe what happened in the transaction. Footings or subtotals (remember, always write the footings smaller than the entries and in pencil) are required to compute the balances of the accounts. The balances are written in the accounts on the side with the larger total.

Assets	=	Liabilities	+	Owner's Equity	+	Revenue	−	Expenses
+ | −		− | +		− | +		− | +		+ | −
Debit | Credit		Debit | Credit		Debit | Credit		Debit | Credit		Debit | Credit

Cash

+	−
Debit	Credit
(a) 82,000	**(b)** 64,000
	(d) 6,000
	70,000
Bal. 12,000	

Accounts Receivable

+	−
Debit	Credit

Prepaid Insurance

+	−
Debit	Credit

Equipment

+	−
Debit	Credit
(b) 64,000	
(c) 10,000	
(e) 6,200	
Bal. 80,200	

Accounts Payable

−	+
Debit	Credit
(d) 6,000	**(c)** 10,000
	Bal. 4,000

R. P. Cline, Capital

−	+
Debit	Credit
	(a) 82,000
	(e) 6,200
	Bal. 88,200

R. P. Cline, Drawing

+	−
Debit	Credit

Income from Services

−	+
Debit	Credit

REMEMBER!

The normal balance of an account classification is on the plus side.

FYI

The T account is not only a learning tool; it will serve you well as a problem-solving device when you need to analyze a transaction prior to recording it—manually or on a computer.

Wages Expense

+	−
Debit	Credit

Rent Expense

+	−
Debit	Credit

Supplies Expense

+	−
Debit	Credit

Advertising Expense

+	−
Debit	Credit

Utilities Expense

+	−
Debit	Credit

Let's pause to see if the two sides of the equation are equal by listing the balances of the accounts:

Account Name	Accounts with Normal Balances on the Left or Debit Side	Accounts with Normal Balances on the Right or Credit Side
	Assets Drawing Expenses	Liabilities Capital Revenue
Cash	$12,000	
Equipment	80,200	
Accounts Payable		$ 4,000
R. P. Cline, Capital		88,200
	$92,200	$92,200

In transaction (f), Cline's Computer Clinic sold services for cash, $3,520. This transaction results in an increase to Cash with a debit and an increase to Income from Services with a credit.

Assets	=	Liabilities	+	Owner's Equity	+	Revenue	−	Expenses
+ | −		− | +		− | +		− | +		+ | −
Debit | Credit		Debit | Credit		Debit | Credit		Debit | Credit		Debit | Credit

Cash		Income from Services
+ | −		− | +
Debit | Credit		Debit | Credit
(f) 3,520		(f) 3,520

In transaction (g), Cline's Computer Clinic paid rent for the month, $900. This transaction results in an increase to Rent Expense with a debit and a decrease to Cash with a credit.

Assets	=	Liabilities	+	Owner's Equity	+	Revenue	−	Expenses
+ | −		− | +		− | +		− | +		+ | −
Debit | Credit		Debit | Credit		Debit | Credit		Debit | Credit		Debit | Credit

Cash		Rent Expense
+ | −		+ | −
Debit | Credit		Debit | Credit
(g) 900		(g) 900

In transaction (h), Cline's Computer Clinic bought CD-R recordable compact discs and holders, manuals, and invoice forms for $870 on account from Freeman Company. This transaction results in an increase to Supplies Expense with a debit and an increase to Accounts Payable with a credit.

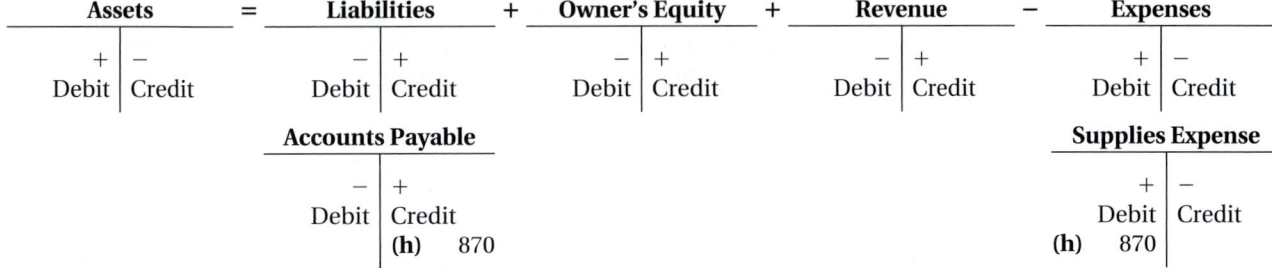

In transaction (i), Cline's Computer Clinic bought a one-year liability insurance policy, $480. This transaction results in an increase to Prepaid Insurance with a debit and a decrease to Cash with a credit.

Assets	=	Liabilities	+	Owner's Equity	+	Revenue	−	Expenses
+ | −		− | +		− | +		− | +		+ | −
Debit | Credit		Debit | Credit		Debit | Credit		Debit | Credit		Debit | Credit

Cash

+	−
Debit	Credit
	(i) 480

Prepaid Insurance

+	−
Debit	Credit
(i) 480	

In transaction (j), Cline's Computer Clinic received a bill for newspaper advertising from the *Daily*, $340. This results in an increase to Advertising Expense with a debit and an increase to Accounts Payable with a credit.

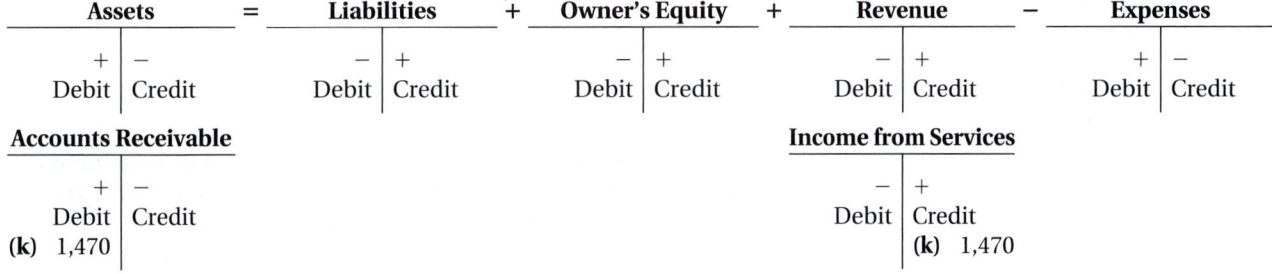

In transaction (k), Cline's Computer Clinic sold services on account to Computer Makeovers, $1,470. This results in an increase to Accounts Receivable with a debit and an increase to Income from Services with a credit.

Assets	=	Liabilities	+	Owner's Equity	+	Revenue	−	Expenses
+ | −		− | +		− | +		− | +		+ | −
Debit | Credit		Debit | Credit		Debit | Credit		Debit | Credit		Debit | Credit

Accounts Receivable

+	−
Debit	Credit
(k) 1,470	

Income from Services

−	+
Debit	Credit
	(k) 1,470

In transaction (l), Cline's Computer Clinic paid on account to Surgo Products, $1,800. This transaction results in a decrease to Accounts Payable with a debit and a decrease to Cash with a credit.

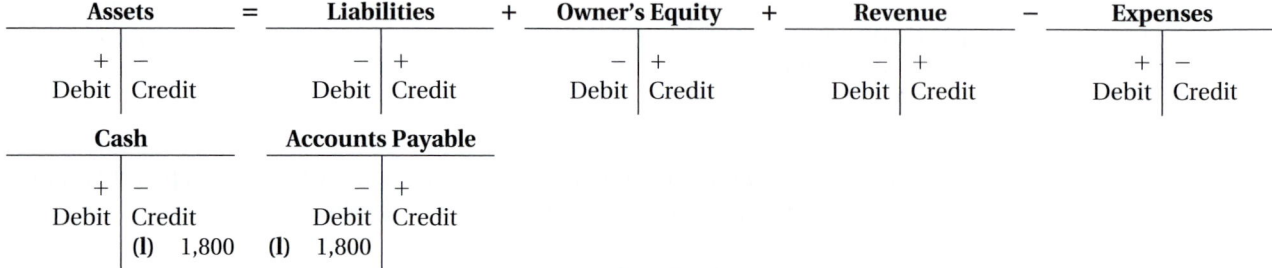

In transaction (m), Cline's Computer Clinic received and paid the electric bill, $320. The result of this transaction is an increase to Utilities Expense with a debit and a decrease to Cash with a credit.

Assets	=	Liabilities	+	Owner's Equity	+	Revenue	−	Expenses
+ | −		− | +		− | +		− | +		+ | −
Debit | Credit		Debit | Credit		Debit | Credit		Debit | Credit		Debit | Credit

Cash

+	−
Debit	Credit
	(m) 320

Utilities Expense

+	−
Debit	Credit
(m) 320	

In transaction (n), Cline's Computer Clinic paid on account to the *Daily*, $340. This transaction results in a decrease to Accounts Payable with a debit and a decrease to Cash with a credit.

Assets	=	Liabilities	+	Owner's Equity	+	Revenue	−	Expenses
+ | −		− | +		− | +		− | +		+ | −
Debit | Credit		Debit | Credit		Debit | Credit		Debit | Credit		Debit | Credit

Cash

+	−
Debit	Credit
	(n) 340

Accounts Payable

−	+
Debit	Credit
(n) 340	

In transaction (o), Cline's Computer Clinic paid the wages of the part-time employee, $2,980. This transaction results in an increase to Wages Expense with a debit and a decrease to Cash with a credit.

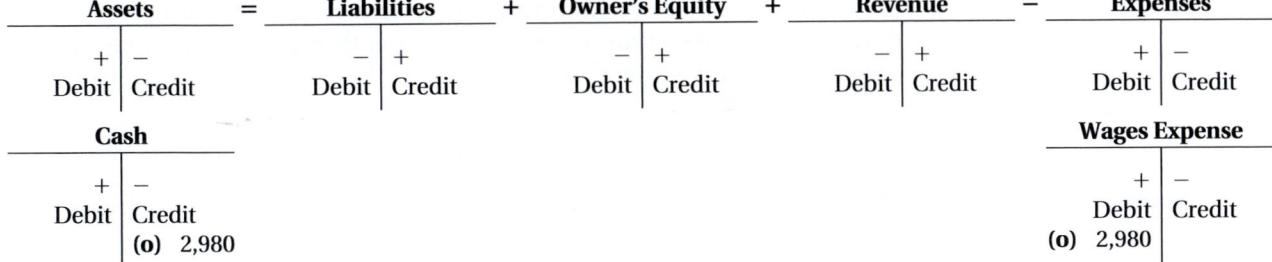

In transaction (p), Cline's Computer Clinic bought additional equipment from Surgo Products, $3,520, paying $620 in cash and placing the balance on account. This transaction results in an increase to Equipment with a debit, an increase to Accounts Payable with a credit, and a decrease to Cash with a credit. This is called a **compound entry**; that is, more than one debit or more than one credit is recorded.

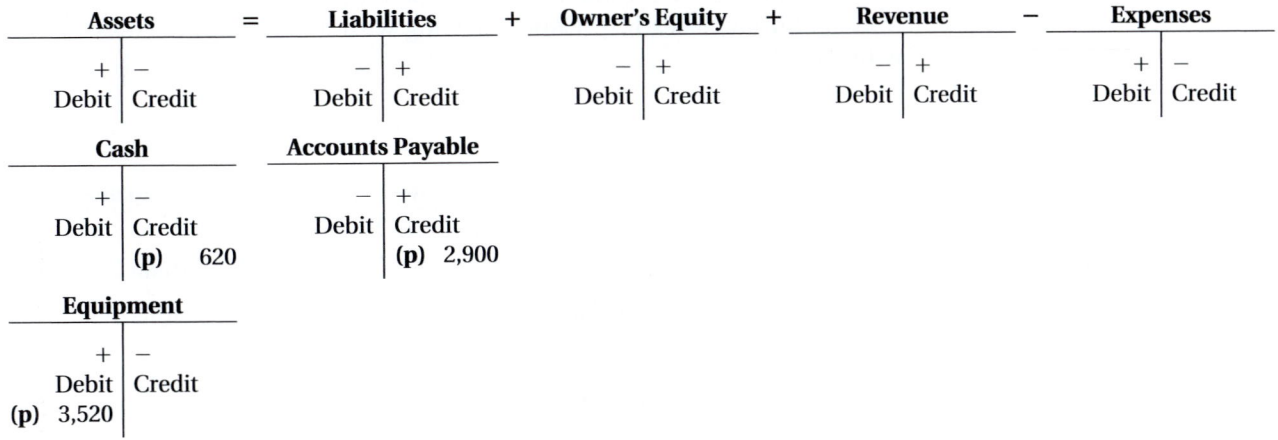

In transaction (q), Cline's Computer Clinic received cash from Computer Makeovers on account, $850. This transaction results in an increase to Cash with a debit and a decrease to Accounts Receivable with a credit.

Assets	=	Liabilities	+	Owner's Equity	+	Revenue	−	Expenses
+ | −		− | +		− | +		− | +		+ | −
Debit | Credit		Debit | Credit		Debit | Credit		Debit | Credit		Debit | Credit

Cash

+	−
Debit	Credit
(q) 850	

Accounts Receivable

+	−
Debit	Credit
	(q) 850

In transaction (r), Cline's Computer Clinic sold services for cash, $6,020. This transaction results in an increase to Cash with a debit and an increase to Income from Services with a credit.

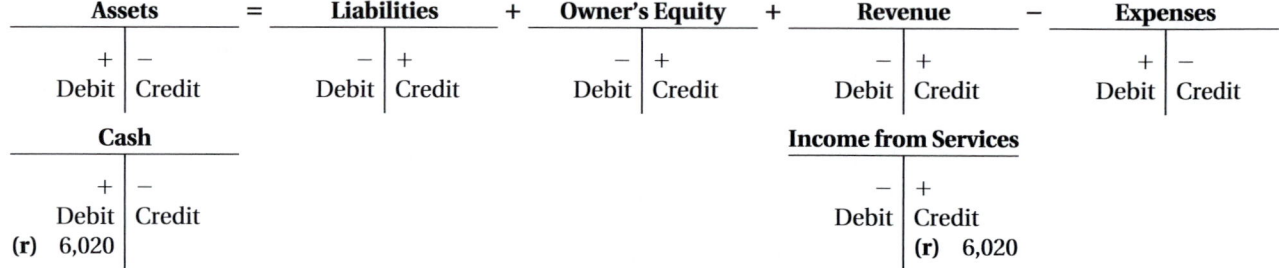

In transaction (s), R. P. Cline withdrew cash for her personal use, $3,000. This transaction increases R. P. Cline, Drawing with a debit and decreases Cash with a credit.

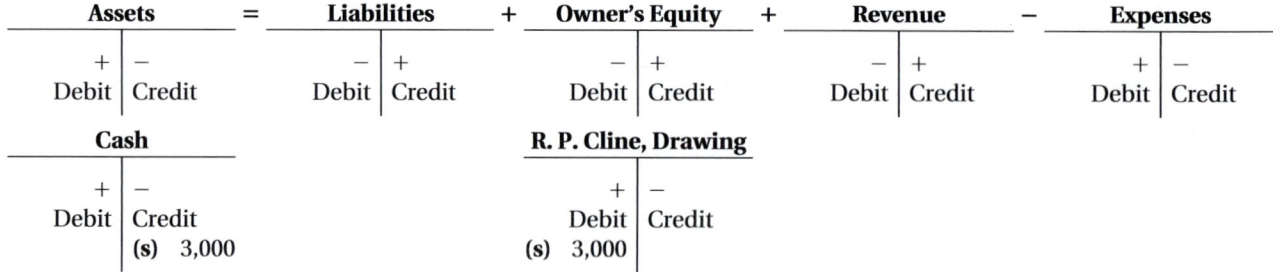

The Drawing account is used to record temporary decreases in Owner's Equity. The owner takes money out of the business for his or her living expenses hoping that the withdrawals will be offset by net income. If, instead, the owner permanently reduces his or her investment in the business, the Capital account is debited.

Summary of Transactions

FYI

Traditionally, accountants use the abbreviations Dr. for Debit and Cr. for Credit.

The following T accounts show the transactions as they are ordinarily recorded. Footings are shown in color. You will notice that the balance of each account is normally on the plus side. Note that, in recording expenses, you place the entries only on the plus, or debit, side. Also, in recording revenue, you place the entries only on the plus, or credit, side.

Assets	=	Liabilities	+	Owner's Equity	+	Revenue	−	Expenses
+ | −		− | +		− | +		− | +		+ | −
Debit | Credit		Debit | Credit		Debit | Credit		Debit | Credit		Debit | Credit

Cash

+		−	
(a)	82,000	(b)	64,000
(f)	3,520	(d)	6,000
(q)	850	(g)	900
(r)	6,020	(i)	480
	92,390	(l)	1,800
		(m)	320
		(n)	340
		(o)	2,980
		(p)	620
		(s)	3,000
			80,440

Bal. 11,950

Accounts Receivable

+		−	
(k)	1,470	(q)	850

Bal. 620

Prepaid Insurance

+		−
(i)	480	

Equipment

+		−
(b)	64,000	
(c)	10,000	
(e)	6,200	
(p)	3,520	

Bal. 83,720

Accounts Payable

−		+	
(d)	6,000	(c)	10,000
(l)	1,800	(h)	870
(n)	340	(j)	340
	8,140	(p)	2,900
			14,110

Bal. 5,970

R. P. Cline, Capital

−		+	
		(a)	82,000
		(e)	6,200
		Bal. 88,200	

R. P. Cline, Drawing

+		−
(s)	3,000	

Income from Services

−		+	
		(f)	3,520
		(k)	1,470
		(r)	6,020
		Bal. 11,010	

Wages Expense

+		−
(o)	2,980	

Rent Expense

+		−
(g)	900	

Supplies Expense

+		−
(h)	870	

Advertising Expense

+		−
(j)	340	

Utilities Expense

+		−
(m)	320	

FYI

A memory tool that helps some students to memorize debits and credits in T accounts is the trial balance equation $A + D + E = L + C + R$.

THE TRIAL BALANCE

OBJECTIVE 5

Prepare a trial balance.

You can now prepare a trial balance by simply recording the balances of the T accounts in two columns. The **trial balance** is a listing of account balances in two columns—one labeled Debit and one labeled Credit—to prove that the total of all the debit balances equals the total of all the credit balances. A trial balance is not considered a financial statement; it is, as the name implies, a trial run by the accountant to prove that the total of the debit balances equals the total of the credit balances. This is evidence of the equality of the two sides of the fundamental accounting equation. The accountant must prove that the accounts are in balance before preparing the company's financial statements.

Cline's Computer Clinic
Trial Balance
June 30, 20—

Column headings identify information in each column

ACCOUNT NAME	DEBIT					CREDIT				
Cash ——————— *Accounts listed*	11	9	5	0	00					
Accounts Receivable *in order of the*		6	2	0	00					
Prepaid Insurance *chart of accounts*		4	8	0	00					
Equipment	83	7	2	0	00					
Accounts Payable						5	9	7	0	00
R. P. Cline, Capital						88	2	0	0	00
R. P. Cline, Drawing	3	0	0	0	00					
Income from Services						11	0	1	0	00
Wages Expense	2	9	8	0	00					
Rent Expense		9	0	0	00					
Supplies Expense		8	7	0	00					
Advertising Expense		3	4	0	00					
Utilities Expense *Single underline beneath*		3	2	0	00					
figures to be added	105	1	8	0	00	105	1	8	0	00

Dollar signs not used on a trial balance

Double underline beneath column totals

FIGURE 1

In preparing a trial balance, shown in Figure 1, record the accounts with balances in the same order as they are listed in the chart of accounts.

- Assets
- Liabilities
- Owner's Equity
- Revenue
- Expenses

The normal balance of each account is on its plus side. Remember that when there is more than one entry in an account, we record the totals in footings and subtract one footing from the other to determine the balance. **Record this balance on the side of the account with the larger footing.** (Here we record the Drawing account balance in the debit column because it has a debit balance. We do not deduct Drawing from the Capital account when we prepare the trial balance.) The following table indicates where each of the account balances would normally be shown in a trial balance.

	Trial Balance	
Account Titles	**Left or Debit Balances**	**Right or Credit Balances**
Assets	Assets	
Liabilities		Liabilities
Capital		Capital
Drawing	Drawing	
Revenue		Revenue
Expenses	Expenses	
Totals	XXXX XX	XXXX XX

MAJOR FINANCIAL STATEMENTS

Earlier we listed summarizing as one of the five basic tasks of the accounting process. To accomplish this task, accountants use financial statements. A **financial statement** is a report prepared by accountants to summarize the financial affairs of a business for managers and others, both inside and outside the business.

Note that the headings of all financial statements require three lines:

1. Name of the company (or owner, if there is no company name)
2. Title of the financial statement
3. Period of time covered by the financial statement, or its date

Also, note that dollar signs are placed at the head of each column and with each total. Single lines (drawn with a ruler) are used to show that the figures above are being added or subtracted. Lines should be drawn across the entire column. A double line is drawn under the final total in a column.

The financial statements are all interconnected. The income statement must be prepared first, followed by the statement of owner's equity, and then the balance sheet.

The Income Statement

The **income statement** shows total revenue minus total expenses, which yields the net income or net loss. The income statement shows the results of business transactions involving revenue and expense accounts—in other words, how the business has performed—over a period of time, usually a month or a year. When total revenue exceeds total expenses over the period, the result is **net income**, or profit. If the total revenue is less than the total expenses, the result is a **net loss**.

The income statement in Figure 2 shows the results of the first month of operations for Cline's Computer Clinic.

For convenience, the individual expense amounts are recorded in the first amount column. Thus, the total expenses ($5,410) may be subtracted directly from the total revenue ($11,010).

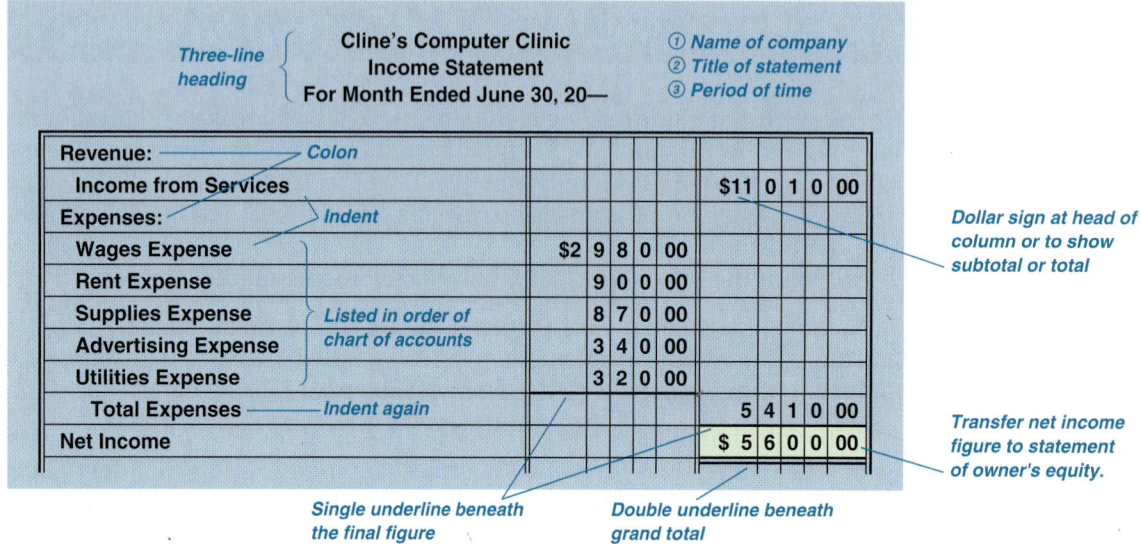

FIGURE 2

FYI

Compare the third line of the income statement heading with the third line of the balance sheet heading shown in Figure 4.

The income statement covers a period of time, whereas the balance sheet has only one date: the end of the financial period. On the income statement, the revenue for June, less the expenses for June, shows the results of operations—a net income of $5,600. To the accountant, the term *net income* means "clear" income, or profit after all expenses have been deducted. Expenses are usually listed in the same order as in the chart of accounts. Revenue and expense amounts are taken directly from the trial balance. If total expenses were greater than the revenue, then a net loss would be recorded.

The Statement of Owner's Equity

OBJECTIVE 6b

Prepare a statement of owner's equity.

We said that revenue and expenses are connected with owner's equity through the financial statements. Now let's demonstrate this by a statement of owner's equity, shown in Figure 3, which the accountant prepares after he or she has determined the net income or net loss on the income statement.

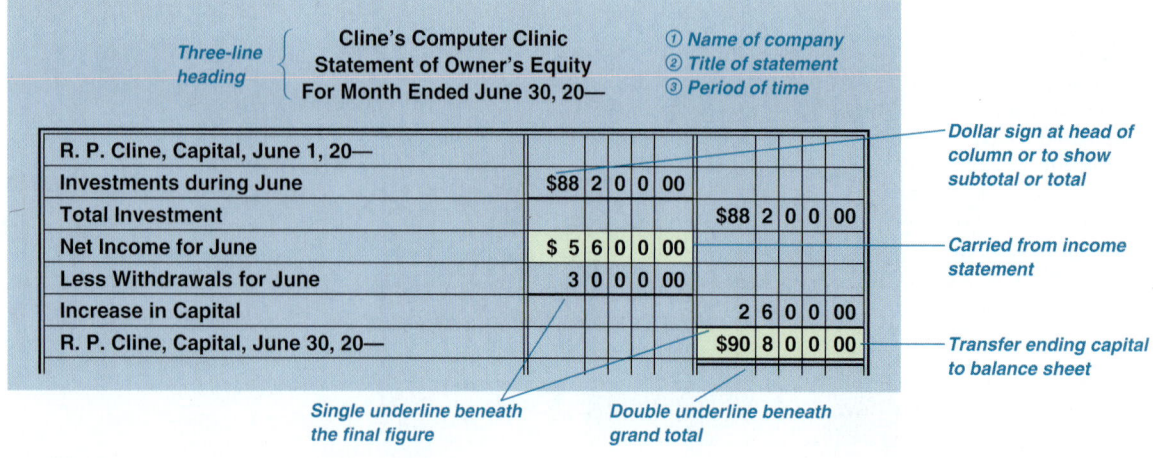

FIGURE 3

The **statement of owner's equity** shows how—and why—the owner's equity, or Capital account, has changed over a stated period of time (in this case, the month of June). Notice the third line in the heading of Figure 3. It shows that the statement of owner's equity covers the same period of time as the income statement.

Now look at the body of the statement. The first line shows the zero balance in the Capital account at the beginning of the month. An investment of $88,200 was made by R. P. Cline: total investment $88,200. Two items have affected owner's equity during the month: A net income of $5,600 was earned, and the owner withdrew $3,000. To perform the calculations smoothly, move to the left-hand column and list these two items, subtracting withdrawals from net income ($5,600 − $3,000 = $2,600). The difference ($2,600) represents an increase in capital. This difference is placed in the right-hand column to be added directly to the total capital. The final figure is the ending amount in the owner's Capital account.

The Balance Sheet

After preparing the statement of owner's equity, we prepare a balance sheet. The **balance sheet** shows the **financial position**, or the condition of a business's assets offset by claims against them as of one particular date. It summarizes the balances of the asset, liability, and owner's equity accounts on a given date (usually the end of a month or year). The balance sheet is, thus, like a snapshot—a picture of the financial condition of the business at that particular date.

The ending capital balance in the balance sheet is taken from the statement of owner's equity. Note that the accounts appear in the same order as in the chart of accounts.

In the **report form** of the balance sheet, the elements in the accounting equation are presented one on top of the other. A balance sheet prepared on June 30 for Cline's Computer Clinic in report form would look like Figure 4.

REMEMBER!

The income statement is prepared first, so that the net income can be recorded in the statement of owner's equity. The statement of owner's equity is prepared second, so that the ending amount of capital can be recorded in the balance sheet, which is prepared last.

OBJECTIVE 6c

Prepare a balance sheet.

Cline's Computer Clinic
Balance Sheet
June 30, 20—

Assets											
Cash	$11	9	5	0	00						
Accounts Receivable		6	2	0	00						
Prepaid Insurance		4	8	0	00						
Equipment	83	7	2	0	00						
Total Assets						$96	7	7	0	00	
Liabilities											
Accounts Payable						$ 5	9	7	0	00	
Owner's Equity											
R. P. Cline, Capital						90	8	0	0	00	— Carried from statement of owner's equity
Total Liabilities and Owner's Equity						$96	7	7	0	00	

FIGURE 4

ERRORS EXPOSED BY THE TRIAL BALANCE

If the debit and credit columns in a trial balance are not equal, then it is evident that we have made an error. Possible mistakes include the following:

- Making errors in arithmetic, such as errors in adding the trial balance columns or in finding the balances of the accounts.
- Recording only half an entry, such as a debit without a corresponding credit, or vice versa.
- Recording both halves of the entry on the same side, such as two debits rather than a debit and a credit.
- Recording one or more amounts incorrectly.

Procedure for Locating Errors

Suppose that you are in a business situation where you have recorded transactions for a month in the account books, and the accounts do not balance. To save yourself time, you need to have a definite procedure for tracking down the errors. The best method is to do everything in reverse, as follows:

- Look at the pattern of balances to see if a normal balance was placed in the wrong column on the trial balance.
- Re-add the trial balance columns.
- Check the transferring of the figures from the accounts to the trial balance.
- Verify the footings and balances of the accounts.

As an added precaution, form the habit of verifying all addition and subtraction as you go along. You can thus correct many mistakes *before* the time comes to prepare a trial balance.

FYI

Even if debits equal credits, this does not necessarily mean that there were no errors in the recording of the transactions. For example, a transaction may have been forgotten, it may have been included twice, or it may have been written for an incorrect amount.

Although using a computer greatly reduces the occurrence of addition and subtraction errors, it does not prevent the occurrence of other kinds of errors, such as recording transactions incorrectly.

When the trial balance totals do not balance, the difference might indicate that you forgot to record half of an entry in the accounts. For example, if the difference in the trial balance totals is $20, you may have recorded $20 on the debit side of one account without recording $20 on the credit side of another account.

Another possibility is to divide the difference by 2; this may provide a clue that you accidentally recorded half an entry twice. For example, if the difference in the trial balance is $600, you may have recorded $300 on the debit side of one account and an additional $300 on the debit side of another account. Look for a transaction that involved $300 and then see if you have recorded both a debit and a credit. By knowing which transactions to check, you can save a lot of time.

Transpositions and Slides

OBJECTIVE 7

Recognize the effect of transpositions and slides on account balances.

If the difference is evenly divisible by 9, the discrepancy may be either a transposition or a slide. A **transposition** means that the digits have been transposed, or switched around, when the numbers were copied from one place to another. For example, one transposition of digits in 916 can be written as 619:

Correct Number	Number Copied	Difference	Difference Divided by 9
916	619	297	297 ÷ 9 = 33

A **slide** is an error in placing the decimal point; in other words, a slide in the decimal point. For example, $27,000 could be inadvertently written as $2,700:

Correct Number	Number Copied	Difference	Difference Divided by 9
27,000	2,700	24,300	24,300 ÷ 9 = 2,700
64,000	6,400	57,600	57,600 ÷ 9 = 6,400

Or the error may be a combination of a transposition and a slide, as when $450 is written as $54:

Correct Number	Number Copied	Difference	Difference Divided by 9
450	54	396	396 ÷ 9 = 44

Again, the difference is evenly divisible by 9 (with no remainder).

CHAPTER REVIEW

Online Study Center
ACE the test!

Review of Performance Objectives

1. **Determine balances of T accounts having entries recorded on both sides of the accounts.**

   Add the amounts listed on each side of the T account. The totals are called footings. To get the account balance, subtract the total of the smaller side from the total of the larger side. Record the account balance on the larger side.

2. Present the fundamental accounting equation with the T account form, and label the plus and minus sides.

Assets	=	Liabilities	+	Owner's Equity	+	Revenue	−	Expenses
+ | −		− | +		− | +		− | +		+ | −
Left | Right		Left | Right		Left | Right		Left | Right		Left | Right

3. Present the fundamental accounting equation with the T account form, and label the debit and credit sides.

Assets	=	Liabilities	+	Owner's Equity	+	Revenue	−	Expenses
+ | −		− | +		− | +		− | +		+ | −
Left | Right		Left | Right		Left | Right		Left | Right		Left | Right
Debit | Credit		Debit | Credit		Debit | Credit		Debit | Credit		Debit | Credit

4. Record directly in T accounts a group of business transactions involving changes in asset, liability, owner's equity, revenue, and expense accounts for a service business.

   The transactions are recorded by first recognizing and classifying the accounts involved. Next, decide whether the accounts involved are increased or decreased, and record the amounts as additions or subtractions in the accounts. The equation must always remain in balance.

5. Prepare a trial balance.

   A trial balance is a list of all account balances in two columns—one labeled Debit and one labeled Credit. The trial balance shows that both sides of the accounting equation are equal. The heading consists of the company name, Trial Balance, and the date.

6. Prepare (a) an income statement, (b) a statement of owner's equity, and (c) a balance sheet.

   (a) An income statement shows the results of operations of a business for a period of time. It includes revenue and expense accounts and reports either a net income or a net loss. (b) A statement of owner's equity shows the activity in the owner's equity, or Capital account, for a period of time. It includes the balance in the Capital account at the beginning of the period plus any additional investments and any increase or decrease in capital as the result of a net income (or a net loss) minus any withdrawals. (c) A balance sheet shows the financial condition of a business at a particular date in time. It summarizes the balances of the asset, liability, and owner's equity accounts on a given date.

7. Recognize the effect of transpositions and slides on account balances.

   An error in a trial balance may be a transposition or a slide. The clue is whether the difference in account balances or trial balance totals is evenly divisible by 9. With a transposition, some digits have been switched around. With a slide, the decimal point has been recorded in the wrong place.

Glossary

Balance sheet A financial statement showing the financial position of an organization on a given date, such as June 30 or December 31. The balance sheet lists the balances in the asset, liability, and owner's equity accounts. (51)

Compound entry A transaction that requires more than one debit or more than one credit to be recorded. (45)

Credit The right side of a T account; to credit is to record an amount on the right side of a T account. Credits represent increases in liability, capital, or revenue accounts and decreases in asset, drawing, or expense accounts. (38)

Debit The left side of a T account; to debit is to record an amount on the left side of a T account. Debits represent increases in asset, drawing, or expense accounts and decreases in liability, capital, or revenue accounts. (38)

Financial position The resources or assets owned by an organization at a point in time, offset by the claims against those resources and owner's equity; shown on a balance sheet. (51)

Financial statement A report prepared by accountants that summarizes the financial affairs of a business. (49)

Footings The totals of each side of a T account, recorded in small, pencil-written figures. (36)

Income statement A financial statement showing the results of business transactions involving revenue and expense accounts over a period of time. (49)

Net income The result when total revenue exceeds total expenses over a period of time. (49)

Net loss The result when total expenses exceed total revenue over a period of time. (49)

Normal balance The plus side of a T account. (36)

Report form The form of the balance sheet in which assets are placed at the top and liabilities and owner's equity are placed below. (51)

Slide An error in placing the decimal point in a number. (53)

Statement of owner's equity A financial statement showing the activity in the owner's equity, or Capital account, over the financial period. (51)

T account form A form of account shaped like the letter T in which increases and decreases in the account may be recorded. One side of the T is for entries on the debit or left side. The other side of the T is for entries on the credit or right side. (36)

Transposition An error that involves interchanging, or switching around, digits during the recording of a number. (53)

Trial balance A list of all account balances to prove that the total of all the debit balances equals the total of all the credit balances. (47)

QUESTIONS, EXERCISES, AND CASES

Discussion Questions

1. Explain how a trial balance and a balance sheet differ.
2. Explain why the term *debit* doesn't always mean "increase" and why the term *credit* doesn't always mean "decrease."
3. What are footings in accounting?
4. How are the three financial statements shown in this chapter connected?
5. What is a compound entry?
6. List two reasons why the debits and credits in the trial balance might not balance.
7. Give an example of a slide and an example of a transposition. Explain how you might decide whether an error is a slide or a transposition.
8. What do we mean when we say that revenue and expense accounts are under the "umbrella" of owner's equity?

Exercises

P.O. 4

Describe transactions.

Exercise 2-1 During the first month of operation, Garza's Craft Supply recorded the following transactions. Describe what has happened in each of the transactions (a) through (k).

Cash	
(a) 3,200	(b) 435
(k) 1,025	(c) 98
	(e) 75
	(g) 900
	(i) 92
	(j) 325

Accounts Receivable	
(h) 615	

Equipment	
(f) 3,720	
(g) 1,835	

Accounts Payable	
(d) 280	
(g) 935	

C. S. Garza, Capital	
	(a) 3,200
	(f) 3,720

C. S. Garza, Drawing	
(j) 325	

Income from Services	
	(h) 615
	(k) 1,025

Rent Expense	
(b) 435	

Utilities Expense	
(i) 92	

Advertising Expense	
(c) 98	

Supplies Expense	
(d) 280	

Miscellaneous Expense	
(e) 75	

P.O. 2,3

Draw T accounts and record the plus and minus signs and debit and credit.

Exercise 2-2 On a sheet of paper, set up the fundamental accounting equation with T accounts under each of the five account classifications, noting plus and minus signs and debit and credit on the appropriate sides of each account. Under each of the five classifications, set up T accounts, again with the correct plus and minus signs and debit and credit, for each of the following accounts of Bevin Engine Repair.

Cash
Accounts Receivable
Equipment
Accounts Payable
A. Bevin, Capital
A. Bevin, Drawing

Income from Services
Rent Expense
Wages Expense
Utilities Expense
Supplies Expense
Miscellaneous Expense

P.O. 2,3,4

Record transactions in T accounts.

Exercise 2-3 R. Casey operates Casey's Cards. The company has the following chart of accounts:

Assets

Cash
Accounts Receivable
Prepaid Insurance
Display Equipment
Van
Office Equipment

Liabilities

Accounts Payable

Owner's Equity

R. Casey, Capital
R. Casey, Drawing

Revenue

Income from Services

Expenses

Wages Expense
Gas Expense
Utilities Expense
Supplies Expense
Advertising Expense

Using the chart of accounts above, record the following transactions in pairs of T accounts. Give the T account to be debited first and the account to be credited to the right. Show debit and credit and plus and minus signs. (Example: Received and paid the bill for the month's rent, $480.)

Rent Expense			Cash	
+	−		+	−
Dr.	Cr.		Dr.	Cr.
480				480

a. Received and paid the electric bill, $85.
b. Bought supplies on account, $245.
c. Paid for insurance for one year, $400.
d. Made a payment on account to a creditor, $555.
e. Received and paid the telephone bill, $96.
f. Sold services on account, $975.
g. Received and paid the gasoline bill for the van, $108.
h. Received cash on account from customers, $1,138.
i. Casey withdrew cash for personal use, $500.

P.O. 4

Classify accounts.

Exercise 2-4 List the classification of each of the following accounts as A (asset), L (liability), OE (owner's equity), R (revenue), or E (expense). Write Debit or Credit to indicate the increase side, the decrease side, and the normal balance side.

Account	Classification	Increase Side	Decrease Side	Normal Balance Side
0. Cash	A	Debit	Credit	Debit
1. Wages Expense				
2. Equipment				
3. J. Roth, Capital				
4. Service Revenue				
5. J. Roth, Drawing				
6. Accounts Receivable				
7. Rent Expense				
8. Fees Earned				
9. Accounts Payable				

P.O. 5

Prepare a corrected trial balance.

Exercise 2-5 At Your Service, owned by L. Mays, hired a new bookkeeper who is not entirely familiar with the process of preparing a trial balance. All the accounts have normal balances. Find the errors, and prepare a corrected trial balance for December 31 of this year.

At Your Service
Trial Balance
December 31, 20—

ACCOUNT NAME	DEBIT	CREDIT
Accounts Receivable		9 5 0 0 00
Cash	3 3 0 0 00	
Accounts Payable		8 6 0 0 00
Equipment	26 0 0 0 00	
L. Mays, Capital		26 6 0 0 00
L. Mays, Drawing		1 8 0 0 00
Prepaid Insurance		1 4 0 0 00
Income from Services		33 0 0 0 00
Rent Expense		3 6 0 0 00
Supplies Expense	1 7 0 0 00	
Utilities Expense	3 5 0 0 00	
Wages Expense	17 4 0 0 00	
	51 9 0 0 00	84 5 0 0 00

P.O. 5,6

Prepare a trial balance and financial statements.

Exercise 2-6 During the first month of operations, Hahn Modeling Agency recorded transactions in T account form. Prepare a trial balance dated March 31 of this year. Prepare an income statement, statement of owner's equity, and balance sheet.

Cash			
Bal.	8,100	**(b)**	350
(c)	8,500	**(d)**	1,600
(i)	7,580	**(f)**	175
		(g)	3,400
		(h)	2,200

Accounts Receivable	
(e)	2,600

Office Furniture	
(b)	350

Office Equipment	
(a)	2,800

Accounts Payable			
		(a)	2,800
		(j)	82

R. Hahn, Capital			
		Bal.	8,100

R. Hahn, Drawing	
(h)	2,200

Modeling Fees			
		(c)	8,500
		(e)	2,600
		(i)	7,580

Salary Expense	
(g)	3,400

Rent Expense	
(d)	1,600

Utilities Expense	
(f)	175

Supplies Expense	
(j)	82

P.O. 7

Determine the effects of errors.

Exercise 2-7 The following errors were made in journalizing transactions. In each case, calculate the amount of the error and indicate whether the debit or the credit column of the trial balance will be understated or overstated.

	Amount of Difference	Debit or Credit Column of Trial Balance Understated or Overstated
0. Example: A $149 debit to Accounts Receivable was not recorded.	$149	Debit column understated
a. A $42 debit to Supplies Expense was recorded as $420.		
b. A $155 debit to Accounts Payable was recorded twice.		
c. A $179 debit to Prepaid Insurance was not recorded.		
d. A $65 credit to Cash was not recorded.		
e. A $190 debit to Equipment was recorded twice.		
f. A $57 debit to Utilities Expense was recorded as $75.		

P.O. 7

Determine the effects of errors.

Exercise 2-8 Which of the following errors would cause a trial balance to have unequal totals? As a result of the errors, which accounts are overstated (by how much) or understated (by how much)?

a. A purchase of office equipment for $480 was recorded as a debit to Office Equipment for $48 and a credit to Cash for $48.

b. A payment of $260 to a creditor was debited to Accounts Receivable and credited to Cash for $260 each.

c. A purchase of supplies for $145 was recorded as a debit to Equipment for $145 and a credit to Cash for $145.

d. A payment of $86 to a creditor was recorded as a debit to Accounts Payable for $86 and a credit to Cash for $68.

LINKS TO ACCOUNTING

Let's review what you've learned in this chapter and apply it to Citigroup, Inc. as you look at the SEC report. Recall the steps in analyzing a business transaction in Performance Objective 4. Citigroup's sale of its insurance companies affected asset accounts, which included an $8.444 billion credit (decrease) to Ownership Interest in the insurance companies, a $10.830 billion debit (increase) to Cash, and a $1 billion debit (increase) to Investments (the other assets received were shares of MetLife stock). Notice that those debits and credits are not equal ($10.830 + $1 does not equal $8.444). The difference is a $3.386 billion gain on the sale. That gain is similar to an increase (credit) to revenue. Now the total amount of debits and the total amount of credits in this transaction are equal. Recall the fundamental accounting equation: Assets = Liabilities + Capital + Revenue − Expenses. The accounting equation has remained in balance after the transaction above. Because total debits and total credits are equal, the equation remained in balance.

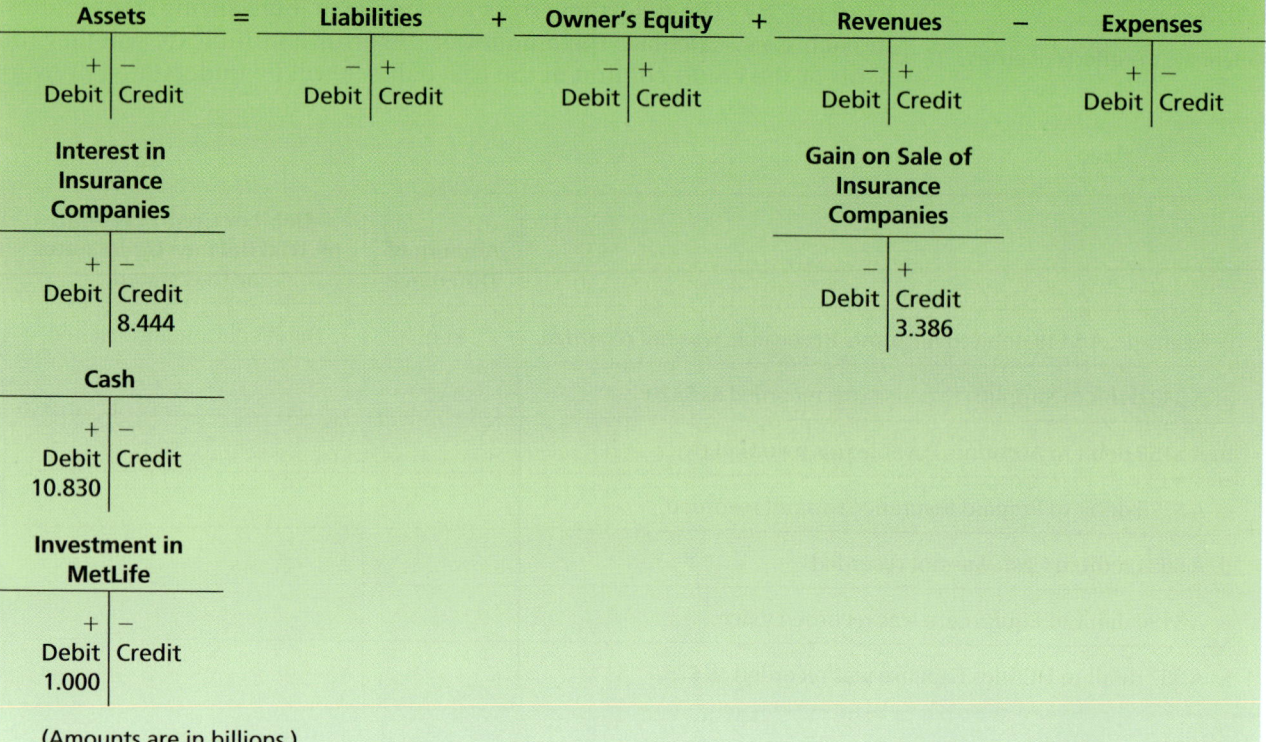

(Amounts are in billions.)

1. Is a trial balance included in the SEC 10-K report? Why or why not?
2. What was Citigroup, Inc.'s Cash and Due From Banks balance for the years ended December 31, 2004, and December 31, 2005? Place these amounts as the beginning and ending balances in a T account for Cash, and then record the sale of the insurance companies in this account. If only one other cash transaction took place during the year, what was the amount, and was it a debit or a credit to Cash?

CONSIDER AND COMMUNICATE

A fellow accounting student has difficulty understanding how the fundamental accounting equation stays in balance when a compound entry with one debit and two credits is recorded. Consider, for example, that a business bought equipment for $7,000, paid $3,000 in cash, and placed the remainder on account.

This means that there are two credits and one debit—one debit and one credit on the left side of the equation and the other credit on the right side of the equation. How does the equation stay in balance?

WHAT'S WRONG WITH THIS PICTURE?

An accounting tutor has drawn the following T accounts for two of her students who are having trouble understanding where the plus and minus signs are placed as well as where the debit and credit go. What would you do to assist these students and their tutor?

Assets	=	Liabilities	+	Owner's Equity	+	Expenses	−	Revenue
+ | −		− | +		− | +		− | +		+ | −
Debit | Credit		Credit | Debit		Credit | Debit		Credit | Debit		Credit | Debit

A QUESTION OF ETHICS

A new bookkeeper can't find the errors that are causing the month-end trial balance for her company to be out of balance. The bookkeeper is too shy to ask for help at the office, so she takes the financial records home and asks her uncle, a retired bookkeeper, to help her locate the errors. Discuss the ethics of the situation in which she has placed herself.

PROBLEM SET A

For additional help, see the demonstration problem at the beginning of each chapter in your Working Papers.

P.O. 1,2,3,4

Problem 2-1A During February of this year, R. Billand established Billand Shoe Repair. The following asset, liability, and owner's equity accounts are included in the chart of accounts:

Cash	Accounts Payable
Shop Equipment	R. Billand, Capital
Store Equipment	Supplies Expense
Office Equipment	

The following transactions occurred during the month of February:

a. Billand deposited $20,000 cash in a bank account in the name of the business.
b. Bought shop equipment for cash, $1,735, Ck. No. 1000.

c. Bought supplies on account from Melland Company, $225.

d. Bought store shelving on account from Isem Hardware, $650.

e. Bought office equipment from Shreeve's Office Supply, $325, paying $125 in cash and placing the balance on account, Ck. No. 1001.

f. Paid on account to Isem Hardware, a creditor, $250, Ck. No. 1002.

g. Billand invested his personal leather working tools with a fair market value of $700 in the business.

Check Figure

Cash balance, $17,890

Instructions

1. Write the account classifications (Assets, Liabilities, Owner's Equity, Revenue, Expense) in the fundamental accounting equation, as well as the plus and minus signs and Debit and Credit.

2. Write the account names on the T accounts under the classifications, place the plus and minus signs for each T account, and label the debit and credit sides of the T accounts.

3. Record the amounts in the proper positions in the T accounts. Write the letter next to each entry to identify the transaction.

4. Foot and balance accounts.

P.O. 1,2,3,4,5

Problem 2-2A J. Cory established Cory Photo Service during June of this year. The accountant prepared the following chart of accounts:

Assets

Cash
Computer Software
Office Equipment
Neon Sign

Liabilities

Accounts Payable

Owner's Equity

J. Cory, Capital
J. Cory, Drawing

Revenue

Income from Services

Expenses

Advertising Expense
Supplies Expense
Rent Expense
Utilities Expense
Wages Expense
Miscellaneous Expense

The following transactions occurred during the month of June:

a. Cory deposited $20,000 cash in a bank account in the name of the business.

b. Bought office equipment for cash, $850, Ck. No. 1001.

c. Bought computer software from Morrison Computer Center, $640, paying $340 in cash and placing the balance on account, Ck. No. 1002.

d. Paid current month's rent, $850, Ck. No. 1003 (Rent Expense).

e. Sold services for cash, $1,476 (Income from Services).

f. Bought a neon sign from The Sign Company, $1,435, paying $435 in cash and placing the balance on account, Ck. No. 1004.

g. Received bill from *The Daily* for advertising, $745 (Advertising Expense).

h. Bought supplies on account from Central Supply, $660.

i. Received and paid the electric bill, $320, Ck. No. 1005.

j. Paid on account to *The Daily*, a creditor, $745, Ck. No. 1006.

k. Sold services for cash, $3,384.

l. Paid wages to an employee, $830, Ck. No. 1007.

m. Cory invested his personal computer (Office Equipment) with a fair market value of $1,100 in the business.

n. Cory withdrew cash for personal use, $900, Ck. No. 1008.
o. Received and paid the bill for city business license, $55, Ck. No. 1009 (Miscellaneous Expense).

Check Figure

Trial balance total, $27,920

Instructions

1. Record the owner's name in the Capital and Drawing T accounts.
2. Correctly place the plus and minus signs for each T account, and label the debit and credit sides of the accounts.
3. Record the transactions in the T accounts. Write the letter of each entry to identify the transaction.
4. Foot the T accounts and show the balances.
5. Prepare a trial balance, with a three-line heading, dated June 30, 20—.

P.O. 1,2,3,4,5,6

Problem 2-3A Dr. D. Juarez, a physical therapist, opened Juarez Physical Therapy Clinic. His accountant provided the following chart of accounts:

Assets

Cash
Accounts Receivable
Office Equipment
Office Furniture

Liabilities

Accounts Payable

Owner's Equity

D. Juarez, Capital
D. Juarez, Drawing

Revenue

Professional Fees

Expenses

Rent Expense
Salary Expense
Utilities Expense
Miscellaneous Expense

The following transactions occurred during July of this year:

a. Juarez deposited $20,000 in a bank account in the name of the business.
b. Bought filing cabinets on account from Miller Office Supply (Office Equipment), $480.
c. Paid cash for chairs and carpets (Office Furniture) for the waiting room, $955, Ck. No. 1000.
d. Bought a photocopier from Rory's Office Equipment, $560, paying $200 in cash and placing the balance on account, Ck. No. 1001.
e. Received and paid the telephone bill, which included installation charges, $195, Ck. No. 1002.
f. Sold professional services on account, $2,245.
g. Received and paid the bill for the state physical therapy convention, $440, Ck. No. 1003 (Miscellaneous Expense).
h. Received and paid the electric bill, $205, Ck. No. 1004.
i. Received cash on account from credit customers, $930.
j. Paid on account to Miller Office Supply, a creditor, $220, Ck. No. 1005.
k. Paid the office rent for the current month, $845, Ck. No. 1006.
l. Sold consulting services for cash, $1,950.
m. Paid the salary of the receptionist, $850, Ck. No. 1007.
n. Juarez withdrew cash for personal use, $1,500, Ck. No. 1008.

Check Figure

Net Income, $1,660

Instructions

1. Record the owner's name in the Capital and Drawing T accounts.
2. Correctly place the plus and minus signs for each T account, and label the debit and credit sides of the accounts.

3. Record the transactions in the T accounts. Write the letter of each entry to identify the transaction.
4. Foot the T accounts and show the balances.
5. Prepare a trial balance as of July 31, 20—.
6. Prepare an income statement for July 31, 20—.
7. Prepare a statement of owner's equity for July 31, 20—.
8. Prepare a balance sheet as of July 31, 20—.

P.O. 1,2,4,5,6

Problem 2-4A On July 1, K. Rossy opened Rossy's Quick Clean. Rossy's accountant listed the following chart of accounts:

Cash
Prepaid Insurance
Equipment
Furniture and Fixtures
Accounts Payable
K. Rossy, Capital
K. Rossy, Drawing
Laundry Revenue
Wages Expense
Supplies Expense
Rent Expense
Utilities Expense
Miscellaneous Expense

During July, the following transactions were completed:

a. Rossy deposited $18,000 in a bank account in the name of the business.
b. Bought tables and chairs for cash, $625, Ck. No. 1200.
c. Paid the rent for the current month, $750, Ck. No. 1201.
d. Bought washers and dryers from Forbes Equipment, $16,500, paying $4,000 in cash and placing the balance on account, Ck. No. 1202.
e. Bought laundry supplies on account from Wicks Distributors, $515.
f. Sold services for cash, $872.
g. Bought insurance for one year, $475, Ck. No. 1203.
h. Paid on account to Forbes Equipment, a creditor, $500, Ck. No. 1204.
i. Received and paid the electric bill, $238, Ck. No. 1205.
j. Paid on account to Wicks Distributors, a creditor, $225, Ck. No. 1206.
k. Sold services to customers for cash for the second half of the month, $1,015.
l. Received and paid the bill for the business license, $65, Ck. No. 1207 (Miscellaneous Expense).
m. Paid wages to an employee, $900, Ck. No. 1208.
n. Rossy withdrew cash for personal use, $700, Ck. No. 1209.

Check Figure

Net Loss, ($581)

Instructions

1. Record the owner's name in the Capital and Drawing T accounts.
2. Correctly place the plus and minus signs for each T account, and label the debit and credit sides of the accounts.
3. Record the transactions in the T accounts. Write the letter of each entry to identify the transaction.
4. Foot the T accounts and show the balances.
5. Prepare a trial balance as of July 31, 20—.
6. Prepare an income statement for July 31, 20—.
7. Prepare a statement of owner's equity for July 31, 20—.
8. Prepare a balance sheet as of July 31, 20—.

PROBLEM SET B

For additional help, see the demonstration problem at the beginning of each chapter in your Working Papers.

P.O. 1,2,3,4

Problem 2-1B During December of this year, G. Eldridge established Gloria's Gym. The following asset, liability, and owner's equity accounts are included in the chart of accounts:

Cash
Exercise Equipment
Office Equipment
Video Equipment
Accounts Payable
G. Eldridge, Capital
Supplies Expense

During December, the following transactions occurred:

a. Eldridge deposited $25,000 in a bank account in the name of the business.
b. Bought exercise equipment for cash, $8,058, Ck. No. 1001.
c. Bought a printer on account from Horizon Company, $105.
d. Bought a computer (Office Equipment) on account from Cyber Center, $690.
e. Bought supplies on account from Office Needs, $175.
f. Eldridge invested her video equipment with a fair market value of $1,500 in the business.
g. Made a payment to Cyber Center, a creditor, $195, Ck. No. 1002.

Check Figure

Balance of Cash, $16,747

Instructions

1. Write the account classifications (Assets, Liabilities, Owner's Equity, Revenue, Expense) in the fundamental accounting equation, as well as the plus and minus signs and Debit and Credit.
2. Write the account names on the T accounts under the classifications, place the plus and minus signs for each T account, and label the debit and credit sides of the T accounts.
3. Record the amounts in the proper positions in the T accounts. Write the letter next to each entry to identify the transaction.
4. Foot and balance accounts.

P.O. 1,2,3,4,5

Problem 2-2B B. Kim established Computing Needs during November of this year. The accountant prepared the following chart of accounts:

Assets

Cash
Computer Software
Office Equipment
Neon Sign

Liabilities

Accounts Payable

Owner's Equity

B. Kim, Capital
B. Kim, Drawing

Revenue

Income from Services

Expenses

Advertising Expense
Supplies Expense
Rent Expense
Utilities Expense
Wages Expense
Miscellaneous Expense

The following transactions occurred during the month:

a. Kim deposited $25,000 in a bank account in the name of the business.
b. Paid the rent for the current month, $800, Ck. No. 2001.
c. Bought office desks and filing cabinets for cash, $785, Ck. No. 2002.
d. Bought a computer and printer (Office Equipment) from Cyber Computer Center for use in the business, $2,500, paying $1,500 in cash and placing the balance on account, Ck. No. 2003.
e. Bought a neon sign on account from Sign Co., $1,200.
f. Kim invested her personal computer software with a fair market value of $800 in the business.
g. Received a bill from *County News* for newspaper advertising, $275.
h. Sold services for cash, $1,045.
i. Received and paid the electric bill, $245, Ck. No. 2004.
j. Paid on account to *County News,* a creditor, $185, Ck. No. 2005.
k. Sold services for cash, $1,355.
l. Paid the wages to the employee, $725, Ck. No. 2006.
m. Received and paid the bill for the city business license, $55, Ck. No. 2007 (Miscellaneous Expense).
n. Kim withdrew cash for personal use, $750, Ck. No. 2008.
o. Bought printer paper and letterhead stationery on account from Office Suppliers, $108.

Check Figure

Trial balance total, $30,598

Instructions

1. Record the owner's name in the Capital and Drawing T accounts.
2. Correctly place the plus and minus signs for each T account, and label the debit and credit sides of the accounts.
3. Record the transactions in T accounts. Write the letter of each entry to identify the transaction.
4. Foot the T accounts and show the balances.
5. Prepare a trial balance, with a three-line heading, dated November 30, 20—.

P.O. 1,2,3,4,5,6

Problem 2-3B R. Morton, a dentist, opened a clinic in the name of Morton Clinic. Her accountant prepared the following chart of accounts:

Assets

Cash
Accounts Receivable
Office Equipment
Office Furniture

Liabilities

Accounts Payable

Owner's Equity

R. Morton, Capital
R. Morton, Drawing

Revenue

Professional Fees

Expenses

Rent Expense
Salary Expense
Utilities Expense
Miscellaneous Expense

The following transactions occurred during June of this year:

a. Morton deposited $28,000 in a bank account in the name of the business.
b. Bought a facsimile/copier/telephone combination from Maxie's Equipment for $495, paying $100 in cash and placing the balance on account, Ck. No. 1001.

c. Bought waiting room chairs and tables (Office Furniture), paying cash, $1,230, Ck. No. 1002.
d. Bought an intercom system on account from Regal Office Supply (Office Equipment), $275.
e. Received and paid the telephone bill, $108, Ck. No. 1003.
f. Sold professional services on account, $1,294.
g. Received and paid the electric bill, $185, Ck. No. 1004.
h. Received and paid the bill for the Regional Dental Convention, $350, Ck. No. 1005 (Miscellaneous Expense).
i. Sold professional services for cash, $1,765.
j. Paid on account to Regal Office Supply, a creditor, $100, Ck. No. 1006.
k. Paid the rent for the current month, $840, Ck. No. 1007.
l. Paid salary of the receptionist, $700, Ck. No. 1008.
m. R. Morton withdrew cash for personal use, $850, Ck. No. 1009.
n. Received $550 on account from patients who were previously billed.

Check Figure

Net Income, $876

Instructions

1. Record the owner's name in the Capital and Drawing T accounts.
2. Correctly place the plus and minus signs for each T account, and label the debit and credit sides of the accounts.
3. Record the transactions in the T accounts. Write the letter of each entry to identify the transaction.
4. Foot the T accounts and show the balances.
5. Prepare a trial balance as of June 30, 20—.
6. Prepare an income statement for June 30, 20—.
7. Prepare a statement of owner's equity for June 30, 20—.
8. Prepare a balance sheet as of June 30, 20—.

P.O. 1,2,4,5,6

Problem 2-4B On May 1, B. Brego opened Self-Service Laundry. His accountant listed the following chart of accounts:

Cash
Prepaid Insurance
Equipment
Furniture and Fixtures
Accounts Payable
B. Brego, Capital
B. Brego, Drawing
Laundry Revenue
Wages Expense
Supplies Expense
Rent Expense
Utilities Expense
Miscellaneous Expense

During May the following transactions were completed:

a. Brego deposited $25,000 in a bank account in the name of the business.
b. Bought chairs and tables (Furniture and Fixtures) paying cash, $670, Ck. No. 1000.
c. Bought laundry supplies on account from Barnes Supply Company, $325.
d. Paid the rent for the current month, $575, Ck. No. 1001.
e. Bought washing machines and dryers from Lahr Equipment Company, $11,500, paying $3,500 in cash and placing the balance on account, Ck. No. 1002.
f. Sold services for cash for the first half of the month, $925.

g. Bought insurance for one year, $560, Ck. No. 1003.
h. Paid on account to Lahr Equipment Company, a creditor, $700, Ck. No. 1004.
i. Received and paid electric bill, $208, Ck. No. 1005.
j. Sold services for cash for the second half of the month, $835.
k. Paid the wages to the employee, $740, Ck. No. 1006.
l. Brego withdrew cash for his personal use, $500, Ck. No. 1007.
m. Paid on account to Barnes Supply Company, a creditor, $275, Ck. No. 1008.
n. Received and paid bill from the county for sidewalk repair assessment, $280, Ck. No. 1009 (Miscellaneous Expense).

Check Figure

Net Loss, ($368)

Instructions

1. Record the owner's name in the Capital and Drawing T accounts.
2. Correctly place the plus and minus signs for each T account, and label the debit and credit sides of the accounts.
3. Record the transactions in the T accounts. Write the letter of each entry to identify the transaction.
4. Foot the T accounts and show the balances.
5. Prepare a trial balance as of May 31, 20—.
6. Prepare an income statement for May 31, 20—.
7. Prepare a statement of owner's equity for May 31, 20—.
8. Prepare a balance sheet as of May 31, 20—.

3

The General Journal and the General Ledger

LINKS TO ACCOUNTING

How do you keep track of the money you earn and spend? It's an important thing to know. If you were keeping the books of Peyton Manning, quarterback for the Indianapolis Colts in 2004, how would you keep track of what he earns? Or, if you were paying his salary, how would you keep track of what you pay him?

You can check out Manning's salary for 2004 at **http://asp.usatoday.com/ sports/football/nfl/salaries/default.aspx.** As you read along in this chapter and learn how to record transactions such as receiving income and paying salaries, think about how you would record Manning's salary. You will learn, as well, about how these data are used in the process of creating financial statements by posting from the journal to the proper accounts and then preparing a trial balance.

Most professional athletes are not NFL superstars. How much are you likely to earn if you are a professional athlete in your state, but you aren't an NFL superstar? You can find out by going to **http://www. collegegrad.com/salaries/salaries.shtml.** Check out this website to see how much the average professional athlete in your area earns. Keep in mind, no matter how much you earn, you can be financially successful as long as you know how to track and manage your money.

Performance Objectives

After you have completed this chapter, you will be able to do the following:

1. Record a group of transactions pertaining to a service enterprise in a two-column general journal.

2. Post entries from a two-column general journal to general ledger accounts.

3. Prepare a trial balance from the ledger accounts.

4. Correct entries using the manual ruling method.

5. Correct entries using the manual or computerized correcting entry method.

Recall that *recording* is a step in the definition of accounting. Here we introduce the *journal* as the official record of business transactions. We have recorded business transactions as debits and credits to T accounts because, in the process of formulating debits and credits for business transactions, it's easier to visualize these debits and credits as the plus and minus sides of the T accounts involved. **Formulating the appropriate**

transaction debits and credits is the most important element in the accounting process. It represents the very basic foundation of accounting, and all the structure represented by financial statements and other reports is entirely dependent upon it. After determining the debits and credits, the accountant records the transaction in a journal and a ledger.

The initial steps in the accounting process are

1. Record business transactions in a journal.
2. Post entries to accounts in the ledger.
3. Prepare a trial balance.

In this chapter, we present the general journal and the posting procedure.

THE GENERAL JOURNAL

We have seen that an accountant must keep a written record of each transaction. You could record the transactions directly in T accounts; however, only part of the transaction would be listed in each T account. A **journal** is a book in which business transactions are recorded as they happen. In the journal, both the debits and the credits of the entire transaction are recorded in one place. Actually, the journal is a diary for the business, in which you record in day-by-day order all the events involving financial affairs. A journal is called a *book of original entry*. In other words, a transaction is always recorded first in the journal. The process of recording a business transaction in the journal is called **journalizing**. The information about transactions comes from business papers, such as checks, invoices, receipts, letters, and memos. These **source documents** furnish proof (objective evidence) that a transaction has taken place, and they should be identified in the journal entry whenever possible. The basic form of journal is the **two-column general journal**. The term *two-column* refers to the two columns used for debit and credit amounts.

As an example of journalizing business transactions, let's use the transactions for Cline's Computer Clinic. The pages of the journal are numbered in consecutive order. This is the first page, and so we write a 1 in the space for the page number. Also, we must write the date of each transaction. Let's begin with the first entry.

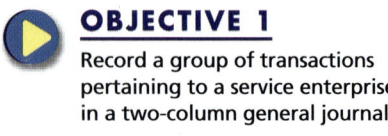

OBJECTIVE 1

Record a group of transactions pertaining to a service enterprise in a two-column general journal.

Transaction (a) June 1: R. P. Cline deposited $82,000 in a bank account in the name of Cline's Computer Clinic. First, we will show the complete journal entry.

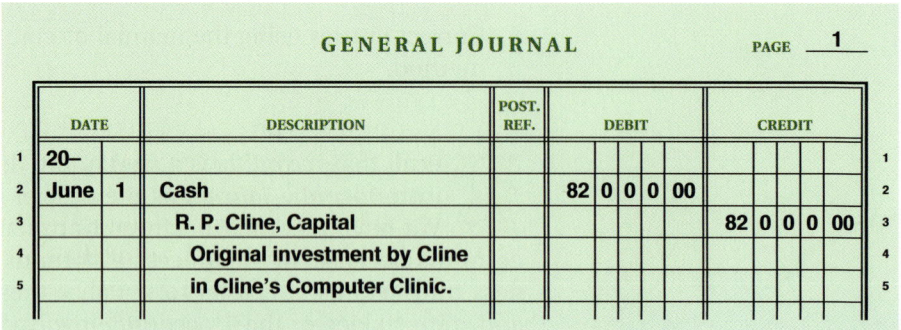

	DATE		DESCRIPTION	POST. REF.	DEBIT	CREDIT	
1	20–						1
2	June	1	Cash		82 0 0 0 00		2
3			R. P. Cline, Capital			82 0 0 0 00	3
4			Original investment by Cline				4
5			in Cline's Computer Clinic.				5

GENERAL JOURNAL   PAGE ___1___

To explain the entry, we break it down line by line. On the first line at the top of the page, we record the page number where indicated. On line one, we record the year in the left part of the Date column. On the second line, we record the month in the left part of the Date column and the day of the month in the right part of the Date column. We don't have to repeat the year and month until we start a new page, or until the year or month changes. (Because our illustrations are separated, however, the month may be repeated to eliminate confusion.)

| | GENERAL JOURNAL | Page number | PAGE 1 |

	DATE	DESCRIPTION	POST. REF.	DEBIT	CREDIT	
1	20–					1
2	June 1	} Date				2
3						3

Decide which accounts should be debited and credited. We do this by first deciding which accounts are involved and whether they are increased or decreased. We then visualize the accounts and their plus and minus sides.

Cash is involved in our example. Cash is an asset because it falls within the definition of "things owned." Cash is increased, and the increase side of Cash is the left or debit side. So we debit Cash $82,000.

R. P. Cline, Capital, is involved. R. P. Cline, Capital, is an owner's equity account because it represents the owner's investment. R. P. Cline, Capital, is increased, and the increase side of Capital is the right or credit side. So we credit R. P. Cline, Capital, $82,000. Let's show these entries by referring to our reliable fundamental accounting equation with the accompanying T accounts:

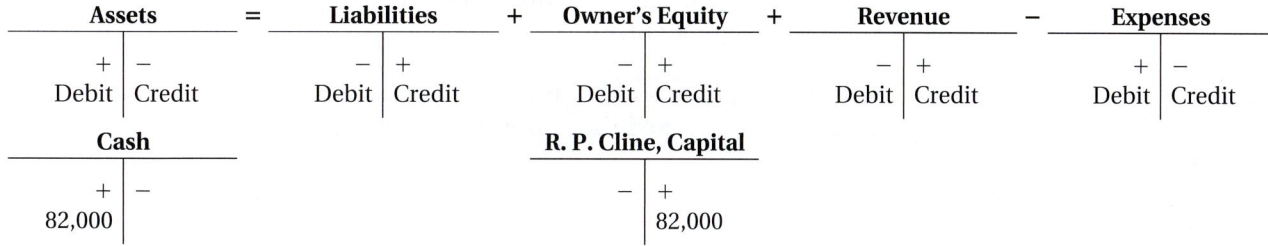

You perform this process mentally. If the transaction is more complicated, draw the T accounts on scratch paper. Using T accounts is the accountant's way of drawing a picture of the transaction. You must get into the T account habit; it will be a great help to you in the future.

Always record the debit part of the entry first. Enter the account title—in this case, Cash—in the Description column. Record the amount—$82,000—in the Debit amount column.

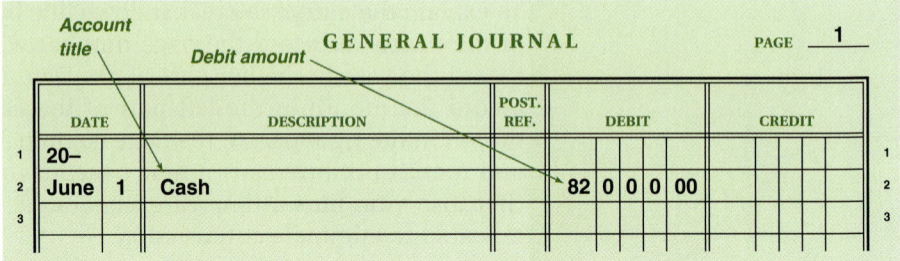

GENERAL JOURNAL PAGE __1__

	DATE		DESCRIPTION	POST. REF.	DEBIT	CREDIT	
1	20–						1
2	June	1	Cash		82 0 0 0 00		2
3							3

FYI

Customarily, accountants don't abbreviate account titles.

Next, record the credit part of the entry. Enter the account title—in this case, R. P. Cline, Capital—on the line below the debit in the Description column, indented about one-half inch. On the same line, write the amount in the Credit column.

GENERAL JOURNAL PAGE __1__

	DATE		DESCRIPTION	POST. REF.	DEBIT	CREDIT	
1	20–						1
2	June	1	Cash		82 0 0 0 00		2
3			R. P. Cline, Capital			82 0 0 0 00	3
4							4
5							5
6							6

Indent the account title that is credited

FYI

The explanation refers to the source document.

You should now write a brief explanation, in which you should refer to business papers, giving such information as check numbers, receipt numbers, or invoice numbers. You may also list names of charge customers or creditors, or terms of payment. Enter the explanation below the credit entry, indented an additional one-half inch.

GENERAL JOURNAL PAGE __1__

	DATE		DESCRIPTION	POST. REF.	DEBIT	CREDIT	
1	20–						1
2	June	1	Cash		82 0 0 0 00		2
3			R. P. Cline, Capital			82 0 0 0 00	3
4			Original investment by Cline				4
5			in Cline's Computer Clinic.				5
6							6

Indent again for the explanation

REMEMBER!

In the transaction, R. P. Cline deposited $82,000 in a bank account in the name of Cline's Computer Clinic.

For an entry in the general journal to be complete, it must contain (1) the date, (2) a debit entry, (3) a credit entry, and (4) an explanation. To anyone thoroughly familiar with the accounts, the explanation may seem quite obvious. Nevertheless, record the explanation as a required, integral part of the entry. To make the journal entries easier to read, leave one blank line between each transaction in your homework.

Transaction (b) June 2: Cline's Computer Clinic bought equipment costing $64,000, paying cash. Decide which accounts are involved. Next, determine which of the five possible classifications each part of the transaction applies to. Visualize the plus and minus signs for each classification. Decide whether the accounts are increased or decreased. When you use T accounts to analyze the transaction, the results are as follows:

Equipment		Cash	
+	–	+	–
Debit	Credit	Debit	Credit
64,000			64,000

Now journalize this analysis below the first transaction. Record the day of the month in the Date column. Remember, you do not have to record the month and year again until the month or year changes or you use a new journal page.

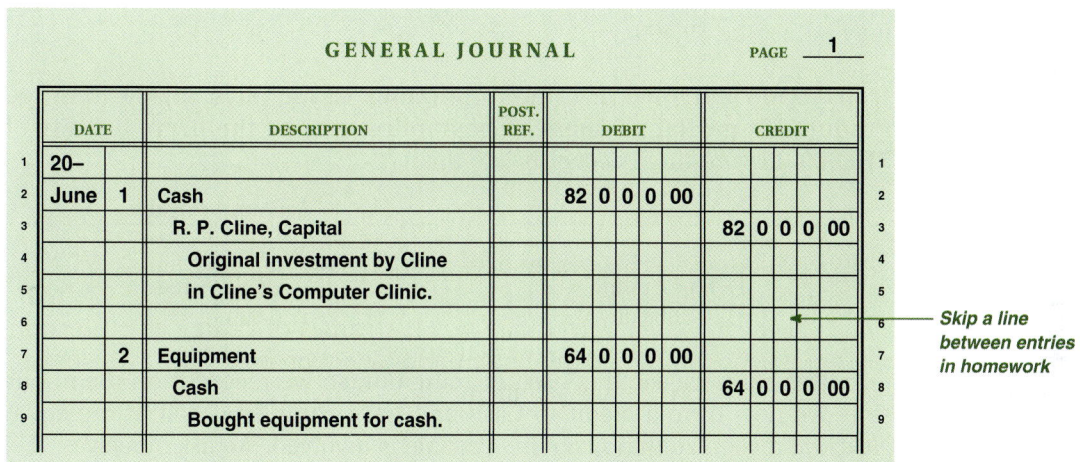

GENERAL JOURNAL   PAGE ___1___

	DATE		DESCRIPTION	POST. REF.	DEBIT	CREDIT	
1	20–						1
2	June	1	Cash		82 0 0 0 00		2
3			R. P. Cline, Capital			82 0 0 0 00	3
4			Original investment by Cline				4
5			in Cline's Computer Clinic.				5
6							6
7		2	Equipment		64 0 0 0 00		7
8			Cash			64 0 0 0 00	8
9			Bought equipment for cash.				9

— Skip a line between entries in homework

Transaction (c) June 3: Cline's Computer Clinic bought equipment costing $10,000 on credit (on account) from Surgo Products. Again start with the T accounts.

Equipment		Accounts Payable	
+	–	–	+
Debit	Credit	Debit	Credit
10,000			10,000

After skipping a line in the journal, record the day of the month and then the entry. In journalizing a transaction involving Accounts Payable, always state the name of the creditor in the explanation. Similarly, in journalizing a transaction involving Accounts Receivable, always state the name of the customer who charged the amount in the explanation.

GENERAL JOURNAL　　PAGE ___1___

	DATE	DESCRIPTION	POST. REF.	DEBIT	CREDIT	
10						10
11	3	Equipment		10 0 0 0 00		11
12		Accounts Payable			10 0 0 0 00	12
13		Bought equipment on				13
14		account from Surgo				14
15		Products.				15

When a business buys an asset, the asset should be recorded at the actual cost (the agreed amount of a transaction). This is called the **cost principle**. For example, suppose that the $10,000 that Cline's Computer Clinic paid for the equipment from Surgo Products was a bargain price, as Surgo Products had been asking $12,500 for the equipment. The day after Cline's Computer Clinic took possession of the equipment, it received an offer of $9,500 from another party, but the offer was declined. Cline's Computer Clinic *should record the cost of the equipment as the actual amount paid in the transaction that occurred,* which is $10,000. This is true even though the fair market value may indeed be $9,500.

Transaction (d) June 4: Cline's Computer Clinic pays $6,000 to Surgo Products as partial payment to be applied against the firm's liability of $10,000. Picture the T accounts like this:

Cash		Accounts Payable	
+	−	−	+
Debit	Credit	Debit	Credit
	6,000	6,000	

In this case, we see that cash is going out, so we record it on the minus side. We now have a credit to Cash and have completed half of the entry. Next, we recognize that Accounts Payable is involved. We ask ourselves, "Do we owe more or less as a result of this transaction?" The answer is "less," so we record it on the minus, or debit, side of the account.

GENERAL JOURNAL　　PAGE ___1___

	DATE	DESCRIPTION	POST. REF.	DEBIT	CREDIT	
16						16
17	4	Accounts Payable		6 0 0 0 00		17
18		Cash			6 0 0 0 00	18
19		Paid Surgo Products				19
20		on account.				20
21						21
22						22
23						23

CAREERS IN YOUR FUTURE

ERICA KENNEDY

Export Development Supervisor for a Global Logistics Company

Without her solid theoretical foundation in accounting fundamentals, Erica Kennedy would not be where she is today. She considers accounting an essential success factor in the business world, one that has provided endless combinations and possibilities for her career.

Erica works for an international global logistics company that has hundreds of offices in over fifty countries—each using the same accounting software, unique to the industry, that is programmed in-house and tailored for the different fiscal and legal requirements of each country. Within the company, Erica has moved from accounting, where she performed internal audits and wrote internal control procedures, to analyzing software issues and finding solutions. She focuses on the company's export software. Branches all over the world report software issues to her; she then supervises a team that tackles the software questions and finds solutions to them.

Erica has carried her accounting and software skills into this new endeavor. She will tell you that accounting trained her for her current position because she has to be very methodical, detail oriented, accurate, and thorough as she moves up in the high-tech world.

Erica also has taught accounting students at a community college. She urged her students to complete all homework, develop productive habits, and learn to write well—writing is essential in business. She also stressed to her students the importance of understanding and making journal entries. She finds that knowing about financial statement preparation and financial statement analysis are two other extremely valuable skills. What other accounting skills might be helpful in Erica's current job?

"I loved geology, but only liked accounting. On the other hand, I felt accounting would provide a better opportunity . . . to start working professionally. And because of accounting, I get to do what I love to do—teach people how to use accounting systems around the world."

Now let's list the transactions for June for Cline's Computer Clinic with the date of each transaction. The journal entries are illustrated in Figures 1, 2, and 3.

June
1   Cline invests $82,000 cash in her new business.
2   Buys equipment costing $64,000, paying cash.
3   Buys equipment costing $10,000 on credit from Surgo Products.
4   Pays $6,000 to Surgo Products to be applied against the firm's liability of $10,000.
4   Cline invests her personal equipment valued at $6,200 in her new business.
7   Receives cash revenue, $3,520.
8   Pays rent for the month, $900.
10   Buys compact discs and holders for storing troubleshooting programs and customer files during installations and repairs, as well as manuals and invoice forms, on account from Freeman Company, $870.
10   Pays for one-year liability insurance policy, $480.

FIGURE 1

	GENERAL JOURNAL				PAGE 1	
	DATE	DESCRIPTION	POST. REF.	DEBIT	CREDIT	
1	20—					1
2	June 1	Cash		82 0 0 0 00		2
3		R. P. Cline, Capital			82 0 0 0 00	3
4		Original investment by Cline				4
5		in Cline's Computer Clinic.				5
6						6
7	2	Equipment		64 0 0 0 00		7
8		Cash			64 0 0 0 00	8
9		Bought equipment for cash.				9
10						10
11	3	Equipment		10 0 0 0 00		11
12		Accounts Payable			10 0 0 0 00	12
13		Bought equipment on				13
14		account from Surgo				14
15		Products.				15
16						16
17	4	Accounts Payable		6 0 0 0 00		17
18		Cash			6 0 0 0 00	18
19		Paid Surgo Products on				19
20		account.				20
21						21
22	4	Equipment		6 2 0 0 00		22
23		R. P. Cline, Capital			6 2 0 0 00	23
24		Investment by Cline in				24
25		Cline's Computer Clinic.				25
26						26
27	7	Cash		3 5 2 0 00		27
28		Income from Services			3 5 2 0 00	28
29		Cash revenue.				29
30						30
31	8	Rent Expense		9 0 0 00		31
32		Cash			9 0 0 00	32
33		For month ended June 30.				33
34						34
35	10	Supplies Expense		8 7 0 00		35
36		Accounts Payable			8 7 0 00	36
37		Bought computer supplies				37
38		on account from Freeman				38
39		Company.				39

Heavy-duty ladders, spray painting machines, and a truck to carry it all in are part of the equipment used by these house painters.

June 14 Receives bill for newspaper advertising from the *Daily*, $340.

15 Cline's Computer Clinic signs a contract with Computer Makeovers to refurbish some of the computers it receives and then bills Computer Makeovers $1,470 for services performed.

15 Pays $1,800 to Surgo Products as a partial payment on account.

GENERAL JOURNAL   PAGE ___2___

	DATE		DESCRIPTION	POST. REF.	DEBIT	CREDIT	
1	20–						1
2	June	10	Prepaid Insurance		4 8 0 00		2
3			Cash			4 8 0 00	3
4			Premium for one-year liability				4
5			insurance policy.				5
6							6
7		14	Advertising Expense		3 4 0 00		7
8			Accounts Payable			3 4 0 00	8
9			Received bill for advertising				9
10			from the *Daily*.				10
11							11
12		15	Accounts Receivable		1 4 7 0 00		12
13			Income from Services			1 4 7 0 00	13
14			Billed Computer Makeovers				14
15			for services performed.				15
16							16
17		15	Accounts Payable		1 8 0 0 00		17
18			Cash			1 8 0 0 00	18
19			Paid Surgo Products on				19
20			account.				20
21							21
22		18	Utilities Expense		3 2 0 00		22
23			Cash			3 2 0 00	23
24			Paid bill for utilities, Regional				24
25			Power, Inc.				25
26							26
27		20	Accounts Payable		3 4 0 00		27
28			Cash			3 4 0 00	28
29			Paid the *Daily* in full.				29
30							30
31		24	Wages Expense		2 9 8 0 00		31
32			Cash			2 9 8 0 00	32
33			Paid wages of part-time				33
34			employee.				34

FIGURE 2

June 18 Receives and pays bill for utilities from Regional Power, Inc., $320.

20 Pays the *Daily* for advertising, $340 in full. (This bill has been previously recorded.)

24 Pays wages of part-time employee, $2,980.

26 Buys additional equipment costing $3,520 from Surgo Products, paying $620 down with the remaining $2,900 on account.

				GENERAL JOURNAL										PAGE ___3___	

	DATE		DESCRIPTION	POST. REF.	DEBIT					CREDIT					
1	20–														1
2	June	26	Equipment		3	5	2	0	00						2
3			Cash								6	2	0	00	3
4			Accounts Payable							2	9	0	0	00	4
5			Bought equipment on												5
6			account from Surgo												6
7			Products.												7
8															8
9		30	Cash			8	5	0	00						9
10			Accounts Receivable								8	5	0	00	10
11			Received from Computer												11
12			Makeovers to apply on												12
13			account.												13
14															14
15		30	Cash		6	0	2	0	00						15
16			Income from Services							6	0	2	0	00	16
17			Cash revenue.												17
18															18
19		30	R. P. Cline, Drawing		3	0	0	0	00						19
20			Cash							3	0	0	0	00	20
21			Withdrawal for personal use.												21

FIGURE 3

June 30   Receives $850 from Computer Makeovers to apply on amount previously billed.
    30   Receives cash revenue, $6,020.
    30   Cline withdraws cash for personal use, $3,000.

POSTING TO THE GENERAL LEDGER

You can see that the journal is the *book of original entry.* Each transaction must first be recorded in the journal in full. However, it is difficult to determine the balance of any one account, such as Cash, from the general journal entries. So the **ledger account** has been devised to give us a complete record of the transactions recorded in each individual account. The **general ledger** contains all the accounts. It may be a loose-leaf binder so that you can add or remove pages. The process of transferring information from the journal to the ledger accounts is called **posting**.

The Chart of Accounts

The accounts in the ledger are arranged according to the chart of accounts, which **is the official list of the ledger accounts in which transactions of a business are recorded.** Assets are listed first, liabilities second, owner's equity

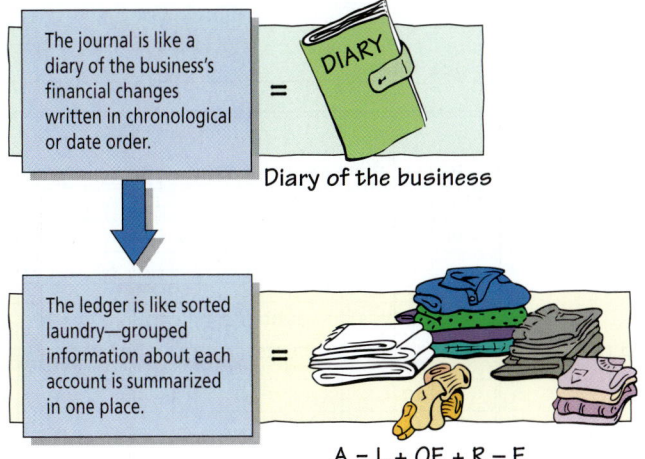

Diary of the business

A = L + OE + R − E

third, revenue fourth, and expenses fifth. The chart of accounts for Cline's Computer Clinic is as follows:

Chart of Accounts

Assets (100–199)

111 Cash
113 Accounts Receivable
117 Prepaid Insurance
124 Equipment

Liabilities (200–299)

221 Accounts Payable

Owner's Equity (300–399)

311 R. P. Cline, Capital
312 R. P. Cline, Drawing

Revenue (400–499)

411 Income from Services

Expenses (500–599)

511 Wages Expense
512 Rent Expense
513 Supplies Expense
514 Advertising Expense
515 Utilities Expense

Notice that the arrangement of the chart of accounts consists of the balance sheet accounts followed by the income statement accounts. The numbers preceding the account titles are the **account numbers**. Accounts in the ledger are kept by numbers rather than by pages because it is hard to tell in advance how many pages to reserve for a particular account. When you use the number system, you can add sheets easily. The digits in the account numbers also indicate account *classifications*. For most companies, assets start with 1, liabilities with 2, owner's equity with 3, revenue with 4, and expenses with 5. The second and third digits indicate the positions of the individual accounts within their respective classifications.

The Ledger Account Form (Running Balance Format)

We have been looking at accounts in the simple T account form primarily because T accounts illustrate situations so well. The debit and credit sides are specifically labeled, making the T account form a good way to picture account activity. However, determining the balance of an account using the T account form is difficult. You must add both columns and subtract the smaller total from the larger. To overcome this disadvantage, accountants generally use the four-column account form with Balance columns in the general ledger. Let's look at the Cash account of Cline's Computer Clinic in four-column form (Figure 4) compared with the T account form. *Leave the Post. Ref. column blank for now.*

Cash			
	+	−	
(a)	82,000	(b)	64,000
(f)	3,520	(d)	6,000
(q)	850	(g)	900
(r)	6,020	(i)	480
	92,390	(l)	1,800
		(m)	320
		(n)	340
		(o)	2,980
		(p)	620
		(s)	3,000
			80,440
Bal.	**11,950**		

GENERAL LEDGER

ACCOUNT **Cash**   ACCOUNT NO. __111__

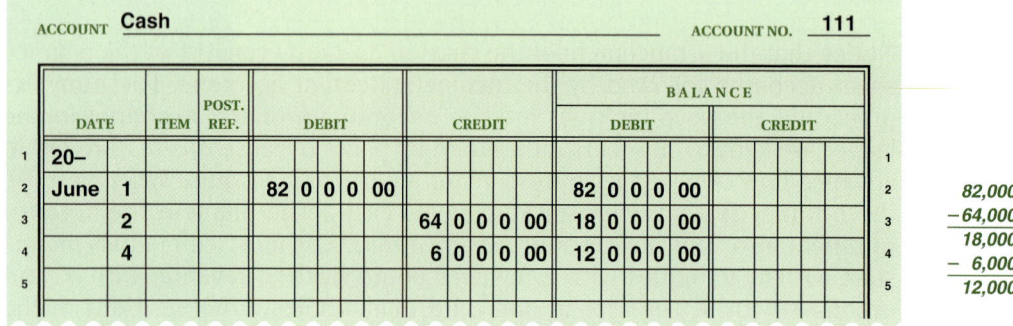

	DATE	ITEM	POST. REF.	DEBIT	CREDIT	BALANCE DEBIT	BALANCE CREDIT	
1	20–							1
2	June 1			82 000 00		82 000 00		2
3	2				64 000 00	18 000 00		3
4	4				6 000 00	12 000 00		4
5	7			3 520 00		15 520 00		5
6	8				900 00	14 620 00		6
7	10				480 00	14 140 00		7
8	15				1 800 00	12 340 00		8
9	18				320 00	12 020 00		9
10	20				340 00	11 680 00		10
11	24				2 980 00	8 700 00		11
12	26				620 00	8 080 00		12
13	30			850 00		8 930 00		13
14	30			6 020 00		14 950 00		14
15	30				3 000 00	11 950 00		15

Transaction Amount   Running Balance

FIGURE 4

Note the calculation of the running balance. In the abbreviated form, it looks like this:

ACCOUNT **Cash**   ACCOUNT NO. __111__

	DATE	ITEM	POST. REF.	DEBIT	CREDIT	BALANCE DEBIT	BALANCE CREDIT	
1	20–							1
2	June 1			82 000 00		82 000 00		2
3	2				64 000 00	18 000 00		3
4	4				6 000 00	12 000 00		4
5								5

```
  82,000
− 64,000
  18,000
−  6,000
  12,000
```

The Posting Process

OBJECTIVE 2

Post entries from a two-column general journal to general ledger accounts.

In the posting process, you must transfer the following information from the journal to the ledger accounts: the *date of the transaction, the debit and credit amounts,* and the *page number* of the journal. Post each account separately, using the following steps. Post the debit part of the entry first. After locating the account in the ledger, you need to do the following steps.

1. Write the date of the transaction in the account's Date column.
2. Write the amount of the transaction in the Debit or Credit column and enter the new balance in the Balance columns under Debit or Credit.

3. Write the page number of the journal in the Post. Ref. column of the ledger account. (This is a **cross-reference**; it tells where the amount came from.)

4. Record the ledger account number in the Post. Ref. column of the journal. (This is also a cross-reference; it tells where the amount was posted.)

Entering the account number in the Post. Ref. column of the journal should be the last step. It acts as a verification of the three preceding steps.

The first transaction for Cline's Computer Clinic is illustrated in Figure 5. Let's look first at the debit part of the entry.

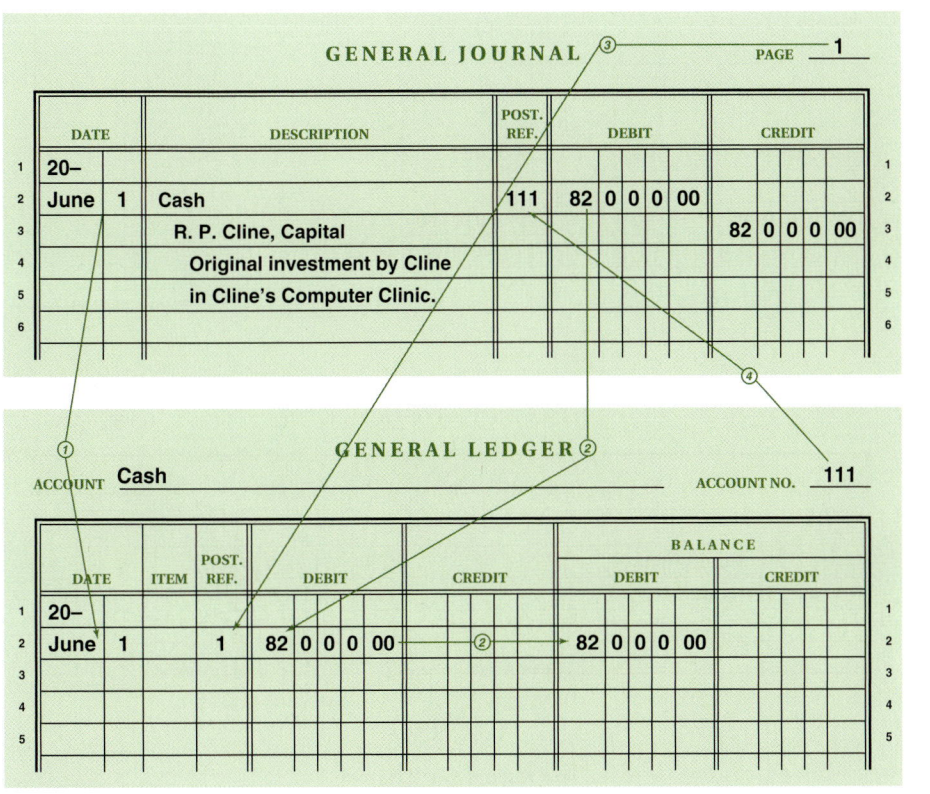

① *Date of transaction*
② *Amount of transaction*
③ *Page number of the journal*
④ *Ledger account number*

FIGURE 5

Next we post the credit part of the entry, as shown in Figure 6.

The accountant usually uses the Item column only at the end of a financial period. The words that may appear in this column are *balance, closing, adjusting,* and *reversing.* We will explain the use of these terms later.

Incidentally, some accountants use running balance–type ledger account forms that have only one balance column. However, we have used the two-balance-column arrangement to show clearly the appropriate balance of an account. For example, in Figure 5, Cash has an $82,000 balance recorded in the Debit column (normal balance). In Figure 6, R. P. Cline, Capital, has a $82,000 balance recorded in the Credit column (normal balance).

In the recording of the second transaction, shown in Figure 7, see if you can identify in order the four steps in the posting process.

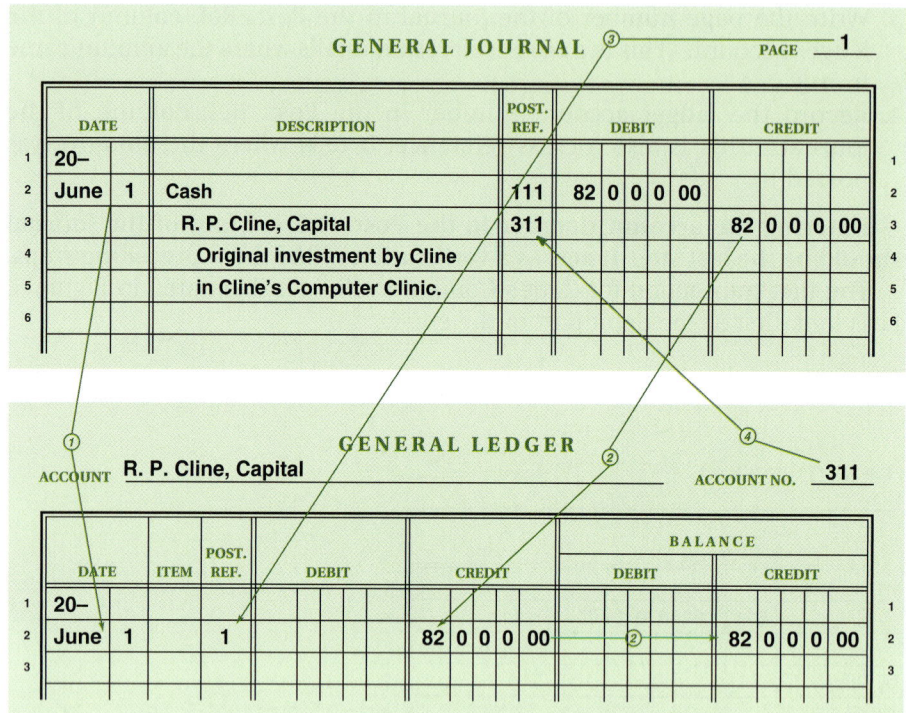

FIGURE 6

FIGURE 7

① Date of transaction
② Amount of transaction
③ Page number of the journal
④ Ledger account number

GENERAL JOURNAL   PAGE ___1___

	DATE		DESCRIPTION	POST. REF.	DEBIT	CREDIT	
7		2	Equipment	124	64 0 0 0 00		7
8			Cash	111		64 0 0 0 00	8
9			Bought equipment for cash.				9
10							10

GENERAL LEDGER

ACCOUNT Cash _____   ACCOUNT NO. ___111___

	DATE		ITEM	POST. REF.	DEBIT	CREDIT	BALANCE DEBIT	BALANCE CREDIT	
1	20–								1
2	June	1		1	82 0 0 0 00		82 0 0 0 00		2
3		2		1		64 0 0 0 00	18 0 0 0 00		3

ACCOUNT Equipment _____   ACCOUNT NO. ___124___

	DATE		ITEM	POST. REF.	DEBIT	CREDIT	BALANCE DEBIT	BALANCE CREDIT	
1	20–								1
2	June	2		1	64 0 0 0 00		64 0 0 0 00		2

REMEMBER!

Do not record account numbers in the Post. Ref. column of the journal until the amounts have been posted to the ledger accounts as either debits or credits.

REMEMBER!

Posting is simply transferring or copying exactly the same date and the debits and credits listed in the journal entry from the journal to the ledger.

Now let's look at the journal entries for the first month of operation for Cline's Computer Clinic. As you can see in Figure 8, the Post. Ref. column has been filled in, because the posting has been completed.

FIGURE 8

GENERAL JOURNAL   PAGE __1__

	DATE		DESCRIPTION	POST. REF.	DEBIT	CREDIT	
1	20–						1
2	June	1	Cash	111	82 0 0 0 00		2
3			R. P. Cline, Capital	311		82 0 0 0 00	3
4			Original investment by Cline				4
5			in Cline's Computer Clinic.				5
6							6
7		2	Equipment	124	64 0 0 0 00		7
8			Cash	111		64 0 0 0 00	8
9			Bought equipment for cash.				9
10							10
11		3	Equipment	124	10 0 0 0 00		11
12			Accounts Payable	221		10 0 0 0 00	12
13			Bought equipment on				13
14			account from Surgo				14
15			Products.				15
16							16
17		4	Accounts Payable	221	6 0 0 0 00		17
18			Cash	111		6 0 0 0 00	18
19			Paid Surgo Products on				19
20			account.				20
21							21
22		4	Equipment	124	6 2 0 0 00		22
23			R. P. Cline, Capital	311		6 2 0 0 00	23
24			Investment by Cline in				24
25			Cline's Computer Clinic.				25
26							26
27		7	Cash	111	3 5 2 0 00		27
28			Income from Services	411		3 5 2 0 00	28
29			Cash revenue.				29
30							30
31		8	Rent Expense	512	9 0 0 00		31
32			Cash	111		9 0 0 00	32
33			For month ended June 30.				33
34							34
35		10	Supplies Expense	513	8 7 0 00		35
36			Accounts Payable	221		8 7 0 00	36
37			Bought computer supplies				37
38			on account from Freeman				38
39			Company.				39
40							40

(continued)

FIGURE 8
(continued)

GENERAL JOURNAL

PAGE ___2___

	DATE		DESCRIPTION	POST. REF.	DEBIT	CREDIT	
1	20–						1
2	June	10	Prepaid Insurance	117	4 8 0 00		2
3			Cash	111		4 8 0 00	3
4			Premium for one-year liability				4
5			insurance policy.				5
6							6
7		14	Advertising Expense	514	3 4 0 00		7
8			Accounts Payable	221		3 4 0 00	8
9			Received bill for advertising				9
10			from the *Daily*.				10
11							11
12		15	Accounts Receivable	113	1 4 7 0 00		12
13			Income from Services	411		1 4 7 0 00	13
14			Billed Computer Makeovers				14
15			for services performed.				15
16							16
17		15	Accounts Payable	221	1 8 0 0 00		17
18			Cash	111		1 8 0 0 00	18
19			Paid Surgo Products on				19
20			account.				20
21							21
22		18	Utilities Expense	515	3 2 0 00		22
23			Cash	111		3 2 0 00	23
24			Paid bill for utilities, Regional				24
25			Power, Inc.				25
26							26
27		20	Accounts Payable	221	3 4 0 00		27
28			Cash	111		3 4 0 00	28
29			Paid the *Daily* in full.				29
30							30
31		24	Wages Expense	511	2 9 8 0 00		31
32			Cash	111		2 9 8 0 00	32
33			Paid wages of part-time				33
34			employee.				34
35							35

GENERAL JOURNAL

PAGE ___3___

	DATE		DESCRIPTION	POST. REF.	DEBIT	CREDIT	
1	20–						1
2	June	26	Equipment	124	3 5 2 0 00		2
3			Cash	111		6 2 0 00	3
4			Accounts Payable	221		2 9 0 0 00	4
5			Bought equipment on				5
6			account from Surgo				6
7			Products.				7

FIGURE 8 (continued)

				POST. REF.	DEBIT	CREDIT	
9		30	Cash	111	8 5 0 0 00		9
10			Accounts Receivable	113		8 5 0 00	10
11			Received from Computer				11
12			Makeovers to apply on				12
13			account.				13
14							14
15		30	Cash	111	6 0 2 0 00		15
16			Income from Services	411		6 0 2 0 00	16
17			Cash revenue.				17
18							18
19		30	R. P. Cline, Drawing	312	3 0 0 0 00		19
20			Cash	111		3 0 0 0 00	20
21			Withdrawal for personal use.				21

FYI

Computerized accounting programs also require journal explanations and will generate posting references.

In making journal entries, you will sometimes find that there are not enough lines at the bottom of a page to record the entire entry. In this case, do not split up the entry; instead, record the entire entry on the next journal page. The ledger accounts and entries for Cline's Computer Clinic are shown in Figure 9.

FIGURE 9

GENERAL LEDGER

ACCOUNT **Cash**   ACCOUNT NO. **111**

	DATE	ITEM	POST. REF.	DEBIT	CREDIT	BALANCE DEBIT	BALANCE CREDIT	
1	20–							1
2	June 1		1	82 0 0 0 00		82 0 0 0 00		2
3	2		1		64 0 0 0 00	18 0 0 0 00		3
4	4		1		6 0 0 0 00	12 0 0 0 00		4
5	7		1	3 5 2 0 00		15 5 2 0 00		5
6	8		1		9 0 0 00	14 6 2 0 00		6
7	10		2		4 8 0 00	14 1 4 0 00		7
8	15		2		1 8 0 0 00	12 3 4 0 00		8
9	18		2		3 2 0 00	12 0 2 0 00		9
10	20		2		3 4 0 00	11 6 8 0 00		10
11	24		2		2 9 8 0 00	8 7 0 0 00		11
12	26		3		6 2 0 00	8 0 8 0 00		12
13	30		3	8 5 0 00		8 9 3 0 00		13
14	30		3	6 0 2 0 00		14 9 5 0 00		14
15	30		3		3 0 0 0 00	11 9 5 0 00		15

ACCOUNT **Accounts Receivable**   ACCOUNT NO. **113**

	DATE	ITEM	POST. REF.	DEBIT	CREDIT	BALANCE DEBIT	BALANCE CREDIT	
1	20–							1
2	June 15		2	1 4 7 0 00		1 4 7 0 00		2
3	30		3		8 5 0 00	6 2 0 00		3

(continued)

FIGURE 9
(continued)

ACCOUNT **Prepaid Insurance**   ACCOUNT NO. **117**

	DATE	ITEM	POST. REF.	DEBIT	CREDIT	BALANCE DEBIT	BALANCE CREDIT	
1	20–							1
2	June 10		2	4 8 0 00		4 8 0 00		2

ACCOUNT **Equipment**   ACCOUNT NO. **124**

	DATE	ITEM	POST. REF.	DEBIT	CREDIT	BALANCE DEBIT	BALANCE CREDIT	
1	20–							1
2	June 2		1	64 0 0 0 00		64 0 0 0 00		2
3	3		1	10 0 0 0 00		74 0 0 0 00		3
4	4		1	6 2 0 0 00		80 2 0 0 00		4
5	26		3	3 5 2 0 00		83 7 2 0 00		5

ACCOUNT **Accounts Payable**   ACCOUNT NO. **221**

	DATE	ITEM	POST. REF.	DEBIT	CREDIT	BALANCE DEBIT	BALANCE CREDIT	
1	20–							1
2	June 3		1		10 0 0 0 00		10 0 0 0 00	2
3	4		1	6 0 0 0 00			4 0 0 0 00	3
4	10		1		8 7 0 00		4 8 7 0 00	4
5	14		2		3 4 0 00		5 2 1 0 00	5
6	15		2	1 8 0 0 00			3 4 1 0 00	6
7	20		2	3 4 0 00			3 0 7 0 00	7
8	26		3		2 9 0 0 00		5 9 7 0 00	8
9								9
10								10
11								11

ACCOUNT **R. P. Cline, Capital**   ACCOUNT NO. **311**

	DATE	ITEM	POST. REF.	DEBIT	CREDIT	BALANCE DEBIT	BALANCE CREDIT	
1	20–							1
2	June 1		1		82 0 0 0 00		82 0 0 0 00	2
3	4		1		6 2 0 0 00		88 2 0 0 00	3

ACCOUNT **R. P. Cline, Drawing**   ACCOUNT NO. **312**

	DATE	ITEM	POST. REF.	DEBIT	CREDIT	BALANCE DEBIT	BALANCE CREDIT	
1	20–							1
2	June 30		3	3 0 0 0 00		3 0 0 0 00		2

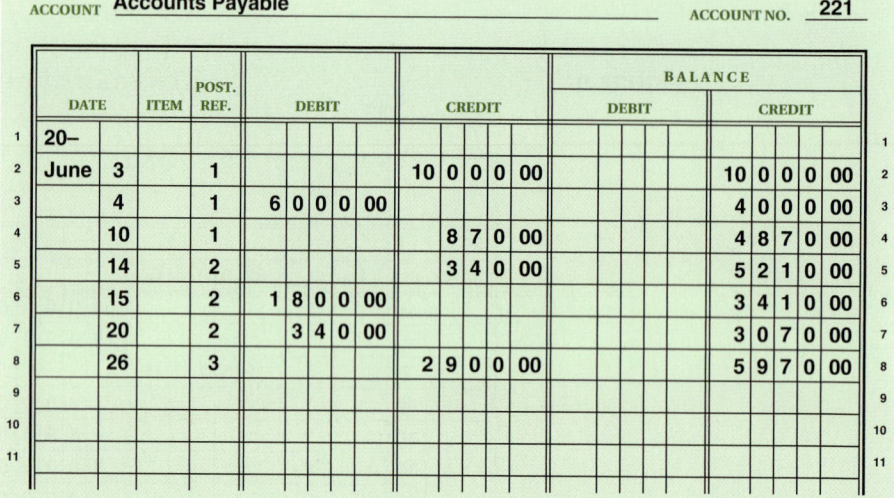
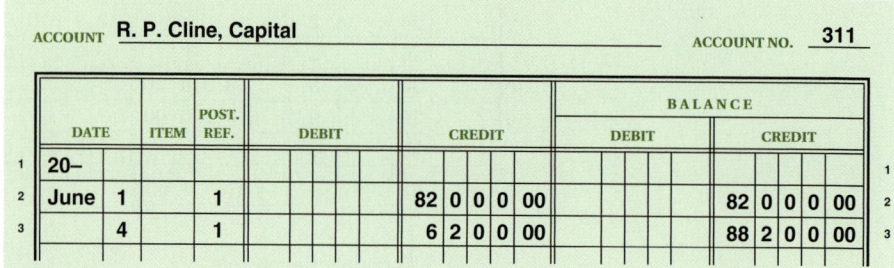

**FIGURE 9
(continued)**

ACCOUNT **Income from Services**   ACCOUNT NO. 411

| | DATE | ITEM | POST. REF. | DEBIT | CREDIT | BALANCE | |
						DEBIT	CREDIT
1	20–							1
2	June 7		1		3 5 2 0 00		3 5 2 0 00	2
3	15		2		1 4 7 0 00		4 9 9 0 00	3
4	30		3		6 0 2 0 00		11 0 1 0 00	4
5								5
6								6

ACCOUNT **Wages Expense**   ACCOUNT NO. 511

| | DATE | ITEM | POST. REF. | DEBIT | CREDIT | BALANCE | |
						DEBIT	CREDIT
1	20–							1
2	June 24		2	2 9 8 0 00		2 9 8 0 00		2
3								3

ACCOUNT **Rent Expense**   ACCOUNT NO. 512

| | DATE | ITEM | POST. REF. | DEBIT | CREDIT | BALANCE | |
						DEBIT	CREDIT
1	20–							1
2	June 8		1	9 0 0 00		9 0 0 00		2

ACCOUNT **Supplies Expense**   ACCOUNT NO. 513

| | DATE | ITEM | POST. REF. | DEBIT | CREDIT | BALANCE | |
						DEBIT	CREDIT
1	20–							1
2	June 10		1	8 7 0 00		8 7 0 00		2
3								3

ACCOUNT **Advertising Expense**   ACCOUNT NO. 514

| | DATE | ITEM | POST. REF. | DEBIT | CREDIT | BALANCE | |
						DEBIT	CREDIT
1	20–							1
2	June 14		2	3 4 0 00		3 4 0 00		2

ACCOUNT **Utilities Expense**   ACCOUNT NO. 515

| | DATE | ITEM | POST. REF. | DEBIT | CREDIT | BALANCE | |
						DEBIT	CREDIT
1	20–							1
2	June 18		2	3 2 0 00		3 2 0 00		2

FIGURE 10

Cline's Computer Clinic
Trial Balance
June 30, 20—

ACCOUNT NAME	DEBIT	CREDIT
Cash	11 9 5 0 00	
Accounts Receivable	6 2 0 00	
Prepaid Insurance	4 8 0 00	
Equipment	83 7 2 0 00	
Accounts Payable		5 9 7 0 00
R. P. Cline, Capital		88 2 0 0 00
R. P. Cline, Drawing	3 0 0 0 00	
Income from Services		11 0 1 0 00
Wages Expense	2 9 8 0 00	
Rent Expense	9 0 0 00	
Supplies Expense	8 7 0 00	
Advertising Expense	3 4 0 00	
Utilities Expense	3 2 0 00	
	105 1 8 0 00	105 1 8 0 00

Preparation of the Trial Balance

OBJECTIVE 3

Prepare a trial balance from the ledger accounts.

The trial balance is simply a list of the ledger accounts that have balances. A trial balance is presented in Figure 10.

Remember that the trial balance proves only that the total ledger debit balances equal the total ledger credit balances. Even when the debit and credit balances are equal, other types of errors may slip through—for example,

1. Posting the correct debit or credit amounts to the incorrect account.
2. Neglecting to journalize or post an entire transaction.

If the temporary balance of an account happens to be zero, insert long dashes through both the Debit Balance and the Credit Balance columns. We'll use another business, the Becker Company, in this example. Its Accounts Receivable ledger account appears below.

ACCOUNT Accounts Receivable   **ACCOUNT NO.** 113

	DATE	ITEM	POST. REF.	DEBIT	CREDIT	BALANCE DEBIT	BALANCE CREDIT	
1	20–							1
2	Oct. 7		96	1 4 0 00		1 4 0 00		2
3	19		97	2 3 8 00		3 7 8 00		3
4	21		97		1 4 0 00	2 3 8 00		4
5	29		98		2 3 8 00	—	—	5
6	31		98	1 6 2 00		1 6 2 00		6
7								7
8								8
9								9
10								10
11								11
12								12

Steps in the Accounting Process

1. **Record the transactions of a business in a journal (book of original entry or the day-by-day record of the transactions of a firm).** An entry should be based on some source document or evidence that a transaction has occurred, such as an invoice, a receipt, or a check.
2. **Post entries to the accounts in the ledger.** Transfer the amounts from the journal to the Debit or Credit columns of the specified accounts in the ledger. Use a cross-reference system. Accounts are organized in the ledger according to the account numbers assigned to them in the chart of accounts.
3. **Prepare a trial balance.** Record the balances of the ledger accounts in the appropriate column, Debit or Credit, of the trial balance form. Prove that the total of the debit balances equals the total of the credit balances.

Source Document

A source document can be an invoice, a receipt, a check, etc. We now add an important detail in the recording of a journal entry. This detail consists of listing the related source document number, which is used as a reference for the proof of a transaction. Figure 11 is an example of a source document followed by the journal entry (Figure 12) and ledger accounts (Figure 13). Note how the explanation differs from the one we showed earlier.

FIGURE 11

FREEMAN COMPANY				No. 4-962
220 East Ames Street				
Detroit, Michigan 48222				

Sold By: __203__   Date: __6/10/20—__

Name: __Cline's Computer Clinic__

Address: __1701 East Delaware Street__

__Detroit, Michigan 48228__

Terms: __Net 30 days__

QUANTITY	DESCRIPTION	UNIT PRICE	AMOUNT
20 bx	Compact discs	16 00	320 00
20 bx	Compact disc holders	8 00	160 00
20 ea	Manuals	10 00	200 00
10 bx	Invoice forms	12 00	120 00
	SUBTOTAL		800 00
	SALES TAX		48 00
	SHIPPING		22 00
	TOTAL		870 00

Record in the journal (Figure 12). Note how the explanation includes important information from the source document presented earlier.

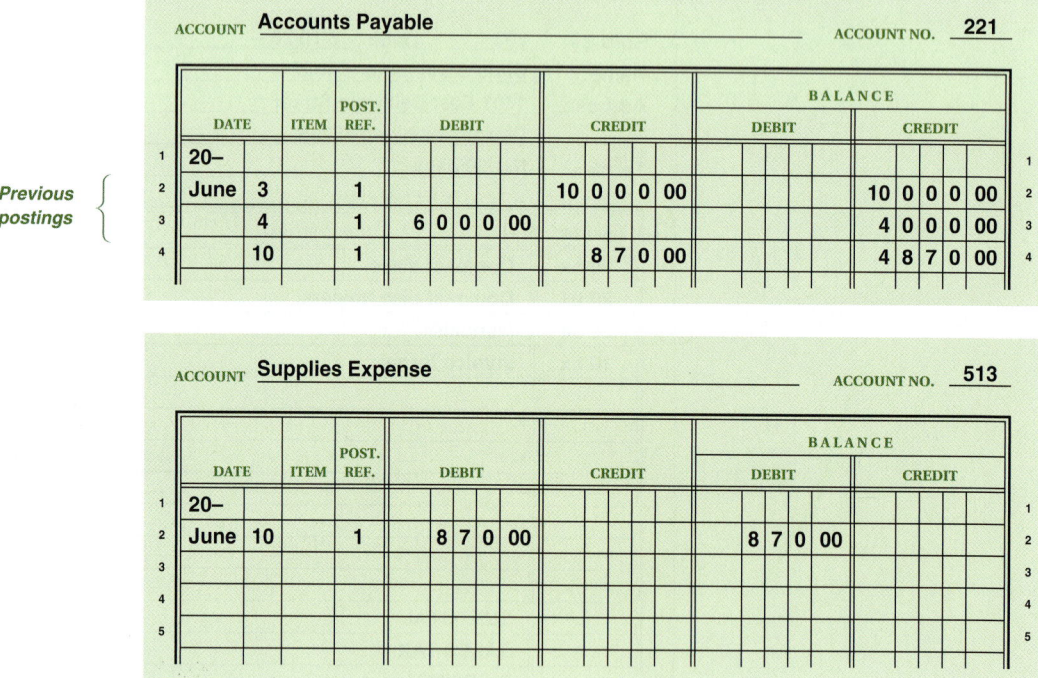

GENERAL JOURNAL

PAGE ___1___

	DATE	DESCRIPTION	POST. REF.	DEBIT	CREDIT	
35	10	Supplies Expense	513	8 7 0 00		35
36		Accounts Payable	221		8 7 0 00	36
37		Bought computer supplies				37
38		on account from Freeman				38
39		Company, Inv. No. 4-962.				39
40						40
41						41
42						42
43						43

FIGURE 12

Post to the ledger (Figure 13).

ACCOUNT **Accounts Payable**   ACCOUNT NO. ___221___

	DATE	ITEM	POST. REF.	DEBIT	CREDIT	BALANCE DEBIT	BALANCE CREDIT	
1	20–							1
2	June 3		1		10 0 0 0 00		10 0 0 0 00	2
3	4		1	6 0 0 0 00			4 0 0 0 00	3
4	10		1		8 7 0 00		4 8 7 0 00	4

Previous postings {

ACCOUNT **Supplies Expense**   ACCOUNT NO. ___513___

	DATE	ITEM	POST. REF.	DEBIT	CREDIT	BALANCE DEBIT	BALANCE CREDIT	
1	20–							1
2	June 10		1	8 7 0 00		8 7 0 00		2
3								3
4								4
5								5

FIGURE 13

CORRECTION OF ERRORS—MANUAL AND COMPUTERIZED

Errors are occasionally made in recording journal entries and posting to the ledger accounts whether recording them manually or on a computer. Never erase them, because it might look as if you were trying to hide something. The method for correcting errors depends on how and when the errors were made. There are two manual methods for correcting errors; they are

1. The ruling method.
2. The correcting entry method.

Manual Ruling Method

OBJECTIVE 4
Correct entries using the manual ruling method.

You can use the ruling method to correct an error in the journal before posting or to correct an error in the ledger after an entry has been posted.

Manually Correcting Errors Before Posting Has Taken Place When an error has been made in recording an account title in a journal entry, draw a line through the incorrect account title in the journal entry, and write the correct account title immediately above. Include your initials with the correction. For example, an entry to record payment of $1,700 rent was incorrectly debited to Salary Expense.

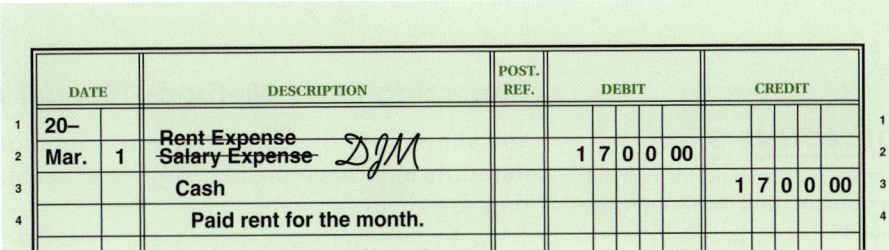

When an error has been made in recording an amount, draw a line through the incorrect amount in the journal entry, and write the correct amount immediately above. For example, an entry for a $230 payment for office supplies was recorded as $320. Include your initials with the correction.

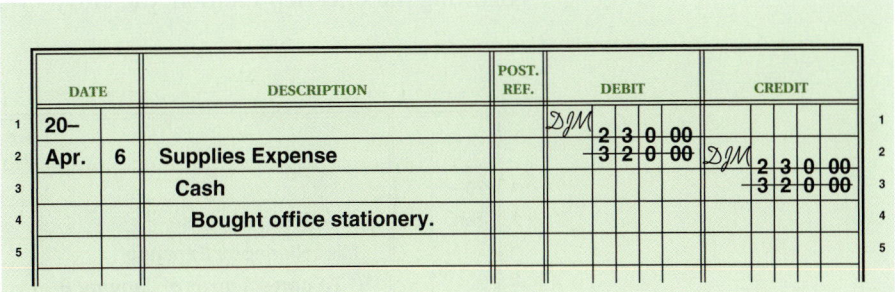

Manually Correcting Errors After Posting Has Taken Place When an entry was journalized correctly but one of the amounts was posted incorrectly,

Whether you are preparing accounting records manually or on computer, accuracy is of primary importance. Rapid and accurate ten-key and computer keyboard skills are a must for the accountant or bookkeeper.

correct the error by drawing a single line through the amount and recording the correct amount above. For example, an entry to record cash received for professional fees was correctly journalized as $400. However, it was posted as a debit to Cash for $400 and a credit to Professional Fees for $4,000. In the Professional Fees account, draw a line through $4,000 and insert $400 above. Change the running balance of the account and initial the corrections.

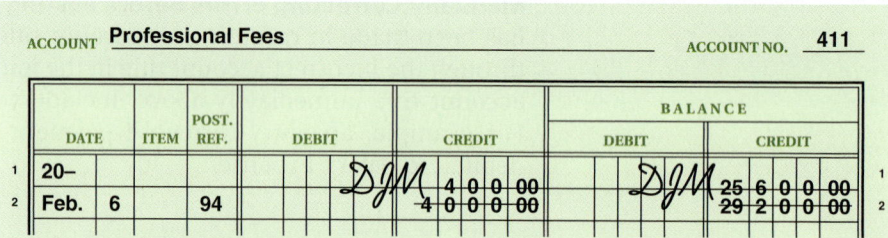

FYI

Use a ruler to draw a line through an error.

Correcting Entry Method—Manual or Computerized

OBJECTIVE 5

Correct entries using the manual or computerized correcting entry method.

You should use the correcting entry method when incorrectly journalized amounts have been posted. There are two manual correcting entry methods; they are

1. One-step method. Simply make one entry that undoes the error and provides the correct account.
2. Two-step method. The first step reverses the error made by the original entry. The second step includes the correct entry.

The correcting entry should *always* include an explanation. For example, on January 9, a $620 payment for advertising was incorrectly journalized and posted as a debit to Miscellaneous Expense for $620 and a credit to Cash for $620. Following the one-step method, the entry would be:

	DATE		DESCRIPTION	POST. REF.	DEBIT	CREDIT	
1	20–						1
2	Jan.	27	Advertising Expense		6 2 0 00		2
3			Miscellaneous Expense			6 2 0 00	3
4			To correct error of January 9				4
5			in which a payment for				5
6			Advertising Expense was				6
7			debited to Miscellaneous				7
8			Expense.				8

Following the two-step method, if the original entry was recorded as a debit to Miscellaneous Expense and a credit to Cash, then reverse this entry by debiting Cash and crediting Miscellaneous Expense, and then record the correct entry.

	DATE		DESCRIPTION	POST. REF.	DEBIT	CREDIT	
1	20–						1
2	Jan.	27	Cash		6 2 0 00		2
3			Miscellaneous Expense			6 2 0 00	3
4			To reverse out an incorrect				4
5			entry recorded January 9.				5
6							6

	DATE		DESCRIPTION	POST. REF.	DEBIT	CREDIT	
1	20–						1
2	Jan.	27	Advertising Expense		6 2 0 00		2
3			Cash			6 2 0 00	3
4			To correct error of January 9				4
5			in which a payment for				5
6			Advertising Expense was				6
7			debited to Miscellaneous				7
8			Expense.				8

Correcting Errors on the Computer Again, never delete an error; most commercial programs will not allow deletion because if you could delete an entry, it would destroy the audit trail that tracks the life of each transaction. The procedure is to make a correcting entry with a brief and appropriate explanation followed by posting.

After the correcting entry has been journalized, the accounts are posted as for any other entry. After posting, the account balances should be correct.

CHAPTER REVIEW

Online Study Center
ACE the test!

Review of Performance Objectives

1. Record a group of transactions pertaining to a service enterprise in a two-column general journal.

   Based on source documents, the transactions are analyzed to determine the accounts involved and whether the accounts are debited or credited. For each transaction, total debits must equal total credits. The journal is a book of original entry in which a day-by-day record of business transactions is maintained. The parts of a journal entry consist of the transaction date, the title of the account(s) debited, the title of the account(s) credited, the amounts recorded in the Debit and Credit columns, and an explanation.

2. Post entries from a two-column general journal to general ledger accounts.

The ledger is a book that contains all the accounts, arranged according to the chart of accounts. Posting is the process of transferring information from the journal to the ledger accounts. The posting process consists of four steps:

1. Write the date of the transaction in the account's Date column.
2. Write the amount of the transaction in the Debit or Credit column, and enter the new balance in the Balance columns under Debit or Credit.
3. Write the page number of the journal in the Post. Ref. column of the ledger account.
4. Record the ledger account number in the Post. Ref. column of the journal.

3. Prepare a trial balance from the ledger accounts.

The trial balance consists of a listing of account balances in two columns, one labeled Debit and one labeled Credit. The balances come from the ledger accounts.

4. Correct entries using the manual ruling method.

The ruling method can be used if an error is discovered before or after an entry has been posted. Draw a line through the incorrect account title or amount, and write the correct account title or amount immediately above. Include your initials with the correction.

5. Correct entries using the manual or computerized correcting entry method.

This method is used if an error is discovered after an incorrectly journalized entry has been posted. If the error consists of the wrong account(s), an entry is made to cancel out or reverse the incorrect account(s) and insert the correct account(s). Initial the correction.

Glossary

Account numbers The numbers assigned to accounts according to the chart of accounts. (79)

Cost principle The principle that a purchased asset should be recorded at its actual cost. (74)

Cross-reference The ledger account number in the Post. Ref. column of the journal and the journal page number in the Post. Ref. column of the ledger account. (81)

General ledger A loose-leaf book containing the activity (by accounts) of a business. (78)

Journal The book in which a person makes the original record of a business transaction; commonly referred to as a *book of original entry*. (70)

Journalizing The process of recording a business transaction in a journal. (70)

Ledger account A complete record of the transactions recorded in an individual account. (78)

Posting The process of transferring figures from the journal to the ledger accounts. (78)

Source documents Business papers, such as checks, invoices, receipts, letters, and memos, that furnish proof that a transaction has taken place. (70)

Two-column general journal A general journal in which there are two amount columns, one used for debit amounts and one used for credit amounts. (70)

QUESTIONS, EXERCISES, AND CASES

Discussion Questions

1. Why is the journal called a book of original entry?

2. How does the journal differ from the ledger?

3. What is the purpose of providing a ledger account for each account?

4. List by account classification the order of the accounts in the general ledger.

5. Arrange the following steps in the posting process in correct order:
    a. Write the ledger account number in the Post. Ref. column of the journal.
    b. Write the amount of the transaction.
    c. Write the date of the transaction.
    d. Write the page number of the journal in the Post. Ref. column of the ledger account.

6. What does cross-referencing mean in the posting process?

7. Why is a source document important?

8. What is the first number for each of the following accounts in a chart of accounts listed by account number?
    a. Professional Fees   d. Accounts Receivable
    b. Utilities Expense   e. Accounts Payable
    c. J. R. Watson, Capital

Exercises

P.O. 1

Label parts of a journal entry.

Exercise 3-1 In the two-column journal below, the capital letters represent where parts of a journal entry appear. Write the numbers 1 through 8 on a piece of paper. After each number, match the capital letter where these items appear with the number of the item.

	DATE		DESCRIPTION	POST. REF.	DEBIT	CREDIT	
1	G						1
2	H	I	J	O	M		2
3			K	P		N	3
4			L				4
5							5

GENERAL JOURNAL   PAGE __1__

1. Year
2. Month
3. Explanation
4. Title of account debited
5. Ledger account number of account credited
6. Amount of debit
7. Day of the month
8. Title of account credited

P.O. 1

Journalize transactions.

Exercise 3-2 Decor Services completed the following transactions. Journalize the transactions in general journal form, including brief explanations.

Oct. 7 Received cash on account from Greg Hinton, a customer, Inv. No. 312, $830.
15 Paid on account to Madera Brothers, a creditor, $260, Ck. No. 2242.
20 M. Kledzik, the owner, withdrew cash for personal use, $800, Ck. No. 2243.
23 Bought store supplies for $88 and office supplies for $74 on account from Wegner Office Supply, Inv. No. 1040.
29 M. Kledzik, the owner, invested $2,500 cash and $3,500 of her personal equipment.

P.O. 1

Journalize transactions.

Exercise 3-3 Montoya Tutoring Service completed the following transactions. Journalize the transactions in general journal form, including brief explanations.

Mar. 1 Bought equipment for $6,075 from Teaching Partners, paying $3,000 in cash and placing the balance on account, Ck. No. 3230.
10 Paid the wages for the first week of March, $1,435, Ck. No. 3231.
15 Sold services for cash to Chandler District, $1,330, Sales Inv. 121.
26 Sold services on account to Clark School, $1,700, Sales Inv. 122.
31 Paid on account to Teaching Partners, $650, Ck. No. 3232.

P.O. 2

Post to a ledger account.

Exercise 3-4 The following May journal entries all involved cash.

Increases to Cash—Debits		Decreases to Cash—Credits	
5/1	9,000	5/3	800
5/9	1,800	5/8	900
5/16	4,400	5/12	2,200
5/23	900	5/25	3,600
5/30	5,200		

Post the amounts to the ledger account for Cash, Account No. 111. Assume that all transactions appeared on page 6 of the general journal.

P.O. 2

Determine steps in the posting process.

Exercise 3-5 Arrange the following steps in the posting process in correct order:

a. The amount of the balance of the ledger account is recorded in the Debit Balance or Credit Balance column.
b. The amount of the transaction is recorded in the Debit or Credit column of the ledger account.
c. The ledger account number is recorded in the Post. Ref. column of the journal.
d. The date of the transaction is recorded in the Date column of the ledger account.
e. The page number of the journal is recorded in the Post. Ref. column of the ledger account.

P.O. 3

Prepare a corrected trial balance.

Exercise 3-6 The bookkeeper for Navarro Company has prepared the following trial balance.

Navarro Company
Trial Balance
June 30, 20—

ACCOUNT NAME	DEBIT	CREDIT
Cash		2 5 0 0 00
Accounts Receivable	8 3 0 0 00	
Prepaid Insurance	6 5 0 00	
Equipment	15 3 0 0 00	
Accounts Payable		2 7 0 0 00
M. Navarro, Capital		12 5 0 0 00
M. Navarro, Drawing	4 8 9 0 00	
Professional Fees		17 5 4 0 00
Supplies Expense	6 0 0 00	
Rent Expense	5 0 0 00	
Miscellaneous Expense	1 8 0 0 00	
	32 0 4 0 00	35 2 4 0 00

The bookkeeper has asked for your help. In examining the company's journal and ledger, you discover the following errors. Use this information to construct a corrected trial balance.

a. The debits to the Cash account total $8,000, and the credits total $3,300.
b. A $500 payment to a creditor was entered in the journal correctly but was not posted to the Accounts Payable account.
c. The first two numbers in the balance of the Accounts Receivable account were transposed in copying the balance from the ledger to the trial balance.
d. The $1,500 amount withdrawn by the owner for personal use was debited to Miscellaneous Expense by mistake—it was correctly credited to Cash.

P.O. 4,5

Determine the effect of errors.

Exercise 3-7 Determine the effect of the following errors on a company's total revenue, total expenses, and net income. Indicate the effect by writing O for "Overstated (too much)"; U for "Understated (too little)"; or NA for "Not Affected."

Transactions	Total Revenue	Total Expenses	Net Income
Example: A check for $325 was written to pay on account. The accountant debited Rent Expense for $325 and credited Cash for $325.	NA	O	U
a. $420 was received on account from customers. The accountant debited Cash for $420 and credited Professional Fees for $420.			
b. The owner withdrew $1,200 for personal use. The accountant debited Wages Expense for $1,200 and credited Cash for $1,200.			
c. A check was written for $1,250 to pay the rent. The accountant debited Rent Expense for $1,520 and credited Cash for $1,520.			
d. $1,800 was received on account from customers. The accountant debited Cash for $1,800 and credited the Capital account for $1,800.			
e. A check was written for $225 to pay the phone bill received and recorded earlier in the month. The accountant debited Phone Expense for $225 and credited Cash for $225.			

P.O. 4,5

Journalize correcting entries.

Exercise 3-8 Journalize correcting entries for each of the following errors and include a brief explanation.

a. A cash purchase of office equipment for $710 was journalized as a cash purchase of store equipment for $710. (Use the ruling method; assume the entry has not been posted.)

b. An entry for a $150 payment for office supplies was journalized as $510. (Use the ruling method; assume the entry has not been posted.)

c. A $520 payment for repairs was journalized and posted as a debit to Equipment instead of a debit to Repair Expense. (Use the correcting entry method to journalize the correction.)

d. A $650 bill for vehicle insurance was received and immediately paid. It was journalized and posted as $560. (Use the correcting entry method to journalize the correction.)

LINKS TO ACCOUNTING

You have just learned how transactions are recorded in a general journal and then posted to the general ledger. Now, let's go back and apply this to Peyton Manning and his salary. He earned $35,037,700 in 2004!

Questions

1. If you were Manning's bookkeeper, how would you record the salary he earned for the year 2004 (assuming he gets it all in one paycheck)?

2. Now, let's look at this transaction from the giving end instead of the receiving end. If you were a bookkeeper for the Indianapolis Colts, show how you would record the payment made to Manning for his 2004 salary.

3. You probably need a reality check about now. How much *does* a professional athlete (this means the average person, not Peyton Manning) earn? To find out, go to **http://www.collegegrad.com/salaries/ salaries.shtml** (or **http://www.collegegrad.com** and select Salaries and then Salary Calculator). In the Salary Wizard, select Sports and Recreation from the Job Category drop-down menu. Then, from the State/Metro Area drop-down menu, choose a listed location that is near you and click the Search button. When the search results appear, scroll through the list to find the professional athlete listing and click on Base Pay for salary information. What is the median pay indicated?

CONSIDER AND COMMUNICATE

You are the new bookkeeper in a small business. The bookkeeper whose job you are taking is training you on the business's manual system. As he journalizes, he writes the account number into the Post. Ref. column because he thinks it's easier. Then, when he posts, he won't have to be bothered writing the account numbers. How would you explain why he should *not* write the account number in the Post. Ref. column immediately and should instead enter the account number after he has posted the amount to the ledger?

CRITICAL THINKING

You work as an accounting clerk. You have received the following information supplied by a client, S. Williamson, from the client's bank statement, the client's tax returns, and a variety of other July documents. The client wants you to prepare an income statement, a statement of owner's equity, and a balance sheet for the month of July for Williamson Company.

Income from Services	8,570	Wages Expense	3,230
Beginning Capital	48,000	Utilities Expense	525
Cash	22,340	Drawing	1,200
Truck	?	Supplies Expense	612
Accounts Payable	?	Equipment	16,148
Rent Expense	1,100	Total Liabilities and Owner's Equity	54,238

PROBLEM SET A

For additional help, see the demonstration problem at the beginning of each chapter in your Working Papers.

P.O. 1

Problem 3-1A The chart of accounts of the Barkley School is shown here, followed by the transactions that took place during October of this year:

Assets

111 Cash
113 Accounts Receivable
115 Prepaid Insurance
124 Equipment
127 Furniture

Liabilities

221 Accounts Payable

Owner's Equity

311 R. Barkley, Capital
312 R. Barkley, Drawing

Revenue

411 Tuition Income

Expenses

511 Salary Expense
512 Rent Expense
513 Gas and Oil Expense
514 Advertising Expense
515 Repair Expense
516 Telephone Expense
517 Utilities Expense
529 Miscellaneous Expense

Oct.		
	1	Bought liability insurance for one year, $1,450, Ck. No. 1527.
	3	Received a bill for advertising from *Business Highlights*, $320.
	4	Paid the rent for the current month, $890, Ck. No. 1528.
	7	Received a bill for equipment repair from Speedy Service, $288, Inv. 436.
	10	Received and deposited tuition from students, $6,250.
	11	Received and paid the telephone bill, $230, Ck. No. 1529.
	15	Bought desks and chairs from Oakley Furniture Company, $1,880, paying $880 in cash and placing the balance on account, Ck. No. 1530.
	18	Paid on account to *Business Highlights*, a creditor, $320, Ck. No. 1531.
	21	R. Barkley withdrew $800 for personal use, Ck. No. 1532.
	24	Received a bill for gas and oil from West's Oil Company, $180, Inv. 682.
	25	Received and deposited tuition from students, $6,140.

Oct.   27   Paid the salary of the office assistant, $1,200, Ck. No. 1533.

28   Bought a photocopier on account from Crest Office Machines, $750, Inv. 417.

29   Received $700 tuition from a student who had charged the tuition on account last month.

30   Received and paid the bill for utilities, $360, Ck. No. 1534.

31   Paid for flower arrangements for front office, $62, Ck. No. 1535.

31   R. Barkley invested his personal computer and printer, with a fair market value of $1,230, in the business.

Instructions

Record these transactions in the general journal, including a brief explanation for each entry. Number the journal pages 31 and 32.

P.O. 2,3

Problem 3-2A The journal entries for August, Casey's Car Care's second month of business, have been journalized in the general journal in your Working Papers. The balances of the accounts as of July 31 have been recorded in the general ledger in your Working Papers. Notice the word *Balance* in the Item column, the check mark in the Post. Ref. column, and that the amount is in the Balance column only.

Check Figure

Net Income, $9,333

Instructions

1. Write the owner's name, M. Casey, in the Capital and Drawing accounts.
2. Post the general journal entries to the general ledger accounts.
3. Prepare a trial balance as of August 31, 20—.
4. Prepare an income statement for the two months ended August 31, 20—.
5. Prepare a statement of owner's equity for the two months ended August 31, 20—.
6. Prepare a balance sheet as of August 31, 20—.

P.O. 1,2,3

Problem 3-3A Following is the chart of accounts of the C. Elson Clinic.

Assets

111 Cash
113 Accounts Receivable
117 Prepaid Insurance
124 Equipment

Liabilities

221 Accounts Payable

Owner's Equity

311 C. Elson, Capital
312 C. Elson, Drawing

Revenue

411 Professional Fees

Expenses

511 Salary Expense
512 Rent Expense
513 Laboratory Expense
514 Utilities Expense
515 Supplies Expense

Dr. Elson completed the following transactions during July:

July   1   Bought laboratory equipment on account from BLM Surgical Supply Company, $3,580, paying $1,500 in cash and placing the remainder on account, Ck. No. 1730.

3   Paid the office rent for the current month, $1,100, Ck. No. 1731.

5   Received cash on account from patients, $850 (temporary abnormal balance).

6   Bought supplies on account from McReady Supply Company, $218, Inv. 3455.

7   Received and paid the bill for laboratory services, $1,110, Ck. No. 1732.

July	8	Bought insurance for one year, $1,400, Ck. No. 1733.
	12	Performed medical services for patients on account, $4,990.
	15	Performed medical services for patients for cash, $3,320.
	16	The equipment purchased on July 1 was found to be broken. Dr. Elson returned the damaged part and received a reduction in his bill, $415, Inv. 3162, Credit Memo No. 141. (Credit Equipment.)
	18	Paid the salary of the part-time nurse, $1,200, Ck. No. 1734.
	24	Received and paid the telephone bill for the month, $252, Ck. No. 1735.
	28	Performed medical services for patients on account, $6,250.
	29	Dr. Elson withdrew cash for his personal use, $1,600, Ck. No. 1736.

Check Figure

Trial balance total, $59,265

Instructions

1. Journalize the transactions for July in the general journal, beginning on page 21.
2. Write the name of the owner next to the Capital and Drawing accounts in the general ledger. The balances of the accounts as of June 30 have been recorded in the general ledger in your Working Papers. Notice the word *Balance* in the Item column, the check mark in the Post. Ref. column, and that the amount is in the Balance column only. This indicates a balance brought forward from a prior page or month.
3. Post the entries to the general ledger accounts.
4. Prepare a trial balance.

Instructions for General Ledger Software

1. Journalize the transactions in the general journal.
2. Post the entries to the general ledger.
3. Print a trial balance as of July 31.

P.O. 1,2,3

Problem 3-4A Robbin's Landscaping Service has the following chart of accounts:

Assets

111 Cash
113 Accounts Receivable
117 Prepaid Insurance
124 Equipment

Liabilities

221 Accounts Payable

Owner's Equity

311 J. Robbin, Capital
312 J. Robbin, Drawing

Revenue

411 Landscaping Income

Expenses

511 Salary Expense
512 Rent Expense
513 Gas and Oil Expense
514 Utilities Expense
515 Supplies Expense

The following transactions were completed by Robbin's Landscaping Service:

Mar.	1	Robbin deposited $20,000 in a bank account in the name of the business.
	4	Robbin invested her personal gardening equipment, with a fair market value of $1,000, in the business.
	6	Bought a used trailer on account from Roth Sales, $850, Inv. 314.
	7	Paid the rent for the current month, $600, Ck. No. 1000.
	9	Bought a used backhoe from Mobile Equipment, $6,200, paying $3,000 in cash and placing the balance on account, Inv. 4166, Ck. No. 1001.

Mar.   10   Bought liability insurance for one year, $900, Ck. No. 1002.

13   Sold landscaping services on account to Franklin's, $3,420, Inv. 100.

14   Bought supplies on account from Office Decor, $240, Inv. 5172.

15   Sold landscaping services on account to C. Clayton, $2,560, Inv. 101.

17   Received and paid the bill from Engine Services for gas and oil for the equipment, $140, Ck. No. 1003.

19   Sold landscaping services for cash to Cass Company, $1,880, Inv. 102.

22   Paid on account to Roth Sales, a creditor, $400, Inv. 314, Ck. No. 1004.

24   Received on account from Franklin's, a customer, $700, Inv. 100.

28   Sold landscaping services on account to Simpson, Inc., $1,625, Inv. 103.

29   Received and paid the telephone bill, $186, Ck. No. 1005.

30   Paid the salary of the employee, $1,340, Ck. No. 1006.

31   Robbin withdrew cash for her personal use, $1,400, Ck. No. 1007.

Check Figure

Trial balance total, $34,375

Instructions

1. Journalize the transactions in the general journal, beginning on page 1. Write a brief explanation for each entry.
2. Write the name of the owner on the Capital and Drawing accounts.
3. Post the journal entries to the general ledger accounts.
4. Prepare a trial balance dated March 31, 20—.

PROBLEM SET B

For additional help, see the demonstration problem at the beginning of each chapter in your Working Papers.

P.O. 1

Problem 3-1B The chart of accounts of Edgar Academy is shown here, followed by the transactions that took place during December of this year:

Assets

111 Cash
113 Accounts Receivable
115 Prepaid Insurance
124 Equipment
127 Furniture

Liabilities

221 Accounts Payable

Owner's Equity

311 R. Edgar, Capital
312 R. Edgar, Drawing

Revenue

411 Tuition Income

Expenses

511 Salary Expense
512 Rent Expense
513 Gas and Oil Expense
514 Advertising Expense
515 Repair Expense
516 Telephone Expense
517 Utilities Expense
518 Supplies Expense
529 Miscellaneous Expense

Dec.   1   Bought liability insurance for one year, $1,260, Ck. No. 1627.

11   Received a bill for advertising from the *District News*, $370, Statement No. 4267.

12   Paid the rent for the current month, $950, Ck. No. 1628.

13   Received a bill for equipment repair from Electrician's Services, $360, Inv. 547.

Dec. 16 Received and deposited tuition from students, $4,860.
  17 Received and paid the telephone bill, $292, Ck. No. 1629.
  18 Bought desks and chairs from Classroom Furniture, $1,520, paying $700 in cash and placing the balance on account, Ck. No. 1630.
  20 Paid on account to the *District News*, a creditor, $370, Statement No. 4267, Ck. No. 1631.
  21 R. Edgar withdrew $900 for personal use, Ck. No. 1632.
  26 Received a bill for gas and oil from Cheapest Oil Company, $194, Inv. 591.
  27 Received and deposited tuition from students, $5,672.
  31 Paid the salary of the office assistant, $975, Ck. No. 1633.
  31 Bought a fax machine on account from OfficeCo, $192, Inv. 529.
  31 Received $910 tuition from a student who had put the tuition on account last month.
  31 Received and paid the bill for utilities, $448, Ck. No. 1634.
  31 R. Edgar invested her personal computer and printer, with a fair market value of $1,275, in the business.
  31 Bought supplies, $284, Ck. No. 1635.

Instructions

Record these transactions in the general journal, including a brief explanation for each entry. Number the journal pages 31 and 32.

P.O. 2,3

Problem 3-2B The journal entries for May, Petite Day Care's second month of business, have been journalized in the general journal in your Working Papers. The balances of the accounts as of April 30 have been recorded in the general ledger in your Working Papers. Notice the word *Balance* in the Item column, the check mark in the Post. Ref. column, and that the amount is in the Balance column only. This indicates a balance brought forward from a prior page or month.

Check Figure

Net Income, $4,994

Instructions

1. Write the owner's name, R. Ochoa, in the Capital and Drawing accounts.
2. Post the general journal entries to the general ledger accounts.
3. Prepare a trial balance as of May 31, 20—.
4. Prepare an income statement for the two months ended May 31, 20—.
5. Prepare a statement of owner's equity for the two months ended May 31, 20—.
6. Prepare a balance sheet as of May 31, 20—.

P.O. 1,2,3

Problem 3-3B Following is the chart of accounts of D. Roe, M.D.

Assets

111 Cash
113 Accounts Receivable
117 Prepaid Insurance
124 Equipment

Liabilities

221 Accounts Payable

Owner's Equity

311 D. Roe, Capital
312 D. Roe, Drawing

Revenue

411 Professional Fees

Expenses

511 Salary Expense
512 Rent Expense
513 Laboratory Expense
514 Utilities Expense
515 Supplies Expense

Dr. Roe completed the following transactions during July:

July   1   Bought laboratory equipment on account from Seger Surgical Supply Company, $6,430, paying $1,530 in cash and placing the remainder on account, Inv. 2071, Ck. No. 1930.
3   Paid the office rent for the current month, $1,250, Ck. No. 1931.
5   Received cash on account from patients, $2,753.
6   Bought supplies on account from Regan Supply, $290, Inv. 3455.
9   Received and paid the bill for laboratory services, $995, Ck. No. 1932.
10   Bought insurance for one year, $1,600, Ck. No. 1933.
12   Performed medical services for patients on account, $4,875.
14   Performed medical services for patients for cash, $3,723.
18   Part of the equipment purchased on July 1 was found to be broken. Dr. Roe returned the damaged part and received a reduction in her bill, $368, Inv. 2071, Credit Memo No. 218. (Credit Equipment.)
20   Paid the salary of the part-time nurse, $1,075, Ck. No. 1934.
22   Received and paid the telephone bill for the month, $235, Ck. No. 1935.
24   Performed medical services for patients on account, $3,857.
30   Dr. Roe withdrew cash for her personal use, $1,400, Ck. No. 1936.

Check Figure

Trial balance total, $43,925

Instructions

1. Journalize the transactions for July in the general journal, beginning on page 21.
2. Write the name of the owner next to the Capital and Drawing accounts in the general ledger. The balances of the accounts as of June 30 have been recorded in the general ledger in your Working Papers. Notice the word *Balance* in the Item column, the check mark in the Post. Ref. column, and that the amount is in the Balance column only. This indicates a balance brought forward from a prior page or month.
3. Post the entries to the general ledger accounts.
4. Prepare a trial balance.

Instructions for General Ledger Software

1. Journalize the transactions in the general journal.
2. Post the entries to the general ledger.
3. Print a trial balance as of July 31.

P.O. 1,2,3

Problem 3-4B Lara's Landscaping Service maintains the following chart of accounts.

Assets

111 Cash
113 Accounts Receivable
117 Prepaid Insurance
124 Equipment

Liabilities

221 Accounts Payable

Owner's Equity

311 J. Lara, Capital
312 J. Lara, Drawing

Revenue

411 Landscaping Income

Expenses

511 Salary Expense
512 Rent Expense
513 Gas and Oil Expense
514 Utilities Expense
515 Supplies Expense

The following transactions were completed by Lara:

Apr.
1 Lara deposited $20,000 in a bank account in the name of the business.

4 Lara invested his personal gardening equipment, with a fair market value of $1,600, in the business.

6 Bought a used trailer on account from Trailer Sales, $1,800, Inv. 415.

7 Paid the rent for the current month, $510, Ck. No. 100.

9 Bought a used bulldozer from Digger's Equipment, $11,000, paying $3,000 in cash and placing the balance on account, Inv. 3255, Ck. No. 101.

10 Bought liability insurance for one year, $800, Ck. No. 102.

13 Sold landscaping services on account to Felton Homes, $4,253, Inv. 100.

14 Bought supplies on account from Padilla Supply, $318, Inv. 4281.

15 Sold landscaping services on account to Britton Inc., $3,878, Inv. 101.

17 Received and paid the bill from The Tanks for gas and oil for the equipment, $105, Ck. No. 103.

19 Sold landscaping services for cash to Scheck Company, $1,214, Inv. 102.

22 Paid on account to Trailer Sales, a creditor, $600, Inv. 415, Ck. No. 104.

24 Received on account from Felton Homes, a customer, $700, Inv. 100.

28 Sold landscaping services on account to Lester Inc., $1,820, Inv. 103.

29 Received and paid the telephone bill, $238, Ck. No. 105.

30 Paid the salary of the employee, $1,650, Ck. No. 106.

30 Lara withdrew cash for his personal use, $1,800, Ck. No. 107.

Check Figure

Trial balance total, $42,283

Instructions

1. Journalize the transactions in the general journal, beginning on page 1. Write a brief explanation for each entry.
2. Write the name of the owner on the Capital and Drawing accounts.
3. Post the journal entries to the general ledger accounts.
4. Prepare a trial balance dated April 30, 20—.

The Computer Clinic

Meet the owner.

Determine owner's needs.

Gather information and make assessment.

Journalizing, Posting, and Preparing a Trial Balance

A friend of yours, Anika Valli, has decided to open a spa to serve her small resort town of about 7,000 people and 4 million tourists annually. She has named the business All About You Spa to convey the idea that the business intends to pamper those who enter its doors. She will operate the spa five days a week, Tuesday through Saturday, but a phone line will always be available to answer questions and take appointments. Hours will be from 8 A.M. to 8 P.M. She has asked you to be the bookkeeper for this new business. At the end of the month of June, the owner, Anika Valli, would like you to provide the following:

1. General journal
2. General ledger
3. Trial balance
4. Income statement
5. Statement of owner's equity
6. Balance sheet

She has kept a checkbook and a file folder with summary evidence of June's spa activity: a check register, a summary report of charges by customers for services provided, all receipts that were issued, and a summary of charges made by All About You Spa. Most of the income from services is received in cash and as charges to credit cards. No checks are accepted, except from approved clients (primarily conference planners and other organizations that book packages as prizes for attendees or gifts for employees, speakers, or other people they want to thank with a spa service or package of services). Anika deposits cash receipts on the 7th, 14th, 21st, and last day of each month.

The first page in the file folder contains the following chart of accounts.

Chart of Accounts for All About You Spa

111	Cash	411	Income from Services
113	Accounts Receivable		
117	Prepaid Insurance	511	Wages Expense
124	Spa Equipment	512	Rent Expense
128	Office Equipment	513	Office Supplies Expense
		514	Spa Supplies Expense
211	Accounts Payable	515	Laundry Expense
		516	Advertising Expense
311	A. Valli, Capital	517	Utilities Expense
312	A. Valli, Drawing	530	Miscellaneous Expense

Clipped to the front of the file folder is a brochure listing the services of All About You Spa. Part of the brochure is shown on the next page.

All About You Spa Services

Massages

Type	Time	Description	Price
Deep-Tissue Destresser	90 min.	Vigorous, prescriptive	$90.00
Herbal Body Sea Wrap	90 min.	Gentle, cleansing	$90.00
Aromatherapy Healing Experience	90 min.	Gentle, relaxing	$90.00
Healing Stones Experience	90 min.	Healing, relaxing	$90.00
Post-Workout Massage	90 min.	Invigorating, prescriptive	$90.00
Exfoliating Ginger and Sea Salt Scrub	90 min.	Cleansing, invigorating	$90.00
Custom Massage	60 min.	Highlights problem areas	$60.00

Other Spa Experiences

Type	Time	Description	Price
Reflexology Points Experience	60 min.	Problem areas, relaxing	$60.00
Reiki Healing Experience	60 min.	Full body, relaxing	$60.00
All About You Women's Facial	60 min.	Relaxing, individualized	$60.00
All About You Men's Facial	60 min.	Relaxing, individualized	$60.00
All About You Pedicure	60 min.	Beautifying, relaxing	$60.00
Day of Beauty	Full day or Half day	Let us help you select a memorable combination of services.	
Body Analysis and Consultation	60 min.	Informative, prescriptive	$60.00
All About You Makeup Consultation	60 min.	Beautifying, individualized	$60.00

Packages and Gift Certificates

Type	Time	Description	Price
Package of three 90-minute services	270 min.	Mix and match to your needs.	$250.00
Package of two 90-minute services	180 min.	Select your favorite duo.	$160.00
Package of three 60-minute services	180 min.	Mix and match to your needs.	$160.00
Package of two 60-minute services	120 min.	Select your favorite duo.	$110.00
Gift certificates available at any price		Reward employees, friends, or relatives.	

WHERE TO START
Enter chart of accounts.

WHAT TO DO FIRST
Enter June's transactions from documents and/or input form.

1. Load and log into your general ledger software.
2. Enter the chart of accounts. In future chapters, other accounts will have to be added as you need them.
3. There are no beginning balances since this is a new business.
4. Journalize and post the transactions prompted by the following documents (save often):

   a. Checkbook entries (deposits made and checks written)

Check No.	Date	Explanation	√	Deposits	Check Amount
	6/1	Invested cash in business.		15,000.00	
1011	6/3	Bought 6-month liability insurance policy.			960.00
1012	6/3	Bought spa equipment for $4,235.00, putting $2,000.00 cash down.			2,000.00
1013	6/3	Paid June rent.			1,650.00
1014	6/5	Bought office supplies.			248.00
1015	6/5	Purchased flowers and balloons for grand opening (Misc. Exp.).			112.00
1016	6/7	Paid first week's wages.			1,847.50
	6/7	Deposited first week's cash revenue.		2,630.00	
1017	6/11	Paid on account payable for spa equipment (June 3).			873.00
	6/14	Deposited second week's cash revenue.		3,703.00	
1018	6/14	Paid second week's wages.			1,847.50
1019	6/18	Paid on account payable for spa equipment (June 3).			1,200.00
	6/21	Deposited third week's cash revenue.		4,758.00	
1020	6/21	Paid third week's wages.			1,847.50
1021	6/25	Paid on account payable for spa equipment (June 3).			73.00
1022	6/28	Paid fourth week's wages.			1,847.50
1023	6/28	Paid month's laundry bill.			84.00
	6/30	Deposited end of month's cash revenue.		5,992.00	
1024	6/30	A. Valli withdrew $1,850 for personal use.			1,850.00
1025	6/30	Paid June telephone bill.			225.00
1026	6/30	Paid June power and water bill.			248.00

b. Other documents that also require journal entries:

Receipt: 6/1

A. Valli, owner of All About You Spa, invested her personal spa equipment valued at $3,158.00.

June Accounts Payable Charges Summary Report:

6/3 Bought spa supplies on account from Spa Supplies, Inv. 804	$492.00
6/5 Bought office equipment on account from Office Equipment, Inv. 3415	$318.00
6/5 Bought advertising pamphlets on account from Adco, Inv. 512	$397.00
6/5 Bought office equipment on account from Office Equipment, Inv. 3445	$832.00
6/5 Bought office supplies on account from Office Staples, Inv. 522	$120.00

June Sales to Customers on Account Summary Report:

6/7	Jill Anson	$325.00
6/14	Jack Morgan	$486.00
6/21	Tory Ligman	$344.00
6/28	Judy Wilcox	$109.00

WHAT TO DO AT THE END OF THE MONTH
Month-end wrap-up.

5. Print a trial balance dated June 30, 20—.
6. Print the income statement for the month ended June 30, 20—.
7. Print the statement of owner's equity for the month ended June 30, 20—.
8. Print the balance sheet dated June 30, 20—.

Note: The trial balance and financial statements are unadjusted. In the next chapter, you will learn that certain accounts need to be adjusted. These adjustments will change some of the figures in these reports.

Check Figures

5. Trial balance total, $38,753
6. Net Income, $7,381
7. Ending balance of A. Valli, Capital, $23,689
8. Total Assets, $25,937

PART I: Multiple-Choice Questions

____ 1. Which of the following is not considered an account?

    a. Cash
    b. Prepaid Insurance
    c. Equipment
    d. Assets
    e. Accounts Receivable

____ 2. In which of the following transactions would an expense be recorded?

    a. Received a bill for advertising.
    b. Paid on an account payable for the utility bill.
    c. Received and paid a bill for repairs.
    d. All of these should be recorded as an expense.
    e. Only a and c should be recorded as an expense.

____ 3. The ending capital balance appears on which of the following statements?

    a. Statement of owner's equity
    b. Balance sheet
    c. Income statement
    d. Statement of owner's equity and balance sheet
    e. Statement of owner's equity and income statement

____ 4. On a statement of owner's equity, if beginning capital is $42,000 and there are an additional investment of $5,000, a net loss of $9,000, and owner withdrawals of $15,000, the ending capital amount would be

    a. $70,000.
    b. $23,000.
    c. $40,000.
    d. $54,000.
    e. none of these.

____ 5. If a $26 cash purchase of supplies is recorded as a $62 debit to Supplies Expense and a $62 credit to Cash, the result will be that

    a. the trial balance will be in balance.
    b. the Supplies Expense account will be overstated.
    c. the Cash account will be understated.
    d. Supplies Expense will be overstated and Cash will be understated.
    e. all of these will be true.

Note: Answers to Before a Test Check begin on page A-1.

____ 6. A person who wanted to know the balance of an account would look in

a. the ledger.
b. the chart of accounts.
c. the journal.
d. the source documents.
e. none of these.

PART II: The Accounting Cycle

Journalizing, Posting, Trial Balance, and Financial Statements

The accounts and their balances, as of December 1 of this year, for Antec Services are listed below:

111	Cash	$18,900	311 J. Dunn, Capital	$49,590
113	Accounts Receivable	6,300	312 J. Dunn, Drawing	11,200
116	Prepaid Insurance	1,230	411 Service Income	39,600
124	Equipment	31,200	511 Wages Expense	10,450
221	Accounts Payable	6,340	512 Utilities Expense	2,760
			513 Rent Expense	12,620
			514 Supplies Expense	870

Check Figure

Net Income, $21,153

Instructions

1. Journalize the following December transactions in general journal form on journal page 31.

   Dec. 1 Sold services for cash, $9,500.
   4 Received and paid the bill for the rent for December, $1,000, Ck. No. 2331.
   11 Received $1,750 on account from customers, Cash Receipt Nos. 1430–1438.
   19 Sold services on account, $2,075, Sales Inv. No. 2591.
   22 Received and paid the bill for utilities, $255, Ck. No. 2332.
   23 Bought supplies on account from Office Works, $292, Inv. No. 2606.
   31 Paid the wages for the month, $1,775, Ck. No. 2333.
   31 Dunn withdrew $1,500 for personal use, Ck. No. 2334.

2. Label T accounts with the above account names.

3. Correctly place the plus and minus signs under all T accounts, and label the debit and credit sides of each T account.

4. Post the entries to the T accounts by date, and foot and balance the accounts.

5. Prepare a trial balance as of December 31.

6. Prepare an income statement for the year ended December 31.

7. Prepare a statement of owner's equity for the year ended December 31.

8. Prepare a balance sheet as of December 31.

Whether a small company is doing all its accounting work manually or a large corporation is using a general ledger software package, the process of transforming the information in a company's accounting records into financial statements is the same. Take for instance Activision, a leading producer of video games for systems such as Sony's PlayStation®2, Microsoft's Xbox™, and Nintendo's GameCube™ and Game Boy® Advance. Activision's annual report for 2005 can be viewed at **http://investor.activision.com/reports.cfm.** Find Activision's balance sheet on page 54 of the annual report. The company reports its property and equipment value as Property and Equipment, net. What does this mean? Review Note 7, Property and Equipment, in the Notes to Consolidated Financial Statements, which begin on page 59. What was the total cost of Activision's property and equipment as of March 31, 2005? How much depreciation had accumulated? As you learn about adjustments for depreciation of equipment, think about the steps that Activision took to determine the amounts reported on the balance sheet in its 2005 annual report. The company used the same process you will learn about here.

In this chapter you will also learn about fiscal periods. After you read about fiscal periods, find out when Activision's fiscal year begins and ends. Where do you find this information in the annual report?

Performance Objectives

After you have completed this chapter, you will be able to do the following:

1. Define *fiscal period* and *fiscal year*.

2. List the classifications of the accounts that occupy each column of a ten-column work sheet.

3. Complete a work sheet for a service enterprise, involving adjustments for expired insurance, depreciation, and accrued wages.

4. Prepare an income statement, a statement of owner's equity, and a balance sheet for a service business directly from the work sheet.

5. Journalize and post the adjusting entries.

6. Prepare (a) an income statement involving more than one revenue account and a net loss, (b) a statement of owner's equity with an additional investment and either a net income or a net loss, (c) a balance sheet for a business having more than one accumulated depreciation account, and (d) a balance sheet containing the statement of owner's equity information.

REMEMBER!

Accounting steps:

Analyzing: Which accounts are involved?

Classifying: assets, liabilities, capital, revenue, and expenses

Recording: journalizing

Summarizing: financial statements

Interpreting: drawing conclusions

As part of the *summarizing* step in the definition of accounting, here we introduce the work sheet and the financial statements. Now that you are familiar with the classifying and recording phases of accounting for a service business, let's look at the remaining steps in the accounting process.

FISCAL PERIOD

OBJECTIVE 1

Define *fiscal period* and *fiscal year.*

A **fiscal period** is any period of time covering a complete accounting cycle. A **fiscal year** is a fiscal period consisting of twelve consecutive months. It does not have to coincide with the calendar year. If a business has seasonal peaks, it is a good idea to complete the accounting operations at the end of the most active season. At that time, management wants to know the results of the year and where the business stands financially. The fiscal year of a resort that operates during the summer may be from October 1 of one year to September 30 of the next. The government has a fiscal year from October 1 of one year to September 30 of the following year. Department stores often use a fiscal period from February 1 of one year to January 31 of the next. For income tax purposes, any period of twelve consecutive months may be selected. However, you have to be consistent and use the same fiscal period each year.

THE ACCOUNTING CYCLE

The **accounting cycle** represents the sequence of steps in the accounting process completed during the fiscal period. Figure 1 shows how we introduce these steps on a chapter-by-chapter basis. This outline brings you up to date on what we have accomplished so far and how each chapter fits into the steps in the accounting cycle.

FIGURE 1

REMEMBER!

The yellow color represents source documents, which are evidence of transactions.

Chapter 1
Analysis of Business Transactions
Assets = Liabilities + Owner's Equity
Analysis of Business Transactions
Assets = Liabilities + Owner's Equity + Revenue − Expenses

Chapter 2
Analysis of Business Transactions
Assets = Liabilities + Owner's Equity + Revenue − Expenses
$$\overline{+\,|\,-} \qquad \overline{-\,|\,+} \qquad \overline{-\,|\,+} \qquad \overline{-\,|\,+} \qquad \overline{+\,|\,-}$$

Chapter 3
Journalize and Post Business Transactions.
Prepare a Trial Balance.

Chapter 4
Gather the Adjustment Data.
Complete a Work Sheet.
Prepare Financial Statements.
Journalize and Post Adjusting Entries.

Chapter 5
Journalize and Post Closing Entries.
Prepare a Post-Closing Trial Balance.

THE WORK SHEET

The **work sheet** is a working paper used by accountants to record necessary adjustments and provide up-to-date account balances needed to prepare the financial statements. **The work sheet is a tool that accountants use to help in preparing the financial statements.** As a tool, the work sheet serves as a central place for bringing together the information needed to record the adjustments. With up-to-date account balances, the accountant can prepare the financial statements.

First, we present the work sheet form so that you can see the big picture. Next, we describe and show examples of adjustments. Finally, we show how the adjustments are entered on the work sheet and how the work sheet is completed.

We will use a ten-column work sheet—so called because two amount columns are provided for each of the work sheet's five major sections. We will explain the function of each of these sections, again basing our discussion on the accounting activities of Cline's Computer Clinic. But first we need to fill in the heading, which consists of three lines: (1) the name of the company, (2) the title of the working paper, and (3) the period of time covered.

Cline's Computer Clinic
Work Sheet
For Month Ended June 30, 20—

ACCOUNT NAME	TRIAL BALANCE		ADJUSTMENTS		ADJUSTED TRIAL BALANCE		INCOME STATEMENT		BALANCE SHEET	
	DEBIT	CREDIT	DEBIT	CREDIT	DEBIT	CREDIT	DEBIT	CREDIT	DEBIT	CREDIT

Next, we want to point out the account classifications that are placed in each column. We start with the Trial Balance columns and then move across the work sheet, discussing each pair of columns separately.

The Columns of the Work Sheet

Trial Balance Columns   When you use a work sheet, you do not have to prepare a trial balance on a separate sheet of paper. Instead, you enter the account balances from the general ledger in the first two amount columns of the work sheet. List the accounts that have balances in the Account Name column in the same order in which they appear in the chart of accounts. Assuming **normal balances,** the account classifications are listed in the Trial Balance Debit and Credit columns of the work sheet as shown at the top of the next page.

As we move along in this chapter, we will discuss the adjustments. The Adjusted Trial Balance columns contain the same account classifications as the Trial Balance columns. **The Adjusted Trial Balance columns are merely extensions of the Trial Balance columns, plus or minus any adjustment amounts.** If an adjustment is required, the amounts are carried from the Trial Balance columns through the Adjustments columns and into the Adjusted Trial Balance columns.

OBJECTIVE 2

List the classifications of the accounts that occupy each column of a ten-column work sheet.

Account Name	Trial Balance		Adjustments		Adjusted Trial Balance		Income Statement		Balance Sheet	
	Debit	Credit	Debit	Credit	Debit	Credit	Debit	Credit	Debit	Credit
	Assets ——————————————→				Assets					
		Liabilities —————————————→				Liabilities				
		Capital ———————————————→				Capital				
	Drawing ————————————————→				Drawing					
		Revenue ———————————————→				Revenue				
	Expenses ———————————————→				Expenses					

Income Statement Columns An income statement contains the revenues minus the expenses. Revenue accounts have credit balances, so they are recorded in the Income Statement Credit column. Expense accounts have debit balances, so they are recorded in the Income Statement Debit column.

Account Name	Trial Balance		Adjustments		Adjusted Trial Balance		Income Statement		Balance Sheet	
	Debit	Credit	Debit	Credit	Debit	Credit	Debit	Credit	Debit	Credit
	Assets ——————————————→				Assets					
		Liabilities —————————————→				Liabilities				
		Capital ———————————————→				Capital				
	Drawing ————————————————→				Drawing					
		Revenue ———————————————→				Revenue ———————→		Revenue			
	Expenses ———————————————→				Expenses ———————→		Expenses			

Balance Sheet Columns As you recall, the balance sheet is a statement showing assets, liabilities, and owner's equity. Asset accounts have debit balances, so they are recorded in the Balance Sheet Debit column. Liability accounts have credit balances, so they are recorded in the Balance Sheet Credit column. The Capital account has a credit balance, so it is recorded in the Balance Sheet Credit column. Because the Drawing account is a deduction from Capital, it has a debit balance and is recorded in the Balance Sheet Debit column (the opposite column from that in which Capital is recorded).

Account Name	Trial Balance		Adjustments		Adjusted Trial Balance		Income Statement		Balance Sheet	
	Debit	Credit	Debit	Credit	Debit	Credit	Debit	Credit	Debit	Credit
	Assets ——————————→				Assets ——————————————————→				Assets	
		Liabilities —————————→				Liabilities ——————————————→				Liabilities
		Capital ——————————→				Capital ———————————————→				Capital
	Drawing ————————————→				Drawing ————————————————→				Drawing	
		Revenue ——————————→				Revenue ——————→		Revenue		
	Expenses ——————————→				Expenses ———————→		Expenses			

ADJUSTMENTS

OBJECTIVE 3

Complete a work sheet for a service enterprise, involving adjustments for expired insurance, depreciation, and accrued wages.

The Financial Picture Before Adjustments | The Financial Picture After Adjustments

Without adjustments, the financial statements would be out of focus.

Adjustments are a way of updating the ledger accounts. They may be considered *internal transactions*. They have not been recorded in the accounts up to this time because no outside party has been involved. Adjustments are determined after the trial balance has been prepared. Adjustments fine-tune the accounts to present a more accurate concept of the accounts.

Only a few accounts are adjusted. To describe the reasons for making adjustments, let's return to Cline's Computer Clinic. First, we select the accounts that require adjustments. Next, we show the adjustments recorded in T accounts so you can see the effect on the accounts. **However, bear in mind that the adjustments are first recorded on the work sheet when using a manual accounting system.** When using general ledger software, adjustments are recorded in the general journal.

Prepaid Insurance

The $480 balance in Prepaid Insurance represents the premium paid in advance for a one-year liability insurance policy. One month of the twelve months of premium has now expired, which amounts to $40.

$$\frac{\$\ 40 \text{ per month}}{12 \text{ months })\$480}$$

In the adjustment, Cline's Computer Clinic deducts the expired or used portion from Prepaid Insurance and adds it to Insurance Expense.

	(a)	**Prepaid Insurance**			**Insurance Expense**	
			+ | −			+ | −
(Old)	Balance	480	**Adjusting** 40	**Adjusting** 40		
(New)	Balance	440				

The new balance of Prepaid Insurance, $440 ($480 − $40), represents the cost of insurance that remains paid in advance and should therefore appear in the Balance Sheet Debit column. The $40 amount in Insurance Expense represents the cost of insurance that has expired and should therefore appear in the Income Statement Debit column.

Depreciation of Equipment

We have recorded durable items, such as appliances and fixtures, under Equipment because they will last longer than one year. The benefits of these assets will eventually be used up (the assets will either wear out or become obsolete). Therefore, we should systematically spread out the cost of these assets over their useful lives. That is, we allocate the cost of the equipment as an expense *over its estimated useful life* and call this **depreciation** because such equipment loses its usefulness. A part of this depreciation expense is allotted to each fiscal period. In the case of Cline's Computer Clinic, the

REMEMBER!

When using a manual accounting system, adjustments are recorded in the work sheet first. They will be journalized and posted later in the accounting cycle.

REMEMBER!

For the adjustment of insurance, you are given the amount used (expired). So, in the adjusting entry, take the amount used directly out of Prepaid Insurance and put it into Insurance Expense.

FYI

There are several methods of depreciation for assets. Straight-line depreciation is shown here—equal amounts are taken each year. There are also accelerated methods that assign larger amounts to expense in the early years of the life of an asset.

Equipment account has a balance of $83,720. Suppose we estimate that the equipment will have a useful life of seven years, with a trade-in (salvage) value of $13,160 at the end of that time. Using **straight-line depreciation**, we can allocate the cost of an asset, less any trade-in value, evenly over the useful life of the asset. Depreciation for one month is figured like this:

1. Subtract the trade-in (salvage) value from the cost to get the full depreciation.

   $83,720 − $13,160 = $70,560

2. Divide the full depreciation by the number of years in the asset's useful life to get the depreciation for one year.

$$\frac{\$10,080 \text{ per year}}{7 \text{ years })\$70,560 \text{ full depreciation}}$$

3. Divide the depreciation for one year by 12 to get the depreciation for one month.

$$\frac{\$\quad 840 \text{ per month}}{12 \text{ months })\$10,080}$$

When depreciation is recorded, we do not subtract it directly from the asset account. In asset accounts, such as Equipment or Building, we must keep the original cost recorded in the account. Consequently, the amount of depreciation has to be recorded in another account; that account is Accumulated Depreciation.

Always record the adjusting entry for depreciation as a debit to Depreciation Expense (an income statement item) and a credit to Accumulated Depreciation (a balance sheet item), which increases both accounts. The adjustment in T account form would appear as follows:

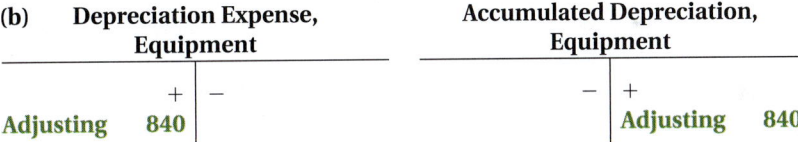

Accumulated Depreciation, Equipment, is contrary to, or a deduction from, Equipment, so we call it a **contra account**. To show the accounts under their proper headings, let's look at the fundamental accounting equation. Brackets indicate that Accumulated Depreciation, Equipment, is a deduction from the Equipment account. Note that the plus and minus signs are opposite.

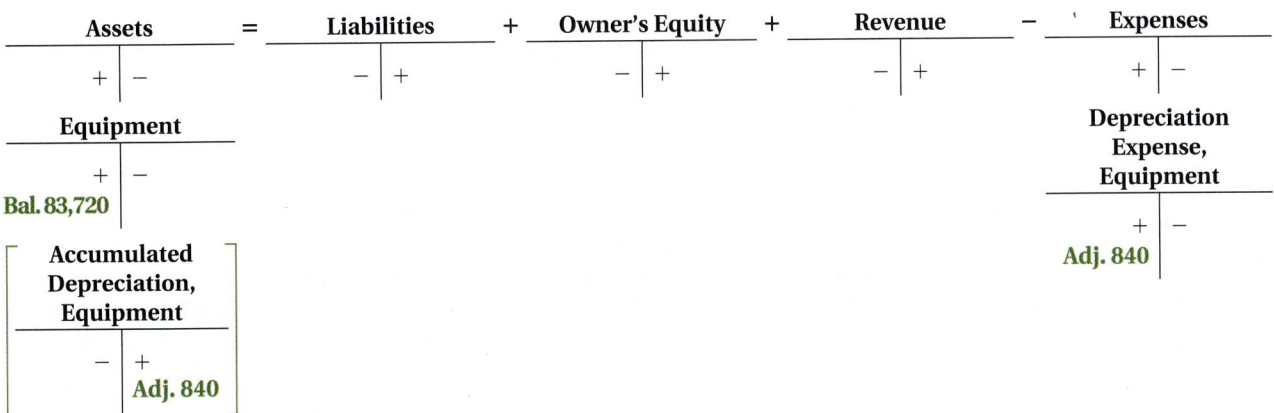

On the work sheet, Equipment (an asset) appears in the Balance Sheet Debit column. Accumulated Depreciation (a deduction from an asset) appears in the opposite column, which is the Balance Sheet Credit column.

Accumulated Depreciation, Equipment, as the title implies, is the total depreciation that the company has taken since the original purchase of the asset. Rather than crediting the Equipment account, Cline's Computer Clinic keeps track of the total depreciation taken since it first acquired the asset in a separate account. The maximum depreciation it could take would be the cost of the equipment, $83,720, less the trade-in value of $13,160. So, for the first year, Accumulated Depreciation, Equipment, will increase at the rate of $840 per month, assuming that no additional equipment has been purchased. For example, at the end of the second month, Accumulated Depreciation, Equipment, will amount to $1,680 ($840 + $840).

On the balance sheet, the balance of Accumulated Depreciation is deducted from the balance of the related asset account as illustrated on the following partial balance sheet for Cline's Computer Clinic. The net amount shown, $82,880, is referred to as the book value of the asset. Thus, **book value** (or **carrying value**) is the cost of an asset minus accumulated depreciation.

FYI

If we had a Building account, the adjusting entry would be a debit to Depreciation Expense, Building, and a credit to Accumulated Depreciation, Building. Building and Accumulated Depreciation, Building, would be listed separately on the balance sheet.

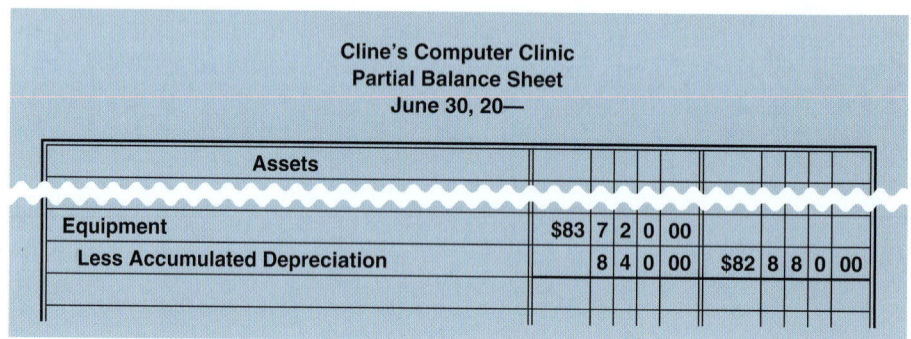

Cline's Computer Clinic
Partial Balance Sheet
June 30, 20—

Assets				
Equipment		$83 7 2 0 00		
Less Accumulated Depreciation		8 4 0 00	$82 8 8 0 00	

Wages Expense

The end of the fiscal period and the end of the employees' payroll period rarely fall on the same day. A diagram of the situation looks like this:

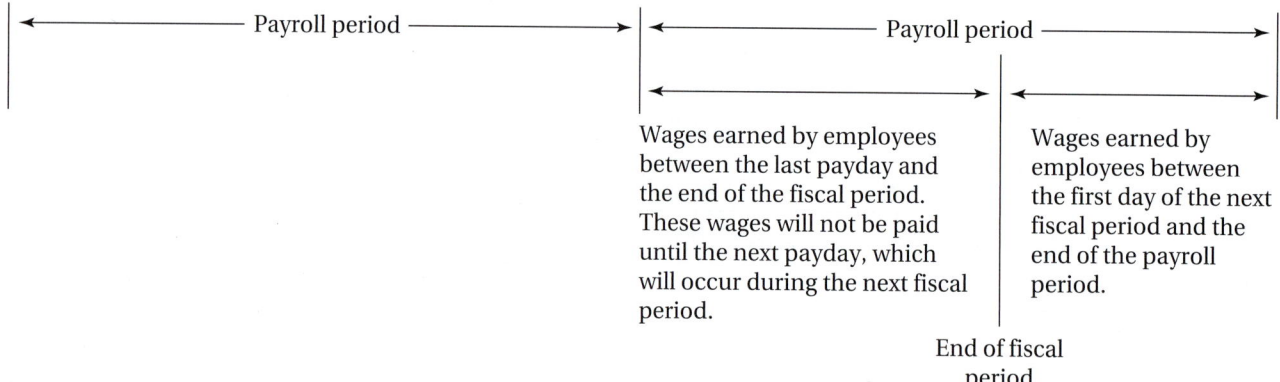

Since the last day of the fiscal period falls in the middle of the payroll period, we have to split up the wages earned in that payroll period between the fiscal period just ending and the next fiscal period. We will use another company for this example.

Assume that Brown Company pays its employees a total of $400 per day and that payday falls on Friday throughout the year. The employees work a five-day week. When the employees pick up their paychecks on Friday, the amount of the checks includes their wages for that day and for the preceding four days. Suppose that the last day of the fiscal period falls on Wednesday, December 31. The diagram below illustrates this situation.

				Dec. 26 Fri	Dec. 29 Mon	Dec. 30 Tue	Dec. 31 Wed	Jan. 1 Thur	Jan. 2 Fri
Mon	Tue	Wed	Thur						
$400	$400	$400	$400	$400	$400	$400	$400	$400	$400

End of Fiscal Period

←———————— Payroll period ————————→   ←———————— Payroll period ————————→

Payday $2,000

Payday $2,000

$1,200 $800

December						
S	M	T	W	T	F	S
	1	2	3	4	⑤	6
7	8	9	10	11	⑫	13
14	15	16	17	18	⑲	20
21	22	23	24	25	㉖	27
28	29	30	31			

Paydays

To have the Wages Expense account show an accurate balance for the fiscal period, you need to add $1,200 for the cost of labor between the last payday, December 26, and the end of the year, December 31 ($400 for December 29; $400 for December 30; $400 for December 31). Because the $1,200 will not be paid at this time but is owed to the employees as of December 31, you also need to add $1,200 to Wages Payable, a liability account, because the company owes this amount to employees.

Wages Expense			Wages Payable	
	+	–	–	+
(Old) Balance 104,000				Adjusting 1,200
Adjusting **1,200**				
(New) Balance 105,200				

Returning to our illustration of Cline's Computer Clinic, the last payday was June 24. Between June 24 and the end of the month, Cline's Computer Clinic owes an additional $240 in wages to its employee. Accountants refer to this extra amount that has not been recorded at the end of the month as **accrued wages**. In accounting terms, **accrual** means recognition of an expense or a revenue that has been incurred (expense) or earned (revenue) but has not yet been recorded.

(c)	Wages Expense			Wages Payable	
	+	−		−	+
(Old) Balance	2,980				**Adjusting** **240**
Adjusting	**240**				
(New) Balance	3,220				

Placement of Accounts on the Work Sheet

We have to enter the adjustments on the work sheet, but before doing so, let's briefly discuss the Drawing and Accumulated Depreciation accounts, as well as net income, and their effect on the work sheet.

Capital and Drawing Account Balances

The Drawing account is a contra account (contrary to Capital). In the statement of owner's equity, Drawing is deducted from Capital. To show one account as a deduction from another, the plus and minus signs are switched around. The T accounts look like this:

R. P. Cline, Capital		R. P. Cline, Drawing	
−	+	+	−
Debit	Credit	Debit	Credit
	Balance	Balance	

The normal balance for the Capital account is recorded in the Credit columns of the Trial Balance, the Adjusted Trial Balance, and the Balance Sheet sections. The normal balance for the Drawing account is recorded in the Debit columns of the Trial Balance, the Adjusted Trial Balance, and the Balance Sheet sections.

Equipment and Accumulated Depreciation, Equipment, Account Balances

The Accumulated Depreciation, Equipment, account is a contra account (contrary to Equipment). In the balance sheet, Accumulated Depreciation, Equipment, is deducted from Equipment. The T accounts look like this:

Equipment		Accumulated Depreciation, Equipment	
+	−	−	+
Debit	Credit	Debit	Credit
Balance			Balance

The normal balance for the Equipment account is recorded in the Debit columns of the Trial Balance, the Adjusted Trial Balance, and the Balance Sheet sections. The normal balance for the Accumulated Depreciation, Equipment, account is recorded in the Credit columns of the Trial Balance, the Adjusted Trial Balance, and the Balance Sheet sections.

Net Income

Net income (or net loss) is the difference between revenue and expenses. It is used to balance the Income Statement columns; since revenue is normally larger than expenses, the balancing amount must be added to the expense side. Net income (or net loss) is also used to balance the Balance Sheet columns. On the statement of owner's equity, you add net income to the owner's beginning Capital balance. Since the Capital balance is located in the Balance Sheet Credit column, net income must also be added to that side. The following diagram shows these relationships:

Account Name	Trial Balance		Adjustments		Adjusted Trial Balance		Income Statement		Balance Sheet	
	Debit	Credit	Debit	Credit	Debit	Credit	Debit	Credit	Debit	Credit
	A + Draw. + E	Accum. Depr. + L + Cap. + R			A + Draw. + E	Accum. Depr. + L + Cap. + R	E	R	A + Draw.	Accum. Depr. + L + Cap.
Net Income							NI			NI

REMEMBER!

A net income amount is entered in the Income Statement Debit column and the Balance Sheet Credit column (same side as the increase side of Capital). A net loss is entered in the Income Statement Credit column and the Balance Sheet Debit column (same side as the decrease side of Capital).

On the other hand, if expenses are larger than revenue, the result is a net loss. You must add net loss to the revenue side to balance the Income Statement columns. Also, because a net loss is deducted from the owner's beginning Capital balance, you must include net loss in the debit side of the Balance Sheet columns, thereby balancing these columns. To show this, let's look at the Income Statement and Balance Sheet columns diagrammed here.

	Income Statement		Balance Sheet	
	Debit	Credit	Debit	Credit
	E	R	A + Draw.	Accum. Depr. + L + Cap.
Net Loss		NL	NL	

Summary of Adjustments by T Accounts

To test your understanding, describe why the following adjustments are necessary. The answers are shown below the accounts.

(a) Prepaid Insurance

	+	−	
Balance	480	Adjusting	40

Insurance Expense

	+	−
Adjusting	40	

(b) Depreciation Expense, Equipment

	+	−
Adjusting	840	

Accumulated Depreciation, Equipment

	−	+	
		Adjusting	840

(c) Wages Expense

	+	−
Balance	2,980	
Adjusting	240	

Wages Payable

	−	+	
		Adjusting	240

a. To record the insurance expired during June, $40.
b. To record the depreciation for the month of June, $840.
c. To record accrued wages owed at the end of June, $240.

Cline's Computer Clinic
Work Sheet
For Month Ended June 30, 20—

	ACCOUNT NAME	TRIAL BALANCE DEBIT A + Draw. + E		TRIAL BALANCE CREDIT Accum. Depr. + L + Cap. + R		ADJUSTMENTS DEBIT		ADJUSTMENTS CREDIT	
1	Cash	11 9 5 0 00							
2	Accounts Receivable	6 2 0 00							
3	Prepaid Insurance	4 8 0 00						(a)	4 0 00
4	Equipment	83 7 2 0 00							
5	Accounts Payable			5 9 7 0 00					
6	R. P. Cline, Capital			88 2 0 0 00					
7	R. P. Cline, Drawing	3 0 0 0 00							
8	Income from Services			11 0 1 0 00					
9	Wages Expense	2 9 8 0 00				(c) 2 4 0 00			
10	Rent Expense	9 0 0 00							
11	Supplies Expense	8 7 0 00							
12	Advertising Expense	3 4 0 00							
13	Utilities Expense	3 2 0 00							
14		105 1 8 0 00		105 1 8 0 00					
15	Insurance Expense					(a) 4 0 00			
16	Depreciation Expense, Equipment					(b) 8 4 0 00			
17	Accumulated Depreciation, Equipment							(b) 8 4 0 00	
18	Wages Payable							(c) 2 4 0 00	
						1 1 2 0 00		1 1 2 0 00	

FIGURE 2

REMEMBER!

Each of the accounts that is adjusted has a companion account. Prepaid Insurance—companion account is Insurance Expense. Depreciation Expense—companion account is Accumulated Depreciation. Wages Expense—companion account is Wages Payable.

Mixed Accounts At this point, take special notice of the fact that each **adjusting entry contains an income statement account (revenue or expense) and a balance sheet account (asset, contra asset, or liability)**. Accountants refer to these accounts as **mixed accounts**—accounts with balances that are partly income statement amounts and partly balance sheet amounts. The income statement and balance sheet accounts involved are separate accounts having a part of their name in common, like Prepaid Insurance and Insurance Expense. Prepaid Insurance is recorded as $480 in the Trial Balance columns but is apportioned as $40 in Insurance Expense in the Income Statement columns and $440 in Prepaid Insurance in the Balance Sheet columns. In other words, portions of these trial balance amounts are recorded in each section.

In the previous examples, we used T accounts to explain how to handle adjustments. T accounts help organize any type of accounting entry into debits and credits. But now it is time to record the adjustments on the work sheet. To help you remember which classifications of accounts appear in each column of the work sheet, we will label the columns with letters specifying each classification of accounts; for example, A for assets, L for liabilities, etc., as shown in Figure 2.

Steps in the Completion of the Work Sheet

A completed work sheet is shown in Figure 3. Before we complete the work sheet, let's list the recommended steps to follow.

REMEMBER!

The Trial Balance columns are exactly the same as they are listed in the Trial Balance presented in Chapter 2.

1. Complete the Trial Balance columns, total, and rule.
2. Complete the Adjustments columns, total, and rule.
3. Complete the Adjusted Trial Balance columns, total, and rule.
4. Record balances in the Income Statement and Balance Sheet columns and total each column.
5. Record net income or net loss in the Income Statement columns by subtracting the smaller side from the larger side and adding the difference to the smaller side, total, and rule.
6. Record net income or net loss in the Balance Sheet columns by subtracting the smaller side from the larger side and adding the difference to the smaller side (the amount should be the same as the difference between the Income Statement column totals—if not, there is an error), total, and rule.

The steps assume the work sheet is prepared manually. The work sheet can also be prepared using a computer spreadsheet program, such as Microsoft Excel®. Whether the work sheet is prepared manually or on a computer, the columns must be completed, totaled, and ruled. An Excel version of the work sheet is shown in Figure 5 on page 128.

Step 1: Trial Balance Columns   Note that the trial balance in Figure 2 is the same trial balance presented earlier for Cline's Computer Clinic. You will be able to follow the completion of the entire work sheet for Cline's Computer Clinic in Figure 3.

REMEMBER!

After the first fiscal period, Accumulated Depreciation will have a balance, so it will be listed immediately below the asset being depreciated (which in this example is Equipment). Consequently, Accumulated Depreciation will not appear at the bottom of next month's work sheet.

Step 2: Adjustments Columns   When we enter the adjustments, we identify them as **(a), (b), (c),** to indicate the relationships between the debit and credit sides and the sequence of the individual adjusting entries (see Figure 3).

Note that Insurance Expense; Depreciation Expense, Equipment; Accumulated Depreciation, Equipment; and Wages Payable did not appear in the trial balance because there were no balances in the accounts at that time. We wrote them below the Trial Balance totals to complete the work sheet.

Here is a brief review of the adjustments:

a. To record the $40 cost of insurance expired during June.
b. To record $840 depreciation for the month of June.
c. To record $240 of accrued wages owed at the end of June.

Now let's look at the work sheet shown in Figure 4. To reinforce the idea of adjusting entries, see the brief explanation of each adjustment at the right of the work sheet. Again, the completed work sheet is shown in Figure 3.

After the first fiscal period, Accumulated Depreciation will always have a balance until the related asset is sold or disposed of. Consequently, it will be listed in the Trial Balance columns immediately below the appropriate asset (Equipment, in this case).

Again, we emphasize that the work sheet is strictly a tool used to gather all the up-to-date information needed to prepare the financial statements. **The adjustments are always recorded in the work sheet first.**

REMEMBER!

Insurance is adjusted by adding the amount expired to Insurance Expense while deducting the same amount from Prepaid Insurance.

Depreciation is added to both Depreciation Expense and Accumulated Depreciation.

Accrued wages are added to both Wages Expense and Wages Payable.

Step 3: Adjusted Trial Balance Columns   Once the Adjustments columns are totaled and ruled, extend each Trial Balance amount, plus or minus any adjustment from the Adjustments columns, to the Adjusted Trial Balance columns as shown in Figure 3.

Step 4: Income Statement and Balance Sheet Columns   Extend the balances in the Adjusted Trial Balance columns to either the Income Statement or the Balance Sheet columns (see Figure 3).

FIGURE 3

Cline's Computer Clinic
Work Sheet
For Month Ended June 30, 20—

	ACCOUNT NAME	TRIAL BALANCE		ADJUSTMENTS	
		DEBIT A + Draw. + E	CREDIT Accum. Depr. + L + Cap. + R	DEBIT	CREDIT
1	Cash	11 9 5 0 00			
2	Accounts Receivable	6 2 0 00			
3	Prepaid Insurance	4 8 0 00			(a) 4 0 00
4	Equipment	83 7 2 0 00			
5	Accounts Payable		5 9 7 0 00		
6	R. P. Cline, Capital		88 2 0 0 00		
7	R. P. Cline, Drawing	3 0 0 0 00			
8	Income from Services		11 0 1 0 00		
9	Wages Expense	2 9 8 0 00		(c) 2 4 0 00	
10	Rent Expense	9 0 0 00			
11	Supplies Expense	8 7 0 00			
12	Advertising Expense	3 4 0 00			
13	Utilities Expense	3 2 0 00			
14		105 1 8 0 00	105 1 8 0 00		
15	Insurance Expense			(a) 4 0 00	
16	Depr. Exp., Equip.	Step 1		(b) 8 4 0 00	
17	Accum. Depr., Equip.				(b) 8 4 0 00
18	Wages Payable				(c) 2 4 0 00
19				1 1 2 0 00	1 1 2 0 00
20	Net Income				
21				Step 2	
22					
23					
24					
25					
26	(a) Insurance expired, $40	Step 1		Step 2	
27	(b) Depr. of equip., $840	In the Account Name column,		Enter the adjustments,	
28	(c) Accrued wages, $240	list the accounts that have		labeling each adjustment	
29		balances. Enter the account		as (a), (b), (c), and so on.	
30		balances in the Trial Balance		Total and rule the columns.	
31		columns. Total and rule the			
32		columns.			
33					
34					
35					
36					

ADJUSTED TRIAL BALANCE		INCOME STATEMENT		BALANCE SHEET		
DEBIT	CREDIT Accum. Depr. +L+Cap.+R	DEBIT	CREDIT	DEBIT	CREDIT Accum. Depr. +L+Cap.	
A+Draw.+E		E	R	A+Draw.		
11 9 5 0 00				11 9 5 0 00		1
6 2 0 00				6 2 0 00		2
4 4 0 00				4 4 0 00		3
83 7 2 0 00				83 7 2 0 00		4
	5 9 7 0 00				5 9 7 0 00	5
	88 2 0 0 00				88 2 0 0 00	6
3 0 0 0 00				3 0 0 0 00		7
	11 0 1 0 00		11 0 1 0 00			8
3 2 2 0 00		3 2 2 0 00				9
9 0 0 00		9 0 0 00				10
8 7 0 00		8 7 0 00				11
3 4 0 00		3 4 0 00				12
3 2 0 00		3 2 0 00				13
						14
4 0 00		4 0 00				15
8 4 0 00		8 4 0 00				16
	8 4 0 00				8 4 0 00	17
	2 4 0 00				2 4 0 00	18
106 2 6 0 00	106 2 6 0 00	6 5 3 0 00	11 0 1 0 00	99 7 3 0 00	95 2 5 0 00	19
		4 4 8 0 00			4 4 8 0 00	20
	Step 3	11 0 1 0 00	11 0 1 0 00	99 7 3 0 00	99 7 3 0 00	21
						22
			Steps 4, 5, 6			23

Step 3

Carry amounts across from
the Trial Balance columns
plus or minus any amounts
appearing in the Adjustments
columns. Total and rule the
columns.

Step 4

From the top of the Adjusted Trial Balance columns, go down line
by line carrying each amount over to the Income Statement or
Balance Sheet columns. Total the columns.

Step 5

Write Net Income or Net Loss in the Account Name column and
the amount in the appropriate Income Statement column. Total
and rule the columns.

Step 6

Enter the net income or loss amount in the appropriate Balance
Sheet column. Total, balance, and rule the columns.

FIGURE 4

		TRIAL BALANCE	
ACCOUNT NAME	**DEBIT** A + Draw. + E	**CREDIT** Accum. Depr. + L + Cap. + R	
1 Cash	11 9 5 0 00		
2 Accounts Receivable	6 2 0 00		
3 Prepaid Insurance	4 8 0 00		
4 Equipment	83 7 2 0 00		
5 Accounts Payable		5 9 7 0 00	
6 R. P. Cline, Capital		88 2 0 0 00	
7 R. P. Cline, Drawing	3 0 0 0 00		
8 Income from Services		11 0 1 0 00	
9 Wages Expense	2 9 8 0 00		
10 Rent Expense	9 0 0 00		
11 Supplies Expense	8 7 0 00		
12 Advertising Expense	3 4 0 00		
13 Utilities Expense	3 2 0 00		
14	105 1 8 0 00	105 1 8 0 00	
15 Insurance Expense			
16 Depreciation Expense, Equipment		Step 1	
17 Accumulated Depreciation, Equipment			
18 Wages Payable			
19			
20 (a) Insurance expired, $40			
21 (b) Depreciation of equipment, $840			
22 (c) Accrued wages, $240			

Depreciation can occur from everyday wear and tear, or assets can simply become obsolete.

Step 5: Net Income or Net Loss—Income Statement Columns Total each of the two Income Statement columns. Subtract the smaller side from the larger side, write the difference under the smaller Income Statement column total, and total and rule as shown in Figure 3.

Step 6: Net Income or Net Loss—Balance Sheet Columns Total the two Balance Sheet columns. Subtract the smaller side from the larger side, write the difference under the smaller Balance Sheet column total (the amount should equal the difference between the Income Statement column totals—if not, there is an error), and total and rule as shown in Figure 3.

If there is a net income, the credit side of the Income Statement columns will be larger than the debit side—more revenue than expenses. In this case, write Net Income in the Account Name column on the same line as the difference you calculated. If there is a net loss, the debit side of the Income Statement columns will be larger than the credit side—more expenses than revenue. In this case, write Net Loss in the Account Name column on the same line as the difference you calculated.

Cline's Computer Clinic
Work Sheet
For Month Ended June 30, 20—

ADJUSTMENTS DEBIT	ADJUSTMENTS CREDIT	ADJUSTED TRIAL BALANCE DEBIT (A + Draw. + E)	ADJUSTED TRIAL BALANCE CREDIT (Accum. Depr. + L + Cap. + R)	INCOME STATEMENT DEBIT (E)	INCOME STATEMENT CREDIT (R)	BALANCE SHEET DEBIT (A + Draw.)	BALANCE SHEET CREDIT (Accum. Depr. + L + Cap.)	
		11 950 00		No adjustment, so carry over amount directly				1
		620 00						2
	(a) 40 00	440 00		Adjustment involved, subtract $40 (expired) from $480				3
		83 720 00		No adjustment, so carry over amount directly				4
			5 970 00					5
			88 200 00					6
		3 000 00						7
			11 010 00					8
(c) 240 00		3 220 00		Adjustment involved, add $240 (accrued) to $2,980				9
		900 00		No adjustment, so carry over amount directly				10
		870 00						11
		340 00						12
		320 00						13
				This line is blank because of the trial balance total				14
(a) 40 00		40 00		Adjustment involved, carry $40 over to the same column				15
(b) 840 00		840 00		Adjustment involved, carry $840 over to the same column				16
	(b) 840 00		840 00	Adjustment involved, carry $840 over to the same column				17
	(c) 240 00		240 00	Adjustment involved, carry $240 over to the same column				18
1 120 00	1 120 00	106 260 00	106 260 00					19
								20
	Step 2		Step 3					21
								22

Work Sheet Requiring Two Pages

If a large number of accounts is involved, it may be necessary to continue the work sheet to a second page.

(First Page)

Account Name	Trial Balance		Adjustments	
Wages Expense	3,240 00		(c) 220 50	
Totals carried forward	98,312 00	91,146 10	962 50	126 50

Note that the totals at the bottom of the first page are labeled "Totals carried forward" in the Account Name column. At the top of the second page, the totals are repeated and labeled "Totals brought forward" in the Account Name column. Continue listing account names and balances below the totals brought forward.

FIGURE 5

Cline's Computer Clinic
Work Sheet
For Month Ended June 30, 20—

ACCOUNT NAME	TRIAL BALANCE DEBIT (A+Draw.+E)	TRIAL BALANCE CREDIT (+L+Cap.+R / Accum. Depr.)	ADJUSTMENTS DEBIT	ADJUSTMENTS CREDIT	ADJUSTED TRIAL BALANCE DEBIT (A+Draw.+E)	ADJUSTED TRIAL BALANCE CREDIT (+L+Cap.+R / Accum. Depr.)	INCOME STATEMENT DEBIT (E)	INCOME STATEMENT CREDIT (R)	BALANCE SHEET DEBIT (A+Draw.)	BALANCE SHEET CREDIT (+L+Cap. / Accum. Depr.)
Cash	11,950.00				11,950.00				11,950.00	
Accounts Receivable	620.00				620.00				620.00	
Prepaid Insurance	480.00			(a) 40.00	440.00				440.00	
Equipment	83,720.00				83,720.00				83,720.00	
Accounts Payable		5,970.00				5,970.00				5,970.00
R. P. Cline, Capital		88,200.00				88,200.00				88,200.00
R. P. Cline, Drawing	3,000.00				3,000.00				3,000.00	
Income from Services		11,010.00				11,010.00		11,010.00		
Wages Expense	2,980.00		(c) 240.00		3,220.00		3,220.00			
Rent Expense	900.00				900.00		900.00			
Supplies Expense	870.00				870.00		870.00			
Advertising Expense	340.00				340.00		340.00			
Utilities Expense	320.00				320.00		320.00			
	105,180.00	105,180.00								
Insurance Expense			(a) 40.00		40.00		40.00			
Depr. Exp., Equip.			(b) 840.00		840.00		840.00			
Accum. Depr., Equip.				(b) 840.00		840.00				840.00
Wages Payable				(c) 240.00		240.00				240.00
			1,120.00	1,120.00	106,260.00	106,260.00	6,530.00	11,010.00	99,730.00	95,250.00
Net Income							4,480.00			4,480.00
							11,010.00	11,010.00	99,730.00	99,730.00

Sheet1 Sheet2 Sheet3

Menu Bar

Function Bar

Format Bar

Arial   12

What you want to do	Button*	Button Name	Where to find it - or how to do it
Center a column heading over two or more cells		Merge and Center	Format toolbar—Highlight cells, then click button
Add numbers in a range of cells	Σ	Auto Sum	Function toolbar—Highlight cell in which you want total to appear, click button, highlight cells to add, then press the enter key
Rule a cell		Borders	Format toolbar—Highlight cell(s), then click arrow on right side of button, make your selection
Add commas to numbers	,	Comma Style	Format toolbar—Highlight cell(s), then click button
Center labels in a cell		Center	Format toolbar—Highlight cell(s), then click button
Adjust column width	Format		Select Format from Menu bar, then Column from drop-down menu, then Width
Format cell contents	Format		Select Format from Menu bar, then click Cells on drop-down menu

Menu Bar
File Edit View Insert Format Tools Data Window Help

* These tools may have additional uses or be accessed in different ways in more sophisticated applications.

	(Second Page)						
Account Name	**Trial Balance**				**Adjustments**		
	Debit		Credit		Debit		Credit	
Totals brought forward	98,312	00	91,146	10	962	50	126	50
Wages Payable							(c) 220	50

Finding Errors in the Income Statement and Balance Sheet Columns

As you have seen, the amount of the net income or net loss must be recorded in both an Income Statement column and a Balance Sheet column. Suppose that, after the net income is added to the Balance Sheet Credit column, the Balance Sheet columns are not equal. To find the error, follow this procedure:

1. Check to see that the amount of the net income or loss is recorded in the correct columns. For example, net income is placed in the Income Statement Debit column and the Balance Sheet Credit column.
2. Verify the addition of all the columns.
3. Look to see if the appropriate amounts have been recorded in the Income Statement and Balance Sheet columns. For example, asset amounts should be listed in the Balance Sheet Debit column, expense amounts should be listed in the Income Statement Debit column, and so forth.
4. Verify, by adding or subtracting across each line, that the amounts carried over from the Trial Balance columns through the Adjustments columns into the Adjusted Trial Balance columns are correct.
5. The correct amounts of the revenue and expense accounts are transferred to the Income Statement columns.
6. The correct amounts of assets, liabilities, and owner's equity accounts are transferred to the Balance Sheet columns.

Generally, one of these steps will expose the error.

Completion of the Financial Statements

OBJECTIVE 4

Prepare an income statement, a statement of owner's equity, and a balance sheet for a service business directly from the work sheet.

As we stated, the purpose of the work sheet is to help the accountant prepare the financial statements. Since we have completed the work sheet for Cline's Computer Clinic, we can now prepare the income statement, the statement of owner's equity, and the balance sheet by taking the figures directly from the work sheet. These statements are shown in Figure 6.

Note that you record Accumulated Depreciation, Equipment, in the asset section of the balance sheet as a direct deduction from Equipment. As we have said, accountants refer to this as a **contra asset account** because it is contrary to its companion account. The difference, $82,880, is called the book value or carrying value because it represents the cost of the asset after Accumulated Depreciation has been deducted.

When preparing the statement of owner's equity, always remember to check the beginning balance of Capital against the balance shown in the Capital account in the general ledger. An additional investment may have been made during the fiscal period, and you need to record any such additional investment in the statement of owner's equity.

Cline's Computer Clinic
Income Statement
For Month Ended June 30, 20—

Revenue:			
Income from Services		$11 0 1 0 00	
Expenses:			
Wages Expense	$3 2 2 0 00		
Rent Expense	9 0 0 00		
Supplies Expense	8 7 0 00		
Advertising Expense	3 4 0 00		
Utilities Expense	3 2 0 00		
Insurance Expense	4 0 00		
Depreciation Expense, Equipment	8 4 0 00		
Total Expenses		6 5 3 0 00	
Net Income		$ 4 4 8 0 00	

Cline's Computer Clinic
Statement of Owner's Equity
For Month Ended June 30, 20—

R. P. Cline, Capital, June 1, 20—		$88 2 0 0 00
Net Income for June	$4 4 8 0 00	
Less Withdrawals for June	3 0 0 0 00	
Increase in Capital		1 4 8 0 00
R. P. Cline, Capital, June 30, 20—		$89 6 8 0 00

Cline's Computer Clinic
Balance Sheet
June 30, 20—

Assets			
Cash		$11 9 5 0 00	
Accounts Receivable		6 2 0 00	
Prepaid Insurance		4 4 0 00	
Equipment	$83 7 2 0 00		
Less Accumulated Depreciation	8 4 0 00	82 8 8 0 00	
Total Assets		$95 8 9 0 00	
Liabilities			
Accounts Payable	$ 5 9 7 0 00		
Wages Payable	2 4 0 00		
Total Liabilities		$ 6 2 1 0 00	
Owner's Equity			
R. P. Cline, Capital		89 6 8 0 00	
Total Liabilities and Owner's Equity		$95 8 9 0 00	

FIGURE 6

JOURNALIZING ADJUSTING ENTRIES

OBJECTIVE 5

Journalize and post the adjusting entries.

To change the balance of a ledger account, you need a journal entry as evidence of the change. So far, we have been listing adjustments only in the Adjustments columns of the work sheet. The work sheet is not a journal, so we must journalize **adjusting entries** to update the ledger accounts. **Take the information for these entries directly from the Adjustments columns of the work sheet, debiting and crediting exactly the same accounts and amounts in the journal entries.**

In the Description column of the general journal, write "Adjusting Entries" before you begin making these entries. This can eliminate the need to write an explanation for each entry. The adjusting entries for Cline's Computer Clinic are shown in Figure 7.

REMEMBER!

Each adjusting entry consists of an income statement account and a balance sheet account.

GENERAL JOURNAL PAGE __4__

	DATE		DESCRIPTION	POST. REF.	DEBIT	CREDIT	
1	20–		**Adjusting Entries**				1
2	June	30	Insurance Expense	516	4 0 00		2
3			Prepaid Insurance	117		4 0 00	3
4							4
5		30	Depr. Expense, Equipment	517	8 4 0 00		5
6			Accum. Depr., Equipment	125		8 4 0 00	6
7							7
8		30	Wages Expense	511	2 4 0 00		8
9			Wages Payable	222		2 4 0 00	9

FIGURE 7

When you post the adjusting entries to the ledger accounts, write the word "Adjusting" in the Item column of the ledger account. The adjusting entry for Prepaid Insurance is posted as follows:

GENERAL LEDGER

ACCOUNT **Prepaid Insurance** ACCOUNT NO. __117__

	DATE		ITEM	POST. REF.	DEBIT	CREDIT	BALANCE DEBIT	BALANCE CREDIT	
1	20–								1
2	June	10		2	4 8 0 00		4 8 0 00		2
3		30	Adj.	4		4 0 00	4 4 0 00		3
4									4

FYI

Many businesses produce monthly financial statements. Adjustments must be made every time a financial statement is produced.

ACCOUNT Insurance Expense						ACCOUNT NO. 516	
		POST.			BALANCE		
DATE	ITEM	REF.	DEBIT	CREDIT	DEBIT	CREDIT	
20–							1
June 30	Adj.	4	4 0 00		4 0 00		2
							3

Accounting Treatment for the Cost of Supplies

In Chapter 1, when Cline's Computer Clinic bought supplies, the amount paid was recorded as an expense. Generally, most service businesses expense supplies when they buy them. An alternative to expensing supplies is to record the cost as an asset (debit to Supplies, credit to Cash). At the end of the accounting period, an inventory is taken to determine the amount of supplies used in operations. The debit would be to Supplies Expense for the amount of supplies used during the accounting period, and the credit would be to Supplies (an asset account). The ending balance in Supplies (asset account) would be the supplies on hand at the end of the accounting period.

If supplies are a major cost to a business and expensing the supplies when they are purchased would distort the income statement, then recording the cost as an asset and adjusting accordingly would be the preferable method of accounting for supplies. **We will continue expensing supplies in this text.**

Income Statement Involving More than One Revenue Account and a Net Loss

OBJECTIVE 6a

Prepare an income statement involving more than one revenue account and a net loss.

When an organization has more than one distinct source of revenue, a separate revenue account is set up for each source. See, for example, the income statement of Haro Miniature Golf presented in Figure 8. Also note that expenses are greater than revenues, resulting in a net loss.

FIGURE 8

Haro Miniature Golf
Income Statement
For Month Ended September 30, 20—

Revenue:		
Admissions Income	$9 6 2 4 00	
Concessions Income	2 7 1 2 00	
Total Revenue		$12 3 3 6 00
Expenses:		
Wages Expense	$4 1 2 3 00	
Advertising Expense	3 1 7 00	
Total Expenses		13 4 7 5 00
Net Loss		($ 1 1 3 9 00)

L. A. Grady Company
Statement of Owner's Equity
For Month Ended April 30, 20—

L. A. Grady, Capital, April 1, 20—						$ 96	0	0	0	00
Additional Investment, April 12, 20—						10	0	0	0	00
Total Investment						$106	0	0	0	00
Net Income for April	$5	2	0	0	00					
Less Withdrawals for April	4	0	0	0	00					
Increase in Capital						1	2	0	0	00
L. A. Grady, Capital, April 30, 20—						$107	2	0	0	00

FIGURE 9

Statement of Owner's Equity with an Additional Investment and a Net Income

OBJECTIVE 6b

Prepare a statement of owner's equity with an additional investment and either a net income or a net loss.

Any additional investment by the owner during the period covered by the financial statements should be shown on the statement of owner's equity, since such a statement should show everything that has affected the Capital account from the *beginning* until the *end* of the period covered by the financial statements. For example, in Figure 9, assume that the following information is true for L. A. Grady Company, which has a net income:

Balance of L. A. Grady, Capital, on April 1	$96,000
Additional investment by L. A. Grady on April 12	10,000
Net income for the month (from income statement)	5,200
Total withdrawals for the month	4,000

The additional investment may be in the form of cash. Or the investment may be in the form of other assets, such as tools, equipment, and similar items. In the case of investments of assets other than cash, the assets should be recorded at their fair market value. Fair market value is the present worth of an asset, or the amount that would be received if the asset were sold to an outsider on the open market. Fair market value may differ greatly from the amount the owner originally paid for the asset.

Statement of Owner's Equity with an Additional Investment and a Net Loss

Assume the following for J. D. Roe Company, which has a net loss:

J. D. Roe, Capital, on Oct. 1	$70,000
Additional investment by J. D. Roe on Oct. 25	6,000
Net loss for the month (from income statement)	2,500
Total withdrawals for the month	5,100

The statement of owner's equity in Figure 10 shows this information.

FIGURE 10

FYI

The information normally shown on the statement of owner's equity is sometimes included as part of the owner's equity section of the balance sheet in computerized general ledger systems.

J. D. Roe Company Statement of Owner's Equity For Month Ended October 31, 20—			
J. D. Roe, Capital, October 1, 20—			$70 0 0 0 00
Additional Investment, October 25, 20—			6 0 0 0 00
Total Investment			$76 0 0 0 00
Less: Net Loss for October	$2 5 0 0 00		
Withdrawals for October	5 1 0 0 00		
Decrease in Capital			7 6 0 0 00
J. D. Roe, Capital, October 31, 20—			$68 4 0 0 00

Businesses with More than One Depreciation Expense Account and More than One Accumulated Depreciation Account

OBJECTIVE 6c

Prepare a balance sheet for a business having more than one accumulated depreciation account.

Figures 11 and 12 show the income statement and the balance sheet for Moen Veterinary Clinic. In Figure 12, note that the company has two assets subject to depreciation: Building and Equipment. In the financial statements, Depreciation Expense and Accumulated Depreciation must be listed for each asset.

In the adjusted accounts, notice that the intent is to make sure that the expenses recorded match up or compare with the revenues for the same period of time. In other words, for the month of June, we record all the revenues for June and all the expenses for June. Thus the revenues and expenses for the same time period are matched. This is called the **matching principle**.

Land supposedly lasts forever, so land is not depreciated. Adjustments would have been made in the work sheet for depreciation of the equipment and the building. The balance sheet for Moen Veterinary Clinic is shown in Figure 12.

FIGURE 11

Moen Veterinary Clinic Income Statement For Year Ended December 31, 20—		
Revenue:		
Professional Fees	$335 1 6 0 00	
Boarding Fees	66 1 8 0 00	
Total Revenue		$401 3 4 0 00
Expenses:		
Salary Expense	$252 0 0 0 00	
Depreciation Expense, Building	19 4 4 0 00	
Depreciation Expense, Equipment	11 5 2 0 00	
Supplies Expense	11 1 6 0 00	
Insurance Expense	2 1 6 0 00	
Miscellaneous Expense	6 4 8 0 00	
Total Expenses		302 7 6 0 00
Net Income		$ 98 5 8 0 00

FIGURE 12

Moen Veterinary Clinic
Balance Sheet
December 31, 20—

Assets													
Cash									$ 18	7	2	0	00
Supplies										6	0	0	00
Land									13	2	0	0	00
Building	$353	1	0	0	00								
Less Accumulated Depreciation	109	2	0	0	00	243	9	0	0	00			
Equipment	$127	8	0	0	00								
Less Accumulated Depreciation	87	6	0	0	00	40	2	0	0	00			
Total Assets						$316	6	2	0	00			
Liabilities													
Accounts Payable						$ 8	4	0	0	00			
Owner's Equity													
R. N. Moen, Capital						308	2	2	0	00			
Total Liabilities and Owner's Equity						$316	6	2	0	00			

Balance Sheet with Statement of Owner's Equity Included

▶ **OBJECTIVE 6d**

Prepare a balance sheet containing the statement of owner's equity information.

The information normally shown in the statement of owner's equity is sometimes included as part of the owner's equity section of the balance sheet, as shown in Figure 13.

FIGURE 13

Cline's Computer Clinic
Balance Sheet
June 30, 20—

Assets													
Cash									$11	9	5	0	00
Accounts Receivable										6	2	0	00
Prepaid Insurance										4	4	0	00
Equipment	$83	7	2	0	00								
Less Accumulated Depreciation		8	4	0	00	82	8	8	0	00			
Total Assets						$95	8	9	0	00			
Liabilities													
Accounts Payable	$ 5	9	7	0	00								
Wages Payable		2	4	0	00								
Total Liabilities						$ 6	2	1	0	00			
Owner's Equity													
R. P. Cline, Capital, June 1, 20—						$88	2	0	0	00			
Net Income	$ 4	4	8	0	00								
Less Withdrawals for June	3	0	0	0	00								
Increase in Capital						1	4	8	0	00			
R. P. Cline, Capital, June 30, 20—						$89	6	8	0	00			
Total Liabilities and Owner's Equity						$95	8	9	0	00			

FYI

Computerized accounting programs frequently do not produce a separate statement of owner's equity.

CHAPTER REVIEW

Online Study Center
ACE the test!

Review of Performance Objectives

1. Define *fiscal period* and *fiscal year*.

   A fiscal period is any period of time covering a complete accounting cycle. A fiscal year consists of twelve consecutive months.

2. List the classifications of the accounts that occupy each column of a ten-column work sheet.

Trial Balance Debit	Assets + Drawing + Expenses
Trial Balance Credit	Accum. Depr. + Liabilities + Capital + Revenue
Adjustments Debit	Expenses
Adjustments Credit	Assets + Liabilities + Contra Assets
Adj. Trial Balance Debit	Assets + Drawing + Expenses
Adj. Trial Balance Credit	Accum. Depr. + Liabilities + Capital + Revenue
Income Statement Debit	Expenses
Income Statement Credit	Revenue
Balance Sheet Debit	Assets + Drawing
Balance Sheet Credit	Accumulated Depreciation + Liabilities + Capital

3. Complete a work sheet for a service enterprise, involving adjustments for expired insurance, depreciation, and accrued wages.

   Adjustment for expired insurance: debit Insurance Expense and credit Prepaid Insurance.
   Adjustment for depreciation: debit Depreciation Expense and credit Accumulated Depreciation.
   Adjustment for accrued wages: debit Wages Expense and credit Wages Payable.

4. Prepare an income statement, a statement of owner's equity, and a balance sheet for a service business directly from the work sheet.

   Prepare the income statement directly from the amounts listed in the Income Statement Debit and Credit columns. The net income should equal the net income previously determined on the work sheet. For the statement of owner's equity, use the amount of the beginning capital listed in the Balance Sheet Credit column after checking the general ledger for any additional investment(s), the amount of the net income from the Balance Sheet Credit column, and the amount of Drawing from the Balance Sheet Debit column. Prepare the balance sheet directly from the amounts listed in the Balance Sheet Debit and Credit columns (except Drawing and Capital).

5. Journalize and post the adjusting entries.

6. Prepare (a) an income statement involving more than one revenue account and a net loss, (b) a statement of owner's equity with an additional investment and either a net income or a net loss, (c) a balance sheet for a business having more than one accumulated depreciation account, and (d) a balance sheet containing the statement of owner's equity information.

   (a) An income statement containing more than one revenue account requires an additional line for each type of revenue, followed by a total amount of revenue.

   (b) A statement of owner's equity involving an additional investment requires a line for each additional investment beneath the beginning capital amount, followed by a total amount of investment.

   (c) Businesses that have more than one source of revenue or more than one type of asset that is subject to depreciation must show a separate account for each on the income statement and the balance sheet.

(d) A balance sheet sometimes contains in the owner's equity section the information normally placed in a separate statement of owner's equity. The section would contain the beginning capital, plus the amount of net income (or minus the net loss), minus total withdrawals. The result is the same amount that would be calculated in a separate statement of owner's equity—the ending capital.

Glossary

Accounting cycle The sequence of steps in the accounting process completed during the fiscal period. (113)

Accrual Recognition of an expense or a revenue that has been incurred or earned but has not yet been recorded. (119)

Accrued wages Unpaid wages owed to employees for the time between the end of the last pay period and the end of the fiscal period. (119)

Adjusting entries Entries that bring the books up to date at the end of the fiscal period. (131)

Adjustments Internal transactions that bring ledger accounts up to date, as a planned part of the accounting procedure. They are first recorded in the Adjustments columns of the work sheet when using a manual accounting system. (116)

Book value or carrying value The cost of an asset minus the accumulated depreciation. (118)

Contra account An account that is contrary to, or a deduction from, another account; for example, Accumulated Depreciation is listed as a deduction from Equipment. (117)

Contra asset account An account that is contrary to or a deduction from its companion asset account. (129)

Depreciation An expense based on the expectation that an asset will gradually decline in usefulness due to time, wear and tear, or obsolescence; the cost of the asset is therefore spread out over its estimated useful life. A part of depreciation expense is apportioned to each fiscal period. (116)

Fiscal period Any period of time covering a complete accounting cycle, generally consisting of twelve consecutive months. (113)

Fiscal year A fiscal period consisting of twelve consecutive months. (113)

Matching principle The principle that the revenue for one time period is matched up with the related expenses for the same time period. (134)

Mixed accounts Certain accounts that appear on the trial balance with balances that are partly income statement amounts and partly balance sheet amounts—for example, Prepaid Insurance and Insurance Expense. (122)

Straight-line depreciation A means of calculating depreciation in which the cost of an asset, less any trade-in value, is allocated evenly over the useful life of the asset. (117)

Work sheet A working paper used by accountants to record necessary adjustments and provide up-to-date account balances needed to prepare the financial statements. (114)

QUESTIONS, EXERCISES, AND CASES

Discussion Questions

1. What is the purpose of a work sheet in a manual system?
2. What is the purpose of adjusting entries?

3. What is a mixed account? A contra account? Give an example of each.

4. In which column of the work sheet—Income Statement (IS) or Balance Sheet (BS)—would the adjusted balances of the following accounts appear?

Account	IS or BS?	Account	IS or BS?
a. Prepaid Insurance		e. Accumulated Depreciation, Equipment	
b. Wages Expense		f. T. Klein, Drawing	
c. Wages Payable		g. Insurance Expense	
d. Income from Services		h. Depreciation Expense, Equipment	

5. Why is it necessary to make an adjustment if wages for work performed for the pay period Monday through Friday are paid on Friday and the accounting period ends on a Wednesday?

6. Define depreciation as it relates to a van you bought for your business.

7. Define an internal transaction and provide an example.

8. Why is it necessary to journalize and post adjusting entries?

Exercises

P.O. 2

List account classifications in work sheet columns.

Exercise 4-1 List the following classifications of accounts in all the columns in which they appear on the work sheet, with the exception of the Adjustments columns. (Example: Assets.)

Assets	Capital
Accumulated Depreciation (with previous balance)	Drawing
Liabilities	Revenue
	Expenses

Write Net Income in the appropriate columns.

Account Name	Trial Balance Debit	Trial Balance Credit	Adjustments Debit	Adjustments Credit	Adjusted Trial Balance Debit	Adjusted Trial Balance Credit	Income Statement Debit	Income Statement Credit	Balance Sheet Debit	Balance Sheet Credit
Assets					Assets				Assets	
Net Income										

P.O. 2

Classify accounts and indicate normal balances and statement columns.

Exercise 4-2 Classify each of the accounts listed below as assets (A), liabilities (L), owner's equity (OE), revenue (R), or expenses (E). Indicate the normal debit or credit balance of each account. Indicate whether each account will appear in the Income Statement columns (IS) or the Balance Sheet columns (BS) of the work sheet. Item 0 is given as an example.

Account	Classification	Normal Balance	IS or BS Columns
0. Example: Wages Expense	E	Debit	IS
a. Prepaid Insurance			
b. Accounts Payable			
c. T. Robley, Capital			
d. Accounts Receivable			
e. Accumulated Depreciation, Building			
f. T. Robley, Drawing			
g. Rental Income			
h. Equipment			
i. Depreciation Expense, Equipment			
j. Supplies Expense			

P.O. 3

Choose accounts that require adjustment.

Exercise 4-3 Place a check mark next to any account(s) requiring adjustment. Explain why those accounts must be adjusted.

✓	Account Name (in trial balance order)	Reason for Adjusting This Account
	a. Cash	
	b. Prepaid Insurance	
	c. Equipment	
	d. Accumulated Depreciation, Equipment	
	e. Accounts Payable	
	f. L. Lawson, Capital	
	g. L. Lawson, Drawing	
	h. Wages Expense	

P.O. 3

Prepare adjustments on the work sheet.

Exercise 4-4 Below is a partial work sheet for Peg's Place. Prepare the following adjustments on this work sheet for the month ended June 30, 20—.

a. Expired or used-up insurance, $350.
b. Depreciation expense on equipment, $750—remember to credit the Accumulated Depreciation account for equipment, not Equipment.
c. Wages accrued or earned since the last payday, $136 (owed and to be paid on the next payday).

	ACCOUNT NAME	TRIAL BALANCE DEBIT	TRIAL BALANCE CREDIT	ADJUSTMENTS DEBIT	ADJUSTMENTS CREDIT
1	Cash	5 6 2 1 00			
2	Prepaid Insurance	9 0 0 00			
3	Equipment	4 6 8 0 00			
4	Accumulated Depreciation, Equipment		1 2 5 0 00		
5	Accounts Payable		2 6 4 9 00		
6	P. Ryan, Capital		4 6 2 4 00		
7	P. Ryan, Drawing	2 2 0 0 00			
8	Service Income		6 8 4 7 00		
9	Rent Expense	9 5 6 00			
10	Supplies Expense	3 8 5 00			
11	Wages Expense	5 6 0 00			
12	Miscellaneous Expense	6 8 00			
13		15 3 7 0 00	15 3 7 0 00		
14					

P.O. 3

Prepare adjustments and adjusted trial balance.

Exercise 4-5 Complete the work sheet through the adjusted trial balance using the following adjustment information:

a. Expired or used-up insurance, $350.
b. Depreciation expense on equipment, $870—remember to credit the Accumulated Depreciation account for equipment, not Equipment.
c. Wages accrued or earned since the last payday, $288 (owed and to be paid on the next payday).

	ACCOUNT NAME	TRIAL BALANCE DEBIT	TRIAL BALANCE CREDIT	ADJUSTMENTS DEBIT	ADJUSTMENTS CREDIT	ADJUSTED TRIAL BALANCE DEBIT	ADJUSTED TRIAL BALANCE CREDIT
1	Cash	4 6 2 0 00					
2	Prepaid Insurance	1 1 0 0 00					
3	Equipment	5 6 7 8 00					
4	Accumulated Depreciation,						
5	Equipment		1 4 5 6 00				
6	Accounts Payable		1 9 7 5 00				
7	D. Lee, Capital		6 1 2 6 00				
8	D. Lee, Drawing	1 8 0 0 00					
9	Service Fees		5 7 3 6 00				
10	Rent Expense	8 6 5 00					
11	Supplies Expense	3 6 7 00					
12	Wages Expense	7 8 5 00					
13	Miscellaneous Expense	7 8 00					
14		15 2 9 3 00	15 2 9 3 00				
15							

P.O. 3

Calculate the missing adjustments.

Exercise 4-6 Journalize the three adjusting entries from the partial work sheet below for the month ended May 31. (*Hint:* Use what you know about opening new accounts for adjusting entries.)

	ACCOUNT NAME	INCOME STATEMENT DEBIT	INCOME STATEMENT CREDIT	BALANCE SHEET DEBIT	BALANCE SHEET CREDIT	
1	Cash			4 7 3 1 00		1
2	Prepaid Insurance			8 4 1 00		2
3	Equipment			5 8 3 2 00		3
4	Accumulated Depreciation, Equipment				1 8 2 0 00	4
5	Accounts Payable				9 8 5 00	5
6	B. Ray, Capital				6 8 1 0 00	6
7	B. Ray, Drawing			2 1 5 0 00		7
8	Professional Fees		8 6 7 3 00			8
9	Salary Expense	2 7 8 7 00				9
10	Rent Expense	1 2 0 0 00				10
11	Supplies Expense	3 8 4 00				11
12	Miscellaneous Expense	1 3 4 00				12
13						13
14	Insurance Expense	1 8 5 00				14
15	Depreciation Expense, Equipment	3 6 4 00				15
16	Salaries Payable				3 2 0 00	16
17		5 0 5 4 00	8 6 7 3 00	13 5 5 4 00	9 9 3 5 00	17
18	Net Income	3 6 1 9 00			3 6 1 9 00	18
19		8 6 7 3 00	8 6 7 3 00	13 5 5 4 00	13 5 5 4 00	19
20						20

P.O. 5

Journalize adjusting entries from the work sheet.

Exercise 4-7 Journalize the adjustments for James Company as of August 31.

	ACCOUNT NAME	TRIAL BALANCE DEBIT	TRIAL BALANCE CREDIT	ADJUSTMENTS DEBIT	ADJUSTMENTS CREDIT	
1	Cash	3 9 7 1 00				1
2	Prepaid Insurance	4 8 7 3 00			(a) 2 6 5 00	2
3	Equipment	5 6 7 8 00				3
4	Accumulated Depreciation, Equipment		6 4 5 00		(b) 2 0 6 00	4
5	Accounts Payable		8 4 3 00			5
6	L. James, Capital		12 7 5 2 00			6
7	L. James, Drawing	2 0 0 0 00				7
8	Service Fees		4 6 8 3 00			8
9	Rent Expense	7 9 5 00				9
10	Supplies Expense	6 6 3 00				10
11	Wages Expense	8 6 5 00		(c) 1 6 8 00		11
12	Miscellaneous Expense	7 8 00				12
13		18 9 2 3 00	18 9 2 3 00			13
14	Insurance Expense			(a) 2 6 5 00		14
15	Depreciation Expense, Equipment			(b) 2 0 6 00		15
16	Wages Payable				(c) 1 6 8 00	16
17				6 3 9 00	6 3 9 00	17
18						18

P.O. 5

Journalize adjusting entries.

Exercise 4-8 Journalize the following adjusting entries that were included on the work sheet for the month ended December 31. Assume the financial statements have been prepared.

Dec. 31 Salaries for two days are unpaid at December 31, $1,800 (verify). Salaries are $4,500 for a five-day week.

31 Insurance was bought on September 1 for $2,400 for 12 months' coverage. Four months' coverage has expired, $800 (verify).

31 Depreciation for the month on equipment, $20, based on an asset costing $3,200 with a trade-in value of $2,000 and an estimated life of 5 years (verify).

As you have learned, companies report the financial results of the year at the end of a twelve-month period called the fiscal year. Businesses with seasonal peaks usually end their accounting cycles at the end of the most active season.

1. Is Activision a company that might have seasonal peaks and that would want a fiscal year that is different from the calendar year? What is its fiscal year and where do you find this information in the annual report? (Access Activision's annual report for 2005 at **http://investor.activision .com/reports.cfm.**)

2. In this chapter, financial information entered into the general journal is transformed into the financial statements. Let's go back to Activision and analyze the Property and Equipment account on its balance sheet. This account is listed as Property and Equipment, *net* on the balance sheet on page 54. What does this mean?

3. If Property and Equipment, net was $30,490,000 as of March 31, 2005, what was the total cost of Activision's property and equipment? (*Hint:* What was Accumulated Depreciation, Property and Equipment as of March 31, 2005? Review Note 7, Property and Equipment, in the Notes to Consolidated Financial Statements, which begin on page 59 of the annual report.)

CONSIDER AND COMMUNICATE

You are the bookkeeper for a small but thriving business. You have asked the owner for the information you need in order to make adjusting entries for depreciation, insurance, and wages. He says he's really busy, and what you've done so far is "close enough." Explain the need for adjusting entries and how they can affect his balance sheet and the "bottom line" on the income statement.

A QUESTION OF ETHICS

Your client is preparing financial statements to show the bank. You know that he has incurred a refrigeration repair expense during the month, but you see no such expense on the books. When you question the client, he tells you that he has not paid the $1,250 bill yet. Your client is on the accrual basis of accounting. He does not want the refrigeration repair expense on the books as of the end of the month because he wants his profits to look good for the bank. Is your client behaving ethically by suggesting that the refrigeration repair expense should not be booked until the $1,250 is paid? Are you behaving ethically if you go along with the client's request? What principle is involved here?

CRITICAL THINKING

Your supervisor just finished a work sheet, but all the columns except the following were destroyed by a spilled latte. You have been asked to journalize the adjusting entries using the surviving partial work sheet.

| | ACCOUNT NAME | INCOME STATEMENT | | BALANCE SHEET | |
		DEBIT	CREDIT	DEBIT	CREDIT
1	Cash			8 4 7 6 00	
2	Accounts Receivable			1 4 8 6 00	
5	Equipment			12 3 6 7 00	
6	Accumulated Depreciation, Equipment				3 6 1 0 00
7	Accounts Payable				2 8 1 3 00
8	G. Kramer, Capital				11 7 0 7 00
9	G. Kramer, Drawing			1 1 0 0 00	
10	Income from Services		11 2 1 6 00		
11	Rent Expense	1 4 0 0 00			
12	Supplies Expense	1 1 1 0 00			
13	Wages Expense	2 4 6 7 00			
14					
15	Insurance Expense	2 1 0 00			
16	Depreciation Expense, Equipment	7 5 0 00			
17	Wages Payable				6 2 0 00
18		5 9 3 7 00	11 2 1 6 00	24 0 2 9 00	18 7 5 0 00

PROBLEM SET A

For additional help, see the demonstration problem at the beginning of each chapter in your Working Papers.

P.O. 3

Problem 4-1A The trial balance for Maxie's Insurance Agency as of August 31, after the firm has completed its first month of operations, follows:

Maxie's Insurance Agency
Trial Balance
August 31, 20—

ACCOUNT NAME	DEBIT	CREDIT
Cash	3 4 2 7 00	
Accounts Receivable	1 3 1 9 00	
Prepaid Insurance	3 6 2 00	
Office Equipment	4 9 3 9 00	
Accounts Payable		1 0 7 1 00
C. Maxie, Capital		9 0 2 0 00
C. Maxie, Drawing	9 0 0 00	
Commissions Earned		2 5 2 0 00
Rent Expense	6 9 5 00	
Travel Expense	2 2 5 00	
Supplies Expense	4 9 2 00	
Utilities Expense	1 9 8 00	
Miscellaneous Expense	5 4 00	
	12 6 1 1 00	12 6 1 1 00

Check Figure

Net Loss, $50

Instructions

1. Record the amounts in the Trial Balance columns of the work sheet.
2. Complete the work sheet by making the following adjustments and lettering each adjustment:
   a. Expired or used-up insurance, $106.
   b. Depreciation expense on office equipment, $800—remember to credit the Accumulated Depreciation account for office equipment, not Office Equipment.

P.O. 4,5

Problem 4-2A The completed work sheet for J. Marquez Design for the month of March is in your Working Papers.

Check Figure

Total Assets, $15,164

Instructions

1. Prepare an income statement.
2. Prepare a statement of owner's equity. Assume that no additional investments were made in March.
3. Prepare a balance sheet.
4. Journalize the adjusting entries.

P.O. 3,5

Problem 4-3A The trial balance of The New Directions Center for the month ended September 30 is presented on the following page.

The New Directions Center
Trial Balance
September 30, 20—

ACCOUNT NAME	DEBIT	CREDIT
Cash	2 3 7 8 00	
Prepaid Insurance	1 3 4 5 00	
Equipment	32 9 7 8 00	
Accumulated Depreciation, Equipment		16 2 3 5 00
Accounts Payable		2 7 5 1 00
C. Bock, Capital		45 2 0 8 00
C. Bock, Drawing	22 4 4 5 00	
Income from Services		43 7 9 1 00
Wages Expense	29 7 6 1 00	
Rent Expense	14 9 3 2 00	
Supplies Expense	8 6 4 00	
Utilities Expense	1 5 7 3 00	
Telephone Expense	1 2 7 1 00	
Miscellaneous Expense	4 3 8 00	
	107 9 8 5 00	107 9 8 5 00

Data for the adjustments are as follows:

a. Expired or used-up insurance, $325.
b. Depreciation expense on equipment, $2,700—remember to credit the Accumulated Depreciation account for equipment, not Equipment.
c. Wages accrued or earned since the last payday, $455 (owed and to be paid on the next payday).

Check Figure

Net Loss, $8,528

P.O. 3,4,5,6

Instructions

1. Complete the work sheet.   2. Journalize the adjusting entries.

Problem 4-4A See the trial balance for Wes's Pitch and Putt on June 30 below.

Wes's Pitch and Putt
Trial Balance
June 30, 20—

ACCOUNT NAME	DEBIT	CREDIT
Cash	4 5 3 2 00	
Prepaid Insurance	1 2 8 4 00	
Equipment	23 6 8 7 00	
Accumulated Depreciation, Equipment		1 2 7 8 00
Repair Equipment	6 2 8 9 00	
Accumulated Depreciation, Repair Equipment		1 4 8 5 00
Accounts Payable		9 6 0 00
W. Wygle, Capital		23 0 1 0 00
W. Wygle, Drawing	1 5 6 5 00	
Golf Fees Income		12 3 8 7 00
Concessions Income		2 8 6 3 00
Wages Expense	2 1 6 3 00	
Rent Expense	1 3 5 0 00	
Utilities Expense	3 5 7 00	
Repair Expense	2 7 1 00	
Supplies Expense	3 4 6 00	
Miscellaneous Expense	1 3 9 00	
	41 9 8 3 00	41 9 8 3 00

Data for month-end adjustments are as follows:

a. Expired or used-up insurance, $370.
b. Depreciation expense on equipment, $950 (remember to credit the Accumulated Depreciation account for equipment, not Equipment).
c. Depreciation expense on repair equipment, $1,350 (remember to credit the Accumulated Depreciation account for repair equipment, not Repair Equipment).
d. Wages accrued or earned since the last payday, $485 (owed and to be paid on the next payday).

Check Figure

Net Income, $7,469

Instructions

1. Complete the work sheet for the month.
2. Prepare an income statement, a statement of owner's equity, and a balance sheet. Assume that no additional investments were made during June.
3. Journalize the adjusting entries.

Instructions for General Ledger Software

1. Journalize the adjusting entries in the general journal. (No work sheet is required.)
2. Post the adjusting entries.
3. Print an income statement, a statement of owner's equity, and a balance sheet. Assume that no additional investments were made during the month.

PROBLEM SET B

For additional help, see the demonstration problem at the beginning of each chapter in your Working Papers.

P.O. 3

Problem 4-1B The trial balance of Marty's Insurance Agency as of September 30, after the firm has completed its first month of operations, follows:

Marty's Insurance Agency
Trial Balance
September 30, 20—

ACCOUNT NAME	DEBIT	CREDIT
Cash	3 5 3 7 00	
Accounts Receivable	1 2 2 8 00	
Prepaid Insurance	6 7 5 00	
Office Equipment	5 2 4 6 00	
Accounts Payable		1 2 6 7 00
S. Marty, Capital		9 6 2 8 00
S. Marty, Drawing	1 1 0 0 00	
Commissions Earned		2 8 4 3 00
Rent Expense	7 8 5 00	
Supplies Expense	3 8 7 00	
Travel Expense	4 8 8 00	
Utilities Expense	2 2 7 00	
Miscellaneous Expense	6 5 00	
	13 7 3 8 00	13 7 3 8 00

P.O. 4,5

P.O. 3,5

Check Figure

Net Income, $41

Check Figure

Total Assets, $20,134

Instructions

1. Record the amounts in the Trial Balance columns of the work sheet.
2. Complete the work sheet by making the following adjustments and lettering each adjustment:
   a. Expired or used-up insurance, $200.
   b. Depreciation expense on office equipment, $650—remember to credit the Accumulated Depreciation account for office equipment, not Office Equipment.

Problem 4-2B The completed work sheet for Delta Decorators for the month of March is in your Working Papers.

Instructions

1. Prepare an income statement.
2. Prepare a statement of owner's equity. Assume no additional investments were made in March.
3. Prepare a balance sheet.
4. Journalize the adjusting entries.

Problem 4-3B The trial balance of Gentle Cleaners for the month ended September 30 is presented below.

Gentle Cleaners
Trial Balance
September 30, 20—

ACCOUNT NAME	DEBIT	CREDIT
Cash	2 4 8 9 00	
Prepaid Insurance	1 2 3 6 00	
Equipment	22 7 5 2 00	
Accumulated Depreciation, Equipment		14 3 5 7 00
Accounts Payable		2 6 4 7 00
D. Nguyen, Capital		28 1 6 9 00
D. Nguyen, Drawing	20 3 5 9 00	
Income from Services		40 8 5 0 00
Wages Expense	24 9 8 3 00	
Rent Expense	10 6 7 3 00	
Utilities Expense	1 1 5 4 00	
Supplies Expense	7 5 2 00	
Telephone Expense	1 2 4 4 00	
Miscellaneous Expense	3 8 1 00	
	86 0 2 3 00	86 0 2 3 00

Data for the adjustments are as follows:

a. Expired or used-up insurance, $685.
b. Depreciation expense on equipment, $2,800 (remember to credit the Accumulated Depreciation account for equipment, not Equipment).
c. Wages accrued or earned since the last payday, $485 (owed and to be paid on the next payday).

Check Figure

Net Loss, $2,307

P.O. 3,4,5,6

Instructions

1. Complete the work sheet.
2. Journalize the adjusting entries.

Problem 4-4B The trial balance for Game Town on July 31 is shown below.

Game Town
Trial Balance
July 31, 20—

ACCOUNT NAME	DEBIT	CREDIT
Cash	3 6 2 1 00	
Prepaid Insurance	1 2 9 5 00	
Equipment	28 6 4 2 00	
Accumulated Depreciation, Equipment		2 3 8 7 00
Repair Equipment	1 8 6 5 00	
Accumulated Depreciation, Repair Equipment		7 8 0 00
Accounts Payable		8 4 2 00
A. Wata, Capital		23 9 7 1 00
A. Wata, Drawing	1 0 0 0 00	
Game Fees Income		8 9 5 4 00
Concessions Income		2 7 5 2 00
Wages Expense	1 2 6 8 00	
Rent Expense	9 8 0 00	
Utilities Expense	2 4 6 00	
Repair Expense	3 8 0 00	
Supplies Expense	2 5 7 00	
Miscellaneous Expense	1 3 2 00	
	39 6 8 6 00	39 6 8 6 00

Data for month-end adjustments are as follows:

a. Expired or used-up insurance, $280.
b. Depreciation expense on equipment, $750 (remember to credit the Accumulated Depreciation account for equipment, not Equipment).
c. Depreciation expense on repair equipment, $350 (remember to credit the Accumulated Depreciation account for repair equipment, not Repair Equipment).
d. Wages accrued or earned since the last payday, $425 (owed and to be paid on the next payday).

Check Figure

Net Income, $6,638

Instructions

1. Complete the work sheet for the month.
2. Prepare an income statement, a statement of owner's equity, and a balance sheet. Assume that no additional investments were made during July.
3. Journalize the adjusting entries.

Instructions for General Ledger Software

1. Journalize the adjusting entries in the general journal. (No work sheet is required.)
2. Post the adjusting entries.
3. Print an income statement, a statement of owner's equity, and a balance sheet. Assume no additional investments were made during the month.

The Computer Clinic

Adjustments

Although you printed the trial balance and financial statements to get an idea of how All About You Spa is doing, some accounts are not accurate. You need to make adjusting entries to provide a clearer picture of how the spa is doing.

How to Compute the Adjustments

1. Compute the adjustment amounts for the month of June, using the following information:

Adjustment (a): Liability insurance for six months was purchased during the first days of the month. That protection for one month has been used or expended (Insurance Expense), and the asset (Prepaid Insurance) is not worth what the balance sheet says. Therefore, since All About You Spa paid $960 for a six-month policy and one month of the coverage has been used, $160 of that policy is no longer an asset and represents an expense to the company. How was the figure $160 computed?

Adjustments (b) and (c): Spa equipment and office equipment have depreciated. That means that they have been in use for a month and have, for accounting purposes, lost some usefulness. This is an estimate, of course, which allows us to expense the depreciation and, in effect, lowers the book value (value on the books) of both types of equipment.

(b) The owner, Anika Valli, invested spa equipment totaling $7,393 in the business ($3,158 of her own spa equipment, plus $4,235 of new spa equipment purchased). The spa equipment will be depreciated using the straight-line method. The spa equipment is estimated to have a trade-in or salvage value of $3,500 and is expected to last five years. Therefore, the spa equipment is estimated to have depreciated $64.88 for the month of June. How was the figure $64.88 computed? Remember, you want to compute the depreciation for one month, not one year.

(c) Anika Valli purchased office equipment totaling $1,150. The office equipment will be depreciated using the straight-line method. The office equipment is estimated to have a trade-in or salvage value of $550 and is expected to last five years. Therefore, the office equipment is estimated to have depreciated $10 for the month of June. How was the figure $10 computed? Remember, you want to compute the depreciation for one month, not one year.

Adjustment (d): All About You Spa owes one day of wages to its employees. The month's total wages paid in June amounted to $7,390. The employees worked twenty-one days, but were paid for only twenty days because payday for the last day worked is in the next pay period. Therefore, the spa owes them one day's pay ($369.50), which also needs to be expensed. How was the figure $369.50 computed?

What to Do with the Adjustment Amounts

Note: You will need to add six new accounts to the chart of accounts:

125 Accumulated Depreciation, Spa Equipment
129 Accumulated Depreciation, Office Equipment
212 Wages Payable
518 Insurance Expense
519 Depreciation Expense, Spa Equipment
520 Depreciation Expense, Office Equipment

2. a. If you are completing a work sheet, enter the adjusting entries and complete the work sheet by extending totals to the Adjusted Trial Balance columns and those totals to either the Income Statement or Balance Sheet columns. Total and compute the adjusted net income or net loss.
   b. Using general ledger software, journalize and post the four adjusting entries.

3. Print an adjusted trial balance.
4. Print an after-adjustment income statement for the month ended June 30, 20—.
5. Print an after-adjustment statement of owner's equity for the month ended June 30, 20—.
6. Print an after-adjustment balance sheet as of June 30, 20—.
7. Compare the statements before adjustments with the statements after adjustments. What do you find?

Methods of Depreciation

Performance Objectives

After you have completed this appendix, you will be able to do the following:

1. Prepare a schedule of depreciation using the straight-line method.

2. Prepare a schedule of depreciation using the double-declining-balance method.

3. Prepare a schedule of depreciation for five-year property under the Modified Accelerated Cost Recovery System.

Two methods of depreciation will be illustrated using the example of a delivery truck. Assume that the truck was bought at the beginning of Year 1 and at a cost of $24,000. The truck is estimated to have a useful life of five years and a trade-in value of $6,000 at the end of the five-year period. The two methods to be described are straight-line and double-declining-balance.

STRAIGHT-LINE METHOD

OBJECTIVE 1

Prepare a schedule of depreciation using the straight-line method.

We showed this method in Chapter 4, providing for an equal amount of depreciation each year.

$$\text{Yearly depreciation} = \frac{\text{Cost of asset} - \text{Trade-in value}}{\text{Years of life}} = \frac{\$24,000 - \$6,000}{5 \text{ years}}$$

$$= \frac{\$18,000}{5 \text{ years}} = \$3,600 \text{ per year}$$

Year	Depreciation for the Year	Accumulated Depreciation	Book Value (Cost Less Accumulated Depreciation)
1	$18,000 ÷ 5 years = $ 3,600	$ 3,600	$24,000 − $ 3,600 = $20,400
2	18,000 ÷ 5 years = 3,600	$ 3,600 + $3,600 = 7,200	24,000 − 7,200 = 16,800
3	18,000 ÷ 5 years = 3,600	7,200 + 3,600 = 10,800	24,000 − 10,800 = 13,200
4	18,000 ÷ 5 years = 3,600	10,800 + 3,600 = 14,400	24,000 − 14,400 = 9,600
5	18,000 ÷ 5 years = 3,600	14,400 + 3,600 = 18,000	24,000 − 18,000 = 6,000
	$18,000		

Double-Declining-Balance Method

OBJECTIVE 2

Prepare a schedule of depreciation using the double-declining-balance method.

The term *double* refers to double the straight-line rate. With an estimated useful life of five years, the straight-line rate is ⅕, or 0.2. Twice, or double, the straight-line rate is ⅖ (⅕ × 2) or 0.4. The trade-in value is not taken into account until the end of the schedule. Multiply *book value* at beginning of year by twice the straight-line rate.

Year	Depreciation for the Year	Accumulated Depreciation	Book Value (Cost Less Accumulated Depreciation)
1	$24,000 × 0.4 = $ 9,600	$ 9,600	$24,000 − $ 9,600 = $14,400
2	$14,400 × 0.4 = 5,760	$ 9,600 + $5,760 = 15,360	24,000 − 15,360 = 8,640
3	$8,640 − $6,000 = 2,640	15,360 + 2,640 = 18,000	24,000 − 18,000 = 6,000
4	0	18,000	24,000 − 18,000 = 6,000
5	0	18,000	24,000 − 18,000 = 6,000
	$18,000		

If the schedule is continued for Year 3, depreciation expense would be $3,456 ($8,640 × 0.4). Accumulated depreciation would be $18,816 ($15,360 + $3,456). And book value would be $5,184 ($24,000 − $18,816). However, the book value cannot drop below the established trade-in value of $6,000. So for Year 3 an adjustment must be made limiting the depreciation for the year to $2,640, which will bring the accumulated depreciation up to $18,000. Consequently, the book value at the end of the year will be $6,000 ($24,000 cost − $18,000 accumulated depreciation).

TAX REQUIREMENT—MACRS

OBJECTIVE 3

Prepare a schedule of depreciation for five-year property under the Modified Accelerated Cost Recovery System.

Modified Accelerated Cost Recovery System (MACRS) is the title given by the Internal Revenue Service for a variety of tax rate schedules. The term *recovery* is used because MACRS is a means of recovering or deducting the cost of an asset. Most small businesses use MACRS for financial statement reporting and tax reporting. MACRS is a combination of the declining-balance and straight-line depreciation methods. For more information, see IRS Publication 946, available at **http://www.irs.gov.**

According to MACRS, property is divided into eight classes, as follows:

3-year property—certain horses and tractor units for use over the road
5-year property—autos, light trucks, computers, office machines, and copiers
7-year property—office furniture and fixtures and any property that does not have a class life and that is not, by law, in any other class
10-year property—vessels, barges, tugs, and similar water transportation equipment
15-year property—land improvements including parking lots and roads
20-year property—certain farm buildings
27.5-year residential rental property—rental houses and apartments
39-year property—office buildings and warehouses (nonresidential real property) placed in service after May 13, 1993

Under MACRS, trade-in value is ignored. The following table lists the depreciation rates that a business typically may use for tax purposes.

	Depreciation for Recovery Period			
Year	3-Year	5-Year	7-Year	10-Year
1	33.33%	20.00%	14.29%	10.00%
2	44.45	32.00	24.49	18.00
3	14.81	19.20	17.49	14.40
4	7.41	11.52	12.49	11.52
5		11.52	8.93	9.22
6		5.76	8.92	7.37
7			8.93	6.55
8			4.46	6.55
9				6.56
10				6.55
11				3.28

Our light truck qualifies as five-year property.

Year	Depreciation for the Year	Accumulated Depreciation	Book Value (Cost Less Accumulated Depreciation)
1	$24,000 × 0.20 = $ 4,800.00	$ 4,800.00	$24,000.00 − $ 4,800.00 = $19,200.00
2	24,000 × 0.32 = 7,680.00	$ 4,800.00 + $7,680.00 = 12,480.00	24,000.00 − 12,480.00 = 11,520.00
3	24,000 × 0.192 = 4,608.00	12,480.00 + 4,608.00 = 17,088.00	24,000.00 − 17,088.00 = 6,912.00
4	24,000 × 0.1152 = 2,764.80	17,088.00 + 2,764.80 = 19,852.80	24,000.00 − 19,852.80 = 4,147.20
5	24,000 × 0.1152 = 2,764.80	19,852.80 + 2,764.80 = 22,617.60	24,000.00 − 22,617.60 = 1,382.40
6	24,000 × 0.0576 = 1,382.40	22,617.60 + 1,382.40 = 24,000.00	24,000.00 − 24,000.00 = 0
	$24,000.00		

PROBLEMS

P.O. 1

Check Figure

Year 1 depreciation, $4,000

P.O. 3

Check Figure

Year 3 depreciation, $3,456

Problem A-1 A delivery van was bought for $18,000. The estimated life of the van is four years. The trade-in value at the end of four years is estimated to be $2,000. Prepare a depreciation schedule for the four-year period using the straight-line method.

Problem A-2 Assume the van is 5-year property. Using the information in Problem A-1, prepare a schedule of depreciation under MACRS. Round figures to the nearest whole dollar.

If you had your own shop and sold something to a customer on credit, when would you record the revenue from that sale? Would you record it when the sale was made, even though you haven't received any cash for the item yet? Or would you wait and record the revenue when you actually received the payment? Your answer to this question depends on what method of accounting you use to record your transactions. As you learn about the different methods in this chapter, think about which method you might use and why. What about Dell, Inc., the computer manufacturer? Look up financial highlights by going to **htpp://www .dell.com** and searching for SEC Reports. Select 2005 and then Form 10-K. Think about the method that Dell uses. Can you tell from looking at its financial statements?

Performance Objectives

After you have completed this chapter, you will be able to do the following:

1. List the steps in the accounting cycle.

2. Journalize and post closing entries for a service enterprise.

3. Prepare a post-closing trial balance.

4. Define the following methods of accounting: cash basis and accrual basis.

5. Prepare interim statements.

Let's review the steps in the accounting cycle for an entire fiscal period. Remember that a fiscal period is generally twelve consecutive months, but it can also consist of other time frames like three months or six months.

OBJECTIVE 1

List the steps in the accounting cycle.

1. **Analyze source documents and record business transactions in a journal.**
2. **Post journal entries to the accounts in the ledger.**
3. **Prepare a trial balance.**
4. **Gather adjustment data and record the adjusting entries on a work sheet.**
5. **Complete the work sheet.**
6. **Prepare financial statements from the data on the work sheet.**
7. **Journalize and post the adjusting entries from the data on the work sheet.**

8. **Journalize and post the closing entries.**
9. **Prepare a post-closing trial balance.**

This chapter explains the procedure for completing the final steps: closing entries and the post-closing trial balance.

Adjusting entries, closing entries, and a post-closing trial balance are prepared at the end of a fiscal period. The number of months in a fiscal period varies. To introduce you to these final steps in the accounting cycle, we assume here that the fiscal period for Cline's Computer Clinic is one month. We make this assumption so that we can thoroughly cover the material and give you a chance to practice its application. The entire accounting cycle is outlined in Figure 1.

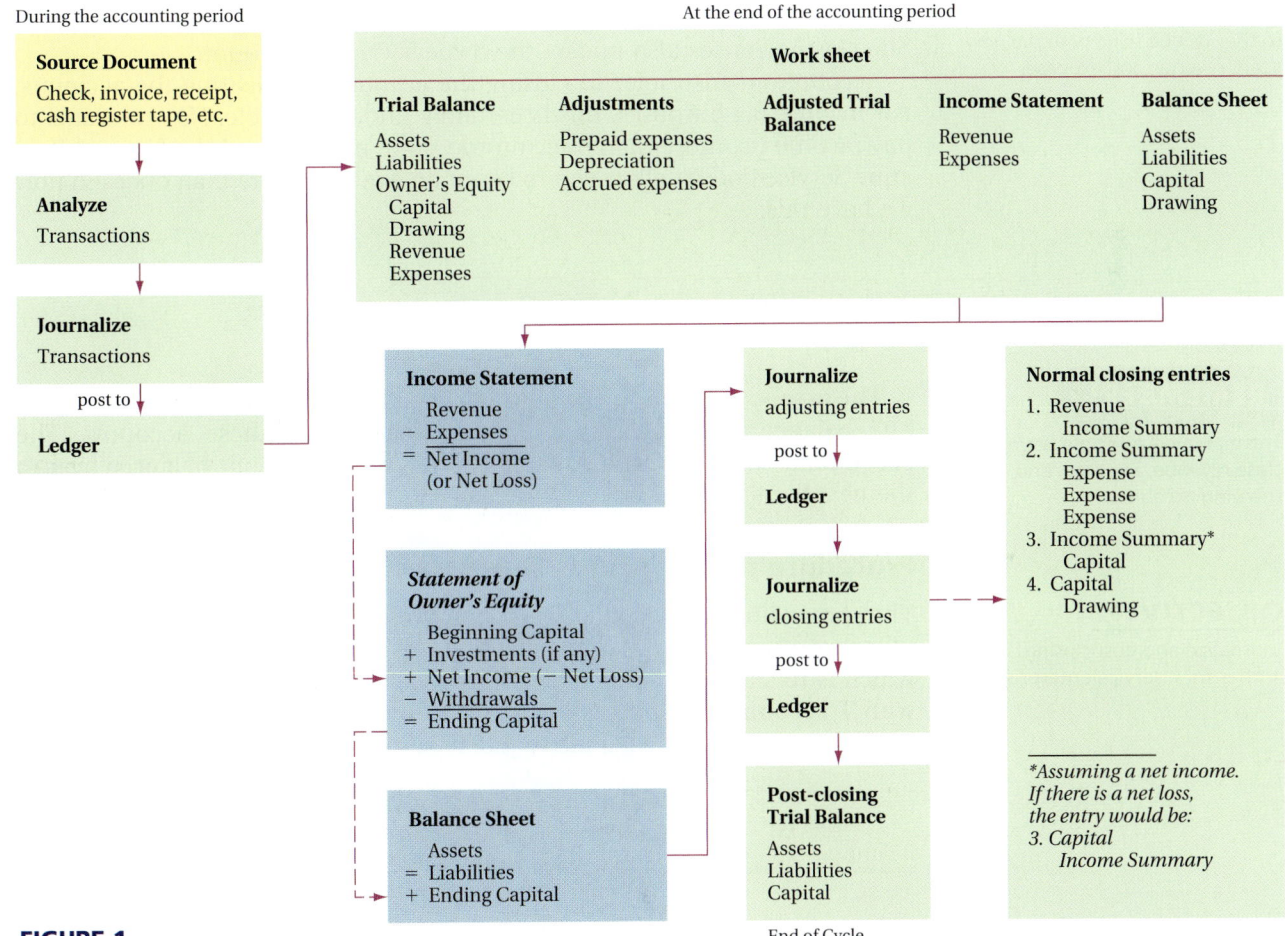

FIGURE 1

CLOSING ENTRIES

To help you understand the reason for the closing entries, let's repeat the fundamental accounting equation:

Assets = Liabilities + Owner's Equity + Revenue − Expenses

Closing entries empty or zero out temporary owner's equity accounts and prepare the accounts for the new accounting period—emptying out folders for one year so they can be filled with the new year's revenue and expenses.

We know that the income statement, as stated in the third line of its heading, covers a period of time. The income statement consists of revenue minus expenses for this period of time only. So, when the next fiscal period begins, we should start with zero balances. We start all over again each period.

Purpose of Closing Entries

This brings us to the *purpose* of the **closing entries**, which is to close (or zero) the temporary-equity or nominal accounts (revenue, expense, and Drawing accounts). We do this because their balances apply to only one fiscal period. Closing entries are made after the last adjusting entry. With the coming of the next fiscal period, we want to start from zero, recording revenue and expenses for the new fiscal period. The closing entries also update the owner's Capital account.

Accountants also refer to closing the accounts as clearing the accounts. For income tax purposes, this is certainly understandable. No one wants to pay income tax more than once on the same income, and the Internal Revenue Service doesn't allow you to count an expense more than once. So now we have this:

$$\text{Assets} = \text{Liabilities} + \underset{\text{(Capital)}}{\text{Owner's Equity}} + \overset{\text{(closed)}}{\cancel{\text{Revenue}}} - \overset{\text{(closed)}}{\cancel{\text{Expenses}}}$$

REMEMBER!

The matching principle is why we close revenue, expense, and Drawing accounts.

The assets, the liabilities, and the owner's Capital account remain open. The balance sheet gives the present balances of these accounts. The accountant carries the asset, liability, and Capital account balances over to the next fiscal period.

Procedure for Closing

 OBJECTIVE 2

Journalize and post closing entries for a service enterprise.

The procedure for closing is simply to balance off the account; in other words, to make the balance *equal to zero*. This meets our objective, which is to start from zero in the next fiscal period. Let's illustrate this first with T accounts. Suppose an account to be closed has a debit balance of $960; then, to make the balance equal to zero, we *credit* the account for $960.

Debit		Credit	
Balance	960	Closing	960

Now suppose an account to be closed has a credit balance of $1,200; then, to make the balance equal to zero, we *debit* the account for $1,200.

Debit		Credit	
Closing	1,200	Balance	1,200

Remember, every entry must have at least one debit and one credit. So, to record the other half of the closing entry, we bring into existence the **Income Summary account**. The Income Summary account does not have plus and minus signs, just debit and credit.

At the end of a fiscal period, closing entries allow a business to start a new income statement period with a clean slate. Revenue and expense accounts are closed.

There are four steps in the closing procedure:

1. **Close the revenue accounts into Income Summary.**
2. **Close the expense accounts into Income Summary.**
3. **Close the Income Summary account into the Capital account, transferring the net income or loss to the Capital account.**
4. **Close the Drawing account into the Capital account.**

To illustrate, we return to Cline's Computer Clinic. For the purpose of the illustration, assume that Cline's Computer Clinic's fiscal period consists of one month. We have the following T account balances in the revenue and expense accounts after the adjustments have been posted.

FYI

Making closing entries using accounting software is frequently an instantaneous procedure. Be sure that all financial statements you require have been printed and saved prior to closing, since the closing procedure causes zero balances in the temporary owner's equity accounts. For example, after closing, all revenue and expense account balances are zero—imagine, then, what the latest income statement would look like. The operator selects the command/function to close the accounting period, and the revenue and expense accounts are automatically closed. The Drawing account may need to be closed with a journal entry. The net income (or loss) is sent to the Capital account. The bad news is that any errors made prior to closing are included. Always make a backup copy of your file prior to closing in case you have made a mistake.

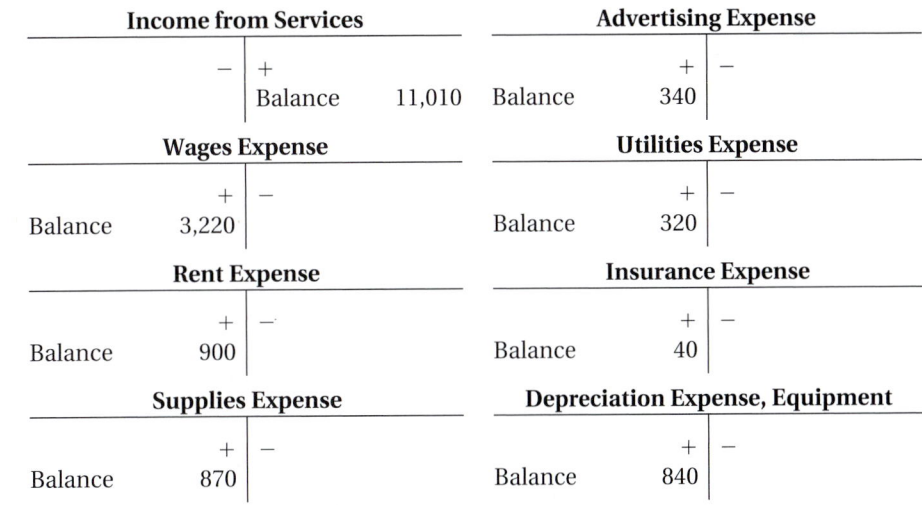

Step 1 **Close the revenue account or accounts into Income Summary.** In order to make the balance of Income from Services equal to zero, we *balance it off,* or debit it, in the amount of $11,010. Because we need an offsetting credit, we credit Income Summary for the same amount. Notice that there

are no signs in Income Summary, only Debit and Credit like the other accounts.

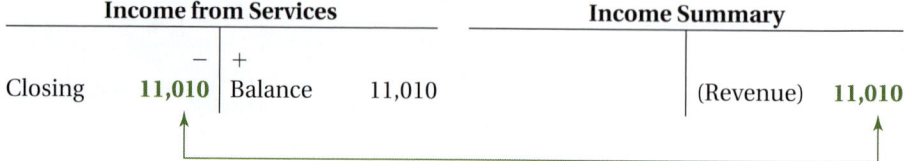

The balance of Income from Services is transferred to Income Summary.

Step 2 **Close the expense accounts into Income Summary.** To make the balances of the expense accounts equal to zero, we need to balance them off, or credit them. Again the T accounts are useful for formulating this journal entry.

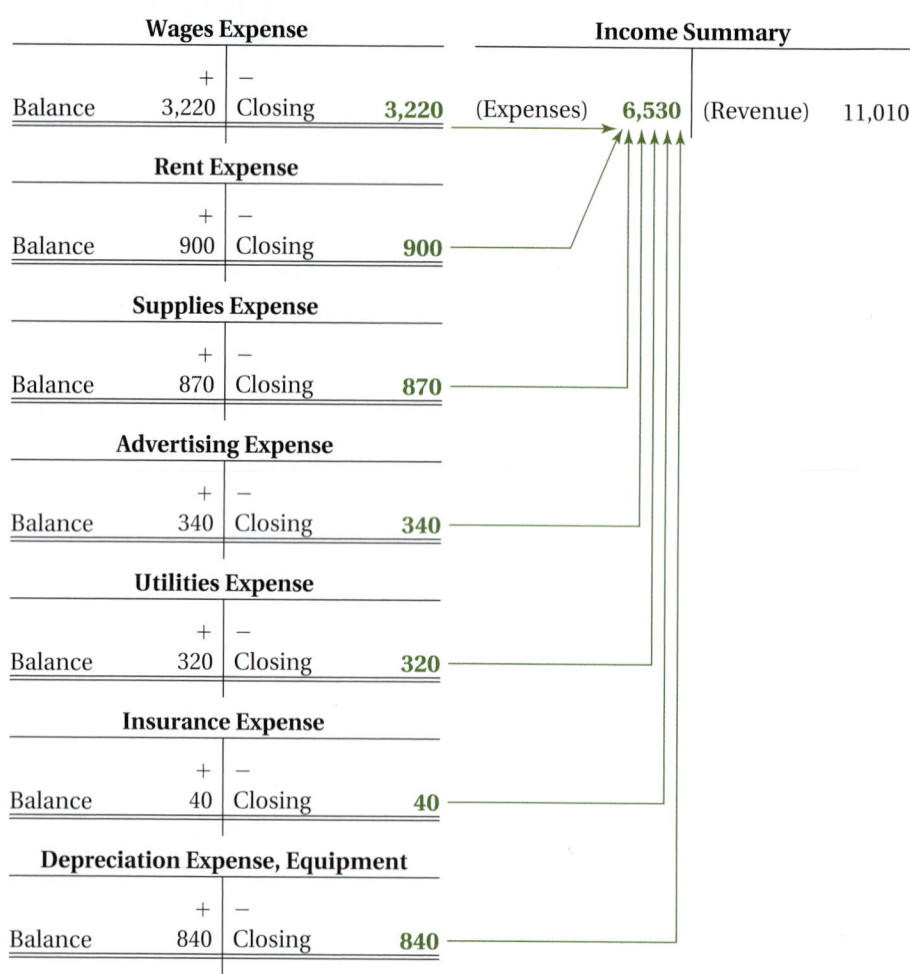

Step 3 Recall that we created Income Summary so that we could have a debit and a credit in each closing entry. Now that it has done its job, we close it out. We use the same procedure as before, in that we make the balance equal to zero, or balance off the account. We transfer, or close, the balance of the Income Summary account into the Capital account, as shown in the T accounts and in Figure 2.

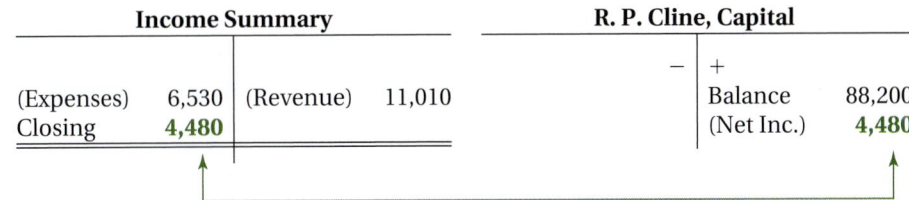

Income Summary is always closed into the Capital account by the amount of the net income (Revenue minus Expenses) or the net loss. Comparing net income or net loss on the work sheet with the closing entry for Income Summary can serve as a check point or verification for you.

FIGURE 2

						GENERAL JOURNAL							PAGE	4		

	DATE		DESCRIPTION	POST. REF.	DEBIT						CREDIT					
14	Step		**Closing Entries**													14
15	1	30	**Income from Services**		11	0	1	0	00							15
16			**Income Summary**							11	0	1	0	00		16
17																17
18		30	**Income Summary**		6	5	3	0	00							18
19			**Wages Expense**							3	2	2	0	00		19
20			**Rent Expense**								9	0	0	00		20
21	Step		**Supplies Expense**								8	7	0	00		21
22	2		**Advertising Expense**								3	4	0	00		22
23			**Utilities Expense**								3	2	0	00		23
24			**Insurance Expense**									4	0	00		24
25			**Depreciation Expense,**													25
26			**Equipment**								8	4	0	00		26
27																27
28		30	**Income Summary**		4	4	8	0	00							28
29			**R. P. Cline, Capital**							4	4	8	0	00		29

Net income is added (credited) to the Capital account because, as shown in the statement of owner's equity, net income is treated as an addition. Net loss, on the other hand, is subtracted from (debited to) the Capital account, because net loss is treated as a deduction in the statement of owner's equity. Here's how to close Income Summary for J. Doe Company (net loss of $200):

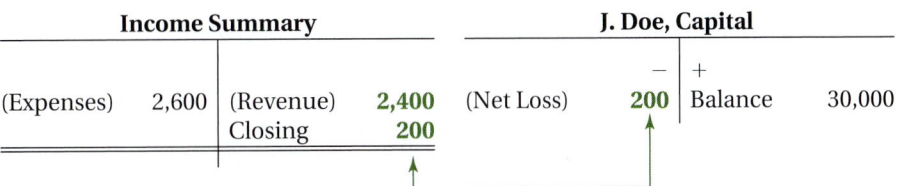

The entry to close Income Summary into J. Doe's Capital account would look like the following.

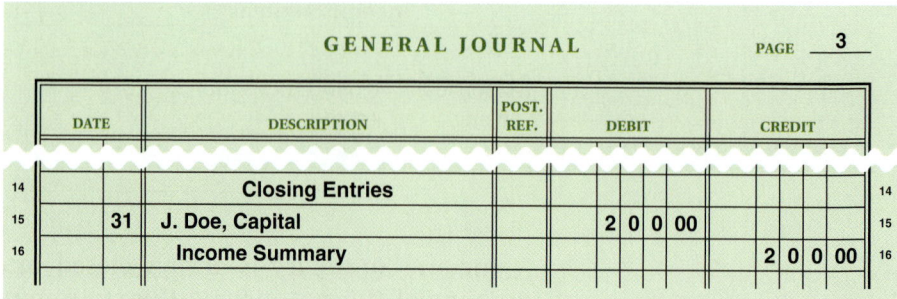

	DATE	DESCRIPTION	POST. REF.	DEBIT	CREDIT	
14		**Closing Entries**				14
15	31	J. Doe, Capital		2 0 0 00		15
16		Income Summary			2 0 0 00	16

GENERAL JOURNAL PAGE 3

Step 4 Let's return to the example of Cline's Computer Clinic. The Drawing account applies to only one fiscal period, and so it too must be closed. Drawing is not an expense because it did not help the business generate revenue. And because Drawing is not an expense, it cannot affect net income or net loss. It appears in the statement of owner's equity as a deduction from the Capital account, so it is closed directly into the Capital account. We balance off the Drawing account, or make the balance of it equal to zero. The balance of Drawing is transferred to the Capital account.

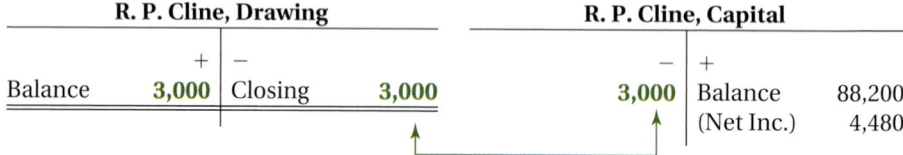

	R. P. Cline, Drawing				R. P. Cline, Capital		
	+	−			−	+	
Balance	**3,000**	Closing	**3,000**	**3,000**		Balance	88,200
						(Net Inc.)	4,480

The journal entries in the closing procedure are shown in Figure 3.

FIGURE 3

GENERAL JOURNAL PAGE 4

		DATE	DESCRIPTION	POST. REF.	DEBIT	CREDIT	
14	Step 1		**Closing Entries**				14
15		30	Income from Services	411	11 0 1 0 00		15
16			Income Summary	313		11 0 1 0 00	16
17							17
18		30	Income Summary	313	6 5 3 0 00		18
19			Wages Expense	511		3 2 2 0 00	19
20			Rent Expense	512		9 0 0 00	20
21	Step 2		Supplies Expense	513		8 7 0 00	21
22			Advertising Expense	514		3 4 0 00	22
23			Utilities Expense	515		3 2 0 00	23
24			Insurance Expense	516		4 0 00	24
25			Depreciation Expense,				25
26			Equipment	517		8 4 0 00	26
27							27
28	Step 3	30	Income Summary	313	4 4 8 0 00		28
29			R. P. Cline, Capital	311		4 4 8 0 00	29
30							30
31	Step 4	30	R. P. Cline, Capital	311	3 0 0 0 00		31
32			R. P. Cline, Drawing	312		3 0 0 0 00	32

FYI

As a memory tool for the sequence of steps in the closing procedure, use the letters of the closing elements, **REID:** Revenue, Expenses, Income Summary, Drawing.

These closing entries show that Cline's Computer Clinic has net income of $4,480, the owner has withdrawn $3,000 for personal expenses, and $1,480 has been retained in the business, thereby increasing capital.

Closing Entries Taken Directly from the Work Sheet

You can gather the information for the closing entries either directly from the ledger accounts or from the work sheet. Since the Income Statement columns of the work sheet consist entirely of revenues and expenses, you can pick up the figures for three of the four closing entries from these columns. Figure 4 shows a partial work sheet for Cline's Computer Clinic.

	ACCOUNT NAME	TRIAL BALANCE DEBIT	TRIAL BALANCE CREDIT	ADJUSTMENTS DEBIT	ADJUSTMENTS CREDIT	INCOME STATEMENT DEBIT	INCOME STATEMENT CREDIT
1	Cash	11 9 5 0 00					
2	Accounts Receivable	6 2 0 00					
3	Prepaid Insurance	4 8 0 00			(a) 4 0 00		
4	Equipment	83 7 2 0 00					
5	Accounts Payable		5 9 7 0 00				
6	R. P. Cline, Capital		88 2 0 0 00				
7	R. P. Cline, Drawing	3 0 0 0 00					
8	Income from Services		11 0 1 0 00				11 0 1 0 00
9	Wages Expense	2 9 8 0 00		(c) 2 4 0 00		3 2 2 0 00	
10	Rent Expense	9 0 0 00				9 0 0 00	
11	Supplies Expense	8 7 0 00				8 7 0 00	
12	Advertising Expense	3 4 0 00				3 4 0 00	
13	Utilities Expense	3 2 0 00				3 2 0 00	
14		105 1 8 0 00	105 1 8 0 00				
15	Insurance Expense			(a) 4 0 00		4 0 00	
16	Depreciation Expense,						
17	Equipment			(b) 8 4 0 00		8 4 0 00	
18							
19	Accumulated Dep.,						
20	Equipment				(b) 8 4 0 00		
21	Wages Payable				(c) 2 4 0 00		
22				1 1 2 0 00	1 1 2 0 00	6 5 3 0 00	11 0 1 0 00
23	Net Income					4 4 8 0 00	
24						11 0 1 0 00	11 0 1 0 00
25							
26							

FIGURE 4

You may plan the closing entries by balancing off all the figures that appear in the Income Statement columns. For example, in the Income Statement Credit column, there is a credit for $11,010 (Income from Services), so we debit that account for $11,010 and credit Income Summary for $11,010.

There are debits for $3,220, $900, $870, $340, $320, $40, and $840 (expense accounts). So now we *credit* these accounts for the same amounts, and we debit Income Summary for their total ($6,530).

Next, we close Income Summary into Capital, using the net income figure already shown on the work sheet in Figure 4.

We do, of course, have to get the last closing entry from the Balance Sheet columns to close Drawing.

Incidentally, accountants call the accounts that are to be closed (such as revenue, expenses, Income Summary, and Drawing) **nominal** or **temporary-equity accounts**. These accounts are *temporary* in that their balances apply to only one fiscal period. The *equity* aspect pertains because these accounts all come under the umbrella of owner's equity.

On the other hand, accountants call the accounts that remain open (such as assets, liabilities, and Capital) **real** or **permanent accounts**. These accounts have balances that will be carried over to the next fiscal period. They are *permanent* because as long as the company exists, there will be balances in these accounts.

Posting the Closing Entries

In the Item column of the ledger account, we write the word *Closing*. To show that the balance of an account is zero, we draw a line through both the Debit Balance and the Credit Balance columns.

After we have posted the closing entries, the Capital, Drawing, Income Summary, revenue, and expense accounts of Cline's Computer Clinic appear as follows:

GENERAL LEDGER

ACCOUNT R. P. Cline, Capital   ACCOUNT NO. 311

	DATE	ITEM	POST. REF.	DEBIT	CREDIT	BALANCE DEBIT	BALANCE CREDIT	
1	20–							1
2	June 1		1		82 0 0 0 00		82 0 0 0 00	2
3	4		1		6 2 0 0 00		88 2 0 0 00	3
4	30	Closing	4		4 4 8 0 00		92 6 8 0 00	4
5	30	Closing	4	3 0 0 0 00			89 6 8 0 00	5

ACCOUNT R. P. Cline, Drawing   ACCOUNT NO. 312

	DATE	ITEM	POST. REF.	DEBIT	CREDIT	BALANCE DEBIT	BALANCE CREDIT	
1	20–							1
2	June 30		3	3 0 0 0 00		3 0 0 0 00		2
3	30	Closing	4		3 0 0 0 00	—	—	3

ACCOUNT Income Summary   ACCOUNT NO. 313

	DATE	ITEM	POST. REF.	DEBIT	CREDIT	BALANCE DEBIT	BALANCE CREDIT	
1	20–							1
2	June 30	Closing	4		11 0 1 0 00		11 0 1 0 00	2
3	30	Closing	4	6 5 3 0 00			4 4 8 0 00	3
4	30	Closing	4	4 4 8 0 00		—	—	4

ACCOUNT **Income from Services**   ACCOUNT NO. __411__

	DATE	ITEM	POST. REF.	DEBIT	CREDIT	BALANCE DEBIT	BALANCE CREDIT	
1	20–							1
2	June 7		1		3 5 2 0 00		3 5 2 0 00	2
3	15		2		1 4 7 0 00		4 9 9 0 00	3
4	30		3		6 0 2 0 00		11 0 1 0 00	4
5	30	Closing	4	11 0 1 0 00				5
6								6

ACCOUNT **Wages Expense**   ACCOUNT NO. __511__

	DATE	ITEM	POST. REF.	DEBIT	CREDIT	BALANCE DEBIT	BALANCE CREDIT	
1	20–							1
2	June 24		2	2 9 8 0 00		2 9 8 0 00		2
3	30	Adj.	4	2 4 0 00		3 2 2 0 00		3
4	30	Closing	4		3 2 2 0 00			4

ACCOUNT **Rent Expense**   ACCOUNT NO. __512__

	DATE	ITEM	POST. REF.	DEBIT	CREDIT	BALANCE DEBIT	BALANCE CREDIT	
1	20–							1
2	June 8		1	9 0 0 00		9 0 0 00		2
3	30	Closing	4		9 0 0 00			3

ACCOUNT **Supplies Expense**   ACCOUNT NO. __513__

	DATE	ITEM	POST. REF.	DEBIT	CREDIT	BALANCE DEBIT	BALANCE CREDIT	
1	20–							1
2	June 10		1	8 7 0 00		8 7 0 00		2
3	30	Closing	4		8 7 0 00			3

ACCOUNT **Advertising Expense**   ACCOUNT NO. __514__

	DATE	ITEM	POST. REF.	DEBIT	CREDIT	BALANCE DEBIT	BALANCE CREDIT	
1	20–							1
2	June 14		2	3 4 0 00		3 4 0 00		2
3	30	Closing	4		3 4 0 00			3

ACCOUNT __Utilities Expense__ ACCOUNT NO. __515__

	DATE		ITEM	POST. REF.	DEBIT	CREDIT	BALANCE DEBIT	BALANCE CREDIT	
1	20–								1
2	June	18		2	3 2 0 00		3 2 0 00		2
3		30	Closing	4		3 2 0 00			3

ACCOUNT __Insurance Expense__ ACCOUNT NO. __516__

	DATE		ITEM	POST. REF.	DEBIT	CREDIT	BALANCE DEBIT	BALANCE CREDIT	
1	20–								1
2	June	30	Adj.	4	4 0 00		4 0 00		2
3		30	Closing	4		4 0 00			3

ACCOUNT __Depreciation Expense, Equipment__ ACCOUNT NO. __517__

	DATE		ITEM	POST. REF.	DEBIT	CREDIT	BALANCE DEBIT	BALANCE CREDIT	
1	20–								1
2	June	30	Adj.	4	8 4 0 00		8 4 0 00		2
3		30	Closing	4		8 4 0 00			3

Office supplies—such as those supplied by major chains like Office Depot and Staples—consist of a wide variety of items that are used up and reordered frequently in the course of doing business.

THE POST-CLOSING TRIAL BALANCE

OBJECTIVE 3

Prepare a post-closing trial balance.

After posting the closing entries and before going on to the next fiscal period, verify the balances of the accounts that remain open. To do so, prepare a **post-closing trial balance**, using the final balance figures from the ledger accounts. The purpose of the post-closing trial balance is to make sure that the debit balances equal the credit balances.

Note that the accounts listed in the post-closing trial balance (assets, liabilities, and Capital) are the *real* or *permanent accounts* (see Figure 5). The accountant carries forward the balances of the permanent accounts from one fiscal period to another.

FIGURE 5

Cline's Computer Clinic
Post-Closing Trial Balance
June 30, 20—

ACCOUNT NAME	DEBIT	CREDIT
Cash	11 9 5 0 00	
Accounts Receivable	6 2 0 00	
Prepaid Insurance	4 4 0 00	
Equipment	83 7 2 0 00	
Accumulated Depreciation, Equipment		8 4 0 00
Accounts Payable		5 9 7 0 00
Wages Payable		2 4 0 00
R. P. Cline, Capital		89 6 8 0 00
	96 7 3 0 00	96 7 3 0 00

Contrast this to the handling of *nominal* or *temporary-equity accounts* (revenue, expenses, Income Summary, and Drawing), which are closed at the end of each fiscal period.

If the total debits and total credits of the post-closing trial balance are not equal, here's a recommended procedure for tracking down the error.

1. Re-add the trial balance columns.
2. Check to see that the figures were correctly transferred from the ledger accounts to the post-closing trial balance.
3. Verify the posting of the adjusting entries and the recording of the new balances.
4. Make sure that the closing entries have been posted and that all revenue, expense, Income Summary, and Drawing accounts have zero balances.

THE BASES OF ACCOUNTING: CASH AND ACCRUAL

OBJECTIVE 4

Define the following methods of accounting: cash basis and accrual basis.

The basis of accounting that a company chooses has a direct effect on the company's net income and the company's income tax. The business must use the same basis of accounting from year to year, and the basis of accounting must clearly reflect the net income of the business.

FYI

For income tax purposes, the availability of the cash method is explained by the IRS in Publication 538. Most service businesses with average annual gross receipts of $5 million or less will be allowed to use the cash method rather than the accrual method, which is more complicated and time consuming. Most businesses use the same method of accounting for their financial statements and income tax reporting. IRS Publication 538 is available on the IRS website at **http://www.irs.gov.**

Under the **cash basis of accounting**, revenue is counted when it is received in cash, and generally expenses are counted when they are paid in cash. If the expenditures have an economic life of more than one year, for example equipment purchases and insurance, then the cost of these items must be prorated or spread out over their useful lives. Many small businesses' and individuals' personal income taxes are recorded on the cash basis.

Under the **accrual basis of accounting**, revenue is recorded when it is earned, and expenses are recorded when they are incurred (when they occur or the bill is received). For example, in the sale of goods, revenue is counted by the seller when the buyer accepts delivery of the goods. Expenses are recorded by the seller of the goods when the costs are incurred. This is called the *matching* principle, since revenue in one fiscal period is matched up with expenses incurred in the same period. If your business produces, purchases, or sells merchandise, the business must keep an inventory and use the accrual method for sales and purchases of merchandise. A business may also use a combination of cash and accrual bases of accounting, called the *hybrid method.*

INTERIM STATEMENTS

OBJECTIVE 5

Prepare interim statements.

The owner of a business understandably does not want to wait until the end of the twelve-month fiscal period to determine whether the company made a profit or a loss. Instead, most owners want financial statements at the end of each month. Financial statements prepared during the fiscal year, for periods of less than twelve months, are called **interim statements**. (They are given this name because they are prepared within the fiscal period.) For example, a business may prepare the income statement, the statement of owner's equity, and the balance sheet *monthly.* These statements provide up-to-date information about the results and status of operations. For example, a company might have the following interim statements:

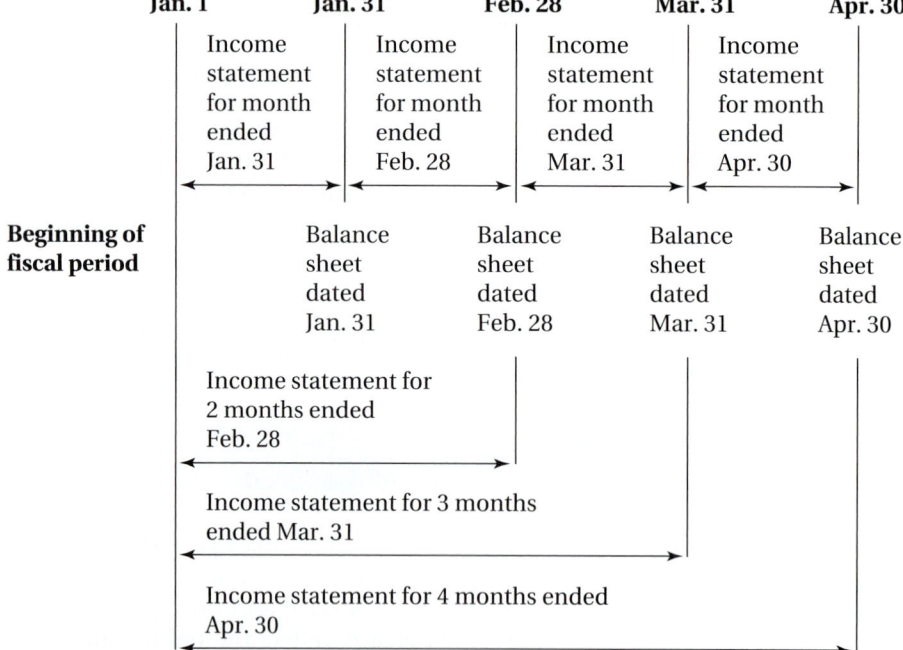

In this case, the accountant would prepare a work sheet at the end of each month. Next, based on these work sheets, he or she would prepare the financial statements. *However, the remaining steps—journalizing the adjusting and closing entries and preparing the post-closing trial balance—would be performed only at the end of the year.*

CHAPTER REVIEW

Online Study Center

ACE the test!

Review of Performance Objectives

1. List the steps in the accounting cycle.

   1. Analyze source documents and record business transactions in a journal.
   2. Post journal entries to the accounts in the ledger.
   3. Prepare a trial balance.
   4. Gather adjustment data and record the adjusting entries on a work sheet.
   5. Complete the work sheet.
   6. Prepare financial statements from the data on the work sheet.
   7. Journalize and post the adjusting entries from the data on the work sheet.
   8. Journalize and post the closing entries.
   9. Prepare a post-closing trial balance.

2. Journalize and post closing entries for a service enterprise.

   The four steps in the closing procedure are as follows:

   1. Close the revenue accounts into Income Summary.
   2. Close the expense accounts into Income Summary.
   3. Close the Income Summary account into the Capital account, transferring the net income or loss to the Capital account.
   4. Close the Drawing account into the Capital account.

3. Prepare a post-closing trial balance.

   A post-closing trial balance consists of the final balances of the accounts remaining open. It is the final proof that the debit balances equal the credit balances before the posting for the new fiscal period begins.

4. Define the following methods of accounting: cash basis and accrual basis.

   Under the *cash basis* of accounting, revenue is recorded when it is received and expenses are generally counted when they are paid in cash. Under the *accrual basis* of accounting, revenue is recorded when earned, even if cash is received at a later date, and expenses are recorded when incurred, even if cash is to be paid at a later date.

5. Prepare interim statements.

   Interim statements consist of year-to-date income statements, statements of owner's equity, and balance sheets as of various dates during the fiscal period.

Glossary

Accrual basis of accounting An accounting method under which revenue is recorded when it is earned, regardless of when it is received, and expenses are recorded when they are incurred, regardless of when they are paid. (166)

Cash basis of accounting An accounting method under which revenue is recorded only when it is received in cash. Most expenses are recorded only when they are paid in cash. However, exceptions are made for expenditures on items having a useful life of more than one year and for certain prepaid items. Expenditures for insurance premiums can be *prorated,* or spread out, over the fiscal periods covered. Expenditures for long-lived items are recorded as assets and later depreciated as an expense over their useful lives. (166)

Closing entries Entries made at the end of a fiscal period to close off the revenue, expense, and Drawing accounts—that is, to make the balances of the temporary-equity accounts equal to zero. Closing is also called *clearing the accounts.* (156)

Income Summary account An account brought into existence in order to have a debit and credit in each closing entry. The revenue and expense account balances are transferred to this account to allow calculations of net income or net loss. (156)

Interim statements Financial statements prepared during the fiscal year, covering a period of time less than twelve months. (166)

Nominal or **temporary-equity accounts** Accounts that apply to only one fiscal period and that are to be closed at the end of that fiscal period, such as revenue, expense, Income Summary, and Drawing accounts. This category may also be described as all accounts except assets, liabilities, and the Capital account. (162)

Post-closing trial balance The listing of the final balances of the real accounts at the end of the fiscal period. (165)

Real or **permanent accounts** The accounts that remain open (assets, liabilities, and the Capital account in owner's equity) and that have balances that will be carried over to the next fiscal period. (162)

QUESTIONS, EXERCISES, AND CASES

Discussion Questions

1. Number in order the following steps in the accounting cycle.
   a. Prepare a trial balance on the first two columns of the work sheet.
   b. Post journal entries to accounts in the ledger.
   c. Journalize and post adjusting entries.
   d. Analyze source documents and record transactions in the journal.
   e. Prepare financial statements.
   f. Gather adjusting data and write adjusting entries on the work sheet.

g. Journalize and post closing entries.

h. Prepare a post-closing trial balance.

i. Complete the work sheet (this assumes a manual system).

2. List the steps in the closing procedure in the correct order.

3. What is the purpose of closing entries? Consider the consequence of forgetting to make closing entries.

4. What happens if you do not print, save, and back up your financial statements before the closing entries occur?

5. What are real accounts? What are nominal accounts? Give examples of each.

6. What is the purpose of the Income Summary account, and how does it relate to the revenue and expense accounts?

7. What is the purpose of the post-closing trial balance? What is the difference between a trial balance and a post-closing trial balance?

8. Write the third closing entry to transfer the profit or loss to the B. Corson, Capital account, assuming the following:

a. A profit of $3,765 during the first quarter (Jan.–Mar.)

b. A loss of $1,689 during the second quarter (Apr.–Jun.)

Exercises

P.O. 2

Classify accounts and show where they are listed on the work sheet.

Exercise 5-1 Classify the accounts listed below as real (permanent) or nominal (temporary), and indicate with an X whether the account is closed. Also, indicate the financial statement in which each account will appear. The Building account is given as an example.

Account Title	Real	Nominal	Closed Yes	Closed No	Income Statement	Balance Sheet
0. Example: Building	X			X		X
a. Prepaid Insurance						
b. Accounts Payable						
c. Wages Payable						
d. Services Income						
e. Rent Expense						
f. Supplies Expense						
g. Accum. Depr.,						

P.O. 2

Journalize closing entries from T account balances.

Exercise 5-2 Number the closing entries as steps 1 through 4. Journalize the closing entries shown on the next page.

Assets	=	Liabilities	+	Owner's Equity	+	Revenue	–	Expenses
Dr. | Cr.		Dr. | Cr.		Dr. | Cr.		Dr. | Cr.		Dr. | Cr.
+ | –		– | +		– | +		– | +		+ | –

Prepaid Insurance

Bal. 990	(c) 360
Bal. 630	

Wages Payable

	(a) 210

J. Ramsey, Capital

560	Bal. 24,000
500	
	Bal. 22,940

Professional Fees

3,650	Bal. 3,650

Wages Expense

Bal. 2,800	
(a) 210	
Bal. 3,010	3,010

Accum. Depr., Equipment

	Bal. 3,200
	(b) 700
	Bal. 3,900

J. Ramsey, Drawing

Bal. 500	500

Income Summary

4,210	3,650
	560

Insurance Expense

(c) 360	360

Depr. Expense, Equipment

(b) 700	700

Misc. Expense

Bal. 140	140

P.O. 2

Journalize closing entries from account balances.

Exercise 5-3 As of December 31, the end of the current year, the ledger of Harris Company contained the following account balances after adjustment. All accounts have normal balances. Journalize the closing entries.

Cash	$ 8,540	H. Harris, Drawing	$1,698
Equipment	11,486	Professional Fees	6,875
Accumulated Depreciation,		Wages Expense	1,468
Equipment	2,687	Rent Expense	990
Accounts Payable	1,574	Depreciation Expense,	
Wages Payable	658	Equipment	1,243
H. Harris, Capital	13,876	Miscellaneous Expense	245

P.O. 2

Journalize closing entries from work sheet columns—a profit.

Exercise 5-4 The Income Statement columns of the work sheet of Dwyer Company for the fiscal year ended June 30 appear below. During the year, N. Dwyer withdrew $4,200. Journalize the closing entries.

	ACCOUNT NAME	INCOME STATEMENT	
		DEBIT	CREDIT
1	Service Income		6 8 9 7 00
2	Rental Income		3 6 7 6 00
3	Rent Expense	2 7 0 0 00	
4	Wages Expense	1 9 5 4 00	
5	Utilities Expense	3 6 5 00	
6	Miscellaneous Expense	1 5 9 00	
7		5 1 7 8 00	10 5 7 3 00
8	Net Income	5 3 9 5 00	
9		10 5 7 3 00	10 5 7 3 00

P.O. 2

Journalize closing entries from work sheet columns—a loss.

Exercise 5-5 The Income Statement columns of the work sheet of Salas Company for the fiscal year ended December 31 appear on the following page. During the year, S. Salas withdrew $18,000. Journalize the closing entries.

	ACCOUNT NAME	INCOME STATEMENT DEBIT	INCOME STATEMENT CREDIT
1	Service Income		32 7 4 0 00
2	Rental Income		12 0 0 0 00
3	Wages Expense	43 5 2 0 00	
4	Utilities Expense	4 6 3 0 00	
5	Miscellaneous Expense	9 2 0 0 00	
6		57 3 5 0 00	44 7 4 0 00
7	Net Loss		12 6 1 0 00
8		57 3 5 0 00	57 3 5 0 00

P.O. 2

Journalize closing entries three and four from account balances.

Exercise 5-6 After all revenue and expenses have been closed at the end of the fiscal period ended December 31, Income Summary has a debit of $46,550 and a credit of $37,520. On the same date, E. Masters, Drawing, has a debit balance of $13,500, and E. Masters, Capital, had a beginning credit balance of $64,410.

a. Journalize the entries to close the remaining temporary accounts.
b. What is the new balance of E. Masters, Capital, after closing the remaining temporary accounts? Show your calculations.

P.O. 5

Place accounts on financial statements.

Exercise 5-7 Indicate with an X whether each of the following would appear on the income statement, statement of owner's equity, or balance sheet. An item may appear on more than one statement. The first item is provided as an example.

Item	Income Statement	Statement of Owner's Equity	Balance Sheet
0. Example: The total liabilities of the business at the end of the year.			X
a. The amount of the owner's Capital balance at the end of the year.			
b. The amount of depreciation expense on equipment during the year.			
c. The amount of the company's net income for the year.			
d. The book value of the equipment.			
e. Total insurance expired during the year.			
f. Total accounts receivable at the end of the year.			
g. Total withdrawals by the owner.			
h. The cost of utilities used during the year.			
i. The amount of the owner's Capital balance at the beginning of the year.			

P.O. 5

Prepare a statement of owner's equity from T accounts.

Exercise 5-8 Prepare a statement of owner's equity for The Dunn Clinic for the year ended December 31. P. Dunn's capital amount on January 1 was $125,000, and there was an additional investment of $8,000 on May 12 and withdrawals of $32,500 for the year. Net income for the year was $21,418.

internet
LINKS TO ACCOUNTING

You just learned about the methods of accounting a company can use when recording transactions, such as sales. This would be a good time to review the methods discussed in Performance Objective 4. Then, see if you can answer some questions about Dell. Go to **http://www.dell.com** and then search for SEC Reports. Select 2005 and then Form 10-K. Use the financial statements that begin on page 33 of the 10-K report.

1. For 2005, how much is net revenue on Dell's income statement? How much are accounts receivable, net, and accounts payable on the balance sheet?

2. What method of accounting does Dell use? How can you tell by looking at its financial statements?

CONSIDER AND COMMUNICATE

Your uncle owns a small sole proprietorship. He does his own bookkeeping, although he didn't finish the chapter on closing entries before he opened his business. He mentions to you that closing entries look like they take a long time. He wonders why he should bother to do them, because all he really looks at is the checkbook anyway. What would you say to convince him that closing entries are necessary?

CRITICAL THINKING

Following is the post-closing trial balance submitted to you by the bookkeeper. Assume that the debit total ($41,048) is correct.

a. Analyze the work and prepare a response to what you have reviewed.
b. Journalize the closing entries.
c. What is the net income or net loss?
d. Is there an increase or a decrease in Capital?
e. What would be the ending amount of Capital?
f. What is the new balance of the post-closing trial balance?

Tafoya Consulting Company
Post-Closing Trial Balance
December 31, 20—

ACCOUNT NAME	DEBIT	CREDIT
Cash	3 4 1 2 00	
Accounts Receivable	1 6 9 3 00	
Prepaid Insurance	2 1 4 7 00	
Accounts Payable		
C. Tafoya, Capital		13 8 1 8 00
C. Tafoya, Drawing	6 3 6 0 00	
Consulting Income		25 6 0 3 00
Wages Expense	11 9 9 4 00	
Rent Expense	9 6 0 0 00	
Advertising Expense	2 5 8 2 00	
Supplies Expense	9 1 4 00	
Insurance Expense	1 6 1 0 00	
Miscellaneous Expense	7 3 6 00	
	41 0 4 8 00	41 0 4 8 00

A QUESTION OF ETHICS

You are preparing a post-closing trial balance for the company where you work, but it doesn't balance. You are tired, and besides, you don't think they pay you for this kind of hassle and extra time. You decide to increase the balance of an asset account to make the totals balance. Discuss this action and whether it is ethical or illegal.

WHAT'S WRONG WITH THIS PICTURE?

The bookkeeper has completed a work sheet and has journalized and posted the closing entries, but he forgot to journalize and post the adjusting entries from the work sheet. What are the effects of these actions and omissions? How would these actions and omissions affect the accounting records and the resulting financial statements?

PROBLEM SET A

For additional help, see the demonstration problem at the beginning of each chapter in your Working Papers.

P.O. 2

Problem 5-1A After the accountant posted the adjusting entries for M. Waldon, Designer, the general ledger contained the following account balances on May 31:

	ACCOUNT NAME	ADJUSTED TRIAL BALANCE	
		DEBIT	CREDIT
		A + Draw. + E	Accum. Deprec. + L + C + R
1	Cash	2 3 1 8 00	
2	Accounts Receivable	1 4 0 8 00	
3	Prepaid Insurance	9 8 7 00	
4	Office Equipment	5 7 9 0 00	
5	Accumulated Depreciation, Office Equipment		1 3 6 4 00
6	Accounts Payable		8 8 0 00
7	M. Waldon, Capital		8 2 4 7 00
8	M. Waldon, Drawing	1 8 0 0 00	
9	Commissions Earned		3 8 9 7 00
10	Rent Expense	7 9 0 00	
11	Supplies Expense	3 8 1 00	
12	Depreciation Expense, Office Equipment	5 2 0 00	
13	Utilities Expense	2 7 6 00	
14	Miscellaneous Expense	1 1 8 00	
15		14 3 8 8 00	14 3 8 8 00

Check Figure

Net Income, $1,812

Instructions

a. Write the owner's name on the Capital and Drawing T accounts.
b. Record the account balances in the T accounts for owner's equity, revenue, and expenses.
c. Journalize the closing entries with the four steps in correct order. Number the closing entries 1 through 4.
d. Post the closing entries to the T accounts right after you journalize each one to see the effect of the closing entries. Number the closing entries 1 through 4.

P.O. 2

Problem 5-2A The partial work sheet for Kessley Consulting for the month of May is shown on the next page.

ACCOUNT NAME	INCOME STATEMENT				BALANCE SHEET					
	DEBIT		CREDIT		DEBIT		CREDIT Accum. Depr.			
	E		R		A + Draw.		+ L + C			
1 Cash					2 2 4 8 00					1
2 Prepaid Insurance					8 5 9 00					2
3 Equipment					5 7 3 1 00					3
4 Accumulated Depreciation, Equipment							2 3 7 9 00			4
5 Accounts Payable							8 4 1 00			5
6 K. Kessley, Capital							2 4 1 5 00			6
7 K. Kessley, Drawing					1 8 0 0 00					7
8 Consulting Income			8 5 4 6 00							8
9 Rent Expense	8 0 0 00									9
10 Wages Expense	1 6 3 3 00									10
11 Supplies Expense	3 6 5 00									11
12 Miscellaneous Expense	1 6 8 00									12
13										13
14 Insurance Expense	2 6 4 00									14
15 Depreciation Expense, Equipment	7 0 0 00									15
16 Wages Payable							3 8 7 00			16
17	3 9 3 0 00		8 5 4 6 00		10 6 3 8 00		6 0 2 2 00			17
18 Net Income	4 6 1 6 00						4 6 1 6 00			18
19	8 5 4 6 00		8 5 4 6 00		10 6 3 8 00		10 6 3 8 00			19
20										20

Check Figure

Debit to Income Summary, second entry, $3,930

Instructions

a. Write the owner's name on the Capital and Drawing T accounts.

b. Record the account balances in the T accounts for owner's equity, revenue, and expenses.

c. Journalize the closing entries with the four steps in correct order. Number the closing entries 1 through 4.

d. Post the closing entries to the T accounts right after you journalize each one to see the effect of the closing entries. Number the closing entries 1 through 4.

P.O. 1,2,3

Problem 5-3A The completed work sheet for Ulmer Tour Company as of December 31 is presented in your Working Papers, along with the general ledger as of December 31 before adjustments.

Check Figure

Post-closing trial balance total, $7,408

Instructions

1. Write the name of the owner, K. Ulmer, in the Capital and Drawing accounts.

2. Write the balances from the unadjusted trial balance in the general ledger.

3. Journalize and post the adjusting entries.

4. Journalize and post the closing entries in the correct order.

5. Prepare a post-closing trial balance.

P.O. 1,2,3

Problem 5-4A The account balances of Morrow's Tutoring Service as of June 30, the end of the current fiscal year, are as follows:

	ACCOUNT NAME	TRIAL BALANCE DEBIT	TRIAL BALANCE CREDIT
1	Cash	5 4 9 1 00	
2	Accounts Receivable	6 2 4 00	
3	Prepaid Insurance	1 2 8 0 00	
4	Equipment	6 4 9 7 00	
5	Accumulated Depreciation, Equipment		2 6 7 2 00
6	Van	18 6 7 4 00	
7	Accumulated Depreciation, Van		4 3 6 8 00
8	Accounts Payable		1 0 3 6 00
9	B. Morrow, Capital		4 8 4 8 00
10	B. Morrow, Drawing	12 0 0 0 00	
11	Fees Earned		53 2 8 0 00
12	Salary Expense	18 0 0 0 00	
13	Advertising Expense	1 2 0 0 00	
14	Van Operating Expense	6 0 5 00	
15	Utilities Expense	1 2 4 8 00	
16	Supplies Expense	3 2 7 00	
17	Miscellaneous Expense	2 5 8 00	
18		66 2 0 4 00	66 2 0 4 00

Check Figure

Net Income, $28,248

Instructions

1. Complete the work sheet:

   Data for the adjustments:

   a. Expired or used up insurance, $350.
   b. Depreciation expense on equipment, $980 (remember to credit the Accumulated Depreciation, Equipment account, not Equipment).
   c. Depreciation expense on the van, $1,690 (remember to credit the Accumulated Depreciation, Van account, not Van).
   d. Salary accrued (earned) since the last payday, $374 (owed and to be paid on the next payday).

2. Prepare an income statement.
3. Prepare a statement of owner's equity; assume there was an additional investment of $2,000 on July 10.
4. Prepare a balance sheet.
5. Journalize the adjusting entries.
6. Journalize the closing entries with the four steps in the correct sequence.

Instructions for General Ledger Software

1. Print a trial balance.
2. Journalize the adjusting entries in the general journal and post to the general ledger. (No work sheet is required on the computer.)

3. Print an income statement, a statement of owner's equity, and a balance sheet.
4. Journalize the closing entries in the general journal.
5. Post the closing entries.
6. Print a post-closing trial balance.

PROBLEM SET B

For additional help, see the demonstration problem at the beginning of each chapter in your Working Papers.

P.O. 2

Problem 5-1B After the accountant posted the adjusting entries for C. Lynn, Designer, the general ledger contained the following account balances on May 31:

ACCOUNT NAME	ADJUSTED TRIAL BALANCE	
	DEBIT	CREDIT Accum. Deprec.
	A + Draw. + E	+ L + C + R
1 Cash	2 4 2 9 00	
2 Accounts Receivable	8 8 6 00	
3 Prepaid Insurance	1 4 6 0 00	
4 Office Equipment	4 6 7 2 00	
5 Accumulated Depreciation, Office Equipment		1 2 5 3 00
6 Accounts Payable		9 4 3 00
7 C. Lynn, Capital		6 5 2 0 00
8 C. Lynn, Drawing	1 6 5 0 00	
9 Commissions Earned		4 6 7 9 00
10 Rent Expense	8 9 5 00	
11 Supplies Expense	5 7 0 00	
12 Depreciation Expense, Office Equipment	4 6 7 00	
13 Utilities Expense	2 6 4 00	
14 Miscellaneous Expense	1 0 2 00	
15	13 3 9 5 00	13 3 9 5 00

Check Figure

Net Income, $2,381

Instructions

a. Write the owner's name on the Capital and Drawing T accounts.
b. Record the account balances in the T accounts for owner's equity, revenue, and expenses.
c. Journalize the closing entries with the four steps in correct order. Number the closing entries 1 through 4.
d. Post the closing entries to the T accounts right after you journalize each one to see the effect of the closing entries. Number the closing entries 1 through 4.

P.O. 2

Problem 5-2B The partial work sheet for Kwan Consulting for the month of June is as follows.

	ACCOUNT NAME	INCOME STATEMENT DEBIT — E	INCOME STATEMENT CREDIT — R	BALANCE SHEET DEBIT A + Draw.	BALANCE SHEET CREDIT Accum. Depr. + L + C	
1	Cash			6 1 0 4 00		1
2	Prepaid Insurance			1 3 4 4 00		2
3	Equipment			6 7 5 1 00		3
4	Accumulated Depreciation, Equipment				3 3 9 3 00	4
5	Accounts Payable				1 3 5 6 00	5
6	L. Kwan, Capital				1 3 6 7 00	6
7	L. Kwan, Drawing			2 4 0 0 00		7
8	Consulting Income		15 0 6 0 00			8
9	Rent Expense	1 1 0 0 00				9
10	Wages Expense	1 9 0 8 00				10
11	Miscellaneous Expense	2 4 0 00				11
12						12
13	Supplies Expense	4 3 2 00				13
14	Insurance Expense	3 4 5 00				14
15	Depreciation Expense, Equipment	9 0 0 00				15
16	Wages Payable				3 4 8 00	16
17		4 9 2 5 00	15 0 6 0 00	16 5 9 9 00	6 4 6 4 00	17
18	Net Income	10 1 3 5 00			10 1 3 5 00	18
19		15 0 6 0 00	15 0 6 0 00	16 5 9 9 00	16 5 9 9 00	19
20						20

Check Figure

Debit to Income Summary, second entry, $4,925

Instructions

a. Write the owner's name on the Capital and Drawing T accounts.
b. Record the account balances in the T accounts for owner's equity, revenue, and expenses.
c. Journalize the closing entries with the four steps in correct order. Number the closing entries 1 through 4.
d. Post the closing entries to the T accounts right after you journalize each one to see the effect of the closing entries. Number closing entries 1 through 4.

P.O. 1,2,3

Problem 5-3B The completed work sheet for Valenti Insurance Agency as of December 31 is presented in your Working Papers, along with the general ledger as of December 31 before adjustments.

Check Figure

Post-closing trial balance total, $8,889.60

Instructions

1. Write the name of the owner, M. Valenti, in the Capital and Drawing accounts.
2. Write the balances from the unadjusted trial balance in the general ledger.
3. Journalize and post the adjusting entries.
4. Journalize and post the closing entries in the correct order.
5. Prepare a post-closing trial balance.

P.O. 1,2,3

Problem 5-4B The account balances of Braden Company as of June 30, the end of the current fiscal year, are as follows.

		TRIAL BALANCE			
	ACCOUNT NAME	DEBIT		CREDIT	
1	Cash	4 3 8 1 00			
2	Accounts Receivable	5 7 8 00			
3	Prepaid Insurance	1 1 3 8 00			
4	Equipment	5 7 1 3 00			
5	Accumulated Depreciation, Equipment			2 4 8 7 00	
6	Van	12 6 7 8 00			
7	Accumulated Depreciation, Van			3 3 1 8 00	
8	Accounts Payable			9 9 7 00	
9	B. Braden, Capital			5 9 6 4 00	
10	B. Braden, Drawing	18 0 0 0 00			
11	Fees Earned			48 3 1 7 00	
12	Salary Expense	16 0 0 0 00			
13	Advertising Expense	8 8 7 00			
14	Supplies Expense	3 9 7 00			
15	Van Operating Expense	4 6 2 00			
16	Utilities Expense	6 8 5 00			
17	Miscellaneous Expense	1 6 4 00			
18		61 0 8 3 00		61 0 8 3 00	

Check Figure

Net income, $26,822

Instructions

1. Complete the work sheet.

   Data for the adjustments:
   a. Expired or used up insurance, $490.
   b. Depreciation expense on equipment, $680 (remember to credit the Accumulated Depreciation, Equipment account, not Equipment).
   c. Depreciation expense on the van, $1,090 (remember to credit the Accumulated Depreciation, Van account, not Van).
   d. Salary accrued (earned) since the last payday, $640 (owed and to be paid on the next payday).

2. Prepare an income statement.
3. Prepare a statement of owner's equity; assume there was an additional investment of $3,000 on October 10.
4. Prepare a balance sheet.
5. Journalize the adjusting entries.
6. Journalize the closing entries with the four steps in the proper sequence.

Instructions for General Ledger Software

1. Print a trial balance.
2. Journalize the adjusting entries in the general journal and post to the general ledger. (No work sheet is required on the computer.)
3. Print an income statement, a statement of owner's equity, and a balance sheet.
4. Journalize the closing entries in the general journal.
5. Post the closing entries.
6. Print a post-closing trial balance.

The Computer Clinic

Closing Entries

Before the Month-End Closing Entries

What to do *before* you perform the closing entries:

1. a. Print out all financial statements.
   b. Make a copy of your pre-closing file.
   c. Add the Income Summary account (399) to the chart of accounts.

Month-End Closing Entries

What to do to *close* (or zero out) the temporary owner's equity accounts (revenue(s), expenses, Income Summary, and Drawing), a process that transfers the net income into or deducts the net loss and the withdrawals from the Capital account. In addition, the closing process prepares the records for the new fiscal period:

2. a. Debit each revenue account and credit the Income Summary account. Now, all revenue accounts have a zero balance and the Income Summary account has a credit representing all revenue earned this fiscal period.
   b. Debit the Income Summary account for the total of all expenses and credit each expense account. Now, all expenses have a zero balance and the Income Summary account has a debit representing all expenses incurred this fiscal period.
   c. The Income Summary account has a larger credit (revenue) than debit (expenses), which indicates that there is a net income. This is consistent with the income statement you printed in Chapter 4. The balance in the Income Summary account is $6,776.62. Therefore, to close the Income Summary account with a credit balance, debit Income Summary for the balance and credit A. Valli, Capital. The balance of the Income Summary account is now zero and the net income of $6,776.62 has been transferred to the Capital account.
   d. Finally, debit A. Valli, Capital for the amount of the A. Valli, Drawing account and credit A. Valli, Drawing. The balance of A. Valli, Drawing is now zero, and you have reduced A. Valli, Capital by the amount of the owner withdrawal.

After the Month-End Closing Entries

What to do *after* the closing entries:

3. a. Print a post-closing trial balance from the general ledger. *Post* means "after," so you are printing a trial balance *after* closing.
   b. Look at the post-closing trial balance. What do you see? How does it differ from the other trial balances you have seen? It should be shorter than the trial balances you are used to seeing. What classifications of accounts are present or open (that is, they have balances over zero)? You should see only assets, liabilities, and the owner's Capital account. Why? Because the purpose of the post-closing trial balance is to be assured that all temporary owner's equity accounts (revenues, expenses, Income Summary, and Drawing) are closed or have zero balances, readying the records to receive revenues, expenses, and drawing entries in the new fiscal period. You have experienced not only accrual-basis accounting, but the matching principle as well.

PART I: Multiple-Choice Questions

___ 1. The net income appears on all of the following statements except

     a. the statement of owner's equity.
     b. the balance sheet.
     c. the income statement.
     d. all of these.
     e. none of these.

___ 2. Which of the following entries records the withdrawal of cash for personal use by Dolan, the owner of a business firm?

     a. Debit Cash and credit Drawing.
     b. Debit Salary Expense and credit Cash.
     c. Debit Cash and credit Salary Expense.
     d. Debit Drawing and credit Cash.
     e. None of these.

___ 3. Which of the following errors, considered individually, would cause the trial balance totals to be unequal?

     a. A payment of $52 for supplies was posted as a debit of $52 to Supplies and a credit of $25 to Cash.
     b. A payment of $625 to a creditor was posted as a debit of $625 to Accounts Payable and a debit of $625 to Cash.
     c. Cash received from customers on account was posted as a debit of $380 to Cash and a credit of $38 to Accounts Receivable.
     d. All of these.
     e. None of these.

___ 4. The balance in the Prepaid Insurance account before adjustment at the end of the year is $600. This represents six months' insurance paid on November 1. The monthly adjusting entry required on December 31 is

     a. debit Insurance Expense, $200; credit Prepaid Insurance, $200.
     b. debit Prepaid Insurance, $100; credit Insurance Expense, $100.
     c. debit Prepaid Insurance, $600; credit Insurance Expense, $600.
     d. debit Insurance Expense, $600; credit Prepaid Insurance, $600.
     e. none of these.

___ 5. If an accountant fails to make an adjusting entry to record expired insurance at the end of a fiscal period, the omission will cause

     a. total expenses to be understated.
     b. total revenue to be understated.
     c. total assets to be understated.
     d. all of these.
     e. none of these.

Note: Answers to Before a Test Check begin on page A-1.

___ 6. Farmer Company bought equipment on January 2 of this year for $9,000. At the time of purchase, the equipment was estimated to have a useful life of eight years and a trade-in value of $1,000 at the end of eight years. Using the straight-line method, the amount of depreciation for the first year is

   a. $900.
   b. $1,000.
   c. $800.
   d. $950.
   e. none of these.

___ 7. If expenses are greater than revenue, the Income Summary account will be closed by a debit to

   a. Cash and a credit to Income Summary.
   b. Income Summary and a credit to Cash.
   c. Capital and a credit to Income Summary.
   d. Income Summary and a credit to Capital.
   e. none of these.

___ 8. In preparing closing entries, it is helpful to refer to which of the following columns of the work sheet first?

   a. The Balance Sheet columns
   b. The Adjusted Trial Balance columns
   c. The Income Statement columns
   d. Both the Adjusted Trial Balance and the Income Statement columns
   e. None of these

PART II: Practical Application

On December 31, the ledger accounts of Kristopher's Upholstery Shop have the following balances after all adjusting entries have been posted.

Cash	$ 1,200
Equipment	15,400
Accumulated Depreciation, Equipment	1,100
Accounts Payable	300
K. Payton, Capital	16,500
K. Payton, Drawing	16,400
Income Summary	
Income from Services	35,900
Wages Expense	11,500
Rent Expense	2,400
Utilities Expense	1,000
Depreciation Expense, Equipment	500
Supplies Expense	4,100
Miscellaneous Expense	900

Instructions

Journalize the four closing entries in the proper order.

PART III: Matching Questions

_____ 1. Creditor

_____ 2. Business entity

_____ 3. Fundamental accounting equation

_____ 4. Income statement

_____ 5. Owner's equity

_____ 6. Accounts Receivable

_____ 7. Net loss

_____ 8. Ledger

_____ 9. Credit

_____ 10. Compound entry

_____ 11. Trial balance

_____ 12. Journalizing

_____ 13. Posting

_____ 14. Cross-reference

_____ 15. Journal

_____ 16. Work sheet

_____ 17. Book value

_____ 18. Depreciation

_____ 19. Accounting cycle

_____ 20. Fiscal year

_____ 21. Contra account

_____ 22. Mixed accounts

_____ 23. Temporary-equity accounts

_____ 24. Real accounts

_____ 25. Debit

a. The book of original entry

b. One to whom money is owed

c. Accounts that are partly income statement and partly balance sheet accounts

d. Assets − Liabilities

e. A listing of the ending balances of all ledger accounts that proves the equality of total debits and total credits

f. The process of recording transactions in a journal

g. The left side of a T account

h. A business enterprise, separate and distinct from the person who owns its assets

i. The process of transferring accounts and amounts from the journal to the ledger

j. An account that is deducted from another account

k. Amounts owed by charge customers

l. Balance sheet accounts

m. Assets = Liabilities + Owner's Equity

n. A bookkeeping device for referring from journal to ledger or ledger to journal

o. The right side of a T account

p. Allocation of the cost of a plant asset over its estimated life

q. Financial statement that shows the net results of operations

r. Accounts that belong to only one fiscal period and are closed out at the end of each fiscal period

s. A transaction that has two or more debits and/or credits

t. Paper used to record adjustments and provide balances to prepare financial statements

u. Excess of total expenses over total revenues

v. A period of twelve consecutive months

w. A book containing all the accounts of a business

x. The cost of an asset minus its accumulated depreciation

y. Steps in the accounting process, completed during the fiscal period

Accounting Cycle Review Problem A

This problem is designed to enable you to apply the knowledge you have acquired in the preceding chapters. In accounting, the ultimate test is being able to handle data in real-life situations. This problem will give you valuable experience.

Chart of Accounts

Assets

111 Cash
112 Accounts Receivable
114 Prepaid Insurance
121 Land
122 Building
123 Accumulated Depreciation, Building
124 Pool/Slide Facility
125 Accumulated Depreciation, Pool/Slide Facility
126 Pool Furniture
127 Accumulated Depreciation, Pool Furniture

Liabilities

221 Accounts Payable
222 Wages Payable
223 Mortgage Payable

Owner's Equity

311 W. Wong, Capital
312 W. Wong, Drawing
313 Income Summary

Revenue

411 Income from Services
412 Concessions Income

Expenses

511 Pool Maintenance Expense
512 Wages Expense
513 Advertising Expense
514 Utilities Expense
515 Interest Expense
517 Insurance Expense
518 Depreciation Expense, Building
519 Depreciation Expense, Pool/Slide Facility
520 Depreciation Expense, Pool Furniture
522 Miscellaneous Expense

You are to record transactions in a two-column general journal. Assume that the fiscal period is one month. You will then be able to complete all the steps in the accounting cycle.

When you are analyzing the transactions, think them through by visualizing the T accounts or by writing them down on scratch paper. For unfamiliar types of transactions, specific instructions for recording them are included. However, reason them out for yourself as well. Check off each transaction as it is recorded.

July 1 Wong deposited $150,000 in a bank account for the purpose of buying Splashdown. The business is a recreation area offering three large waterslides (called "tubes"), one children's slide, an inner tube run, and a looping extreme slide.

2 Bought Splashdown in its entirety for a total price of $540,800. The assets include pool furniture, $3,800; the pool/slide facility (includes filter system, pools, pump, and slides), $148,800; building, $96,200; and land, $292,000. Paid $120,000 down and signed a mortgage note for the remainder. (Debit the assets, and credit Cash and Mortgage Payable.)

July   2   Received and paid the bill for a one-year premium for insurance, $12,240.

2   Bought 125 inner tubes from Worn Tires for $1,225, paying $500 down, with the remainder due in twenty days. (Debit Pool/Slide Facility.)

3   Signed a contract with a video game company to lease space for video games and to provide a food concession. The rental income agreed upon is 10 percent of the revenues generated from the machines and food, with the estimated monthly rental income paid in advance. Received cash payment for July, $250. (Debit Cash and credit Concessions Income.)

5   Received bills totaling $1,320 for the grand opening/Fourth of July party. The bill from Party Rentals for the promotional hand-outs, balloons, decorations, and prizes was $620, and the newspaper advertising bills from the *City Star* were $700. (These expenses should all be considered advertising expense.)

6   Signed a one-year contract for the pool maintenance with All-Around Maintenance and paid the maintenance fee for July of $800.

6   Paid cash for employee picnic food and beverages, $128. (Debit Miscellaneous Expense.)

7   Received $12,086 in cash as income for the use of the facilities.

9   Bought parts for the filter system on account from Arlen's Pool Supply, $646. (Debit Pool Maintenance Expense.)

14   Received $10,445 in cash as income for the use of the facilities.

15   Paid wages to employees for the period ending July 14, $8,460.

16   Paid $1,150 on account for promotional expenses recorded on July 5.

16   Wong withdrew cash for personal use, $2,500.

17   Bought additional pool furniture from Pool Suppliers for $2,100; payment due in thirty days.

18   Paid cash to seamstress for alterations and repairs to the character costumes, $248. (Debit Miscellaneous Expense.)

21   Received $10,330 in cash as income for the use of the facilities.

21   Paid cash to Worn Tires as partial payment on account, $600.

23   Received a $225 reduction of our account from Pool Suppliers for lawn chairs received in damaged condition.

25   Received and paid telephone bill, $292.

29   Paid wages for the period July 15 through 28 of $8,227.

31   Received $11,870 in cash as income for the use of the facilities.

31   Paid cash to Arlen's Pool Supply to apply on account, $360.

31   Received and paid water bill, $684.

31   Paid cash as an installment payment on the mortgage, $3,890. Of this amount, $1,910 represents a reduction in the principal, and the remainder is interest. (Debit Mortgage Payable, debit Interest Expense, and credit Cash.)

31   Received and paid electric bill, $824.

31   Bought additional inner tubes from Worn Tires for $480, paying $100 down, with the remainder due in thirty days.

31   Wong withdrew cash for personal use, $2,200.

31   Sales for the video and food concessions amounted to $4,840, and 10 percent of $4,840 equals $484. Since you have already recorded $250 as concessions income, record the additional $234 revenue due from the concessionaire (cash was not received).

Check Figures

Trial balance total, $616,941; net income, $18,391

Instructions

1. Journalize the transactions, starting on page 1 of the general journal.
2. Post the transactions to the ledger accounts.
3. Prepare a trial balance in the first two columns of the work sheet.
4. Complete the work sheet. Data for the adjustments are as follows:
   a. Insurance expired during the month, $1,020.
   b. Depreciation of building for the month, $480.
   c. Depreciation of pool/slide facility for the month, $675.
   d. Depreciation of pool furniture for the month, $120.
   e. Wages accrued at July 31, $920.
5. Prepare the income statement.
6. Prepare the statement of owner's equity.
7. Prepare the balance sheet.
8. Journalize adjusting entries.
9. Post adjusting entries to the ledger accounts.
10. Journalize closing entries.
11. Post closing entries to the ledger accounts.
12. Prepare a post-closing trial balance.

Accounting Cycle Review Problem B

This problem is designed to enable you to apply the knowledge you have acquired in the preceding chapters. In accounting, the ultimate test is being able to handle data in real-life situations. This problem will give you valuable experience.

Chart of Accounts

Assets

111 Cash
112 Accounts Receivable
114 Prepaid Insurance
121 Land
125 Pool Structure
126 Accumulated Depreciation, Pool Structure
127 Fan System
128 Accumulated Depreciation, Fan System
129 Sailboats
130 Accumulated Depreciation, Sailboats

Liabilities

221 Accounts Payable
222 Wages Payable
223 Mortgage Payable

Owner's Equity

311 R. Erdmon, Capital
312 R. Erdmon, Drawing
313 Income Summary

Revenue

411 Income from Services
412 Concessions Income

Expenses

511 Sailboat Rental Expense
512 Wages Expense
513 Advertising Expense
514 Utilities Expense
515 Interest Expense
516 Insurance Expense
517 Depreciation Expense, Pool Structure
518 Depreciation Expense, Fan System
519 Depreciation Expense, Sailboats
522 Miscellaneous Expense

You are to record transactions in a two-column general journal. Assume that the fiscal period is one month. You will then be able to complete all the steps in the accounting cycle.

When you are analyzing the transactions, think them through by visualizing the T accounts or by writing them down on scratch paper. For unfamiliar types of transactions, specific instructions for recording them are included. However, reason them out for yourself as well. Check off each transaction as it is recorded.

June 1 Erdmon deposited $85,000 in a bank account for the purpose of buying Wind Riders, a business offering the use of small sailboats to the public at a large indoor pool with a fan system that provides wind.

2 Bought Wind Riders in its entirety for a total price of $216,100. The assets include sailboats, $25,800; fan system, $13,300; pool structure, $140,000; land, $37,000. Paid $60,000 down, and signed a mortgage note for the remainder. (Debit each asset and credit Cash and Mortgage Payable.)

June   3   Received and paid bill for newspaper advertising, $350.

3   Received and paid bill for a one-year premium for insurance, $12,000.

3   Bought additional boats from Larkin Manufacturing Co. for $7,200, paying $3,200 down, with the remainder due in thirty days.

3   Signed a contract with a vending machine service to lease space for vending machines. The rental income agreed upon is 10 percent of the sales generated from the machines, with the estimated total rental income payable in advance. Received estimated cash payment for June, $150. (Debit Cash and credit Concessions Income.)

3   Received bill from Quick Printing for promotional handouts, $460 (Advertising Expense).

3   Signed a contract for leasing sailboats from K. Erdmon Boat Co. and paid rental fee for June, $700.

5   Paid cash for miscellaneous expenses, $96.

8   Received $2,855 in cash as income for the use of the boats.

9   Bought an addition for the fan system on account from Stark Pool Supply, $745.

15   Paid wages to employees for the period ending June 14, $3,900.

16   Paid on account for promotional handouts already recorded on June 3, $460.

16   Erdmon withdrew cash for personal use, $1,200.

16   Bought additional sails from Canvas Products, Inc., $850; payment due in thirty days. (Debit Sailboats.)

16   Received $4,850 in cash as income for the use of the boats.

19   Paid cash for miscellaneous expenses, $40.45.

20   Paid cash to Larkin Manufacturing Co. as part payment on account, $1,300.

22   Received $8,260 in cash for the use of the boats (Income from Services).

23   Received a reduction in the outstanding bill from Larkin Manufacturing Co. for a boat received in a damaged condition, $380. (Debit Accounts Payable, credit Sailboats.)

24   Received and paid telephone bill, $284.

29   Paid wages for period June 15 through 28, $4,973.

30   Paid cash to Stark Pool Supply to apply on account, $475.

30   Received and paid electric bill, $345.

30   Paid cash as an installment payment on the mortgage, $1,848. Of this amount, $497 represents a reduction in the principal, and the remainder is interest. (Debit Mortgage Payable, debit Interest Expense, and credit Cash.)

30   Received and paid water bill, $590.

30   Bought additional boats from Ranger and Son for $5,320, paying $1,550 down, with the remainder due in thirty days.

30   Erdmon withdrew cash for personal use, $1,500.

30   Received $5,902 in cash as income for the use of the boats.

30   Sales from vending machines for the month amounted to $1,780. Ten percent of $1,780 equals $178. Since you have already recorded $150 as concessions income, list the additional $28 revenue earned from the vending machine operator. (Cash was not received.)

Check Figures

Net income, $5,290.55; total of post-closing trial balance, $253,068.55

Instructions

1. Journalize the transactions, starting on page 1 of the general journal.
2. Post the transactions to the ledger accounts.
3. Prepare a trial balance in the first two columns of the work sheet.
4. Complete the work sheet. Data for the adjustments are as follows:
    a. Insurance expired during the month, $1,000.
    b. Depreciation of pool structure for the month, $715.
    c. Depreciation of fan system for the month, $260.
    d. Depreciation of sailboats for the month, $900.
    e. Wages accrued at June 30, $790.
5. Prepare the income statement.
6. Prepare the statement of owner's equity.
7. Prepare the balance sheet.
8. Journalize adjusting entries.
9. Post adjusting entries to the ledger accounts.
10. Journalize closing entries.
11. Post closing entries to the ledger accounts.
12. Prepare a post-closing trial balance.

Accounting systems for professional companies such as architecture firms, law firms, and physician's offices require users to document such items as fees for services rendered, utility bills, travel expenses, supplies, and insurance. But each type of profession uses an individualized set of accounts to record business transactions. These professionals would probably find that a combined journal, which has special columns to record frequently used accounts, is more efficient than a general journal. As you learn about combined journals in this chapter, think about how the accounts you would commonly use in your accounting records might differ if you were an architect or a doctor.

A little later in this chapter, you will also learn how the entries in the combined journal (or general journal) are transformed into financial statements, which are prepared for professional enterprises as well as major corporations. How does Dr. Hanna's balance sheet in this chapter differ from Best Buy's balance sheet? How is it the same? You can find Best Buy's 2005 balance sheet by going to **http://www.sec.gov/edgar/searchedgar/companysearch.html**. Search by company name (Best Buy Co Inc) and either scroll through the listing or search for Form 10-K. Select the 2005 filing. You will find the 2005 balance sheet on page 58 of Form 10-K.

Performance Objectives

After you have completed this chapter, you will be able to do the following:

1. Describe the accounting records for a professional enterprise.

2. Record transactions for both a professional enterprise and a service enterprise in a combined journal.

3. Post from the combined journal and determine the cash balance.

4. Prepare a work sheet for a professional enterprise.

5. Prepare financial statements for a professional enterprise.

6. Record adjusting and closing entries in a combined journal.

Aprofessional enterprise offers a specialized service for a fee. The fee may be charged on a per hour basis, a per visit basis, or a per job or task basis. **Professional enterprises** include practices of medicine, dentistry, law, architecture, engineering, accounting, and so forth. Your knowledge of accounting procedures can be readily applied to professional enterprises. Professional enterprises generally use the cash basis of accounting.

EXAMPLE: RECORDS OF A DENTIST

 OBJECTIVE 1

Describe the accounting records for a professional enterprise.

To understand the cash basis of accounting used by a professional enterprise, let's look at the records of Dr. S. A. Hanna, a dentist. The basic records used in his office are the appointment record and the patient's ledger record. We will assume the patient records are kept manually. Specialized computer software is available for professional businesses, such as dentists, that combines the accounting for patient records and the accounting records of the business. Following is the chart of accounts for the office:

Chart of Accounts

Assets

111 Cash
115 Prepaid Insurance
121 Dental Equipment
122 Accumulated Depreciation, Dental Equipment
123 Office Furniture and Equipment
124 Accumulated Depreciation, Office Furniture and Equipment

Liabilities

211 Notes Payable

Owner's Equity

311 S. A. Hanna, Capital
312 S. A. Hanna, Drawing
313 Income Summary

Revenue

411 Professional Fees

Expenses

511 Dental Instruments Expense
512 Laundry and Cleaning Expense
513 Salary Expense
514 Laboratory Expense
515 Dental Supplies Expense
516 Rent Expense
517 Depreciation Expense, Dental Equipment
518 Depreciation Expense, Office Furniture and Equipment
519 X-ray Supplies Expense
521 Office Supplies Expense
522 Insurance Expense
523 Telephone Expense
524 Utilities Expense
525 Repairs and Maintenance Expense
526 Miscellaneous Expense

Appointment Record

The dentist's receptionist keeps a daily appointment record, showing the time of each appointment and the name of the patient, and gives a copy of the appointment record to the dentist the day before the scheduled appointments. Dr. Hanna's appointment record is shown in Figure 1.

FIGURE 1

APPOINTMENT RECORD

DATE 12/1/20—

HOUR	PATIENT	SERVICE RENDERED	FEES	RECEIPTS
8:00	Edna Dixon			
15	John Freed			
30				
45	Carlos Flores			
9:00				
15				
30				
45	Rita Irvine			
10:00	M. L. Lilly			
15				
30				
45	R. D. Petrie			
11:00	Carl Ryan			
15				
30				
45				
1:00	Glen C. Smith			
15				
30	C. K. Wyse			
45				
2:00	Alice Cheney			
15				
30	Ralph Farr			
45	Paul Hayes			
3:00				
15	Nancy Kirby			
30				
45	C. L. McKoy			
4:00				
15	Juan Tyra			

Patient's Ledger Record

The receptionist also maintains a **patient's ledger record** card for each patient. One side of this card shows a daily record of the services performed, amount of any cost estimate given, plan of payment, and information regarding collections. This side of the card is shown in Figure 2.

The other side of the card contains a diagram of the patient's teeth and a space for personal information about the patient.

After Dr. Hanna completes the work, he (or an assistant) describes the services performed and writes the amount of the fees in the Debit column. The card is returned to the receptionist, who records the services rendered and the fees charged on the appointment record.

The patient's ledger record for M. L. Lilly is shown in Figure 2. **As with Accounts Receivable, debits mean increases in the amounts owed by patients, and credits mean decreases in the amounts owed by patients.** The

FIGURE 2

M. L. Lilly
2416 Bryan Ave., E
Chicago, IL 60644

360-365-2619
Account No. 46-4128

DATE		SERVICE RENDERED	TIME	DEBIT	CREDIT	BALANCE
June	15	#31—M.O.D. (4)	10:00	1 5 7 00		1 5 7 00
July	4	Ck.			1 5 7 00	
	16	#27—D.O. (Amal.)	9:15	1 4 1 00		1 4 1 00
Aug.	5	Ck.			1 4 1 00	
Sept.	24	#25—P.J.C.	10:00	1 1 1 0 00		1 1 1 0 00
Oct.	6	Ck.			1 8 0 00	9 3 0 00
	18	#24—D. (Porc.)	9:00	1 2 0 00		1 0 5 0 00
Nov.	3	Ck.			1 8 0 00	8 7 0 00
	9	#18—full gold crown	10:00	8 2 5 00		1 6 9 5 00
Dec.	1	B. W. X-rays (6)	10:00	1 4 4 00		1 8 3 9 00
		Full upper denture		1 3 5 0 00		3 1 8 9 00
	1	Ck.			3 0 0 00	2 8 8 9 00

PLAN OF SERVICE	PLAN OF PAYMENT	COLLECTION EFFORTS
1–2 surf. ⎫ amalgam	30-day basis	
2–3 surf. ⎬ 1 full gold crown	or $150 per month	
1–1 surf. ⎭ 1 ceramic crown		
2 anterior porcelain		

ESTIMATE IF ANY		
$900 upper denture (6 appt.)	$225 per month	

Balance column shows the amount owed by the patient at the time of the latest entry.

The services to be performed may require a number of appointments. Some patients may make partial payments each time they have an appointment. Others may pay the entire amount at—or after—the last appointment. Patients' bills are compiled directly from the patient's ledger record. The dentist or receptionist regularly reviews the patients' ledger records to determine which accounts are past due. Figure 3 on page 194 shows the statement that was mailed to M. L. Lilly at the end of December.

Receipt of Payments from Patients

REMEMBER!

The fees charged are not recorded in the Professional Fees account until they are received in cash when using the cash basis.

Depending on the size of the office, the person who receives payments may be the receptionist or the cashier in the accounting office. Whoever receives the payments issues a written receipt for all incoming cash, filled out in duplicate, giving the first copy to the patient and filing the second copy as evidence of the transaction. Receipts should be prenumbered so that they can be accounted for. The payment is recorded in the Receipts column of the appointment record.

When a patient sends in a payment, the receptionist records the amount on the appointment record and on the patient's ledger record in the Credit column on the day the payment was received.

FIGURE 3

S. A. HANNA, D.D.S.
1710 CARTER AVE., E
CHICAGO, IL 60642

STATEMENT

M. L. Lilly
2416 Bryan Ave., E
Chicago, IL 60644

December 31, 20—
Account No. 46-4128

DATE	PROFESSIONAL SERVICE	CHARGES		PAYMENTS		BALANCE	
6/15	#31—MOD (4)	157	00			157	00
7/4	Ck.			157	00		
7/16	#27—DO (Amal.)	141	00			141	00
8/5	Ck.			141	00		
9/24	#25—PJC	1,110	00			1,110	00
10/6	Ck.			180	00	930	00
10/18	#24—D (Porc.)	120	00			1,050	00
11/3	Ck.			180	00	870	00
11/9	#18—full gold crown	825	00			1,695	00
12/1	B.W. X-rays (6)	144	00			1,839	00
	Full upper denture	1,350	00			3,189	00
12/1	Ck.			300	00	2,889	00

PAY LAST AMOUNT IN BALANCE COLUMN. ◄

The form in Figure 4 is a typical appointment record for a day, showing services rendered, fees (recorded by the dentist on the patients' ledger records), and payments received (recorded by the receptionist). The receptionist deposits $2,048 in the bank. A journal entry would now be made debiting Cash and crediting Professional Fees for $2,048.

Summary of Procedures

1. Patients request appointments.
2. Receptionist records appointments on appointment record: date, time, and name of patient.
3. Receptionist furnishes dentist with appointment record for the day, plus the patients' ledger records.
4. Dentist performs services and records descriptions of the services performed on each patient's ledger card, listing the fees to be charged in the Debit column.
5. Receptionist accepts payments from patients both in the office and through the mail and records receipt of payments in the Receipts column of the appointment record. Any difference between the fee charged amount and the insurance company approved amount for the services rendered can be shown in the Debit column and a note made in the Service Rendered column. (For purposes of this text, cash receipts are recorded weekly.)
6. At the end of the day, receptionist deposits cash received in the bank.

FIGURE 4

APPOINTMENT RECORD

DATE 12/1/20—

HOUR	PATIENT	SERVICE RENDERED	FEES		RECEIPTS	
8:00	Edna Dixon	Extraction	90	00		
15	John Freed	Three amalgam fillings				
30		D.O. (3)	460	00	130	00
45	Carlos Flores	Gold inlay filling	632	00		
9:00						
15						
30						
45	Rita Irvine	Amalgam filling D.O.	138	00		
10:00	M. L. Lilly	B.W. X-rays (6)	144	00	300	00
15		Full upper denture				
30		(6 appointments)	1,350	00		
45	R. D. Petrie	Prophylaxis	108	00	108	00
11:00	Carl Ryan	Endodontia treatment	338	00	75	00
15						
30						
45						
1:00	Glen C. Smith	Amalgam filling M.O.D.	156	00	78	00
15						
30	C. K. Wyse	Ceramco crown	870	00		
45						
2:00	Alice Cheney	Extraction	75	00		
15						
30	Ralph Farr	Amalgam filling 1 surf.	112	00		
45	Paul Hayes	Prophylaxis and full-				
3:00		mouth X-ray (14)	196	00		
15	Nancy Kirby	Fixed bridge 3 units				
30		(Gold) (5 appointments)	2,460	00	187	00
45	C. L. McKoy	Prophylaxis & bitewing				
4:00		X-rays	138	00		
15	Juan Tyra	Periodontal treatment	426	00		
	Robert L. Moyer				180	00
	Rita Davis				165	00
	Gene Roxang				204	00
	Sidney Woods				81	00
	N. T. Wyatt				279	00
	S. T. Mendoza				111	00
	Gilbert Lamont				150	00
			7,693	00	2,048	00

7. Receptionist lists the description of services and the amount charged on the appointment record.
8. Receptionist records payments received on the patients' ledger cards in the Credit column. The source is the appointment record.

9. Receptionist compiles monthly statements directly from patient's ledger records.

This procedure may vary, depending on the size of the office staff. Also, the monthly statement may consist of a duplicate copy of the patient's ledger card. If the size of the office staff is sufficiently large, the function of accepting and depositing money should be separated from the function of recording payments.

Here is a list of Dr. Hanna's transactions for December, the last month of the fiscal period. **To save time and space, cash receipts are recorded on a weekly basis.**

Dec.	1	Issued Ck. No. 416 for rent for December, $3,000.
	1	Issued Ck. No. 417 for telephone bill for November, $107.
	1	Issued Ck. No. 418 for electric bill for November, $168.
	3	Issued Ck. No. 419 to First-Rate Printing for patient statement forms, $198.
	5	Issued Ck. No. 420 to Milner Dental Supply for drills, $381.
	5	Total cash received from patients during the week, $10,716.
	8	Issued Ck. No. 421 to Monroe Office Supply for repair of copier, $138.
	9	Issued Ck. No. 422 to S. A. Hanna for personal use, $1,125.
	11	Issued Ck. No. 423 to Ready Cleaning Service for janitorial service, $210.

We will first record these transactions in general journal form (Figure 5). However, since our objective is to introduce the combined journal, we will also record the same transactions in a combined journal.

FIGURE 5

GENERAL JOURNAL

DATE		DESCRIPTION	POST. REF.	DEBIT	CREDIT
20—					
Dec.	1	Rent Expense		3 0 0 0 00	
		Cash			3 0 0 0 00
		Rent for December,			
		Ck. No. 416.			
	1	Telephone Expense		1 0 7 00	
		Cash			1 0 7 00
		Telephone bill for November,			
		Ck. No. 417.			
	1	Utilities Expense		1 6 8 00	
		Cash			1 6 8 00
		Electric bill for November,			
		Ck. No. 418.			
	3	Office Supplies Expense		1 9 8 00	
		Cash			1 9 8 00
		First-Rate Printing for			
		statement forms, Ck. No. 419.			

**FIGURE 5
(continued)**

5	Dental Instruments Expense				3	8	1	00						
	Cash									3	8	1	00	
	Milner Dental Supply for													
	drills, Ck. No. 420.													
5	Cash		10	7	1	6	00							
	Professional Fees								10	7	1	6	00	
	For period Dec. 1 through 5.													
8	Repairs and Maint. Expense				1	3	8	00						
	Cash									1	3	8	00	
	Monroe Office Supply, for													
	repair of copier, Ck. No. 421.													
9	S. A. Hanna, Drawing			1	1	2	5	00						
	Cash									1	1	2	5	00
	For personal use, Ck. No. 422.													
11	Laundry and Cleaning Expense				2	1	0	00						
	Cash									2	1	0	00	
	Ready Cleaning Service,													
	Ck. No. 423.													

THE COMBINED JOURNAL

 OBJECTIVE 2

Record transactions for both a professional enterprise and a service enterprise in a combined journal.

The **combined journal** is designed to make the recording and posting of transactions more efficient. It is used widely by professional and service enterprises, where **it replaces the general journal.** No explanations are given in the combined journal. **Special columns** are set up to record accounts that are used frequently by a particular business. Most transactions can be recorded on one line.

Compare the first nine transactions in the combined journal in Figure 6 (pages 198–199) with the same transactions recorded in the general journal in Figure 5. In the first transaction (paid rent for the month, $3,000), the entry is a debit to Rent Expense and a credit to Cash. There is a Cash Credit column in the combined journal, so $3,000 is listed in this column; that $3,000 will be posted as part of the column total. The Other Accounts columns are used to record any accounts for which there are no special columns. Since there is no Rent Expense Debit column, the $3,000 debit to Rent Expense must be recorded in the Other Accounts Debit column. Notice that the Other Accounts column does not tell you where to post the $3,000. Therefore, you need to write the title of the account to be posted in the Account Name column. This amount is posted separately.

In the December 5 entry to record professional fees received in cash, special columns are available to handle both the debit to Cash and the credit to Professional Fees. In cases where the special columns can handle both the entire debit and credit amounts, it is not necessary to use the Account Name

COMBINED JOURNAL

	CASH								
	DEBIT	CREDIT	CK. NO.	DATE	ACCOUNT NAME	POST. REF.	OTHER ACCOUNTS DEBIT		OTHER ACCOUNTS CREDIT
1				20—					
2		3 0 0 0 00	416	Dec. 1	Rent Expense	516	3 0 0 0 00		
3		1 0 7 00	417	1	Telephone Expense	523	1 0 7 00		
4		1 6 8 00	418	1	Utilities Expense	524	1 6 8 00		
5		1 9 8 00	419	3	Office Supplies Expense	521	1 9 8 00		
6		3 8 1 00	420	5	Dental Instruments Expense	511	3 8 1 00		
7	10 7 1 6 00			5	————————————	–			
8		1 3 8 00	421	8	Repairs and Maintenance Expense	525	1 3 8 00		
9		1 1 2 5 00	422	9	S. A. Hanna	–			
10		2 1 0 00	423	11	Ready Cleaning Service	–			
11	3 6 1 6 00			12	————————————	–			
12		6 4 8 00	424	16	Davies Dental Supply	–			
13		1 4 5 5 00	425	16	C. R. Jarvis	–			
14		1 4 5 5 00	426	16	D. C. Yang	–			
15				19	Dental Equipment	121	8 6 6 8 00		
16		2 6 6 8 00	427	19	Notes Payable	211		6 0 0 0 00	
17	1 8 3 0 00			19	————————————	–			
18		1 2 1 5 00	428	22	S. A. Hanna	–			
19		4 4 4 00	429	23	Nollen Dental Laboratory	–			
20		6 0 0 00	430	23	Notes Payable	211	6 0 0 00		
21	2 0 9 4 00			27	————————————	–			
22		3 3 9 00	431	29	Briggs Automotive	–			
23		3 2 8 00	432	31	Milner Dental Supply	–			
24		1 4 5 5 00	433	31	C. R. Jarvis	–			
25		1 4 5 5 00	434	31	D. C. Yang	–			
26		1 7 8 5 00	435	31	S. A. Hanna	–			
27		8 1 00	436	31	Jersey Publishers Service	–			
28		1 2 6 00	437	31	Clement Linen Supply	–			
29	2 9 6 4 00			31	————————————	–			
30	21 2 2 0 00	19 3 8 1 00		31			13 2 6 0 00		6 0 0 0 00
31	(1 1 1)	(1 1 1)					(X)		(X)

END OF MONTH
Post the column totals to the Cash account in the general ledger at the end of the month. The account number in parentheses at the foot of each column indicates that posting has been completed.

DAILY
Post each amount in the Other Accounts columns to an account in the general ledger. The account number recorded in the Post. Ref. column indicates that posting has been completed. The (X) indicates that the column total is not to be posted.

FIGURE 6

PAGE **12**

	S. A. HANNA, DRAWING	PROFESSIONAL FEES	LAUNDRY AND CLEANING EXPENSE	SALARY EXPENSE	LABORATORY EXPENSE	DENTAL SUPPLIES EXPENSE	MISC. EXPENSE	
	DEBIT	CREDIT	DEBIT	DEBIT	DEBIT	DEBIT	DEBIT	
1								
2								
3								
4								
5								
6								
7		10 7 1 6 00						
8								
9	1 1 2 5 00							
10			2 1 0 00					
11		3 6 1 6 00						
12						6 4 8 00		
13				1 4 5 5 00				
14				1 4 5 5 00				
15								
16								
17		1 8 3 0 00						
18	1 2 1 5 00							
19					4 4 4 00			
20								
21		2 0 9 4 00						
22	3 3 9 00							
23						3 2 8 00		
24				1 4 5 5 00				
25				1 4 5 5 00				
26	1 7 8 5 00							
27							8 1 00	
28			1 2 6 00					
29		2 9 6 4 00						
30	4 4 6 4 00	21 2 2 0 00	3 3 6 00	5 8 2 0 00	4 4 4 00	9 7 6 00	8 1 00	
31	(3 1 2)	(4 1 1)	(5 1 2)	(5 1 3)	(5 1 4)	(5 1 5)	(5 2 6)	
32								
33								
34								

END OF MONTH
Post the column totals to
their general ledger accounts.
Account numbers in
parentheses indicate that
posting has been completed.

Owners of dry cleaners and service stations as well as doctors and lawyers can buy premade combined journals targeted directly for their own professions. These combined journals are set up to help channel routine transactions into the journal.

column except to write the name of the check payee. To show that the Account Name column has not been overlooked, we draw a long line through it and put a dash in the Post. Ref. column. The individual amounts are posted as parts of the totals of the special columns. The rest of the month's transactions follow:

Dec. 12   Total cash received from patients during the week, $3,616.
16   Issued Ck. No. 424 to Davies Dental Supply for miscellaneous dental supplies, $648.
16   In payment of salaries, issued Ck. No. 425 to C. R. Jarvis, $1,455 and Ck. No. 426 to D. C. Yang, $1,455. (Use two lines.)
19   Bought new dental chair from Milner Dental Supply, $8,668. Issued Ck. No. 427 as a down payment, $2,668. The balance is to be paid in ten monthly payments of $600 each (Notes Payable). (Use two lines.)
19   Total cash received from patients during the week, $1,830.
22   Issued Ck. No. 428 to S. A. Hanna for personal use, $1,215.
23   Issued Ck. No. 429 to Nollen Dental Laboratory for laboratory expense, $444.
23   Issued Ck. No. 430 to Milner Dental Supply as the first contract payment (Notes Payable) on dental equipment purchased on December 19, $600.
27   Total cash received from patients during the week, $2,094.
29   Hanna wrote Ck. No. 431 payable to Briggs Automotive for repairing his car, $339 (to be recorded as Drawing).
31   Issued Ck. No. 432 to Milner Dental Supply for miscellaneous dental supplies, $328.
31   In payment of salaries, issued Ck. No. 433 to C. R. Jarvis, $1,455 and Ck. No. 434 to D. C. Yang, $1,455. (Use two lines.)
31   Issued Ck. No. 435 to S. A. Hanna for personal use, $1,785.
31   Issued Ck. No. 436 to Jersey Publishers Service for magazines for the office, $81.
31   Issued Ck. No. 437 to Clement Linen Supply for laundry services, $126.
31   Total cash received from patients this week up until last day of year, $2,964.

After you have added all columns at the end of the month, prove on scratch paper that the sum of the debit totals equals the sum of the credit totals.

Column	Debit totals	Credit totals
Cash	$21,220.00	$19,381.00
Other Accounts	13,260.00	6,000.00
S. A. Hanna, Drawing	4,464.00	
Professional Fees		21,220.00
Laundry and Cleaning Expense	336.00	
Salary Expense	5,820.00	
Laboratory Expense	444.00	
Dental Supplies Expense	976.00	
Miscellaneous Expense	81.00	
	$46,601.00	$46,601.00

OBJECTIVE 3

Post from the combined journal and determine the cash balance.

REMEMBER!

Special columns are posted as one total. Amounts in Other Accounts columns are posted individually.

Posting from the Combined Journal

The person who keeps records posts items in the Other Accounts columns individually, usually daily, using the specific transaction date. **After posting the ledger account, the person records the ledger account number in the Post. Ref. column of the combined journal.** This procedure is similar to posting from a general journal.

Special columns, used only for debits or credits to specific accounts, are posted as totals at the end of the month. **After posting the ledger account, the ledger account number is recorded in the special column immediately below the total.** The account number is placed in parentheses. The total of the Cash Debit column in Figure 6 on pages 198–199 is an example. After the Cash account in the general ledger has been debited for $21,220.00, the account number of Cash (111) is placed in parentheses below the total of the Cash Debit column in the combined journal. Notice the X's in parentheses below the totals of the Other Accounts columns. These totals were not posted because the individual amounts recorded in the columns were posted separately. The separate amounts listed in the Other Accounts columns should not be posted twice.

The Cash, Dental Supplies Expense, and Rent Expense accounts from Dr. Hanna's completed general ledger are shown in Figure 7 to illustrate the posting process.

FIGURE 7

GENERAL LEDGER

ACCOUNT **Cash**   ACCOUNT NO. **111**

	DATE	ITEM	POST. REF.	DEBIT	CREDIT	BALANCE DEBIT	BALANCE CREDIT	
1	20—							1
2	Dec. 1	Balance	✓			9 9 3 0 00		2
3	31		12	21 2 2 0 00		31 1 5 0 00		3
4	31		12		19 3 8 1 00	11 7 6 9 00		4

ACCOUNT **Dental Supplies Expense**   ACCOUNT NO. **515**

	DATE	ITEM	POST. REF.	DEBIT	CREDIT	BALANCE DEBIT	BALANCE CREDIT	
1	20—							1
2	Dec. 1	Balance	✓			7 2 4 4 00		2
3	31		12	9 7 6 00		8 2 2 0 00		3

ACCOUNT **Rent Expense**   ACCOUNT NO. **516**

	DATE	ITEM	POST. REF.	DEBIT	CREDIT	BALANCE DEBIT	BALANCE CREDIT	
1	20—							1
2	Dec. 1	Balance	✓			24 0 0 0 00		2
3	1		12	3 0 0 0 00		27 0 0 0 00		3

FIGURE 8

	ACCOUNT NAME	TRIAL BALANCE DEBIT	TRIAL BALANCE CREDIT
1	Cash	11 7 6 9 00	
2	Prepaid Insurance	3 6 7 2 00	
3	Dental Equipment	172 8 5 1 00	
4	Accumulated Depreciation, Dental Equipment		25 8 0 0 00
5	Office Furniture and Equipment	11 7 0 0 00	
6	Accum. Depr., Office Furniture and Equipment		6 3 0 0 00
7	Notes Payable		11 4 0 0 00
8	S. A. Hanna, Capital		107 2 4 7 00
9	S. A. Hanna, Drawing	69 4 2 0 00	
10	Professional Fees		241 5 3 6 00
11	Dental Instruments Expense	2 9 7 3 00	
12	Laundry and Cleaning Expense	4 5 3 6 00	
13	Salary Expense	61 2 0 0 00	
14	Laboratory Expense	8 7 8 4 00	
15	Dental Supplies Expense	8 2 2 0 00	
16	Rent Expense	27 0 0 0 00	
17	X-ray Supplies Expense	1 9 6 2 00	
18	Office Supplies Expense	4 1 4 3 00	
19	Telephone Expense	6 1 8 00	
20	Utilities Expense	1 1 6 7 00	
21	Repairs and Maintenance Expense	1 3 3 2 00	
22	Miscellaneous Expense	9 3 6 00	
23		392 2 8 3 00	392 2 8 3 00
24	Depreciation Expense, Dental Equipment		
25	Depreciation Expense, Office Furn. and Equipment		
26	Insurance Expense		
27			
28	Net Income		
29			
30			

A combined journal allows businesses to set up special columns for frequently used accounts, such as Dental Supplies Expense, for this professional firm.

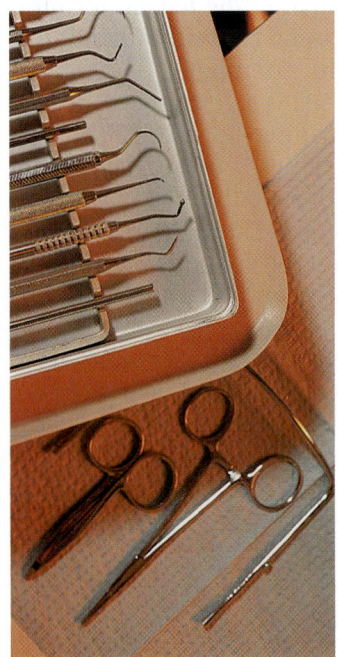

Determining Cash Balance

The cash balance may be determined at any time during the month by taking the beginning balance of cash, adding the total cash debits so far during the month, and subtracting the total cash credits so far during the month. For example, to determine the balance of cash on December 5:

Beginning balance (Dec. 1)	$ 9,930
Add cash debits	10,716
Total	$20,646
Less cash credits	3,854
Ending balance (Dec. 5)	$16,792

COMBINED JOURNAL PAGE 12

	CASH DEBIT	CASH CREDIT	CK. NO.	DATE		ACCOUNT NAME
1				20—		
2		3 0 0 0 00	416	Dec.	1	Rent Expense
3		1 0 7 00	417		1	Telephone Expense
4		1 6 8 00	418		1	Utilities Expense
5		1 9 8 00	419		3	Office Supplies Expense
6		3 8 1 00	420		5	Dental Instruments Expense
7	10 7 1 6 00				5	
8	10 7 1 6 00	3 8 5 4 00				

S. A. Hanna, D.D.S.
Work Sheet
For Year Ended December 31, 20—

ADJUSTMENTS Debit	ADJUSTMENTS Credit	ADJUSTED TRIAL BALANCE Debit	ADJUSTED TRIAL BALANCE Credit	INCOME STATEMENT Debit	INCOME STATEMENT Credit	BALANCE SHEET Debit	BALANCE SHEET Credit	
		11 7 6 9 00				11 7 6 9 00		1
	(c) 2 7 5 4 00	9 1 8 00				9 1 8 00		2
		172 8 5 1 00				172 8 5 1 00		3
	(a)12 6 0 0 00		38 4 0 0 00				38 4 0 0 00	4
		11 7 0 0 00				11 7 0 0 00		5
	(b) 2 2 8 0 00		8 5 8 0 00				8 5 8 0 00	6
			11 4 0 0 00				11 4 0 0 00	7
			107 2 4 7 00				107 2 4 7 00	8
		69 4 2 0 00				69 4 2 0 00		9
			241 5 3 6 00		241 5 3 6 00			10
		2 9 7 3 00		2 9 7 3 00				11
		4 5 3 6 00		4 5 3 6 00				12
		61 2 0 0 00		61 2 0 0 00				13
		8 7 8 4 00		8 7 8 4 00				14
		8 2 2 0 00		8 2 2 0 00				15
		27 0 0 0 00		27 0 0 0 00				16
		1 9 6 2 00		1 9 6 2 00				17
		4 1 4 3 00		4 1 4 3 00				18
		6 1 8 00		6 1 8 00				19
		1 1 6 7 00		1 1 6 7 00				20
		1 3 3 2 00		1 3 3 2 00				21
		9 3 6 00		9 3 6 00				22
								23
(a)12 6 0 0 00		12 6 0 0 00		12 6 0 0 00				24
(b) 2 2 8 0 00		2 2 8 0 00		2 2 8 0 00				25
(c) 2 7 5 4 00		2 7 5 4 00		2 7 5 4 00				26
17 6 3 4 00	17 6 3 4 00	407 1 6 3 00	407 1 6 3 00	140 5 0 5 00	241 5 3 6 00	266 6 5 8 00	165 6 2 7 00	27
				101 0 3 1 00			101 0 3 1 00	28
				241 5 3 6 00	241 5 3 6 00	266 6 5 8 00	266 6 5 8 00	29
								30

OBJECTIVE 4

Prepare a work sheet for a professional enterprise.

Work Sheet for a Professional Enterprise

Assume that Dr. Hanna's receptionist posted the journal entries to the ledger accounts and recorded the trial balance in the first two columns of the work sheet. Dr. Hanna uses the cash basis of accounting, recording revenue only when he has received it in cash and recording expenses only when he has paid for them in cash. However, when Dr. Hanna buys an item that is going to last a number of years, he records this item as an asset and writes it off or depreciates it by making an adjusting entry each year of its useful life. He also makes adjusting entries for expired insurance. Data for the adjustments are given below.

a. Additional depreciation on dental equipment, $12,600.
b. Additional depreciation on office furniture and equipment, $2,280.
c. Insurance expired, $2,754.

With these adjusting entries, the rest of the work sheet can be completed as shown in Figure 8. First the balances of the accounts that were adjusted are brought up to date in the Adjusted Trial Balance columns. Then these amounts are carried forward to the remaining columns.

Medical professionals have their uniforms or lab coats cleaned by outside services. Their work sheets are likely to include an account for Laundry and Cleaning Expense.

Financial Statements

OBJECTIVE 5

Prepare financial statements for a professional enterprise.

From the work sheet, Dr. Hanna's accountant prepares the financial statements shown in Figure 9. In this case, there was no additional investment made by S. A. Hanna during the year.

FIGURE 9

S. A. Hanna, D.D.S.
Income Statement
For Year Ended December 31, 20—

Revenue:			
Professional Fees		$241 5 3 6 00	
Expenses:			
Dental Instruments Expense	$ 2 9 7 3 00		
Laundry and Cleaning Expense	4 5 3 6 00		
Salary Expense	61 2 0 0 00		
Laboratory Expense	8 7 8 4 00		
Dental Supplies Expense	8 2 2 0 00		
Rent Expense	27 0 0 0 00		
Depreciation Expense, Dental Equipment	12 6 0 0 00		
Depreciation Expense, Office Furniture and Equipment	2 2 8 0 00		
X-ray Supplies Expense	1 9 6 2 00		
Office Supplies Expense	4 1 4 3 00		
Insurance Expense	2 7 5 4 00		
Telephone Expense	6 1 8 00		
Utilities Expense	1 1 6 7 00		
Repairs and Maintenance Expense	1 3 3 2 00		
Miscellaneous Expense	9 3 6 00		
Total Expenses		140 5 0 5 00	
Net Income		$101 0 3 1 00	

**FIGURE 9
(continued)**

Whenever you are preparing a statement of owner's equity, always check the Capital account in the general ledger to see if any additional investment was recorded.

**S. A. Hanna, D.D.S.
Statement of Owner's Equity
For Year Ended December 31, 20—**

S. A. Hanna, Capital, January 1, 20—		$107 2 4 7 00
Net Income for Year	$101 0 3 1 00	
Less Withdrawals for Year	69 4 2 0 00	
Increase in Capital		31 6 1 1 00
S. A. Hanna, Capital, December 31, 20—		$138 8 5 8 00

**S. A. Hanna, D.D.S.
Balance Sheet
December 31, 20—**

Assets		
Cash		$ 11 7 6 9 00
Prepaid Insurance		9 1 8 00
Dental Equipment	$172 8 5 1 00	
Less Accumulated Depreciation	38 4 0 0 00	134 4 5 1 00
Office Furniture and Equipment	$ 11 7 0 0 00	
Less Accumulated Depreciation	8 5 8 0 00	3 1 2 0 00
Total Assets		$150 2 5 8 00
Liabilities		
Notes Payable		$ 11 4 0 0 00
Owner's Equity		
S. A. Hanna, Capital		138 8 5 8 00
Total Liabilities and Owner's Equity		$150 2 5 8 00

OBJECTIVE 6

Record adjusting and closing entries in a combined journal.

Adjusting and Closing Entries

Dr. Hanna (or his receptionist) records the adjusting and closing entries entirely in the Other Accounts columns of the combined journal. These entries must be posted individually, so the special columns are never used for them.

The adjusting and closing entries are shown in Figure 10 on page 206, two pages of a shortened combined journal. These adjusting and closing entries are shown here on two pages to make the concept clear. In practice, the closing entries would be written right below the adjusting entries. Be careful not to split up any individual entry between two pages. The totals are included because it is customary to show totals of all columns of a combined journal. In the Account Name column, accounts to be credited do not have to be indented.

COMBINED JOURNAL

CASH DEBIT	CASH CREDIT	CK. NO.	DATE	ACCOUNT NAME	POST. REF.	OTHER ACCOUNTS DEBIT	OTHER ACCOUNTS CREDIT
			20—	**Adjusting Entries**			
			Dec. 31	Depr. Expense, Dental Equipment	517	12 6 0 0 00	
				Accum. Depr., Dental Equipment	122		12 6 0 0 00
			31	Depreciation Expense, Office			
				Furniture and Equipment	518	2 2 8 0 00	
				Accumulated Depreciation, Office			
				Furniture and Equipment	124		2 2 8 0 00
			31	Insurance Expense	522	2 7 5 4 00	
				Prepaid Insurance	115		2 7 5 4 00
			31			17 6 3 4 00	17 6 3 4 00
						(X)	(X)

COMBINED JOURNAL

CASH DEBIT	CASH CREDIT	CK. NO.	DATE	ACCOUNT NAME	POST. REF.	OTHER ACCOUNTS DEBIT	OTHER ACCOUNTS CREDIT
			20—	**Closing Entries**			
			Dec. 31	Professional Fees	411	241 5 3 6 00	
				Income Summary	313		241 5 3 6 00
			31	Income Summary	313	140 5 0 5 00	
				Dental Instruments Expense	511		2 9 7 3 00
				Laundry and Cleaning Expense	512		4 5 3 6 00
				Salary Expense	513		61 2 0 0 00
				Laboratory Expense	514		8 7 8 4 00
				Dental Supplies Expense	515		8 2 2 0 00
				Rent Expense	516		27 0 0 0 00
				Depr. Expense, Dental Equipment	517		12 6 0 0 00
				Depr. Expense, Office Furniture			
				and Equipment	518		2 2 8 0 00
				X-ray Supplies Expense	519		1 9 6 2 00
				Office Supplies Expense	521		4 1 4 3 00
				Insurance Expense	522		2 7 5 4 00
				Telephone Expense	523		6 1 8 00
				Utilities Expense	524		1 1 6 7 00
				Repairs and Maintenance Expense	525		1 3 3 2 00
				Miscellaneous Expense	526		9 3 6 00
			31	Income Summary	313	101 0 3 1 00	
				S. A. Hanna, Capital	311		101 0 3 1 00
			31	S. A. Hanna, Capital	311	69 4 2 0 00	
				S. A. Hanna, Drawing	312		69 4 2 0 00
			31			552 4 9 2 00	552 4 9 2 00
						(X)	(X)

FIGURE 10

DESIGNING A COMBINED JOURNAL

REMEMBER!

A combined journal can be used for either the accrual or the cash basis of accounting.

Since the combined journal is widely used in professional offices and service business firms, it is interesting to look over the varieties of combined journals available at stores selling office supplies. Some are bound journals; others are loose-leaf books. The number of columns varies from six to twenty, and they are available with or without column headings. Those that have printed column headings represent a "canned" type of combined journal. These journals are available for service stations, dry cleaners, doctors' offices, and many other types of businesses.

Combined journals with blank columns can be customized to meet the specific requirements of a given business. Prior to labeling the columns, first study the operations of the business and make up a chart of accounts. Next, identify those accounts that are likely to be used frequently to record typical transactions of the business. Naturally, if these accounts are used over and over, you need to set up special columns for them.

CHAPTER REVIEW

Online Study Center
ACE the test!

Review of Learning Objectives

1. **Describe the accounting records for a professional enterprise.**

   The records for a professional enterprise generally consist of an appointment record, a recording of charges levied for services rendered, and patients' or clients' (customers') ledger cards. A combined journal is generally used to record transactions that are posted to a general ledger.

2. **Record transactions for both a professional enterprise and a service enterprise in a combined journal.**

   Special columns are set up to record transactions involving frequently used accounts. Transactions involving other accounts are recorded in the Other Accounts columns. A long line in the Account Name column and a dash in the Post. Ref. column indicate that all debits and credits for a transaction have been entered in special columns.

3. **Post from the combined journal and determine the cash balance.**

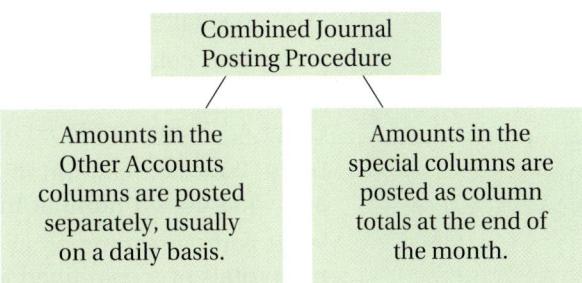

An account number in the Post. Ref. column indicates that the amount in the Other Accounts column has been posted; a dash in that column indicates that the amount is being posted as part of a column total. Below the totals of the Other Accounts columns, an X in parentheses indicates that the column total was not posted; accounts were posted individually. Below the totals of the special columns, the account numbers in parentheses indicate that each column has been posted.

4. Prepare a work sheet for a professional enterprise.

   The work sheet for a professional enterprise is the same as the work sheet presented in Chapter 4 for a service enterprise.

5. Prepare financial statements for a professional enterprise.

   The financial statements for professional enterprises are the same as the financial statements presented previously for service enterprises, except for some new account titles.

6. Record adjusting and closing entries in a combined journal.

   Adjusting and closing entries are recorded in the Account Name column and the Other Accounts Debit and Credit columns. The closing entries may be recorded immediately below the adjusting entries. However, if it is necessary to carry over any one entry to a second page, you should not split up the entry.

Glossary

Combined journal A journal format widely used by professional and service enterprises in place of a general journal; designed to make the recording and posting of transactions more efficient. (197)

Patient's ledger record A record of amounts charged to patients, amounts received from patients, estimates given, and the remaining amounts owed by patients, which are called debit balances. In the event that a patient overpaid, the remainder is called a credit balance, which indicates a liability exists to the patient. (192)

Professional enterprise A business that provides a highly specialized service for a fee. (191)

Special columns Columns in a journal that are used to record amounts that occur frequently. (197)

QUESTIONS, EXERCISES, AND CASES

Discussion Questions

1. Why do small businesses find the combined journal convenient to use?
2. Name four columns that should always appear in a combined journal.
3. What types of transactions are recorded in the Other Accounts Debit and Other Accounts Credit columns?
4. In the Post. Ref. column of a combined journal, what does a dash signify and what does a number indicate?
5. What is the meaning of an X or a number in parentheses under the column totals of a combined journal?
6. When an amount is placed in the Other Accounts Debit or Other Accounts Credit column, what would be written in the Account Name column?
7. You have been asked to design a combined journal for Jody's Hair Salon. Customers pay in cash only. The business buys supplies on account from

creditors. Rent and utilities are paid monthly. Employees are paid wages weekly. The owner, Jody Wallace, makes withdrawals weekly. The firm advertises frequently. List the special columns needed plus the four columns that always appear in a combined journal.

8. Describe the process of proving the combined journal at the end of the month.

Exercises

P.O. 1

Record receipt of cash under the cash basis.

Exercise 6-1 On June 4, the appointment record for a psychiatrist shows that the total of the Fees column is $926 and the total of the Receipts column is $287. At the end of the day, $287 is deposited in the bank. Record the journal entry for the deposit in the general journal. Assume that the cash basis is used.

P.O. 2

List the columns to record transactions.

Exercise 6-2 Zambrano Advertising Agency uses a combined journal with the following columns. Assume that the accrual basis of accounting is used.

Cash Debit	Accounts Receivable Debit
Cash Credit	Accounts Receivable Credit
Ck. No.	Accounts Payable Debit
Date	Accounts Payable Credit
Account Name	Commissions Earned Credit
Post. Ref.	Salary Expense Debit
Other Accounts Debit	Utilities Expense Debit
Other Accounts Credit	

For each of the following, (a) list all of the columns that would be used to record the transaction and (b) describe what would be shown in each of the columns. (You do not have to indicate the Date column, since it would be used in the same way for each of the transactions.)

a. Payment of rent for the month.
b. Charge of commission to a client.
c. Payment of an electric bill.
d. Investment of equipment by the owner.

P.O. 2

Designate columns to record transactions.

Exercise 6-3 J. L. Larson, an attorney, uses a combined journal with the columns listed below.

a. Cash Debit
b. Cash Credit
c. Other Accounts Debit
d. Other Accounts Credit
e. Accounts Receivable Debit
f. Accounts Receivable Credit
g. Fees Earned Credit
h. Office Supplies Expense Debit
i. Salary Expense Debit
j. Travel Expense Debit

For each of the following, (a) list all of the columns that would be used to record the transaction and (b) describe what would be shown in each of the columns.

1. Issued a check for $235 for the purchase of a filing cabinet.
2. Sold services on account, $4,680.

3. Received and paid the electric bill, $168.
4. Received and paid the bill for airline ticket, $485.
5. Sold services for cash, $600.
6. Received and paid the bill for rent for the month, $1,600.
7. Received $3,300 on account from customers.
8. J. L. Larson withdrew $2,000 for personal use.
9. Issued a check for $250 payment of court fees on behalf of a client (client owes J. L. Larson).

P.O. 2

Designate columns to record transactions.

Exercise 6-4 The books of Baylor and Associates, Certified Public Accountants, are kept on a cash basis. The client record of Alice Benson is presented below.

BAYLOR AND ASSOCIATES
CERTIFIED PUBLIC ACCOUNTANTS
242 SELVA AVENUE
MIAMI, FLORIDA 32906

CLIENT RECORD

Alice Benson
1429 Garfield Avenue
Miami, Florida 32909

DATE		SERVICE	CHG		REC		BAL	
20—								
May	6	Tax prep.	164	00			164	00
June	2				90	00	74	00

Record the June 2 transaction in a combined journal.

P.O. 2

Journalize a withdrawal.

Exercise 6-5 Assume that on June 14, Baylor and Associates issues business check number 311 for $1,950 to Miami National Bank for payment on N. Baylor's home mortgage. Explain how the transaction would be recorded in a combined journal.

P.O. 2

List the special columns to accommodate a situation.

Exercise 6-6 Ahmad Dental Laboratory maintains charge accounts for eight dentists. The owner is R. A. Ahmad. Frequent payments include supplies, salaries, delivery, and owner's withdrawals. List the most important special columns for the company's combined journal.

P.O. 3

Describe the posting procedure.

Exercise 6-7 Clayton Landscaping Services uses a combined journal that includes the following columns:

Cash Debit
Cash Credit
Other Accounts Debit
Other Accounts Credit
Fees Earned Credit

Truck Expense Debit
Supplies Expense Debit
Wages Expense Debit
Miscellaneous Expense Debit

Indicate the columns that are posted individually and those that are posted as a column total. Indicate the columns that are posted daily and those that are posted at the end of the month.

P.O. 3

Determine up-to-date cash balance.

Exercise 6-8 Determine the cash balance after November 11.

Cash

Beginning Nov. 1 Bal. 642.50	

	CASH		CK. NO.	DATE	
	DEBIT	CREDIT			
1				20—	
2	9 2 1 64			Nov.	1
3		7 5 42	121		3
4	3 8 9 00				5
5		4 1 6 20	122		8
6	8 4 0 00	2 1 9 00	123		9
7		8 4 59	124		11

---

internet

LINKS TO ACCOUNTING

Now that you have learned about recording transactions in a combined journal and preparing financial statements, let's go back to the questions we asked at the beginning of the chapter.

1. How would the accounts you would commonly use in a combined journal for a doctor differ from the accounts for an architect?
2. Give some examples of how Dr. Hanna's balance sheet in this chapter differs from Best Buy's balance sheet (found on page 58 of the 2005 Form 10-K report) by going to **http://www.sec.gov/edgar/searchedgar/companysearch.html** and searching for Best Buy Co Inc. Then, either scroll through the listing or do a search for Form 10-K. Select the 2005 filing.
3. The information found on the Internet seems endless. Choose any professional/service enterprise you know about and see if you can find its financial statements online.

CONSIDER AND COMMUNICATE

You do the bookkeeping for a small animal veterinarian. She has no formal accounting system yet, but she does save all source documents.

1. Convince her of the benefits of a combined journal.
2. Design the format for a combined journal with Debit and Credit columns and headings to accommodate the entries for a small animal veterinarian using the cash basis.

WHAT'S WRONG WITH THIS PICTURE?

Your friend, a psychotherapist, has been using a general journal for his sole proprietorship practice. He needs a better journal solution because he does the accounting himself. Discuss how you think a combined journal could save him time.

A QUESTION OF ETHICS

It is Friday at 6 P.M. It is your responsibility to count the money in the cash register, prepare the deposit slip for the bank, and lock up. You have counted the money, prepared the bank deposit, and cleared the cash register, when a customer comes in to buy something. You finish the sale for $19.50. The customer has the exact change. You are in a hurry and do not want to redo the deposit, so you put the $19.50 in your bag (the safe is locked and you don't have the combination). You intend to add it to Monday's deposit. Over the weekend you have a flat tire and need the $19.50 for repairs and lunch. Discuss the possible problems that arise from this action.

PROBLEM SET A

For additional help, see the demonstration problem at the beginning of each chapter in your Working Papers.

P.O. 2

Problem 6-1A M. L. Green, M.D., uses the following chart of accounts:

Assets

111 Cash
121 Medical Equipment
122 Accumulated Depreciation, Medical Equipment
123 Office Furniture and Equipment
124 Accumulated Depreciation, Office Furniture and Equipment
125 Vehicle
126 Accumulated Depreciation, Vehicle

Liabilities

211 Notes Payable

Owner's Equity

311 M. L. Green, Capital
312 M. L. Green, Drawing
313 Income Summary

Revenue

411 Professional Fees

Expenses

511 Nurse Salary Expense
512 Office Salary Expense
513 Equipment Rental Expense
514 Rent Expense
515 Medical Supplies Expense
516 X-ray Supplies Expense
517 Laboratory Expense
518 Cleaning Expense
519 Office Supplies Expense
521 Depreciation Expense, Medical Equipment
522 Depreciation Expense, Office Furniture and Equipment
523 Depreciation Expense, Vehicle
524 Vehicle Expense
525 Insurance Expense
526 Telephone Expense
527 Utilities Expense
528 Miscellaneous Expense

Dr. Green's records consist of an appointment record book, examination and charge reports, patients' ledger records, a combined journal, and a general ledger. The doctor fills out an examination and charge report each time a patient visits. The report contains a listing of the treatments and tests administered, coded for insurance purposes, as well as the amounts of the charges. The charges are then recorded in the patient's ledger record. Monthly statements based on the patient's ledger record are mailed to the patient. Dr. Green's books are kept on the cash basis. These transactions took place during April:

Apr.		
	1	Paid April's rent, $1,790 (Ck. No. 636).
	2	Paid salary for the part-time office person, $775 (Ck. No. 637).
	4	Bought medical supplies for cash from Park Medical Supply, $670 (Ck. No. 638).
	6	Received cash from patients during week, $7,680.
	9	Paid telephone bill, $170 (Ck. No. 639).
	12	Paid Technical Labs for laboratory expense, $855 (Ck. No. 640).
	13	Received cash from patients during week, $6,593.
	15	Dr. M. L. Green withdrew $1,050 for personal use (Ck. No. 641).
	17	Bought x-ray supplies for cash, $214 (Ck. No. 642).
	18	Paid for gas and oil for vehicle used in business, $135 (Vehicle Expense) (Ck. No. 643).
	20	Received cash from patients during week, $3,742.
	23	Bought postage stamps for cash, $30 (Miscellaneous Expense) (Ck. No. 644).
	24	Paid $110 to Carson Laundry for laundry service (Cleaning Expense) (Ck. No. 645).
	27	Paid Kramer News for waiting room magazines, $86.50 (Miscellaneous Expense) (Ck. No. 646).
	30	Paid nurse's salary for the month, $2,010 (Ck. No. 647).
	30	Paid A-One Cleaning for janitorial services, $132 (Cleaning Expense) (Ck. No. 648).
	30	Received cash from patients (April 21 through 30), $3,246.
	30	Dr. M. L. Green withdrew $1,750 for personal use (Ck. No. 649).

Check Figure

Total debits, $31,038.50

Instructions

1. Record these transactions on page 9 of the combined journal. Insert the name of the Drawing account.
2. Prove the equality of the debit and credit totals in the Account Name column below the totals.

P.O. 6

Problem 6-2A The completed work sheet for S. R. Lindell, Psychologist, is shown in Figure 11 on pages 214 and 215.

Check Figure

Total Other Accounts Debit column, $172,626.20

Instructions

Record the adjusting and closing entries on page 5 of the combined journal. Remember to total the columns and insert an X in parentheses below each total.

P.O. 2,3

Problem 6-3A Dr. Terrence T. Cascone operates the Cascone Allergy Clinic. The transactions were completed during September of this year. Following is his chart of accounts.

FIGURE 11

	ACCOUNT NAME	TRIAL BALANCE DEBIT					TRIAL BALANCE CREDIT				
1	Cash		6	2	7	0	00				
2	Office Equipment	56	4	1	0	25					
3	Accumulated Depreciation, Office Equipment							16	9	8	4	16
4	S. R. Lindell, Capital							38	8	7	2	94
5	S. R. Lindell, Drawing	24	7	8	5	00					
6	Professional Fees							70	9	2	9	20
7	Salary Expense	16	3	2	4	60					
8	Advertising Expense		4	5	7	5	10				
9	Rent Expense		7	6	7	0	00				
10	Vehicle Expense		2	0	6	2	75				
11	Travel Expense		2	2	4	1	32				
12	Entertainment Expense			7	9	6	12				
13	Supplies Expense		5	2	6	0	00				
14	Miscellaneous Expense			3	9	1	16				
15		126	7	8	6	30	126	7	8	6	30
16	Depreciation Expense, Office Equipment										
17											
18	Net Income										
19											
20											

Assets

111 Cash
112 Accounts Receivable
114 Prepaid Insurance
121 Equipment
122 Accumulated Depreciation,
    Equipment

Liabilities

221 Accounts Payable

Owner's Equity

311 T. T. Cascone, Capital
312 T. T. Cascone, Drawing
313 Income Summary

Revenue

411 Professional Fees

Expenses

511 Salary Expense
512 Rent Expense
513 Laboratory Expense
514 Utilities Expense
515 Depreciation Expense,
    Equipment
516 Supplies Expense
517 Miscellaneous Expense

Sept. 2 Bought medical equipment on account from Wing Medical Supplies, $1,560. (Use two lines.)

2 Paid office rent for month, $1,200 (Ck. No. 516).

2 Received cash on account from patients, $5,129: D. R. Crain, $1,152.50; Deanne Skeller, $1,372; Jason Neeles, $1,317; Terense Garner, $1,287.50. These patients were billed last month for services performed in August. (Dr. Cascone uses the

S. R. Lindell, Psychologist
Work Sheet
For Year Ended December 31, 20—

ADJUSTMENTS		ADJUSTED TRIAL BALANCE		INCOME STATEMENT		BALANCE SHEET		
DEBIT	CREDIT	DEBIT	CREDIT	DEBIT	CREDIT	DEBIT	CREDIT	
		6 2 7 0 00				6 2 7 0 00		1
		56 4 1 0 25				56 4 1 0 25		2
	(a) 5 9 8 2 80		22 9 6 6 96				22 9 6 6 96	3
			38 8 7 2 94				38 8 7 2 94	4
		24 7 8 5 00				24 7 8 5 00		5
			70 9 2 9 20		70 9 2 9 20			6
		16 3 2 4 60		16 3 2 4 60				7
		4 5 7 5 10		4 5 7 5 10				8
		7 6 7 0 00		7 6 7 0 00				9
		2 0 6 2 75		2 0 6 2 75				10
		2 2 4 1 32		2 2 4 1 32				11
		7 9 6 12		7 9 6 12				12
		5 2 6 0 00		5 2 6 0 00				13
		3 9 1 16		3 9 1 16				14
								15
(a) 5 9 8 2 80		5 9 8 2 80		5 9 8 2 80				16
5 9 8 2 80	5 9 8 2 80	132 7 6 9 10	132 7 6 9 10	45 3 0 3 85	70 9 2 9 20	87 4 6 5 25	61 8 3 9 90	17
				25 6 2 5 35			25 6 2 5 35	18
				70 9 2 9 20	70 9 2 9 20	87 4 6 5 25	87 4 6 5 25	19
								20

accrual basis. Use four lines, recording individual amounts in both the Cash Debit column and the Accounts Receivable Credit column. List each patient's name in the Account Name column.)

Sept. 3 Received cash for professional services rendered, $3,229.

5 Received and paid electric bill to Mid-State Power, $258.40 (Ck. No. 517).

8 Received and paid telephone bill to Western Telephone Company for month, $183 (Ck. No. 518).

9 Recorded fees charged to patients on account for professional services rendered, $830.50: F. Radewan, $484.50; M. Parkhill, $346. (Use two lines.)

15 Paid salary of L. Mance (assistant), $847.50 (Ck. No. 519).

19 Received cash for professional services, $1,608.

23 Returned part of the equipment purchased on September 2 and received a reduction on the bill, $184.

28 Billed patients on account for professional services rendered, $2,045: C. R. Roberts, $1,486; Marnie Lendal, $516.50; Dave Hensen, $42.50.

30 Paid salary of C. Barnes (part-time assistant), $720.75 (Ck. No. 520).

30 Paid salary of R. Carson (receptionist), $942 (Ck. No. 521).

30 Dr. Cascone withdrew $1,700 cash for personal use (Ck. No. 522).

Check Figure

Total debits (combined journal), $20,437.15

Instructions

1. Record these transactions in the combined journal, page 37.
2. Prove the equality of the debit and credit totals in the Account Name column below the totals.
3. Fill in owner's equity accounts and post to the accounts in the general ledger.
4. Prepare a trial balance.

P.O. 2

Problem 6-4A On September 1 of this year, T. W. Baptiste started a limousine service serving the local area. The following transactions related to Luscious Limousine Service were completed during September.

Sept.	1	Baptiste opened an account at the Golden State Bank in the name of the business and deposited $34,000.
	2	Bought two used limousines from Laughlin Motors for $80,900, paying $20,900 down, with the balance payable in 30 days (Ck. No. 1).
	3	Bought heavy-duty vacuum and car-cleaning equipment for $380, paying cash (Ck. No. 2).
	4	Paid Valley Service for gas and oil for limousines, $243 (Ck. No. 3).
	5	Paid rent for subletting office space, $725 (Ck. No. 4).
	7	Paid wages to G. Baugh, $540 (Ck. No. 5).
	7	Received revenue for the week, $2,315.
	9	Paid for city business license, $175 (Ck. No. 6).
	11	Bought desk and filing cabinet on account from Murray Office Supply, $480.
	14	Paid for telephone answering service for the month, $225 (Ck. No. 7).
	14	Paid wages to G. Baugh, $540 (Ck. No. 8).
	14	Baptiste withdrew $1,800 for personal use (Ck. No. 9).
	14	Received revenue for the week, $2,784.
	17	Paid Laughlin Motors $2,800 as part payment on account (Ck. No. 10).
	18	Paid $342 for advertising in the telephone directory (Ck. No. 11).
	18	Paid Valley Service for gas and oil for limousines, $295 (Ck. No. 12).
	20	Paid utilities for the month, $208 (Ck. No. 13).
	21	Received revenue for the week, $2,405.
	23	Paid wages to G. Baugh, $540 (Ck. No. 14).
	30	Received revenue for the period September 22–30, $2,010.
	30	Paid Security Insurance Agency for vehicle insurance for six months, $857 (Ck. No. 15).
	30	Paid wages to G. Baugh, $540 (Ck. No. 16).
	30	Baptiste withdrew $1,500 for personal use (Ck. No. 17).

Check Figure

Total debits (combined journal), $136,604

Instructions

1. Review the transactions for Luscious Limousine Service and then develop an appropriate chart of accounts. The company uses the cash basis. All revenue is in the form of cash.
2. Label the appropriate columns in the combined journal. Next to the Date column, list a Ck. No. column and record checks beginning with number 1.
3. Record the transactions in the combined journal beginning with page 1.
4. Show proof of the equality of debit and credit totals in the Account Name column below the totals.

PROBLEM SET B

For additional help, see the demonstration problem at the beginning of each chapter in your Working Papers.

P.O. 2

Problem 6-1B L. Swanson, M.D., uses the following chart of accounts:

Assets

111 Cash
121 Medical Equipment
122 Accumulated Depreciation, Medical Equipment
123 Office Furniture and Equipment
124 Accumulated Depreciation, Office Furniture and Equipment
125 Vehicle
126 Accumulated Depreciation, Vehicle

Liabilities

211 Notes Payable

Owner's Equity

311 L. Swanson, Capital
312 L. Swanson, Drawing
313 Income Summary

Revenue

411 Professional Fees

Expenses

511 Salary Expense
512 Rent Expense
513 Equipment Rental Expense
514 Medical Supplies Expense
515 X-ray Supplies Expense
516 Laboratory Expense
517 Cleaning Expense
518 Office Supplies Expense
519 Depreciation Expense, Medical Equipment
521 Depreciation Expense, Office Furniture and Equipment
522 Depreciation Expense, Vehicle
523 Vehicle Expense
524 Insurance Expense
525 Telephone Expense
526 Utilities Expense
527 Miscellaneous Expense

Dr. Swanson's records consist of an appointment record book, examination and charge reports, patients' ledger records, a combined journal, and a general ledger. The doctor fills out an examination and charge report each time a patient visits. The reports contain a listing of the treatments and tests administered, coded for insurance purposes, as well as the amounts of the charges. The charges are then recorded in the patient's ledger record. Monthly statements based on the patients' ledger records are mailed to patients. Dr. Swanson's books are kept on the cash basis. These transactions took place during November:

Nov. 1 Bought medical supplies for cash from Martin Surgical Supply, $679.50 (Ck. No. 214).

1 Paid November's rent, $1,450 (Ck. No. 215).

4 Paid salary for the part-time office person, $820 (Ck. No. 216).

6 Received cash from patients during the week, $7,325.

7 Bought an examination table from Martin Surgical Supply, costing $1,560, paying $560 in cash and agreeing by contract to pay the balance in four monthly installments of $250 each (credit Notes Payable) (Ck. No. 217).

8 Paid Runyan Laboratories for laboratory expense, $854 (Ck. No. 218).

9 Paid telephone bill, $184 (Ck. No. 219).

FIGURE 12

	ACCOUNT NAME	TRIAL BALANCE			
		DEBIT		CREDIT	
1	Cash	8 1 0 5 00			
2	Equipment	35 2 1 9 00			
3	Accumulated Depreciation, Equipment			7 4 9 0 00	
4	T. R. Berman, Capital			27 9 4 5 40	
5	T. R. Berman, Drawing	14 8 8 0 00			
6	Professional Fees			65 9 5 2 00	
7	Salary Expense	31 3 1 5 00			
8	Advertising Expense	1 0 6 0 80			
9	Rent Expense	1 8 3 0 00			
10	Vehicle Expense	1 9 7 5 00			
11	Travel Expense	3 1 2 4 60			
12	Entertainment Expense	9 3 5 00			
13	Supplies Expense	2 2 4 2 40			
14	Miscellaneous Expense	7 0 0 60			
15		101 3 8 7 40		101 3 8 7 40	
16	Depreciation Expense, Equipment				
17					
18	Net Income				
19					
20					

Nov. 13 Received cash from patients during the week, $5,230.

16 Dr. L. Swanson withdrew $1,500 for personal use (Ck. No. 220).

16 Bought x-ray supplies for cash, $398 (Ck. No. 221).

20 Received cash from patients during the week, $3,622.

23 Bought postage stamps for cash, $30 (Miscellaneous Expense) (Ck. No. 222).

26 Paid for gas and oil for vehicle used in business, $100.25 (Vehicle Expense) (Ck. No. 223).

28 Paid Selton and Company for janitorial services, $195 (Cleaning Expense) (Ck. No. 224).

30 Paid nurse's salary for the month, $2,100 (Ck. No. 225).

30 Dr. L. Swanson withdrew $1,500 for personal use (Ck. No. 226).

30 Received cash from patients (November 21 through 30), $3,450.

30 Paid $112 to Pro Laundry for laundry service through November 30 (Cleaning Expense) (Ck. No. 227).

Check Figure

Total debits, $31,109.75

Instructions

1. Record these transactions in the combined journal, page 26. Insert the name in the Drawing account.
2. Prove the equality of the debits and credits in the Account Name column below the totals.

P.O. 6

Problem 6-2B The completed work sheet for Berman Development Company is shown in Figure 12 above.

Berman Development Company
Work Sheet
For Month Ended December 31, 20—

	ADJUSTMENTS			ADJUSTED TRIAL BALANCE			INCOME STATEMENT			BALANCE SHEET		
	DEBIT		CREDIT	DEBIT		CREDIT	DEBIT		CREDIT	DEBIT		CREDIT	
				8 1 0 5 00						8 1 0 5 00			1
				35 2 1 9 00						35 2 1 9 00			2
			(a) 1 2 2 1 00			8 7 1 1 00						8 7 1 1 00	3
						27 9 4 5 40						27 9 4 5 40	4
				14 8 8 0 00						14 8 8 0 00			5
						65 9 5 2 00			65 9 5 2 00				6
				31 3 1 5 00			31 3 1 5 00						7
				1 0 6 0 80			1 0 6 0 80						8
				1 8 3 0 00			1 8 3 0 00						9
				1 9 7 5 00			1 9 7 5 00						10
				3 1 2 4 60			3 1 2 4 60						11
				9 3 5 00			9 3 5 00						12
				2 2 4 2 40			2 2 4 2 40						13
				7 0 0 60			7 0 0 60						14
													15
(a) 1 2 2 1 00				1 2 2 1 00			1 2 2 1 00						16
1 2 2 1 00		1 2 2 1 00		102 6 0 8 40		102 6 0 8 40	44 4 0 4 40		65 9 5 2 00	58 2 0 4 00		36 6 5 6 40	17
							21 5 4 7 60					21 5 4 7 60	18
							65 9 5 2 00		65 9 5 2 00	58 2 0 4 00		58 2 0 4 00	19
													20

Check Figure

Total Other Accounts Debit column, $148,005

P.O. 2,3

Instructions

Record the adjusting and closing entries on page 6 of the combined journal. Remember to total the columns and insert an X in parentheses below each total.

Problem 6-3B Tara Eng, D.C., operates the Eng Chiropractic Clinic. The transactions described on page 220 were completed during September of this year. Her chart of accounts is as follows:

Assets

111 Cash
112 Accounts Receivable
114 Prepaid Insurance
121 Equipment
122 Accumulated Depreciation, Equipment

Liabilities

221 Accounts Payable

Owner's Equity

311 T. Eng, Capital
312 T. Eng, Drawing
313 Income Summary

Revenue

411 Professional Fees

Expenses

511 Salary Expense
512 Rent Expense
513 Laboratory Expense
514 Utilities Expense
515 Depreciation Expense, Equipment
516 Supplies Expense
517 Miscellaneous Expense

Sept. 1 Bought x-ray equipment on account from Radiological Associates, $1,640. (Use two lines.)

2 Paid office rent for the month, $1,725 (Ck. No. 423).

2 Received cash on account from patients, $926: R. Whitten, $375; Ellen Briggs, $412; Andy Corde, $139. These patients were billed last month for services performed in August. (Dr. Eng uses the accrual basis. Use three lines, recording individual amounts in both the Cash Debit column and the Accounts Receivable Credit column. List each patient's name in the Account Name column.)

4 Received cash for professional services rendered, $2,790.75.

6 Received and paid electric bill to Universal Electric, $145.50 (Ck. No. 424).

7 Received and paid telephone bill for month to Southern Telephone Company, $151 (Ck. No. 425).

9 Recorded fees charged to patients on account for professional services rendered, $945.50: T. Wang, $335; H. Carver, $610.50. (Use two lines.)

15 Paid salary of K. Olsen (assistant), $1,230 (Ck. No. 426).

19 Received cash for professional services, $1,581.

22 Returned part of equipment purchased on September 1 and received a reduction on the bill, $265.

27 Billed patients on account for professional services rendered, $1,532: N. Carol, $280; J. Ortiz, $390; S. Archer, $862.

30 Paid salary of D. Canton (part-time assistant), $625 (Ck. No. 427).

30 Paid salary of J. Grand (receptionist), $1,155 (Ck. No. 428).

30 Dr. Eng withdrew $1,500 cash for personal use (Ck. No. 429).

Check Figure

Total debits (combined journal), $16,211.75

Instructions

1. Record these transactions in the combined journal, page 43.
2. Prove the equality of the debit and credit totals in the Account Name column below the totals.
3. Fill in owner's equity accounts and post to the accounts in the general ledger.
4. Prepare a trial balance.

P.O. 2

Problem 6-4B On July 1 of this year, K. A. Bremer started a landscaping business. The following transactions related to Bremer's Landscaping were completed during July.

July 1 Bremer opened an account at the Carter National Bank in the name of the business and deposited $18,000.

1 Paid rent for office and warehouse space for the month, $1,425 (Ck. No. 1).

2 Bought a used truck from Nelson Motors for $15,200, paying $5,000 as a down payment, with the balance on account due in 30 days (Ck. No. 2).

3 Bought landscaping equipment from Glade Equipment for $3,750, paying $1,750 as a down payment, with the balance due in 30 days (Ck. No. 3).

3 Paid Zelda's Fast Serve for gas and oil for the truck, $136 (Ck. No. 4).

4 Received and paid bill for advertising from the *City Review*, $248 (Ck. No. 5).

July   4   Bought fertilizers on account from Drager's Lawn and Garden Store, $1,145 (Supplies Expense).

4   Bought beauty bark from R&L Distributing Company on account, $430 (Supplies Expense).

6   Received revenue for the week, $2,392.

7   Paid wages to part-time employee, $492 (Ck. No. 6).

7   Paid for telephone answering service for the month, $244 (Ck. No. 7).

10   Paid Zelda's Fast Serve for gas and oil for the truck, $185 (Ck. No. 8).

13   Received revenue for the week, $2,515.

17   Bremer withdrew $1,020 for personal use (Ck. No. 9).

20   Received revenue for the week, $2,368.

21   Paid wages to part-time employee, $412 (Ck. No. 10).

27   Paid for city business license, $157 (Ck. No. 11).

27   Paid utilities for the month, $228 (Ck. No. 12).

30   Paid Nelson Motors $2,500 to apply on account (Ck. No. 13).

30   Paid Zelda's Fast Serve for gas and oil for the truck, $145, plus $115 for a tune-up (Ck. No. 14).

31   Received revenue for the period July 21–31, $2,525.

31   Paid wages to part-time employee, $415 (Ck. No. 15).

31   Bremer withdrew $1,850 for personal use (Ck. No. 16).

Check Figure

Total debits (combined journal), $57,897

Instructions

1. Review the transactions for Bremer's Landscaping and then develop an appropriate chart of accounts. Bremer uses the cash basis of accounting. All revenue is in the form of cash.

2. Label the appropriate columns in the combined journal. Next to the Date column, list a Ck. No. column and record checks beginning with number 1.

3. Record the transactions in the combined journal beginning with page 1.

4. Show proof of the equality of debit and credit totals in the Account Name column below the totals.

7 Bank Accounts and Cash Funds

Managing your money online is easier than ever. You can manage your checking and savings accounts, apply for loans, pay bills, and handle your investments over the Internet. Most banks and credit unions offer remote banking online. But, how do you find out which institutions provide the best online customer service or are easiest to use? The Bankrate.com website explains the advantages and disadvantages of online banking. This information can help consumers decide whether online banking is right for them. The information can be found at **http://www.bankrate.com/brm/olbstep2.asp.**

What factors would be important to you when deciding whether to bank online?

Performance Objectives

After you have completed this chapter, you will be able to do the following:

1. Describe the procedure for depositing checks.

2. Reconcile a bank statement.

3. Record the required journal entries from the bank reconciliation.

4. Record journal entries to establish and reimburse a Petty Cash Fund.

5. Complete petty cash vouchers and petty cash payments records.

6. Record the journal entries to establish a Change Fund.

7. Record journal entries for transactions involving Cash Short and Over.

A very important aspect of any system of financial accounting, either for an individual or for a business enterprise, is the accurate and efficient management of cash. For a business of any size, all cash received during a work day should be deposited at the end of the day, and all disbursements—with the exception of payments from Petty Cash—should be made by check or paid electronically. The handling of cash in this manner is an example of **internal control**. Internal control is the system of policies and procedures to (1) protect assets against fraud and waste, (2) provide for accurate accounting data, (3) promote an efficient operation, and (4) encourage adherence to management policies.

When we talk about cash, we mean currency, coins, checks, money orders, traveler's checks, and bank drafts or bank cashier's checks. Personal checks are accepted conditionally—that is, based on the condition that they are valid. In other words, we consider checks to be good until they are otherwise proven not to be good.

Internal control of cash is a critical activity in a business. Divide the cash activities among several people to deter mishandling.

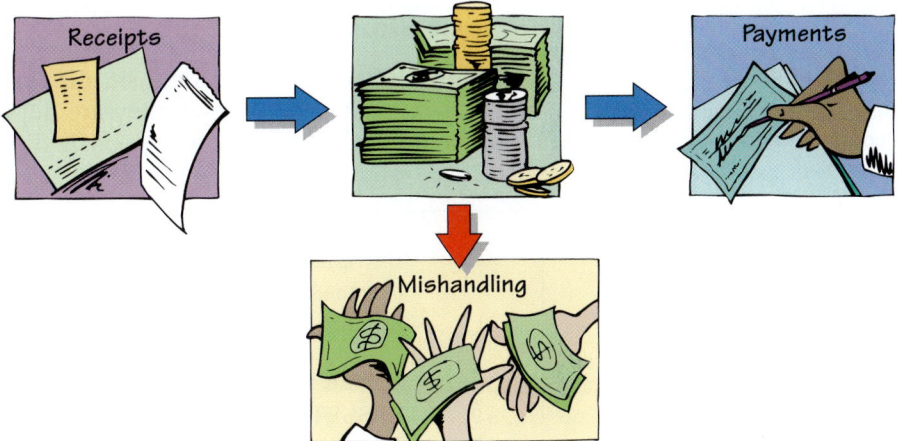

In this chapter, besides discussing bank accounts, we are going to talk about **cash funds**—petty cash funds and change funds—which are separately held reserves of cash set aside for specific purposes.

USING A CHECKING ACCOUNT

Although you may be familiar with the process of opening a checking account, making deposits, and writing checks, let's review these and other procedures associated with opening and maintaining a business checking account. We will discuss signature cards, deposit slips, automated teller machines, electronic funds transfer, night deposits, and endorsements.

Signature Card

FYI

As a means of preventing employee theft, many companies require more than one signature on checks over a certain dollar amount.

When Paula C. Boyd founded Bay Cleaners, she opened a checking account in the name of the business. When she opened the account, she filled out a **signature card** for the bank's files. Because Boyd gave her assistant Maria R. Ruiz the right to sign checks too, the assistant also signed the card. The signature card gives the bank a copy of the official signatures of any persons authorized to sign checks. The bank can use it to verify the signatures on any checks of Bay Cleaners presented for payment. This card helps the bank detect forgeries. Figure 1 shows a typical signature card.

FIGURE 1

Title	Account Number
Bay Cleaners	5008-3007

In consideration of the acceptance by   BESSETT NATIONAL BANK   of my/our account of the type indicated below, I/we agree to be bound by such rules and regulations and/or such schedules of interest, fees and charges applicable to such account as may now or hereafter be adopted by and in effect at said Bank, and also by the provisions printed hereon. It is understood that the acceptance by said Bank of my/our account is subject to the receipt by said Bank of satisfactory credit information.

(1) Sign Here   *Paula C. Boyd*

(2) Sign Here   *Maria R. Ruiz*

Address   **625 Montes Avenue**

City   **San Diego**   State   **California**   Zip   **92109**

☑ CHECKING   ☐ MULTIPLE MATURITY   ☐ CASH MANAGER

☐ SAVINGS   ☐ GUARANTEED INTEREST (Multiple Maturity)   ☐ SAFE DEPOSIT   ☐ OTHER _____

IF THIS IS A JOINT ACCOUNT, BOTH OWNERS MUST SIGN ABOVE

Each of the signers guarantees the genuineness of the signature of the other. Each signer also agrees with the other and the Bank that deposits now or hereafter made to this account may be withdrawn in whole or part by either or survivor, and that each may endorse for deposit to this account any instrument payable to the order of either or both. Provisions respecting this agreement shall be modified only upon receipt by the Bank of written notice, signed by both.

Deposit Slips

OBJECTIVE 1

Describe the procedure for depositing checks.

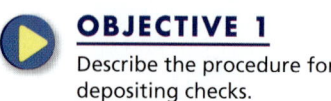

The bank provides printed **deposit slips** on which customers record the amount of coins and currency they are depositing and list each individual check being deposited. A typical deposit slip is shown in Figure 2.

FIGURE 2

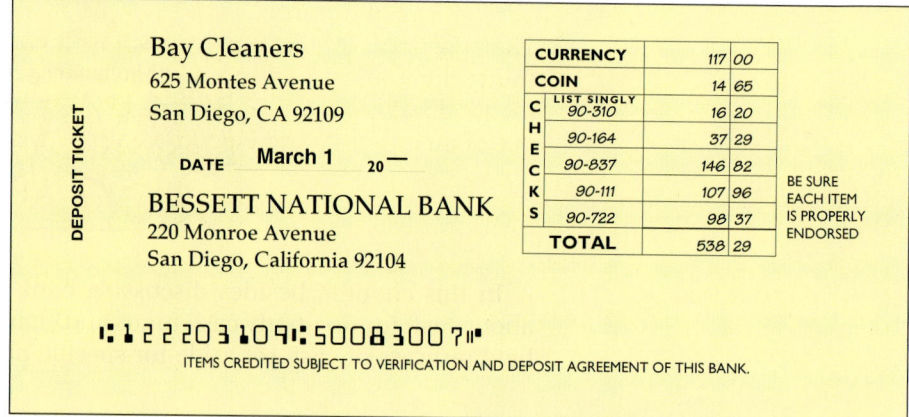

Each check should be listed according to its American Bankers Association (ABA) transit number. The **ABA number** is the small fraction located in the upper right corner of a check. The numerator (top of the fraction) indicates the city or state in which the bank is located and the specific bank on which the check is drawn. The denominator (bottom of the fraction) indicates the Federal Reserve District in which the check is cleared and the routing number used by the Federal Reserve Bank. For example,

$$\frac{90\text{-}310}{1222}$$

FYI

The 12 in the denominator represents the Twelfth Federal Reserve District, and the 22 represents the routing number used by the Federal Reserve Bank.

The 90 identifies the city or state, and the 310 indicates the specific bank within that area (see Figures 3 and 5).

For a business account, the depositor fills out the deposit slip in duplicate, giving the original to the bank teller and keeping the copy. (This procedure may vary from bank to bank.)

The bank prints the amount of each deposited check on the lower right side of the check in a distinctive script called **MICR**, which stands for *magnetic ink character recognition*. The routing number (as well as the depositor's number) used by the Federal Reserve Bank was printed on the lower left side of the blank check before it was sent to the account holder. The electronic equipment used to process the checks is able to rapidly read the script identifying the bank on which the check is drawn and the amount of the check.

Automated Teller Machines

Deposits, withdrawals, and transfers can be made at all hours at banks with **ATMs (automated teller machines)**. Each depositor uses a plastic card that contains a code number and has a personal identification number (PIN). The amount to be deposited, withdrawn, or transferred is keyed in by the depositor. To make a deposit, the customer inserts an envelope containing cash and/or checks and, if required, a copy of the deposit slip into the ATM. To make a withdrawal, the customer requests an amount, the ATM dispenses it, and the customer removes the cash. In addition to deposits and withdrawals, a customer may transfer amounts from one account to another (for example, from savings to checking).

Electronic Funds Transfer

A transfer of funds initiated through an electronic terminal, such as a telephone, computer, or magnetic tape, is an **Electronic Funds Transfer (EFT)**. There is no paper document, such as a check or deposit slip, starting the transaction. The monthly bank statement will list the EFT deposits and payments. Examples of EFTs include an ATM transaction, a wire transfer in or out of an account, and electronic bill paying.

Night Deposits

Most banks provide night depositories so that businesses and individuals can make deposits after regular hours. These are secured chutes into which a business's representative can drop a bag of cash and checks, knowing that the day's receipts will be safe until the bank opens in the morning.

Endorsements

The bank may not accept for deposit a check made out to a business until someone from the business has endorsed the check by signature or by stamp. The endorsement should appear on the back of the left end of a check, as it does in Figure 3. The **endorsement** (1) transfers title to the money and (2) authorizes the payment of the check. In other words, if the check is not good, NSF (not sufficient funds), then the bank, in order to protect itself, will deduct the amount of the check from the depositor's account.

FIGURE 3

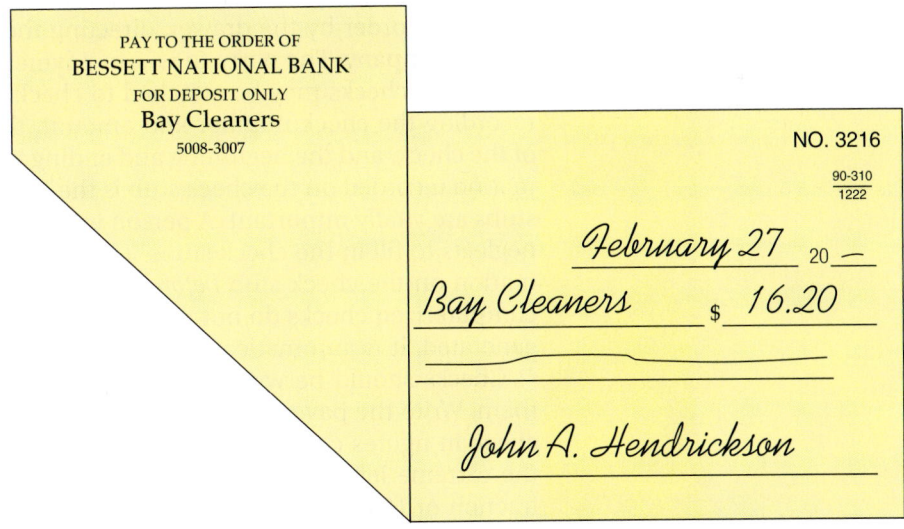

Restrictive Endorsement   All checks made payable to Bay Cleaners are endorsed by stamping on the back of the checks "Pay to the Order of Bessett National Bank, For Deposit Only, Bay Cleaners." This is called a **restrictive endorsement** because it restricts or limits any further transfer of the check. This endorsement also forces the deposit of the check, because the endorsement is not valid for any other purpose.

Blank Endorsement   When the party to whom a check is made payable (the payee) endorses the check by signing only her or his name on the back

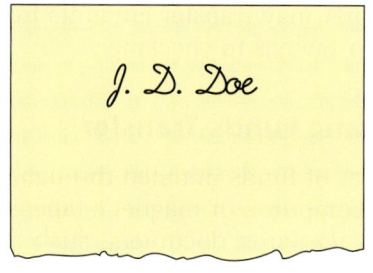

Restrictive Endorsement
(with rubber stamp)

Blank Endorsement

Qualified Endorsement

FIGURE 4

of the check, this is known as a **blank endorsement** (Figure 4). With a blank endorsement, there are no restrictions attached.

Qualified Endorsement A third type of endorsement is a **qualified endorsement** (see Figure 4), which generally includes the phrase "Pay to the order of," followed by the name of the person to whom the check is being transferred, and then followed by the phrase "without recourse." Such an endorsement frees the endorser from future liability in case the drawer of the check does not have sufficient funds to cover the check.

WRITING CHECKS

People generally use a check to withdraw money from a bank checking account. The party who writes the check is called the **drawer**. A check represents an order by the drawer, directing the bank to pay a designated person or company. The party to whom payment is to be made is the **payee**.

Manual checks may be attached to check stubs. Each stub has spaces for recording the check number and amount, the date and payee, the purpose of the check, and the beginning and ending balances of cash. *Note:* The information recorded on the check stub is the basis for the journal entry, so check stubs are vitally important. A person in a hurry or under pressure sometimes neglects to fill in the check stubs. Therefore, it is best to record all the information on the check stub *before making out the check*. Businesses that use computerized checks do not need check stubs. When the check is computer generated, it is automatically entered into the accounting system.

Checks should be written carefully so that no one can successfully alter them. Write the payee's name on the first long line. Write the amount of the check in figures close to the dollar sign, then write the amount in words at the extreme left of the line provided for this information. Write cents as a fraction of 100. For example, write $727.50 as "seven hundred twenty-seven and 50/100," or $89.00 as "eighty-nine and NO/100." Legally, if there is a discrepancy between the amount in figures and the written amount, the written amount prevails. However, generally, the bank gets in touch with the drawer and asks what the correct amount should be.

Finally, the drawer's signature on the face of the check should match that on the signature card on file at the drawer's bank.

Figure 5 is a manual check, with the accompanying stub, drawn on the account of Bay Cleaners. A description of the script appears in Figure 6.

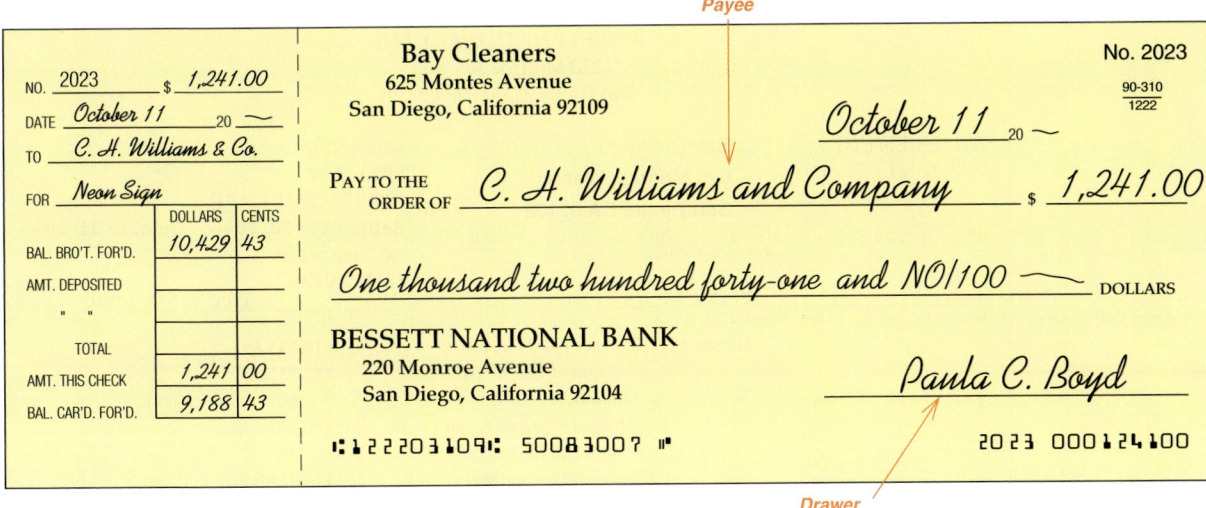

FIGURE 5

FIGURE 6

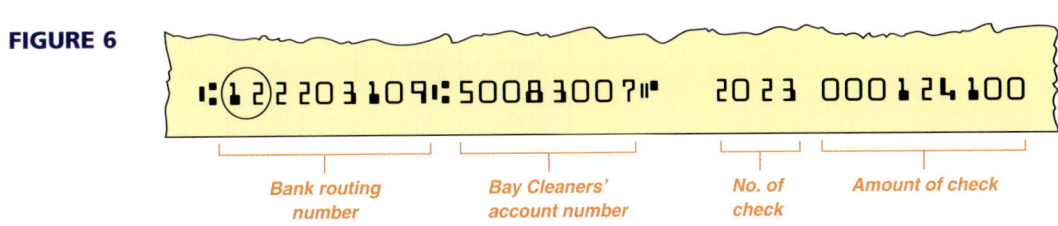

Bank routing number   Bay Cleaners' account number   No. of check   Amount of check

BANK STATEMENTS

The bank prepares the **bank statement**, which is created from the bank's viewpoint. Keep in mind that, to the bank, a customer's account is a liability and, therefore, has a credit balance. Once a month, the bank sends each of its customers the following information with the bank statement:

- The balance at the beginning of the month
- Additions in the form of deposits and credit memos
- Deductions in the form of checks and debit memos
- Electronic transactions
- The final balance at the end of the month

A bank statement for Bay Cleaners is shown in Figure 7 on page 228. The following legend of symbols is listed on the bottom of the statement:

- **CM (credit memo)** Increases in or credits to the account, such as notes or accounts left with the bank for collection and interest income earned.
- **DM (debit memo)** Decreases in or debits to the account, such as NSF checks and service charges. Service charges are based on the number of items processed and the average account balance. Special charges may also be levied against the account for collections and other services performed, including check printing.

BESSETT NATIONAL BANK
220 Monroe Avenue
San Diego, California 92104

STATEMENT OF
ACCOUNT

Bay Cleaners
625 Montes Avenue
San Diego, CA 92109

ACCOUNT NUMBER
5008-3007
STATEMENT DATE
September 30, 20 — – October 31, 20 —
TAX ID NUMBER
83-424 9732

SUMMARY		
Balance Last Statement	$10,633.69
Amount of Checks and Debits	$37,732.36
Number of Checks	66
Amount of Deposits and Credits	$40,547.67
Number of Deposits	23
Balance This Statement	$13,449.00

CHECKS/ OTHER DEBITS

CHECKS

CHECK NUMBER	DATE POSTED	AMOUNT	CHECK NUMBER	DATE POSTED	AMOUNT
1952	10-01	50.00	1988	10-17	61.22
1953	10-01	200.00	1989	10-17	463.29
1954	10-01	400.00	1990	10-18	520.00
1955	10-02	46.00	1991	10-19	14.57
1956	10-02	174.23	1992	10-19	23.98
1957	10-02	671.74	1993	10-19	115.16
1958	10-03	846.20	1994	10-20	117.37
1984	10-14	664.56	2018	10-30	126.70
1985	10-15	719.00	2019	10-30	943.64
1986	10-16	61.68	2020	10-31	843.17
1987	10-16	591.84	2021	10-31	21.92

OTHER DEBITS

DESCRIPTION	DATE POSTED	AMOUNT
DM NSF check from A. L. Sanders	10-15	193.00
DM Automated Teller Trans. 062142 customer N3162241 at terminal 30962—cash	10-16	20.00
DM Service charge	10-31	9.50

DEPOSITS/ OTHER CREDITS

DEPOSITS

DATE POSTED	AMOUNT	DATE POSTED	AMOUNT
10-01	921.00	10-17	873.19
10-02	1,476.22	10-18	946.78
10-03	463.62	10-21	329.49
10-04	789.44	10-22	1,116.27
10-07	1,063.14	10-23	734.13
10-08	1,211.96	10-26	227.69
10-14	992.27	10-28	439.45
10-15	759.41	10-29	611.12
10-16	641.33	10-30	764.35

OTHER CREDITS

DESCRIPTION	DATE POSTED	AMOUNT
CM Note collected, principal $900, interest $9	10-29	909.00

PLEASE EXAMINE THIS STATEMENT CAREFULLY. REPORT ANY POSSIBLE ERRORS IN 10 DAYS.

CODE SYMBOLS

CM Credit Memo	OD Overdraft
DM Debit Memo	EC Error Correction

FIGURE 7

- **OD (overdraft)** The withdrawal of more than the cash balance in the account, resulting in a negative balance.
- **EC (error correction)** Corrections of errors made by the bank, such as encoding mistakes.

The bank statement is a valuable aid to efficiency and accuracy because it provides a double record of the Cash account. If a business entity deposits all cash receipts in the bank and makes all payments by check, then the bank is keeping an independent record of the business's cash. You might think that the two balances—the business's and the bank's—should be equal, but this is unlikely. Some transactions may have been recorded in the business's account before being entered in the bank's records. In addition, there are unavoidable delays (by either the business or the bank) in recording transactions. Ordinarily, there is a delay of one or more days between the date on which a check is written and the date when it is presented to the bank for payment. Also, banks may not record deposits until the following business day. During this time lag, deposits made or checks written are recorded in the business's check register, but they are not yet listed on the bank statement.

The bank mails statements to its depositors each month. The **canceled checks** (checks that have been paid or cleared by the bank) are listed on the bank statement. They are called *canceled checks* because they are canceled by a stamp on the back, indicating that they have been paid. Debit or credit memos are generally described on the bank statement.

Recording Deposits or Withdrawals

Each business entity keeps its accounts from its *own* point of view. As far as the bank is concerned, each customer's deposits are liabilities, in that the bank owes the customer the amount of the deposits. Using T accounts, it looks like this:

Liabilities

−	+
Debits	Credits

Deposits Payable

	−	+	
	Debits	Credits	
	Checks written	Deposits	
	Service charges	Notes	
Debit	NSF checks	collected	**Credit**
memos	ATM withdrawals	Interest income	**memos**
	Electronic	Wire transfers	
	payments made	received	

When the bank receives a cash deposit from a customer, the bank credits Deposits Payable, because it owes more to its customer. When the bank cashes a check (pays out) for a customer, the bank debits Deposits Payable, because it owes less to its customer.

The customer, on the other hand, uses the account titled Cash, or Cash in Bank, or simply the name of the bank. Deposits are recorded as debits and withdrawals are recorded as credits in the account. On a bank reconciliation, the balance of the account is listed as the **ledger balance of cash** before reconciliation with the bank statement.

CAREERS IN YOUR FUTURE

JERRY DUNN

Co-founder, Co-owner, and President of Aviation Finance Group

How do you go from reconciling bank statements to owning a company that finances private jets for high-net-worth individuals on a nationwide basis? Jerry Dunn says you apply common sense and problem-solving skills as you learn accounting rather than relying on rote memorization. He believes that the successful accounting student and businessperson must understand the "big picture" of the business transaction before applying accounting procedures and principles. In other words, you mustn't get buried in the procedures and lose sight of what the numbers mean, where they are going, and what impact they have on the business as a whole.

"The statement of cash flows is king in business along with the fundamental foundation of successful business—INTEGRITY."

Jerry believes that *cash flow is king* in business and that *integrity is essential*—beliefs shared by many successful businesses and individuals. Integrity is a fundamental foundation of a successful business. And building on these beliefs,

Jerry's career has taken an exciting path. After working on Wall Street in the finance industry, he later became an entrepreneur. Although he has never prepared financial statements, he certainly uses them almost every day. There's that solid accounting foundation and big-picture combination again; they are inseparable.

Besides selling jets to high-net-worth people, as president of the Aviation Finance Group, Jerry is responsible for the day-to-day internal operations of the company—human resources, operations, and systems. Part of that responsibility includes managing the financial health of the company. It is very hard to stay in any business without a healthy cash flow. And without his accounting and finance background, he wouldn't be able to balance the responsibilities involved with financing jets and keeping up his own company's cash flow and monetary return.

Need for Reconciling Bank Balance and Ledger Balance

OBJECTIVE 2
Reconcile a bank statement.

Since the bank statement balance and the ledger balance of cash are not equal, a business prepares a **bank reconciliation** to uncover the reasons for the difference between the two balances and to correct any errors that may have been made by either the bank or the business. This makes it possible to arrive at the same balance in each account, which is called the *adjusted balance*, or *true balance*, of the Cash account.

Because identity theft and white-collar crimes are potential problems for a business, another purpose of the bank reconciliation is to make sure all of the amounts paid out from the account are proper disbursements for the business. It is a mark of good internal control to have the bank reconciliation prepared by someone other than the check signer (if someone other than the business owner is signing checks). The person performing the bank reconciliation will be making sure (a) the dollar amount of each check has not been altered, (b) all of the charges, checks, and electronic transfers belong to the company, and (c) deposits are made in a timely way.

There are a variety of reasons for differences between the bank statement balance and the customer's cash balance. Here are some of the more common ones:

- **Deposit in transit** A deposit made after the bank statement was issued. The depositor has already added the amount to the Cash account in his or her books, but the deposit has not been recorded by the bank (this is also called a *late deposit*).
- **Outstanding checks** Checks that have been written by the company but not yet received for payment by the time the bank sends out its statement. The company employee, when preparing the checks, deducted the amounts from the Cash account in the company's books, which explains the difference.
- **Collections** Money collected by the bank for the customer. When the bank acts as a collection point for its customers by accepting payments on their behalf, it adds the proceeds to the customer's bank account and sends a credit memorandum to notify the customer of the transaction or includes it on the next bank statement.
- **Interest income** Interest earned for keeping cash in the bank account. Some checking accounts are interest bearing or earning. The depositor will not learn how much interest the bank has credited to the bank account until the bank statement is received.
- **NSF (not sufficient funds) check** A deposited check that the bank cannot process because the check writer's account does not contain enough money. When a bank customer deposits a check, it is recorded as cash on the customer's books. Occasionally, however, a check is not paid (bounces). When the bank notifies the customer of this, the customer must make a deduction from the Cash account. Simultaneously, the depositor records an increase in accounts receivable because the client's debt to the depositor remains unpaid. An NSF check may also be called a *dishonored check.*
- **Service charge** A bank charge for services rendered: for handling checks, for collecting money, for receiving payment of notes turned over to it by the customer for collection, for check printing, and for other such services. The bank immediately deducts the fee from the balance of the bank account and identifies the charges on the bank statement.
- **Errors** Mistakes made by the customer or the bank. In spite of internal controls and systems designed to double-check to prevent errors, sometimes either the customer or the bank makes a mistake. Often these errors do not become evident until the bank reconciliation is performed.

Steps in Reconciling the Bank Statement

Follow these steps to reconcile a bank statement:

1. **Canceled checks**
   a. Compare the amount of each canceled check with the bank statement and note any differences. The amount of the machine-readable characters should appear at the lower right-hand corner of the check, which should match the amount written on the check and the bank statements.
   b. In the checkbook beside the check number, list the date of the bank statement. In some cases, a bank may not pay a check until one or two months after it was written. If a question arises as to whether or not you have paid a particular bill, you can look at the checkbook. Then you can refer directly to the bank statement to pick up the accompanying canceled check as proof of payment.

Besides their core activities of providing financial transactions, many banks are actively committed to community service by supporting various causes, such as the JPMorgan Chase. The bank sponsors the JPMorgan Chase Corporate Challenge, which is run in various locations all over the world. Learn more about the race at **http://www .jpmorganchaseco.com.**

2. **Deposits**
   a. Compare the deposits in transit (not recorded by the bank at the time of the statement) listed on last month's bank reconciliation with the deposits shown on the bank statement. All of last month's deposits in transit should be listed on this month's bank statement. If they are not, notify the bank immediately.
   b. Compare the remaining deposits listed on this month's bank statement with deposits written in the company's accounting records. Consider any deposits not shown on the bank statement as deposits in transit.

3. **Outstanding checks**
   a. Arrange the canceled checks in order by check number.
   b. Look over the list of outstanding checks left over from last month's bank reconciliation, and note the checks that have now been returned or cleared.
   c. For each canceled check, compare the amount recorded in MICR numbers at the lower right-hand corner of the check with the amount recorded in the checkbook. Next, compare the canceled check with the numerical listing in the statement. Use a check mark (✓) to indicate that the check has been paid and that the amount is correct. Any payments that have not been marked off, including the outstanding checks from last month's bank reconciliation, are the present outstanding checks.
   d. Review the endorsements on the backs of the checks to verify that money has been sent to the correct payee.

4. **Bank memoranda** Trace the credit memos and debit memos to the journal. If the memos have not been recorded, make separate entries for them.

For businesses that have computerized check registers, the bank reconciliation can also be done on the computer. The procedures are similar as there is still the need to compare canceled checks, compare deposits, identify outstanding checks and deposits, and record adjustments.

The Check Clearing for the 21st Century Act (Check 21), a federal law that became effective in 2004, enables banks to create a new negotiable instrument called a *substitute check*. Substitute checks, which are special paper copies of the front and back of the original checks, are easily converted into an electronic form that can be processed quickly and inexpensively. The banks are also allowed to return copies of substitute checks rather than original checks with the bank statement. The Federal Reserve's website (**http://www .federalreserve.gov/pubs/check21/consumer_guide.htm**) provides more information about Check 21.

Examples of Bank Reconciliations

Let's go through the reconciliation process for two businesses, M. K. Young Company and Bay Cleaners.

M. K. Young Company   The bank statement of M. K. Young Company indicates a balance of $6,357 as of March 31. The balance of the Cash account in Young's ledger as of that date is $4,656. Young's accountant has taken the following steps:

1. Verified that canceled checks were recorded correctly on the bank statement.
2. Noted that the deposit made on March 31 was not recorded on the bank statement, $2,286.
3. Noted outstanding checks: no. 921, $1,878; no. 985, $207; no. 986, $1,314.
4. Noted credit memo: note collected by the bank from T. Chang, $600, not recorded in the journal.
5. Noted debit memo: collection charge and service charge not recorded in the journal, $12.

The note received from T. Chang is called a promissory note. A **promissory note** is a written promise to pay a definite amount at a definite future time. Let's assume that M. K. Young Company received the sixty-day non-interest-bearing note from T. Chang for services performed. In recording the transaction, Young's accountant debited Notes Receivable and credited Income from Services. (The account Notes Receivable is similar to Accounts Receivable. However, Accounts Receivable is reserved for customer charge accounts, with payments usually due in thirty days.) Next, M. K. Young Company turned the note over to its bank for collection.

The bank will use a credit memo form to notify M. K. Young Company that the note has been collected and that the company's bank account has been increased by the amount of the note. Based on the credit memo, Young's accountant will make a journal entry debiting Cash and crediting Notes Receivable.

Think of the bank reconciliation in terms of the following:

1. Bring the bank statement balance up to date by recording the events that we knew about but the bank did not know about when it prepared the statement (deposits in transit and outstanding checks as shown in our checkbook, for example).
2. Bring the balance of the Cash account up to date by recording the events that the bank knew about but we did not know about until we received the statement (debit memos and credit memos as shown on the bank statement, for example).

Figure 8 shows M. K. Young Company's bank reconciliation. The items in the reconciliation that require journal entries are shown in color, and the entries are shown below.

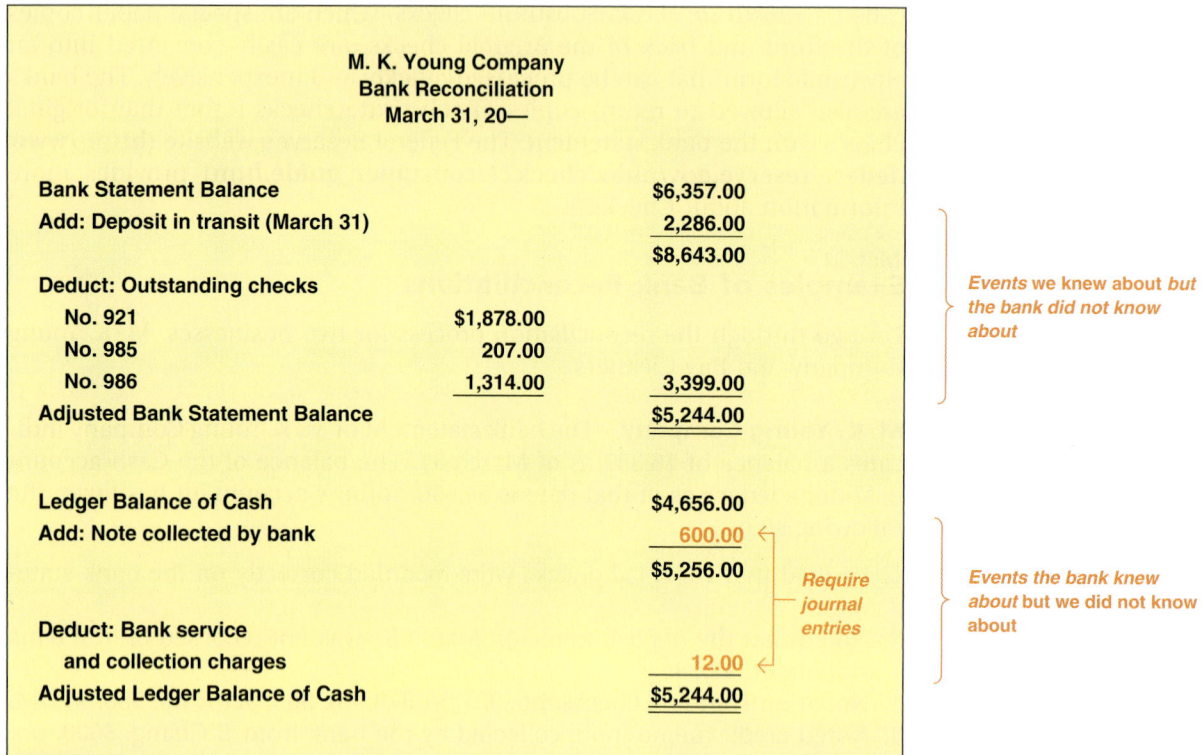

M. K. Young Company
Bank Reconciliation
March 31, 20—

Bank Statement Balance		$6,357.00
Add: Deposit in transit (March 31)		2,286.00
		$8,643.00
Deduct: Outstanding checks		
No. 921	$1,878.00	
No. 985	207.00	
No. 986	1,314.00	3,399.00
Adjusted Bank Statement Balance		$5,244.00
Ledger Balance of Cash		$4,656.00
Add: Note collected by bank		600.00
		$5,256.00
Deduct: Bank service		
and collection charges		12.00
Adjusted Ledger Balance of Cash		$5,244.00

Events we knew about but the bank did not know about

Require journal entries

Events the bank knew about but we did not know about

FIGURE 8

OBJECTIVE 3

Record the required journal entries from the bank reconciliation.

Note that the journal entries are based on the items used to adjust the ledger balance of Cash. These items represent the transactions that the bank has knowledge of but the business does not. According to the bank reconciliation, the true balance of Cash is $5,244, which is the balance we wish to show on the business's books. We can't change the balance of an account unless we first make a journal entry and then post the entry to the accounts involved. **Consequently, we have to make journal entries for items in the Ledger Balance of Cash section of the bank reconciliation.** The additions are debited to the Cash account, and the deductions are credited to the Cash account. M. K. Young Company records the entries in its general journal:

	GENERAL JOURNAL		PAGE _____	
DATE	DESCRIPTION	POST. REF.	DEBIT	CREDIT
20—				
Mar. 31	Cash		6 0 0 00	
	Notes Receivable			6 0 0 00
	Non-interest-bearing note			
	signed by T. Chang was			
	collected by the bank.			
31	Miscellaneous Expense		1 2 00	
	Cash			1 2 00
	Service charge and collection			
	charge levied by bank.			

Here bank service and collection charges are recorded in Miscellaneous Expense because the amounts are relatively small. Some accountants may use a separate expense account, such as Bank Charge Expense. After the entries have been posted, the T account for Cash looks like this:

Cash

Balance	4,656	Mar. 31	12
Mar. 31	600		
Bal.	**5,244**		

Note that the balance in the T account is now equal to both the adjusted bank statement balance and the adjusted ledger balance of cash.

Form of Bank Reconciliation

Now that you have seen an example of a bank reconciliation, let's look at the standard form of a bank reconciliation for an imaginary company.

Bank Statement Balance (last figure on the statement)		$4,000
Add		
Deposits in transit (deposits made after the bank statement was issued and already added to the ledger balance of Cash)	$300	
Bank errors (that understate balance)	20	320
		$4,320
Deduct		
Outstanding checks and transfers (they have already been deducted from the Cash account)	$960	
Bank errors (that overstate balance)	40	1,000
Adjusted Bank Statement Balance (the true balance of Cash)		$3,320
Ledger Balance of Cash (the latest balance of the Cash account if it has been posted up to date; otherwise take the beginning balance of Cash, plus cash receipts, minus cash payments)		$2,850
Add		
Credit memos (additions by the bank not recorded in the Cash account, such as collections of notes)	$500	
Book errors (that understate balance)	40	540
		$3,390
Deduct		
Debit memos (deductions by the bank not recorded in the Cash account, such as service charges or collection charges and NSF checks)	$ 20	
Book errors (that overstate balance)	50	70
Adjusted Ledger Balance of Cash (the true balance of Cash)		$3,320

Bay Cleaners The bank statement of Bay Cleaners shows a final balance of $13,449 as of October 31 (see Figure 7). The present balance of the Cash account in the ledger, after Bay Cleaners' accountant has posted from the journal, is $12,495.50. The accountant took the following steps:

1. Verified that canceled checks were recorded correctly on the bank statement.
2. Discovered that a deposit of $1,955 made on October 31 was not recorded on the bank statement.
3. Noted outstanding checks: no. 1916, $692; no. 2022, $179; no. 2023, $1,241; no. 2024, $101.
4. Noted that a credit memo for a note collected by the bank from Lee and Camara, $900 principal plus $9 interest, was not recorded in the journal.
5. Found that check no. 2001 for $845, payable to Dennis, Inc., on account, was recorded in the journal as $854. (The correct amount is $845.)
6. Noted that a debit memo for a collection charge and service charge of $9.50 was not recorded in the journal.
7. Noted that a debit memo for an NSF check for $193 from A. L. Sanders was not recorded.
8. Noted that a $20 personal withdrawal by Paula C. Boyd, the owner, using an ATM, was not recorded.

Look at Figure 9 to see how each step relates to the bank reconciliation.

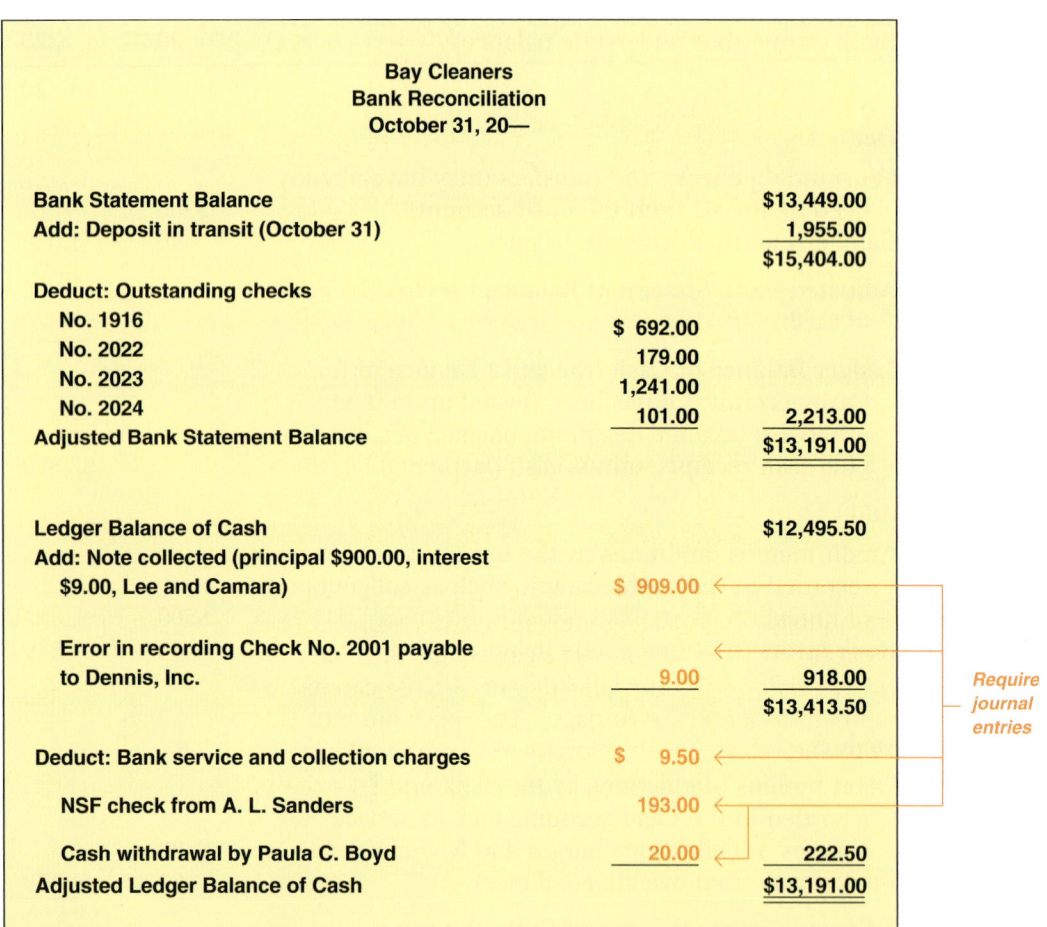

Bay Cleaners		
Bank Reconciliation		
October 31, 20—		
Bank Statement Balance		$13,449.00
Add: Deposit in transit (October 31)		1,955.00
		$15,404.00
Deduct: Outstanding checks		
No. 1916	$ 692.00	
No. 2022	179.00	
No. 2023	1,241.00	
No. 2024	101.00	2,213.00
Adjusted Bank Statement Balance		$13,191.00
Ledger Balance of Cash		$12,495.50
Add: Note collected (principal $900.00, interest		
$9.00, Lee and Camara)	$ 909.00	
Error in recording Check No. 2001 payable		
to Dennis, Inc.	9.00	918.00
		$13,413.50
Deduct: Bank service and collection charges	$ 9.50	
NSF check from A. L. Sanders	193.00	
Cash withdrawal by Paula C. Boyd	20.00	222.50
Adjusted Ledger Balance of Cash		$13,191.00

Require journal entries

FIGURE 9

FIGURE 10

DATE		DESCRIPTION	POST. REF.	DEBIT	CREDIT
20—					
Oct.	31	Cash		9 0 9 00	
		Notes Receivable			9 0 0 00
		Interest Income			9 00
		Bank collected note signed			
		by Lee and Camara.			
	31	Cash		9 00	
		Accounts Payable			9 00
		Error in recording Ck. No.			
		2001 payable to Dennis, Inc.			
	31	Miscellaneous Expense		9 50	
		Cash			9 50
		Bank service charge and			
		collection charge.			
	31	Accounts Receivable		1 9 3 00	
		Cash			1 9 3 00
		NSF check received from			
		A. L. Sanders.			
	31	P. C. Boyd, Drawing		2 0 00	
		Cash			2 0 00
		Withdrawal for personal use.			

GENERAL JOURNAL   PAGE ____

The accountant makes journal entries for the items indicated in Figure 9 to change the balance of the Cash account from its present balance of $12,495.50 to the true balance of $13,191.00. Again, those items that require journal entries are highlighted in Figure 9 and shown in Figure 10.

The account Interest Income is classified as a revenue account. It represents the amount received on the promissory note that is over and above the face value of the note.

As for the NSF check, upon being notified by the bank, Bay Cleaners calls its customer (A. L. Sanders). Sanders can now take steps to cover the check. Review Bay Cleaners' transaction with A. L. Sanders. In return for service provided, Bay Cleaners received Sanders's check for $193. At that time, Bay Cleaners' accountant recorded the transaction as a debit to Cash for $193 and a credit to Income from Services for $193. Then the bank, through its debit memorandum, notified Bay Cleaners about Sanders's NSF check. To avoid overdrawing its own bank account, Bay Cleaners makes an entry crediting Cash (to correct its earlier debit to Cash) and debiting Accounts Receivable (to put the amount into Accounts Receivable). Since A. L. Sanders owes the money, it is logical to add the amount to Accounts Receivable.

A bank reconciliation form is ordinarily printed on the back of the bank statement. The adjusted balance of the ledger balance of cash has already been determined. Consequently, the bank form is provided only for calculating the adjusted bank statement balance of the bank reconciliation. The bank form for Bay Cleaners is shown in Figure 11 on page 238.

REMEMBER!

When you are reconciling a bank statement, always double-check for any outstanding checks or deposits from previous statements that have been carried forward. Also double-check for any bank service charges.

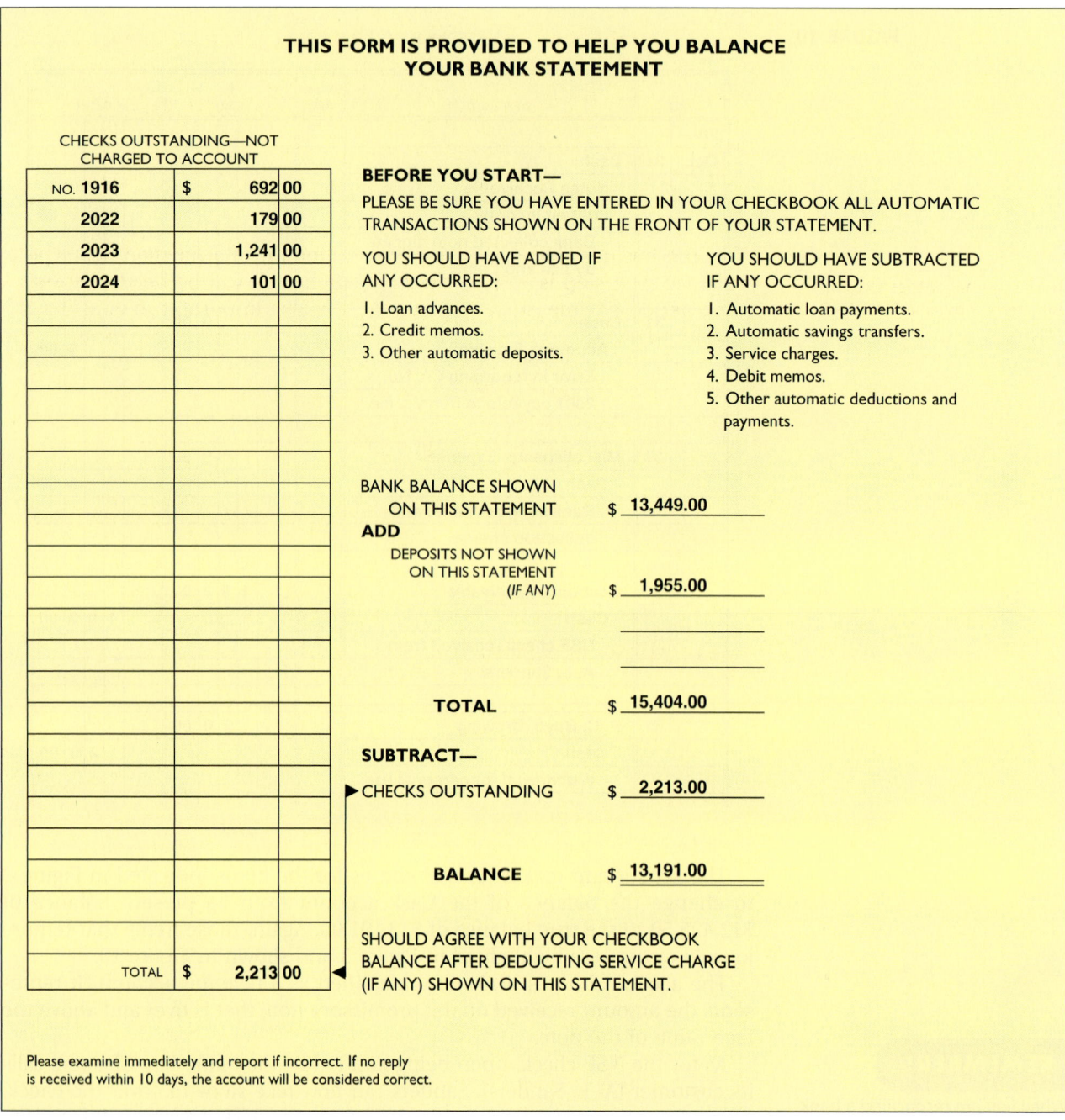

**THIS FORM IS PROVIDED TO HELP YOU BALANCE
YOUR BANK STATEMENT**

CHECKS OUTSTANDING—NOT
CHARGED TO ACCOUNT

NO. 1916	$	692	00
2022		179	00
2023		1,241	00
2024		101	00
TOTAL	$	2,213	00

BEFORE YOU START—

PLEASE BE SURE YOU HAVE ENTERED IN YOUR CHECKBOOK ALL AUTOMATIC TRANSACTIONS SHOWN ON THE FRONT OF YOUR STATEMENT.

YOU SHOULD HAVE ADDED IF ANY OCCURRED:

1. Loan advances.
2. Credit memos.
3. Other automatic deposits.

YOU SHOULD HAVE SUBTRACTED IF ANY OCCURRED:

1. Automatic loan payments.
2. Automatic savings transfers.
3. Service charges.
4. Debit memos.
5. Other automatic deductions and payments.

BANK BALANCE SHOWN
ON THIS STATEMENT $ 13,449.00
ADD

DEPOSITS NOT SHOWN
ON THIS STATEMENT
(IF ANY) $ 1,955.00

TOTAL $ 15,404.00

SUBTRACT—

►CHECKS OUTSTANDING $ 2,213.00

BALANCE $ 13,191.00

SHOULD AGREE WITH YOUR CHECKBOOK
BALANCE AFTER DEDUCTING SERVICE CHARGE
(IF ANY) SHOWN ON THIS STATEMENT.

Please examine immediately and report if incorrect. If no reply
is received within 10 days, the account will be considered correct.

FIGURE 11

THE PETTY CASH FUND

Day after day, businesses are confronted with transactions requiring small immediate payments, such as paying for delivery charges, birthday cards, or pizza for after-hours workers. If the business had to make all payments by check, the time consumed would be frustrating and the whole process would be unduly expensive. For many businesses, the cost of writing each check is more than $10; this includes the cost of an employee's time for writing and reconciling the check. Suppose you buy five stamps from an employee for $1.95, and you want to reimburse her. To write a check would not be practical. It only makes sense to pay in cash, using the **Petty Cash Fund**. *Petty* means "small," so the business sets a maximum amount that can be paid immediately out of petty cash. Payments that exceed this maximum must be processed by regular check through the journal.

Establishing the Petty Cash Fund

OBJECTIVE 4

Record journal entries to establish and reimburse a Petty Cash Fund.

After the business has set the maximum amount of a payment from petty cash, the next step is to estimate how much cash will be needed during a given period of time, such as a month. It is also important to consider the element of security when keeping cash in the office. If the risk is great, the amount kept in the fund should be small. Bay Cleaners decides to establish a Petty Cash Fund of $100 and put it under the control of the assistant. Accordingly, Bay Cleaners' accountant writes a check, cashes it at the bank, and records this transaction in the journal as follows:

					GENERAL JOURNAL				PAGE ____		
	DATE		DESCRIPTION	POST. REF.		DEBIT			CREDIT		
1	20—										1
2	Sept.	1	Petty Cash Fund			1 0 0 00					2
3			Cash						1 0 0 00		3
4			Established a Petty Cash								4
5			Fund, Ck. No. 1880.								5

T accounts for the entry look like this:

Petty Cash Fund		Cash	
+	−	+	−
100			100

Because the Petty Cash Fund is an asset account, it is listed on the balance sheet immediately below Cash.

Once the fund has been created, it is not debited again unless the original amount is not large enough to handle the necessary transactions. In that case, the accountant has to increase the Petty Cash Fund—perhaps from $100 to $200. **But, if no change is made in the size of the fund, Petty Cash Fund is debited only once.**

The check is written to the assistant, "Maria Ruiz, Petty Cash Fund." She converts it into convenient **denominations**, which are varieties of coins and currency, such as quarters and dimes and $1 and $5 bills. Then the assistant puts the money in a locked drawer and will not pay anything larger than $20 (or whatever is the agreed-upon amount) out of petty cash.

REMEMBER!

The Petty Cash Fund account is debited only once, and this happens when the fund is first established.

Payments from the Petty Cash Fund

OBJECTIVE 5

Complete petty cash vouchers and petty cash payments records.

The assistant is designated as the only person who can make payments from the Petty Cash Fund. In case of her illness, another employee should be named as stand-in. A **petty cash voucher** must be used to account for every payment from the fund. The voucher constitutes a receipt signed by the person who authorized the payment and by the person who received payment as well as the purpose of the payment. Thus, even for small payments of $20 or less, there would have to be collusion between the payee and the assistant for any theft to occur. Figure 12 is a petty cash voucher.

FIGURE 12

PETTY CASH VOUCHER

No. __1__   Date __September 2, 20—__

Paid to __Mark Delivery Service__ $ __10.00__

For __Delivery__

Account __Delivery Expense__

Approved by   *Payment received by*

M. Ruiz   D. Stanton

Petty Cash Payments Record

Some businesses prefer to have a written record on one sheet of paper, so they keep a **petty cash payments record**. In a petty cash payments record,

FIGURE 13

Petty Cash Payments Record
Month of September 20—

	DATE	VOU. NO.	EXPLANATION	PAYMENTS	OFFICE SUPPLIES EXPENSE	
1	Sept. 1		Establish fund, Ck. No. 1880, $100			
2	2	1	Mark Delivery Service	1 0 00		
3	3	2	Pencils and pens	4 59	4 59	
4	5	3	Local newspapers	2 00		
5	7	4	Postage on incoming packages	3 70		
6	10	5	Paula C. Boyd	2 0 00		
7	14	6	Reimburse employee for stamps	1 95		
8	21	7	Stick-on tabs	4 10	4 10	
9	22	8	Mark Delivery Service	1 4 00		
10	26	9	Postage for mailings	3 60		
11	27	10	Fast Way Delivery	9 00		
12	29	11	Memo pads	4 40	4 40	
13	29	12	Making duplicate keys	3 19		
14	30	13	Mark Delivery Service	8 20		
15	30	14	Trash removal	5 00		
16	30		Totals	9 3 73	1 3 09	
17			Balance in Fund $ 6.27			
18			Reimburse fund, Ck. No. 1926 93.73			
19			Total $100.00			
20						
21						

petty cash vouchers and the accounts that are to be charged are listed as well as the purpose of the expenditure. Special columns for frequent types of expenditures are included in the Distribution of Payments section. The petty cash payments record is not a journal.

Bay Cleaners made the following payments from its Petty Cash Fund during September:

Sept. 2   Paid $10 to Mark Delivery Service, voucher no. 1.
    3   Bought pencils and pens, $4.59, voucher no. 2.
    5   Bought local newspapers for article related to Bay Cleaners, $2, voucher no. 3.
    7   Paid postage on incoming packages, $3.70, voucher no. 4.
    10 Paula C. Boyd, the owner, withdrew $20 for personal use, voucher no. 5.
    14 Reimbursed employee for stamps, $1.95, voucher no. 6.
    21 Bought stick-on tabs, $4.10, voucher no. 7.
    22 Paid $14 to Mark Delivery Service, voucher no. 8.
    26 Paid for mailing packages, $3.60, voucher no. 9.
    27 Paid $9 to Fast Way Delivery, voucher no. 10.
    29 Bought memo pads, $4.40, voucher no. 11.
    29 Paid for making duplicate keys, $3.19, voucher no. 12.
    30 Paid $8.20 to Mark Delivery Service, voucher no. 13.
    30 Paid for trash removal, $5, voucher no. 14.

Figure 13 below shows how these payments are recorded.

PAGE ___1___

		DISTRIBUTION OF PAYMENTS			
DELIVERY EXPENSE	MISCELLANEOUS EXPENSE	OTHER ACCOUNTS			
		ACCOUNT		AMOUNT	
					1
10 00					2
					3
	2 00				4
3 70					5
		P. C. Boyd, Drawing		20 00	6
	1 95				7
					8
14 00					9
3 60					10
9 00					11
					12
	3 19				13
8 20					14
	5 00				15
48 50	12 14			20 00	16
					17
					18
					19
					20
					21

A petty cash fund is an effective and efficient way to deal with small cash payments that need to be made immediately. These caterers, delivering food for an office party, can be paid on the spot, saving their own company the expense of billing and the recipient the expense of writing a check.

Reimbursement of the Petty Cash Fund

To bring the fund back up to the original amount when it is nearly exhausted (for instance, at the end of the month), the accountant reimburses the fund for expenditures made. Consequently, the Petty Cash Fund may be considered a revolving fund. If the amount initially put in the Petty Cash Fund is $100 and at the end of the month only $6.27 is left, the accountant puts $93.73 in the fund as a reimbursement, thereby bringing the fund back up to $100 to start the new month.

Bear in mind that the petty cash payments record is only a supplementary record for gathering information. A less formal way of compiling the information concerning petty cash payments might consist of collecting one month's petty cash vouchers, then sorting them by accounts, such as Office Supplies Expense, Delivery Expense, and the like. Then run a calculator tape for each account. At the end of the month, the accountant makes a summarizing entry to officially journalize the transactions that have taken place. The journal and T accounts of Bay Cleaners are shown below.

Note that, in the summarizing entry, the accountant debits the accounts for which the payments were made and credits the Cash account. No entry is made to the Petty Cash Fund account alone. Then the assistant cashes a check for $93.73 and puts the cash in a locked place, thereby restoring the amount in the Petty Cash Fund to the original $100.

REMEMBER!

The petty cash payments record is not a journal; it is simply used as a basis for compiling information for the journal entry. Remember, to change an account, we have to make a journal entry.

GENERAL JOURNAL PAGE _____

	DATE		DESCRIPTION	POST. REF.	DEBIT	CREDIT	
1	20—						1
2	Sept.	30	Office Supplies Expense		1 3 09		2
3			Delivery Expense		4 8 50		3
4			Miscellaneous Expense		1 2 14		4
5			P. C. Boyd, Drawing		2 0 00		5
6			Cash			9 3 73	6
7			Reimbursed the Petty Cash				7
8			Fund, Ck. No. 1926.				8
9							9
10							10

Cash		P. C. Boyd, Drawing		Miscellaneous Expense	
+	−	+	−	+	−
	93.73		20.00		12.14

Office Supplies Expense		Delivery Expense	
+	−	+	−
	13.09		48.50

THE CHANGE FUND

Anyone who has tried to pay for a small item with a $20 bill knows that any business that carries out numerous cash transactions needs a **Change Fund**.

Establishing the Change Fund

OBJECTIVE 6

Record the journal entries to establish a Change Fund.

Before setting up a Change Fund, you have to decide two things: (1) how much money needs to be in the fund, and (2) what denominations of bills and coins are needed. Like the Petty Cash Fund, **the Change Fund is debited only once: when it is established.** It is left at the initial figure unless the person in charge decides to make it larger. The Change Fund account, like the Petty Cash Fund account, is an asset. It is recorded in the balance sheet immediately below Cash. If the Petty Cash Fund account is larger than the Change Fund account, it precedes the Change Fund.

The owner of Bay Cleaners, Paula C. Boyd, decides to establish a Change Fund; she decides this at the same time she sets up the company's Petty Cash Fund. The entries for the two transactions look like this:

GENERAL JOURNAL   PAGE _____

	DATE		DESCRIPTION	POST. REF.	DEBIT	CREDIT	
1	20—						1
2	Sept.	1	Petty Cash Fund		1 0 0 00		2
3			Cash			1 0 0 00	3
4			Established a Petty Cash Fund.				4
5							5
6		1	Change Fund		1 5 0 00		6
7			Cash			1 5 0 00	7
8			Established a Change Fund.				8
9							9

The T accounts for establishing the Change Fund are as follows:

Change Fund	Cash
+ | −	+ | −
150 |	| 150

Boyd cashes a check for $150 and gets the money in several denominations. She is now prepared to make change for any normal business transactions.

Depositing Cash

At the end of each business day, Bay Cleaners' accountant deposits the cash taken in during the day but holds back the amount of the Change Fund, being sure that it is in convenient denominations. Let's say that on September 1, Bay Cleaners had $1,475 on hand at the end of the day.

$1,475 Total cash count
−   150 Change Fund
─────
$1,325 New cash deposit

The T accounts look like this:

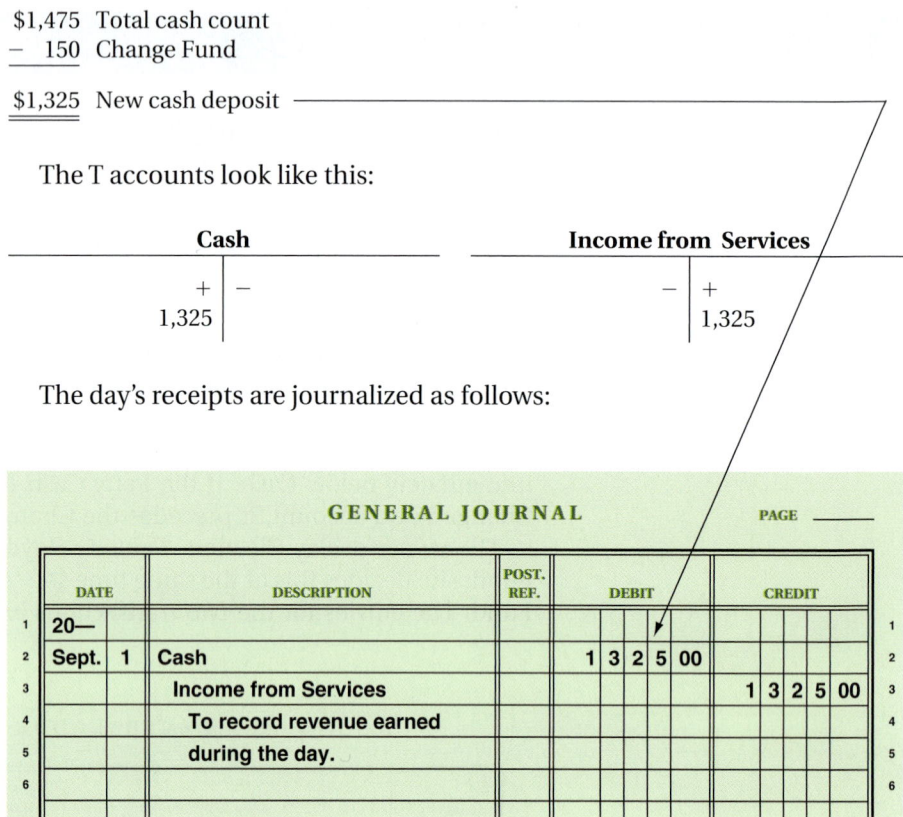

Cash			Income from Services		
+	−		−	+	
1,325				1,325	

The day's receipts are journalized as follows:

GENERAL JOURNAL   PAGE _____

	DATE		DESCRIPTION	POST. REF.	DEBIT	CREDIT	
1	20—						1
2	Sept.	1	Cash		1 3 2 5 00		2
3			Income from Services			1 3 2 5 00	3
4			To record revenue earned				4
5			during the day.				5
6							6

The amount of the cash deposit is the total cash count less the amount of the Change Fund. This should be equal to the income earned.

On September 9, the cash count is $1,583. So the accountant deposits $1,433 ($1,583 − $150). Bay Cleaners' accountant makes the following entry to record the day's receipts:

GENERAL JOURNAL   PAGE _____

	DATE		DESCRIPTION	POST. REF.	DEBIT	CREDIT	
1	20—						1
2	Sept.	9	Cash		1 4 3 3 00		2
3			Income from Services			1 4 3 3 00	3
4			To record revenue earned				4
5			during the day.				5
6							6

Some businesses label the Cash account *Cash in Bank* and label the Change Fund *Cash on Hand.*

CASH SHORT AND OVER

OBJECTIVE 7

Record journal entries for transactions involving Cash Short and Over.

FYI

The Cash Short and Over account may also be used to handle shortages and overages in the Petty Cash Fund.

FYI

Like the Income Summary account, which has no normal balance, the Cash Short and Over account has no signs.

There is an inherent danger in making change: Human beings make mistakes, especially when there are many customers to be waited on or when the business is temporarily short-handed. Because mistakes do happen, accounting records must be set up to cope with the situation. One reason that a business uses a cash register is to detect mistakes in handling cash. **If, after removing the Change Fund, the day's receipts are less than the register reading, then a cash shortage exists. Conversely, when the day's receipts are greater than the register reading, a cash overage exists.** Both shortages and overages are recorded in the same account, which is called Cash Short and Over. Shortages are considered an expense of operating a business, and therefore shortages are recorded on the debit side of the account. Overages are treated as another form of revenue, and therefore overages are recorded on the credit side of the account.

Let's say that on September 14, Bay Cleaners is faced with the following situation:

Cash Register Tape	Cash Count	Amount of the Change Fund
$1,515	$1,661	$150

After deducting the $150 in the Change Fund, Boyd will deposit $1,511 ($1,661 − $150). Note that this amount is $4 less than the amount indicated by the cash register ($1,515 − $1,511); therefore, a $4 cash shortage exists. The following T accounts show how the accountant entered this transaction into the books:

Cash		Income from Services		Cash Short and Over	
+	−	−	+		
1,511			1,515	4	

The next day, September 15, the pendulum happens to swing in the other direction:

Cash Register Tape	Cash Count	Amount of the Change Fund
$1,574	$1,726	$150

The amount to be deposited is $1,576 ($1,726 − $150). This figure is $2 greater than the $1,574 in income from services indicated by the cash register tape. Thus, there is a $2 cash overage ($1,576 − $1,574). The analysis of this transaction is shown in the following T accounts:

Cash		Income from Services		Cash Short and Over	
+	−	−	+		
1,576			1,574		2

Bay Cleaners' revenue for September 14 and 15 is recorded in the general journal as follows:

	DATE		DESCRIPTION	POST. REF.	DEBIT	CREDIT	
1	20—						1
2	Sept.	14	Cash		1 5 1 1 00		2
3			Cash Short and Over		4 00		3
4			Income from Services			1 5 1 5 00	4
5			To record revenue earned				5
6			for the day involving a				6
7			cash shortage of $4.				7
8							8
9		15	Cash		1 5 7 6 00		9
10			Income from Services			1 5 7 4 00	10
11			Cash Short and Over			2 00	11
12			To record revenue earned				12
13			during the day involving a				13
14			cash overage of $2.				14

GENERAL JOURNAL   PAGE _____

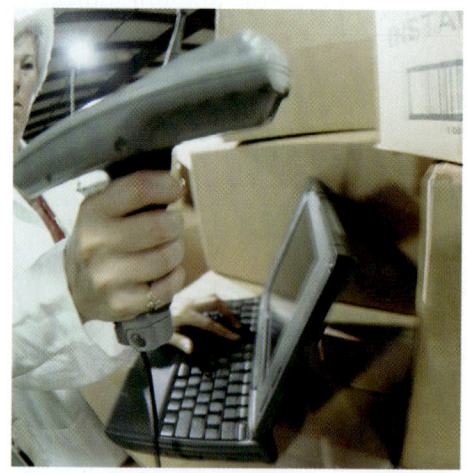

A scanner can speed customer checkout or taking inventory of goods still on the shelves. The scanner, however, is only as accurate as the amount for each item entered in the computer.

As far as errors are concerned, one would think that shortages would be offset by overages. However, customers receiving change are more likely to report shortages than overages. **Consequently, the business usually experiences a greater number of shortages.** A business may set a tolerance level for the cashiers. If the shortages consistently exceed the level of tolerance, either fraud is being committed or somebody is making entirely too many careless mistakes.

Now let's summarize our discussion of the Cash Short and Over account by drawing the following conclusions from the illustration:

1. At the close of the business day, the business deposits the difference between the amount in the cash drawer and the amount in the Change Fund.
2. The business records the amount shown on the cash register tape as its income from services.
3. If the amount of the cash deposit disagrees with the record of receipts, Cash Short and Over makes up the difference. In the first situation just described, there was a shortage of $4, and so there was a debit to Cash Short and Over. In the second situation, there was an overage of $2, and so there was a credit to Cash Short and Over. It is apparent that, as a result of these transactions, the account looks like this:

Cash Short and Over		
Shortage	4	2	Overage

Throughout any fiscal period, the accountant must continually record shortages and overages in the Cash Short and Over account. Let's say that

Bay Cleaners' final balance is $21 on the debit side. Bay Cleaners winds up with a net shortage of $21.

At the end of the fiscal period, **if the account has a debit balance or net shortage, the accountant classifies it as an expense and credits Cash Short and Over and debits Miscellaneous Expense, so that the amount is put in the income statement under Miscellaneous Expense.** The T account would look like this:

Cash Short and Over

Shortage	4	2	Overage	
	4	1		
	3	2		
	7	2		
	5	1		
	2	2		
	3	1		
	4			
Bal.	**21**			

Conversely, **if the account has a credit balance or net overage, the accountant classifies it as a revenue account and debits Cash Short and Over and credits Miscellaneous Income, so that the amount is put in the income statement under Miscellaneous Income.** This is an exception to the policy of recording accounts under their exact account title in financial statements. Rather than attaching plus and minus signs to the Cash Short and Over account immediately, we wait until we find out its final balance, then make a journal entry to send the balance to the correct account classification.

CHAPTER REVIEW

Online Study Center
ACE the test!

Review of Performance Objectives

1. Describe the procedure for depositing checks.

   The procedure for depositing checks consists of first endorsing each check and then completing a deposit slip. On the deposit slip, record the date, the amount of currency to be deposited, the amount and ABA number of each check, and the total amount to be deposited. The checks to be deposited should accompany the deposit slip.

2. Reconcile a bank statement.

   The standard form for a bank reconciliation is as follows:

   Bank Statement Balance

   Add

   Deposits in transit
   Bank errors that understate bank statement balance

   Deduct

   Outstanding checks or electronic transfers
   Bank errors that overstate bank statement balance

   Adjusted Bank Statement Balance

Ledger Balance of Cash

Add

Notes collected
Interest income earned
Checkbook errors that understate the ledger balance of cash
Bank credit memos

Deduct

Bank service charges
Checkbook errors that overstate the ledger balance of cash
NSF checks
Bank debit memos

Adjusted Ledger Balance of Cash

3. **Record the required journal entries from the bank reconciliation.**

   Journal entries for the Ledger Balance of Cash section are required. The entry for notes and interest collected is a debit to Cash and credits to Notes Receivable and Interest Income. The entry for a bank service charge is a debit to Miscellaneous Expense and a credit to Cash. The entry for an NSF check is a debit to Accounts Receivable and a credit to Cash.

4. **Record journal entries to establish and reimburse a Petty Cash Fund.**

   The entry to establish a Petty Cash Fund is a debit to Petty Cash Fund and a credit to Cash. The entry to reimburse the Petty Cash Fund consists of debits to the items for which payments from the Petty Cash Fund were made and one credit to Cash for the total payments.

5. **Complete petty cash vouchers and petty cash payments records.**

   A petty cash voucher is made out for each payment from the Petty Cash Fund. In the petty cash payments record, each voucher is listed and a notation is made concerning the accounts involved; also, an explanation of why the money was paid out is recorded. The petty cash payments record is used as a source of information for making the journal entry to reimburse the Petty Cash Fund.

6. **Record the journal entries to establish a Change Fund.**

   The entry to establish the Change Fund is a debit to Change Fund and a credit to Cash.

7. **Record journal entries for transactions involving Cash Short and Over.**

   The Cash Short and Over account provides a way to keep a record of errors in making change. A debit balance in Cash Short and Over denotes a shortage, which is listed as Miscellaneous Expense; the entry is a debit to Miscellaneous Expense and a credit to Cash Short and Over. A credit balance in Cash Short and Over denotes an overage, which becomes Miscellaneous Income; the entry is a debit to Cash Short and Over and a credit to Miscellaneous Income.

Glossary

ABA number The number assigned by the American Bankers Association to a given bank. The first part of the numerator denotes the city or state in which the bank is located; the second part denotes the bank on which the check is drawn. The denominator indicates the Federal Reserve District in which the check is cleared and the routing number used by the Federal Reserve Bank. (224)

ATM (automated teller machine) A machine that enables depositors to make deposits, withdrawals, and transfers using a coded plastic card. (224)

Bank reconciliation A process by which an accountant determines whether and why there is a difference between the balance shown on the bank statement and the balance of the Cash account in the business's general ledger. The object is to determine the adjusted (or true) balance of the Cash account. (230)

Bank statement A periodic statement that a bank sends to the drawer/depositor of a checking account listing deposits received and checks paid by the bank, debit and credit memos, electronic transactions, and beginning and ending balances. (227)

Blank endorsement An endorsement in which the holder (payee) of a check simply signs her or his name on the back of the check. There are no restrictions attached. (226)

Canceled checks Checks issued by the depositor that have been paid (cleared) by the bank and listed on the bank statement. They are called canceled checks because they are canceled by a stamp or perforation, indicating that they have been paid. (229)

Cash funds Separately held reserves of cash set aside for specific purposes. (223)

Change Fund A cash fund used by a business to make change for customers who pay cash for goods or services. (243)

Collections Payments collected by the bank and added to the customer's bank account in the form of a credit memorandum. (231)

Denominations Varieties of coins and currency, such as quarters, dimes, and nickels and $1 and $5 bills and so on. (239)

Deposit in transit A deposit not recorded on the bank statement because the deposit was made between the time of the bank's closing date for compiling items for its statement and the time the statement is received by the depositor; also known as a *late deposit*. (231)

Deposit slips Printed forms provided by a bank on which customers can list all items being deposited; also known as *deposit tickets*. (224)

Drawer The party who writes the check. (226)

Electronic Funds Transfer (EFT) A transfer of funds initiated through an electronic terminal, such as a telephone, computer, or magnetic tape. (225)

Endorsement The process by which the payee transfers ownership of the check to a bank or another party. A check must be endorsed when deposited in a bank, because the bank must have legal title to it in order to collect payment from the drawer of the check (the person or firm who wrote the check). In case the check cannot be collected, the endorser guarantees all subsequent holders (*exception:* an endorsement "without recourse"). (225)

Interest income The amount earned from lending money to another person or business. (231)

Internal control Plans and procedures built into the accounting system with the following objectives: (1) to protect assets against fraud and waste; (2) to provide accurate accounting data; (3) to promote an efficient operation; and (4) to encourage adherence to management policies. (222)

Ledger balance of cash The balance of the Cash account in the general ledger before it is reconciled with the bank statement. (229)

MICR Magnetic ink character recognition; the characters the bank uses to print the number of the depositor's account and the bank's number at the bottom of checks and deposit slips. The bank also prints the amount of the check in MICR when the check is deposited. A number written in these characters can be read by electronic equipment used by banks in clearing checks. (224)

NSF (not sufficient funds) checks Checks drawn against an account in which there are *not sufficient funds* and returned by the payee's bank to the drawer's bank because of nonpayment; also known as *dishonored checks*. (231)

Outstanding checks Checks that have been written by the drawer and deducted on his or her records but have not reached the bank for payment and are not deducted from the bank balance by the time the bank issues its statement. (231)

Payee The person to whom a check is payable. (226)

Petty Cash Fund A cash fund used to make small, immediate cash payments. (239)

Petty cash payments record A record indicating the amount of each petty cash voucher, the accounts to which it should be charged, and the purpose of the expenditure. (240)

Petty cash voucher A form stating who requested cash from the Petty Cash Fund, signed by (1) the person in charge of the fund and (2) the person who received the cash, and indicating the purpose of the petty cash payment. (240)

Promissory note A written promise to pay a definite sum at a definite future time. (233)

Qualified endorsement An endorsement in which the holder (payee) of a check avoids future liability, in case the drawer of the check does not have sufficient funds to cover the check, by adding the words "Pay to the order of" and "without recourse" to the endorsement on the back of the check. (226)

Restrictive endorsement An endorsement, such as "Pay to the order of (name of bank), for deposit only," that restricts or limits any further negotiation of a check. It forces the check's deposit, because the endorsement is not valid for any other purpose. (225)

Service charge The fee the bank charges for handling checks, collections, and other items. It is in the form of a debit memorandum. (231)

Signature card The form a depositor signs to give the bank a copy of the official signatures of any persons authorized to sign checks. The bank can use it to verify the depositors' signatures on checks. (223)

QUESTIONS, EXERCISES, AND CASES

Discussion Questions

1. Why does a bank keep a signature card on file for your account(s)?
2. What is the purpose of endorsing a check?

3. Why is there generally a difference between the balance in the Cash account on the company's books and the balance on the bank statement?

4. Indicate whether the following items in a bank reconciliation should be (1) added to the Cash account balance, (2) deducted from the Cash account balance, (3) added to the bank statement balance, or (4) deducted from the bank statement balance.
   a. NSF check
   b. Deposit in transit
   c. Outstanding check
   d. Bank error charging the business's account with another company's check
   e. Bank service charge

5. Why is it necessary to make general journal entries for the ledger balance side of the bank reconciliation?

6. a. Why would a business use a Petty Cash Fund?
   b. Describe the entry needed to establish a $50 Petty Cash Fund and an entry to reimburse the fund.

7. a. What does a debit balance in Cash Short and Over mean?
   b. Where does a debit balance in Cash Short and Over appear in the financial statements?
   c. What does a credit balance in Cash Short and Over mean?
   d. Where does a credit balance in Cash Short and Over appear in the financial statements?

Exercises

P.O. 2

Determine missing amounts on a bank reconciliation.

Exercise 7-1 Fill in the missing amounts for the following bank reconciliation:

Bank Reconciliation
March 31, 20—

Bank Statement Balance		$3,754.00
Add: Deposit in transit		(a)
		$4,021.00
Deduct: Outstanding checks		
No. 210	$210.00	
No. 224	(b)	
No. 227	320.00	851.00
Adjusted Bank Statement Balance		(c)
Ledger Balance of Cash		$2,840.00
Add: Note collected by bank		427.00
		(d)
Deduct: Bank service and collection charge	(e)	
NSF check from customer	85.00	97.00
Adjusted Ledger Balance of Cash		(f)

P.O. 3

Journalize entries from a bank reconciliation.

Exercise 7-2 The Ledger Balance of Cash section of the bank reconciliation for Jeon Company for July 31 is shown on the following page.

Ledger Balance of Cash		$6,357.00
Add: Note collected (principal, $700, interest		
$41, signed by L. Diaz)	$741.00	
Error in recording Ck. No. 2225 payable to		
Fenton Company (recorded check for		
$18 too much)	18.00	759.00
		$7,116.00
Deduct: NSF check from J. Kelton	$ 85.00	
Bank service and collection charges	21.00	106.00
Adjust Ledger Balance of Cash		$7,010.00

Journalize the entries required to bring the general ledger up to date as of July 31 of this year.

P.O. 2

Determine amount of outstanding checks.

Exercise 7-3 When the bank statement is received on December 3, it shows a balance, before reconciliation, of $3,000 as of November 30. After reconciliation, the adjusted balance is $2,500. If there was one deposit in transit amounting to $500, what was the total of the outstanding checks, assuming that there were no other adjustments to be made to the bank statement?

P.O. 2

Place items on a bank reconciliation.

Exercise 7-4 Write a check mark in the column that indicates the location of each item that would be found on a bank reconciliation. The checks are written correctly.

Item	Add to Bank Statement Balance	Subtract from Bank Statement Balance	Add to Ledger Balance of Cash	Subtract from Ledger Balance of Cash
a. A check-printing charge				
b. An outstanding check				
c. A deposit for $187 listed incorrectly on the bank statement as $178				
d. A collection charge the bank made for a note it collected for its depositor				
e. A check written for $40.73 and recorded incorrectly in the checkbook as $40.37				
f. A deposit in transit				
g. An NSF check received from a customer				
h. A check written for $72.39 and recorded incorrectly in the checkbook as $720.39				

P.O. 2

Determine the adjusted ledger balance of cash.

Exercise 7-5 Mysung Company's Cash account shows a balance of $752 as of August 31 of this year. The balance on the bank statement on that date is $1,250.50. Checks for $263.70, $437.05, and $327 are outstanding. The bank statement shows a check issued by another depositor for $237.25 (in other words, the bank made an error and charged Mysung Company for a check written by another company). The bank statement also shows an NSF check for $280 received from one of Mysung's customers. Service charges for the month were $12. What is the adjusted ledger balance of cash as of August 31?

P.O. 4

Journalize entries pertaining to a Petty Cash Fund.

Exercise 7-6 Record entries in general journal form to record the following:

a. Established a Petty Cash Fund, $150. Issued Ck. No. 857.
b. Reimbursed the Petty Cash Fund for expenditures of $102: Store Supplies Expense, $28; Office Supplies Expense, $36; Miscellaneous Expense, $38. Issued Ck. No. 889.
c. Increased the amount of the fund by an additional $25. Issued Ck. No. 891.
d. Reimbursed the Petty Cash Fund for expenditures of $91.84: Store Supplies Expense, $45.92; Delivery Expense, $36; Miscellaneous Expense, $9.92. Issued Ck. No. 936.

P.O. 7

Journalize entry for the receipt of cash.

Exercise 7-7 At the end of the day, the cash register tape lists $827.27 as total income from services. Cash on hand consists of $15.27 in coins, $694 in currency, $80 in traveler's checks, and $236 in customers' checks. The amount of the Change Fund is $200. In general journal form, record the entry to record the day's cash revenue.

P.O. 6,7

Describe entries related to the Change Fund and Cash Short and Over.

Exercise 7-8

a. Describe the entries that have been posted to the following accounts after the Change Fund was established.

Change Fund		Sales		Cash	
200		1,521 Jan. 3	Jan. 3	1,523	
		1,420 4	4	1,419	
		1,663 6	6	1,660	

Cash Short and Over			
Jan. 4	1	2	Jan. 3
6	3		

b. How will the balance of Cash Short and Over be reported on the income statement?

internet
LINKS TO ACCOUNTING

You have just learned about checking accounts, reconciling bank statements, and managing Petty Cash Funds. Using an online banking service can provide many advantages to managing your cash.

1. What advantages are there to having access to your bank statement online?
2. What are the disadvantages, if any?

CONSIDER AND COMMUNICATE

As the new bookkeeper at a small business, you find the Petty Cash Fund is accessed by several people, usually without anyone leaving any written explanation of what the money was used for. The amount of cash does not match the recorded amount of the fund. Explain how the Petty Cash Fund operation can be made more efficient in order to maintain an accurate accounting of how the money is used.

CRITICAL THINKING

Jamal Page, a college student, plans to provide keyboarding services to graduate students at the university near his home. He must determine how much money to deposit initially in his business account to cover the start-up of the new business. The deposit must cover the start-up costs and leave him with a balance of $5,000 in his business account. He plans to buy a computer/printer and a copier for $4,500 cash. The fax machine and the telephone system he needs are available for $2,500, and he will put down $300. He will buy paper for the copier for $275 on account.

1. Determine the required amount of the beginning investment Jamal needs to make if he is to meet his goal of having $5,000 in his business account after his anticipated transactions.
2. Use the practice grid to complete each transaction. Balance the fundamental accounting equation after each transaction.

	Quality Keyboarding Service				
	Cash	+ Equipment =	Accounts Payable	+ J. Page, Capital	− Supplies Expense
(a) Make needed beginning investment.					
Balance					
(b) Buy equipment for cash, $4,500.					
Balance					
(c) Buy equipment, $2,500, paying $300 down.					
Balance					
(d) Buy supplies on account, $275.					
Balance					

3. Prepare a balance sheet for Jamal's business as of June 10, 20—.

WHAT'S WRONG WITH THIS PICTURE?

You work as a cashier in a service business. Some days you are short of cash at the end of the day, and some days you have more cash than the cash register tape says was earned. You are embarrassed when your cash is short and don't want the owner to know, so you use your own money to make up the difference. On days when you are over, you keep the difference to help pay back what you paid to cover your shortages. What do you think of this practice and why?

PROBLEM SET A

P.O. 2,3

Problem 7-1A Amelio's Men's Shop deposits all receipts in the bank each evening and makes all payments by check. On November 30 its ledger balance of cash is $2,370.65. The bank statement balance of cash as of November 30 is $2,235.25. Use the following information to reconcile the bank statement:

a. The reconciliation for October, the previous month, showed three checks outstanding on October 31: no. 1416 for $85, no. 1419 for $75.75, and no. 1420 for $126. Checks no. 1416 and 1420 were returned with the November bank statement; however, check no. 1419 was not returned.

b. Checks no. 1499 for $40, no. 1516 for $22, no. 1517 for $115, and no. 1518 for $24.85 were written during November and have not been returned by the bank.

c. A deposit of $810 was placed in the night depository on November 30 and did not appear on the bank statement.

d. The canceled checks were compared with the entries in the checkbook, and it was observed that check no. 1487, for $78, was written correctly, payable to M. A. Garson, the owner, for personal use, but was recorded in the checkbook as $87.

e. A bank debit memo for service charges, $24.

f. A bank credit memo for collection of a note signed by T. R. Ritz, $412, including $400 principal and $12 interest.

Check Figure

Adjusted ledger balance of cash, $2,767.65

Instructions

1. Prepare a bank reconciliation as of November 30, assuming that the debit and credit memos have not been recorded.
2. Record the necessary entries in general journal form.

P.O. 4,5

Problem 7-2A On May 1 of this year, Estes and Company established a Petty Cash Fund. The following petty cash transactions took place during the month:

May 1 Cashed check no. 956 for $80 to establish a Petty Cash Fund, and put the $80 in a locked drawer in the office.

3 Bought postage stamps, $7.80, voucher no. 1 (Miscellaneous Expense).

4 Issued voucher no. 2 for taxi fare, $8 (Miscellaneous Expense).

6 Issued voucher no. 3 for delivery charges on outgoing parts, $5.

9 N. Estes, the owner, withdrew $10 for personal use, voucher no. 4.

13 Paid $8.15 for postage, voucher no. 5 (Miscellaneous Expense).

19 Bought pens for office, $6.58, voucher no. 6.

May 23 Paid $1.98 for a box of staples, voucher no. 7.
28 Paid $12 for window cleaning service, voucher no. 8 (Miscellaneous Expense).
29 Paid $1.85 for pencils for office, voucher no. 9.
31 Issued for cash check no. 1098 for $61.36 to reimburse Petty Cash Fund.

Check Figure

Office Supplies Expense, $10.41

Instructions

1. Journalize the entry establishing the Petty Cash Fund in the general journal.
2. Record the disbursements of petty cash in the petty cash payments record.
3. Journalize the summarizing entry to reimburse the Petty Cash Fund.

P.O. 7

Problem 7-3A Emie Harold, owner of Harold's Dry Cleaners, makes bank deposits in the night depository at the close of each business day. The following information for the last four days of July is available.

	July			
	28	**29**	**30**	**31**
Cash register tape	$785.20	$ 965.70	$894.50	$1,021.60
Cash count	883.50	1,068.40	992.60	1,124.40

Check Figure

Cash Short and Over, July 31, $2.80 cash overage

Instructions

In general journal form, record the cash deposit for each day, assuming that there is a $100 Change Fund.

P.O. 2,3

Problem 7-4A On August 31, Bronski and Company receives its bank statement (on the following page). The company deposits its receipts in the bank and makes all payments by check. The debit memo for $49 is for an NSF check written by N. Corday. Check no. 924 for $37, payable to Jackson Company (a creditor), was recorded in the checkbook and journal as $73.

The ledger balance of cash as of August 31 is $1,321. Outstanding checks as of August 31 are: no. 928, $140; no. 929, $245. The accountant notes that the deposit of August 31 for $368 did not appear on the bank statement.

Check Figure

Adjusted ledger balance of cash, $1,306

Instructions

1. Prepare a bank reconciliation as of August 31, assuming that the debit memos have not been recorded.
2. Record the necessary journal entries.
3. Complete the bank form to determine the adjusted balance of cash.

Instructions for General Ledger Software

1. Prepare a bank reconciliation as of August 31. Errors made by the company or the bank, as well as service charges, must be entered as debit or credit memos.
2. Print the bank reconciliation.
3. Record the necessary journal entries.
4. Print the journal entries.

PEABODY NATIONAL BANK

Bronski and Company
416 Seneca Avenue
Kansas City, Missouri 64102

ACCOUNT NO.
152-6 55-217

STATEMENT DATE
August 1–31, 20—

SUMMARY		
Balance Last Statement	$ 961.00
Amount of Checks and Debits	$2,289.00
Number of Checks	11
Amount of Deposits and Credits	$2,651.00
Number of Deposits	7
Balance This Statement	$1,323.00

CHECKS/OTHER DEBITS

CHECKS	CHECK NUMBER	DATE POSTED	AMOUNT	CHECK NUMBER	DATE POSTED	AMOUNT
	917	8-04	172.00	923	8-09	621.00
	918	8-04	76.00	924	8-17	37.00
	919	8-05	146.00	925	8-17	14.00
	920	8-07	206.00	926	8-23	533.00
	921	8-07	139.00	927	8-28	94.00
	922	8-08	200.00			

OTHER DEBITS	DESCRIPTION	DATE POSTED	AMOUNT
	DM NSF check	8-31	49.00
	DM Service charge	8-31	2.00

DEPOSITS/OTHER CREDITS

DEPOSITS	DATE POSTED	AMOUNT	DATE POSTED	AMOUNT
	8-02	326.00	8-18	419.00
	8-05	412.00	8-24	398.00
	8-09	437.00	8-28	291.00
	8-14	368.00		

PLEASE EXAMINE THIS STATEMENT CAREFULLY. REPORT ANY POSSIBLE ERRORS IN 10 DAYS.

CODE SYMBOLS

CM Credit Memo   DM Debit Memo   OD Overdraft   EC Error Correction

---

PROBLEM SET B

P.O. 2,3

Problem 7-1B Madox Company deposits all receipts in the bank each evening and makes all payments by check. On November 30 its ledger balance of cash is $3,219.72. The bank statement balance of cash as of November 30 is $3,185.90. You are given the following information with which to reconcile the bank statement:

a. A deposit of $518.32 was placed in the night depository on November 30 and did not appear on the bank statement.

b. The reconciliation for October, the previous month, showed three checks outstanding on October 31: no. 727 for $81.30, no. 730 for $127.40, and no. 732 for $46.84. Checks no. 727 and 730 were returned with the November bank statement; however, check no. 732 was not returned.

c. Checks no. 742 for $27, no. 743 for $20.20, no. 744 for $101, and no. 745 for $15.46 were written during November but were not returned by the bank.

d. A $36 personal withdrawal by C. R. Madox, the owner, using an ATM, was not recorded in the checkbook.

e. Included in the bank statement was a bank debit memo for service charges, $18.

f. A bank credit memo was also enclosed for the collection of a note signed by L. B. Leonard, $256, including $250 principal and $6 interest.

Check Figure

Adjusted ledger balance of cash, $3,493.72

Instructions

1. Prepare a bank reconciliation as of November 30, assuming that the debit and credit memos have not been recorded.
2. Record the necessary entries in general journal form.

P.O. 4,5

Problem 7-2B On March 1 of this year, Stein Company established a Petty Cash Fund, and the following petty cash transactions took place during the month:

Mar.	1	Cashed check no. 314 for $70 to establish a Petty Cash Fund, and put the $70 in a locked drawer in the office.
	4	Issued voucher no. 1 for taxi fare, $7 (Miscellaneous Expense).
	7	Issued voucher no. 2 for memo pads, $8.20 (Office Supplies Expense).
	9	Paid $11.50 for an advertisement in a college basketball program, voucher no. 3.
	16	Bought postage stamps, $7.80, voucher no. 4 (Miscellaneous Expense).
	20	Paid $10 to have snow removed from office front sidewalk, voucher no. 5 (Miscellaneous Expense).
	25	Issued voucher no. 6 for delivery charge, $5.55.
	28	R. C. Stein, the owner, withdrew $10 for personal use, voucher no. 7.
	29	Paid $3.82 for postage, voucher no. 8 (Miscellaneous Expense).
	30	Paid $5.60 for delivery charge, voucher no. 9.
	31	Issued for cash check no. 372 for $69.47 to reimburse Petty Cash Fund.

Check Figure

Office Supplies Expense, $8.20

Instructions

1. Journalize the entry establishing the Petty Cash Fund in the general journal.
2. Record the disbursements of petty cash in the petty cash payments record.
3. Journalize the summarizing entry to reimburse the Petty Cash Fund.

P.O. 7

Problem 7-3B Betty Ferrari, owner of Betty's Beauty Salon, makes bank deposits in the night depository at the close of each business day. The following information for the first four days of April is available.

	April			
	1	**2**	**3**	**4**
Cash register tape	$374.75	$580.25	$586.65	$633.25
Cash count	473.50	681.25	685.75	732.15

Check Figure

Cash Short and Over, April 3, $0.90 cash shortage

Instructions

In general journal form, record the cash deposit for each day, assuming that there is a $100 Change Fund.

P.O. 2,3

Problem 7-4B On August 2, Northway Hotel receives its bank statement (below). The company deposits its receipts in the bank and makes all payments by check. The debit memo for $37 is for an NSF check written by T. N. Ross. Check no. 1617 for $72.50, payable to Michaels Company (a creditor), was incorrectly recorded in the checkbook and journal as $27.50.

The balance of the Cash account as of July 31 is $1,877.46. Outstanding checks as of July 31 are: no. 1631, $115.35; no. 1632, $75.10; no. 1633, $173.25. The accountant notes that the July 31 deposit of $580 did not appear on the bank statement.

Check Figure

Adjusted ledger balance of cash, $1,792.36

Instructions

1. Prepare a bank reconciliation as of July 31, assuming that the debit memos have not been recorded.
2. Record the necessary journal entries.
3. Complete the bank form to determine the adjusted balance of cash.

STANTON NATIONAL BANK

Northway Hotel
410 W. Lang Street
Rockford, Illinois 61104

ACCOUNT NO.
761-145-792
STATEMENT DATE
July 1–31, 20—

SUMMARY		
Balance Last Statement	$1,153.80	
Amount of Checks and Debits	$2,105.91	
Number of Checks	14	
Amount of Deposits and Credits	$2,528.17	
Number of Deposits	7	
Balance This Statement	$1,576.06	

CHECKS/OTHER DEBITS	CHECKS	CHECK NUMBER	DATE POSTED	AMOUNT	CHECK NUMBER	DATE POSTED	AMOUNT
		1617	7-03	72.50	1624	7-08	120.00
		1618	7-03	167.00	1625	7-09	429.60
		1619	7-03	124.20	1626	7-12	37.40
		1620	7-05	137.20	1627	7-14	38.49
		1621	7-06	236.25	1628	7-22	182.71
		1622	7-06	159.89	1629	7-25	96.87
		1623	7-08	244.50	1630	7-26	19.20

OTHER DEBITS	DESCRIPTION	DATE POSTED	AMOUNT
	DM NSF check	7-22	37.00
	DM Service charge	7-31	3.10

DEPOSITS/OTHER CREDITS	DEPOSITS	DATE POSTED	AMOUNT	DATE POSTED	AMOUNT
		7-03	491.50	7-15	291.76
		7-06	415.72	7-18	142.90
		7-09	439.16	7-28	368.93
		7-11	378.20		

PLEASE EXAMINE THIS STATEMENT CAREFULLY. REPORT ANY POSSIBLE ERRORS IN 10 DAYS.

CODE SYMBOLS

CM Credit Memo   DM Debit Memo   OD Overdraft   EC Error Correction

Instructions for General Ledger Software

1. Prepare a bank reconciliation as of July 31. Errors made by the company or the bank, as well as service charges, must be entered as debit or credit memos.
2. Print the bank reconciliation.
3. Record the necessary journal entries.
4. Print the journal entries.

Bad Debts

Performance Objectives

After you have completed this appendix, you will be able to do the following:

1. Prepare the adjusting entry for bad debts using the allowance method, based on a percentage of credit sales.

2. Prepare the entry to write off an account as uncollectible when the allowance method is used.

3. Prepare the entry to write off an account as uncollectible when the specific charge-off method is used.

As you know, not all credit customers pay their bills. In this appendix, we turn our attention to the accounts receivable that will not be collected. There are two basic methods of providing for writing or charging off credit customers' accounts that are considered uncollectible. They are the allowance method and the specific charge-off method.

ALLOWANCE METHOD

The allowance method provides for bad debt losses in advance, by estimating them. Though there are a number of ways to estimate the amount of future losses from open accounts, we will base our estimate on a percentage of credit sales.

For example, based on its experience with bad debt losses, Miami Printing estimates that 1 percent of its revenue from services on account for the year will be uncollectible. Obviously, Miami Printing does not know which credit customers will not pay their bills. If the company were certain that a particular customer would not pay his or her bill, then it wouldn't perform services without requiring cash in advance.

Adjusting Entry and Writing Off an Account

OBJECTIVE 1

Prepare the adjusting entry for bad debts using the allowance method, based on a percentage of credit sales.

Miami Printing's total income from services on account for last year was $500,000. One percent of $500,000 is $5,000. On its work sheet, Miami Printing makes an adjusting entry. We show this in T account form.

Bad Debts Expense				Allowance for Doubtful Accounts		
	+	−		−	+	
Dec. 31						Dec. 31
Adjusting	5,000				5,000	Adjusting

Allowance for Doubtful Accounts is treated as a deduction from Accounts Receivable. Consequently, Allowance for Doubtful Accounts is a contra account. The adjusting entry is similar to the entry for depreciation in that there is a debit to an expense account and a credit to a contra-asset account. In T account form, the adjustment for depreciation looks like this:

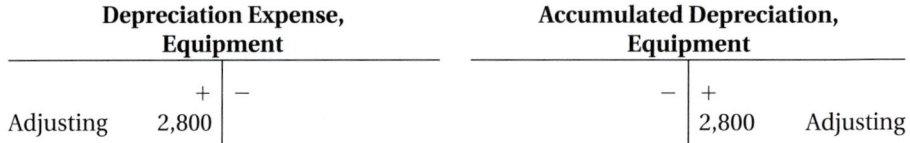

	Depreciation Expense, Equipment			Accumulated Depreciation, Equipment	
	+	−	−	+	
Adjusting	2,800			2,800	Adjusting

Assume that Miami Printing's Accounts Receivable balance is $90,000 and its Equipment balance is $75,000. Let's show the accounts and the adjusting entries in T account form.

Assets	=	Liabilities	+	Owner's Equity	+	Revenue	−	Expenses
+ | −		− | +		− | +		− | +		+ | −

Accounts Receivable

+	−
Bal. 90,000	

Allowance for Doubtful Accounts

−	+
	Bal. 170
	Adj. 5,000
	Bal. 5,170

Equipment

+	−
Bal. 75,000	

Accumulated Depreciation, Equipment

−	+
	Bal. 7,000
	Adj. 2,800
	Bal. 9,800

Income from Services

−	+
	Bal. 500,000

Bad Debts Expense

+	−
Adj. 5,000	

Depreciation Expense, Equipment

+	−
Adj. 2,800	

The Depreciation Expense, Equipment, account comes into existence as an adjusting entry at the end of the year. It is closed immediately after being brought into existence. The same thing happens to Bad Debts Expense; it comes into existence as an adjusting entry, and then it is immediately closed during the closing process.

FYI

Companies generally have a credit balance left in the Allowance account.

OBJECTIVE 2

Prepare the entry to write off an account as uncollectible when the allowance method is used.

As certain charge customers' accounts are determined to be uncollectible and are written off, the losses are taken out of Allowance for Doubtful Accounts. Think of the Allowance for Doubtful Accounts as a reservoir. By means of the adjusting entry, the account is filled up at the end of the year and then is gradually drained off (reduced) during the next year by write-offs of charge customer accounts. The $170 balance in Allowance for Doubtful Accounts at the end of the year indicates that less accounts receivable were actually written off as uncollectible during the year than previously estimated. As a result, Bad Debts Expense in the period was overstated and therefore net income understated.

Let's go on to the next year. On January 2, Miami Printing finally gives up on its attempts to collect $720 from its credit customer Ace Computer, which is included in Accounts Receivable. Miami Printing now writes off the account in the amount of $720, shown below in T account form.

Accounts Receivable				Allowance for Doubtful Accounts			
	+	−			−	+	
Bal.	90,000		Jan. 2	Jan. 2		5,170	Bal.
		720	(write-off)	(write-off)	720		
Bal.	**89,280**					**4,450**	**Bal.**

As you can see, the write-off has reduced both the balance of Accounts Receivable and the balance of Allowance for Doubtful Accounts but has not changed the net realizable value of accounts receivable. The general journal entry is shown below.

PAGE _____

	DATE		DESCRIPTION	POST. REF.	DEBIT	CREDIT	
1	20—						1
2	Jan.	2	Allowance for Doubtful Accounts		7 2 0 00		2
3			Accounts Receivable			7 2 0 00	3
4			Wrote off the account of				4
5			Ace Computer as uncollectible.				5
6							6

An Advantage and a Disadvantage of the Allowance Method

The allowance method is consistent with the accrual basis of accounting in that it matches revenues of one year with expenses of the same year. The bad-debt loss potential is provided in the same year in which the revenue is earned. The conformity with the matching principle places the allowance method in compliance with generally accepted accounting principles as recognized by the FASB. However, the allowance method cannot be used for federal income tax purposes. This means that if a business uses the allowance method, the net income shown on the company's income statement will differ from the net income shown on its federal income tax return. The tax return shows a reconciliation between income reported for book purposes and income reported for tax purposes.

SPECIFIC CHARGE-OFF METHOD

OBJECTIVE 3

Prepare the entry to write off an account as uncollectible when the specific charge-off method is used.

Under the specific charge-off method, when a credit customer's account is determined to be uncollectible, the account is simply written off. The terms *write-off* and *charge-off* mean the same thing. No allowance account is used with the specific charge-off method because no estimate of uncollectible accounts receivable is calculated. As an illustration, Walter Company uses the specific charge-off method. On May 5, Walter Company writes off the account of Garber Construction, $1,220. For the purpose of this example, we will use a separate Accounts Receivable account for Garber Construction. T accounts pertaining to Garber's account look like this:

Accounts Receivable		Bad Debts Expense	
+ | −		+ | −	
Balance 1,220	May 5	May 5	
	1,220 (write-off)	(write-off) 1,220	

The general journal entry is shown below.

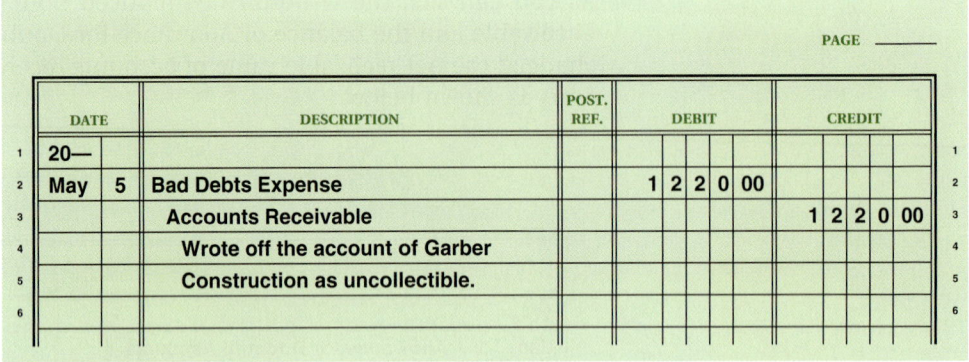

Under this method, entries will be made directly into the Bad Debts Expense account during the year. No adjusting entry is needed, and Allowance for Doubtful Accounts is not used.

Advantages of the Specific Charge-off Method

The main advantage is that the method may be used for federal income tax purposes. It is not necessary to make an adjusting entry. Also, one less account (Allowance for Doubtful Accounts) is required.

Disadvantage of the Specific Charge-off Method

This method is not consistent with the accrual basis of accounting (recognizing revenue when it is earned and expenses when they are incurred). The method does not match up the revenue of one year with the expense of the same year. This lack of conformity with the matching principle places the specific charge-off method in violation of generally accepted accounting principles. For example, the sale of services on account to Garber Construction could have been made two years ago. Since the account receivable will never be collected, the revenue for that year was too high (overstated). Consequently, net income is also overstated during that year. Now, two years later, $1,220 is written off as an expense. So net income for this year is too low (understated) because of the added expense.

PROBLEMS

P.O. 1,2

Check Figure

Adjusting entry amount, $3,270

Problem B-1 Regis Company's total sales on account for the year amounted to $327,000. The company, which uses the allowance method, estimated bad debts at 1 percent of its charge sales. Journalize the following selected entries:

20X8
Dec. 31 The adjusting entry.

20X9
Mar. 2 Write-off of the account of B. L. Giroux as uncollectible, $584.

June 6 Write-off of the account of A. P. Bollard as uncollectible, $492.

P.O. 1,2

Check Figure

Adjusting entry amount, $1,366.03

Problem B-2 Harron's Landscape Service's total revenue on account for 2008 amounted to $273,205. The company, which uses the allowance method, estimates bad debts at ½ percent of total revenue on account. Journalize the following selected entries:

20X8
Dec. 12 Performed services on account for D. A. Wallace, $245.
         31 The adjusting entry for Bad Debts Expense.
         31 The closing entry for Bad Debts Expense.

20X9
Feb. 18 Wrote off the account of D. A. Wallace as uncollectible, $245.

P.O. 3

Check Figure

Total amount debited to Bad Debts Expense in 20X8, $677

Problem B-3 Spin City uses the specific charge-off method for recording bad debts. Journalize the following selected entries:

20X8
Apr. 10 Write-off of the account of J. C. Sargent as uncollectible, $286.

July 27 Write-off of the account of B. R. Warner as uncollectible, $391.

8 Employee Earnings and Deductions

Performance Objectives

After you have completed this chapter, you will be able to do the following:

1. Understand the role of laws that affect payroll deductions and contributions.

2. Calculate total earnings based on an hourly, piece-rate, or commission basis.

3. Determine deductions using tables of employees' income tax withholding.

4. Complete a payroll register.

5. Journalize the payroll entry from a payroll register.

6. Maintain employees' individual earnings records.

Up to now, we've been recording employees' earnings as a debit to Salary or Wages Expense and a credit to Cash, but we've really been talking only about **gross pay**: the total amount of an employee's pay before deductions. We haven't mentioned the various deductions that we all know are taken out of our gross pay before we get to the **net pay**, or take-home pay. In this chapter, we will talk about types of deductions and how to enter them in the payroll records, and about journal entries to record the payroll and pay the employees.

OBJECTIVES OF PAYROLL RECORDS AND ACCOUNTING

There are two primary reasons to maintain accurate payroll records. First, we must collect the data necessary to compute the compensation for each employee for each payroll period.

Second, we must provide the information needed to complete the various government reports—federal and state—required of all employers. All business enterprises, both large and small, are required by law to withhold certain amounts from employees' pay for taxes, to make payments to government agencies by specific deadlines, and to submit reports on official forms. Because governments impose penalties if the requirements are not met, employers are vitally concerned with payroll accounting.

The employer is required to keep records of the following information:

1. **Personal data on employee** Name, address, Social Security number, date of birth
2. **Data on wage payments** Dates and amounts of payments, and payroll periods
3. **Amount of taxable wages paid** Dates and amount earned year to date for the calendar year involved
4. **Amount of tax withheld from each employee's earnings by pay period**

Many companies use software, such as Excel or Quickbooks, or outside payroll services, such as ADP or Paychex, to assist with their payroll acounting.

EMPLOYER/EMPLOYEE RELATIONSHIPS

FYI

Examples of independent contractors include a self-employed appliance repair person, plumber, or CPA.

Payroll accounting is concerned with employees and their compensation, withholdings, records, reports, and taxes. There is a distinction between an employee and an independent contractor. An **employee** is one who is under the direction and control of the employer, such as a bookkeeper, salesclerk, assistant, vice president, controller, and so on. An **independent contractor** is engaged for a definite job or service and may choose his or her own means of doing the work. Payments made to independent contractors are in the form of fees or charges. Independent contractors submit bills or invoices for the work they do. The payment is not subject to any withholding or payroll taxes by the person or firm paying that invoice. Such taxes are the responsibility of the independent contractor.

LAWS AFFECTING EMPLOYEES' PAY DEDUCTIONS

Both federal and state laws require the employer to act as a collecting agent and deduct specified amounts from employees' gross earnings. The employer sends the withholdings to the appropriate government agencies, along with reports substantiating the figures. Let's look at some of the more important laws that pertain to employees' pay.

Fair Labor Standards Act

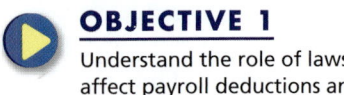

OBJECTIVE 1

Understand the role of laws that affect payroll deductions and contributions.

The **Fair Labor Standards Act** of 1938 is referred to as "the Act" or "FLSA." The Act provides for minimum standards for both wages and overtime. Included in the Act are also provisions related to child labor and equal pay for equal work. In addition, the Act exempts specified employees or groups of employees from the application of certain of its provisions. Details of the Act may be read at **http://www.opm.gov.**

Federal Income Tax Withholding

The **Current Tax Payment Act**, passed in 1943, requires employers not only to withhold the tax and then pay it to the U.S. Treasury but also to keep records of the names and addresses of persons employed, their earnings and withholdings, and the amounts and dates of payment. The employer has to submit reports to the Internal Revenue Service on a quarterly basis (Form 941) and to the employee on an annual basis (W-2 form). With few exceptions, this requirement applies to employers of one or more persons. We will discuss these reports and the related deposits in Chapter 9.

FICA Tax (Employees' Share)

The **Social Security Act of 1935** began as an attempt to provide retired workers with benefits based upon their work history. Several amendments have added benefits for spouses and minor children of retired workers, disability insurance, lowering the age when benefits may be collected, Medicare, and supplemental security income.

Currently, FICA consists of Social Security and Medicare. At the writing of this text, employees contribute 6.2 percent (.062) on the first $94,200 earned in a calendar year for Social Security. Employees contribute 1.45 percent (.0145) on all earnings in a calendar year with no limit for Medicare. Throughout this chapter, we will use these percentages and earnings limitations for our calculations.

LAWS AFFECTING EMPLOYER'S PAYROLL TAX CONTRIBUTIONS (PAYROLL TAX EXPENSE)

Certain payroll taxes, based on the total wages paid to employees, are levied on the employer. Let's look at some of the more important laws that pertain to the pay of employees.

FICA Tax (Employer's Share)

The employer has to match the amount of FICA tax withheld from the employees' wages, and the employer's share is recorded under Payroll Tax Expense. Every three months the employer has to submit reports to the U.S. Treasury, recording the information on Form 941, the same form that is used to report the income tax withheld. The employer's payment to the Internal Revenue Service consists of (1) the employee's share of the FICA tax, (2) the employer's matching portion of the FICA tax, and (3) the employee's income tax withheld. We will talk about this in detail in Chapter 9.

State Unemployment Taxes (SUTA)

Each state is responsible for paying its own unemployment compensation benefits. The revenue provided by **state unemployment taxes** is used exclusively for this purpose. However, there is considerable variation among the states concerning the tax rates and the amount of taxable income. **This tax is paid by employers only.** Most states, under a State Unemployment Tax Act, charge their employers a percentage of the first $7,000 based on the taxable income stipulated in the Federal Unemployment Tax Act. In this text, we will use 5.4 percent (.054) of the first $7,000. States require employers to file reports on a quarterly, or three-month, basis. Included in these reports are a listing of employees' names, Social Security numbers, amounts of wages paid to each employee, and computations of unemployment taxes.

Federal Unemployment Tax Act (FUTA)

The purpose of the Federal Unemployment Tax Act is to provide financial support for the maintenance of government-run employment offices throughout the country. **FUTA taxes are paid by employers only.** Generally this includes all employers except nonprofit schools and charities.

The federal unemployment tax is based on the total earnings of each employee during the calendar year. Congress has frequently changed the rates and the taxable income base.

For the examples and problems in this text, we will assume that employers pay an effective federal unemployment tax rate of 0.8 percent (.008) of the first $7,000 of earnings of each employee during the calendar year.

Reports to the federal government (Form 940) must be submitted annually. We will discuss these reports in Chapter 9.

Workers' Compensation Laws

Workers' compensation laws protect employees and their dependents against losses due to death or injury incurred on the job. Most states require employers either to contribute to a state compensation insurance fund or to buy similar insurance from a private insurance company. The employer ordinarily pays the cost of the insurance premiums. The premium rates vary according to the degree of danger inherent in each job category and the employer's number of accidents. The employer has to keep records of job descriptions and classifications as well as claims of insured persons.

HOW EMPLOYEES GET PAID

Employees may be paid salaries or wages, depending on the type of work and the period of time covered. Money paid to a person for managerial or administrative services is usually called a salary, and the time period covered is generally a month or a year. Money paid for either skilled or unskilled labor is usually called wages, and the time period covered is hours or weeks. Wages may also be paid on a piecework basis. A company may supplement an employee's salary or wage by commissions, bonuses, cost-of-living adjustments, and profit-sharing plans. As a rule, employees are paid by check, in cash, or by a direct deposit to their bank account. However, their compensation may take the form of merchandise, lodging, meals, or other property as well. When the compensation is in these forms, you have to determine the fair value of the property or service given in payment for an employee's labor.

Calculating Total Earnings

OBJECTIVE 2

Calculate total earnings based on an hourly, piece-rate, or commission basis.

When compensation is based on the amount of time worked, the accountant has to have a record of the number of hours worked by each employee. When there are only a few employees, this can be accomplished by means of a time book. When there are many employees, time clocks or other electronic time-keeping systems are used.

Employees may be paid weekly, biweekly, semimonthly, or monthly. Biweekly is every two weeks. Semimonthly is twice a month.

Wages

Consider Mark E. Amano, who works for Goren Company. His regular rate of pay is $22.95 per hour. The company pays time-and-a-half for hours worked in excess of 40 per week. In addition, it pays him double time for any work he does on Sundays and holidays. Amano has a ½-hour lunch break during an 8½-hour day. He is not paid for the lunch break nor is he paid for minutes before 8 AM or after 4:30 PM unless hours of overtime are authorized in advance. His time card for the week is shown in Figure 1.

Although wages are more often paid by check or direct deposit, some industries or companies still pay employees in cash. From an internal control point of view, however, it is better to have a permanent record, which a check or direct deposit slip provides.

TIME CARD

Name Amano, Mark E.

Week ending Oct. 7, 20—

Day	In	Out	In	Out	Hours Worked Regular	Hours Worked Overtime
M	7:57	12:00	12:20	4:32	8	
T	7:56	12:06	12:36	4:37	8	
W	7:57	12:02	12:31	4:31	8	
T	8:00	12:11	12:40	6:32	8	2
F	8:00	12:03	12:33	5:33	8	1
S	7:59	11:02				3
S						

FIGURE 1

Amano's gross wages can be computed by one of two methods. The first method works like this:

40 hours at straight time	40 × $22.95 per hour =	$ 918.00
2 hours overtime on Thursday ($22.95 × 1.5 = $34.43)	2 × $34.43 per hour =	68.86
1 hour overtime on Friday	1 × $34.43 per hour =	34.43
3 hours overtime on Saturday	3 × $34.43 per hour =	103.29
Total gross wages	46	$1,124.58

The second method of calculating gross wages is often used when it is necessary to identify or track overtime premium.

FYI

Minimum wages are set by Congress or state legislature—whichever is higher. Originally, in 1938, the minimum wage was $.25 per hour.

46 hours at straight time: 46 × $22.95 per hour = $1,055.70
Overtime premium:
6 hours × $11.48 per hour premium =   68.88

Total gross wages $1,124.58

Salaries

Employees who are paid a regular salary may also be entitled to extra pay for overtime. It is necessary to figure out their regular hourly rate of pay before you can determine their overtime rate. Consider R. Henry, who gets a salary of $2,350 per month. She is entitled to overtime pay for all hours worked in excess of 40 during a week at the rate of 1½ times her regular hourly rate. This past week she worked 44 hours, so we calculate her gross pay as follows:

$2,350 per month × 12 months = $28,200 per year
$28,200 per year ÷ 52 weeks = $542.31 per week
$542.31 per week ÷ 40 hours = $13.56 per regular hour
$13.56 × 1.5 = $20.34 per overtime hour

Earnings for 44 hours:
40 hours at straight time, as calculated above = $542.31
4 hours overtime   4 × $20.34 =   81.36

Total gross earnings $623.67

Piece Rate

Workers under the piece-rate system are paid at the rate of so much per unit of production. For example, Ben Frost, a pear picker, gets paid $8 for picking a bin of pears. If he picks 6 bins during the day, his total earnings are 6 × $8 = $48.

Workers paid by the piece-rate system are paid according to how much they produce. The number of heads of lettuce picked or flags sewn determines the worker's total compensation.

Commissions

Some salespersons are paid on a purely commission basis. However, a more common arrangement is a salary plus a commission or bonus. Assume that Lori Borsca receives an annual salary of $22,000. Her employer agrees to pay her a 5 percent commission on all sales during the year in excess of $100,000. Her sales for the year total $245,000. Her commission is $7,250 ($145,000 × 0.05). Therefore, her total earnings are $29,250 ($22,000 + $7,250).

DEDUCTIONS FROM TOTAL EARNINGS

Anyone who has ever earned a paycheck has encountered some of the many types of deductions. Total earnings minus deductions equal net pay. The most common deductions are for

1. Federal income tax withholding
2. State income tax withholding
3. FICA tax (Social Security and Medicare), employee's share
4. Union dues
5. Medical and life insurance premiums
6. Contributions to a charitable organization
7. Repayment of personal loans from the company credit union or retirement savings
8. Savings through the company credit union or retirement savings
9. Purchase of U.S. savings bonds

FYI

For purposes of this text, medical insurance premiums are treated as an after-tax deduction, similar to union dues and charitable contributions. However, in the real world, medical insurance premiums as usually deducted *pre-tax*. If a pre-tax deduction, the employee does not have to pay income tax, nor does the employee or employer have to pay payroll taxes, on the amount of the premium.

FYI

Federal tax rates change frequently, but the procedure stays the same. We will use the tax table given in this chapter for all computations.

Employees' Federal Income Tax Withholding

Employers are required not only to withhold employees' taxes and then pay them to the U.S. Treasury but also to keep records of the names and addresses of persons employed, their **taxable earnings** (the earnings subject to tax) and withholdings, and the amounts and dates of payment.

The amount of federal income tax withheld from an employee's earnings depends on the amount of her or his total earnings, marital status, and number of withholding allowances claimed. A **withholding allowance** is an amount of an individual's earnings that is exempt from income taxes (nontaxable). An employee is entitled to one personal allowance for the taxpayer, one for his or her spouse, and one for each dependent. An **exemption** is an amount of an employee's annual earnings not subject to income tax. Each employee has to fill out an **Employee's Withholding Allowance Certificate (Form W-4)**, shown in Figure 2.

The employer retains this form as authorization to withhold money for the employee's federal income tax.

Publication 15 (Circular E), Employer's Tax Guide

OBJECTIVE 3
Determine deductions using tables of employees' income tax withholding.

Publication 15 (Circular E) contains withholding tables for federal income, Social Security, and Medicare taxes, along with the rules for depositing these taxes. It is regularly updated to reflect changes in tax laws and withholding rates. It also describes filing requirements for official employer reports. Publication 15 (Circular E) is provided free of charge by the Internal Revenue Service. Accountants responsible for preparation of payroll registers and forms should be familiar with the contents of Publication 15 (Circular E).

Form **W-4**	**Employee's Withholding Allowance Certificate**	OMB No. 1545-0074
Department of the Treasury Internal Revenue Service	▶ Whether you are entitled to claim a certain number of allowances or exemption from withholding is subject to review by the IRS. Your employer may be required to send a copy of this form to the IRS.	20**XX**

1 Type or print your first name and middle initial.	Last name	**2** Your social security number
Mark E.	Amano	543 : 24 : 1680

Home address (number and street or rural route)	**3** ☐ Single ☑ Married ☐ Married, but withhold at higher Single rate.
6357 Boston Lane	**Note.** If married, but legally separated, or spouse is a nonresident alien, check the "Single" box.
City or town, state, and ZIP code	**4** If your last name differs from that shown on your social security ☐
Bangor, Maine 04401	card, check here. You must call 1-800-772-1213 for a new card. ▶

5	Total number of allowances you are claiming (from line **H** above **or** from the applicable worksheet on page 2)	**5**	0
6	Additional amount, if any, you want withheld from each paycheck	**6** $	

7 I claim exemption from withholding for 2006, and I certify that I meet **both** of the following conditions for exemption.
- Last year I had a right to a refund of **all** federal income tax withheld because I had **no** tax liability **and**
- This year I expect a refund of **all** federal income tax withheld because I expect to have **no** tax liability.

If you meet both conditions, write "Exempt" here . . . . ▶ | **7** |

Under penalties of perjury, I declare that I have examined this certificate and to the best of my knowledge and belief, it is true, correct, and complete.

Employee's signature
(Form is not valid
unless you sign it.) ▶ *Mark E. Amano*　　　　　Date ▶ *January 2, 20--*

8 Employer's name and address (Employer: Complete lines 8 and 10 only if sending to the IRS.)	**9** Office code (optional)	**10** Employer identification number (EIN)

For Privacy Act and Paperwork Reduction Act Notice, see page 2. | Cat. No. 10220Q | Form **W-4** (20XX)

FIGURE 2

FYI

Publication 15 (Circular E) is available in paper form or can be downloaded from the Internet at **www.irs.gov**.

The **wage-bracket tax tables** cover monthly, semimonthly, biweekly, weekly, and daily payroll periods. The tables are also subdivided on the basis of marital status. First locate the wage bracket in the first two columns of the table. Next, find the column for the number of allowances claimed and read down this column until you get to the appropriate wage-bracket line. A portion of the weekly federal income tax withholding table for married persons is reproduced in Figure 3 on page 274.

Assume that Mark E. Amano, who claims zero allowances as of the October 7 payroll, has gross wages of $1,124.58 for the week. As $1,124.58 falls in the $1,120–$1,130 bracket, you can see from the table that $131 should be withheld.

Note the headings of the bracket columns: "At least" and "But less than." A strict interpretation of the $1,120–$1,130 bracket really means $1,120–$1,129.99. Therefore, if Amano's salary were $1,130, it would fall into the $1,130–$1,140 bracket.

Employees' State Income Tax Withholding

Many states that levy state income taxes also furnish employers with withholding tables. Other states use a fixed percentage of the federal income tax withholding as the amount to be withheld for state taxes. In our illustration, we assume that the amount of each employee's state income tax deduction is 20 percent (.20) of that employee's federal income tax deduction.

Employees' FICA Tax Withholding (Social Security and Medicare)

The Federal Insurance Contributions Act provides for retirement pensions after a worker reaches age 62, disability benefits for any worker who becomes disabled (and for her or his dependents), and a health insurance program

MARRIED Persons—WEEKLY Payroll Period
(For Wages Paid in 2006)

If the wages are—		And the number of withholding allowances claimed is—										
At least	But less than	0	1	2	3	4	5	6	7	8	9	10
		The amount of income tax to be withheld is—										
$740	$750	$74	$65	$55	$46	$36	$27	$21	$15	$8	$2	$0
750	760	76	66	57	47	38	28	22	16	9	3	0
760	770	77	68	58	49	39	30	23	17	10	4	0
770	780	79	69	60	50	41	31	24	18	11	5	0
780	790	80	71	61	52	42	33	25	19	12	6	0
790	800	82	72	63	53	44	34	26	20	13	7	1
800	810	83	74	64	55	45	36	27	21	14	8	2
810	820	85	75	66	56	47	37	28	22	15	9	3
820	830	86	77	67	58	48	39	29	23	16	10	4
830	840	88	78	69	59	50	40	31	24	17	11	5
840	850	89	80	70	61	51	42	32	25	18	12	6
850	860	91	81	72	62	53	43	34	26	19	13	7
860	870	92	83	73	64	54	45	35	27	20	14	8
870	880	94	84	75	65	56	46	37	28	21	15	9
880	890	95	86	76	67	57	48	38	29	22	16	10
890	900	97	87	78	68	59	49	40	30	23	17	11
900	910	98	89	79	70	60	51	41	32	24	18	12
910	920	100	90	81	71	62	52	43	33	25	19	13
920	930	101	92	82	73	63	54	44	35	26	20	14
930	940	103	93	84	74	65	55	46	36	27	21	15
940	950	104	95	85	76	66	57	47	38	28	22	16
950	960	106	96	87	77	68	58	49	39	30	23	17
960	970	107	98	88	79	69	60	50	41	31	24	18
970	980	109	99	90	80	71	61	52	42	33	25	19
980	990	110	101	91	82	72	63	53	44	34	26	20
990	1,000	112	102	93	83	74	64	55	45	36	27	21
1,000	1,010	113	104	94	85	75	66	56	47	37	28	22
1,010	1,020	115	105	96	86	77	67	58	48	39	29	23
1,020	1,030	116	107	97	88	78	69	59	50	40	31	24
1,030	1,040	118	108	99	89	80	70	61	51	42	32	25
1,040	1,050	119	110	100	91	81	72	62	53	43	34	26
1,050	1,060	121	111	102	92	83	73	64	54	45	35	27
1,060	1,070	122	113	103	94	84	75	65	56	46	37	28
1,070	1,080	124	114	105	95	86	76	67	57	48	38	29
1,080	1,090	125	116	106	97	87	78	68	59	49	40	30
1,090	1,100	127	117	108	98	89	79	70	60	51	41	32
1,100	1,110	128	119	109	100	90	81	71	62	52	43	33
1,110	1,120	130	120	111	101	92	82	73	63	54	44	35
1,120	1,130	131	122	112	103	93	84	74	65	55	46	36
1,130	1,140	133	123	114	104	95	85	76	66	57	47	38
1,140	1,150	134	125	115	106	96	87	77	68	58	49	39
1,150	1,160	136	126	117	107	98	88	79	69	60	50	41
1,160	1,170	137	128	118	109	99	90	80	71	61	52	42
1,170	1,180	139	129	120	110	101	91	82	72	63	53	44
1,180	1,190	140	131	121	112	102	93	83	74	64	55	45
1,190	1,200	142	132	123	113	104	94	85	75	66	56	47
1,200	1,210	143	134	124	115	105	96	86	77	67	58	48
1,210	1,220	145	135	126	116	107	97	88	78	69	59	50
1,220	1,230	146	137	127	118	108	99	89	80	70	61	51
1,230	1,240	148	138	129	119	110	100	91	81	72	62	53
1,240	1,250	149	140	130	121	111	102	92	83	73	64	54
1,250	1,260	151	141	132	122	113	103	94	84	75	65	56
1,260	1,270	152	143	133	124	114	105	95	86	76	67	57
1,270	1,280	154	144	135	125	116	106	97	87	78	68	59
1,280	1,290	155	146	136	127	117	108	98	89	79	70	60
1,290	1,300	157	147	138	128	119	109	100	90	81	71	62
1,300	1,310	158	149	139	130	120	111	101	92	82	73	63
1,310	1,320	161	150	141	131	122	112	103	93	84	74	65
1,320	1,330	163	152	142	133	123	114	104	95	85	76	66
1,330	1,340	166	153	144	134	125	115	106	96	87	77	68
1,340	1,350	168	155	145	136	126	117	107	98	88	79	69
1,350	1,360	171	156	147	137	128	118	109	99	90	80	71
1,360	1,370	173	158	148	139	129	120	110	101	91	82	72
1,370	1,380	176	160	150	140	131	121	112	102	93	83	74
1,380	1,390	178	162	151	142	132	123	113	104	94	85	75
1,390	1,400	181	165	153	143	134	124	115	105	96	86	77

$1,400 and over   Use Table 1(b) for a **MARRIED person** on page 36. Also see the instructions on page 34.

FIGURE 3

after age 65 (Medicare). Both the employee and the employer have to pay **FICA taxes**, which are commonly referred to as **Social Security taxes** and **Medicare taxes**. The employer withholds FICA taxes from employees' wages and pays them to the U.S. Treasury.

FICA tax rates apply to the gross earnings of an employee during the **calendar year** (January 1 through December 31). After an employee has paid Social Security tax on the maximum taxable earnings, the employer stops deducting Social Security tax until the next calendar year begins. Congress has frequently changed the schedule of rates and taxable incomes.

In this text, we assume a Social Security rate of 6.2 percent (.062) of the first $94,200 for each employee and a Medicare rate of 1.45 percent (.0145) of all earnings for each employee. Both tax rates apply to earnings during the calendar year. (Tables for Social Security and Medicare tax withholdings are available in the Internal Revenue Service Publication 15 (Circular E), Employer's Tax Guide.)

Let's return to Mark E. Amano, who had gross wages of $1,124.58 for the week ending October 7. Suppose that his total accumulated gross wages earned this year *prior to this payroll period* are $44,960. Amano's total gross wages including this payroll period were $46,084.58 ($44,960 + $1,124.58). Since the Social Security tax applies to the first $94,200 and the Medicare tax applies to all earnings, Amano's earnings are subject to both taxes. For Amano's Social Security tax, multiply $1,124.58 by 6.2 percent ($1,124.58 × 0.062 = $69.72). For Amano's Medicare tax, multiply $1,124.58 by 0.0145 = $16.31.

Here's another example. At the beginning of the pay period, Susan Walker had cumulative earnings of $91,300, which is $2,900 less than $94,200. During this pay period, she earned $3,010.35, which is greater than $2,900. Thus, she must pay Social Security tax of $179.80 ($2,900 × 0.062) on $2,900. However, because the Medicare tax applies to all earnings, she is not exempt from any Medicare tax. Her Medicare tax is $43.65 ($3,010.35 × 0.0145).

FYI

At one time, Social Security and Medicare were not separated for tax computation and there was a limit on Medicare taxable earnings. Now ALL earnings are taxable for Medicare.

PAYROLL REGISTER

OBJECTIVE 4
Complete a payroll register.

The **payroll register** is a multicolumn form prepared for each payroll period listing the earnings, deductions, and net pay for each employee. In Figure 4 (shown on the next page) we see a payroll register that shows the data for each employee on a separate line. This would be suitable for a firm, like Goren Company, that has a small number of employees.

First, we'll show the entire payroll register; then, we'll break it down and explain it column by column. The number at the foot of each column refers to the related text description.

The payroll period shown in Figure 4 covers October 1 through October 7. The first part consists of employees' names, hours worked, beginning cumulative earnings, and taxable earnings.

(1) Total Hours—Taken from employees' time cards.

(2) Beginning Cumulative Earnings—The amount each employee has earned between January 1 and September 30 (the last day of the previous payroll period). It is taken from each employee's individual earnings record. (See Figure 7, pages 282–283.)

(3) Regular Earnings—Earnings for hours worked up to and including 40. In other words, the first 40 hours multiplied by each employee's regular hourly rate.

	NAME	TOTAL HOURS	BEGINNING CUMULATIVE EARNINGS	EARNINGS REGULAR	EARNINGS OVERTIME	EARNINGS TOTAL	ENDING CUMULATIVE EARNINGS	UNEMPLOYMENT
1	Amano, Mark E.	46	44 9 6 0 00	9 1 8 00	2 0 6 58	1 1 2 4 58	46 0 8 4 58	
2	Barkov, Anna E.	45	5 9 8 7 00	6 2 6 20	1 1 8 00	7 4 4 20	6 7 3 1 20	7 4 4 20
3	Dorn, David L.	49	6 7 8 6 00	6 8 6 00	2 3 0 00	9 1 6 00	7 7 0 2 00	2 1 4 00
4	Felding, Sarah H.	40	38 4 6 2 00	1 0 8 4 50	0 00	1 0 8 4 50	39 5 4 6 50	
5	Graham, Jason W.	40	68 6 0 0 00	1 7 9 8 45	0 00	1 7 9 8 45	70 3 9 8 45	
6	Kilmer, Richard B.	40	68 5 0 0 00	1 8 9 5 58	0 00	1 8 9 5 58	70 3 9 5 58	
7	Mankowitz, Jim L.	55	37 8 5 0 00	1 2 6 4 30	5 8 0 00	1 8 4 4 30	39 6 9 4 30	
8	Orlene, Barbara A.	40	45 8 2 0 00	1 4 8 7 20	0 00	1 4 8 7 20	47 3 0 7 20	
9	Parker, William R.	44	46 4 3 0 00	1 5 8 1 58	1 9 4 70	1 7 7 6 28	48 2 0 6 28	
10	Rumberg, Shelly L.	45	54 8 6 7 00	1 6 7 4 16	2 7 5 00	1 9 4 9 16	56 8 1 6 16	
11	Tabor, Annette G.	40	42 7 4 0 00	1 1 6 8 83	0 00	1 1 6 8 83	43 9 0 8 83	
12	Walker, Susan	52	91 3 0 0 00	2 2 1 5 15	7 9 5 20	3 0 1 0 35	94 3 1 0 35	
13			552 3 0 2 00	16 3 9 9 95	2 3 9 9 48	18 7 9 9 43	571 1 0 1 43	9 5 8 20
14		(1)	(2)	(3)	(4)	(5)	(6)	(7A)
15								

16,399.95 + 2,399.48 = 18,799.43

552,302.00 + 18,799.43 = 571,101.43

FIGURE 4

(4) **Overtime Earnings**—Hours in excess of 40 (relative to a 40-hour week) worked by each employee, multiplied by that employee's overtime rate.

(5) **Total Earnings**—Regular earnings plus overtime earnings.

(6) **Ending Cumulative Earnings**—Beginning Cumulative Earnings plus Total Earnings.

(7) **Taxable Earnings**—The amount of earnings subject to taxation, **not the tax itself.** We'll use these columns later to figure the amount of each tax. In other words, **Taxable Earnings is the base on which to figure the tax. Taxable Earnings multiplied by the tax rate equals the amount of the tax.**

(7A) **Unemployment Taxable Earnings**—In our illustration, we are using a maximum of $7,000 for unemployment tax liability on the employer for each employee. This column represents the previously untaxed portion remaining of the $7,000 for the individual employees. **Unemployment tax is paid only by the employer in most states. An unemployment tax may be paid both to the state and to the federal government.** Actually, states may use different maximum earnings and different rates than does the federal government. However, many states use $7,000, which at the time of this writing is the amount used by the federal government. There are three possibilities for Unemployment Taxable Earnings, as follows:

a. **Employee's cumulative earnings including this pay period have not reached $7,000.** When an employee's cumulative earnings so far during the calendar year (since January 1) are less than $7,000, we record the total earnings for the payroll period in the Unemployment Taxable Earnings column. For example, Anna E. Barkov's cumulative earnings before this

PAYROLL REGISTER FOR WEEK ENDED October 7, 20—

| (7) TAXABLE EARNINGS | | (8) DEDUCTIONS | | | | | |
SOCIAL SECURITY	MEDICARE	FEDERAL INCOME TAX	STATE INCOME TAX	SOCIAL SECURITY TAX	MEDICARE TAX	MEDICAL INSURANCE	OTHER
1 1 2 4 58	1 1 2 4 58	1 3 1 00	2 6 20	6 9 72	1 6 31	1 8 50	0 00
7 4 4 20	7 4 4 20	7 4 00	1 4 80	4 6 14	1 0 79	1 1 50	UW 3 5 00
9 1 6 00	9 1 6 00	1 0 0 00	2 0 00	5 6 79	1 3 28	1 5 50	UW 2 5 00
1 0 8 4 50	1 0 8 4 50	1 1 6 00	2 3 20	6 7 24	1 5 73	1 7 20	0 00
1 7 9 8 45	1 7 9 8 45	2 8 1 00	5 6 20	1 1 1 50	2 6 08	3 0 50	0 00
1 8 9 5 58	1 8 9 5 58	3 0 6 00	6 1 20	1 1 7 53	2 7 49	3 2 00	UW 1 5 00
1 8 4 4 30	1 8 4 4 30	2 9 3 00	5 8 60	1 1 4 35	2 6 74	3 0 00	UW 1 5 00
1 4 8 7 20	1 4 8 7 20	2 0 4 00	4 0 80	9 2 21	2 1 56	2 5 00	UW 2 0 00
1 7 7 6 28	1 7 7 6 28	2 7 6 00	5 5 20	1 1 0 13	2 5 76	3 0 50	0 00
1 9 4 9 16	1 9 4 9 16	3 1 9 00	6 3 80	1 2 0 85	2 8 26	3 5 00	AR 3 0 00
1 1 6 8 83	1 1 6 8 83	1 3 7 00	2 7 40	7 2 47	1 6 95	2 0 00	UW 2 5 00
2 9 0 0 00	3 0 1 0 35	6 0 1 00	1 2 0 20	1 7 9 80	4 3 65	5 5 00	UW 5 0 00
18 6 8 9 08	18 7 9 9 43	2 8 3 8 00	5 6 7 60	1 1 5 8 73	2 7 2 60	3 2 0 70	2 1 5 00
(7 B)	(7 C)	(8 A)	(8 B)	(8 C)	(8 D)	(8 E)	(8 F)

2,838.00 + 567.60 + 1,158.73 + 272.60 + 320.70 + 215.00 = 5,372.63

PAGE 56

| | (9) PAYMENTS | | | (10) EXPENSE ACCOUNT DEBITED | |
TOTAL	NET AMOUNT	CK. NO.	SALES WAGES EXPENSE	OFFICE WAGES EXPENSE	
2 6 1 73	8 6 2 85	931	1 1 2 4 58		1
1 9 2 23	5 5 1 97	932	7 4 4 20		2
2 3 0 57	6 8 5 43	933	9 1 6 00		3
2 3 9 37	8 4 5 13	934		1 0 8 4 50	4
5 0 5 28	1 2 9 3 17	935	1 7 9 8 45		5
5 5 9 22	1 3 3 6 36	936		1 8 9 5 58	6
5 3 7 69	1 3 0 6 61	937	1 8 4 4 30		7
4 0 3 57	1 0 8 3 63	938		1 4 8 7 20	8
4 9 7 59	1 2 7 8 69	939	1 7 7 6 28		9
5 9 6 91	1 3 5 2 25	940	1 9 4 9 16		10
2 9 8 82	8 7 0 01	941	1 1 6 8 83		11
1 0 4 9 65	1 9 6 0 70	942	3 0 1 0 35		12
5 3 7 2 63	13 4 2 6 80		14 3 3 2 15	4 4 6 7 28	13
(8 G)	(9 A)	(9B)	(1 0 A)	(1 0 B)	14
					15

5,372.63 + 13,426.80 = 18,799.43   14,332.15 + 4,467.28 = 18,799.43

FYI

Social Security and Medicare taxes are recorded separately in the payroll register because there is no limit on Medicare as there is on Social Security.

week were $5,987. Barkov's cumulative earnings after this week are $6,731.20 ($5,987 + $744.20). Because Barkov's cumulative earnings are still less than $7,000 (after the current check of $744.20), her entire $744.20 in wages earned during this pay period is listed in the Unemployment Taxable Earnings column.

b. **Employee's cumulative earnings were less than $7,000 before this week and are more than $7,000 after this week.** Look at the line for David L. Dorn and notice that his cumulative earnings before this week were $6,786. Dorn's new cumulative earnings (ending) are $7,702 ($6,786 + $916), putting him over the $7,000 maximum. Therefore, to bring Dorn up to the $7,000 limit, $214 ($7,000 − $6,786) of his earnings for the week are taxable. After this week, none of Dorn's earnings for the remainder of this calendar year will be taxable for unemployment.

c. **Employee's cumulative earnings before this week were more than $7,000.** After an employee's earnings top $7,000 during the calendar year, record a dash in the Unemployment Taxable Earnings column to indicate that the column has not been forgotten or overlooked. For example, Mark Amano's total earnings before the payroll period ended October 7 (beginning) were $44,960 (as shown in his individual earnings record in Figure 7). Since he had previously earned more than $7,000 this year, we record a dash in the Unemployment Taxable Earnings column.

(7B) Social Security Taxable Earnings—The first $94,200 for each employee. We assume a Social Security tax rate of 6.2 percent of the first $94,200 paid to each employee during the calendar year.

a. **Employee's cumulative earnings including this pay period have not reached $94,200.** When an employee's cumulative earnings so far during the year are less than $94,200, we record the total earnings for the payroll period in the Social Security Taxable Earnings column. For example, Anna Barkov's cumulative earnings so far this year amount to $6,731.20. Because Barkov's total earnings are less than $94,200, the entire $744.20 of wages earned during this pay period is listed in the Social Security Taxable Earnings column. Note that this is true of all the employees except Susan Walker.

b. **Employee's cumulative earnings were less than $94,200 before this week and are more than $94,200 after this week.** The line for Susan Walker shows her cumulative earnings before the payroll period ended October 7 were $91,300. However, the cumulative earnings including those of this payroll period total $94,310.35, which is greater than the $94,200 limit. That means only $2,900 ($94,200 − $91,300) of her current pay period earnings is recorded in the Social Security Taxable Earnings column. After an employee's earnings top $94,200 during the calendar year, record a dash to indicate that the column has not been forgotten or overlooked. (Use the same procedure as for the Unemployment Taxable Earnings column.)

(7C) Medicare Taxable Earnings—All earnings for this period. We have assumed a Medicare tax rate of 1.45 percent (.0145) on all earnings that are paid to each employee during the calendar year. Therefore, all earnings for this period are taxable and are recorded in the Medicare Taxable Earnings column.

(8) Deductions—Amounts taken away (withheld) from total earnings.

(8A) **Federal Income Tax Deductions**—The amount of the federal income tax deduction for each employee can be located directly on the wage bracket tables or calculated on a percentage basis.

(8B) **State Income Tax Deductions**—States that impose income taxes also provide wage-bracket tables. The state tax deduction for each employee can be located directly in the appropriate table. As stated previously, we are assuming a rate of 20 percent of the federal income tax.

(8C) **Social Security Tax Deductions**—For each employee's Social Security tax deduction, we first go to the Social Security Taxable Earnings column and note the amount subject to tax. Next, we multiply the Social Security taxable earnings by 6.2 percent (.062). For example, Barkov's taxable earnings are $744.20, and her Social Security tax deduction is $46.14 ($744.20 × .062).

(8D) **Medicare Tax Deductions**—For each employee's Medicare tax deduction, we go to the Medicare Taxable Earnings column and note the amount subject to tax. Next, we multiply the Medicare taxable earnings by 1.45 percent. For example, Barkov's taxable earnings are $744.20, and her Medicare tax deduction is $10.79 ($744.20 × .0145).

(8E) **Medical Insurance Deductions**—Premiums paid by the employee through payroll withholding. The amount of the premium for each employee depends on the number of dependents claimed, among other things. For example, Barkov's premium is $11.50 per week.

(8F) **Other Deductions**—Employees' voluntary withholdings. In our illustration, UW represents the United Way, and AR stands for Accounts Receivable (employee pays off charge account to the company). For example, Shelly Rumberg paid $30 on her charge account.

(8G) **Total Deductions**—The combined total of each employee's deductions for taxes, insurance, and other. For example, Barkov's total deduction is $192.23 ($74.00 + $14.80 + $46.14 + $10.79 + $11.50 + $35.00).

(9) **Payments**—The amount of each employee's payroll check (take-home pay).

(9A) **Net Amount**—Each employee's Total Earnings minus Total Deductions. For example, Barkov's net amount is $551.97 ($744.20 − $192.23).

(9B) **Ck. No.**—The number of each employee's payroll check.

(10) **Expense Account Debited**—Columns used for distributing each amount into the appropriate wages expense account. Goren Company uses Sales Wages Expense and Office Wages Expense. The sum of these two columns equals the total earnings.

(10A) **Sales Wages Expense**—Amounts earned by employees involved in sales activities.

(10B) **Office Wages Expense**—Amounts earned by employees involved in office activities.

THE PAYROLL ENTRY

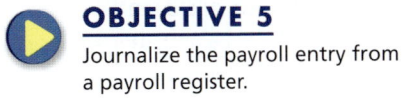

OBJECTIVE 5

Journalize the payroll entry from a payroll register.

Because the payroll register summarizes the payroll data for the period, it is used as the basis for recording the payroll in the ledger accounts. Since the payroll register does not have the status of a journal, a journal entry is necessary. Figure 5 on page 280 shows the entry in general journal form.

GENERAL JOURNAL   PAGE ___31___

	DATE		DESCRIPTION	POST. REF.	DEBIT	CREDIT	
1	20–						1
2	Oct.	7	Sales Wages Expense		14 3 3 2 15		2
3			Office Wages Expense		4 4 6 7 28		3
4			Employees' Federal Income				4
5			Tax Payable			2 8 3 8 00	5
6			FICA Tax Payable			1 4 3 1 33	6
7			Employees' State Income Tax				7
8			Payable			5 6 7 60	8
9			Employees' Medical Insurance				9
10			Payable			3 2 0 70	10
11			Employees' United Way				11
12			Payable			1 8 5 00	12
13			Accounts Receivable			3 0 00	13
14			Wages Payable			13 4 2 6 80	14
15			Payroll register, page 56,				15
16			for week ended October 7.				16

FIGURE 5

Note that the accountant records the total cost to the company for services of employees as debits to the Wages Expense accounts.

Also note that the total Social Security tax deductions ($1,158.73) and the total Medicare tax deductions ($272.60) are combined to become FICA Tax Payable of $1,431.33 ($1,158.73 + $272.60). The two tax deductions are combined into the one liability account because they are paid together at the same time. Social Security and Medicare taxes are recorded separately in the payroll register because they must be listed separately on each employee's W-2 form (Wage and Tax Statement).

To pay the employees from the company's regular checking account, the accountant now makes the following journal entry:

			DESCRIPTION	DEBIT	CREDIT	
17		8	Wages Payable	13 4 2 6 80		17
18			Cash—M. Amano		8 6 2 85	18
19			Cash—A. Barkov		5 5 1 97	19
20			Cash—D. Dorn		6 8 5 43	20
21			Cash—S. Felding		8 4 5 13	21
22			Cash—J. Graham		1 2 9 3 17	22
23			Cash—R. Kilmer		1 3 3 6 36	23
24			Cash—J. Mankowitz		1 3 0 6 61	24
25			Cash—B. Orlene		1 0 8 3 63	25
26			Cash—W. Parker		1 2 7 8 69	26
27			Cash—S. Rumberg		1 3 5 2 25	27
28			Cash—A. Tabor		8 7 0 01	28
29			Cash—S. Walker		1 9 6 0 70	29

Special Payroll Bank Account—An Alternative

A firm with a large number of employees would probably open a special **payroll bank account** with its bank. One check drawn on the regular bank account is made payable to the special payroll account for the amount of the total net pay for a payroll period. All payroll checks for the period are then written on the special payroll account. To record this, the accountant makes the following journal entry. In this book, assume the entry to debit Cash—Payroll Bank Account and to credit Cash has already been made.

GENERAL JOURNAL   PAGE 1

DATE	DESCRIPTION	POST. REF.	DEBIT	CREDIT
8	Wages Payable		13 4 2 6 80	
	Cash—Payroll Bank Account			13 4 2 6 80
	Paid wages for week			
	ended October 7.			

Paycheck

All the data needed to make out a payroll check are available in the payroll register. Mark E. Amano's paycheck is shown in Figure 6.

FIGURE 6

EMPLOYEE	TOTAL HOURS	O.T. HOURS	REG. PAY	O.T. PREM. PAY	GROSS PAY	FED INC. TAX	STATE INC. TAX	SOCIAL SECURITY TAX	MEDICARE TAX	MEDICAL INSURANCE	OTHER	TOTAL DED.	NET PAY
Mark E. Amano	46	6	918.00	206.58	1,124.58	131.00	26.20	69.72	16.31	18.50	—	261.73	862.85

CENTRAL NATIONAL BANK 98-461/252

Payroll Account

Goren Company
610 First Avenue
Bangor, Maine 04401

October 8 20 — No. 931

PAY TO THE ORDER OF Mark E. Amano $ 862.85

Eight hundred sixty-two and 85/100 — DOLLARS

Eileen Goren

⑆252⑈046⑆

EMPLOYEE'S INDIVIDUAL EARNINGS RECORD

NAME **Mark E. Amano**

ADDRESS **6357 Boston Lane**

Bangor, Maine 04401

MALE **X**   FEMALE _____

MARRIED **X**   SINGLE _____

PHONE NO. **663-2556**   DATE OF BIRTH **9/19/72**

EMPLOYEE NO. **5**

SOC. SEC. NO. **543-24-1680**

PAY RATE **$22.95**

EQUIVALENT HOURLY RATE **$22.95**

DATE TERMINATED _____

CLASSIFICATION FOR WORKERS' COMPENSATION INSURANCE _____ **Sales floor**

PERIOD ENDED	DATE PAID	HOURS WORKED REG	HOURS WORKED O.T.	EARNINGS REGULAR	EARNINGS OVERTIME	EARNINGS TOTAL	ENDING CUMULATIVE EARNINGS	FEDERAL INCOME TAX	STATE INCOME TAX
9/2	9/3	40	8	9 1 8 00	2 7 5 44	1 1 9 3 44	40 7 7 1 55	1 4 2 00	2 8 40
9/9	9/10	40	2	9 1 8 00	6 8 86	9 8 6 86	41 7 5 8 41	1 1 0 00	2 2 00
9/16	9/17	40	2	9 1 8 00	6 8 86	9 8 6 86	42 7 4 5 27	1 1 0 00	2 2 00
9/23	9/24	40	5	9 1 8 00	1 7 2 15	1 0 9 0 15	43 8 3 5 42	1 2 7 00	2 5 40
9/30	10/1	40	6	9 1 8 00	2 0 6 58	1 1 2 4 58	44 9 6 0 00	1 3 1 00	2 6 20
10/7	10/8	40	6	9 1 8 00	2 0 6 58	1 1 2 4 58	46 0 8 4 58	1 3 1 00	2 6 20

FIGURE 7

Employees' Individual Earnings Records

To comply with government regulations, a firm has to keep current data on each employee's accumulated earnings, deductions, and net pay. The information contained in the payroll register is recorded each payday in each **employee's individual earnings record**. Figure 7 shows a portion of the earnings record for Mark E. Amano.

CHAPTER REVIEW

Review of Performance Objectives

1. Understand the role of laws that affect payroll deductions and contributions.

   Those employees and employers involved in the computation and paying of employees for their work must understand the laws, know the percentages and limits involved, and when and to whom to submit the funds deducted from employees and contributed by employees.

2. Calculate total earnings based on an hourly, piece-rate, or commission basis.

   Earnings calculated on an *hourly basis* equal the hourly rate multiplied by the number of hours worked. Earnings calculated on a *piece-rate basis* equal the total number of products produced multiplied by the rate per unit of product. Earnings calculated on a *commission basis* equal the total number of units sold or the price of units sold multiplied by the commission rate.

3. Determine deductions using tables of employees' income tax withholding.

   Using the appropriate income tax withholding table in IRS Publication 15 (Circular E), first determine marital status and payroll period and then locate the wage bracket containing the amount of earnings. Next, on the same horizontal line, select the vertical column containing the number of allowances claimed.

4. Complete a payroll register.

   List the employees' names, hours worked, and beginning cumulative earnings. Add the total earnings to the beginning cumulative earnings to get ending cumulative earnings. The Unemployment Taxable Earnings column is used for the first

DATE EMPLOYED __2/1/—__

NO. OF EXEMPTIONS __0__

PER HOUR __X__   PER DAY _____

PER WEEK _____   PER MONTH _____

	SOCIAL SECURITY TAX	MEDICARE TAX	MEDICAL INSURANCE	OTHER CODE	AMOUNT	TOTAL	NET AMOUNT	CK. NO.
	73 99	17 30	18 50	UW	5 00	285 19	908 25	871
	61 19	14 31	18 50	UW		226 00	760 86	883
	61 19	14 31	18 50	UW	5 00	231 00	755 86	895
	67 59	15 81	18 50	UW		254 30	835 85	907
	69 72	16 31	18 50	UW	5 00	266 73	857 85	919
	69 72	16 31	18 50	UW		261 73	862 85	931

$7,000 of each employee's earnings for FUTA and SUTA. The Social Security Taxable Earnings column is used for an assumed first $94,200. The Medicare Taxable Earnings column is used for all earnings. Under the Deductions columns, list the income taxes withheld, the Social Security taxes withheld, the Medicare taxes withheld, and other deductions. The Social Security tax deduction equals the Social Security taxable earnings multiplied by an assumed rate of 6.2 percent. The Medicare tax deduction equals the Medicare taxable earnings multiplied by an assumed rate of 1.45 percent. Net amount equals total (gross) earnings minus total deductions. The Expense Account Debited columns are used to distribute salaries and wages expense to the appropriate accounts.

5. Journalize the payroll entry from a payroll register.

   Totals are taken directly from the payroll register. Refer to the general journal illustrations on pages 280 and 281 for an example of the first payroll entry and examples of two ways to journalize the payment of the payroll—one from the company's regular checking account, and one from a special payroll bank account.

6. Maintain employees' individual earnings records.

   In the employees' individual earnings records, list the personal data for each employee. Based on the information contained in the payroll register, record the earnings and deductions for each payroll period.

Glossary

Calendar year A twelve-month period beginning on January 1 and ending on December 31 of the same year. (275)

Current Tax Payment Act (Income Tax Withholding) An act to require employers to withhold and pay to the U.S. Treasury employee funds. (268)

Employee One who works for compensation under the direction and control of the employer. (267)

Employee's individual earnings record A supplementary record for each employee showing personal payroll data and yearly cumulative earnings, deductions, and net pay. (282)

Employee's Withholding Allowance Certificate (Form W-4) A form that specifies the number of allowances claimed by each employee and gives the employer the authority to withhold money for an employee's federal income taxes and FICA taxes. (272)

Exemption An amount of an employee's annual earnings not subject to income tax for the taxpayer, taxpayer's spouse, and dependents (usually children). (272)

Fair Labor Standards Act (FLSA) The act of 1938 that provides for minimum standards for wages and overtime, including provisions related to child labor and equal pay for equal work. (268)

FICA taxes Social Security taxes plus Medicare taxes, paid by both employee and employer under the provisions of the Federal Insurance Contributions Act. The proceeds are used to pay old-age and disability pensions and to fund the Medicare program. (275)

Gross pay The total amount of an employee's pay before any deductions. (266)

Independent contractor Someone who is engaged for a definite job or service, and who may choose his or her own means of doing the work. This person is not an employee of the firm for which the service is provided. (267)

Medicare taxes Federal government taxes levied on employees and employers; proceeds are used for medical insurance for eligible people age 65 or over. (275)

Net pay Gross pay minus deductions. Also called *take-home pay*. (266)

Payroll bank account A special checking account used to pay a company's employees. (281)

Payroll register A multicolumn form prepared for each payroll period listing the earnings, deductions, and net pay for each employee. (275)

Social Security Act of 1935 An act to provide for worker retirement funding through deductions from their wages and matching amounts from the employers. (268)

Social Security taxes Federal government taxes levied on employees and employers; proceeds are used for old-age pensions and disability benefits. (275)

Taxable earnings The amount of an employee's earnings subject to a tax. (272)

Wage-bracket tax tables A chart providing the amounts to be deducted for income taxes based on amount of earnings, marital status, and number of allowances claimed. (273)

Withholding allowance An amount of an employee's annual earnings not subject to income tax. (272)

Workers' compensation laws Laws that protect employees and dependents against losses due to death or injury incurred on the job. (269)

QUESTIONS, EXERCISES, AND CASES

Discussion Questions

1. Why must employers maintain employees' individual earnings records?
2. What information is included in an employee's individual earnings record?

3. What is the purpose of the payroll register?

4. Explain the difference between gross earnings and net earnings for a payroll period.

5. Describe how a special payroll bank account is useful in paying the wages and salaries of employees.

6. List three required deductions and four voluntary deductions from an employee's total earnings.

7. What is the difference between an employee and an independent contractor? List two examples of an independent contractor.

8. What information is included in a wage-bracket withholding table? Are there overlapping amounts of gross earnings in the table?

Exercises

P.O. 1,2

Calculate gross pay.

Exercise 8-1 Determine the gross pay for each employee listed below.

a. Gary Dale is paid time-and-a-half for all hours over forty. He worked forty-four hours during the week. His regular pay rate is $10.80 per hour.

b. Moira Nole worked fifty hours during the week. She is entitled to time-and-a-half for all hours in excess of forty per week. Her regular pay rate is $12.50 per hour.

c. Lora Mikel is paid a commission of 8 percent of her sales, which amounted to $10,885.

d. Margo Best's yearly salary is $40,800. During the week, Best worked forty-three hours, and she is entitled to time-and-a-half for all hours over forty.

P.O. 1,2,3

Determine gross pay and withholding.

Exercise 8-2 Lisa Meilo works for Palo Company, which pays its employees time-and-a-half for all hours worked in excess of forty per week. Meilo's pay rate is $18.50 per hour. Her wages are subject to federal income tax, a Social Security tax deduction at the rate of 6.2 percent, and a Medicare tax deduction at the rate of 1.45 percent. She is married and claims three allowances. Meilo has an unpaid half-hour lunch break during an eight-and-one-half-hour day. In the most recent pay period, she worked fifty hours. Meilo's beginning cumulative earnings are $36,827.

Complete the following using Meilo's most recent time card shown at the top of page 286.

a. _____ hours at straight time × $_____
   per hour $_____

b. _____ hours overtime × $_____
   per hour   _____

c. Total gross pay $_____

d. Federal income tax withholding (from tax
   tables in Figure 3, page 274) $_____

e. Social Security tax withholding at 6.2 percent   _____

f. Medicare tax withholding at 1.45 percent   _____

g. Total withholding   _____

h. Net pay $_____

TIME CARD

Name   Meilo, Lisa

Week ending   March 11, 20—

Day	In	Out	In	Out	Hours Worked Regular	Hours Worked Overtime
M	756	12 09	12 39	432	8	
T	752	12 05	12 35	504	8	½
W	759	12 20	12 40	503	8	½
T	800	12 08	12 38	434	8	
F	756	12 09	12 39	633	8	2
S	800	12 01	12 40	340		7
S						

P.O. 1,2,3,4

Determine net pay.

Exercise 8-3 Using the income tax withholding table in Figure 3, page 274, for each employee of Miles Company, determine the net pay for the week ended January 21. Assume a Social Security tax of 6.2 percent and a Medicare tax of 1.45 percent. All employees have cumulative earnings, including this pay period, of less than $94,200. Assume all employees are married.

Employee	Allowances	Total Earnings	Social Security Tax Withheld	Medicare Tax Withheld	Federal Income Tax Withheld	Union Dues Withheld	Medical Insurance Withheld	Net Pay
a. Aston, F. B.	1	$ 900	$	$	$	$ 25	$ 35	$
b. Dwyer, S. J.	2	920				25	35	
c. Flynn, K. A.	3	1,110				25	40	
d. Harden, J. L.	0	1,025				25	40	
e. Nguyen, H.	2	925				25	35	
Totals		$4,880	$	$	$	$125	$185	$

FIGURE 8

NAME	BEGINNING CUMULATIVE EARNINGS	EARNINGS REGULAR	EARNINGS OVERTIME	EARNINGS TOTAL	ENDING CUMULATIVE EARNINGS	TAXABLE EARNINGS UNEMPLOYMENT	TAXABLE EARNINGS SOCIAL SECURITY	TAXABLE EARNINGS MEDICARE
	245 7 5 4 00	6 7 2 4 00	1 2 2 0 00	7 4 9 4 00	253 2 4 8 00	2 4 5 6 00	7 9 4 4 00	7 9 4 4 00

P.O. 1,4

Locate errors in a payroll register.

Exercise 8-4 For the week ended September 7, the totals of the payroll register for Benton, Inc., are presented in Figure 8. The regular and overtime earnings are correct. List six errors that exist. All earnings are subject to Social Security and Medicare taxes.

P.O. 1,4

Determine taxable earnings.

Exercise 8-5 For tax purposes, assume that the maximum taxable earnings are $94,200 for Social Security and $7,000 for the unemployment tax, and that all earnings are taxable for Medicare. For the payroll register for the month of November in Figure 9, determine the taxable earnings for each employee.

EMPLOYEE	BEGINNING CUMULATIVE EARNINGS	TOTAL EARNINGS	ENDING CUMULATIVE EARNINGS	TAXABLE EARNINGS		
				UNEMPLOYMENT	SOCIAL SECURITY	MEDICARE
Axton, C.	94 0 0 0 00	7 6 9 1 00	101 6 9 1 00			
Edgar, E.	45 4 6 5 00	3 6 8 0 00	49 1 4 5 00			
Gorman, L.	36 8 7 9 00	3 0 6 4 00	39 9 4 3 00			
Jolson, R.	24 6 3 4 00	2 3 2 5 00	26 9 5 9 00			
Nixel, P.	6 8 5 0 00	2 4 6 3 00	9 3 1 3 00			

FIGURE 9

P.O. 1,4,5

Determine FICA withholdings and journalize the payroll entry.

Exercise 8-6 On January 21, the column totals of the payroll register for Cory Company showed that its sales employees had earned $14,960, its trucking employees had earned $10,692, and its office employees had earned $8,670. Social Security taxes were withheld at an assumed rate of 6.2 percent, and Medicare taxes were withheld at an assumed rate of 1.45 percent. Other deductions consisted of federal income tax, $3,975; medical insurance, $1,480; union dues, $560. Determine the amount of Social Security and Medicare taxes withheld, and record the general journal entry for the payroll, crediting Salaries Payable for the net pay. All earnings were taxable.

	DEDUCTIONS						PAYMENTS		WAGES EXPENSE
FEDERAL INCOME TAX	SOCIAL SECURITY TAX	MEDICARE TAX	UNION DUES	MEDICAL INSURANCE	TOTAL		NET AMOUNT	CK. NO.	DEBIT
9 4 9 00	4 2 9 53	1 1 5 19	1 9 3 00	2 9 2 00	2 0 8 3 00		5 4 5 6 00		7 4 9 4 00

P.O. 1,2,3

Determine missing amounts.

Exercise 8-7 Lehn Labs has two employees. The information shown below was taken from its individual earnings records for the month of September. Determine the missing amounts, assuming that the Social Security tax is 6.2 percent and the Medicare tax is 1.45 percent. All earnings are subject to Social Security and Medicare taxes. Round amounts to nearest penny.

	Barton	Ringness	Total
Regular earnings	$1,750.00	$?	$?
Overtime earnings	?	120.00	?
Total earnings	$1,860.00	$?	$?
Federal income tax withheld	$ 335.00	$?	$?
State income tax withheld	?	92.00	?
Social Security tax withheld	115.32	111.60	?
Medicare tax withheld	25.38	26.10	?
Medical insurance withheld	26.97	97.00	?
Total deductions	$ 688.88	$ 554.70	$?
Net pay	$?	$1,245.30	$?

P.O. 5

Journalize the payroll entry.

Exercise 8-8 Assume that the employees in Exercise 8-7 are paid from the company's regular bank account (check numbers 981 and 982). Prepare the entry to record and pay the payroll in general journal form, dated September 30.

internet
LINKS TO ACCOUNTING

As you've learned about recording payroll taxes in this chapter, have you thought about how they affect you?

Find out whether you would have more or less deducted from your paycheck if you moved from Massachusetts to Oklahoma. Then, consider moving to Wyoming. Use the paycheck calculator provided at Payroll-Taxes.com (http://www.paycheckcity.com/copayroll-taxes/netpaycalculator.asp). For each state, assume it is the 2006 tax year, you are single, you would make $2,000 per week, and you claim no federal or state exemptions or other deductions. If the amounts differ, explain how they differ.

CONSIDER AND COMMUNICATE

Norton Company pays its employees weekly by issuing checks on its regular bank account. The owner thinks it would be too much trouble to have a second checking account. Explain to the owner why this might be worth the additional effort.

WHAT'S WRONG WITH THIS PICTURE?

You have just completed the payroll register for this week's payroll. You have crossfooted the register—that is, you have added the columns vertically and horizontally to see if you come up with the same totals both ways. There is just one problem: The total of the Net Amount column does not equal the total of the Gross Amount column minus the total of the Total Deductions column. How could this happen? What would you do to obtain correctly crossfooted totals?

A QUESTION OF ETHICS

An employee who is married and has three children submits a W-4 form to his employer and checks the box that says "Single," and writes zero in the "Deductions Claimed" box. Is this action ethical, unethical, or illegal? Explain your reasoning.

PROBLEM SET A

For additional help, see the demonstration problem at the beginning of each chapter in your Working Papers.

P.O. 1,2,3

Problem 8-1A Violet Ross, an employee of Hofman Company, worked forty-eight hours during the week of February 9 through 15. Her rate of pay is $16.50 per hour, and she gets time-and-a-half for work in excess of forty hours per week. She is married and claims two allowances on her W-4 form. Her wages are subject to the following deductions:

a. Federal income tax (use the table in Figure 3, page 274).
b. Social Security tax at 6.2 percent.
c. Medicare tax at 1.45 percent.
d. Union dues, $30.00.
e. Medical insurance, $32.00.

Check Figure

Net pay, $658.36

Instructions

Compute her regular pay, overtime pay, gross pay, and net pay.

P.O. 1,2,4,5

Problem 8-2A Payroll information for Ridge Homes for the week ended February 21 is shown at the top of page 290.

Taxable earnings for Social Security are based on the first $94,200. Taxable earnings for Medicare are based on all earnings. Taxable earnings for federal and state unemployment are based on the first $7,000. Employees are paid time-and-a-half for work in excess of forty hours per week.

Name	Earnings at End of Previous Week	Daily Time							Pay Rate	Federal Income Tax
		S	M	T	W	T	F	S		
Arms, P.	1,950.00	8	8	8	8	8			12.00	125.00
Bill, D.	2,060.00			8	8	8	8	8	12.50	138.00
Carn, W.	2,085.00	8	8	8			8	8	12.95	155.00
Dorf, J.	748.00				8	8			22.00	130.00
Edgar, L.	2,687.00	8	8	8			8	8	12.90	178.00
Fitz, G. W.	2,075.00	8	8		8	8	8	8	12.45	140.00

Check Figure

Net amount, $1,916.88

Instructions

1. Complete the payroll register, page 37. The Social Security tax rate is 6.2 percent, and the Medicare tax rate is 1.45 percent. Begin payroll checks with No. 208.
2. Prepare a general journal entry to record the payroll. The firm's general ledger contains a Wages Expense account and a Wages Payable account.
3. Assuming that the firm has transferred funds from its regular bank account to its special payroll bank account, and that this entry has been made, prepare a general journal entry to record the payment of wages.

P.O. 1,2,3,4,5

Problem 8-3A Austin Company pays its employees time-and-a-half for hours worked in excess of forty per week. The information available from time cards and employees' individual earnings records for the pay period ended October 14 is shown in the chart below.

Name	Earnings at End of Previous Week	Daily Time						Pay Rate	Income Tax Allowances
		M	T	W	T	F	S		
Bardin, J.	43,627.00	8	8	8	8	8	2	21.30	2
Caris, A.	44,340.00	8	8	8	8	8	8	21.60	1
Drew, W.	43,845.00	8	10	10	8	8	0	21.50	1
Garen, S.	93,030.00	8	8	8	8	8	0	49.00	3
North, M.	43,875.00	8	8	8	8	8	5	21.40	3
Ovid, N.	40,150.00	8	8	8	8	8	0	21.50	1
Ross, J.	6,430.00	8	8	8	8	8	4	20.50	1
Springer, O.	44,175.00	8	8	8	8	8	3	21.25	2

Taxable earnings for Social Security are based on the first $94,200. Taxable earnings for Medicare are based on all earnings. Taxable earnings for federal and state unemployment are based on the first $7,000.

Check Figure

Net amount, $7,167.58

Instructions

1. Complete the payroll register, page 72, using the wage-bracket income tax withholding table in Figure 3 (page 274). The Social Security tax rate is 6.2 percent, and the Medicare tax rate is 1.45 percent. Assume that all employees are married. Garen's federal income tax is $312. In the payroll register, begin payroll checks with No. 945.
2. Prepare a general journal entry to record the payroll. The firm's general ledger contains a Wages Expense account and a Wages Payable account.
3. Assuming that the firm has transferred funds from its regular bank account to its special payroll bank account, and that this entry has been made, prepare a general journal entry to record the payment of wages.

P.O. 1,4,5

Problem 8-4A The information for Tanger Company, shown in the chart below, is available from Tanger's time cards and the employees' individual earnings records for the pay period ended December 22.

Name	Hours Worked	Earnings at End of Previous Week	Total Earnings	Class.	Federal Income Tax	Other Deduct.	
Cgo, C.	44	31,670	1,650	Sales	199.00	UW	25.00
Don, V.	42	36,410	1,940	Sales	218.00	AR	95.00
Fine, J.	40	36,860	1,868	Sales	222.00	UW	25.00
Ginny, N.	46	33,590	1,785	Office	190.00	UW	35.00
John, M.	47	36,980	1,835	Office	210.00	UW	25.00
Lund, D.	43	93,240	2,100	Office	325.00	UW	20.00
Maya, R.	42	36,860	1,846	Sales	238.00	AR	70.00
Nord, P.	41	36,750	1,850	Sales	224.00	UW	20.00
Oscar, T.	43	33,480	1,750	Sales	208.00	UW	25.00
Troy, B.	40	47,250	1,170	Sales	116.00	UW	20.00

Taxable earnings for Social Security are based on the first $94,200. Taxable earnings for Medicare are based on all earnings. Taxable earnings for federal and state unemployment are based on the first $7,000.

Check Figure

Net amount, $13,993.41

Instructions

1. Complete the payroll register, page 56, using a Social Security tax rate of 6.2 percent and a Medicare tax rate of 1.45 percent. Concerning Other Deductions, AR refers to Accounts Receivable and UW refers to United Way. Begin payroll checks in the payroll register with No. 914.

2. Prepare the general journal entry to record the payroll. The firm's general ledger contains a Salary Expense account and a Salaries Payable account.
3. Prepare the general journal entry to pay the payroll. Assume that funds for this payroll have been transferred to Cash—Payroll Bank Account and that this entry has been made.

PROBLEM SET B

For additional help, see the demonstration problem at the beginning of each chapter in your Working Papers.

P.O. 1,2,3

Problem 8-1B Ina Provo, an employee of Gellen Company, worked forty-four hours during the week of October 11 through 17. Her rate of pay is $17.50 per hour, and she receives time-and-a-half for all work in excess of forty hours per week. Provo is married and claims two allowances on her W-4 form. Her wages are subject to the following deductions:

a. Federal income tax (use the table in Figure 3, page 274).
b. Social Security tax at 6.2 percent.
c. Medicare tax at 1.45 percent.
d. Union dues, $32.00.
e. Medical insurance, $44.75.

Check Figure

Net pay, $602.67

Instructions

Compute her regular pay, overtime pay, gross pay, and net pay.

P.O. 1,2,4,5

Problem 8-2B Harris Company has the following payroll information for the pay period ended May 14:

| Name | Earnings at End of Previous Week | Daily Time | | | | | | Pay Rate | Federal Income Tax |
		M	T	W	T	F	S		
Grant, L.	7,536.00	8	8	8	8	8	0	18.00	132.00
Hamn, R.	6,496.00	8	8	8	8	8	0	18.10	124.00
Lisk, J.	6,798.00	0	8	8	8	8	8	17.80	126.00
Myre, G.	9,589.00	8	8	8	0	8	8	19.25	155.00
Segel, T.	6,585.00	8	8	8	8	8	6	17.95	135.00
Torgel, I.	7,501.00	0	8	8	8	8	8	18.70	133.00

Taxable earnings for Social Security are based on the first $94,200. Taxable earnings for Medicare are based on all earnings. Taxable earnings for federal and state unemployment are based on the first $7,000. Employees are paid time-and-a-half for work in excess of forty hours per week.

P.O. 1,2,3,4,5

Instructions

1. Complete the payroll register, page 34. The Social Security tax rate is 6.2 percent, and the Medicare tax rate is 1.45 percent. Begin payroll checks with No. 744.
2. Prepare a general journal entry to record the payroll. The firm's general ledger contains a Wages Expense account and a Wages Payable account.
3. Assuming that the firm has transferred funds from its regular bank account to its special payroll bank account, and that this entry has been made, prepare a journal entry to record the payment of wages.

Problem 8-3B Wilke Company pays its employees time-and-a-half for hours worked in excess of forty per week. The information available from time cards and employees' individual earnings records for the pay period ended September 21 is shown in the chart below.

Name	Earnings at End of Previous Week	Daily Time						Pay Rate	Income Tax Allowances
		M	T	W	T	F	S		
Bolt, D.	6,745.00	8	8	8	10	8	0	19.50	1
Dore, C.	36,240.00	8	8	8	8	8	0	25.00	2
Gayle, A.	32,730.00	8	10	8	8	8	0	24.50	2
Hale, R.	92,250.00	8	8	8	8	8	4	53.00	3
Jilly, B.	35,154.00	8	8	8	8	8	0	49.50	0
Karn, S.	29,938.00	8	8	9	8	8	0	20.50	2
Ober, N.	6,795.00	8	8	8	9	9	4	21.00	1
Wong, J.	27,252.00	8	8	10	8	8	0	20.00	2

Taxable earnings for Social Security are based on the first $94,200. Taxable earnings for Medicare are based on all earnings. Taxable earnings for federal and state unemployment are based on the first $7,000.

Instructions

1. Complete the payroll register, page 72, using the wage-bracket income tax withholding table in Figure 3 (page 274). The Social Security tax rate is 6.2 percent, and the Medicare tax rate is 1.45 percent. Assume that all employees are married. Note: Hale's federal income tax deduction is $393. Jilly's federal income tax deduction is $295. In the payroll register, begin payroll checks with No. 863.
2. Prepare a general journal entry to record the payroll. The firm's general ledger contains a Wages Expense account and a Wages Payable account.
3. Assuming that the firm has transferred funds from its regular bank account to its special payroll bank account, and that this entry has been made, prepare a general journal entry to record the payment of wages.

P.O. 1,4,5

Problem 8-4B For Morley Company, the information available from the time books and employees' individual earnings records for the pay period ended December 29 is shown in the chart below.

Name	Hours Worked	Earnings at End of Previous Week	Total Earnings	Class.	Federal Income Tax	Other Deduct.	
Chang, C.	44	33,900.00	1,740.00	Sales	180.00	AR	80.00
Dugan, T.	42	38,270.00	1,935.00	Sales	212.00	UW	20.00
Fancher, K.	40	37,680.00	1,848.00	Sales	200.00	UW	25.00
Gannon, T.	44	33,245.00	1,740.00	Office	187.00		——
Jones, L.	48	37,789.00	1,845.00	Office	289.00	UW	25.00
Lange, M.	40	93,700.00	2,005.00	Office	302.00	UW	35.00
Milton, D.	43	37,684.00	1,938.00	Sales	206.00	UW	20.00
Naylor, B.	40	37,499.00	1,856.00	Sales	209.00		——
Orton, A.	44	34,338.00	1,780.00	Sales	201.00	AR	70.00
Tiosha, J.	42	48,120.00	1,065.00	Sales	190.00	UW	25.00

Taxable earnings for Social Security are based on the first $94,200. Taxable earnings for Medicare are based on all earnings. Taxable earnings for federal and state unemployment are based on the first $7,000.

Check Figure

Net amount, $14,011.28

Instructions

1. Complete the payroll register, page 56, using a Social Security tax rate of 6.2 percent and a Medicare tax rate of 1.45 percent. Concerning Other Deductions, AR refers to Accounts Receivable and UW refers to United Way. Begin payroll checks in the payroll register with No. 914.
2. Prepare the general journal entry to record the payroll. The firm's general ledger contains a Salary Expense account and a Salaries Payable account.
3. Prepare the general journal entry to pay the payroll. Assume that funds for this payroll have been transferred to Cash—Payroll Bank Account and that this entry has been made.

LINKS TO ACCOUNTING

Not only do you pay payroll taxes, but your employers pay their share, also! They deposit the federal taxes they withhold from your paycheck, as well as the FICA taxes they are required to pay, in an authorized commercial bank or in the Federal Reserve Bank using federal tax deposit coupons (Form 8109-B). Electronic deposits are required for companies with larger payrolls. The whole process of withholding and paying taxes can often seem complicated and confusing. As a service to taxpayers, the Internal Revenue Service (IRS) website provides convenient access to tax information, forms, and publications. Employers' requirements for making deposits begin on page 19 of Publication 15 (Circular E), which can be found at **http://www.irs.gov/pub/irs-pdf/p15.pdf.** You might be surprised at the extent of the requirements for something as simple as making a deposit!

Performance Objectives

After you have completed this chapter, you will be able to do the following:

1. Calculate the amount of payroll tax expense and journalize the entry.

2. Journalize the entry for the deposit of employees' federal income taxes withheld and FICA taxes (both employees' withheld and employer's matching share) and prepare the deposit coupon.

3. Journalize the entries for the payment of employer's state and federal unemployment taxes.

4. Journalize the entry for the deposit of employees' state income taxes withheld.

5. Complete Employer's Quarterly Federal Tax Return, Form 941.

6. Prepare W-2 and W-3 forms and Form 940.

7. Calculate the premium for workers' compensation insurance, and prepare the entry for payment in advance.

8. Determine the amount of the end-of-the-year adjustments for (a) workers' compensation insurance and (b) accrued salaries and wages, and record the adjustments.

We have talked about computing and recording such payroll data as gross pay, employees' income tax withheld, employees' FICA tax withheld, and various deductions requested by employees. Now we will pay these withholding liabilities and the taxes levied on the employer.

EMPLOYER IDENTIFICATION NUMBER

Everyone who works must have a Social Security number, a vital part of federal income tax returns. An employer's counterpart to the Social Security number is the **employer identification number** assigned by the Internal Revenue Service. Employers of one or more persons are required to have such a number, and it must be listed on all reports and payments of employees' federal income tax withholding and FICA taxes.

EMPLOYER'S PAYROLL TAXES

An employer's payroll taxes are based on the gross wages paid to employees. Payroll taxes—like property taxes—are an expense of doing business. Goren Company records these taxes in the **Payroll Tax Expense** account and debits the account for the company's portion of FICA taxes and for state and federal unemployment taxes. In T account form, Payroll Tax Expense for Goren Company would look like the following example.

Payroll Tax Expense

+	−
FICA tax (employer's matching portion)	Closed at the end of the year along with all other expense accounts
State unemployment tax	
Federal unemployment tax	

As you can see, **FICA tax (employer's share), state unemployment tax, and federal unemployment tax are included under the Payroll Tax Expense heading.** In most states, the unemployment taxes are levied on the employer only.

The skyrocketing costs of Medicare have caused Congress and the president to try to make sweeping reforms. The issues are far-reaching. Medicare affects a large percentage of the population—who fear their benefits may be reduced.

Employer's Matching Portion of FICA Tax (Social Security Plus Medicare)

FICA tax is imposed equally on both employer and employee. After the firm's accountant deducts the employee's share from gross wages and records it in the payroll entry under FICA Tax Payable, he or she then determines the employer's share by multiplying the employer's tax rates (assumed to be 6.2 percent (.062) for Social Security and 1.45 percent (.0145) for Medicare) by the taxable earnings (assumed to be a maximum of $94,200 for Social Security and all earnings for Medicare). The same tax rates apply to both the employer and the employees.

The accountant gets the Social Security and Medicare taxable earnings amounts from the payroll register. In Figure 1, on the following page, we present the Taxable Earnings columns taken from the payroll register for the week ended October 7.

NAME	TOTAL HOURS	TOTAL	ENDING CUMULATIVE EARNINGS	(7) TAXABLE EARNINGS		
				UNEMPLOYMENT	SOCIAL SECURITY	MEDICARE
1 Amano, Mark E.	46	1 1 2 4 58	46 0 8 4 58	—	1 1 2 4 58	1 1 2 4 58
2 Barkov, Anna E.	45	7 4 4 20	6 7 3 1 20	7 4 4 20	7 4 4 20	7 4 4 20
3 Dorn, David L.	49	9 1 6 00	7 7 0 2 00	2 1 4 00	9 1 6 00	9 1 6 00
4 Felding, Sarah H.	40	1 0 8 4 50	39 5 4 6 50	—	1 0 8 4 50	1 0 8 4 50
5 Graham, Jason W.	40	1 7 9 8 45	70 3 9 8 45	—	1 7 9 8 45	1 7 9 8 45
6 Kilmer, Richard B.	40	1 8 9 5 58	70 3 9 5 58	—	1 8 9 5 58	1 8 9 5 58
7 Mankowitz, Jim J.	55	1 8 4 4 30	39 6 9 4 30	—	1 8 4 4 30	1 8 4 4 30
8 Orlene, Barbara A.	40	1 4 8 7 20	47 3 0 7 20	—	1 4 8 7 20	1 4 8 7 20
9 Parker, William R.	44	1 7 7 6 28	48 2 0 6 28	—	1 7 7 6 28	1 7 7 6 28
10 Rumberg, Shelly L.	45	1 9 4 9 16	56 8 1 6 16	—	1 9 4 9 16	1 9 4 9 16
11 Tabor, Annette G.	40	1 1 6 8 83	43 9 0 8 83	—	1 1 6 8 83	1 1 6 8 83
12 Walker, Susan	52	3 0 1 0 35	94 3 1 0 35	—	2 9 0 0 00	3 0 1 0 35
13		18 7 9 9 43	571 1 0 1 43	9 5 8 20	18 6 8 9 08	18 7 9 9 43

Amount of employees' earnings for the period that has not, as yet, been taxed as part of the $7,000 maximum liability

Amount of employees' earnings that are less than $94,200 per employee for the year

Amount of all employees' earnings

FIGURE 1

Employer's state unemployment tax $958.20 × .054 = $51.74

Employer's Social Security tax $18,689.08 × .062 = $1,158.72

Employer's Medicare tax $18,799.43 × .0145 = $272.59

Employer's federal unemployment tax $958.20 × .008 = $7.67

Combined Employer's FICA tax (Social Security $1,158.72 + Medicare $272.59) = $1,431.31

Before we look at the journal entry to record the employer's share of FICA tax, let's look at the entry in T account form.

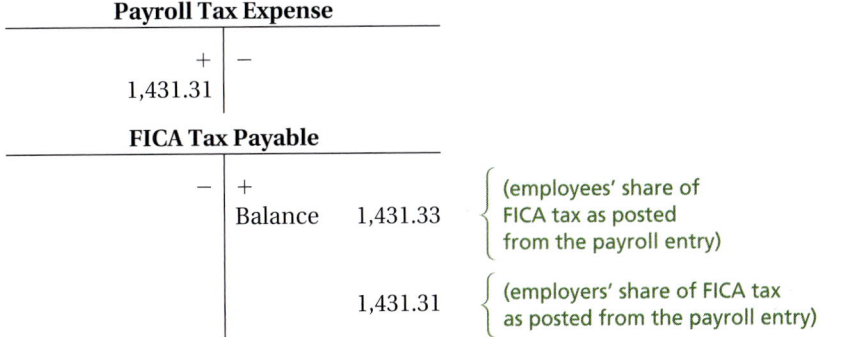

Payroll Tax Expense

+	−
1,431.31	

FICA Tax Payable

−	+
	Balance 1,431.33 — (employees' share of FICA tax as posted from the payroll entry)
	1,431.31 — (employers' share of FICA tax as posted from the payroll entry)

Note particularly that the FICA Tax Payable account is often used for both the tax liability of the employer and the amounts withheld from the employees. This is logical because both FICA taxes are paid at the same time and to the same place. There may be a slight difference between the employer's and the employees' share of FICA taxes because of the rounding process. For the employees' share, the accountant uses the total of the employees' Social Security and Medicare tax deductions. For the employer's share, the accountant multiplies the total taxable earnings (Social Security and Medicare) by the tax rates.

Employer's State Unemployment Tax

The proceeds of the state unemployment tax (SUTA), which is levied only on the employer in most states, are used to pay subsistence benefits to unemployed workers. The rate of the state unemployment tax varies considerably among the states. Assume that Goren Company is subject to a rate of 5.4 percent (.054) of the first $7,000 of each employee's earnings (the same base amount as for the federal unemployment tax). As shown in the portion of the payroll register illustrated in Figure 1, $958.20 of earnings are subject to the state unemployment tax. Accordingly, by T accounts, the state unemployment tax based on taxable earnings is as follows:

Payroll Tax Expense		State Unemployment Tax Payable	
+	−	−	+
(958.20 × .054)			(958.20 × .054)
51.74			51.74

Employer's Federal Unemployment Tax

The federal unemployment tax (FUTA) is paid only by the employer. Congress may from time to time change the rate. Let's assume a rate of 0.8 percent (.008) of the first $7,000 earned by each employee during the calendar year. For the weekly payroll period for Goren Company, the tax liability is $7.67 ($958.20 of unemployment taxable earnings, taken from the payroll register, multiplied by .008, the tax rate). The T account is as follows:

Payroll Tax Expense		Federal Unemployment Tax Payable	
+	−	−	+
(958.20 × .008)			(958.20 × .008)
7.67			7.67

OBJECTIVE 1

Calculate the amount of payroll tax expense and journalize the entry.

To make things clearer, figures for the employer's three payroll taxes have been presented separately. Now let's combine all of this information into one entry, which follows the regular payroll entry. Goren Company pays its employees weekly, so it also makes its Payroll Tax Expense entry weekly.

	DATE		DESCRIPTION	POST. REF.	DEBIT	CREDIT	
17	Oct.	7	Payroll Tax Expense		1 4 9 0 72		17
18			FICA Tax Payable			1 4 3 1 31	18
19			State Unemployment Tax				19
20			Payable			5 1 74	20
21			Federal Unemployment Tax				21
22			Payable			7 67	22
23			To record employer's share				23
24			of FICA tax and employer's				24
25			state and federal				25
26			unemployment taxes.				26
27							27
28							28

JOURNAL ENTRIES FOR RECORDING PAYROLL

At this point, let's restate in general journal form the entries that have already been recorded. We'll do this so that you can see the sequence of the payroll entries. First, the entry to record the payroll is journalized.

	DATE		DESCRIPTION	POST. REF.	DEBIT	CREDIT	
1	20–						1
2	Oct.	7	Sales Wages Expense		14 3 3 2 15		2
3			Office Wages Expense		4 4 6 7 28		3
4			Employees' Federal Income				4
5			Tax Payable			2 8 3 8 00	5
6			FICA Tax Payable			1 4 3 1 33	6
7			Employees' State Income Tax				7
8			Payable			5 6 7 60	8
9			Employees' Medical Insurance				9
10			Payable			3 2 0 70	10
11			Employees' United Way				11
12			Payable			1 8 5 00	12
13			Accounts Receivable			3 0 00	13
14			Wages Payable			13 4 2 6 80	14
15			Payroll register, page 56,				15
16			for week ended October 7.				16
17							17

Next, the entry to record the employer's payroll taxes is journalized.

REMEMBER!

The sequence of steps for recording the payroll entries is: (1) record the payroll for the present period in the payroll register; (2) based on the payroll register, record the payroll entry in the journal; (3) based on the Taxable Earnings columns of the payroll register, record Payroll Tax Expense in the journal; (4) make a journal entry to pay the employees.

	DATE		DESCRIPTION	POST. REF.	DEBIT	CREDIT	
18		7	Payroll Tax Expense		1 4 9 0 72		18
19			FICA Tax Payable			1 4 3 1 31	19
20			State Unemployment Tax				20
21			Payable			5 1 74	21
22			Federal Unemployment Tax				22
23			Payable			7 67	23
24			To record employer's share				24
25			of FICA tax and employer's				25
26			state and federal				26
27			unemployment taxes.				27
28							28

Finally, the entry to pay the employees is journalized. Goren Company issues one check payable to a payroll bank account. To pay its employees, it will draw separate payroll checks on this payroll account. (The entry to transfer cash to the payroll bank account is not shown here.)

	DATE		DESCRIPTION	POST. REF.	DEBIT	CREDIT	
29		8	Wages Payable		13 4 2 6 80		29
30			Cash—Payroll Bank Account			13 4 2 6 80	30
31			Paid salaries for week				31
32			ended October 7.				32
33							33

As stated previously, in the first payroll entry, small employers will credit Cash directly instead of Wages Payable. These employers issue separate checks out of their regular bank accounts for each employee.

Next, we describe the entries for paying withholdings for employees' federal income tax and FICA tax and the employer's matching share of FICA tax. We also show the entries for paying the federal and state unemployment taxes and the withholdings for employees' state income tax.

PAYMENTS OF FICA TAX AND EMPLOYEES' FEDERAL INCOME TAX WITHHOLDING

OBJECTIVE 2

Journalize the entry for the deposit of employees' federal income taxes withheld and FICA taxes (both employees' withheld and employer's matching share) and prepare the deposit coupon.

There are penalties applied for late deposits of federal taxes.

After paying employees, the employer must make payments in the form of federal tax deposits. A deposit includes the combined total of three items: (1) employees' federal income taxes withheld, (2) employees' FICA taxes withheld, and (3) employer's share of FICA taxes. Employers make these deposits on a pay-as-you-go basis.

Deposits are made to authorized commercial banks or Federal Reserve banks and handled through automated clearing-houses. Electronic deposits are required for companies with larger payrolls. The timing of these deposits depends on the amounts owed. The calendar year is broken into days, semi-weekly periods, months, and **quarters** (3 consecutive months).

Employers submit a return, Form 941, every quarter. The due dates for filing this return are as follows:

Quarter	Ending Date of Quarter	Due Date for Form 941
January–February–March	March 31	April 30
April–May–June	June 30	July 31
July–August–September	September 30	October 31
October–November–December	December 31	January 31

We will show a Form 941 later in this chapter.

Federal Tax Deposit Coupon

Let's go back to Goren Company, where tax payments were up to date. From the payroll of October 7, the following federal taxes are owed:

Employees' federal income taxes withheld	$2,838.00
Employees' FICA taxes withheld	1,431.33
Employer's share of FICA taxes	1,431.31
Total federal undeposited taxes	$5,700.64

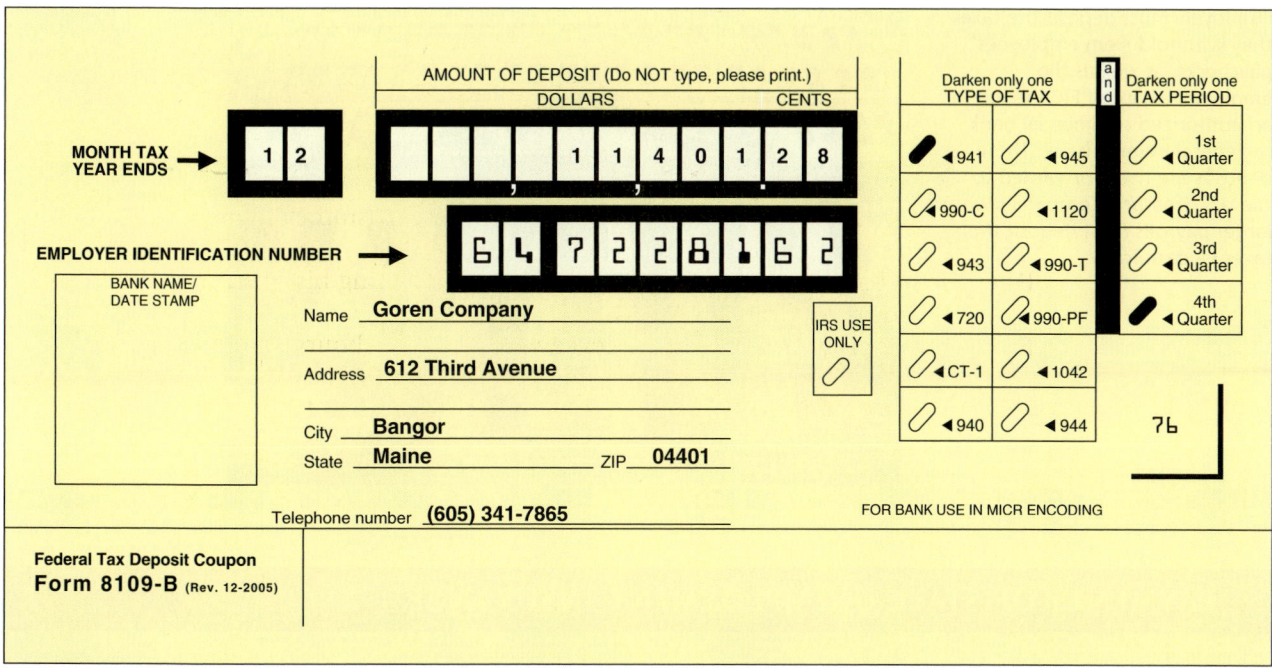

FIGURE 2

We continue on for the next payroll period, ended October 14. Assuming the payroll information for the week is the same as it was for the week ended October 7, the two periods would be:

	Oct. 7	Oct. 14	Total
Employees' federal income taxes withheld	$2,838.00	$2,838.00	$ 5,676.00
Employees' FICA taxes withheld	1,431.33	1,431.33	2,862.66
Employer's share of FICA taxes	1,431.31	1,431.31	2,862.62
Total federal undeposited taxes	$5,700.64	$5,700.64	$11,401.28

Goren Company, which deposits taxes semiweekly, receives a federal tax deposit card (printed with the company's name and employer identification number) from the Internal Revenue Service (Figure 2).

The accountant records the amount of the deposit, the employer identification number (unless preprinted), the type of tax, the tax period, and the name and address of the company. The entry in general journal form to record the deposit of two weeks' taxes looks like the following.

FYI

Because of rounding differences, the employee and employer amounts of FICA taxes may differ slightly. Line 7a of the 941 Form accommodates this difference.

	DATE		DESCRIPTION	POST. REF.	DEBIT	CREDIT	
1	20–						1
2	Oct.	15	Employees' Federal Income Tax				2
3			Payable		5 6 7 6 00		3
4			FICA Tax Payable		5 7 2 5 28		4
5			Cash			11 4 0 1 28	5
6			Issued check for federal tax				6
7			deposit, Bangor Bank.				7

Employers must deposit the taxes they withhold from employees' paychecks, as well as the employer's share of FICA taxes, in an authorized commercial bank or Federal Reserve bank. These deposits are then forwarded to the U.S. Treasury. Companies with larger payrolls must deposit their taxes electronically.

PAYMENTS OF STATE UNEMPLOYMENT INSURANCE

OBJECTIVE 3

Journalize the entries for the payment of employer's state and federal unemployment taxes.

As we stated before, states differ with regard to both the rate and the taxable base for unemployment insurance. In our example, we assume that the state tax is 5.4 percent (.054) of the first $7,000 paid to each employee during the calendar year. **The state tax is usually paid quarterly and is due by the end of the month following the end of the quarter (the same as the due dates for Form 941).** Here's the entry in general journal form made by Goren Company for the first quarter (covering the months of January, February, and March). We assume that $60,325 was taxable for the quarter. The amount of the tax is $3,257.55 ($60,325 × 0.054).

	DATE		DESCRIPTION	POST. REF.	DEBIT	CREDIT	
1	20–						1
2	Apr.	30	State Unemployment Tax				2
3			Payable		3 2 5 7 55		3
4			Cash			3 2 5 7 55	4
5			Issued check for payment of				5
6			state unemployment tax.				6

The T accounts are as follows:

Cash				**State Unemployment Tax Payable**		
+	–			–	+	
	Apr. 30	3,257.55			Mar. 31	
			Apr. 30	3,257.55	Balance	3,257.55

The March 31 balance in State Unemployment Tax Payable is the result of weekly entries recording the state unemployment portion of payroll tax expense. After the payment is made on April 30, the balance is shown as zero for illustrative purposes. However, throughout the month of April, the company would be making weekly entries to record the tax liability and tax expense.

PAYMENTS OF FEDERAL UNEMPLOYMENT TAX

The FUTA tax is calculated quarterly, during the month following the end of each calendar quarter. **If the accumulated tax liability is greater than $100, the tax is deposited in a commercial bank or Federal Reserve bank, accompanied by a preprinted federal tax deposit card** like that used to deposit employees' federal income tax withholding and FICA taxes. The deposit may also be made electronically. The due date for this deposit is the last day of the month following the end of the quarter, the same as the due dates for the Employer's Quarterly Federal Tax Return and for state unemployment taxes.

Here is the entry in general journal form made by Goren Company for the first quarter. In our example, since the FUTA and state unemployment taxable earnings are the same (the first $7,000 for each employee), we assume that $60,325 was taxable for the quarter. The amount of the tax is $482.60 ($60,325 × 0.008).

	DATE		DESCRIPTION	POST. REF.	DEBIT	CREDIT	
1	20–						1
2	Apr.	30	Federal Unemployment Tax				2
3			Payable		4 8 2 60		3
4			Cash			4 8 2 60	4
5			Issued check for deposit of				5
6			federal unemployment tax.				6
7							7

The T accounts are as follows:

Cash		Federal Unemployment Tax Payable	
+	–	–	+
	Apr. 30 482.60		Mar. 31
		Apr. 30 482.60	Balance 482.60

The balance in Federal Unemployment Tax Payable is the result of weekly entries recording the federal unemployment portion of payroll tax expense.

DEPOSITS OF EMPLOYEES' STATE INCOME TAX WITHHOLDING

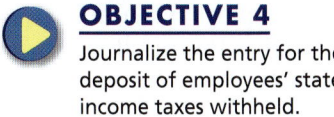

OBJECTIVE 4

Journalize the entry for the deposit of employees' state income taxes withheld.

Assume that the withholdings for employees' state income taxes are deposited on a quarterly basis, payable at the same time as state unemployment tax. Also, as of March 31, the credit balance of Employees' State Income Tax Payable is $1,674.10. The entry in general journal form to record the payment for the first quarter takes the following form.

	DATE		DESCRIPTION	POST. REF.	DEBIT	CREDIT	
1	20–						1
2	Apr.	30	Employees' State Income Tax				2
3			Payable		1 6 7 4 10		3
4			Cash			1 6 7 4 10	4
5			Issued check for state				5
6			income tax deposit.				6
7							7

The T accounts are as follows:

Cash		Employees' State Income Tax Payable	
+	−	−	+
	Apr. 30 1,674.10	Apr. 30 1,674.10	Mar. 31
			Balance 1,674.10

EMPLOYER'S QUARTERLY FEDERAL TAX RETURN (FORM 941)

OBJECTIVE 5

Complete Employer's Quarterly Federal Tax Return, Form 941.

If you are an employer, you must file a quarterly **Form 941**, Employer's Quarterly Federal Tax Return. The purpose of Form 941 is to report the tax liability for withholdings of employees' federal income tax and FICA taxes, and also the employer's share of FICA taxes. Total tax deposits are also listed. As the title implies, the time period is three months. Remember that the due dates for the calendar year are: first quarter, April 30; second quarter, July 31; third quarter, October 31; fourth quarter, January 31.

A completed Form 941 for Goren Company is shown in Figure 3. There are six parts to this form. Figure 3 shows the information for Goren Company for Parts 1 and 2. Part 3 is used when you close your business and stop paying wages—this will also stop the IRS from automatically sending 941 forms. Part 4 is for you to give the IRS permission—or not—to speak with your third-party designee (employee, paid tax preparer for example). Part 5 is the signature, title, and date block for the employer. Part 6 is the signature, firm information, employer identification number (EIN), and date block for any paid preparer of the 941 form. You can go online at **http://www.irs.gov** and enter Form 941 into the search window. For the instructions, type 941 instructions into the search window.

The top of the form contains basic information about the employer. Once an employer has secured an identification number and has filed the first return, the Internal Revenue Service automatically sends forms directly to the employer. These subsequent forms will have the employer's name, address, and identification number filled in.

Now let's look at completed Parts 1 and 2 of an Employer's Quarterly Federal Tax Return (Form 941) starting with its heading.

Form 941 for 2006: Employer's **QUARTERLY** Federal Tax Return

(Rev. January 2006)   Department of the Treasury — Internal Revenue Service

990106

OMB No. 1545-0029

(EIN)
Employer identification number   6 4 – 7 2 2 8 1 6 2

Name (not your trade name)

Trade name (if any)   **Goren Company**

Address   **612 Third Avenue**
Number   Street   Suite or room number

Bangor   **ME**   **04401**
City   State   ZIP code

Report for this Quarter ...
(Check one.)

☐ **1:** January, February, March

☐ **2:** April, May, June

☐ **3:** July, August, September

☒ **4:** October, November, December

Read the separate instructions before you fill out this form. Please type or print within the boxes.

Part 1: Answer these questions for this quarter.

1 Number of employees who received wages, tips, or other compensation for the pay period
including: *Mar. 12* (Quarter 1), *June 12* (Quarter 2), *Sept. 12* (Quarter 3), *Dec. 12* (Quarter 4)   **1** | **12**

2 Wages, tips, and other compensation . . . .   **2** | **216,252 . 00**

3 Total income tax withheld from wages, tips, and other compensation . . . .   **3** | **39,768 . 00**

4 If no wages, tips, and other compensation are subject to social security or Medicare tax . .   ☐ Check and go to line 6.

5 Taxable social security and Medicare wages and tips:

	Column 1		Column 2
5a Taxable social security wages	130,080 . 00	× .124 =	16,129 . 92
5b Taxable social security tips	.	× .124 =	.
5c Taxable Medicare wages & tips	216,252 . 00	× .029 =	6,271 . 31

5d Total social security and Medicare taxes (*Column 2,* lines 5a + 5b + 5c = line 5d) . .   **5d** | **22,401 . 23**

6 Total taxes before adjustments (lines 3 + 5d = line 6) . . . .   **6** | **62,169 . 23**

7 **TAX ADJUSTMENTS** (Read the instructions for line 7 before completing lines 7a through 7h.):

7a Current quarter's fractions of cents . . . . | — .

7b Current quarter's sick pay . . . . | — .

7c Current quarter's adjustments for tips and group-term life insurance | — .

7d Current year's income tax withholding (attach Form 941c) . . | — .

7e Prior quarters' social security and Medicare taxes (attach Form 941c) | — .

7f Special additions to federal income tax (attach Form 941c) . . . | — .

7g Special additions to social security and Medicare (attach Form 941c) | — .

7h **TOTAL ADJUSTMENTS** (Combine all amounts: lines 7a through 7g.) . . . .   **7h** | — .

8 Total taxes after adjustments (Combine lines 6 and 7h.) . . . .   **8** | **62,169 . 23**

9 Advance earned income credit (EIC) payments made to employees . . . .   **9** | — .

10 Total taxes after adjustment for advance EIC (line 8 – line 9 = line 10) . . . .   **10** | **62,169 . 23**

11 Total deposits for this quarter, including overpayment applied from a prior quarter . . .   **11** | **62,169 . 23**

12 **Balance due** (If line 10 is more than line 11, write the difference here.) . . . .   **12** | **–0– .**
Make checks payable to *United States Treasury.*

13 **Overpayment** (If line 11 is more than line 10, write the difference here.) | — .   Check one ☐ Apply to next return
☐ Send a refund.

▶ You **MUST** fill out both pages of this form and **SIGN** it.   Next ➡

Part 2: Tell us about your deposit schedule and tax liability for this quarter.

If you are unsure about whether you are a monthly schedule depositor or a semiweekly schedule depositor, see *Pub. 15
(Circular E),* section 11.

14   **M E**   Write the state abbreviation for the state where you made your deposits OR write "MU" if you made your
deposits in *multiple* states.

15 Check one: ☐ **Line 10 is less than $2,500.** Go to Part 3.

☐ You were a **monthly schedule depositor** for the entire quarter. Fill out your tax
liability for each month. Then go to Part 3.

Tax liability: Month 1 | .

Month 2 | .

Month 3 | .

Total liability for quarter | .   Total must equal line 10.

☒ You were a **semiweekly schedule depositor** for any part of this quarter. Fill out *Schedule B (Form 941):
Report of Tax Liability for Semiweekly Schedule Depositors,* and attach it to this form.

FIGURE 3

Questions Listed on Form 941 (Figure 3)

Tax forms can be somewhat intimidating. The best approach to completing a tax form is to have accurate and complete records, read and complete the form line by line, and don't look ahead. Goren Company's fourth quarter form, shown in Figure 3, has been completed as follows. Note that the employees at Goren earn wages. Had they also earned tips or other compensation, such as bonuses, those would have been included in the form.

Part 1:

1. Line 1 indicates the number of employees (12) who received wages.
2. Line 2 shows the total of those wages for the quarter ($216,252.00).
3. Line 3 shows the total income tax withheld from wages for the quarter ($39,768.00).
4. Line 4 is not checked because all wages during the quarter are subject to Medicare tax.
5. Lines 5a–d provide information that indicates how the total of the Social Security and Medicare taxes ($16,129.92 + $6,271.31 = $22,401.23) is calculated. Note that the multipliers represent the combined employee and employer contributions (for Social Security, .062 × 2 = .124; for Medicare, .0145 × 2 = .029).
6. Line 6 ($62,169.23) is the total of the income taxes withheld (line 3) and the Social Security and Medicare taxes (line 5d), before adjustments.
7. Lines 7a–h indicate any tax adjustments that may be needed. Goren Company did not have any of those for the quarter. Note that these adjustments may be for fractions of cents due to rounding (line 7a), corrections of errors in earlier filings of Form 941 (lines 7b–e), or as a result of a notice from the IRS (lines 7f and 7g).
8. Line 8 shows the total taxes after adjustments (line 6 plus line 7h = $62,169.23).
9. Line 9 discloses any payments of advanced earned income credit (EIC), a refundable federal income tax credit for low-income working individuals and families, that may have been made to employees. Goren Company did not have any this quarter.
10. Line 10 is the total of lines 8 and 9 ($62,169.23).
11. Line 11 shows the total deposits ($62,169.23) made by Goren Company for this quarter and includes any overpayments from prior quarters. As indicated, the company has made deposits equaling the total due for this quarter.
12. Lines 12 (underpayment) and 13 (overpayment), which indicate the difference between lines 10 and 11, show that the company's balance for the quarter is zero.

Part 2:

13. Line 14 shows ME, the abbreviation for Maine, the state in which the deposits were made.
14. Line 15 shows a checkmark in the third box because Goren Company was a semiweekly scheduled depositor for part of this quarter.

As stated earlier, the remaining parts of the 941 form require stating whether your business is closing, permission to allow third-party inquiries, signatures and titles of the preparer, and the date Form 941 is submitted. For thorough instructions to assist you in filling out any IRS form, go to **http://www.irs.gov** and enter the form or descriptive words into the search box.

a Control number				
	22222	OMB No. 1545-0008	Safe, accurate, FAST! Use IRS e~file	Visit the IRS website at www.irs.gov/efile.

b Employer identification number (EIN)	1 Wages, tips, other compensation	2 Federal income tax withheld
64-7228162	58,404.58	10,920.00

c Employer's name, address, and ZIP code	3 Social security wages	4 Social security tax withheld
	58,404.58	3,621.08
Goren Company	5 Medicare wages and tips	6 Medicare tax withheld
612 Third Avenue	58,404.58	846.87
Bangor, Maine 04401	7 Social security tips	8 Allocated tips
	0	

d Employee's social security number	9 Advance EIC payment	10 Dependent care benefits
543-24-1680	0	0

e Employee's first name and initial Last name Suff.	11 Nonqualified plans	12a See instructions for box 12
	0	
Mark E. Amano	13 Statutory employee ☐ Retirement plan ☐ Third-party sick pay ☐	12b
6357 Boston Lane		
Bangor, Maine 04401	14 Other	12c
		12d

f Employee's address and ZIP code

15 State	Employer's state ID number	16 State wages, tips, etc.	17 State income tax	18 Local wages, tips, etc.	19 Local income tax	20 Locality name
ME	464-729	58,404.58	2,184.00	0	0	0

Form **W-2** Wage and Tax Statement   **20____**   Department of the Treasury—Internal Revenue Service

Copy B—To Be Filed With Employee's FEDERAL Tax Return.
This information is being furnished to the Internal Revenue Service.

FIGURE 4

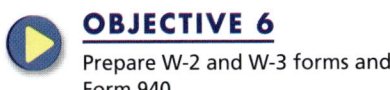

OBJECTIVE 6

Prepare W-2 and W-3 forms and Form 940.

Wage Withholding Statements for Employees (Form W-2)

After the end of a year (December 31) and by the following January 31, the employer must furnish for each employee a Wage and Tax Statement, known as **Form W-2**. This form contains information about the employee's earnings and tax deductions for the year. The source of the information used to complete Form W-2 is the employee's individual earnings record. The amounts used to complete Mark E. Amano's W-2 form (in Figure 4) represent the amounts taken from his earnings record at the end of the calendar year, December 31.

Box 9 shows the total paid to the employee as advance earned income credit (EIC) payments. Box 13 is used for miscellaneous items, such as sick pay that is not included in income because the employee contributed to the sick pay plan. This box is also used for employer-provided group term life insurance in excess of $50,000. Statutory employees are life insurance and traveling salespersons. Box 14 may include the value of noncash fringe benefits, such as providing a vehicle for the employee.

FYI

A copy is also sent (if applicable) to the state and/or local tax department, and a copy is given to the employee to attach to the state/local tax return.

The accountant will prepare at least four copies of the W-2 form for each employee.

Copy A—Employer sends to the Social Security Administration.
Copy B—Employer gives to employee to be attached to the employee's individual federal income tax return.
Copy C—Employer gives to employee to be kept for his or her personal records.
Copy D—Employer keeps this copy as a record of payments made.

If state and local income taxes are withheld, the employer prepares additional copies to be sent to the appropriate tax agency.

Employer's Annual Federal Income Tax Reports (Form W-3)

Accompanying copy A of the employees' W-2 forms, Goren Company sends **Form W-3**, Transmittal of Wage and Tax Statements, to the Social Security Administration. This form is due on February 28, following the end of the calendar year.

For all employees, Form W-3 shows the total wages and tips, total federal income tax withheld, total Social Security and Medicare taxable wages, total Social Security and Medicare tax withheld, and other information. These amounts must be the same as the grand totals of the W-2 forms and the four quarterly 941 forms for the year. Goren Company's completed Form W-3 is presented in Figure 5.

Some boxes deserve an explanation. Box d, establishment number, may be used for a company that has separate establishments, with each establishment filing W-2 and W-3 forms separately. Box 9 is used for recording the amount of advance earned income credits shown on W-2 forms for qualified employees. Box h is used by a company that had more than one employer identification number (EIN) during the year.

To sum up thus far: The employer must submit the following at the end of the calendar year: Employer's Quarterly Federal Tax Return, Form 941, for the fourth quarter by January 31; Wage and Tax Statements, Form W-2, for all employees by January 31; Transmittal of Wage and Tax Statements, Form W-3, by February 28.

REPORTS AND PAYMENTS OF FEDERAL UNEMPLOYMENT TAX

REMEMBER!

If the accumulated FUTA tax liability at the end of a quarter is greater than $100, a deposit must be made.

As we stated previously, generally all employers are subject to the Federal Unemployment Tax Act. These employers must submit an Employer's Annual Federal Unemployment Tax Return, Form 940, not later than January 31 following the close of the calendar year. This deadline may be extended until February 10 if the employer has made deposits paying the FUTA tax liability in full. **Form 940** shows total wages paid to employees, total wages subject to federal unemployment tax, and other information.

DO NOT STAPLE

a Control number	33333	For Official Use Only ▶ OMB No. 1545-0008

b Kind of Payer ▶	941 [X] Military [ ] 943 [ ] 944 [ ] CT-1 [ ] Hshld. emp. [ ] Medicare govt. emp. [ ] Third-party sick pay [ ]	1 Wages, tips, other compensation **861,530.00**	2 Federal income tax withheld **103,383.60**
		3 Social security wages **775,358.00**	4 Social security tax withheld **48,072.20**
c Total number of Forms W-2 **12**	d Establishment number – – – – – –	5 Medicare wages and tips **861,530.00**	6 Medicare tax withheld **12,492.19**
e Employer identification number (EIN) **64-7228162**		7 Social security tips **0**	8 Allocated tips **0**
f Employer's name **Goren Company** **612 Third Avenue** **Bangor, Maine 04401**		9 Advance EIC payments **0**	10 Dependent care benefits **0**
		11 Nonqualified plans **0**	12 Deferred compensation **0**
		13 For third-party sick pay use only	
		14 Income tax withheld by payer of third-party sick pay **0**	
g Employer's address and ZIP code			
h Other EIN used this year **0**			
15 State Employer's state ID number **464-729**		16 State wages, tips, etc.	17 State income tax
		18 Local wages, tips, etc.	19 Local income tax
Contact person **Eileen Goren**		Telephone number **(605) 341-1465**	For Official Use Only
Email address **egoren@fastlink.net**		Fax number **(605) 341-1477**	

Under penalties of perjury, I declare that I have examined this return and accompanying documents, and, to the best of my knowledge and belief, they are true, correct, and complete.

Signature ▶ *Eileen Goren*   Title ▶ *Owner*   Date ▶ *2/27/20--*

Form **W-3** **Transmittal of Wage and Tax Statements**   20___   Department of the Treasury
Internal Revenue Service

FIGURE 5

Using Goren Company as our example, federal unemployment taxable earnings by quarter are as follows:

Federal Unemployment Tax	1st Quarter	2nd Quarter	3rd Quarter	4th Quarter	Cumulative Total
Taxable earnings	$60,325	$9,485	$10,316	$3,520	$83,646
Tax rate	× .008	× .008	× .008	× .008	× .008
Tax liability	$482.60	$75.88	$ 82.53	$28.16	$669.17

We now repeat the journal entry for the first quarter, in which $482.60 was deposited on April 30.

	DATE		DESCRIPTION	POST. REF.	DEBIT	CREDIT	
1	20–						1
2	Apr.	30	Federal Unemployment Tax				2
3			Payable		4 8 2 60		3
4			Cash			4 8 2 60	4
5			Issued check for deposit of				5
6			federal unemployment tax.				6
7							7

During the second quarter, many employees' total earnings passed the $7,000 limit of taxable earnings, and the firm's tax liability was reduced accordingly. Because Goren's total accumulated liability ($75.88) was less than $100, a deposit covering that quarter was not made. However, because of an expansion of the company, three new employees were hired during the middle of the quarter.

For the third quarter, the tax liability amounted to $82.53. The total cumulative tax liability was now $158.41 ($75.88 second quarter plus $82.53 third quarter). Consequently, $158.41 was deposited on October 31.

By the end of the fourth quarter, each of the twelve employees' earnings passed the $7,000 mark. The total liability for the quarter is $28.16. This amount will be paid by January 31, accompanied by the completed Employer's Annual Federal Unemployment Tax Return, Form 940.

The T account for Federal Unemployment Tax Payable follows. The credits to the account were part of the entries to record the federal unemployment tax portion of Payroll Tax Expense for each payroll period.

Federal Unemployment Tax Payable

	−	+	
Apr. 30 deposit	482.60	1st quarter (liability)	482.60
Oct. 31 deposit	158.41	2nd quarter (liability)	75.88
		3rd quarter (liability)	82.53
Jan. 31 deposit	28.16	4th quarter (liability)	28.16

Employer's Annual Federal Unemployment (FUTA) Tax Return (Form 940)

Figure 6 shows a completed Form 940-EZ for Goren Company. This form has three sections. (Bear in mind that all forms change from time to time. Go to **http://www.irs.gov** for updates.)

Form **940-EZ**		Employer's Annual Federal Unemployment (FUTA) Tax Return			OMB No. 1545-1110	
Department of the Treasury Internal Revenue Service		▶ See the separate Instructions for Form 940-EZ for information on completing this form.			20__	

	Name (as distinguished from trade name)	Calendar year	T
You must complete this section. ▶		**20--**	FF
	Trade name, if any	Employer identification number (EIN)	FD
	Goren Company	**64-7228162**	FP
	Address (number and street)	City, state, and ZIP code	I
	612 Third Avenue	**Bangor, ME 04401**	T

*Answer the questions under **Who May Use Form 940-EZ** on page 2. If you cannot use Form 940-EZ, you must use Form 940.*

A Enter the amount of contributions paid to your state unemployment fund (see the separate instructions) . . ▶ $ ....

B (1) Enter the name of the state where you have to pay contributions . . . . ▶ ....

(2) Enter your state reporting number as shown on your state unemployment tax return. ▶

If you will not have to file returns in the future, check here (see **Who Must File** in separate instructions) **and complete and sign the return.** ▶ ☐

If this is an Amended Return, check here (see **Amended Returns** in the separate instructions) . . . . ▶ ☐

Part I	**Taxable Wages and FUTA Tax**				
1	Total payments (including payments shown on lines 2 and 3) during the calendar year for services of employees	1	**861,530**	**00**	
2	Exempt payments. (Explain all exempt payments, attaching additional sheets if necessary.) ▶	2	**—**		
3	Payments of more than $7,000 for services. Enter only amounts over the first $7,000 paid to each employee **(see the separate instructions)**	3	**777,884**	**00**	
4	Add lines 2 and 3	4	**777,884**	**00**	
5	**Total taxable wages** (subtract line 4 from line 1) . . . . ▶	5	**83,646**	**00**	
6	**FUTA tax.** Multiply the wages on line 5 by .008 and enter here. **(If the result is over $500, also complete Part II.)**	6	**669**	**17**	
7	Total FUTA tax deposited for the year, including any overpayment applied from a prior year	7	**669**	**17**	
8	**Balance due** (subtract line 7 from line 6). Pay to the "United States Treasury." . . . . ▶	8	**—**		
	If you owe more than $500, see **Depositing FUTA tax** in the separate instructions.				
9	**Overpayment** (subtract line 6 from line 7). Check if it is to be: ☐ **Applied to next return** or ☐ **Refunded** ▶	9	**—**		

Part II	**Record of Quarterly Federal Unemployment Tax Liability** (Do not include state liability.) **Complete only if line 6 is over $500.**				
Quarter	First (Jan. 1 – Mar. 31)	Second (Apr. 1 – June 30)	Third (July 1 – Sept. 30)	Fourth (Oct. 1 – Dec. 31)	Total for year
Liability for quarter	**482.60**	**75.88**	**82.53**	**28.16**	**669.17**

Third-Party Designee	Do you want to allow another person to discuss this return with the IRS (see the separate instructions)? ☐ **Yes.** Complete the following. ☒ **No**		
	Designee's name ▶	Phone no. ▶ ( )	Personal identification number (PIN) ☐☐☐☐☐

Under penalties of perjury, I declare that I have examined this return, including accompanying schedules and statements, and, to the best of my knowledge and belief, it is true, correct, and complete, and that no part of any payment made to a state unemployment fund claimed as a credit was, or is to be, deducted from the payments to employees.

Signature ▶ *Eileen Goren*   Title (Owner, etc.) ▶ *Owner*   Date ▶ *1/31/20--*

For Privacy Act and Paperwork Reduction Act Notice, see the separate instructions.   ▼ **DETACH HERE** ▼   Cat. No. 10983G   Form **940-EZ** (2005)

FIGURE 6

Part I: Taxable Wages and FUTA Tax.

Line 1 Record total wages paid.

Line 2 Record certain exempt wages—this includes such items as agricultural labor, family employment, and the value of meals and lodging.

Line 3 Record exempt wages paid—wages paid to each employee over and above $7,000 for the calendar year.

Line 4 Total exempt payments.

Line 5 Total taxable wages.

Line 6 Computation of tax due.

Line 7 Total FUTA tax deposited.

Line 8 Balance due.

Line 9 Overpayment.

Part II: Record of Quarterly Federal Unemployment Tax Liability.

WORKERS' COMPENSATION INSURANCE

OBJECTIVE 7

Calculate the premium for workers' compensation insurance, and prepare the entry for payment in advance.

Most states require employers to provide **workers' compensation insurance** or industrial accident insurance for employees killed or injured on the job, either through plans administered by the state or through private insurance companies authorized by the state. The employer usually has to pay all the premiums. The premium rate varies with the amount of risk the job entails and the company's claims history. For example, handling molten steel ingots is much more dangerous than typing reports. Thus, it is very important that employees be identified properly in terms of the insurance premium classifications. The rates as percentages of the payroll may be 0.15 percent for office work, 0.5 percent for sales work, and 3.5 percent for industrial labor in heavy manufacturing. These same rates may be expressed as $0.15 per $100 of the salaries or wages for office work, $0.50 per $100 for sales work, and $3.50 per $100 for industrial labor.

REMEMBER!

Workers' compensation for the year is first estimated based on the anticipated year's payroll; debit Prepaid Insurance, Workers' Compensation, and credit Cash. At the end of the year, when the actual payroll is known, the exact insurance premium is calculated; debit Workers' Compensation Insurance Expense and credit Prepaid Insurance, Workers' Compensation, for the amount paid at the beginning of the year.

If the amount of the estimated payroll is less than the actual payroll, debit Workers' Compensation Insurance Expense and credit Workers' Compensation Insurance Payable for the difference between the actual premium and the estimated premium.

Generally, the employer pays a premium in advance, based on the estimated payroll for the year. After the year ends, the employer knows the exact amount of the payroll and can calculate the exact premium. At that time, depending on the difference between the estimated and exact premiums, the employer either pays an additional premium or gets a credit for having made an overpayment.

At Goren Company, there are two work classifications: office work and sales work. At the beginning of the year, the firm's accountant computed the estimated annual premium as follows:

Classification	Predicted Payroll	Rate (Percent)	Estimated Premium
Office work	$182,000	.15	$182,000 × .0015 = $ 273.00
Sales work	660,000	.50	660,000 × .0050 = 3,300.00
			Total estimated premium $3,573.00

As shown by T accounts, the accountant made the following entry.

Prepaid Insurance, Workers' Compensation			Cash	
+	−		+	−
Jan. 10 3,573.00				3,573.00 Jan. 10

Workers' compensation premiums are based on the level of risk involved. A decimal rating is given to the employer for each type of job.

Then, at the end of the calendar year, the accountant calculated the exact premium:

Classification	Actual Payroll	Rate (Percent)	Estimated Premium
Office work	$188,990	.15	$188,990 × .0015 = $ 283.49
Sales work	672,540	.50	672,540 × .0050 = 3,362.70
			Total estimated premium $3,646.19

Therefore, the amount of the unpaid premium is

$3,646.19	Total exact premium
3,573.00	Less total estimated premium paid
$ 73.19	Additional premium owed

OBJECTIVE 8a

Determine the amount of the end-of-the-year adjustment for workers' compensation insurance, and record the adjustment.

Now the accountant makes an adjusting entry, similar to the adjusting entry for expired insurance; this entry appears on the work sheet. The accountant then makes an additional adjusting entry for the extra premium owed. By T accounts, the entries are as follows:

Prepaid Insurance, Workers' Compensation				
	+	–		
Jan. 10				
Balance	3,573.00		Dec. 31	
		3,573.00	Adj.	

Workers' Compensation Insurance Payable			
	–	+	
			Dec. 31
	73.19		Adj.

Workers' Compensation Insurance Expense		
	+	–
Dec. 31		
Adj.	3,573.00	
Dec. 31		
Adj.	73.19	

Goren Company will pay $73.19, the amount of unpaid premium, in January, together with the estimated premium for the next year.

ADJUSTING FOR ACCRUED SALARIES AND WAGES

OBJECTIVE 8b

Determine the amount of the end-of-the-year adjustment for accrued salaries and wages, and record the adjustment.

Assume that $1,200 of salaries accrue for the time between the last payday and the end of the year. An adjusting entry is necessary.

	DATE		DESCRIPTION	POST. REF.	DEBIT	CREDIT	
1	20–		**Adjusting Entry**				1
2	Dec.	31	Salary Expense		1 2 0 0 00		2
3			Salaries Payable			1 2 0 0 00	3
4							4

Salaries Payable is considered a liability account, as are employees' withholding taxes and deductions payable. Federal income tax and FICA tax levied on employees do not become legal obligations until the employees are paid. Therefore, for the purpose of recording the adjusting entry, the entire liability of the gross salaries and wages is included under Salaries Payable or Wages Payable. In other words, in the adjusting entry, such accounts as Employees' Federal Income Tax Payable, FICA Tax Payable (employees' share), and Employees' Union Dues Payable are not used.

Adjusting Entry for Accrual of Payroll Taxes

As you have seen, the following taxes come under the umbrella of the Payroll Tax Expense account: the employer's share of the FICA tax, the state unemployment tax, and the federal unemployment tax. The employer becomes liable for these taxes only when the employees are actually paid, rather than at the time the liability to the employees is incurred. From the standpoint of legal liability, there should be no adjusting entry for Payroll Tax Expense.

TAX CALENDAR

Now let's put it all together. To keep up with the task of paying and reporting the various taxes, the accountant compiles a chronological list of the due dates. We are including only the payroll taxes here, but sales taxes and property taxes should also be listed. When you think about the penalties for nonpayment of taxes by the due dates, this chronological list seems to be well worth the effort. The employer is a monthly depositor for the federal tax deposit.

Jan. 10 Pay estimated annual premium for workers' compensation insurance. (This is an approximate date, as it varies among the states.)

Compiling a chronological list of tax due dates helps accountants keep up with paying and reporting the various taxes.

Jan. 15 Make federal tax deposit for employees' income tax withholding, employees' FICA taxes withheld, and employer's FICA taxes for wages paid during the month of December.

31 Complete Employer's Quarterly Federal Tax Return, Form 941, for the fourth quarter.

31 Issue copies B and C of Wage and Tax Statement, Form W-2, to employees.

31 Pay state unemployment tax liability for the previous quarter, and submit state return, employer's tax report.

31 Pay any remaining federal unemployment tax liability for the previous year, and submit Form 940, Employer's Annual Federal Unemployment Tax Return.

31 Make state deposit for employees' state income tax withholding and submit any required state payroll reports. (Timing and required reports may differ from state to state.)

Feb. 15 Make federal tax deposit for employees' income tax withholding, employees' FICA tax withholding, and employer's FICA tax for wages paid during the month of January.

28 Complete Transmittal of Wage and Tax Statements, Form W-3, and attach copy A of W-2 forms for employees.

Mar. 15 Make federal tax deposit for employees' income tax withholding, employees' FICA tax withholding, and employer's FICA tax for wages paid during the month of February.

Apr. 15 Make federal tax deposit for employees' income tax withholding, employees' FICA tax withholding, and employer's FICA tax for wages paid during the month of March.

30 Pay state unemployment tax liability for the previous quarter and submit state return, employer's tax report.

30 Complete Employer's Quarterly Federal Tax Return, Form 941, for the first quarter.

30 Make federal tax deposit for federal unemployment tax liability if it exceeds $100.

30 Make state deposit for employees' state income tax withholding.

CHAPTER REVIEW

Online Study Center
ACE the test!

Review of Performance Objectives

1. **Calculate the amount of payroll tax expense and journalize the entry.**

   Payroll tax expense consists of the employer's matching portion of FICA taxes, plus the state unemployment tax, plus the federal unemployment tax. The *FICA tax* consists of Social Security and Medicare taxes. *Social Security tax* equals total Social Security taxable earnings multiplied by .062 (6.2 percent assumed rate) on the taxable earnings. For this text, the maximum taxable is assumed to be $94,200. Total *Medicare tax* equals Medicare taxable earnings multiplied by .0145 (1.45 percent assumed rate). There is no maximum limit for Medicare—all earnings are taxable. *State unemployment tax* equals unemployment taxable earnings multiplied by .054 (5.4 percent assumed rate). *Federal unemployment tax* equals unemployment taxable earnings multiplied by .008 (.8 percent assumed rate). Refer to the related journal entry on page 298.

2. **Journalize the entry for the deposit of employees' federal income taxes withheld and FICA taxes (both employees' withheld and employer's matching share) and prepare the deposit coupon.**

   Refer to this journal entry on page 301.

3. **Journalize the entries for the payment of employer's state and federal unemployment taxes.**

   State unemployment tax is paid on a quarterly basis. Payment is due by the end of the next month following the end of the calendar quarter. Refer to this journal entry on page 302.
      If the amount of the accumulated federal unemployment tax liability exceeds $100 at the end of any quarter, the tax is due by the end of the next month following the end of the quarter. If the federal unemployment tax payable is less than $100 at the end of the year, it is due by January 31 of the next year. Refer to this journal entry on page 303.

4. **Journalize the entry for the deposit of employees' state income taxes withheld.**

   Employees' state income taxes withheld are paid on a quarterly basis or as required by the state. Payment may be due by the end of the next month following the end of the calendar quarter. Refer to this journal entry on page 304.

5. **Complete Employer's Quarterly Federal Tax Return, Form 941.**

   Form 941 is illustrated on page 305.

6. **Prepare W-2 and W-3 forms and Form 940.**

   W-2 form (Wage and Tax Statement) is illustrated on page 307. W-3 form (Transmittal of Wage and Tax Statements) is illustrated on page 309. Form 940 is illustrated on page 311.

7. **Calculate the premium for workers' compensation insurance, and prepare the entry for payment in advance.**

   Rates vary depending on the degree of physical risk involved in different occupations. The amount of the premium equals the predicted annual payroll multiplied by the premium rate. The entry is a debit to Prepaid Insurance, Workers' Compensation, and a credit to Cash.

8. Determine the amount of the end-of-the-year adjustments for (a) workers' compensation insurance and (b) accrued salaries and wages, and record the adjustments.

When the total annual payroll is known, the exact cost of workers' compensation insurance can be determined by multiplying the total payroll by the premium rate. Two adjusting entries are required. The first adjusting entry records the expired insurance as a debit to Workers' Compensation Insurance Expense and a credit to Prepaid Insurance, Workers' Compensation. The second adjusting entry records the difference between the estimated and the actual premiums. If the actual premium is greater than the premium that was paid in advance, the entry is a debit to Workers' Compensation Insurance Expense and a credit to Workers' Compensation Insurance Payable. The adjustment for accrued salaries and wages accounts for the additional amount of salaries or wages paid in the next payroll that are incurred in the current fiscal period—a debit to Wages (or Salary) Expense. The credit to Wages (or Salaries) Payable accounts for the additional amount of liability incurred in the current period that will be paid with the next payroll that occurs in the following fiscal period.

Glossary

Employer identification number The number assigned each employer by the Internal Revenue Service for use in the submission of reports and payments for FICA taxes and federal income tax withheld. (296)

Federal unemployment tax (FUTA) A tax levied only on the employer, equal to 0.8 percent of the first $7,000 of total earnings paid to each employee during the calendar year. This tax is used to administer the funds. (298)

Form 940 An annual report filed by employers showing total wages paid to employees, total wages subject to federal unemployment tax, total federal unemployment tax, and other information. Also called the *Employer's Annual Federal Unemployment Tax Return*. (308)

Form 941 A quarterly report showing the tax liability for withholdings of employees' federal income tax and FICA tax and the employer's share of FICA tax. Total tax deposits made in the quarter are also listed on this *Employer's Quarterly Federal Tax Return*. (304)

Form W-2 A form containing information about employee earnings and tax deductions for the year. Also called *Wage and Tax Statement*. (307)

Form W-3 An annual report sent to the Social Security Administration listing the total wages and tips, total federal income tax withheld, total Social Security and Medicare taxable wages, total Social Security and Medicare tax withheld, and other information for all employees of a firm. Also called the *Transmittal of Wage and Tax Statements*. (308)

Payroll Tax Expense A general expense account used for recording the employer's matching portion of the FICA tax, the federal unemployment tax, and the state unemployment tax. (296)

Quarters Three consecutive months, also referred to as *calendar quarters*. (300)

State unemployment tax (SUTA) A tax levied only on the employer in most states. Rates differ among the various states; however, they are generally 5.4 percent or higher of the first $7,000 of total earnings paid to each employee during the calendar year. The proceeds are used to pay subsistence benefits to unemployed workers. (298)

Workers' compensation insurance This insurance, primarily paid for by the employer, provides benefits for employees injured or killed on the job. The rates vary according to the degree of risk inherent in the job. The plans may be sponsored by states or by private firms. The employer pays the premium in advance at the beginning of the year, based on the estimated payroll. The rates are adjusted after the exact payroll is known. (312)

QUESTIONS, EXERCISES, AND CASES

Discussion Questions

1. What taxes are employers accounting for that increase the debit to Payroll Tax Expense?
2. Describe the journal entry to
   a. record the payroll.
   b. record the employer's payroll tax contributions.
   c. pay the payroll.
3. Explain the deposit requirement for federal unemployment tax.
4. What is the purpose of Form 941? How often is it prepared, and what are the due dates?
5. How many copies are made of a Form W-2, and who uses the copies of the W-2 form?
6. What is the purpose of Form 940? How often is it prepared, and what is the due date?
7. Generally, what is the time schedule for payment of workers' compensation insurance premiums?
8. Explain the advantage of establishing a tax calendar.

Exercises

P.O. 1

Journalize the entry for payroll tax expense.

Exercise 9-1 Salerno Company's partial payroll register for the week ended January 7 is shown below.

	NAME	BEGINNING CUMULATIVE EARNINGS	TOTAL EARNINGS	ENDING CUMULATIVE EARNINGS	TAXABLE EARNINGS		
					UNEMPLOYMENT	SOCIAL SECURITY	MEDICARE
1	Bonney, R. S.		932 00	932 00	932 00	932 00	932 00
2	Fisk, M. C.		567 00	567 00	567 00	567 00	567 00
3	Hayes, W. O.		483 00	483 00	483 00	483 00	483 00
4	Lee, L. B.		679 00	679 00	679 00	679 00	679 00
5	Parks, S. J.		578 00	578 00	578 00	578 00	578 00
6	Tempy, E. B.		546 00	546 00	546 00	546 00	546 00
7			3785 00	3785 00	3785 00	3785 00	3785 00
8							
9							
10							
11							

Assume that the payroll is subject to a Social Security tax of 6.2 percent of the first $94,200 and a Medicare tax of 1.45 percent on all earnings. Also assume that the federal unemployment tax is 0.8 percent of the first $7,000, and the state unemployment tax is 5.4 percent of the first $7,000. Give the entry in general journal form to record the payroll tax expense.

P.O. 1

Journalize the entry for payroll tax expense.

Exercise 9-2 On January 14, at the end of the second week of the year, the totals of Carson Company's payroll register showed that its store employees' wages amounted to $33,482 and its warehouse wages amounted to $13,560. Withholdings consisted of federal income taxes, $5,110; Social Security taxes at the rate of 6.2 percent of the first $94,200 and no employee has reached the limit; Medicare taxes at the rate of 1.45 percent on all earnings; union dues, $845.

a. Calculate the amount of Social Security and Medicare taxes to be withheld, and write the general journal entry to record the payroll.
b. Write the general journal entry to record the employer's payroll taxes, assuming that the federal unemployment tax is 0.8 percent of the first $7,000, that the state unemployment tax is 5.4 percent of the same base, and that no employee has surpassed the $7,000 limit.

P.O. 1

Journalize the payroll entries.

Exercise 9-3 Fennell Systems had the following payroll data for wages for the week ended February 5. These calculations for state income tax (20% of federal income tax) are exceptions.

| | | TAXABLE EARNINGS | | | DEDUCTIONS | | | |
TOTAL EARNINGS	ENDING CUMULATIVE EARNINGS	UNEMPLOYMENT	SOCIAL SECURITY	MEDICARE	FEDERAL INCOME TAX	STATE INCOME TAX	SOCIAL SECURITY TAX	MEDICARE TAX
6 7 0 0 00	72 8 5 0 00	6 7 0 0 00	6 7 0 0 00	6 7 0 0 00	8 2 4 00	1 5 7 00	4 1 9 74	9 8 17

a. Write the general journal entry to record the payroll.
b. Write the general journal entry to record the employer's payroll taxes. Assume rates of 0.8 percent for federal unemployment tax and 5.4 percent for state unemployment tax based on the first $7,000 for each employee and that no employee has earned more than $7,000.

P.O. 1

Journalize the entry for payroll tax expense.

Exercise 9-4 The information on earnings and deductions for the pay period ended December 14 from Larry Company's payroll records is shown on the following page.

For each employee, the Social Security tax is 6.2 percent of the first $94,200 and the Medicare tax is 1.45 percent on all earnings. The federal unemployment tax is 0.8 percent of the first $7,000 of earnings of each employee. The state unemployment tax is 5.4 percent of the same base. Determine the total taxable earnings for unemployment, Social Security, and Medicare. Prepare a general journal entry to record the employer's payroll taxes.

Name	Gross Pay	Beginning Cumulative Earnings
Biliken, J. L.	$ 410	$ 6,750
Clayton, M. E.	785	40,200
Drugden, T. F.	860	38,500
Rich, L. W.	990	39,700
Sparks, C. R.	2,094	93,650
Stevers, D. H.	850	6,810

P.O. 2

Journalize entries for payment of federal payroll taxes.

Exercise 9-5 Selected columns of Linch Company's payroll register for the month of January are as follows. The employees' FICA taxes are matched by the employer.

Payment Date	Employees' Federal Income Tax	Employees' Social Security Tax	Employees' Medicare Tax
Jan. 7	1,192.00	475.00	112.25
14	1,135.00	518.14	122.31
21	1,245.00	572.62	124.24
28	1,452.00	561.27	143.26

Linch Company deposits taxes monthly. In general journal form, record the entry for the February 15 payment of FICA and federal income taxes for employees and employer.

P.O. 2,3

Journalize entries for payment of payroll taxes.

Exercise 9-6 On September 30, Kaplin Company's selected account balances are as follows:

Employees' Federal Income Tax Payable	$ 2,369.00
FICA Tax Payable (employer and employee)	2,604.46
State Unemployment Tax Payable	1,250.00 } (Some employees have
Federal Unemployment Tax Payable	195.00 } reached the limit.)

In general journal form, prepare the entries to record the following:

Oct. 15 Payment of liabilities for FICA and federal income tax.
    31 Payment of liability for state unemployment tax.
    31 Payment of liability for federal unemployment tax.

P.O. 2,3

Journalize entries for payment of payroll taxes.

Exercise 9-7 On September 30, Mitchel Company's selected payroll accounts are as follows:

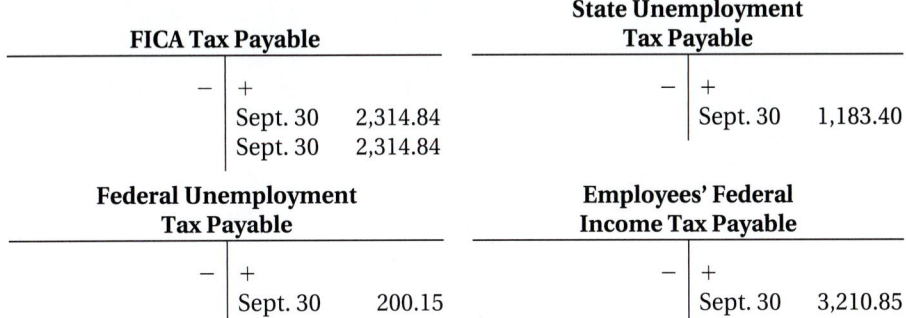

FICA Tax Payable		
−	+	
	Sept. 30	2,314.84
	Sept. 30	2,314.84

State Unemployment Tax Payable		
−	+	
	Sept. 30	1,183.40

Federal Unemployment Tax Payable		
−	+	
	Sept. 30	200.15

Employees' Federal Income Tax Payable		
−	+	
	Sept. 30	3,210.85

Prepare general journal entries to record the following:

Oct. 15 Payment of federal tax deposit of FICA and federal income tax.
 31 Payment of state unemployment tax.
 31 Payment of federal unemployment tax.

P.O. 7,8

Journalize entries for workers' compensation insurance.

Exercise 9-8 Megan Company received and paid a premium notice on January 2 for workers' compensation insurance stating the rates for the new year. Estimated employees' earnings for the year are as follows:

Classification	Estimated Wages and Salaries	Rate Per Hundred	Estimated Premium
Office clerical	$ 92,000	.11	$ 101.20
Warehouse work	29,000	.92	266.80
Manufacturing	264,000	1.20	3,168.00
			$3,536.00

At the end of the year, the exact figures for the payroll are as follows:

Classification	Estimated Wages and Salaries	Rate Per Hundred	Exact Premium
Office clerical	$ 93,000	.11	$ 102.30
Warehouse work	30,000	.92	276.00
Manufacturing	267,000	1.20	3,204.00
			$3,582.30

a. Record the entry in general journal form for payment of the estimated premium.
b. Record the adjusting entries on December 31 for the insurance expired and for the additional premium.

internet
LINKS TO ACCOUNTING

The previous chapter covered payroll taxes, collected by the employer, that the employee pays. In this chapter, you learned about the taxes the employer must pay. The whole process can be very complicated and confusing for the employer!

Are any methods other than Form 8109-B available for making deposits? See if you can find out by visiting the IRS website at **www.irs.gov.** If so, what are they and how are they used?

WHAT'S WRONG WITH THIS PICTURE?

The payroll clerk is working on the payroll for May 31. Several employees' gross earnings are about to exceed the limits for unemployment and FICA taxes. For each employee whose cumulative earnings were near the limit, the payroll clerk multiplied the tax rate by the amount by which the employee's earnings exceeded the tax ceiling (not the amount between the beginning cumulative earnings and the tax limit). Comment on this procedure.

CRITICAL THINKING

It is December 15, and you are the payroll clerk for Lincoln Company. The owner has come to you for help; two employees have asked for a 3 percent pay raise, and the owner wants to know how much more such a raise will cost her next year. Present gross salaries are as follows:

Employee A
$40,000/year   Married, with 2 allowances   Paid weekly
Employee B
$42,000/year   Married, with 1 allowance   Paid weekly

Assume the following tax rates and limits:

Social Security, 6.2 percent with a limit of $94,200
Medicare, 1.45 percent with no limit (all earnings taxable)
SUTA, 5.4 percent with a limit of $7,000
FUTA, 0.8 percent with a limit of $7,000

What will be the cost to the employer of giving Employee A and Employee B the pay raise?

A QUESTION OF ETHICS

Between the end of one month and the fifteenth day of the next month, the balance in the employer's business bank account has been getting smaller and smaller. An employee prepares the next payroll and correctly computes the necessary withholding taxes. The employer is supposed to pay accumulated employment taxes on the fifteenth of the next month. Payday is the last day of the month. However, the employer has used the funds withheld from employees to pay some of the business's bills. He hopes that enough of the customers who owe him money will pay their outstanding debts. If his assumption is true, the checking account will have enough in it to pay the federal deposit on the fifteenth of the month. Is the employer acting ethically? After all, he says he intends to have enough money in the account for the deposit.

PROBLEM SET A

For additional help, see the demonstration problem at the beginning of each chapter in your Working Papers.

P.O. 1

Problem 9-1A Migiro Labs had the following payroll for the week ended February 28:

Salaries		Deductions	
Technicians' salaries	$6,955.00	Federal income tax withheld	$ 695.00
Office salaries	2,260.00	Social Security tax withheld	571.33
		Medicare tax withheld	133.62
Total	$9,215.00	Union dues withheld	165.00
		Medical insurance	450.00
		Total	$2,014.95

Assumed tax rates are as follows:

a. FICA: Social Security, 6.2 percent (.062) on the first $94,200 for each employee, and Medicare, 1.45 percent (.0145) on all earnings for each employee.
b. State unemployment tax, 5.4 percent (.054) on the first $7,000 for each employee.
c. Federal unemployment tax, 0.8 percent (.008) on the first $7,000 for each employee.

Check Figure

Payroll Tax Expense, $1,107.33

Instructions

Record the following entries in general journal form:

1. The payroll entry as of February 28.
2. The entry to record the employer's payroll taxes as of February 28, assuming that the total payroll is subject to the FICA tax (combined Social Security and Medicare) and that $6,490.00 is subject to unemployment taxes.
3. The payment to the employees on March 2. (Assume that the company has transferred cash to Cash—Payroll Bank Account for this payroll.)

P.O. 1

Problem 9-2A Timely Services has the following payroll information for the week ended December 7. State income tax is computed as 20% of federal income tax.

	NAME	BEGINNING CUMULATIVE EARNINGS	TOTAL EARNINGS	DEDUCTIONS	
				FEDERAL INCOME TAX	STATE INCOME TAX
1	Delong, T.	6 8 2 0 00	4 8 0 00	3 9 00	7 80
2	Herrera, M.	6 8 4 0 00	4 7 0 00	3 7 00	7 40
3	Joyner, J.	36 3 2 0 00	7 4 0 00	4 6 00	9 20
4	King, L.	26 2 0 0 00	5 4 0 00	5 0 00	1 0 00
5	Wisniewski, M.	93 3 6 0 00	1 7 2 0 00	2 8 9 00	5 7 80
6	Yee, N.	28 4 2 6 00	6 0 5 00	6 4 00	1 2 80
7					
8					
9					
10					
11					
12					
13					
14					

Assumed tax rates are as follows:

a. FICA: Social Security, 6.2 percent (.062) on the first $94,200 for each employee, and Medicare, 1.45 percent (.0145) on all earnings for each employee.
b. State unemployment tax, 5.4 percent (.054) on the first $7,000 for each employee.
c. Federal unemployment tax, 0.8 percent (.008) on the first $7,000 for each employee.

Check Figure

Payroll Tax Expense, $314.98

Instructions

1. Complete the payroll register, page 72. Payroll checks begin with Ck. No. 714 in the payroll register.
2. Prepare a general journal entry to record the payroll as of December 7. The company's general ledger contains a Salary Expense account and a Salaries Payable account.
3. Prepare a general journal entry to record the payroll taxes as of December 7.
4. Journalize the entry to pay the payroll on December 9. (Assume that the company has transferred cash to the Cash—Payroll Bank Account for this payroll.)

P.O. 5

Problem 9-3A For the third quarter of the year, Jackson Company, 415 Circle Avenue, Chicago, Illinois 60652, received Form 941 from the Internal Revenue Service. The identification number of Jackson Company is 76-4213171. Its payroll for the quarter ended September 30 is as follows.

	NAME	TOTAL EARNINGS	TAXABLE EARNINGS SOCIAL SECURITY	MEDICARE	DEDUCTIONS FEDERAL INCOME TAX	SOCIAL SECURITY TAX	MEDICARE TAX
1	Barker, D. D.	6 6 2 9 00	6 6 2 9 00	6 6 2 9 00	8 4 3 00	4 1 1 00	9 6 12
2	Carey, L. R.	8 5 2 8 00	8 5 2 8 00	8 5 2 8 00	8 2 5 00	5 2 8 74	1 2 3 66
3	Domzalski, T. P.	4 6 6 5 00	4 6 6 5 00	4 6 6 5 00	6 8 9 00	2 8 9 23	6 7 64
4	Grisson, R. O.	3 7 2 1 00	3 7 2 1 00	3 7 2 1 00	4 7 8 00	2 3 0 70	5 3 95
5	Tyler, J. L.	7 4 0 6 00	7 4 0 6 00	7 4 0 6 00	8 6 5 00	4 5 9 17	1 0 7 39
6	Vardic, K. R.	5 2 8 7 00	5 2 8 7 00	5 2 8 7 00	7 9 5 00	3 2 7 79	7 6 66
7		36 2 3 6 00	36 2 3 6 00	36 2 3 6 00	4 4 9 5 00	2 2 4 6 63	5 2 5 42
8							

The company has had six employees throughout the year. Assume that the Social Security tax is 6.2 percent of the first $94,200 and that the Medicare tax is 1.45 percent of all earnings. The employer matches the employees' FICA (Social Security and Medicare) taxes. There are no taxable tips, adjustments, backup withholding, or earned income credits. Jackson Company has submitted the following federal tax deposits and written the accompanying checks:

On August 15 for the July Payroll		**On September 15 for the August Payroll**		**On October 15 for the September Payroll**	
Employees' income tax withheld	$1,380.00	Employees' income tax withheld	$1,892.00	Employees' income tax withheld	$1,223.00
Employees' Social Security and Medicare tax withheld	851.10	Employees' Social Security and Medicare tax withheld	875.92	Employees' Social Security and Medicare tax withheld	1,045.03
Employer's Social Security and Medicare tax contributed	851.10	Employer's Social Security and Medicare tax contributed	875.92	Employer's Social Security and Medicare tax contributed	1,045.03
	$3,082.20		$3,643.84		$3,313.06

Check Figure

Total taxes, $10,039.10

P.O. 1,2,3

Instructions

Complete Part 1 of Form 941 for the third quarter for the owner, Maxwell Jackson.

Problem 9-4A Leidel Company has the following balances in its general ledger as of June 1 of this year:

a. FICA Tax Payable (liability for May), $1,719.40 (employee and employer).
b. Employees' Federal Income Tax Payable (liability for May), $995.00.
c. Federal Unemployment Tax Payable (liability for April and May), $180.00.
d. State Unemployment Tax Payable (liability for April and May), $1,205.75.
e. Employees' Medical Insurance Payable (liability for April and May), $1,289.00.

The company completed the following transactions involving the payroll during June and July:

June 13 Issued check for $2,709.40 payable to Security Bank, for the monthly deposit of May FICA taxes and employees' federal income tax withheld.

30 Recorded the payroll entry in the general journal from the payroll register for June. The payroll register has the following column totals:

Sales salaries	$11,490.00	
Office salaries	5,147.00	
Total earnings		$16,637.00
Employees' federal income tax deductions	$ 1,725.00	
Employees' Social Security tax deductions	1,031.49	
Employees' Medicare tax deductions	241.24	
Employees' medical insurance deductions	755.00	
Total deductions		3,752.73
Net pay		$12,884.27

30 Recorded payroll taxes. Employer matches the employees' FICA taxes. State unemployment tax is 5.4 percent, and federal unemployment tax is 0.8 percent. At this time, all employees' earnings are taxable for FICA and unemployment taxes.

30 Issued check for $12,884.27 from Cash—Payroll Bank Account to pay salaries for the month.

July 14 Issued check for $2,044, payable to Carson Insurance Company, in payment of employees' medical insurance for April, May, and June.

14 Issued check for $4,270.46, payable to Security Bank, for the monthly deposit of June FICA taxes (employee and employer matching) and employees' federal income tax withheld.

31 Issued check for $2,104.15, payable to the State Tax Commission, for state unemployment tax for April, May, and June. The check was accompanied by the quarterly tax return.

31 Issued check for $313.10, payable to Security Bank, for the deposit of federal unemployment tax for the months of April, May, and June.

Check Figure

Payroll Tax Expense, $2,304.23

Instructions

Record the transactions in the general journal, pages 77–78.

Instructions for General Ledger Software

1. Record the transactions in the general journal.
2. Print the journal entries.

PROBLEM SET B

For additional help, see the demonstration problem at the beginning of each chapter in your Working Papers.

P.O. 1

Problem 9-1B Kovich Company had the following payroll for the week ended March 21:

Salaries		Deductions	
Sales salaries	$7,620.00	Federal income tax withheld	$ 894.00
Office salaries	1,790.00	Social Security tax withheld	583.42
		Medicare tax withheld	136.45
Total	$9,410.00	Union dues withheld	153.00
		Medical insurance	200.00
		Total	$1,966.87

Assumed tax rates are as follows:

a. FICA: Social Security, 6.2 percent (.062) on the first $94,200 for each employee, and Medicare, 1.45 percent (.0145) on all earnings for each employee.
b. State unemployment tax, 5.4 percent (.054) on the first $7,000 for each employee.
c. Federal unemployment tax, 0.8 percent (.008) on the first $7,000 for each employee.

Check Figure

Payroll Tax Expense, $1,027.70

Instructions

Record the following entries in general journal form:

1. The payroll entry as of March 21.
2. The entry to record the employer's payroll taxes as of March 21, assuming that the total payroll is subject to the FICA tax (combined Social Security and Medicare) and that $4,965 is subject to unemployment taxes.
3. The payment of the employees on March 23. (Assume that the company has transferred cash to Cash—Payroll Bank Account for this payroll.)

P.O. 1

Problem 9-2B Kyle Agency has the following payroll information for the week ended December 14. State income tax is computed as 20% of federal income tax.

	NAME	BEGINNING CUMULATIVE EARNINGS	TOTAL EARNINGS	DEDUCTIONS FEDERAL INCOME TAX	STATE INCOME TAX
1	Abraham, R.	10 6 5 0 00	4 6 0 00	3 5 00	7 00
2	Baca, T.	38 8 2 0 00	9 7 0 00	1 0 9 00	2 1 80
3	Eubanks, E.	93 2 5 5 00	1 7 9 0 00	2 0 5 00	4 1 00
4	Ling, D.	6 7 5 0 00	3 8 5 00	2 8 00	5 60
5	Metcalf, S.	31 6 7 0 00	6 9 4 00	5 2 00	1 0 40
6	Quinn, D.	48 9 6 1 00	1 0 4 0 00	1 1 0 00	2 2 00
7					

Assumed tax rates are as follows:

a. FICA: Social Security, 6.2 percent (.062) on the first $94,200 for each employee, and Medicare, 1.45 percent (.0145) on all earnings for each employee.
b. State unemployment tax, 5.4 percent (.054) on the first $7,000 for each employee.
c. Federal unemployment tax, 0.8 percent (.008) on the first $7,000 for each employee.

Check Figure

Payroll Tax Expense, $371.55

Instructions

1. Complete the payroll register, page 72. Payroll checks begin with Ck. No. 923 in the payroll register.
2. Prepare a general journal entry to record the payroll as of December 14. The company's general ledger contains a Salary Expense account and a Salaries Payable account.
3. Prepare a general journal entry to record the payroll taxes as of December 14.
4. Journalize the entry to pay the payroll on December 16. (Assume that the company has transferred cash to the Cash—Payroll Bank Account for this payroll.)

P.O. 5

Problem 9-3B For the third quarter of the year, Farley Construction, of 715 Red Rock Boulevard, San Francisco, California 94421, received Form 941 from the District Office of the Internal Revenue Service. The identification number for Farley Construction is 78-7382476. Its payroll for the quarter ended September 30 is as follows:

| | | TAXABLE EARNINGS | | | DEDUCTIONS | | |
NAME	TOTAL EARNINGS	SOCIAL SECURITY	MEDICARE	FEDERAL INCOME TAX	SOCIAL SECURITY TAX	MEDICARE TAX
1 Brinnon, D. L.	3 3 8 7 00	3 3 8 7 00	3 3 8 7 00	3 1 0 00	2 0 9 99	4 9 11
2 Finn, J. A.	6 7 5 3 00	6 7 5 3 00	6 7 5 3 00	7 0 4 00	4 1 8 69	9 7 92
3 Harrell, N. E.	7 7 8 0 00	7 7 8 0 00	7 7 8 0 00	8 2 0 00	4 8 2 36	1 1 2 81
4 Kelly, T. L.	6 2 4 3 00	6 2 4 3 00	6 2 4 3 00	6 6 0 00	3 8 7 07	9 0 52
5 Morton, S. M.	4 2 1 5 00	4 2 1 5 00	4 2 1 5 00	3 8 4 00	2 6 1 33	6 1 12
6 Rieck, A. J.	10 2 6 4 00	10 2 6 4 00	10 2 6 4 00	1 2 2 4 00	6 3 6 37	1 4 8 83
7	38 6 4 2 00	38 6 4 2 00	38 6 4 2 00	4 1 0 2 00	2 3 9 5 81	5 6 0 31

The company has had six employees throughout the year. Assume that the Social Security tax is 6.2 percent of the first $94,200, and that the Medicare tax is 1.45 percent of all earnings. The employer matches the employees' FICA (Social Security and Medicare) taxes. There are no taxable tips, adjustments, backup withholding, or earned income credits. Farley Construction has submitted the following federal tax deposits and written the accompanying checks:

On August 15 for the July Payroll		On September 15 for the August Payroll		On October 15 for the September Payroll	
Employees' income tax withheld	$1,440.00	Employees' income tax withheld	$1,394.00	Employees' income tax withheld	$1,268.00
Employees' Social Security and Medicare tax withheld	984.80	Employees' Social Security and Medicare tax withheld	1,138.40	Employees' Social Security and Medicare tax withheld	832.92
Employer's Social Security and Medicare tax contributed	984.80	Employer's Social Security and Medicare tax contributed	1,138.40	Employer's Social Security and Medicare tax contributed	832.92
	$3,409.60		$3,670.80		$2,933.84

Check Figure

Total taxes, $10,014.24

P.O. 1,2,3

Instructions

Complete Part 1 of Form 941 for the third quarter for the owner, Tom Farley.

Problem 9-4B Degrande Company has the following balances in its general ledger as of March 1 of this year:

a. FICA Tax Payable (liability for February), $1,459.80 (employee and employer).
b. Employees' Federal Income Tax Payable (liability for February), $915.00.
c. State Unemployment Tax Payable (liability for January and February), $965.20.
d. Federal Unemployment Tax Payable (liability for January and February), $151.40.
e. Employees' Medical Insurance Payable (liability for January and February), $935.00.

The company completed the following transactions involving the payroll during March and April:

Mar. 12 Issued check for $2,374.80 payable to Coastal Bank, for monthly deposit of February FICA taxes and employees' federal income tax withheld.

31 Recorded the payroll entry in the general journal from the payroll register for March. The payroll register had the following column totals:

Sales salaries	$7,654.00	
Office salaries	1,982.00	
Total earnings		$9,636.00
Employees' federal income tax deductions	$ 795.00	
Employees' Social Security tax deductions	597.43	
Employees' Medicare tax deductions	139.72	
Employees' medical insurance deductions	485.00	
Total deductions		2,017.15
Net pay		$7,618.85

Mar.   31   Recorded payroll taxes. Employer matches the employees' FICA taxes. State unemployment tax is 5.4 percent. Federal unemployment tax is 0.8 percent. At this time, all employees' earnings are taxable for FICA and unemployment taxes.

   31   Issued check for $7,618.85 from Cash—Payroll Bank Account to pay the salaries for the month.

Apr.   3   Issued check for $1,420, payable to Orange Insurance Company, for employees' medical insurance for January, February, and March.

   14   Issued check for $2,269.30, payable to Coastal Bank, for monthly deposit of March FICA taxes and employees' federal income tax withheld.

   30   Issued check for $1,485.54, payable to State Department of Revenue, for state unemployment tax for January, February, and March. The check was accompanied by the quarterly tax return.

   30   Issued check for $228.49, payable to Coastal Bank, for deposit of federal unemployment tax for January, February, and March.

Check Figure

Payroll Tax Expense, $1,334.58

Instructions

Record the transactions in the general journal, pages 77 and 78.

Instructions for General Ledger Software

1. Record the transactions in the general journal.
2. Print the journal entries.

PART I: Completion

1. Checks issued by the depositor that have been paid or have cleared the bank are called _____ checks.

2. A deposit that is not recorded on the bank statement because it was made after the bank's closing date for preparation of bank statements is called a(n) _____.

3. The process by which the payee transfers ownership of the check to a bank or other party is called a(n) _____.

4. The person to whom a check is payable is called the _____.

5. A cash fund used to make small immediate cash payments is called a(n) _____.

PART II: Application

1. Clara Thompson's salary is $1,775 per month. If she works more than 40 hours in one week, she is entitled to overtime pay at the rate of 1½ times her regular hourly rate. During the current week, she worked 45 hours. Calculate her gross pay.

2. On June 30, the column totals of Midtown Cleaning's payroll register showed that its cleaning employees had earned $9,000 and its office employees had earned $3,000. Social Security taxes were withheld at 6.2 percent, and Medicare taxes were withheld at 1.45 percent. All earnings are taxable. Other deductions consisted of federal income tax, $1,500; U.S. savings bonds, $500; and medical insurance, $962. Determine the amount of Social Security and Medicare taxes that should be withheld. Record the general journal entry to record the payroll, crediting Salaries Payable for the net pay.

3. Roxy Company's payroll for the week ended December 31 is as follows:

Gross earnings of employees	$155,000
Social Security taxable earnings	143,000
Medicare taxable earnings	155,000
Federal unemployment taxable earnings	22,000
State unemployment taxable earnings	22,000

Assume that the payroll is subject to Social Security tax of 6.2 percent (.062), Medicare tax of 1.45 percent (.0145), federal unemployment tax of 0.8 percent (.008), and state unemployment tax of 5.4 percent (.054). Write the entry in general journal form to record the employer's payroll tax expense.

Note: Answers to Before a Test Check begin on page A-1.

PART III: True/False

T   F   1. There is no limit on the amount of taxable earnings for Medicare.

T   F   2. When journalizing the entry to reimburse the Petty Cash Fund, include a credit to Petty Cash Fund.

T   F   3. When journalizing the entry to account for a customer's NSF check, debit Accounts Payable.

T   F   4. An employee's net pay is the result of subtracting his or her deductions from gross pay.

T   F   5. The gross pay for an employee who works 45 hours, earns $8.50 per hour, and receives time and a half for hours worked over 40 hours is $402.75.

10

The Sales Journal and the Purchases Journal

How many times have you purchased something from Target, only to return it later because you changed your mind? How does this affect Target's sales figures? As you learn about sales transactions in this chapter, think about what accounts might be involved to record the sale and return of merchandise. You can view Target's financial statements at **http://www.target.com.** (At the bottom of the site, click on Investors. Select Annual Reports. Once you open up one of the annual reports, you will be able to select the statement of operations from a pull-down menu.) Can you tell the amount of sales returns from looking at the financial statements?

Performance Objectives

After you have completed the chapter, you will be able to do the following:

1. Describe the specific accounts used by a merchandising firm.

2. Journalize transactions in a sales journal.

3. Post sales journal transactions to an accounts receivable ledger and a general ledger.

4. Prepare a schedule of accounts receivable.

5. Journalize sales returns and allowances, including credit memorandums and returns involving sales tax, in a general journal, and post to the accounts receivable ledger and general ledger.

6. Journalize transactions in a three-column purchases journal.

7. Post purchases journal transactions to an accounts payable ledger and a general ledger.

8. Prepare a schedule of accounts payable.

9. Journalize transactions involving purchases returns and allowances in a general journal, and post to the accounts payable ledger and general ledger.

10. Describe the procedures for handling freight charges on merchandise and other goods.

W e begin this chapter by briefly introducing four special journals that are helpful when accounting for merchandising businesses. A **merchandising business** is one that buys and sells goods. It can be a wholesale or a retail business. A **wholesale business**, which is sometimes called a "middleman" or a "distributor," buys goods from manufacturers and sells them to retailers. A **retail business** sells goods directly to consumers ("the public"). An example of a wholesaler is a business that supplies Target with soaps, shampoos, and other "health and beauty" items. Target, then, is a retailer of those same products.

SPECIAL JOURNALS

Special journals are books of original entry used to simplify the recording process. One or more of these journals may be used in a manual accounting system, or they may be used in certain computerized systems designed to facilitate specialized types of repetitive transactions. The four most commonly used special journals are:

Sales journal (S) Used to record sales of merchandise sold on account *only*. For example, if a wholesale business sells televisions to Best Buy (the retailer), on account, the wholesaler could use this journal to record that sale. However, if Best Buy paid cash for the televisions, the sale would not be recorded in this journal. Also, if a company sells some of its old computer equipment, on account, this journal would not be used because the equipment was not part of the business's merchandise sales.

Purchases journal (P) Used to record purchases of merchandise purchased for resale on account *only*. For example, this journal could be used by a shoe store for its purchase, on account, of a supply of shoes to resell to customers. However, this journal would not be used by a company buying a copy machine or supplies for the office, even though purchased on account, because those goods are not intended for resale to customers.

Cash receipts journal (CR) Used to record all transactions that include a debit to Cash, such as cash sales, checks received, or interest earned on a checking account.

Cash payments journal (CP) Used to record all transactions that include a credit to Cash, such as payments by check or bank service charges.

All other transactions are recorded in the general journal (J). A business would use only those journal(s) that it needs.

SPECIFIC ACCOUNTS FOR MERCHANDISING FIRMS

OBJECTIVE 1

Describe the specific accounts used by a merchandising firm.

Merchandise inventory consists of a stock of goods that a company buys and intends to resell at a profit. Merchandise should be differentiated from other assets, such as furniture and equipment, that are acquired for use in the business and are not for resale. Here is the fundamental accounting equation with the T accounts for merchandising businesses.

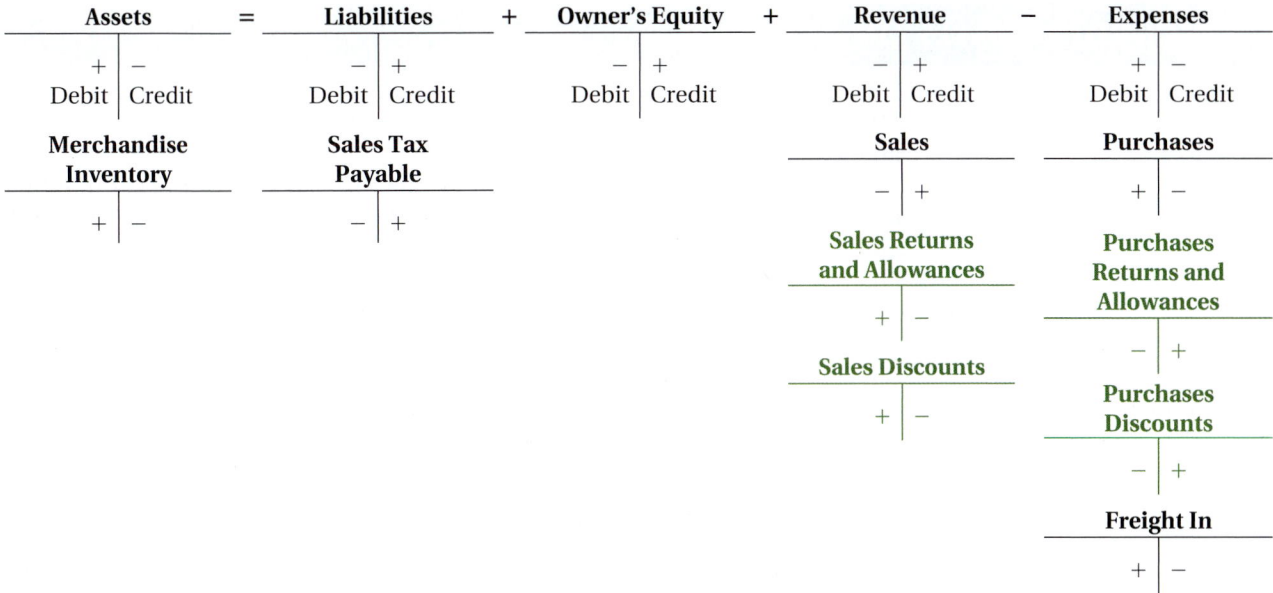

The **Sales account** is a revenue account used for recording sales of merchandise.

The **Purchases account** is used strictly to record the cost of merchandise bought for resale. The plus and minus signs are the same as the signs for Merchandise Inventory. The Purchases account is placed under the Expenses heading because the accountant closes it along with the expense accounts at the end of the fiscal period. (This is explained more in Chapter 17.)

The **Sales Returns and Allowances account** is used to record the physical return of merchandise by customers or a reduction in a bill because merchandise was damaged. It is treated as a deduction from Sales.

The **Sales Tax Payable account** is used to record a tax levied by a state or city government on the retail sale of goods and services. The tax is paid by the consumer but collected by the retailer.

The **Purchases Returns and Allowances account** is used to record the company's returns of merchandise it had purchased from suppliers or reductions in bills because of damaged merchandise. It is treated as a deduction from Purchases.

The **Sales Discounts account** and **Purchases Discounts account** are used to record cash discounts granted for prompt payments, in accordance with the credit terms.

The **Freight In account** is used to record the transportation charges on incoming merchandise intended for resale. Debits to this account increase the cost of purchases.

The T accounts for returns and allowances and for discounts are shown in green to emphasize that we are treating them as deductions from the related accounts placed above them. We list these accounts as deductions because they appear as deductions in the financial statements. Their relationship is similar to that between the Drawing account and the Capital account; remember that we deduct Drawing from Capital in the statement of owner's equity. These same types of accounts pertain to both retail and wholesale businesses.

RECORDING SALES ON ACCOUNT

A sale of merchandise on account is recorded as a debit to Accounts Receivable and a credit to Sales.

In a retail business, a salesperson usually prepares a sales ticket in either duplicate or triplicate for a sale on account. One copy goes to the customer and another to the accounting department, where it serves as the basis for an entry in the sales journal. A third copy may be used as a record of sales—to compute sales commissions or control inventory, for example.

In a wholesale business, the company usually receives a written order directly from a customer or through a salesperson who obtained the order from the customer. The credit department approves the order, and then sends it to the billing department, where the sales invoice is prepared.

Invoices are prepared in multiple copies. Figure 1 shows one possible distribution of sales invoice copies to various parties.

Just as we used Cline's Computer Clinic as a continuous example of a service business, we will use Rainier Plumbing Supply as a continuous example of a merchandising business. Rainier Plumbing Supply is a wholesaler.

FIGURE 1

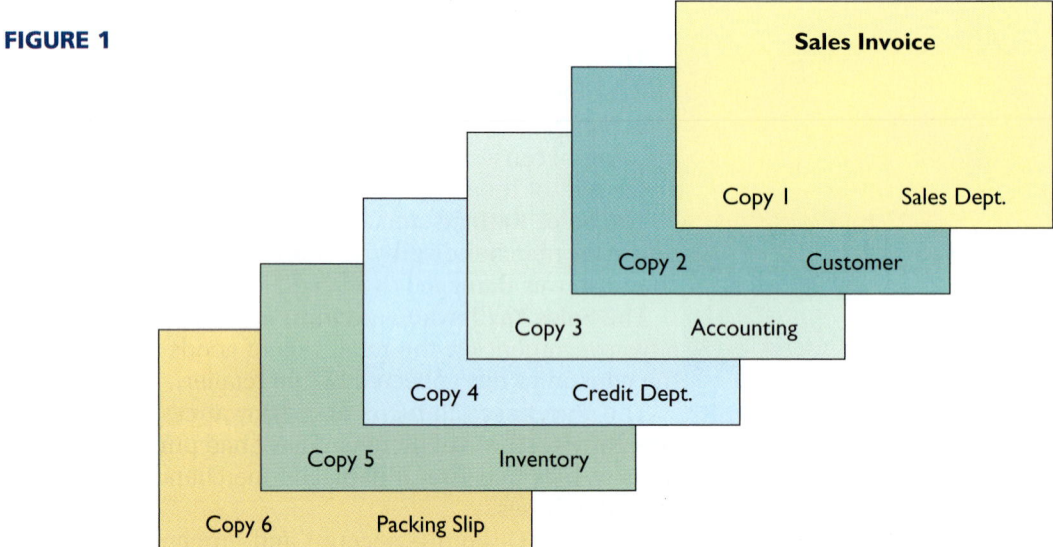

We will introduce the sales journal by looking at three transactions on the books of Rainier Plumbing Supply:

Aug. 1 Sold merchandise on account to Betterbuilt Homes Co., invoice no. 1320, $1,564.86.
     3 Sold merchandise on account to Arnold, Inc., invoice no. 1321, $1,116.
     6 Sold merchandise on account to Gonzales Construction, invoice no. 1322, $1,394.

Here's how the accounts appear in the fundamental accounting equation.

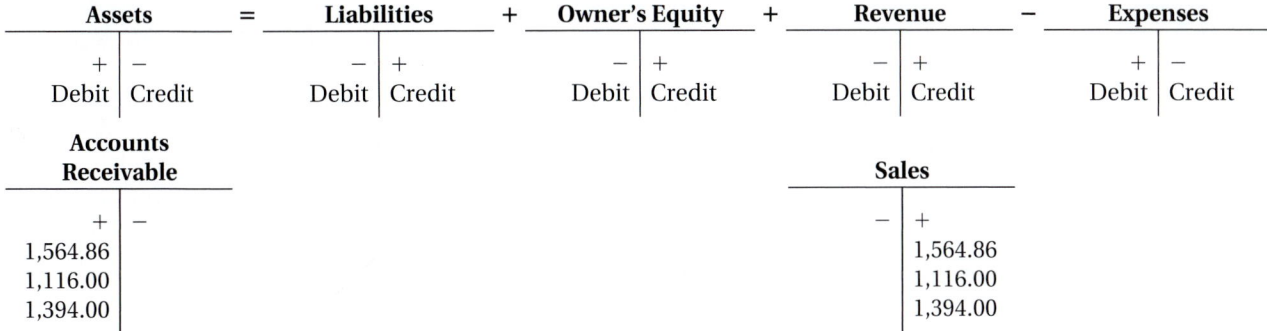

Assets	=	Liabilities	+	Owner's Equity	+	Revenue	−	Expenses
+ | −		− | +		− | +		− | +		+ | −
Debit | Credit		Debit | Credit		Debit | Credit		Debit | Credit		Debit | Credit

Accounts Receivable		Sales
+ | −		− | +
1,564.86		1,564.86
1,116.00		1,116.00
1,394.00		1,394.00

The sales invoice for the sale to Betterbuilt Homes Co. is shown in Figure 2.

FIGURE 2

Rainier Plumbing Supply
1400 Front Street
Seattle, WA 98101

INVOICE

SOLD TO Betterbuilt Homes Co.
5120 Gilman Avenue
Portland, OR 97202

DATE: August 1, 20–
INVOICE NO.: 1320
ORDER NO.: 5384
SHIPPED BY: Their truck
TERMS: 2/10, n/30

QUANTITY	DESCRIPTION	UNIT PRICE	TOTAL
6	Olin single-control tub shower faucet #44B652	61 50	369 00
6	Olin dual-control washerless lavoratory faucet #59B641	22 20	133 20
6	Olin massage shower head, antique brass #37B411	79 06	474 36
6	Olin single pedestal porcelain sink #42B782	98 05	588 30
	TOTAL		1,564 86

CAREERS IN YOUR FUTURE

TRACY L. NEWKIRK

Marketing Manager, Microsoft Corporation

Tracy's accounting skills—along with marketing positions in three large and small, public and private corporations (GE, CareWise, Inc., and Experience Music Project)—have launched her into her dream career with Microsoft in Redmond, Washington. Unlike her last position with a non-profit museum, she now works in a far larger and more global company.

Tracy works as a marketing manager in a relatively small, product-incubation-like group within Microsoft. But her responsibilities are not all related to marketing. Along with all the marketing efforts comes greater fiscal responsibility, including showing the return on investment (ROI) for marketing campaign efforts and being able to justify the next project. Each day brings something new.

Tracy enjoys accounting because she loves the number crunching. The outcome is clear—you either have money to spend on a project or you don't. Although she is not journalizing or preparing financial statements in her current position, her accounting experience sets her apart from many in the marketing field.

"Absorb all that you can in accounting and hang onto it so that you can apply it in your everyday life. Put it on your resume. If you can sit in a room with the controller and/or director of finance and hold your own during a budget discussion, you'll be doing very well. Not many people can do that."

THE SALES JOURNAL

OBJECTIVE 2
Journalize transactions in a sales journal.

The **sales journal** records sales of merchandise **on account only.** This specialized type of transaction calls for debits to Accounts Receivable and credits to Sales. As shown here, Rainier Plumbing Supply uses the sales journal *instead of* the general journal to record the three transactions.

REMEMBER!

The sales journal is a book of original entry. Do not duplicate the transaction in the general journal.

SALES JOURNAL   PAGE __38__

	DATE	INV. NO.	CUSTOMER'S NAME	POST. REF.	ACCOUNTS RECEIVABLE DR. SALES CR.	
1	20–					1
2	Aug. 1	1320	Betterbuilt Homes Co.		1 5 6 4 86	2
3	3	1321	Arnold, Inc.		1 1 1 6 00	3
4	6	1322	Gonzales Construction		1 3 9 4 00	4
5						5
6						6
7						7
8						8
9						9

Because *one* column is headed Accounts Receivable Dr./Sales Cr., each transaction requires only a single line. Repetition is avoided, and all entries for sales of merchandise on account are found in one place. Listing the invoice number makes it easier to check the details of a particular sale at a later date.

The amount of each sale will be posted daily to the account of each charge customer in the accounts receivable ledger. The accounts receivable ledger is introduced on page 341.

Posting from the Sales Journal

OBJECTIVE 3
Post sales journal transactions to an accounts receivable ledger and a general ledger.

Using the sales journal also saves time and space in posting to the ledger accounts. The transactions involving the sales of merchandise on account for the entire month of August are shown in Figure 3 on page 340.

Because every entry is a debit to Accounts Receivable and a credit to Sales, you can make a single posting to these accounts for the amount of the total as of the last day of the month. This entry is called a **summarizing entry** because it summarizes one month's transactions. In the Post. Ref. columns of the ledger accounts, the letter S designates the sales journal.

REMEMBER!

The T accounts look like this:

Accounts Receivable	
+	−
32,973.82	

Sales	
−	+
	32,973.82

GENERAL LEDGER

ACCOUNT __Accounts Receivable__ ACCOUNT NO. __113__

	DATE	ITEM	POST. REF.	DEBIT	CREDIT	BALANCE DEBIT	BALANCE CREDIT	
1	20–							1
2	Aug. 31		S38	32 9 7 3 82		32 9 7 3 82		2
3								3
4								4
5								5

ACCOUNT __Sales__ ACCOUNT NO. __411__

	DATE	ITEM	POST. REF.	DEBIT	CREDIT	BALANCE DEBIT	BALANCE CREDIT	
1	20–							1
2	Aug. 31		S38		32 9 7 3 82		32 9 7 3 82	2
3								3
4								4
5								5

REMEMBER!

The purpose of posting reference numbers is to tell where in the ledger an amount was posted or the journal from which it came.

After posting the total of the sales journal to the Accounts Receivable account in the general ledger, write the account number of Accounts Receivable at the left below the total of the sales journal. Repeat the process of posting for the total of the sales journal to the Sales account in the general ledger, placing the account number of Sales at the right below the total of the sales journal. **Don't record these account numbers until you have completed the postings.**

	DATE	INV. NO.	CUSTOMER'S NAME	POST. REF.	ACCOUNTS RECEIVABLE DR. SALES CR.	
1	20–					1
2	Aug. 1	1320	Betterbuilt Homes Co.		1 5 6 4 86	2
3	3	1321	Arnold, Inc.		1 1 1 6 00	3
4	6	1322	Gonzales Construction		1 3 9 4 00	4
5	9	1323	Harris Service Company		5 9 6 1 00	5
6	11	1324	Carmel Hardware		3 7 7 2 24	6
7	16	1325	Howard and Sons, Inc.		2 4 4 1 00	7
8	20	1326	Green Plumbing and Heating		1 7 1 0 00	8
9	23	1327	Chin Building Supplies		3 3 8 4 00	9
10	24	1328	Carmel Hardware		1 2 9 3 22	10
11	28	1329	Howard and Sons, Inc.		2 4 8 7 00	11
12	30	1330	Chin Building Supplies		3 6 1 4 00	12
13	31	1331	Betterbuilt Homes Co.		1 3 7 5 50	13
14	31	1332	Quality Builders, Inc.		2 8 6 1 00	14
15	31				32 9 7 3 82	15
16					(113)(411)	16
17						17

SALES JOURNAL   PAGE __38__

Sales Journal Provision for Sales Tax

Most states and some cities levy a sales tax on retail sales of goods and services. The retailer collects the sales tax from customers and later pays it to the tax authorities.

When goods or services are sold on credit, the sales tax is charged to the customer and recorded at the time of the sale. The sales journal must be designed to handle this type of transaction. For example, if a retail store sells an item for $500 and the sales tax is 8 percent, the transaction would be recorded in T accounts like this:

Accounts Receivable	Sales	Sales Tax Payable
+ –	– +	– +
540	500	40

Incidentally, when the sales tax is paid to the state, the accountant debits Sales Tax Payable and credits Cash.

Because we want to illustrate a sales journal for a retail merchandising firm operating in a state that has a sales tax, we will talk about the transactions of Dixon Office Furniture Co., another company. Its sales journal is shown in Figure 4.

Column totals would be posted as a debit to Accounts Receivable, a credit to Sales Tax Payable, and a credit to Sales. After posting, the respective account numbers are recorded in parentheses below the totals.

FIGURE 4

	DATE	INV. NO.	CUSTOMER'S NAME	POST. REF.	ACCOUNTS RECEIVABLE DEBIT			SALES TAX PAYABLE CREDIT			SALES CREDIT			
1	20–													1
2	Apr. 1	9382	C. D. Barnes		1 6 7 4	00		1 2 4	00		1 5 5 0	00		2
3	1	9383	Best Child Care		1 1 0 3	76		8 1	76		1 0 2 2	00		3
4	1	9384	Land Use Planners		2 2 1 4	00		1 6 4	00		2 0 5 0	00		4
5	2	9385	R. M. Allen		3 3 6 0	96		2 4 8	96		3 1 1 2	00		5
18	30	10121	Link Accountants		1 2 0 9	60		8 9	60		1 1 2 0	00		18
19	30				49 9 1 7	60		3 6 9 7	60		46 2 2 0	00		19
20					(1 1 3	)		(2 1 4	)		(4 1 1	)		20
21														21
22														22

SALES JOURNAL　　PAGE ___96___

THE ACCOUNTS RECEIVABLE LEDGER

In order to know how much each charge customer owes a business, the firm maintains an **accounts receivable ledger**. This ledger is a separate book or record containing a list of the charge customers with their respective balances listed in either alphabetical order or by account number. If the company's accounting system is not computerized, accountants prefer a loose-leaf binder, so that they can insert accounts for new customers and remove closed accounts.

The Accounts Receivable account in the general ledger should still be maintained. When all the postings are up to date, the balance of this account should equal the total of all the charge customers' individual account balances. The Accounts Receivable account in the general ledger is called a **controlling account**. The accounts receivable *ledger*, containing the accounts of all the charge customers, is really a special type of ledger, called a **subsidiary ledger**. Figure 5 diagrams the interrelationship of these ledgers.

The accountant posts the individual amounts to the accounts receivable ledger every day, so that this ledger will have up-to-date information. At the end of the month, the accountant posts the sales journal total of $12,900 (in Figure 5) to the general ledger accounts as a debit to the Accounts Receivable controlling account and a credit to the Sales account. The schedule of accounts receivable is merely a listing of charge customers' individual account balances.

In the simplified illustration in Figure 5, it just so happens that, since no payments were received from charge customers, the total of the sales journal equals the balance of Accounts Receivable. However, if $1,200 had been received from charge customers, both the balance of the Accounts Receivable controlling account and the total of the schedule of accounts receivable would be $11,700 ($12,900 − $1,200). The total of the sales journal would still be $12,900.

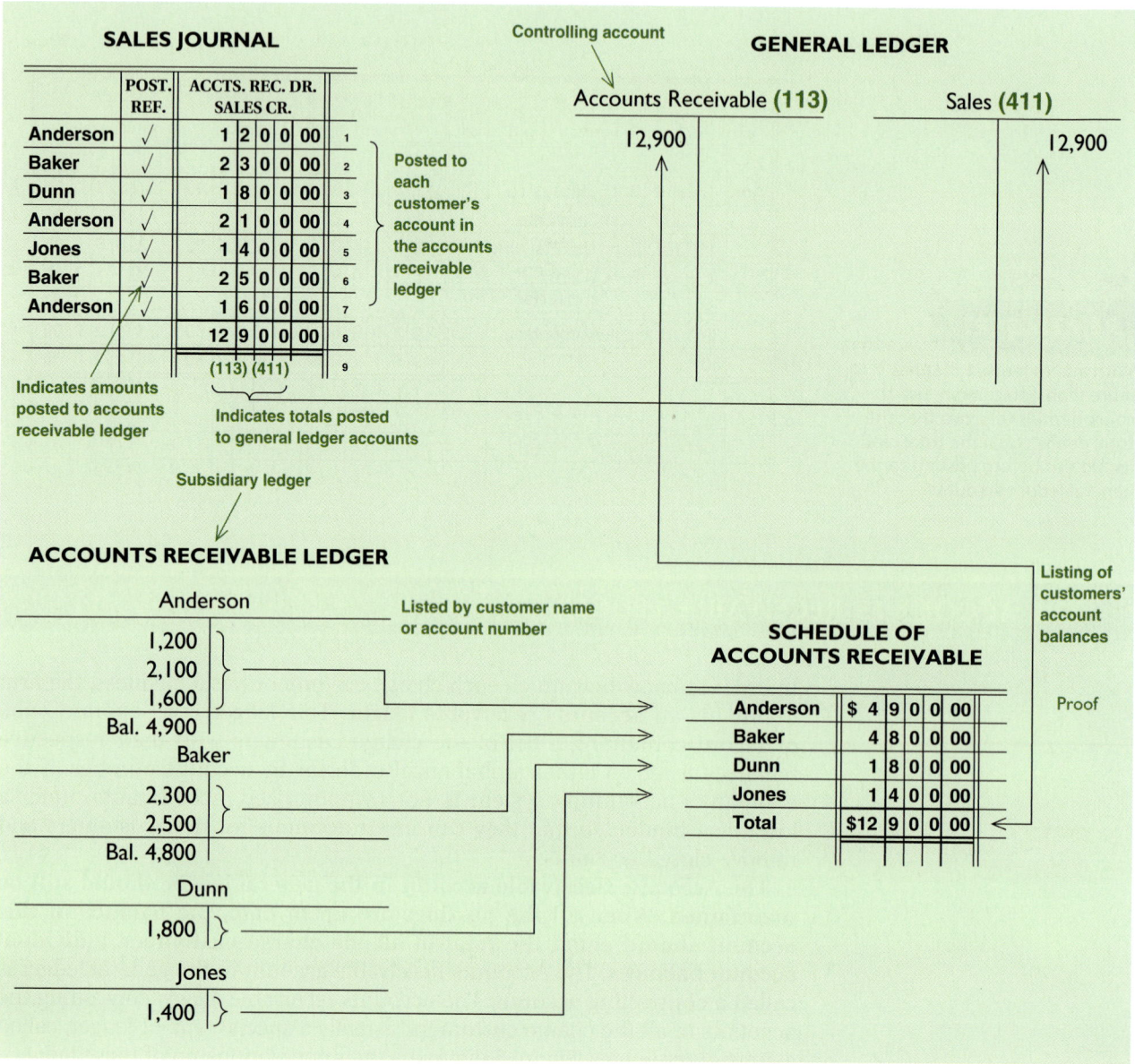

FIGURE 5

After you post an amount from the sales journal to a charge customer's account in the accounts receivable ledger, put a check mark (✓) in the Post. Ref. column of the sales journal. Figure 6 shows the posting procedure for a single-column sales journal.

Let's go back to the sales journal of Rainier Plumbing Supply for August. We will cover the daily postings that its accountant has made to the accounts receivable ledger. Then we'll see the schedule of accounts receivable. These entries are shown in Figure 6 and the ledger accounts that follow. Note that the ruling consists of a single line under the amount column and double lines extended through the Date, Post. Ref., and amount columns. The last day of the month is recorded on the same line as the total.

FIGURE 6

		INV. NO.	CUSTOMER'S NAME	POST. REF.	ACCOUNTS RECEIVABLE DR. SALES CR.	
	DATE					
1	20–					1
2	Aug. 1	1320	Betterbuilt Homes Co.	✓	1 5 6 4 86	2
3	3	1321	Arnold, Inc.	✓	1 1 1 6 00	3
4	6	1322	Gonzales Construction	✓	1 3 9 4 00	4
5	9	1323	Harris Service Company	✓	5 9 6 1 00	5
6	11	1324	Carmel Hardware	✓	3 7 7 2 24	6
7	16	1325	Howard and Sons, Inc.	✓	2 4 4 1 00	7
8	20	1326	Green Plumbing and Heating	✓	1 7 1 0 00	8
9	23	1327	Chin Building Supplies	✓	3 3 8 4 00	9
10	24	1328	Carmel Hardware	✓	1 2 9 3 22	10
11	28	1329	Howard and Sons, Inc.	✓	2 4 8 7 00	11
12	30	1330	Chin Building Supplies	✓	3 6 1 4 00	12
13	31	1331	Betterbuilt Homes Co.	✓	1 3 7 5 50	13
14	31	1332	Quality Builders, Inc.	✓	2 8 6 1 00	14
15	31				32 9 7 3 82	15
16					(113)(411)	16

SALES JOURNAL   PAGE 38

REMEMBER! The check marks (✓) indicate that each amount has been posted to a charge customer's account.

ACCOUNTS RECEIVABLE LEDGER

NAME **Arnold, Inc.**
ADDRESS **1457 Lincoln Street**
Seattle, WA 98101

DATE	ITEM	POST. REF.	DEBIT	CREDIT	BALANCE
20–					
Aug. 3		S38	1 1 1 6 00		1 1 1 6 00

NAME **Betterbuilt Homes Co.**
ADDRESS **5120 Gilman Avenue**
Portland, OR 97202

DATE	ITEM	POST. REF.	DEBIT	CREDIT	BALANCE
20–					
Aug. 1		S38	1 5 6 4 86		1 5 6 4 86
31		S38	1 3 7 5 50		2 9 4 0 36

REMEMBER! The normal balance in the accounts receivable ledger is a debit, because the customer accounts represent assets.

(continued)

FIGURE 6
(continued)

NAME __Carmel Hardware__

ADDRESS __2168 Tenth Street__

__Seattle, WA 98101__

DATE		ITEM	POST. REF.	DEBIT	CREDIT	BALANCE
20–						
Aug.	11		S38	3 7 7 2 24		3 7 7 2 24
	24		S38	1 2 9 3 22		5 0 6 5 46

NAME __Chin Building Supplies__

ADDRESS __2242 Lakeside Avenue__

__Seattle, WA 98101__

DATE		ITEM	POST. REF.	DEBIT	CREDIT	BALANCE
20–						
Aug.	23		S38	3 3 8 4 00		3 3 8 4 00
	30		S38	3 6 1 4 00		6 9 9 8 00

NAME __Gonzales Construction__

ADDRESS __3680 Paseo Avenue__

__Seattle, WA 98115__

DATE		ITEM	POST. REF.	DEBIT	CREDIT	BALANCE
20–						
Aug.	6		S38	1 3 9 4 00		1 3 9 4 00

NAME __Green Plumbing and Heating__

ADDRESS __1620 Salazar Road__

__Tacoma, WA 98405__

DATE		ITEM	POST. REF.	DEBIT	CREDIT	BALANCE
20–						
Aug.	20		S38	1 7 1 0 00		1 7 1 0 00

**FIGURE 6
(continued)**

NAME **Harris Service Company**

ADDRESS **5196 Eighteenth Street**

Seattle, WA 98102

DATE	ITEM	POST. REF.	DEBIT	CREDIT	BALANCE
20–					
Aug. 9		S38	5 9 6 1 00		5 9 6 1 00

NAME **Howard and Sons, Inc.**

ADDRESS **4142 Adams Avenue**

Tacoma, WA 98422

DATE	ITEM	POST. REF.	DEBIT	CREDIT	BALANCE
20–					
Aug. 16		S38	2 4 4 1 00		2 4 4 1 00
28		S38	2 4 8 7 00		4 9 2 8 00

NAME **Quality Builders, Inc.**

ADDRESS **424 Fifteenth Street**

Seattle, WA 98115

DATE	ITEM	POST. REF.	DEBIT	CREDIT	BALANCE
20–					
Aug. 31		S38	2 8 6 1 00		2 8 6 1 00

OBJECTIVE 4

Prepare a schedule of accounts receivable.

Next, the accountant prepares a schedule of accounts receivable, like the one shown in Figure 7, on page 346, listing each charge customer's account balance.

We assume that there were no previous balances in the customers' accounts. Under this circumstance, the Accounts Receivable controlling account in the general ledger will have the same balance, $32,973.82, as the schedule of accounts receivable.

REMEMBER!

Posting to the Accounts Receivable account from the sales journal took place at the end of the month.

GENERAL LEDGER

ACCOUNT **Accounts Receivable**   ACCOUNT NO. **113**

	DATE	ITEM	POST. REF.	DEBIT	CREDIT	BALANCE DEBIT	BALANCE CREDIT	
1	20–							1
2	Aug. 31		S38	32 9 7 3 82		32 9 7 3 82		2
3								3

FIGURE 7

Rainier Plumbing Supply
Schedule of Accounts Receivable
August 31, 20—

Arnold, Inc.	$ 1 1 1 6	00
Betterbuilt Homes Co.	2 9 4 0	36
Carmel Hardware	5 0 6 5	46
Chin Building Supplies	6 9 9 8	00
Gonzales Construction	1 3 9 4	00
Green Plumbing and Heating	1 7 1 0	00
Harris Service Company	5 9 6 1	00
Howard and Sons, Inc.	4 9 2 8	00
Quality Builders, Inc.	2 8 6 1	00
Total Accounts Receivable	$ 32 9 7 3	82

SALES RETURNS AND ALLOWANCES

OBJECTIVE 5

Journalize sales returns and allowances, including credit memorandums and returns involving sales tax, in a general journal, and post to the accounts receivable ledger and general ledger.

The Sales Returns and Allowances account handles two types of transactions related to merchandise that has previously been sold. A *return* is a physical return of the goods. An *allowance* is a reduction from the original price because the goods were defective or damaged. It may not be economically worthwhile to have customers return the goods; each situation is a special case. To avoid writing a separate letter each time to inform customers of their account adjustments, businesses use a special form called a **credit memorandum**. A credit memorandum (Figure 8) is a written statement indicating a seller's willingness to reduce the amount of a buyer's debt.

FIGURE 8

Rainier Plumbing Supply
1400 Front Street
Seattle, WA 98101

CREDIT MEMORANDUM No. 1069

CREDIT TO: *Chin Building Supplies*
2242 Lakeside Avenue
Seattle, WA 98101

DATE: *September 2, 20–*

WE CREDIT YOUR ACCOUNT AS FOLLOWS:

QUANTITY	DESCRIPTION	TOTAL	
50	*Olin pop-up tub drain antique finish* *1¹/₂-inch brass overflow tube #46C72*	254	00

The Sales Returns and Allowances account is a deduction from Sales. Using an account separate from Sales provides a better record of the total returns and allowances. Accountants deduct Sales Returns and Allowances from Sales on the income statement.

Using T accounts, here's an example of a return. The original sale is shown first, followed by the issuance of a credit memorandum.

Transaction (a)   On August 30, Rainier Plumbing Supply sold merchandise on account to Chin Building Supplies, $3,614, and recorded the sale in the sales journal.

Transaction (b)   On September 2, Chin Building Supplies returned $254 worth of the merchandise. Rainier Plumbing Supply issued credit memorandum no. 1069 (see Figure 8).

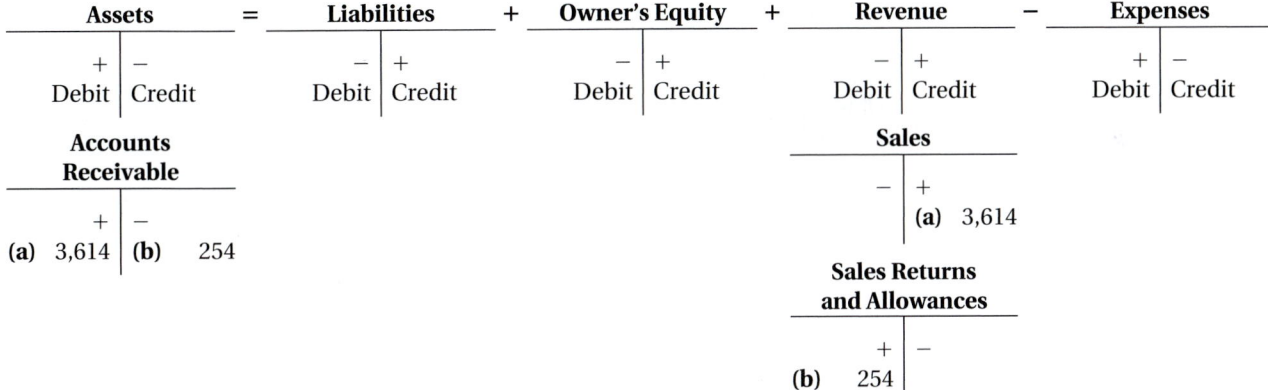

Rainier Plumbing Supply's accountant debits Sales Returns and Allowances to increase it; then, the accountant credits Accounts Receivable to decrease it because the charge customer, Chin Building Supplies, owes less than before.

The general journal entry serves as the posting source for crediting the Accounts Receivable controlling account in the general ledger. It also serves as the posting source for updating the accounts receivable ledger and therefore includes the name of the charge customer. If the balance of the Accounts Receivable controlling account is to equal the total of the individual account balances in the accounts receivable ledger, one must post to *both* the Accounts Receivable account in the general ledger *and* the account of Chin Building Supplies in the accounts receivable ledger. To take care of this double posting, the accountant draws a slanted line in the Post. Ref. column. When the amount has been posted as a credit to the general ledger account, the accountant writes the account number of Accounts Receivable in the left part of the Post. Ref. column. After the account of Chin Building Supplies has been posted as a credit, the accountant puts a check mark in the right portion of the Post. Ref. column. Sales Returns and Allowances is posted in the usual manner. The entry after posting is complete is shown on the following page.

GENERAL JOURNAL

PAGE **27**

	DATE		DESCRIPTION	POST. REF.	DEBIT	CREDIT	
1	20–						1
2	Sept.	2	Sales Returns and Allowances	412	2 5 4 00		2
3			Accounts Receivable, Chin				3
4			Building Supplies	113 ✓		2 5 4 00	4
5			Issued credit memo no. 1069.				5
6							6

GENERAL LEDGER

ACCOUNT **Accounts Receivable**   ACCOUNT NO. **113**

	DATE	ITEM	POST. REF.	DEBIT	CREDIT	BALANCE DEBIT	BALANCE CREDIT	
1	20–							1
2	Aug. 31		S38	32 9 7 3 82		32 9 7 3 82		2
3	Sept. 2		J27		2 5 4 00	32 7 1 9 82		3
4								4

ACCOUNT **Sales Returns and Allowances**   ACCOUNT NO. **412**

	DATE	ITEM	POST. REF.	DEBIT	CREDIT	BALANCE DEBIT	BALANCE CREDIT	
1	20–							1
2	Sept. 2		J27	2 5 4 00		2 5 4 00		2
3								3

ACCOUNTS RECEIVABLE LEDGER

NAME **Chin Building Supplies**
ADDRESS **2242 Lakeside Avenue**
Seattle, WA 98101

DATE		ITEM	POST. REF.	DEBIT	CREDIT	BALANCE
20–						
Aug.	23		S38	3 3 8 4 00		3 3 8 4 00
	30		S38	3 6 1 4 00		6 9 9 8 00
Sept.	2		J27		2 5 4 00	6 7 4 4 00

Sales Return Involving a Sales Tax

If a customer who returns merchandise to a retail store was originally charged a sales tax, the sales tax must be returned to the customer. Refer back to the sales journal of Dixon Office Furniture Company on page 341, which included sales taxes. On April 3, assume that C. D. Barnes returns the furniture bought on April 1 for $1,550 plus $124 sales tax. Following is the general journal entry required for this type of return:

	DATE		DESCRIPTION	POST. REF.	DEBIT	CREDIT	
1	20–						1
2	Apr.	3	Sales Returns and Allowances		1 5 5 0 00		2
3			Sales Tax Payable		1 2 4 00		3
4			Accounts Receivable, C. D. Barnes			1 6 7 4 00	4
5			Issued credit memo no. 1371.				5
6							6
7							7

GENERAL JOURNAL   PAGE **12**

PURCHASING PROCEDURES

In a small retail store, the owner may do the buying. In large retail and whole-sale businesses, department heads or division managers do the buying, after which the Purchasing Department goes into action: It places purchase orders, follows up the orders, and sees that deliveries are made to the right departments. The Purchasing Department also acts as a source of information on current prices, price trends, quality of goods, prospective suppliers, and reliability of suppliers.

The Purchasing Department normally requires that any requests to buy merchandise be in writing, in the form of a **purchase requisition**. After the purchase requisition is approved, the Purchasing Department sends a purchase order to the supplier. A **purchase order** is the company's written offer to buy certain goods. The accountant does not make any entry at this point because the supplier has not yet indicated acceptance of the order. A purchase order has at least four copies. The original goes to the supplier; copies go to the Purchasing Department (as proof of what was ordered), the department that issued the requisition (telling it that the goods it wanted have been ordered), the Accounting Department, and a blind copy (with quantities omitted) goes to Receiving.

To continue with the accounts of Rainier Plumbing Supply, the Fixtures Department submits a purchase requisition to the Purchasing Department, as shown in Figure 9 on page 350.

FIGURE 9

Rainier Plumbing Supply

1400 Front Street
Seattle, WA 98101

No. C-726

PURCHASE REQUISITION

DEPARTMENT _Fixtures_

ADVISE ON DELIVERY _C. Fenwick_

DATE OF REQUEST _July 2, 20–_

DATE REQUIRED _Aug. 5, 20–_

QUANTITY	DESCRIPTION
50	Drominex shower heads #772R

APPROVED BY _D. M. Bruce_   REQUESTED BY _J. C. Garcia_

FOR PURCHASING DEPT. USE ONLY

PURCHASE ORDER NO. _7918_

DATE _July 5, 20–_

ISSUED TO: _Collins, Inc._
1614 Olivera Street
San Francisco, CA 94129

The Purchasing Department completes the rest of the purchase requisition and then sends out the purchase order shown in Figure 10.

FIGURE 10

Rainier Plumbing Supply

1400 Front Street
Seattle, WA 98101

PURCHASE ORDER

TO: _Collins, Inc._
1614 Olivera Street
San Francisco, CA 94129

DATE: _July 5, 20–_

ORDER NO.: _7918_

SHIPPED BY:

TERMS: _2/10, n/30_

QUANTITY	DESCRIPTION	UNIT PRICE		TOTAL	
50	Drominex shower heads #772R	34	20	1,710	00
	Total			1,710	00

D. M. Bruce

The seller then sends an invoice to the buyer as shown in Figure 11. This invoice should arrive in advance of the goods (or at least *with* the goods).

FIGURE 11

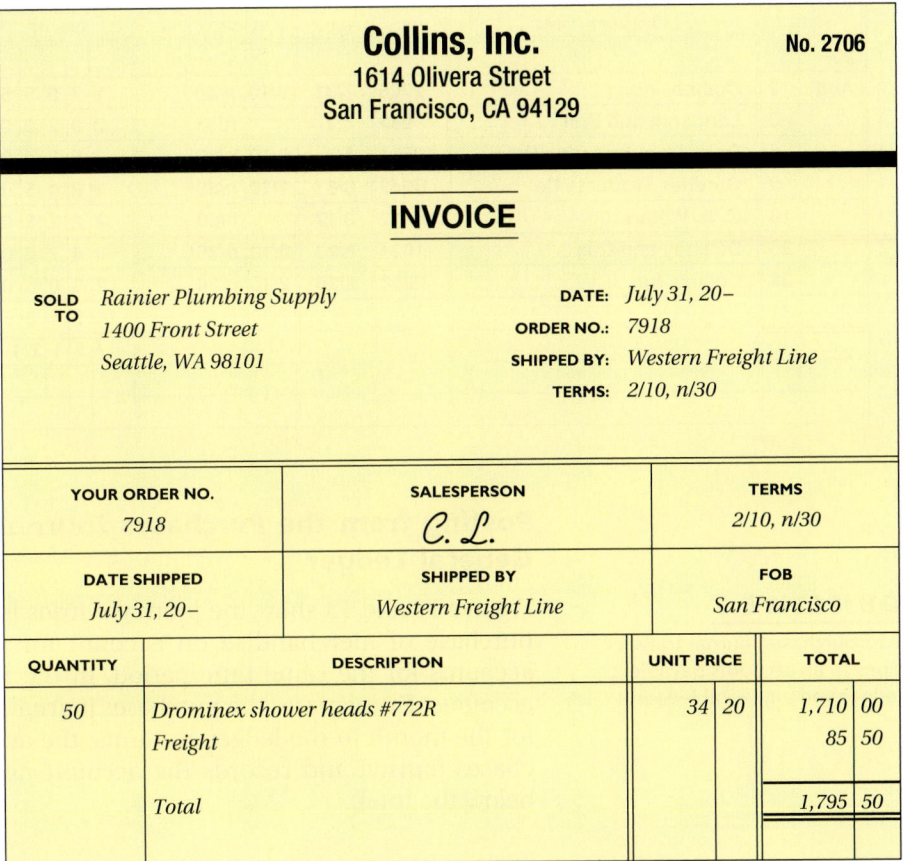

Collins, Inc. (the seller) prepaid the freight cost and added the $85.50 to the bill, listing it separately; this is similiar to buying something by mail order or through the Internet. Freight In is discussed in more detail on pages 358–360. The transaction is recorded in T accounts below. Note that the transaction is recorded on August 2, the day the merchandise is received.

Purchases		Freight In		Accounts Payable	
+	−	+	−	−	+
Aug. 2 1,710.00		Aug. 2 85.50			Aug. 2 1,795.50

PURCHASES JOURNAL (THREE-COLUMN)

OBJECTIVE 6

Journalize transactions in a three-column purchases journal.

The **purchases journal** for Rainier Plumbing Supply for the month of August appears on page 352. By including a separate column for each account, we can record a typical purchase of merchandise on account on one line.

Terms means the terms of payment. For example, 2/10, n/30 means that if we pay the amount due within 10 days, we will receive a 2 percent discount; otherwise, the entire amount is due in 30 days.

PURCHASES JOURNAL   PAGE ___29___

	DATE		SUPPLIER'S NAME	INVOICE NO.	INVOICE DATE	TERMS	POST. REF.	ACCOUNTS PAYABLE CREDIT	FREIGHT IN DEBIT	PURCHASES DEBIT	
1	20–										1
2	Aug.	2	Collins, Inc.	2706	7/31	2/10, n/30		1 7 9 5 50	8 5 50	1 7 1 0 00	2
3		3	Langseth and Son	982	8/2	n/30		2 9 2 9 00	1 5 7 00	2 7 7 2 00	3
4		5	Dana Manufacturing Co.	10611	8/3	2/10, n/30		5 6 4 00		5 6 4 00	4
5		9	Gardner Products Co.	B643	8/6	1/10, n/30		1 2 4 5 00	9 0 00	1 1 5 5 00	5
6		18	C. A. Waters	46812	8/17	n/60		2 2 2 8 00		2 2 2 8 00	6
7		25	Delaney and Cox	1024	8/23	2/10, n/30		3 4 7 6 00	1 1 4 00	3 3 6 2 00	7
8		26	Collins, Inc.	2801	8/25	2/10, n/30		2 6 0 6 00	2 2 2 00	2 3 8 4 00	8
9		31						14 8 4 3 50	6 6 8 50	14 1 7 5 00	9
10								(2 1 2)	(5 1 4)	(5 1 1)	10
11											11
12											12

Posting from the Purchases Journal to the General Ledger

OBJECTIVE 7

Post purchases journal transactions to an accounts payable ledger and a general ledger.

Figures 12 and 13 show the journal entries for all transactions involving the purchase of merchandise on account for August and the related ledger accounts for the same time period. In the Post. Ref. column of the ledger accounts, P designates the purchases journal. After posting the column totals for the month to the ledger accounts, the accountant goes back to the purchases journal and records the account numbers in parentheses directly below the total.

FIGURE 12

REMEMBER!

Transactions involving the buying of supplies or other assets should not be journalized in the three-column purchases journal, because this purchases journal may be used only for purchases of merchandise for resale.

GENERAL LEDGER

ACCOUNT ___Accounts Payable___   ACCOUNT NO. ___212___

	DATE	ITEM	POST. REF.	DEBIT	CREDIT	BALANCE DEBIT	BALANCE CREDIT	
1	20–							1
2	Aug. 1	Balance	✓				1 5 0 4 00	2
3	31		P29		14 8 4 3 50		16 3 4 7 50	3
4								4

ACCOUNT ___Purchases___   ACCOUNT NO. ___511___

	DATE	ITEM	POST. REF.	DEBIT	CREDIT	BALANCE DEBIT	BALANCE CREDIT	
1	20–							1
2	Aug. 1	Balance	✓			89 9 0 4 00		2
3	31		P29	14 1 7 5 00		104 0 7 9 00		3
4								4

**FIGURE 12
(continued)**

| | | | POST. | | | | BALANCE | | |
DATE	ITEM	REF.	DEBIT	CREDIT	DEBIT		CREDIT	
ACCOUNT Freight In						**ACCOUNT NO.** 514		
20–								1
Aug.	1	Balance	✓			4 6 7 9 50		2
	31		P29	6 6 8 50		5 3 4 8 00		3
								4

PURCHASES JOURNAL   PAGE __29__

	DATE	SUPPLIER'S NAME	INVOICE NO.	INVOICE DATE	TERMS	POST. REF.	ACCOUNTS PAYABLE CREDIT	FREIGHT IN DEBIT	PURCHASES DEBIT	
1	20–									1
2	Aug. 2	Collins, Inc.	2706	7/31	2/10, n/30	✓	1 7 9 5 50	8 5 50	1 7 1 0 00	2
3	3	Langseth and Son	982	8/2	n/30	✓	2 9 2 9 00	1 5 7 00	2 7 7 2 00	3
4	5	Dana Manufacturing Co.	10611	8/3	2/10, n/30	✓	5 6 4 00		5 6 4 00	4
5	9	Gardner Products Co.	B643	8/6	1/10, n/30	✓	1 2 4 5 00	9 0 00	1 1 5 5 00	5
6	18	C. A. Waters	46812	8/17	n/60	✓	2 2 2 8 00		2 2 2 8 00	6
7	25	Delaney and Cox	1024	8/23	2/10, n/30	✓	3 4 7 6 00	1 1 4 00	3 3 6 2 00	7
8	26	Collins, Inc.	2801	8/25	2/10, n/30	✓	2 6 0 6 00	2 2 2 00	2 3 8 4 00	8
9	31						14 8 4 3 50	6 6 8 50	14 1 7 5 00	9
10							(2 1 2)	(5 1 4)	(5 1 1)	10

FIGURE 13

THE ACCOUNTS PAYABLE LEDGER

Previously, we called the Accounts Receivable account in the general ledger a **controlling** account, and we saw that the accounts receivable ledger consists of an individual account for each charge customer. We also saw that the accountant posts to the accounts receivable ledger every day.

Accounts Payable is a parallel case; it, too, is a controlling account in the general ledger. **The accounts payable ledger is a subsidiary ledger, and it consists of individual accounts for all the creditors.** Again, posting to the accounts payable ledger is usually done daily. After posting to the individual creditors' accounts, the accountant puts a check mark (✓) in the Post. Ref. column of the purchases journal. After the accountant has finished the posting to the controlling account at the end of the period, the total of the schedule of accounts payable should equal the balance of the Accounts Payable (controlling) account. The three-column form is used for the accounts payable ledger.

Now let's look at the purchases journal (Figure 13) and the postings to the ledger. Note that in the accounts payable ledger—as in the accounts receivable ledger—the accounts of the individual creditors are listed in either alphabetical or numerical order. Firms that handle all of their bookkeeping and accounting on computer may assign an account number to each individual account.

REMEMBER!

Signs for Accounts Payable

Debit	Credit
−	+

Columns for Accounts Payable Ledger

DEBIT	CREDIT	BALANCE
−	+	

ACCOUNTS PAYABLE LEDGER

NAME   Collins, Inc.

ADDRESS   1614 Olivera Street
San Francisco, CA 94129

DATE		ITEM	POST. REF.	DEBIT	CREDIT	BALANCE
20–						
Aug.	2		P29		1 7 9 5 50	1 7 9 5 50
	26		P29		2 6 0 6 00	4 4 0 1 50

NAME   Dana Manufacturing Company

ADDRESS   254 Calle Mancha
Los Angeles, CA 90025

DATE		ITEM	POST. REF.	DEBIT	CREDIT	BALANCE
20–						
Aug.	5		P29		5 6 4 00	5 6 4 00

NAME   Delaney and Cox

ADDRESS   2426 Reilly Way, N.E.
Los Angeles, CA 90101

DATE		ITEM	POST. REF.	DEBIT	CREDIT	BALANCE
20–						
Aug.	25		P29		3 4 7 6 00	3 4 7 6 00

NAME   Gardner Products Company

ADDRESS   2154 Springer St.
Boston, MA 02107

DATE		ITEM	POST. REF.	DEBIT	CREDIT	BALANCE
20–						
Aug.	9		P29		1 2 4 5 00	1 2 4 5 00

NAME   Langseth and Son

ADDRESS   142 Grant Road
Cleveland, OH 44102

DATE		ITEM	POST. REF.	DEBIT	CREDIT	BALANCE
20–						
July	27		P28		1 1 8 0 00	1 1 8 0 00
Aug.	3		P29		2 9 2 9 00	4 1 0 9 00

NAME C. A. Waters
ADDRESS 1620 Minard St.
San Jose, CA 95101

DATE		ITEM	POST. REF.	DEBIT	CREDIT	BALANCE
20–						
July	29		P28		1 3 2 4 00	1 3 2 4 00
Aug.	18		P29		2 2 2 8 00	3 5 5 2 00

Schedule of Accounts Payable

OBJECTIVE 8
Prepare a schedule of accounts payable.

Assuming that no other transactions involved Accounts Payable, the schedule of accounts payable would appear as shown in Figure 14. Note that the balance of Dana Manufacturing Company is taken from the accounts payable ledger.

The posting to the Accounts Payable controlling account in the general ledger below is now up to date.

GENERAL LEDGER

ACCOUNT Accounts Payable   ACCOUNT NO. 212

	DATE		ITEM	POST. REF.	DEBIT	CREDIT	BALANCE DEBIT	BALANCE CREDIT	
1	20–								1
2	Aug.	1	Balance	✓				2 5 0 4 00	2
3		31		P29		14 8 4 3 50		17 3 4 7 50	3
4									4

FIGURE 14

Rainier Plumbing Supply
Schedule of Accounts Payable
August 31, 20—

Collins, Inc.	$ 4 4 0 1 50
Dana Manufacturing Company	5 6 4 00
Delaney and Cox	3 4 7 6 00
Gardner Products Company	1 2 4 5 00
Langseth and Son	4 1 0 9 00
C. A. Waters	3 5 5 2 00
Total Accounts Payable	$17 3 4 7 50

PURCHASES RETURNS AND ALLOWANCES

OBJECTIVE 9

Journalize transactions involving purchases returns and allowances in a general journal, and post to the accounts payable ledger and general ledger.

As its title implies, the Purchases Returns and Allowances account handles either a return of merchandise previously purchased or an allowance made for merchandise that arrived in damaged condition. In both cases, there is a reduction in the amount owed to the supplier. The buyer sends a letter or printed form to the supplier, who acknowledges the reduction by sending a credit memorandum. The buyer should wait for notice of the agreed deduction before making an entry.

The Purchases Returns and Allowances account is considered to be a deduction from Purchases. Using a separate account provides a better record of the total returns and allowances. Purchases Returns and Allowances is deducted from the Purchases account on the income statement. (We'll talk about this point later.) For now, let's look at an example consisting of a return on the books of Rainier Plumbing Supply.

Transaction (a) On September 2, bought merchandise on account from Dana Manufacturing Company, $830. Journalized this entry as a debit to Purchases and a credit to Accounts Payable.

Transaction (b) On September 8, received credit memorandum no. 1629 from Dana Manufacturing Company for $270. Journalized this as a debit to Accounts Payable and a credit to Purchases Returns and Allowances.

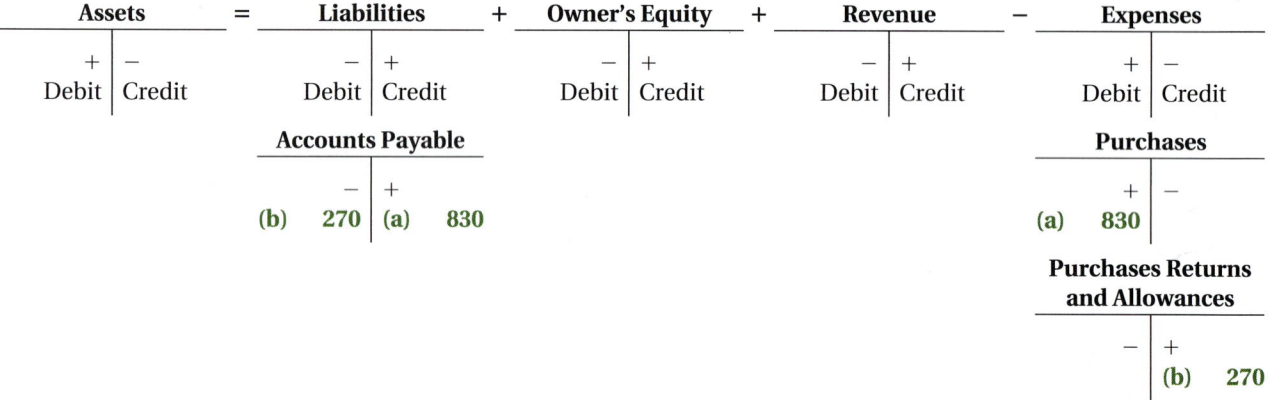

Purchases Returns and Allowances is credited because Rainier Plumbing Supply has more returns and allowances than before. Accounts Payable is debited because Rainier Plumbing Supply owes less than before. The related entry including the postings is shown on the next page. Note that Accounts Payable is followed by the name of the individual creditor's account. **The accountant must post the amount to both the Accounts Payable controlling account and the individual creditor's account in the accounts payable ledger.** The account numbers in the Post. Ref. column indicate postings to the accounts in the general ledger, and the check marks indicate postings to the accounts in the accounts payable ledger.

GENERAL JOURNAL

PAGE __27__

	DATE		DESCRIPTION	POST. REF.	DEBIT	CREDIT	
1	20–						1
2	Sept.	8	Accounts Payable, Dana				2
3			Manufacturing Company	212 ✓	2 7 0 00		3
4			Purchases Returns and				4
5			Allowances	512		2 7 0 00	5
6			Credit memo no. 1629 for				6
7			return of merchandise.				7
8							8

GENERAL LEDGER

ACCOUNT __Accounts Payable__   ACCOUNT NO. __212__

	DATE		ITEM	POST. REF.	DEBIT	CREDIT	BALANCE DEBIT	BALANCE CREDIT	
1	20–								1
2	Sept.	1	Balance	✓				17 3 4 7 50	2
3		8		J27	2 7 0 00			17 0 7 7 50	3
4									4

ACCOUNT __Purchases Returns and Allowances__   ACCOUNT NO. __512__

	DATE		ITEM	POST. REF.	DEBIT	CREDIT	BALANCE DEBIT	BALANCE CREDIT	
1	20–								1
2	Sept.	1	Balance	✓				1 6 4 0 00	2
3		8		J27		2 7 0 00		1 9 1 0 00	3
4									4

ACCOUNTS PAYABLE LEDGER

NAME __Dana Manufacturing Company__
ADDRESS __254 Calle Mancha__
__Los Angeles, CA 90025__

	DATE		ITEM	POST. REF.	DEBIT	CREDIT	BALANCE
	20–						
	Sept.	1	Balance	✓			5 6 4 00
		2		P30		8 3 0 00	1 3 9 4 00
		8		J27	2 7 0 00		1 1 2 4 00

FREIGHT CHARGES ON INCOMING MERCHANDISE

OBJECTIVE 10

Describe the procedures for handling freight charges on merchandise and other goods.

FYI

Some accountants call the Freight In account *Transportation In*.

Companies use the Freight In account to keep a record of all separately charged delivery costs on incoming merchandise.

Freight costs are expressed as FOB (free on board) destination or shipping point. **(Destination is the buyer's location; shipping point is the seller's location.)** In both cases, the supplier loads the goods free on board the carrier. Beyond that point, there must be an understanding as to who is responsible for paying the freight charges. **If the seller assumes the entire cost of transportation, without any reimbursement from the buyer, the terms are FOB destination.** In this case, title or ownership changes hands when the buyer receives the goods. **If the buyer is responsible for paying the freight cost, the shipping terms are called FOB shipping point.** In this case, title or ownership changes hands when goods are transferred to a common carrier (freight company).

Briefly, when goods are shipped FOB destination, the freight charges are not stated, and the seller simply pays the amount of the freight. Suppose Rainier Plumbing Supply, which is in Seattle, buys merchandise from a supplier in Chicago with shipping terms of FOB Seattle listed on the invoice. The total of the invoice is $1,740, and there is no separate listing of freight charges. In other words, the seller has included the transportation costs in the price.

When goods are shipped FOB shipping point, with the buyer responsible for paying the freight charges, transportation costs may be handled in two ways:

1. The buyer may pay the freight charges directly to the transportation company. For example, an automobile dealer in Houston buys cars FOB Detroit. In this case, the automobile dealer makes one check payable to the manufacturer and another check payable to the carrier for the freight charges. (FOB Detroit is the same as FOB shipping point.)
2. The transportation or shipping costs may be listed separately on the invoice. For example, suppose a person orders a computer from an Internet company. The Internet company has prepaid (paid in advance) the freight charges as a favor or convenience for the buyer. However, the

To record the transportation costs of merchandise purchased for resale, such as automobiles, accountants use an expense account called Freight In (also called Transportation In).

freight charges are listed on the bill or invoice, and the buyer is responsible for reimbursing the Internet company for the freight charges. Similarly, when a business buys merchandise, the amount of the freight charges may be prepaid by the seller and listed separately on the invoice.

Look again at the invoice from Collins, Inc., on page 351. Note that the freight cost is listed separately, and the terms are FOB shipping point (San Francisco). Collins paid the transportation cost; Rainier must reimburse Collins for this cost.

Let's proceed with three transactions for Rainier Plumbing Supply. We first record the transactions in a general journal. Then, as a means of reemphasizing the advantages of special journals as opposed to a general journal, we record the same transactions in a special journal. In practice, the transactions would be recorded *in only one journal, not both*.

During the first week in August, the following transactions took place:

Aug. 2 Bought merchandise on account from Collins, Inc., invoice no. 2706, $1,710; terms 2/10, n/30; dated July 31; FOB San Francisco, freight prepaid and added to the invoice, $85.50 (total $1,795.50).

3 Bought merchandise on account from Langseth and Son, invoice no. 982, $2,772; terms net 30 days; dated August 2; FOB Cleveland, freight prepaid and added to the invoice, $157 (total $2,929).

5 Bought merchandise on account from Dana Manufacturing Company, invoice no. 10611, $564; terms 2/10, n/30; dated August 3; FOB Los Angeles.

Notice that the transactions with Collins, Inc., and Langseth and Son are both FOB shipping point with the freight charges listed separately. Consequently, the buyer (Rainier) must reimburse the sellers for the transportation costs by paying the total of the invoices. However, in the transaction with Dana Manufacturing Company, which is FOB shipping point without freight charges listed, the buyer (Rainier) must pay the freight costs separately, perhaps when the goods are delivered.

TRANSPORTATION CHARGES ON THE BUYING OF GOODS AND SERVICES OTHER THAN MERCHANDISE

Any freight charges incurred when buying any other assets, such as supplies or equipment, should be debited to the respective asset accounts. Let's return to Rainier Plumbing Supply and assume that this company bought display cases on account from Carter Cabinet Shop, at a cost of $2,700 plus freight charges of $290. The seller of the display cases prepaid the transportation costs for Rainier Plumbing Supply and then added the $290 to the invoice price of the cases. Let's visualize this with T accounts.

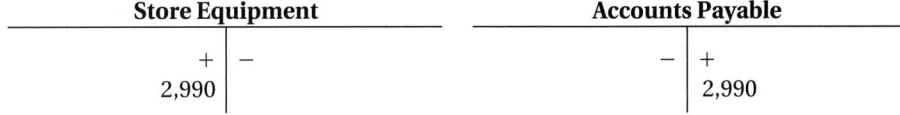

Store Equipment		Accounts Payable	
+	−	−	+
2,990			2,990

If Rainier Plumbing Supply had paid the freight charges separately, the entry for the payment would be a debit to Store Equipment for $290 and a credit to Cash for $290.

INTERNAL CONTROL OF PURCHASES

Purchases is one of the areas in which internal control is essential. Efficiency and security require most companies to work out careful procedures for buying and paying for goods. This is understandable, as large sums of money are usually involved. The control aspect generally involves the following measures:

1. Purchases are made only after proper authorization is given. Purchase requisitions and purchase orders are all prenumbered, so that each form can be accounted for.
2. The receiving department carefully checks all goods upon receipt for count, damages, and description. Later, the report of the receiving department is verified against the purchase order and the purchase invoice.
3. The person who authorizes the payment is neither the person doing the ordering nor the person actually writing the check. Payment is authorized only after verifying the purchase invoice data against the receiving report and purchase order.
4. The person who actually writes the check has not been involved in any of the foregoing purchasing procedures.

CHAPTER REVIEW

Online Study Center
ACE the test!

Picture the T accounts involved in transactions. Here are examples of transactions. Sold merchandise on account to Chin Building Supplies, $3,384.

Assets	=	Liabilities	+	Owner's Equity	+	Revenue	−	Expenses
+ | −		− | +		− | +		− | +		+ | −
Debit | Credit		Debit | Credit		Debit | Credit		Debit | Credit		Debit | Credit

Accounts Receivable		Sales
+ | −		− | +
3,384 |		| 3,384

REMEMBER!

Always think of the T accounts involved in each transaction. Get and stay in the T account habit.

Sold merchandise on account to C. D. Barnes, $1,550 plus sales tax $124.

Assets	=	Liabilities	+	Owner's Equity	+	Revenue	−	Expenses
+ | −		− | +		− | +		− | +		+ | −
Debit | Credit		Debit | Credit		Debit | Credit		Debit | Credit		Debit | Credit

Accounts Receivable	Sales Tax Payable	Sales
+ | −	− | +	− | +
1,674 |	| 124	| 1,550

Chin Building Supplies returned $254 of merchandise.

Assets	=	Liabilities	+	Owner's Equity	+	Revenue	−	Expenses
+ | −		− | +		− | +		− | +		+ | −
Debit | Credit		Debit | Credit		Debit | Credit		Debit | Credit		Debit | Credit

Accounts Receivable		Sales Returns and Allowances
+ | −	**REMEMBER!** Sales Returns and Allowances are a deduction from Sales.	+ | −
| 254		254 |

Purchased merchandise from Gardner Products Co., $1,155 plus $90 freight, total $1,245.

Assets	=	Liabilities	+	Owner's Equity	+	Revenue	−	Expenses
+ | −		− | +		− | +		− | +		+ | −
Debit | Credit		Debit | Credit		Debit | Credit		Debit | Credit		Debit | Credit

	Accounts Payable		Purchases
	− | +		+ | −
	| 1,245		1,155 |

Freight In

+ | −
90 |

Returned merchandise to Dana Manufacturing Co., $270, and received a credit memorandum.

Assets	=	Liabilities	+	Owner's Equity	+	Revenue	−	Expenses
+ | −		− | +		− | +		− | +		+ | −
Debit | Credit		Debit | Credit		Debit | Credit		Debit | Credit		Debit | Credit

	Accounts Payable		Purchases Returns and Allowances
	− | +		− | +
	270 |		| 270

Review of Performance Objectives

1. **Describe the specific accounts used by a merchandising firm.**

   The Merchandise Inventory account is an asset account representing the cost of goods bought for resale.

   The Sales Tax Payable account is a liability account representing amounts owed to state or city governments.

   The Sales account is a revenue account representing the total sales of merchandise.

   The Sales Returns and Allowances account is a deduction from the Sales account, representing amounts allowed for returns of merchandise and damaged goods.

   The Sales Discounts account is a deduction from the Sales account, representing amounts deducted for prompt payments.

   The Purchases account is a cost (expense) account representing the costs of goods bought for resale.

   The Purchases Returns and Allowances account is a deduction from the Purchases account, representing amounts granted by suppliers for the return of merchandise or damaged goods.

   The Purchases Discounts account is a deduction from the Purchases account, representing amounts suppliers allow for prompt payments.

   The Freight In account is a cost (expense) representing the transportation charges on incoming merchandise.

2. **Journalize transactions in a sales journal.**

   The sales journal is used to record only sales of merchandise on account.

   The entries are posted daily to the accounts receivable ledger. At the end of the month, the total is posted to the general ledger as a debit to the Accounts Receivable controlling account and a credit to the Sales account.

3. **Post sales journal transactions to an accounts receivable ledger and a general ledger.**

   During the month, as customers charge merchandise, the amounts must be posted to their individual accounts as debits and a running balance maintained.

   At the end of the month, the total of the amounts charged by customers for purchase of merchandise must be posted to the general ledger as a debit to Accounts Receivable and a credit to Sales.

4. **Prepare a schedule of accounts receivable.**

   The schedule of accounts receivable consists of a listing of the individual account balances of the charge customers taken from the accounts receivable ledger.

5. **Journalize sales returns and allowances, including credit memorandums and returns involving sales tax, in a general journal, and post to the accounts receivable ledger and general ledger.**

   When a customer returns merchandise, or when his or her bill is reduced owing to an allowance for defective or damaged merchandise, the Sales Returns and Allowances account is debited and the Accounts Receivable account is credited. The entry is recorded in the general journal and posted to both the general ledger and the accounts receivable ledger.

6. **Journalize transactions in a three-column purchases journal.**

   The three-column purchases journal handles the purchase of merchandise on account and freight charges that are prepaid by the seller and included in the invoice total.

7. Post purchases journal transactions to an accounts payable ledger and a general ledger.

   Amounts in the Accounts Payable Credit column are posted daily to the accounts payable ledger. At the end of the month, the totals are posted to the general ledger as a debit to Purchases, a debit to Freight In, and a credit to Accounts Payable.

8. Prepare a schedule of accounts payable.

   A schedule of accounts payable, listing the balance of each individual creditor's account, is prepared from the accounts payable ledger.

9. Journalize transactions involving purchases returns and allowances in a general journal, and post to the accounts payable ledger and general ledger.

   When a credit memo is received for the return of merchandise or as an allowance for damaged merchandise, the buyer credits Purchases Returns and Allowances. If the merchandise was bought on account, the buyer debits Accounts Payable. The transaction is journalized in the general journal.

10. Describe the procedures for handling freight charges on merchandise and other goods.

    The Freight In account is debited for the cost of transportation charges on incoming merchandise intended for resale. Freight costs that apply to nonmerchandise assets purchased are added to the asset account that applies. For example, $300 freight on a large freezer for a restaurant would be debited to that freezer account as part of the cost of that asset.

Glossary

Accounts payable ledger A subsidiary ledger that lists the individual accounts of creditors in either alphabetical or numerical order with their respective balances. (353)

Accounts receivable ledger A subsidiary ledger that lists the individual accounts of charge customers in either alphabetical or numerical order, with their respective transactions and balances. (341)

Controlling account An account in the general ledger that summarizes the balances of a subsidiary ledger. (341)

Credit memorandum A written statement indicating a seller's willingness to reduce the amount of a buyer's debt. The seller records the amount of the credit memorandum in the Sales Returns and Allowances account. (346)

FOB destination Shipping terms under which the seller pays the freight charges and includes them in the selling price. Title or ownership changes hands when the buyer receives the goods. (358)

FOB shipping point Shipping terms under which the buyer pays the freight charges between the point of shipment and the destination. Payment may be made directly to the carrier upon receiving the goods or to the supplier if the supplier prepaid the freight charges on behalf of the buyer. Title or ownership changes hands when goods are transferred to the freight company. (358)

Freight In account The account used to record transportation charges on incoming merchandise intended for resale. (335)

Invoices Business forms prepared by the seller that list the items shipped, their cost, the terms of the sale, and the mode of shipment. They may also state the freight charges. The buyer considers them purchase invoices; the seller considers them sales invoices. (336)

Merchandise inventory A stock of goods (an asset account) that a company buys and intends to resell at a profit. (334)

Merchandising business A business that buys and sells goods. (334)

Purchase order A written order from the buyer of goods to the supplier, listing the items wanted and the terms of the transaction. (349)

Purchase requisition A form used to request that the Purchasing Department buy something. This form is intended for internal use within a company. (349)

Purchases account An account for recording the cost of merchandise acquired for resale. (335)

Purchases Discounts account An account that records cash discounts granted by suppliers in return for prompt payment; it is treated as a deduction from Purchases. (335)

Purchases journal A special journal used to record only the buying of goods on account. It may be used to record the purchase of merchandise only. (351)

Purchases Returns and Allowances account An account that records a company's return of merchandise it has purchased or a reduction in the bill because of damaged merchandise; it is treated as a deduction from Purchases. (335)

Retail business A business that sells goods directly to consumers. (334)

Sales account A revenue account for recording the sale of merchandise. (335)

Sales Discounts account An account that records a deduction from the original price, granted by the seller to the buyer for the prompt payment of an invoice. (335)

Sales journal A special journal for recording only the sale of merchandise on account. (338)

Sales Returns and Allowances account The account a seller uses to record the physical return of merchandise by customers or a reduction in a bill because merchandise was damaged. Sales Returns and Allowances is treated as a deduction from Sales. This account is usually evidenced by a credit memorandum issued by the seller. (335)

Sales Tax Payable account An account used to record a tax levied by a state or city government on the retail sale of goods and services. The tax is paid by the consumer but collected by the retailer. (335)

Special journals Books of original entry in which specialized types of repetitive transactions are recorded. (334)

Subsidiary ledger A group of accounts representing individual subdivisions showing the debits and credits of a controlling account. (341)

Summarizing entry An entry made to post the column totals of a special journal to the appropriate accounts in the general ledger. (339)

Wholesale business A business that buys goods from manufacturers and sells those goods (normally in large quantities) to retailers for resale. (334)

Discussion Questions

1. Describe the posting procedures and rules for totaling and ruling the:

   a. Sales journal   b. Purchases journal

2. What is the purpose of a:

   a. Schedule of accounts receivable?
   b. Schedule of accounts payable?

3. Describe the procedure for posting:

   a. From the sales journal to the accounts receivable ledger.
   b. From the purchases journal to the accounts payable ledger.

4. With regard to goods sold and purchased, explain how sales returns and allowances and purchases returns and allowances are different from each other.

5. Explain the meaning and importance of the shipping terms FOB destination and FOB shipping point. Who has title to the goods once they have been shipped?

6. Why is an accounts receivable ledger or an accounts payable ledger necessary for a business with large numbers of charge customers or large numbers of vendors/suppliers?

7. Why is it a good practice to post daily to the accounts receivable or accounts payable ledgers?

8. Describe the four procedures that most companies follow to maintain internal control of purchases of merchandise.

Exercises

P.O. 3,4,7,8

Post to general and subsidiary ledgers; prepare schedules of accounts receivable and accounts payable.

Exercise 10-1 Milcer Company has completed October's sales and purchases journals (see below and on the following page). Your job is to:

a. Total and post the journals to T accounts for the general ledger and the accounts receivable and accounts payable ledgers.
b. Complete a schedule of accounts receivable for October 31, 20—.
c. Complete a schedule of accounts payable for October 31, 20—.
d. Compare the balances of the schedules with their respective general ledger accounts. If they are not the same, find and correct the error(s).

			SALES JOURNAL		PAGE 18	

	DATE	INV. NO.	CUSTOMER'S NAME	POST. REF.	ACCOUNTS RECEIVABLE DR. SALES CR.	
1	20–					1
2	Oct. 3	414	Anderson Company		4 43 24	2
3	4	415	R. T. Holcomb		1 4 26 90	3
4	7	416	Gray and Malo		1 6 47 00	4
5	11	417	Mercer Mobil		3 1 12 16	5
6	16	418	J. L. Anthony		2 1 30 00	6
7	22	419	C. A. Goldschmidt		1 9 44 05	7
8	31	420	F. A. Baumann		2 7 91 00	8
9	31					9
10					( )( )	10

PURCHASES JOURNAL PAGE 10

	DATE		SUPPLIER'S NAME	INVOICE NO.	INVOICE DATE	TERMS	POST. REF.	ACCOUNTS PAYABLE CREDIT	FREIGHT IN DEBIT	PURCHASES DEBIT	
1	20–										1
2	Oct.	2	Colter, Inc.	2706	7/31	2/10, n/30		7 5 9 00	4 9 00	7 1 0 00	2
3		3	Thomas and Son	982	8/2	n/30		8 2 9 00	5 7 00	7 7 2 00	3
4		5	Archer Manufacturing Co.	10611	8/3	2/10, n/30		5 6 4 00		5 6 4 00	4
5		9	Spence Products Co.	B643	8/6	1/10, n/30		1 6 5 00	1 0 00	1 5 5 00	5
6		18	L. C. Walter	46812	8/17	n/60		2 2 8 00		2 2 8 00	6
7		25	Delaney and Cox	1024	8/23	2/10, n/30		3 7 6 00	1 4 00	3 6 2 00	7
8		26	Colter, Inc.	2801	8/25	2/10, n/30		4 0 6 00	2 2 00	3 8 4 00	8
9		31									9
10								( )	( )	( )	10

P.O. 3,5

Describe transactions involving a sale, a return, and a payment.

Exercise 10-2 Describe the transactions recorded in the following T accounts:

Cash	
(c) 358.75	

Sales Tax Payable	
(b) 3.75	(a) 67.50

Sales Returns and Allowances	
(b) 49.95	

Accounts Receivable	
(a) 967.50	(b) 53.70
	(c) 358.75

Sales	
	(a) 900.00

P.O. 3,5

Record entries involving a sale, a return, and a receipt of cash.

Exercise 10-3 Record the following transactions in general journal form:

a. Sold merchandise on account to C. Heald, $560 plus $48.80 sales tax (invoice no. D446).

b. Heald returned $81 of the merchandise. Issued credit memo no. 114 for $87.48 ($81 for the amount of the sale plus $6.48 for the amount of the sales tax).

c. Received $517.32 from C. Heald in full payment of account.

P.O. 5

Post to general and accounts receivable ledgers.

Exercise 10-4 Post the following entry to the general ledger and subsidiary ledger:

GENERAL JOURNAL PAGE 52

	DATE		DESCRIPTION	POST. REF.	DEBIT	CREDIT	
1	20–						1
2	June	16	Sales Returns and Allowances		2 4 1 27		2
3			Accounts Receivable, R. D. Moen			2 4 1 27	3
4			Issued credit memo no. 131.				4
5							5

GENERAL LEDGER

ACCOUNT Accounts Receivable   ACCOUNT NO. 113

DATE		ITEM	POST. REF.	DEBIT	CREDIT	BALANCE	
						DEBIT	CREDIT
20–							
June	1	Balance	✓			6 5 1 1 19	

ACCOUNT Sales Returns and Allowances   ACCOUNT NO. 412

DATE		ITEM	POST. REF.	DEBIT	CREDIT	BALANCE	
						DEBIT	CREDIT
20–							
June	1	Balance	✓			3 1 4 60	

ACCOUNTS RECEIVABLE LEDGER

NAME R. D. Moen

ADDRESS 416 Fifth Avenue

Dallas, Texas 75204

DATE		ITEM	POST. REF.	DEBIT	CREDIT	BALANCE
20–						
May	31		S26	3 1 2 60		3 1 2 60

P.O. 5,9

Record a sales return and a purchases return.

Exercise 10-5 Using the following source document (credit memo issued by Akura Electronics), record the transaction in general journal form on the books of Akura Electronics, then on the books of The Merchandise Market.

Akura Electronics
4160 Broad Street
Chicago, Illinois 60627

CREDIT MEMORANDUM   No.   121

DATE: November 6, 20—

CREDIT TO:

The Merchandise Market

2241 Sullivan Street

Chicago, Illinois   60632

Your account has been credited for:

    1 CPU tower $725.50

P.O. 9

Describe entries involving a purchase and return.

Exercise 10-6 Describe the transactions recorded in the following T accounts:

Cash				Purchases		
	(c)	1,024		**(a)**	1,100	

Accounts Payable				Purchases Returns and Allowances		
(b)	160	**(a)**	1,184		**(b)**	160
(c)	1,024					

Freight In		
(a)	84	

P.O. 9

Record journal entries for a purchase and return.

Exercise 10-7 Journalize the following transactions in general journal form:

a. Bought merchandise on account from Jabari, Inc., invoice no. C3009; net 30 days; FOB destination, $1,125.
b. Received credit memo no. 117 from Jabari, Inc., for merchandise returned, $127.
c. Issued a check to Jabari, Inc., in full payment of account.

P.O. 9

Post to accounts payable ledger and general ledger.

Exercise 10-8 Post the following entry to the general ledger and the subsidiary ledger:

GENERAL JOURNAL   PAGE 92

	DATE		DESCRIPTION	POST. REF.	DEBIT	CREDIT	
1	20–						1
2	July	14	Accounts Payable, Bullock and				2
3			Hendricks		1 9 2 30		3
4			Purchases Returns and				4
5			Allowances			1 9 2 30	5
6			Credit memo no. 942 for				6
7			return of merchandise.				7
8							8

GENERAL LEDGER

ACCOUNT **Accounts Payable**   ACCOUNT NO. **212**

	DATE	ITEM	POST. REF.	DEBIT	CREDIT	BALANCE DEBIT	BALANCE CREDIT	
1	20–							1
2	July 1	Balance	✓				2 7 6 1 24	2
3								3

| ACCOUNT | Purchases Returns and Allowances | | | | | ACCOUNT NO. | 512 |

| | | | POST. REF. | DEBIT | CREDIT | BALANCE | |
| | | | | | | DEBIT | CREDIT |
DATE	ITEM						
1	20–							1
2	July 1	Balance	✓				2 3 0 16	2
3								3

ACCOUNTS PAYABLE LEDGER

NAME **Bullock and Hendricks**

ADDRESS **542 Roselle Blvd.**

Richmond, CA 94879

DATE	ITEM	POST. REF.	DEBIT	CREDIT	BALANCE
20–					
June 13		P73		2 1 8 00	2 1 8 00

You have just learned about recording transactions related to a company's sales. Sales returns and allowances, as well as discounts, affect the amount of a company's net sales.

1. Can you tell from looking at Target's financial statements, how much merchandise was returned during a year? You can view Target's financial statements at **http://www.target.com/.**

2. Target is a retail merchandising company. The company purchases merchandise inventory and then resells it. In Target's chart of accounts, which accounts are related to the purchase and sale of merchandise inventory? (Hint: Look at the statement of operations and the statement of financial position.)

3. In Chapter 5, we discussed the net sales and accounts receivable amounts of Dell, Inc. Now that you have learned about recording sales on account, let's go back to the same question and take another look. Use the financial statements that begin on page 35 of the 2006 10-K report. For 2006, what is the net sales amount (assume that all revenue is from sales) on Dell's income statement (statement of income)? How much is accounts receivable on the balance sheet (statement of financial position)? What can you tell from these two amounts? What is their relation to each other?

CONSIDER AND COMMUNICATE

You are the bookkeeper at a small merchandising firm. You are comparing the income statements from the last three years. You notice that the Purchases Returns and Allowances account (as a percentage of net sales) has been increasing at an alarming rate. If you were a manager, who would you speak to in the organization to help you understand why so much merchandise is being returned?

CRITICAL THINKING

TO: Accounting Clerk   SUBJECT: Errors in trial balance
FROM: Senior Accountant   DATE: April 1, 20—

Following is a trial balance prepared just before you were hired. There are two accounts missing, and the amount for Sales is off. Here are a few facts to consider. Our business is in a state that collects sales tax. I ran some totals, and we collected $1,800 in sales tax. Customers returned $900 in goods, which would reduce the above sales tax by $70. Our books need to reflect these events. The former accounting clerk said she did record everything—somewhere. She said she may have credited the $1,800 sales tax to Sales and not to Sales Tax Payable. Plus, she looked confused when Sales Returns and Allowances was mentioned. She asked, "Why not just debit Sales?" Please determine the two missing accounts and correct the accounts that are off.

Cox Retail Outlet
Trial Balance
March 31, 20—

ACCOUNT NAME	DEBIT	CREDIT
Cash	8 9 4 0 00	
Accounts Receivable	4 8 0 00	
Supplies	1 7 5 00	
Store Equipment	9 4 6 0 00	
Accounts Payable		9 5 8 00
D. Cox, Capital		11 9 5 9 00
D. Cox, Drawing	4 4 8 0 00	
Sales		18 0 0 0 00
Rent Expense	2 4 0 0 00	
Wages Expense	4 8 6 4 00	
Miscellaneous Expense	1 1 8 00	
	30 9 1 7 00	30 9 1 7 00

1. Think about where these amounts might have been put, think about what accounts are missing, and use T accounts to solve the problems.
2. Prepare a corrected trial balance.

A QUESTION OF ETHICS

Ms. Winters, an employee, accidentally dropped a pallet of boxes containing televisions off the forklift she was driving in the warehouse. No one saw what happened. She couldn't see (or hear) any damage to the televisions, so she reloaded the boxes and did not tell her supervisor. Is Ms. Winters behaving in an ethical manner when she withholds this information? Assume that the televisions were damaged and were delivered to customers. How might this damage affect the income statement?

PROBLEM SET A

For additional help, see the demonstration problem at the beginning of each chapter in your Working Papers.

P.O. 2,3,4,5

Problem 10-1A Brandmeir Company sells electrical supplies on a wholesale basis. The following transactions took place during April of this year:

Apr.	1	Sold merchandise on account to Meyer Company, invoice no. 761, $570.40.
	5	Sold merchandise on account to L. R. Feldman Company, invoice no. 762, $486.10.
	6	Issued credit memo no. 50 to Meyer Company for merchandise returned, $40.70.
	10	Sold merchandise on account to Danton Hardware, invoice no. 763, $293.35.
	14	Sold merchandise on account to Blair and Barnes, invoice no. 764, $640.16.
	17	Sold merchandise on account to Pope and Rogers, invoice no. 765, $582.12.
	21	Issued credit memo no. 51 to Blair and Barnes for merchandise returned, $68.44.
	24	Sold merchandise on account to Oberman Company, invoice no. 766, $652.87.
	26	Sold merchandise on account to Danton Hardware, invoice no. 767, $832.19.
	30	Issued credit memo no. 52 to Danton Hardware for damage to merchandise, $98.50.

Check Figure

Accounts Receivable account balance, $5,018.97 debit

Instructions

1. Record these sales of merchandise on account in the sales journal (page 39). Record the sales returns and allowances in the general journal (page 74).
2. Immediately after recording each transaction, post to the accounts receivable ledger.
3. Post the amounts from the general journal daily. Post the sales journal amounts as a total at the end of the month; Accounts Receivable 113, Sales 411, Sales Returns and Allowances 412.
4. Prepare a schedule of accounts receivable. Compare the balance of the Accounts Receivable controlling account with the total of the schedule of accounts receivable.

Instructions for General Ledger Software

1. Record these transactions in either the sales journal or the general journal and post.
2. Print the entries from the general journal.
3. Print the entries from the sales journal.
4. Print a schedule of accounts receivable and compare its total with the balance of the Accounts Receivable controlling account.

P.O. 2,3,4,5

Problem 10-2A Marconi Florists sells flowers on a retail basis. Most of the sales are for cash; however, a few steady customers have charge accounts. Marconi's sales staff fills out a sales slip for each sale. There is a state retail sales tax of 5 percent, which is collected by the retailer and submitted to the state. The following represent Marconi Florists' charge sales for March:

Mar.		
	4	Sold potted plant on account to C. Marlo, sales slip no. 242, $27, plus sales tax of $1.35, total $28.35.
	6	Sold floral arrangement on account to R. Dresher, sales slip no. 267, $54, plus sales tax of $2.70, total $56.70.
	12	Sold corsage on account to B. Carter, sales slip no. 279, $16, plus sales tax of $0.80, total $16.80.
	16	Sold wreath on account to American Legion, sales slip no. 296, $104, plus sales tax of $5.20, total $109.20.
	18	Sold floral arrangements on account to Turner Funeral Home, sales slip no. 314, $260, plus sales tax of $13, total $273.00.
	21	Turner Funeral Home complained about a wrinkled ribbon on the floral arrangement. Marconi Florists allowed a $30 credit and the sales tax of $1.50, credit memo no. 27.
	23	Sold flower arrangements on account to Ponderosa Savings and Loan Association for their fifth anniversary, sales slip no. 337, $180, plus sales tax of $9, total $189.
	24	Allowed Ponderosa Savings and Loan Association credit, $25, plus sales tax of $1.25, because of a few withered blossoms in floral arrangements, credit memo no. 28.

Check Figure

Schedule of Accounts Receivable total, $726.52

Instructions

1. Record these transactions in either the sales journal (page 23) or the general journal (page 57).
2. Immediately after recording each transaction, post to the accounts receivable ledger.
3. Post the amounts from the general journal daily. Post the sales journal amounts as a total at the end of the month; Accounts Receivable 113, Sales Tax Payable 214, Sales 411, Sales Returns and Allowances 412.
4. Prepare a schedule of accounts receivable and compare its total with the balance of the Accounts Receivable controlling account.

P.O. 6,7,8

Problem 10-3A Bhanu Appliance uses a three-column purchases journal. The company is located in Fresno, California. On January 1 of this year, the balances of the ledger accounts are Accounts Payable, $559.06; Purchases, zero; Freight In, zero. In addition to a general ledger, Bhanu Appliance also uses an accounts payable ledger. Transactions for January related to the purchase of merchandise are as follows:

Jan. 2 Bought eighty 12-inch, 3-speed Brighton Oscillating Fans from Sweet and Alyn, $1,890, invoice no. 268J, dated January 2; terms net 60 days; FOB Fresno.

4 Bought ten 35-pint-capacity Crystal Humidifiers from Shasta Company, $2,300, invoice no. 39426, dated January 2; terms 2/10, n/30; FOB Durango, freight prepaid and added to the invoice, $90 (total $2,390).

7 Bought ten 16-inch Axel Window Fans from Teter, Inc., $360, invoice no. 452AD, dated January 6; terms 1/10, n/30; FOB Fresno.

10 Bought twenty-four 4-blade Tiempo Ceiling Fans, Model 2760, from Ukele Company, $3,550, invoice no. D7742, dated January 7; terms 2/10, n/30; FOB Sacramento, freight prepaid and added to the invoice, $84 (total $3,634).

14 Bought four Charger Electric Hedge Trimmers from Famous Products Company, $186, invoice no. 2542, dated January 13; terms net 30 days; FOB Fresno.

22 Bought forty Lindon Electric Bug Killers from Sweet and Alyn, $2,265, invoice no. 392J, dated January 22; terms net 60 days; FOB Fresno.

28 Bought ten Charger Electric Blowers from Famous Products Company, $830, invoice no. 2691, dated January 27; terms net 30 days; FOB Fresno.

30 Bought ten Kole Powered Attic Ventilators from Pinder Company, $446, invoice no. 664CC, dated January 27; terms 2/10, n/30; FOB Seattle, freight prepaid and added to the invoice, $48 (total $494).

Check Figure

Accounts Payable account balance, $12,608.06 credit

Instructions

1. Open the following accounts in the accounts payable ledger and record the January 1 balances, if any, as given: Famous Products Company; Pinder Company, $163.17; Shasta Company, $167.19; Sweet and Alyn; Teter, Inc., $228.70; Ukele Company. For the accounts having balances, write "Balance" in the Item column and place a check mark in the Post. Ref. column.

2. Record the balance of $559.06 in the Accounts Payable controlling account as of January 1. Write "Balance" in the Item column and place a check mark in the Post. Ref. column.

3. Record the transactions in the purchases journal beginning on page 81.

4. Post to the accounts payable ledger daily.

5. Post to the general ledger at the end of the month.

6. Prepare a schedule of accounts payable, and compare the balance of the Accounts Payable controlling account with the total of the schedule of accounts payable.

P.O. 2,3,4,5,6,7,8,9

Problem 10-4A The following transactions relate to Brady Company during April of this year. Terms of sale are 2/10, n/30. The company is located in Atlanta.

Apr. 2 Sold merchandise on account to Slover Company, invoice no. 1126, $1,746.

4 Bought merchandise on account from Pedro Company, invoice no. 16521, $800; terms 1/10, n/30; dated April 2; FOB Atlanta.

9 Sold merchandise on account to Pima and Lane, invoice no. 1127, $860.

Apr. 12 Bought merchandise on account from Varder Company, invoice no. L8552, $2,482; terms 2/10, n/30; dated April 11; FOB Rome, freight prepaid and added to the invoice, $49 (total $2,531).

15 Received credit memo no. 79 for merchandise returned to Kraig and Company, for $120.

17 Sold merchandise on account to C. N. Hague, invoice no. 1128, $1,015.

19 Issued credit memo no. 34 to Pima and Lane for merchandise returned, $86.

26 Bought merchandise on account from M. R. Parker, Inc., invoice no. 7447, $1,482; terms 2/10, n/30; dated April 23; FOB Macon, freight prepaid and added to the invoice, $45 (total $1,527).

29 Bought office supplies on account from Tillman Stationery Company, invoice no. S336, $152; terms net 30 days; dated April 29.

30 Sold merchandise on account to Schilling and Mark, invoice no. 1129, $2,601.

30 Issued credit memo no. 35 to Schilling and Mark for merchandise returned, $153.

Check Figure

Accounts Payable account balance, $5,268 credit

Instructions

1. Open the following accounts in the accounts receivable ledger and record the balances as of April 1: C. N. Hague; Pima and Lane, $426; Schilling and Mark, $974; Slover Company. For the accounts having balances, write "Balance" in the Item column and place a check mark in the Post. Ref. column.
2. Open the following accounts in the accounts payable ledger and record the balances as of April 1: Kraig and Company, $262; M. R. Parker, Inc., $116; Pedro Company; Tillman Stationery Company; Varder Company. For the accounts having balances, write "Balance" in the Item column and place a check mark in the Post. Ref. column.
3. Record the transactions in the sales, purchases, or general journal, as appropriate.
4. Post the entries to the accounts receivable ledger daily.
5. Post the entries to the accounts payable ledger daily.
6. Post the entries in the general journal immediately after you make each journal entry.
7. Post the totals from the special journals at the end of the month.
8. Prepare a schedule of accounts receivable.
9. Prepare a schedule of accounts payable.
10. Compare the totals of the schedules with the balances of the controlling accounts.

Instructions for General Ledger Software

1. Record the transactions in the sales, purchases, or general journal.
   a. For efficiency, analyze the transactions, indicate into which journal each transaction goes, and key the entries in three batches—the sales journal, the purchases journal, and the general journal.
   b. If the program uses a single-column purchases journal, add the amount of the freight to the amount of the purchases.
2. Print the journals.
3. Post the amounts from the sales, purchases, and general journals.
4. Print the general ledger.
5. Print a schedule of accounts receivable and compare the total with the balance of the Accounts Receivable controlling account.

6. Print a schedule of accounts payable and compare the total with the balance of the Accounts Payable controlling account.

PROBLEM SET B

For additional help, see the demonstration problem at the beginning of each chapter in your Working Papers.

P.O. 2,3,4,5

Problem 10-1B C. H. Barton Company sells electrical supplies on a wholesale basis. The following transactions took place during April of this year.

Apr. 3 Sold merchandise on account to Meyer Company, invoice no. 822, $652.80.
 7 Sold merchandise on account to L. R. Feldman Company, invoice no. 823, $462.15.
 8 Sold merchandise on account to Danton Hardware, invoice no. 824, $205.60.
 13 Issued credit memo no. 61 to L. R. Feldman Company for merchandise returned, $136.50.
 15 Sold merchandise on account to Blair and Barnes, invoice no. 825, $831.47.
 21 Sold merchandise on account to Pope and Rogers, invoice no. 826, $590.34.
 24 Issued credit memo no. 62 to Blair and Barnes for merchandise returned, $80.45.
 26 Sold merchandise on account to Oberman Company, invoice no. 827, $569.90.
 28 Issued credit memo no. 63 to Danton Hardware for damage to merchandise, $52.48.
 30 Sold merchandise on account to Danton Hardware, invoice no. 828, $735.50.

Check Figure

Accounts Receivable account balance, $4,947.75 debit

Instructions

1. Record these sales of merchandise on account in the sales journal (page 39). Record the sales returns and allowances in the general journal (page 74).
2. Immediately after recording each transaction, post to the accounts receivable ledger.
3. Post the amounts from the general journal daily. Post the sales journal amount as a total at the end of the month; Accounts Receivable 113, Sales 411, Sales Returns and Allowances 412.
4. Prepare a schedule of accounts receivable. Compare the balance of the Accounts Receivable controlling account with the total of the schedule of accounts receivable.

Instructions for General Ledger Software

1. Record these transactions in either the sales journal or the general journal and post.
2. Print the entries from the general journal.
3. Print the entries from the sales journal.
4. Print a schedule of accounts receivable and compare its total with the balance of the Accounts Receivable controlling account.

P.O. 2,3,4,5

Problem 10-2B Marconi Florists sells flowers on a retail basis. Most of the sales are for cash; however, a few steady customers have charge accounts. Marconi's sales staff fills out a sales slip for each sale. There is a state retail tax of 5 percent, which is collected by the retailer and submitted to the state. Marconi Florists' charge sales for March are as follows:

Mar. 4 Sold floral arrangement on account to R. Dresher, sales slip no. 236, $45, plus sales tax of $2.25, total $47.25.

7 Sold potted plant on account to C. Marlo, sales slip no. 272, $61, plus sales tax of $3.05, total $64.05.

12 Sold wreath on account to American Legion, sales slip no. 294, $63, plus sales tax of $3.15, total $66.15.

17 Sold floral arrangements on account to Turner Funeral Home, sales slip no. 299, $170, plus sales tax of $8.50, total $178.50.

20 Turner Funeral Home returned a flower spray, complaining that there were dead blooms. Marconi Florists allowed a credit of $36 and the sales tax of $1.80, credit memo no. 27.

21 Sold flower arrangements on account to Ponderosa Savings and Loan Association for their anniversary, sales slip no. 310, $236, plus sales tax of $11.80, total $247.80.

22 Allowed Ponderosa Savings and Loan Association credit, $25, plus sales tax of $1.25, because of withered blossoms in floral arrangements, credit memo no. 28.

27 Sold corsage on account to B. Carter, sales slip no. 332, $30, plus sales tax of $1.50, total $31.50.

Check Figure

Schedule of Accounts Receivable total, $682.42

Instructions

1. Record these transactions in either the sales journal (page 23) or the general journal (page 57).
2. Immediately after recording each transaction, post to the accounts receivable ledger.
3. Post the amounts from the general journal daily. Post the sales journal amount as a total at the end of the month; Accounts Receivable 113, Sales Tax Payable 214, Sales 411, Sales Returns and Allowances 412.
4. Prepare a schedule of accounts receivable and compare its total with the balance of the Accounts Receivable controlling account.

P.O. 6,7,8

Problem 10-3B Urban Bicycle Shop uses a three-column purchases journal. The company is located in Topeka, Kansas. On January 1 of this year, the balances of the ledger accounts are Accounts Payable, $423.08; Purchases, zero; Freight In, zero. In addition to a general ledger, the company also uses an accounts payable ledger. Transactions for January related to the purchase of merchandise are as follows:

Jan. 4 Bought fifty 10-speed bicycles from Nakita Company, $4,775, invoice no. 26145, dated January 3; terms net 60 days; FOB Topeka.

7 Bought tires from Bergen Tire Company, $792, invoice no. 9763, dated January 5; terms 2/10, n/30; FOB Topeka.

8 Bought bicycle lights and reflectors from Goodwin Products Company, $384, invoice no. 17317, dated January 6; terms net 30 days; FOB Topeka.

11 Bought hand brakes from Barlow, Inc., $470, invoice no. 291GE, dated January 9; terms 1/10, n/30; FOB Kansas City, freight prepaid and added to the invoice, $36 (total $506).

Jan. 19 Bought handle grips from Goodwin Products Company, $96.50, invoice no. 17520, dated January 17; terms net 30 days; FOB Topeka.

24 Bought thirty 5-speed bicycles from Nakita Company, $1,487, invoice no. 26942, dated January 23; terms net 60 days; FOB Topeka.

29 Bought knapsacks from Dunn Manufacturing Company, $304.80, invoice no. 762AC, dated January 26; terms 2/10, n/30; FOB Topeka.

31 Bought locks from Lincoln Safety Net, $415.47, invoice no. 27712, dated January 26; terms 2/10, n/30; FOB Dodge City, freight prepaid and added to the invoice, $22 (total $437.47).

Check Figure

Accounts Payable account balance, $9,205.85 credit

Instructions

1. Open the following creditor accounts in the accounts payable ledger and record the January 1 balances, if any, as given: Bergen Tire Company, $156; Barlow, Inc.; Dunn Manufacturing Company, $82.88; Goodwin Products Company; Lincoln Safety Net, $184.20; Nakita Company. For the accounts having balances, write "Balance" in the Item column and place a check mark in the Post. Ref. column.
2. Record the balance of $423.08 in the Accounts Payable controlling account as of January 1. Write "Balance" in the Item column and place a check mark in the Post. Ref. column.
3. Record the transactions in the purchases journal beginning with page 81.
4. Post to the accounts payable ledger daily.
5. Post to the general ledger at the end of the month.
6. Prepare a schedule of accounts payable, and compare the balance of the Accounts Payable controlling account with the total of the schedule of accounts payable.

P.O. 2,3,4,5,6,7,8,9

Problem 10-4B The following transactions relate to Kelly Metal Products during April of this year. Terms of sale are 2/10, n/30. The company is located in Los Angeles.

Apr. 1 Sold merchandise on account to Helpful Hardware, invoice no. 5522, $607.40.

4 Bought merchandise on account from Rama Manufacturing Company, invoice no. C1142, $556; terms 1/10, n/30; dated April 2; FOB San Diego, freight prepaid and added to the invoice, $34 (total $590).

9 Sold merchandise on account to Bocci Stores, invoice no. 5523, $1,025.30.

11 Bought merchandise on account from Bali Products Company, invoice no. 8990, $1,756.80; terms 2/10, n/30; dated April 11; FOB San Francisco, freight prepaid and added to the invoice, $75 (total $1,831.80).

16 Sold merchandise on account to C. D. Alvarez, invoice no. 5524, $921.56.

19 Issued credit memo no. 32 to Bocci Stores for merchandise returned, $86.

24 Bought merchandise on account from Ashley Manufacturing Company, invoice no. P1981, $1,432.80; terms 2/10, n/30; dated April 22; FOB Santa Rosa, freight prepaid and added to the invoice, $76 (total $1,508.80).

Apr. 27 Bought office supplies on account from China and Duncan, invoice no. E621A, $84.40; terms net 30 days; dated April 25.

28 Sold merchandise on account to Grady Specialty Company, invoice no. 5525, $3,598.70.

29 Issued credit memo no. 33 to C. D. Alvarez for allowance on damaged merchandise, $80.

30 Received credit memo no. 79 for merchandise returned to Bjorn, Inc., for $115.20.

Check Figure

Accounts Payable account balance, $4,277.80 credit

Instructions

1. Open the following accounts in the accounts receivable ledger and record the balances as of April 1: C. D. Alvarez; Bocci Stores, $352.50; Grady Specialty Company, $225.50; Helpful Hardware, $822. For the accounts having balances, write "Balance" in the Item column and place a check mark in the Post. Ref. column.

2. Open the following accounts in the accounts payable ledger and record the balances as of April 1: Ashley Manufacturing Company; Bali Products Company, $122.46; Bjorn, Inc., $255.54; China and Duncan; Rama Manufacturing Company. For the accounts having balances, write "Balance" in the Item column and place a check mark in the Post Ref. column.

3. Record the transactions in the sales, purchases, or general journal, as appropriate.

4. Post the entries to the accounts receivable ledger daily.

5. Post the entries to the accounts payable ledger daily.

6. Post the entries in the general journal immediately after you make each journal entry.

7. Post the totals from the special journals at the end of the month.

8. Prepare a schedule of accounts receivable.

9. Prepare a schedule of accounts payable.

10. Compare the totals of the schedules with the balances of the controlling accounts.

Instructions for General Ledger Software

1. Record the transactions in the sales, purchases, or general journal.

   a. For efficiency, analyze the transactions, indicate into which journal each transaction goes, and key the entries in three batches—the sales journal, the purchases journal, and the general journal.

   b. If the program uses a single-column purchases journal, add the amount of the freight to the amount of the purchases.

2. Print the journals.

3. Post the amounts from the sales, purchases, and general journals.

4. Print the general ledger.

5. Print a schedule of accounts receivable and compare the total with the balance of the Accounts Receivable controlling account.

6. Print a schedule of accounts payable and compare the total with the balance of the Accounts Payable controlling account.

The Computer Clinic

Sales and Purchases Journals

Ms. Valli of All About You Spa has decided to expand her business by adding two lines of merchandise—a selection of products used in the salon for the body, the feet, and the face, as well as logo mugs, T-shirts, and baseball caps that can provide advertising benefits. She believes she will be able to increase her profits significantly. She has provided paper copies and computer files that report her revenues, operating expenses, and other accounting activity that occurred in June.

The first thing you want to do is to look at the post-closing trial balance as of June 30, 20— shown below. As you look at the post-closing trial balance for the spa, answer the question, "Why is the trial balance so short?"

Why is the trial balance so short?

ACCOUNT NAME	DEBIT	CREDIT
All About You Spa		
Post-Closing Trial Balance		
June 30, 20—		
Cash	15 1 7 0 00	
Accounts Receivable	1 2 6 4 00	
Prepaid Insurance	8 0 0 00	
Spa Equipment	7 3 9 3 00	
Accumulated Depreciation, Spa Equipment		6 4 88
Office Equipment	1 1 5 0 00	
Accumulated Depreciation, Office Equipment		1 0 00
Accounts Payable		2 2 4 8 00
Wages Payable		3 6 9 50
A. Valli, Capital		23 0 8 4 62
	25 7 7 7 00	25 7 7 7 00

If you answered "There are no revenue, expense, or drawing accounts," you are correct. But why are there no revenue, expense, or drawing accounts? What happened to them?*

Directions for July Journal Entries

What do I do next?

1. If you are beginning the Computer Clinic problem at Chapter 10, journalize the post-closing trial balance accounts and amounts in the general journal. Do this as one big compound entry prior to recording the July journal entries.

---

*Answer: There are no temporary owner's equity accounts (revenue, expense, or drawing accounts) because they were closed; their balances were made zero to prepare the books for the next fiscal period. The only accounts remaining open (having a balance) are the real accounts—assets, liabilities, and Owner's Capital.

These amounts are the June 30 balances that become the beginning balances for July.

2. Then, make the following reversing entry, dated July 1. (The purpose of this entry is to reverse or undo the adjusting entry you made in Chapter 4. Reversing entries are explained in Chapter 13.)

Wages Payable		Wages Expense	
+	−	+	−
369.50			369.50

So that you can complete the journal entries for the month of July, Ms. Valli has also left the information you will need and directions on how to proceed.

3. Add new accounts to the chart of accounts as needed (for example, Merchandise Sales). Since All About You Spa now needs a Purchases account, the chart of accounts needs to be modified as follows: All expense accounts need to be in the 600–699 range; for example, Wages Expense changes from 511 to 611. The 500–599 range is now used for the purchase-related accounts; for example, make Purchases 511 and Freight In 515. (*Hint:* Four new accounts need to be added to the chart of accounts.)

4. a. Journalize the checks written in July and shown in the checkbook register, which also shows deposits made to the account. Record these events in the *general journal*. (*Notes:* Payroll taxes related to wages will be ignored here for purposes of simplification. All About You Spa is located in a state that levies sales tax on both merchandise and services. Some states do not tax services.)

   b. Journalize in the *purchases journal* all of the July purchases of merchandise on account, which are shown in the list of invoices provided.

   c. Journalize in the *sales journal* all of the July sales of merchandise on account, which are shown in the list of merchandise sales invoices provided.

> Remember to journalize a transaction in only one journal—either the sales journal *or* the purchases journal *or* the general journal.

5. Set up an accounts receivable ledger and an accounts payable ledger. Use the following opening balances. All other accounts have a zero opening balance.

Accounts Receivable Ledger		Accounts Payable Ledger	
Jill Anson	$325.00	Adco, Inc.	$ 397.00
Troy Ligman	344.00	Golden Spa Supplies	492.00
Jack Morgan	486.00	Office Staples	120.00
Judy Wilcox	109.00	Spa Equipment, Inc.	89.00
		Superior Equipment	1,150.00

6. After journalizing and posting all transactions to the general ledger and subsidiary ledgers, print a trial balance dated July 31, 20—. Do not include those accounts that have a zero balance at the end of the month.

7. Print a schedule of accounts receivable dated July 31, 20—.

8. Print a schedule of accounts payable dated July 31, 20—.

Checkbook Register

Check No.	Date	Explanation	✔	Deposits	Check Amount
	7/1	Owner invested cash in business.		25,000.00	
1027	7/3	Bought additional spa equipment from Spa Equipment, Inc., for $8,235.00, paying $2,000.00 cash down, invoice no. 2731; terms 2/10, n/60.			2,000.00
1028	7/3	Paid July's rent.			1,650.00
1029	7/3	Paid on account to Spa Equipment, Inc., invoice no. 2013, dated June 3 (no discount). Paid in full.			89.00
1030	7/5	Paid on account to Golden Spa Supplies, invoice no. 804, dated June 3 (no discount). Paid in full.			492.00
1031	7/5	Paid on account to Office Staples, invoice no. 522, dated June 5 (no discount). Paid in full.			120.00
1032	7/5	Paid Celebrate, Inc., for flowers and balloons for lobby (Miscellaneous Expense).			98.00
1033	7/5	Paid on account to Adco, Inc., invoice no. 512, dated June 5 (no discount). Paid in full.			397.00
1034	7/5	Paid week's wages.			1,845.50
	7/7	Deposited first week's cash sales: merchandise $1,410.00; services $3,110.00; sales tax collected $361.60. (Open new accounts Merchandise Sales 412 and Sales Tax Payable 215.)		4,881.60	
	7/7	Deposited check from Jill Anson, invoice no. 10, dated June 7 (balance due in August, $175.00).		150.00	
1035	7/12	Paid week's wages.			1,845.50
	7/14	Deposited check from Jack Morgan, invoice no. 11, dated June 14 (balance due in August, $286.00).		200.00	
	7/14	Deposited second week's cash sales: merchandise $1,220.00; services $2,630.00; sales tax collected $308.00.		4,158.00	

Check No.	Date	Explanation	✔	Deposits	Check Amount
1036	7/18	Paid on account to Superior Equipment, invoice no. 3140, dated June 5 (no discount). Paid in full.			1,150.00
1037	7/19	Paid week's wages.			1,840.50
	7/21	Deposited check from Tory Ligman, invoice no. 12, dated June 21 (balance due in August, $164.00).		180.00	
	7/21	Deposited third week's cash sales: merchandise $1,940.00; services $2,920.00; sales tax collected $388.80.		5,248.80	
1038	7/25	Bought new nail cart for cash (debit Spa Equipment).			173.00
1039	7/26	Paid week's wages.			1,842.00
1040	7/28	Paid month's laundry bill.			84.00
	7/28	Deposited check from Judy Wilcox, invoice no. 13, dated June 28 (paid in full).		109.00	
	7/31	Deposited end of month's cash sales: merchandise $1,930.00; services $4,062.00; sales tax collected $479.36.		6,471.36	
1041	7/31	Owner withdrew cash for personal use.			2,500.00
1042	7/31	Paid July telephone bill.			225.00
1043	7/31	Paid July power and water bill.			248.00

Purchases Invoices for Merchandise Bought on Account During July

All About You Spa will pay all freight costs associated with purchases of merchandise to the supplier. Two new accounts are needed: Purchases 511 and Freight In 515.

Date of Purchase	Transaction Information	Amount
July 1	Bought aromatherapy products from Spa Goods; invoice no. 312, dated 7/1; terms 2/10, n/60.	$5,300.00 plus $145.00 freight
1	Bought logo merchandise from Logo Products; invoice no. 1579, dated 7/1; terms 2/10, n/60.	$3,692.00 plus $104.00 freight
2	Bought bath and beauty products from Spa Magic; invoice no. 5033, dated 7/2; 2/10, n/30.	$2,623.00 plus $98.00 freight
5	Bought logo merchandise from Giftco; invoice no. 316, dated 7/5; terms 2/10, n/60.	$1,253 plus $56.00 freight

Sales Invoices for Gift Certificates Sold on Account During July

All About You Spa is responsible for collecting and paying the sales tax on merchandise that it sells. The sales tax rate where All About You Spa does business is 8 percent of each sale; for example, $325.00 $\times$ 0.08 = $26.00.

Date of Sale	Transaction Information	Sales Amount (Before Tax)
July 2	Los Obrigados Lodge, invoice no.14.	$ 325.00
4	Chaco's, invoice no.15.	481.50
5	Pleasant Spa, invoice no.16.	1,815.95
10	Holmes Condos, invoice no.17.	340.25
10	Mini Spa, invoice no.18.	206.00
12	About Face Spa, invoice no.19.	482.95

Note: All certificates for services were redeemed and the services were provided by the end of the month.

Other July Transactions

There were five other transactions in July. None involved cash.

Date	Transaction Information	Amount
July 1	Bought spa supplies on account from Golden Spa Supplies, invoice no. 1836, terms n/45.	$490.00
5	Bought office equipment on account from Superior Equipment, invoice no. 3608, terms 2/10, n/60.	$420.00
5	Bought self-help books for the waiting room on account (Miscellaneous Expense) from Office Staples, invoice no. 1417, n/30.	$186.00
5	Bought office supplies on account from Office Staples, invoice no. 1418, terms n/30.	$118.00
31	Owner invested additional personal spa equipment (treadmill and bicycle) valued at $1,800.00.	

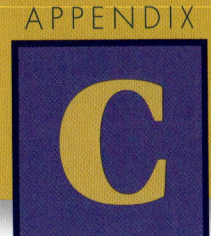

Sales and Purchases on Account: An Alternative to Special Journals

Performance Objectives

After you have completed this appendix, you will be able to do the following:

1. Record transactions pertaining to the sale and purchase of merchandise in a general journal.

2. Maintain an accounts receivable ledger and an accounts payable ledger.

3. Prepare schedules of accounts receivable and accounts payable.

Although most merchandising enterprises set up special journals, some businesses elect to record sales and purchases of merchandise on account in the general journal because of personal preference or the desire to record all transactions chronologically in one place.

JOURNALIZING SALES OF MERCHANDISE ON ACCOUNT

Refer to Figures 1 (page 336), 2 (page 337), and 8 (page 346) in Chapter 10, which illustrate the forms that drive and support the merchandising transactions to be journalized.

Here are the merchandising accounts in T account form. Refer to the glossary at the end of Chapter 10 on pages 363 and 364 for definitions of these accounts. The same accounts are used whether transactions are journalized in special journals (as in Chapter 10) or in a general journal. The outcomes will be the same.

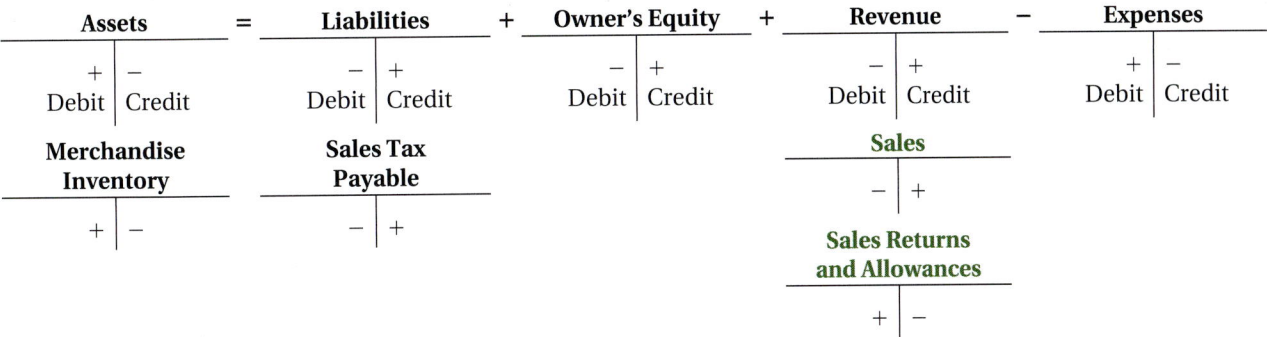

RECORDING SALES ON ACCOUNT IN A GENERAL JOURNAL

OBJECTIVE 1a

Record transactions pertaining to the sale of merchandise in a general journal.

We will introduce journalizing sales of merchandise on account in a general journal by looking at three transactions on the books of Rainier Plumbing Supply:

Aug. 1 Sold merchandise on account to Betterbuilt Homes Co., invoice no. 1320, $1,564.86.

3 Sold merchandise on account to Arnold, Inc., invoice no. 1321, $1,116.

6 Sold merchandise on account to Gonzales Construction, invoice no. 1322, $1,394.

			GENERAL JOURNAL		PAGE 26	
	DATE		DESCRIPTION	POST. REF.	DEBIT	CREDIT
1	20–					
2	Aug.	1	Accounts Receivable, Betterbuilt			
3			Homes Co.		1 5 6 4 86	
4			Sales			1 5 6 4 86
5			Sold merchandise to Betterbuilt			
6			Homes Co., invoice no. 1320.			
7						
8		3	Accounts Receivable, Arnold, Inc.		1 1 1 6 00	
9			Sales			1 1 1 6 00
10			Sold merchandise to Arnold,			
11			Inc., invoice no. 1321.			
12						
13		6	Accounts Receivable, Gonzales			
14			Construction		1 3 9 4 00	
15			Sales			1 3 9 4 00
16			Sold merchandise to Gonzales			
17			Construction, invoice no. 1322.			
18						
19						

Posting to the General Ledger and Subsidiary Ledger

OBJECTIVE 2a

Maintain an accounts receivable ledger.

Post each entry to Accounts Receivable and Sales in the general ledger. Also, post the amount owed by the customer to the subsidiary accounts receivable ledger to maintain a running balance of the amount each customer owes.

Journalizing Sales Tax

In states where sales tax is collected, it is necessary to compute and include the amount of the sales tax for each transaction. That is, the customer owes the amount of the sale plus the applicable sales tax.

Following are three transactions that include sales tax computed on the amount of the sale of merchandise on account in a state that requires sales tax to be collected:

Apr. 1 Sold merchandise on account to C. D. Barnes, invoice no. 9382, $1,550, plus sales of tax $124, total $1,674.
1 Sold merchandise on account to Best Child Care, invoice no. 9383, $1,022, plus sales tax of $81.76, total $1,103.76.
1 Sold merchandise on account to Land Use Planners, invoice no. 9384, $2,050, plus sales tax of $164, total $2,214.

	GENERAL JOURNAL			PAGE 10	
DATE	DESCRIPTION	POST. REF.	DEBIT	CREDIT	
1	20–				1
2	Apr. 1 Accounts Receivable, C. D. Barnes		1 6 7 4 00		2
3	Sales			1 5 5 0 00	3
4	Sales Tax Payable			1 2 4 00	4
5	Sold merchandise to C. D.				5
6	Barnes, invoice no. 9382.				6
7					7
8	1 Accounts Receivable, Best Child Care		1 1 0 3 76		8
9	Sales			1 0 2 2 00	9
10	Sales Tax Payable			8 1 76	10
11	Sold merchandise to Best Child				11
12	Care, invoice no. 9383.				12
13					13
14	1 Accounts Receivable, Land Use				14
15	Planners		2 2 1 4 00		15
16	Sales			2 0 5 0 00	16
17	Sales Tax Payable			1 6 4 00	17
18	Sold merchandise to Land Use				18
19	Planners, invoice no. 9384.				19
20					20

Posting to the General Ledger and Subsidiary Ledger

Post each entry to Accounts Receivable, Sales, and Sales Tax Payable in the general ledger. Also, post the amount owed by the customer to the subsidiary accounts receivable ledger to maintain a running balance of the amount each customer owes.

Schedule of Accounts Receivable

OBJECTIVE 3a
Prepare a schedule of accounts receivable.

At the end of the month, the accountant lists the customer names and amounts owed and totals the amounts. This listing is called the schedule of accounts receivable. The total of this schedule should equal the total of the Accounts Receivable controlling account in the general ledger. If the two amounts are different, reverse the process of adding and posting to discover and correct the error.

Sales Returns and Allowances

Refer to pages 346–348 in Chapter 10 for information on journalizing and posting credit memorandums, which give customers permission to return all or part of the goods sold to them. Since we debited the customer's Accounts

Receivable account and credited Sales and Sales Tax Payable, we must undo or reverse the accounts for the amount the customer is returning in addition to the sales tax on that amount.

JOURNALIZING PURCHASES OF MERCHANDISE (FOR RESALE) ON ACCOUNT

Refer to Figures 9 (page 350), 10 (page 350), and 11 (page 351) in Chapter 10, which illustrate the forms that drive and support the merchandising transactions to be journalized.

Here are the merchandising accounts in T account form. Refer to the glossary at the end of Chapter 10 on pages 363 and 364 for definitions of these accounts. The same accounts are used whether transactions are journalized in special journals (as in Chapter 10) or in a general journal. The outcomes will be the same.

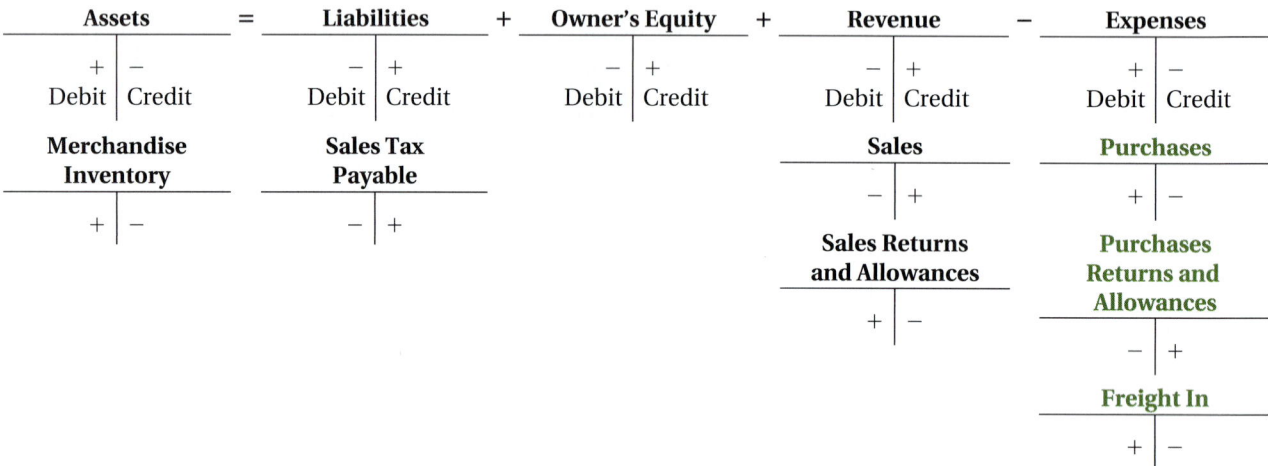

RECORDING PURCHASES ON ACCOUNT IN A GENERAL JOURNAL

OBJECTIVE 1b

Record transactions pertaining to the purchase of merchandise in a general journal.

We will introduce journalizing purchases of merchandise on account in a general journal by looking at three transactions on the books of Rainier Plumbing Supply. These transactions include the cost of delivering the merchandise, called Freight In.

Aug. 2 Bought merchandise on account from Collins, Inc., invoice no. 2706, $1,710; terms 2/10, n/30; dated July 31; FOB San Francisco, freight prepaid and added to the invoice, $85.50 (total $1,795.50).

3 Bought merchandise on account from Langseth and Son, invoice no. 982, $2,772; terms net 30 days; dated August 2; FOB Cleveland, freight prepaid and added to the invoice, $157 (total $2,929).

5 Bought merchandise on account from Dana Manufacturing Company, invoice no. 10611, $564; terms 2/10, n/30; dated August 3; FOB Los Angeles.

		GENERAL JOURNAL									PAGE	26					
	DATE	DESCRIPTION	POST. REF.	DEBIT					CREDIT							
1	20–															1
2	Aug. 2	Purchases		1	7	1	0	00								2
3		Freight In				8	5	50								3
4		Accounts Payable, Collins, Inc.							1	7	9	5	50		4
5		Purchased merchandise from														5
6		Collins, Inc., invoice no. 2706,														6
7		invoice dated 7/31, terms 2/10, n/30.														7
8																8
9	3	Purchases		2	7	7	2	00								9
10		Freight In			1	5	7	00								10
11		Accounts Payable, Langseth and Son							2	9	2	9	00		11
12		Purchased merchandise from														12
13		Langseth and Son, invoice no. 982,														13
14		invoice dated 8/2, terms n/30.														14
15																15
16	5	Purchases			5	6	4	00								16
17		Accounts Payable, Dana Mfg. Co.								5	6	4	00		17
18		Purchased merchandise from														18
19		Dana Mfg. Co., invoice no. 10611,														19
20		invoice dated 8/3, terms 2/10, n/30.														20
21																21
22																22

Posting to the General Ledger and Subsidiary Ledger

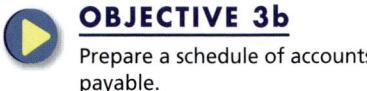

OBJECTIVE 2b

Maintain an accounts payable ledger.

Post each entry to Accounts Payable, Purchases, and Freight In in the general ledger. Also, post the amount owed to the vendor to the subsidiary accounts payable ledger to maintain a running balance of the amount owed to each vendor.

Schedule of Accounts Payable

OBJECTIVE 3b

Prepare a schedule of accounts payable.

At the end of the month, the accountant lists the vendor names and amounts owed and totals the amounts. This listing is called the schedule of accounts payable. The total of this schedule should equal the total of the Accounts Payable controlling account in the general ledger. If the two amounts are different, reverse the process of adding and posting to discover and correct the error.

Purchases Returns and Allowances

Refer to pages 356–357 in Chapter 10 for information on journalizing and posting credit memorandums, which give the purchaser permission from the vendor to return all or part of the goods purchased from them. Since we debited Purchases and sometimes Freight In and credited the customer's Accounts Payable account, we must undo or reverse these accounts for the amount we are returning.

PROBLEMS

P.O. 1, 2, 3

Check Figures

Schedule of Accounts Receivable total, $7,383; Schedule of Accounts Payable total, $5,268

Problem C-1A Complete Problem 10-4A on pages 373–375 *except* journalize transactions in a general journal instead of in special journals.

P.O. 1, 2, 3

Check Figures

Schedule of Accounts Receivable total, $7,386.96; Schedule of Accounts Payable total, $4,277.80

Problem C-1B Complete Problem 10-4B on pages 377–378 *except* journalize transactions in a general journal instead of in special journals.

LINKS TO ACCOUNTING

Most Americans have at least one credit card. Many have more than one. Are you aware of the different charges that are paid when you use a credit card? Online, you can find many websites explaining how credit card use affects you as a consumer. Check out *How Stuff Works,* **http://money .howstuffworks.com/credit-card.htm** for some very useful information.

Even though consumers don't have to pay cash up front for a purchase, using their credit card starts a series of transactions that involve cash. Go to **http://wfhummel.cnchost.com/creditcards.html** to learn all about the transactions involved in a credit card purchase. After reading this article, and as you read this chapter, think about who receives cash and who pays cash for credit card transactions, and how the different parties involved might record these transactions.

Performance Objectives

After you have completed this chapter, you will be able to do the following:

1. Journalize transactions for a merchandising business in a cash receipts journal.

2. Post from a cash receipts journal to a general ledger and an accounts receivable ledger.

3. Determine cash discounts according to credit terms, and record cash receipts from charge customers who are entitled to deduct the cash discount.

4. Journalize transactions in a cash payments journal for a service enterprise.

5. Post from a cash payments journal to a general ledger and an accounts payable ledger.

6. Journalize transactions involving cash discounts in a cash payments journal for a merchandising enterprise.

7. Journalize transactions in a check register.

8. Journalize transactions involving trade discounts.

We have seen that using a sales journal and a purchases journal enables an accountant to carry out the journalizing and posting processes much more efficiently. These special journals make it possible to post column totals rather than individual figures. They also make the division of labor more efficient because the journalizing functions can be delegated to different persons. The *cash receipts journal* and the *cash payments journal* further extend these advantages.

THE CASH RECEIPTS JOURNAL

OBJECTIVE 1

Journalize transactions for a merchandising business in a cash receipts journal.

The **cash receipts journal** contains all transactions in which cash is received, or increases. When a cash receipts journal is used, all transactions in which cash is debited *must* be recorded in it. It may be used for a service as well as a merchandising business. Let's list some typical transactions of a retail merchandising business that result in an increase in cash. To get a better picture of the transactions, let's first record them in T accounts.

May 3 Sold merchandise for cash, $500, plus $40 sales tax.

Cash		Sales Tax Payable		Sales	
+	−	−	+	−	+
540			40		500

May 4 Sold merchandise, $500, plus $40 sales tax, and the customer used a bank charge card. The bank issuing the card bills the customer directly each month. The business, on the other hand, deposits the bank credit card receipts every day. The bank *deducts a discount* and credits the firm's account with cash. We will assume that the discount is 4 percent. The firm therefore records the amount of the discount under Credit Card Expense: $540.00 × .04 = $21.60 credit card expense; $500.00 + $40.00 − $21.60 = $518.40.

Cash		Sales Tax Payable		Sales		Credit Card Expense	
+	−	−	+	−	+	+	−
518.40			40.00		500.00	21.60	

May 5 Collected cash on account from L. R. Ray, a charge customer, $416.

Cash		Accounts Receivable	
+	−	+	−
416			416

May 7 The owner, J. R. Hall, invested cash in the business, $10,000.

Cash		J. R. Hall, Capital	
+	−	−	+
10,000			10,000

Cash transactions can take place anywhere in the world through ATM machines, with clients never entering their banks.

May 8 Sold computer equipment for cash at cost, $500.

Cash		Computer Equipment	
+	−	+	−
500			500

The same transactions are shown in general journal form as follows:

GENERAL JOURNAL   PAGE _____

	DATE		DESCRIPTION	POST. REF.	DEBIT	CREDIT	
1	20–						1
2	May	3	Cash		5 4 0 00		2
3			Sales			5 0 0 00	3
4			Sales Tax Payable			4 0 00	4
5			Sold merchandise for cash.				5
6							6
7		4	Cash		5 1 8 40		7
8			Credit Card Expense		2 1 60		8
9			Sales			5 0 0 00	9
10			Sales Tax Payable			4 0 00	10
11			Sold merchandise involving				11
12			a bank charge card.				12
13							13
14		5	Cash		4 1 6 00		14
15			Accounts Receivable, L. R. Ray			4 1 6 00	15
16			Collected cash on account.				16
17							17
18		7	Cash		10 0 0 0 00		18
19			J. R. Hall, Capital			10 0 0 0 00	19
20			Owner invested cash.				20
21							21
22		8	Cash		5 0 0 00		22
23			Computer Equipment			5 0 0 00	23
24			Sold computer equipment				24
25			at cost.				25
26							26

Now let's analyze these five transactions: The first three would occur frequently; the last two would occur less frequently. When designing a cash receipts journal, it is logical to include a Cash Debit column because all the transactions involve an increase in cash. If a business regularly collects cash from charge customers, there should be an Accounts Receivable Credit column. If a firm often sells merchandise for cash and collects a sales tax, there should be a Sales Credit column and a Sales Tax Payable Credit column. If the business accepts bank charge cards and wants to record the amount of the discount at the time of each transaction, there should be a Credit Card Expense Debit column for the amount deducted by the bank.

However, the credit to J. R. Hall, Capital, and the credit to Computer Equipment do not occur very often, so it would not be practical to set up

CASH RECEIPTS JOURNAL

PAGE __41__

	DATE		ACCOUNT CREDITED	POST. REF.	CASH DEBIT	CREDIT CARD EXPENSE DEBIT	ACCOUNTS RECEIVABLE CREDIT	SALES CREDIT	SALES TAX PAYABLE CREDIT	OTHER ACCOUNTS CREDIT	
1	20–										1
2	May	3	————		5 4 0 00			5 0 0 00	4 0 00		2
3		4	————		5 1 8 40	2 1 60		5 0 0 00	4 0 00		3
4		5	L. R. Ray		4 1 6 00		4 1 6 00				4
5		7	J. R. Hall,								5
6			Capital		10 0 0 0 00					10 0 0 0 00	6
7		8	Computer								7
8			Equipment		5 0 0 00					5 0 0 00	8
9											9

FIGURE 1

special columns for these credits. They can be handled adequately by an Other Accounts Credit column, which can be used for credits to all accounts that have no special column.

Now let's record these transactions in a cash receipts journal (see Figure 1). First, we repeat the transactions:

May 3 Sold merchandise for cash, $500, plus $40 sales tax.
4 Sold merchandise, $500, plus $40 sales tax, and the customer used a bank charge card. Discount charged by the bank is 4 percent of the total of sales plus sales tax.
5 Collected cash on account from L. R. Ray, a charge customer, $416.
7 The owner, J. R. Hall, invested cash in the business, $10,000.
8 Sold computer equipment for cash at cost, $500.

REMEMBER!

The amount of credit card expense is based on the total of sales *plus* sales tax payable.

REMEMBER!

Special journals include a sales journal, a purchases journal, a cash receipts journal, and a cash payments journal. They are used to save time by posting totals of the special columns rather than individual amounts to the general ledger.

As an alternative, many businesses postpone recording the amount of bank credit card expense until they actually receive notification from their bank on their bank statement. For example, total credit card sales for a restaurant for a time period amount to $10,600 plus 8 percent sales tax. The entry is as follows:

Cash		Sales Tax Payable		Sales	
+	–	–	+	–	+
11,448			848		10,600

The restaurant's next bank statement includes a debit memorandum for credit card charges of $457.92, using an assumed 4 percent discount rate ($11,448 × .04). The business handles this in a similar manner to a check service charge:

Credit Card Expense		Cash	
+	–	+	–
457.92			457.92

Posting from the Cash Receipts Journal

Here are some other transactions made during the month that involve increases in cash. (Remember that these transactions are for a retail business.)

May 11 Borrowed $9,000 from the bank, receiving cash and giving the bank a promissory note.

16 Sold merchandise for cash, $200, plus $16 sales tax.

21 Sold merchandise, $100, plus $8 sales tax; customer used a bank charge card. Credit card expense charge is 4 percent of sales plus sales tax.

26 Collected cash from B. Sanchez, a charge customer, on account, $262.40.

28 Sold merchandise for cash, $160, plus $12.80 sales tax.

31 Sold merchandise, $150, plus $12 sales tax; customer used a bank charge card. Credit card expense charge is 4 percent of sales plus sales tax.

31 Collected cash from T. Nguyen, a charge customer, on account, $140.

In the transaction of May 11, in which $9,000 was borrowed from the bank, the bank was given a **promissory note** (a written promise to pay a specified amount at a specified time) as evidence of the debt. The account **Notes Payable**, instead of Accounts Payable, is used to represent the amount owed on the promissory note. The Accounts Payable account is reserved for charge accounts with creditors, which are normally paid on a thirty-day basis.

Let's assume that all the month's transactions involving debits to Cash have now been recorded in the cash receipts journal. The cash receipts journal (see Figure 2 on the following page) and the T accounts following it illustrate the postings to the general ledger and the accounts receivable ledger.

Individual amounts in the Accounts Receivable Credit column of the cash receipts journal are usually posted daily to the accounts receivable ledger. Individual amounts in the Other Accounts Credit column are usually posted daily.

At the end of the month, we can post the special column totals in the cash receipts journal to the general ledger accounts. These columns include Cash Debit, Credit Card Expense Debit, Accounts Receivable Credit, Sales Credit, and Sales Tax Payable Credit.

In the Post. Ref. column, the check marks (✓) indicate that the amounts in the Accounts Receivable Credit column have been posted to the individual charge customers' accounts as credits. The account numbers show that the amounts in the Other Accounts Credit column have been posted separately to the accounts described in the Account Credited column. An (X) goes under the total of the Other Accounts Credit column; it means "do not post—the figures have already been posted separately." This column is totaled to make it easier to prove that the debits equal the credits.

Note the ruling. A single rule is placed above the column totals, and double rules extend through all but the Account Credited column. Also, on the last line, the last day of the month is recorded in the Date column.

Let's say it's the end of the month. Total the columns first. Then begin crossfooting the journal by proving that the sum of the debit totals equals the sum of the credit totals. This process must be completed before you post the totals to the general ledger accounts.

OBJECTIVE 2
Post from a cash receipts journal to a general ledger and an accounts receivable ledger.

FYI
The dash is a placeholder indicating that nothing has been left out or forgotten.

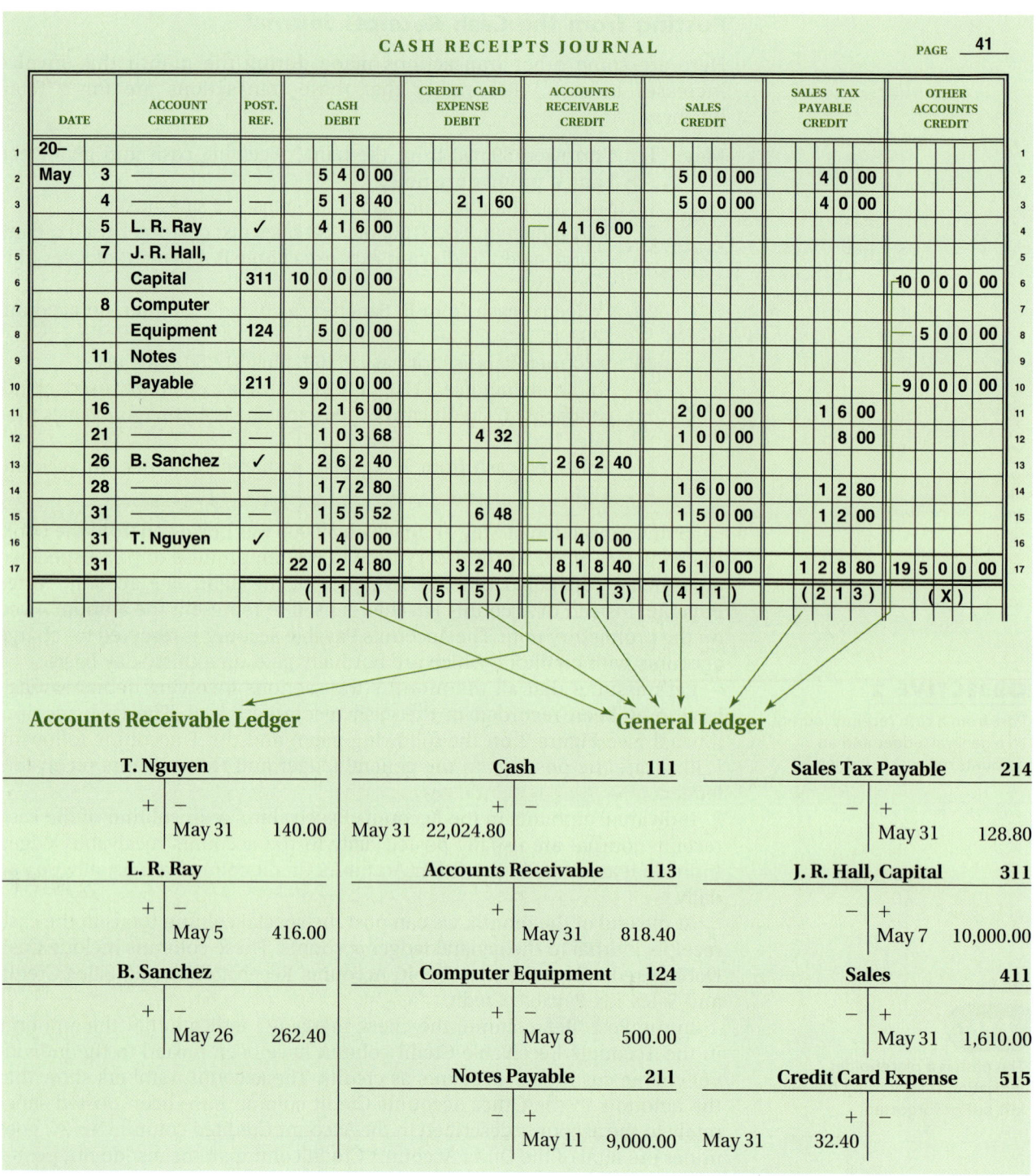

FIGURE 2

Debit Totals		Credit Totals	
Cash	$22,024.80	Accounts Receivable	$ 818.40
Credit Card Expense	32.40	Sales	1,610.00
		Sales Tax Payable	128.80
		Other Accounts	19,500.00
	$22,057.20		$22,057.20

Post the special column totals to the general ledger, using the letters CR as the posting reference. Next, write the general ledger account number in parentheses below the total in the appropriate column.

Advantages of a Cash Receipts Journal

1. Transactions generally can be recorded on one line.
2. All transactions involving debits to Cash are recorded in one place.
3. It eliminates much repetition in posting when there are numerous transactions involving Cash debits. The Cash Debit side can be posted as one total.
4. Special columns can be used for specialized transactions and posted as one total.

CREDIT TERMS

OBJECTIVE 3

Determine cash discounts according to credit terms, and record cash receipts from charge customers who are entitled to deduct the cash discount.

The cash receipts journal and the cash payments journal are used by both service and merchandising businesses to record all transactions in which cash comes into or goes out of the business.

The seller always stipulates credit terms: How much credit can a customer be allowed? And, how much time should the customer be given to pay the full amount? The **credit period** is the time the seller allows the buyer before full payment has to be made. Retailers generally allow twenty-five to thirty days.

Wholesalers and manufacturers often specify a **cash discount** in their credit terms. A cash discount is an amount that a customer can deduct if a bill is paid within a specified time. The discount is based on the *total amount of the invoice after any returns and allowances and freight charges billed on the invoice have been deducted.* Naturally, this discount acts as an incentive for charge customers to pay their bills promptly.

Let's say that a wholesaler offers customers credit terms of 2/10, n/30. These terms mean that the customer gets a 2 percent discount if the bill is paid within ten days after the invoice date. The discount period begins the day after the invoice date. If the bill is not paid within the ten days, the entire amount is due within thirty days after the invoice date. Other types of cash discounts that may be used are the following:

- **1/15, n/60** The seller offers a 1 percent discount if the bill is paid within fifteen days after the invoice date, and the whole bill must be paid within sixty days after the invoice date.
- **2/10, EOM, n/60** The seller offers a 2 percent discount if the bill is paid within ten days after the end of the month, and the whole bill must be paid within sixty days after the last day of the month.

A wholesaler or manufacturer that offers a cash discount adopts a single cash discount as a credit policy and makes this available to all its customers. The seller considers cash discounts as sales discounts; the buyer, on the other hand, considers cash discounts as purchases discounts. In this section we are concerned with the sales discount. *The Sales Discounts account, like Sales Returns and Allowances, is a deduction from Sales.*

To illustrate, we return to Rainier Plumbing Supply. We will record the following transactions in T accounts.

Transaction (a) August 1: Sold merchandise on account to Betterbuilt Homes Co., invoice no. 1320, $1,564.86; terms 2/10, n/30.

Transaction (b) August 10: Received check from Betterbuilt Homes Co. for $1,533.56 in payment of invoice no. 1320, less cash discount ($1,564.86 × .02 = $31.30; $1,564.86 − $31.30 = $1,533.56).

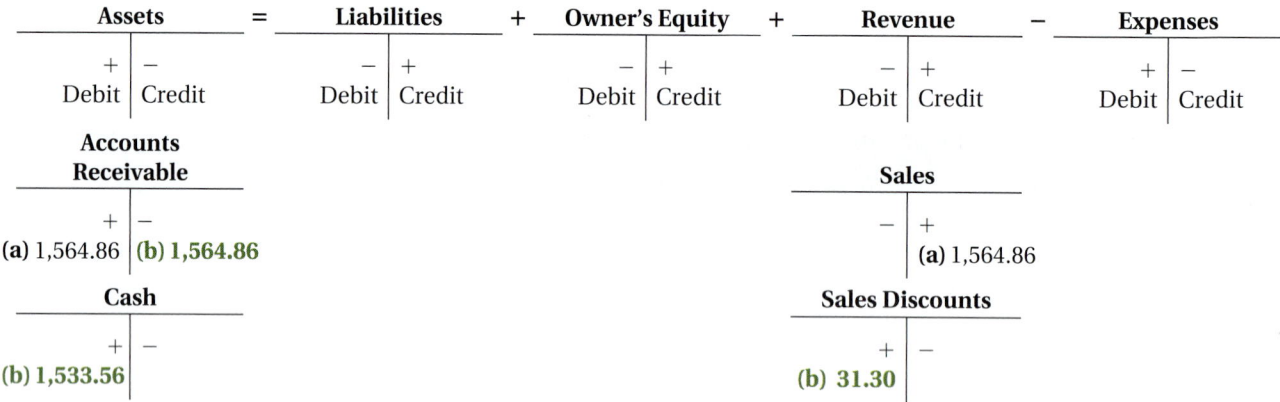

Since Rainier Plumbing Supply offers this cash discount to all its customers, and since charge customers often pay their bills within the discount period, Rainier Plumbing Supply sets up a Sales Discounts Debit column in the cash receipts journal. Note that Rainier Plumbing Supply is a wholesaler. Therefore, a column for Sales Tax Payable is not used since few states levy a tax on sales at the wholesale level.

CASH RECEIPTS JOURNAL   PAGE __18__

	DATE		ACCOUNT CREDITED	POST. REF.	CASH DEBIT	SALES DISCOUNTS DEBIT	ACCOUNTS RECEIVABLE CREDIT	SALES CREDIT	OTHER ACCOUNTS CREDIT	
1	20–									1
2	Aug.	10	Betterbuilt Homes Co.		1 5 3 3 56	3 1 30	1 5 6 4 86			2
3										3

Several other transactions of Rainier Plumbing Supply involve increases in cash during August. Remember that the standard credit terms for all charge customers are 2/10, n/30.

Aug. 15 Cash sales for first half of the month, $2,460.
16 Received check from Gonzales Construction for $1,366.12 in payment of invoice no. 1322, less cash discount ($1,394.00 − $27.88 = $1,366.12).
17 Received payment on a promissory note given by John R. Bryant, $500 principal, plus $10 interest. (The amount of the interest is recorded in Interest Income.)

Aug. 21 Received check from Carmel Hardware for $3,696.80 in payment of invoice no. 1324, less cash discount ($3,772.24 − $75.44 = $3,696.80).

23 Sold equipment for cash at cost, $126.

26 C. F. Rainier, the owner, invested an additional $4,000 cash in the business.

26 Received a check from Howard and Sons, Inc., for $2,392.18 in payment of invoice no. 1325, less cash discount ($2,441.00 − $48.82 = $2,392.18).

30 Received check from Green Plumbing and Heating for $1,675.80 in payment of invoice no. 1326, less cash discount ($1,710.00 − $34.20 = $1,675.80).

31 Cash sales for second half of the month, $2,620.

31 Received check from Arnold, Inc., for $1,116 in payment of invoice no. 1321. (This is longer than the ten-day period, so the cash discount is not allowed.)

Rainier Plumbing Supply records these transactions in its cash receipts journal (Figure 3).

After that has been done, the company's accountant proves the equality of debits and credits:

> **REMEMBER!**
>
> When journalizing a cash receipt involving a sales discount, be sure to credit Accounts Receivable for the total amount of the sales transaction.

Debit Totals	
Cash	$21,496.46
Sales Discounts	217.64
	$21,714.10

Credit Totals	
Accounts Receivable	$11,998.10
Sales	5,080.00
Other Accounts	4,636.00
	$21,714.10

FIGURE 3

CASH RECEIPTS JOURNAL PAGE __18__

DATE	ACCOUNT CREDITED	POST. REF.	CASH DEBIT	SALES DISCOUNTS DEBIT	ACCOUNTS RECEIVABLE CREDIT	SALES CREDIT	OTHER ACCOUNTS CREDIT
20–							
Aug. 10	Betterbuilt Homes Co.	✓	1 5 3 3 56	3 1 30	1 5 6 4 86		
15	————	—	2 4 6 0 00			2 4 6 0 00	
16	Gonzales Construction	✓	1 3 6 6 12	2 7 88	1 3 9 4 00		
17	Notes Receivable	112					5 0 0 00
	Interest Income	422	5 1 0 00				1 0 00
21	Carmel Hardware	✓	3 6 9 6 80	7 5 44	3 7 7 2 24		
23	Equipment	124	1 2 6 00				1 2 6 00
26	C. F. Rainier, Capital	311	4 0 0 0 00				4 0 0 0 00
26	Howard and Sons, Inc.	✓	2 3 9 2 18	4 8 82	2 4 4 1 00		
30	Green Plumbing and Heating	✓	1 6 7 5 80	3 4 20	1 7 1 0 00		
31	————	—	2 6 2 0 00			2 6 2 0 00	
31	Arnold, Inc.	✓	1 1 1 6 00		1 1 1 6 00		
31			21 4 9 6 46	2 1 7 64	11 9 9 8 10	5 0 8 0 00	4 6 3 6 00
			(1 1 1)	(4 1 3)	(1 1 3)	(4 1 1)	(X)

SALES RETURNS AND ALLOWANCES AND SALES DISCOUNTS ON AN INCOME STATEMENT

In the fundamental accounting equation, to be consistent with the income statement, we placed Sales Returns and Allowances and Sales Discounts under Sales with the plus and minus signs reversed. Both accounts are contra revenue accounts, so we subtract their totals from Sales on the income statement. Here is the Revenue from Sales section of the annual income statement of Rainier Plumbing Supply.

Rainier Plumbing Supply
Income Statement
For Year Ended December 31, 20—

Revenue from Sales:			
Sales		$255 1 8 0 00	
Less: Sales Returns and Allowances	$ 8 4 0 00		
Sales Discounts	1 8 8 0 00	2 7 2 0 00	
Net Sales			$252 4 6 0 00

THE CASH PAYMENTS JOURNAL: SERVICE ENTERPRISE

The **cash payments journal**, as the name implies, is a special journal used to record all transactions in which cash goes out, or decreases. When the cash payments journal is used, all transactions in which cash is credited *must* be recorded in it. This journal may be used for either a service or a merchandising business.

To get acquainted with the cash payments journal, let's list some typical transactions of a professional service firm (such as an attorney's office) that result in a decrease in cash. To illustrate, we record the following transactions in T accounts:

May 2 Paid Brown Paper Co., a creditor, on account, Ck. No. 2063, $1,220.

Accounts Payable		Cash	
−	+	+	−
1,220			1,220

May 4 Paid cash for liability insurance, Ck. No. 2064, $4,890.

Prepaid Insurance		Cash	
+	−	+	−
4,890			4,890

May 5 Paid wages for two weeks, Ck. No. 2065, $6,220 (previously recorded in the payroll entry).

Wages Payable		Cash	
−	+	+	−
6,220			6,220

May 6 Paid rent for the month, Ck. No. 2066, $2,950.

Rent Expense		Cash	
+	−	+	−
2,950			2,950

The same transactions are now shown in general journal form.

	DATE		DESCRIPTION	POST. REF.	DEBIT	CREDIT	
	\multicolumn{7}{l}{GENERAL JOURNAL PAGE ____}					
1	20–						1
2	May	2	Accounts Payable,				2
3			Brown Paper Co.		1 2 2 0 00		3
4			Cash			1 2 2 0 00	4
5			Paid on account, Ck. No. 2063.				5
6							6
7		4	Prepaid Insurance		4 8 9 0 00		7
8			Cash			4 8 9 0 00	8
9			Paid cash for liability				9
10			insurance, Ck. No. 2064.				10
11							11
12		5	Wages Payable		6 2 2 0 00		12
13			Cash			6 2 2 0 00	13
14			Paid wages for two weeks,				14
15			Ck. No. 2065.				15
16							16
17		6	Rent Expense		2 9 5 0 00		17
18			Cash			2 9 5 0 00	18
19			Paid rent for month,				19
20			Ck. No. 2066.				20

Let's analyze these four transactions. The first one would occur frequently, as payments to creditors are made several times a month. Of the last three transactions, the debit to Wages Payable might occur twice a month, the debit to Rent Expense once a month, and the debit to Prepaid Insurance only occasionally.

It is logical to include a Cash Credit column in a cash payments journal because all transactions recorded in this journal involve a decrease in cash. Since payments to creditors are made often, there should also be an

OBJECTIVE 4

Journalize transactions in a cash payments journal for a service enterprise.

Accounts Payable Debit column. You can set up any other column that is used often enough to warrant it. Otherwise, an Other Accounts Debit column takes care of all the other transactions.

Now let's record these same transactions in a cash payments journal and include a column titled Ck. No. If you think a moment, you will see that this is consistent with good management of cash. All expenditures except Petty Cash expenditures should be paid for by check. Let's repeat the transactions.

May   2   Paid Brown Paper Co., a creditor, on account, Ck. No. 2063, $1,220.
         4   Paid cash for liability insurance, Ck. No. 2064, $4,890.
         5   Paid wages for two weeks, Ck. No. 2065, $6,220 (previously recorded in the payroll entry).
         6   Paid rent for the month, Ck. No. 2066, $2,950.

CASH PAYMENTS JOURNAL   PAGE __62__

	DATE	CK. NO.	ACCOUNT DEBITED	POST. REF.	OTHER ACCOUNTS DEBIT	ACCOUNTS PAYABLE DEBIT	CASH CREDIT	
1	20–							1
2	May 2	2063	Brown Paper Co.			1 2 2 0 00	1 2 2 0 00	2
3	4	2064	Prepaid Insurance		4 8 9 0 00		4 8 9 0 00	3
4	5	2065	Wages Payable		6 2 2 0 00		6 2 2 0 00	4
5	6	2066	Rent Expense		2 9 5 0 00		2 9 5 0 00	5
6								6

Other transactions involving decreases in cash during May are as follows:

May   7   Paid a one-year premium for fire insurance, Ck. No. 2067, $360.
         9   Paid Morris, Inc., a creditor, on account, Ck. No. 2068, $418.
       11   Issued Ck. No. 2069 in payment of delivery expense, $62.
       14   Paid Russet and Son, a creditor, on account, Ck. No. 2070, $110.
       16   Issued Ck. No. 2071 to the Logan State Bank for a Note Payable, $6,396, $6,000 on the principal and $396 interest.
       19   Voided Ck. No. 2072.
       19   Bought equipment from Snyder Company, Ck. No. 2073, $200.
       20   Paid wages for two weeks, Ck. No. 2074, $3,340 (previously recorded in the payroll entry).
       22   Issued Ck. No. 2075 to Scheel Advertising Agency for advertising, $94 (not previously recorded).
       26   Paid telephone bill, Ck. No. 2076, $326.
       31   Issued Ck. No. 2077 for freight bill on equipment purchased on May 19, $58.
       31   Paid Trask & Co., a creditor, on account, Ck. No. 2078, $160.

You should list all checks in consecutive order, even those checks that must be voided. In this way, *every* check is accounted for, which is necessary for internal control.

These transactions are recorded in the cash payments journal illustrated in Figure 4. Notice that an (X) is placed under the Other Accounts column. That means "do not post—the individual figures have already been posted."

TRADE DISCOUNTS

OBJECTIVE 8

Journalize transactions involving trade discounts.

Manufacturers and wholesalers of many lines of products publish annual catalogs listing their products at retail prices. These organizations offer their customers substantial reductions (often as much as 40 percent) from the list or catalog prices. The reductions from the list prices are called **trade discounts**. Trade discounts are not journalized. Remember, firms grant cash discounts for prompt payment of invoices. Trade discounts are *not related* to cash payments. Manufacturers and wholesalers use trade discounts to avoid the high cost of reprinting catalogs when selling prices change. To change prices, the manufacturer or wholesaler simply issues a sheet showing a new list of trade discounts to be applied to the catalog prices. Trade discounts can also be used to differentiate between classes of customers. For example, a manufacturer may use one schedule of trade discounts for wholesalers and another schedule for retailers.

Firms may quote trade discounts as a single percentage. *Example:* A distributor of furnaces grants a single discount of 40 percent off the listed catalog price of $8,000. In this case, the selling price is calculated as follows:

List or catalog price	$8,000
Less trade discount of 40% ($8,000 × .40)	3,200
Selling price	$4,800

Neither the seller nor the buyer records trade discounts in the accounts; they enter only the selling price. Using T accounts, the furnace distributor records the sale like this:

Accounts Receivable		Sales	
+	−	−	+
4,800			4,800

The buyer records the purchase as follows:

Purchases		Accounts Payable	
+	−	−	+
4,800			4,800

Firms may also quote trade discounts as a chain, or series, of percentages. For example, a distributor of automobile parts grants discounts of 30 percent, 10 percent, and 10 percent off the listed catalog price of $900. In this case, the selling price is calculated as follows:

List or catalog price	$900.00
Less first trade discount of 30% ($900 × .30)	270.00
Remainder after first discount	$630.00
Less second trade discount of 10% ($630 × .10)	63.00
Remainder after second discount	$567.00
Less third discount of 10% ($567 × .10)	56.70
Selling price	$510.30

Using T accounts, the automobile parts distributor records the sale as follows:

Accounts Receivable		Sales	
+	−	−	+
510.30			510.30

The buyer records the purchase as follows:

Purchases		Accounts Payable	
+	−	−	+
510.30			510.30

In the situation involving a chain of discounts, the additional discounts are granted for large-volume transactions, either in dollar amount or in size of shipment, such as carload lots.

Cash discounts could also apply in situations involving trade discounts. *Example:* Suppose that the credit terms of the preceding sale include a cash discount of 2/10, n/30, and that the buyer pays the invoice within ten days. The seller applies the cash discount to the selling price. The seller records the transaction as shown in the following T accounts:

Cash		Sales Discounts		Accounts Receivable	
+	−	+	−	+	−
500.09		10.21			510.30

The buyer records the transaction as follows:

Cash		Purchases Discounts		Accounts Payable	
+	−	−	+	−	+
	500.09		10.21	510.30	

COMPARISON OF THE FIVE TYPES OF JOURNALS

We have now looked at four special journals and the general journal. It is very important for a business to select and use the journals that provide the most efficient accounting system possible. Figure 8 summarizes the applications of the journals we have discussed and the correct procedures for using them.

Recommended Order of Posting to the Subsidiary Ledgers and the General Ledger

To avoid errors and negative balances in accounts, post from the special journals in this order:

1. Sales journal
2. Purchases journal
3. Cash receipts journal
4. Cash payments journal

Types of Transactions

| Sale of merchandise on account | Purchase of merchandise on account | Receipt of cash | Payment of cash | All other |

Evidenced by Source Documents

| Sales invoice | Purchase invoice | Credit card receipts
Cash
Checks | Check stub | Miscellaneous |

Types of Journals

| Sales journal | Purchases journal | Cash receipts journal | Cash payments journal | General journal |

Posting to Ledger Accounts

| *Individual amounts posted daily to the accounts receivable ledger and the total posted monthly to the general ledger.* | *Individual amounts posted daily to the accounts payable ledger and the totals of the special columns posted monthly to the general ledger.* | *Individual amounts in the Accounts Receivable Credit column posted daily to the accounts receivable ledger.*

Individual amounts in the Other Accounts columns posted daily to the general ledger.

Totals of special columns posted monthly to the general ledger. | *Individual amounts in the Accounts Payable Debit column posted daily to the accounts payable ledger.*

Individual amounts in the Other Accounts columns posted daily to the general ledger.

Totals of special columns posted monthly to the general ledger. | *Entries posted daily to the subsidiary ledgers and the general ledger.* |

FIGURE 8

Posting of general journal entries depends on the dates of the specific transactions.

Picture the T accounts involved in transactions. Here are examples of the transactions we have introduced.

REMEMBER!

Again, always think of the T accounts involved in each transaction.

Sold merchandise, $500, plus $40 sales tax, and the customer used a bank charge card. Bank discount rate is 4 percent.

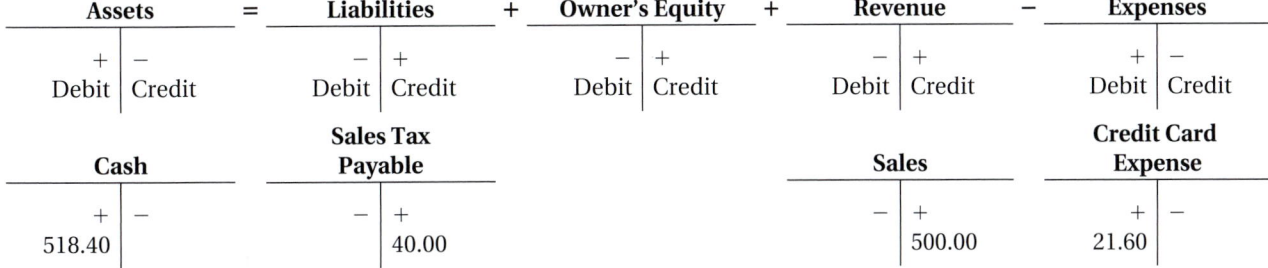

Assets		=	Liabilities		+	Owner's Equity		+	Revenue		−	Expenses	
+	−		−	+		−	+		−	+		+	−
Debit	Credit		Debit	Credit		Debit	Credit		Debit	Credit		Debit	Credit
Cash			**Sales Tax Payable**						**Sales**			**Credit Card Expense**	
+	−		−	+					−	+		+	−
518.40				40.00						500.00		21.60	

Received check from Betterbuilt Homes Co. for $1,533.56 in payment of $1,564.86 invoice less $31.30 cash discount.

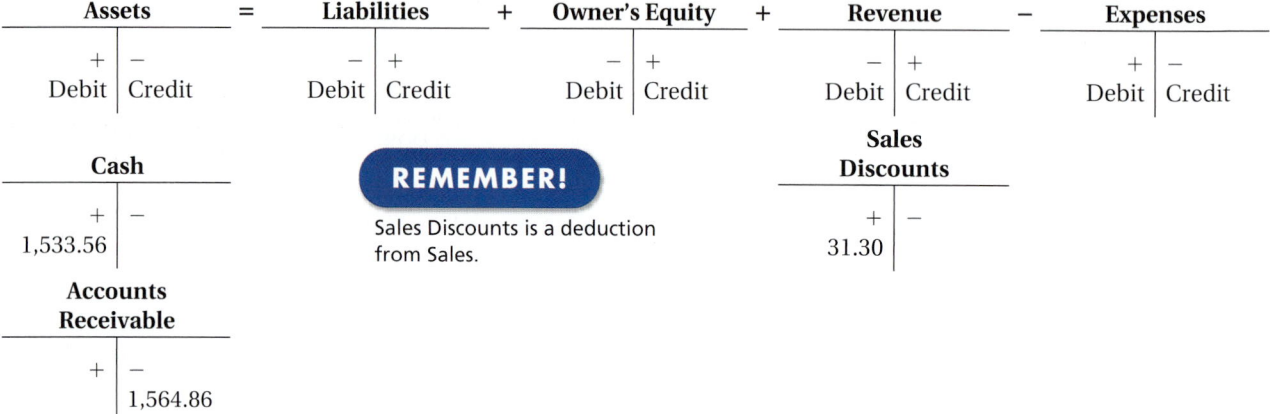

Issued check to Collins, Inc., in payment of $1,795.50 invoice less $34.20 cash discount.

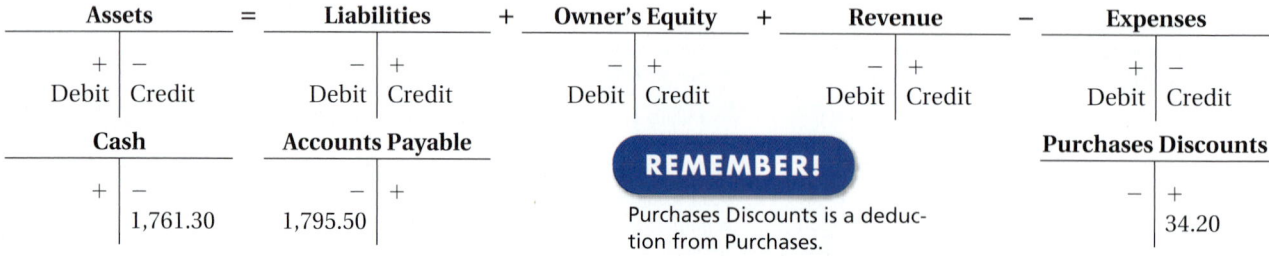

CHAPTER REVIEW

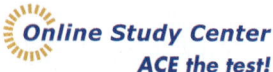

Online Study Center
ACE the test!

Review of Performance Objectives

1. Journalize transactions for a merchandising business in a cash receipts journal.

   A transaction for a retail merchandising business can be recorded on one line in a cash receipts journal. The cash receipts journal usually contains the following columns: Date, Account Credited, Post. Ref., Cash Debit, Credit Card Expense Debit, Accounts Receivable Credit, Sales Credit, Sales Tax Payable Credit, and Other Accounts Credit.

2. Post from a cash receipts journal to a general ledger and an accounts receivable ledger.

   The accountant posts daily from the Accounts Receivable Credit column to the individual charge customers' accounts in the accounts receivable ledger. After posting, the accountant puts a check mark (✓) in the Post. Ref. column. The accountant also posts the amounts in the Other Accounts Credit column daily and records the account numbers in the Post. Ref. column. The special columns are posted as totals at the end of the month. The accountant then writes the account numbers in parentheses under the totals. An (X) below the total of the Other Accounts Credit column shows that amounts are posted individually and the total is not posted.

3. Determine cash discounts according to credit terms, and record cash receipts from charge customers who are entitled to deduct the cash discount.

The same cash discount is available to all the supplier's customers. The amount of the discount is determined by multiplying the invoice total (excluding freight charges and any returns and allowances) by the cash discount rate (usually 1 or 2 percent). The amount of the discount is recorded as a debit to Sales Discounts.

4. Journalize transactions in a cash payments journal for a service enterprise.

A cash payment by a service enterprise can be handled on one line in a cash payments journal. The cash payments journal usually contains the following columns: Date, Ck. No., Account Debited, Post. Ref., Other Accounts Debit, Accounts Payable Debit, and Cash Credit.

5. Post from a cash payments journal to a general ledger and an accounts payable ledger.

The accountant posts daily from the Accounts Payable Debit column to the individual suppliers' accounts in the accounts payable ledger. After posting, the accountant puts a check mark (✓) in the Post. Ref. column. The accountant also posts the amounts in the Other Accounts Debit column daily and records the account numbers in the Post. Ref. column. The special columns are posted as totals at the end of the month. The accountant then writes the account numbers in parentheses under the totals. An (X) below the total of the Other Accounts Debit column shows that amounts are posted individually and the total is not posted.

6. Journalize transactions involving cash discounts in a cash payments journal for a merchandising enterprise.

A cash payment by a merchandising enterprise that includes a purchase discount can be recorded on one line in a cash payments journal. The cash payments journal usually contains the following columns: Date, Ck. No., Account Debited, Post. Ref., Other Accounts Debit, Accounts Payable Debit, Purchases Discounts Credit, and Cash Credit.

7. Journalize transactions in a check register.

Transactions can be recorded on one line in a check register. The check register is similar to the cash payments journal. However, the check register has an additional column entitled Payee, and instead of a Cash Credit column there is often a column with the name of the bank (City Bank Credit, for example).

8. Journalize transactions involving trade discounts.

In transactions involving trade discounts, the trade discounts are deducted from the list prices to arrive at the selling prices. Both sellers and buyers record the transactions at the selling prices.

Glossary

Bank charge card A bank credit card, like the credit cards used by millions of private citizens. The cardholder pays what she or he owes directly to the issuing bank. The business deposits the credit card receipts; the amount of the deposit equals the total of the receipts, less a discount deducted by the bank. (392)

Cash discount The amount a customer can deduct for paying a bill within a specified period of time; used to encourage prompt payment. Not all sellers offer cash discounts. (397)

Cash payments journal A special journal used to record all transactions involving cash payments or decreases. (400)

Cash receipts journal A special journal used to record all transactions involving cash receipts or increases. (392)

Check register A journal in which checks are listed as they are written. A check register replaces a cash payments journal. (407)

Credit period The time the seller allows the buyer before full payment on a charge sale has to be made. (397)

Notes Payable The account containing the balance of promissory notes. (395)

Promissory note A written promise to pay a specified amount at a specified time. (395)

Trade discount A substantial discount from the list or catalog prices of goods, granted by the seller; not recorded by the buyer or the seller. (409)

QUESTIONS, EXERCISES, AND CASES

Discussion Questions

1. What are the normal balances of (a) Purchases? (b) Sales Discounts? (c) Purchases Returns and Allowances? (d) Sales? (e) Purchases Discounts? (f) Sales Returns and Allowances?

2. What does an X under the total of a special journal's Other Accounts column signify?

3. Explain the following credit terms: (a) n/30; (b) 2/10, n/60; (c) 1/15, EOM, n/30.

4. In a cash receipts journal, both the Accounts Receivable Credit column and the Cash Debit column were mistakenly underadded by $700. How will this error be discovered?

5. If a cash payments journal is supposed to save writing, why are there so many entries in the Other Accounts Debit column?

6. Describe the posting procedure for a cash payments journal with an Other Accounts Debit column and several special columns, including an Accounts Payable Debit column.

7. An electronics business purchased speakers for resale. The total of the invoice is $2,580, and it is subject to trade discounts of 15 percent, 10 percent, and 5 percent. Compute the amount the dealer will pay for the speakers.

8. What is the difference between a cash discount and a trade discount?

Exercises

P.O. 1

Describe a recorded transaction involving sale of merchandise with sales tax, paid by credit card.

Exercise 11-1 Describe the transaction recorded.

Cash	Sales Tax Payable	Sales	Credit Card Expense
322.56	16.00	320.00	13.44

P.O. 1,3

Label column headings.

Exercise 11-2 Label the blanks in the column heads as either debit or credit.

CASH RECEIPTS JOURNAL   PAGE _____

DATE	ACCOUNT CREDITED	POST. REF.	OTHER ACCOUNTS	ACCOUNTS RECEIVABLE	SALES	SALES DISCOUNTS	CASH

P.O. 5,6

Describe posted transactions.

Exercise 11-3 Describe the transactions recorded in the following T accounts:

Cash			Accounts Payable			Purchases	
(c)	1,176	(b)	150	(a)	1,350	(a)	1,350
		(c)	1,200				

Purchases Returns and Allowances		Purchases Discounts	
(b)	150	(c)	24

P.O. 6

Calculate amounts paid for merchandise purchases involving returns and cash discounts.

Exercise 11-4 For the following purchases of merchandise, determine the amount of cash to be paid:

Purchase	Invoice Date	Credit Terms	FOB	Amount of Purchase	Freight Charges	Total Invoice Amount	Returns and Allowances	Date Paid
a.	June 1	2/10, n/30	Destination	$550	—	$ 550	—	June 30
b.	June 12	1/10, n/30	Destination	700	—	700	$100	June 21
c.	June 14	2/10, n/30	Shipping point	940	$60	1,000	—	June 20
d.	June 21	n/30	Shipping point	830	70	900	130	July 20
e.	June 24	1/10, n/30	Shipping point	760	50	810	90	July 3

P.O. 1,6

Designate the appropriate journal.

Exercise 11-5 Indicate the journal in which each of the following transactions should be recorded. Assume a three-column purchases journal.

Transaction	Journal				
	S	P	CR	CP	J
a. Paid a creditor on account.					
b. Bought merchandise on account.					
c. Sold merchandise for cash.					
d. Adjusted for insurance expired.					
e. Received payment on account from a charge customer.					
f. Received a credit memo for merchandise returned.					
g. Bought equipment on credit.					
h. Sold merchandise on account.					
i. Recorded a customer's NSF check.					
j. Invested personal noncash assets in the business.					
k. Withdrew cash for personal use.					

Exercise 11-6 Record the following transactions in general journal form:

May	4	Sold merchandise on account to Seymour, Inc., $640; terms 2/10, n/30.
	10	Bought merchandise on account from Mann Company, $750; terms 1/10, n/60; FOB shipping point.
	11	Paid Gordon Freight Lines for freight charges on merchandise purchased from Mann Company, $22.
	13	Received full payment from Seymour, Inc.
	14	Received a credit memo from Mann Company for defective merchandise returned, $104.
	19	Paid Mann Company in full within the discount period.
	28	Bought merchandise on account from Bean Company, $900; terms 2/10, n/30; freight prepaid and added to the invoice, $47 (total $947).

Exercise 11-7 Record the following transactions in general journal form, first on the books of the seller (Fry Company) and then on the books of the buyer (Lee Company).

Fry Company

a. Sold merchandise on account to Lee Company, $1,500; terms 2/10, n/30.
b. Issued a credit memo to Lee Company for damaged merchandise, $100.
c. Lee Company paid the account in full within the discount period.

Lee Company

a. Purchased merchandise on account from Fry Company, $1,500; terms 2/10, n/30.
b. Received a credit memo from Fry Company for damaged merchandise, $100.
c. Paid Fry Company in full within the discount period.

Exercise 11-8 Record general journal entries to correct the errors described below. Assume that the incorrect entries were posted in the same period in which the errors occurred.

a. A freight cost of $57 incurred on equipment purchased for use in the business was debited to Freight In.
b. The issuance of a credit memo to Merino Company for $126 for merchandise returned was recorded as a debit to Purchases Returns and Allowances and a credit to Accounts Receivable, Merino Company.
c. A cash purchase of $114 of store supplies for the business was recorded as office supplies.
d. A cash sale of $92 to M. A. Marx was recorded as a sale on account.
e. A purchase of merchandise from Ames Company in the amount of $1,000 with a 30 percent trade discount was recorded as a debit to Purchases and a credit to Accounts Payable of $1,000 each.

1. Who pays for and who receives money from a credit card transaction?
2. If Arcadia Bank pays the merchant 98 percent of the sale amount, how might the grocer record the sale in its cash receipts journal?

CONSIDER AND COMMUNICATE

You are the manager of the Accounts Receivable Department for a merchandising business. Your billing clerk sent a bill for $2 to a customer who had charged $100 in goods (including sales tax) with terms 2/10, n/30. The customer has called and indicated his displeasure; he can't understand an error like this, since he paid on time. Explain to your billing clerk why Accounts Receivable is credited for $100 and not $98. How was permission given to send less than the full amount?

WHAT'S WRONG WITH THIS PICTURE?

Suppose we collected cash from a charge customer, and our debit was to Cash and the credit to Sales. How and when would this error be discovered?

CRITICAL THINKING

You work for Garson Plumbing Supply. You are responsible for training a new accounting clerk. He has the following questions for you to answer about this invoice:

Garson Plumbing Supply
14 Indiana Avenue
Chicago, Illinois 60612

No. 320

INVOICE

SOLD TO **C. P. Lund Company**
5210 Gilman Avenue
San Diego, CA 92102

DATE: **August 1, 20–**
ORDER NO.: **5384**
SHIPPED BY: **Faster Freight**
TERMS: **2/10, n/30**
SALESPERSON: **H. T.**

QUANTITY	DESCRIPTION	UNIT PRICE	TOTAL
6	Olin single-control tub shower faucet #44B652	51 50	309 00
6	Olin dual-control washerless lavatory faucet #59B641	22 20	133 20
12	Olin massage shower head, antique brass #37B411	11 56	138 72
	Subtotal		580 92
	Freight		63 80
	Total		644 72

1. Who is the buyer?
2. Who is paying the freight?

3. What is the customer's order number?
4. What percentage of the goods bought is the cost of the freight?
5. What are the credit terms and what do they mean?
6. How much will the buyer actually have to pay if the money is received within ten days?
7. What is the dollar amount of the discount?
8. Who receives the discount?
9. What is the due date for payment to get the discount?
10. Why would a seller give a buyer a discount?

A QUESTION OF ETHICS

When the new accountant started to work, the owner took him out to lunch each Friday to discuss problems, progress, and suggestions to improve the business. One Friday, the owner couldn't go to lunch with the accountant. The accountant took the money for his lunch from petty cash and charged it to the owner's drawing account. He reasoned that the owner always took him to lunch on Friday, and he didn't have money for lunch. This happened several Fridays during the year. Was this a fair assumption for the accountant to make? Was it ethical?

PROBLEM SET A

For additional help, see the demonstration problem at the beginning of each chapter in your Working Papers.

P.O. 1,2

Problem 11-1A Winters and Company, a retail flooring store, sells on the bases of (1) cash, (2) charge accounts, and (3) bank credit cards. The following transactions involved cash receipts for the firm during May of this year. The state imposes a 7 percent sales tax on retail sales. The bank charges 4 percent on the total of the credit card sales plus sales tax. (For all sales involving credit cards, record credit card expense at the time of the sale.)

May
8   Total cash sales for the week, $1,248, plus $87.36 sales tax.
8   Total sales for the week paid for by bank credit cards, $1,560, plus $109.20 sales tax.
11 D. C. Winters, the owner, invested an additional $2,500.
11 Collected cash from N. D. Payson, a charge customer, $71.70.
12 Sold store equipment at cost for cash, $360.
15 Total cash sales for the week, $1,780, plus $124.60 sales tax.
15 Total sales for the week paid for by bank credit cards, $1,130, plus $79.10 sales tax.
19 Borrowed $2,300 from the bank, receiving the same in cash and giving the bank a promissory note.
21 Collected cash from R. Binder, a charge customer, $85.
22 Total cash sales for the week, $2,834, plus $198.38 sales tax.
22 Total sales for the week paid for by bank credit cards, $1,385, plus $96.95 sales tax.
24 Received cash as refund for the return of merchandise purchased, $127.
26 Collected cash from C. Fisher, a charge customer, $147.

May 31 Total sales for the week paid for by bank credit cards, $362, plus $25.34 sales tax.

31 Collected cash from R. D. Thompson, a charge customer, $120.

31 Total cash sales for the remainder of the month, $2,892, plus $202.44 sales tax.

Check Figure

Total Sales Credit, $13,191

Instructions

1. Open the following accounts in the accounts receivable ledger and record the May 1 balances as given: R. Binder, $85; C. Fisher, $147; N. D. Payson, $71.70; S. R. Potts, $114.72; R. D. Thompson, $176.47; F. N. Warren, $79.52. Place a check mark in the Post. Ref. column.
2. Record a balance of $674.41 in the Accounts Receivable controlling account as of May 1.
3. Record the transactions in the cash receipts journal beginning with page 62.
4. Post daily to the accounts receivable ledger.
5. Total and rule the cash receipts journal.
6. Prove the equality of debit and credit totals.
7. Post to the Accounts Receivable controlling account in the general ledger.

P.O. 1,3

Problem 11-2A Parker Company sells candy wholesale to vending machine operators. Terms of sales on account are 2/10, n/30, FOB shipping point. The following transactions involving cash receipts and sales of merchandise took place in May of this year:

May 1 Received $1,960 cash from L. Reagon in payment of April 22 invoice of $2,000, less cash discount.

4 Received $896 cash in payment of $800 note receivable and interest of $96.

7 Received $784 cash from K. L. Shaw in payment of April 29 invoice of $800, less cash discount.

8 Sold merchandise on account to D. Pang, invoice no. 272, $396.

16 Cash sales for first half of May, $3,367.

17 Received cash from D. Pang in payment of invoice no. 272, less cash discount.

20 Received $325 cash from L. N. Saranden in payment of April 16 invoice, no discount.

21 Sold merchandise on account to R. O. Winston, invoice no. 285, $935.

24 Received $220 cash refund for return of defective equipment that was originally bought for cash.

27 Sold merchandise on account to R. James, invoice no. 292, $450.

31 Cash sales for second half of May, $3,956.

Check Figure

Total sales on account, $1,781

Instructions

1. Journalize the transactions for May in the cash receipts journal and the sales journal.
2. Total and rule the journals.
3. Prove the equality of debit and credit totals.

P.O. 7

Problem 11-3A Martinson Bookshop uses a check register to keep track of expenditures. The following transactions occurred during February of this year.

Feb. 3 Issued Ck. No. 4312, $804.68, to Kendall Company for invoice no. 68172, recorded previously for $821.10, less 2 percent cash discount.

4 Issued Ck. No. 4313 to King Express Company for freight charges, $46, for books purchased.

6 Issued Ck. No. 4314 to Morton Land Company for monthly rent, $590.

11 Received and paid bill for advertising in the *Ballard News,* $98, Ck. No. 4315.

11 Issued Ck. No. 4316, $970.20, to Corwin Book Company for invoice no. A3322, recorded previously for $980, less 1 percent cash discount.

17 Paid wages recorded previously for first half of February, $598; Ck. No. 4317.

21 R. D. Martinson, the owner, withdrew $800 for personal use; Ck. No. 4318.

26 Issued Ck. No. 4319 to First National Bank for payment on bank loan, $560, consisting of $500 on the principal and $60 interest.

27 Issued Ck. No. 4320, $877, to Grayson Publishing Company for invoice no. 7768, recorded previously (no discount).

28 Voided Ck. No. 4321.

28 Paid wages recorded previously for second half of February, $552; Ck. No. 4322.

Check Figure

Total First Nat'l Bank Credit, $5,895.88

Instructions

1. Record the transactions in the check register.
2. Total and rule the check register.
3. Prove the equality of the debit and credit totals.

P.O. 1,2,3,5,6

Problem 11-4A The following transactions were completed by Hammel Auto Supply during January, which is the first month of this fiscal year. Terms of sale are 2/10, n/30.

Jan. 2 Issued Ck. No. 6981 for monthly rent, $775.

2 J. Hammel, the owner, invested an additional $3,500 in the business.

4 Bought merchandise on account from Vaughn and Company, $2,930, invoice no. A691, dated January 2; terms 2/10, n/30.

4 Received check from Vessey Appliance for $980 in payment of $1,000 invoice less discount.

4 Sold merchandise on account to L. Parker, invoice no. 6483, $850.

6 Received check from Peterson, Inc., $637, in payment of $650 invoice less discount.

7 Issued Ck. No. 6982, $588, to Franklin and Son, in payment of invoice no. C1272 for $600 less discount.

7 Bought supplies on account from Duncan Office Supply, $108, invoice no. 1906B; terms net 30 days. (Debit Supplies Expense—Chapter 12 explains when to use the asset account Supplies.)

7 Sold merchandise on account to English and Cole, invoice no. 6484, $787.

9 Issued credit memo no. 43 to L. Parker, $54, for merchandise returned.

11 Cash sales for January 1 through January 10, $4,863.20.

11 Issued Ck. No. 6983, $2,871.40, to Vaughn and Company, in payment of $2,930 invoice less discount.

Jan. 14 Sold merchandise on account to Vessey Appliance, invoice no. 6485, $2,050.

18 Bought merchandise on account from Crosby Products, $4,854, invoice no. 7281D, dated January 16; terms 2/10, n/60; FOB shipping point, freight prepaid and added to the invoice, $147 (total $5,001).

21 Issued Ck. No. 6984, $194, to *The Newsline* for advertising not recorded previously. (Miscellaneous Expense)

21 Cash sales for January 11 through January 20, $4,591.

23 Issued Ck. No. 6985 to Fastest Freight, $96, for freight charges on merchandise purchased on January 4.

23 Received credit memo no. 163, $376, from Crosby Products for merchandise returned.

29 Sold merchandise on account to Bryan Supply, invoice no. 6486, $1,835.

31 Cash sales for January 21 through January 31, $4,428.

31 Issued Ck. No. 6986, $53, to M. Doore for miscellaneous expenses not recorded previously.

31 Recorded payroll entry from the payroll register: total salaries, $6,200; employees' federal income tax withheld, $872; FICA tax withheld, $474.30.

31 Recorded the payroll taxes: FICA, $474.30; state unemployment tax, $334.80; federal unemployment tax, $49.60.

31 Issued Ck. No. 6987, $4,853.70, for salaries for the month.

31 J. Hammel, the owner, withdrew $1,000 for personal use, Ck. No. 6988.

Check Figure

Trial balance totals, $65,288.80

Instructions

1. Record the transactions for January, using a sales journal, page 73; a purchases journal, page 56; a cash receipts journal, page 38; a cash payments journal, page 45; a general journal, page 100. The chart of accounts is as follows:

111	Cash	311	J. Hammel, Capital
113	Accounts Receivable	312	J. Hammel, Drawing
114	Merchandise Inventory		
116	Prepaid Insurance	411	Sales
121	Equipment	412	Sales Returns and Allowances
		413	Sales Discounts
212	Accounts Payable		
215	Salaries Payable	511	Purchases
216	Employees' Federal Income Tax Payable	512	Purchases Returns and Allowances
		513	Purchases Discounts
217	FICA Tax Payable	514	Freight In
218	State Unemployment Tax Payable		
		621	Salary Expense
219	Federal Unemployment Tax Payable	622	Payroll Tax Expense
		625	Supplies Expense
		627	Rent Expense
		631	Miscellaneous Expense

2. Post daily all entries involving customer accounts to the accounts receivable ledger.

3. Post daily all entries involving creditor accounts to the accounts payable ledger.

4. Post daily those entries involving the Other Accounts columns and the general journal to the general ledger. Write the owner's name in the Capital and Drawing accounts.

5. Add the columns of the special journals, and prove the equality of debit and credit totals on scratch paper.
6. Post the appropriate totals of the special journals to the general ledger.
7. Prepare a trial balance.
8. Prepare a schedule of accounts receivable and a schedule of accounts payable. Do the totals equal the balances of the related controlling accounts?

Instructions for General Ledger Software

1. Record the transactions in the sales journal, purchases journal, cash receipts journal, cash payments journal, and general journal.
   a. For efficiency, analyze the transactions, indicate what journal each transaction goes into, and key the entries in five groups or batches, one for each journal.
   b. Because the program uses a single-column purchases journal, add the amount of the freight to the amount of purchases.
2. Print the journals.
3. Post the amounts from the sales, purchases, cash receipts, cash payments, and general journals.
4. Print a trial balance.
5. Print a schedule of accounts receivable and compare the total with the balance of the Accounts Receivable controlling account.
6. Print a schedule of accounts payable and compare the total with the balance of the Accounts Payable controlling account.

PROBLEM SET B

For additional help, see the demonstration problem at the beginning of each chapter in your Working Papers.

P.O. 1,2

Problem 11-1B Bilden Furniture, a home furnishings store, sells on the bases of (1) cash, (2) charge accounts, and (3) bank credit cards. The following transactions involve cash receipts for the firm for November of this year. The state imposes a 7 percent sales tax on retail sales. The bank charges 4 percent of the total credit card sales plus sales tax. (For all sales involving credit cards, record credit card expense at the time of the sale.)

Nov.   7   Total cash sales for the week, $1,800, plus $126 sales tax.
     7   Total sales from bank credit cards for the week, $1,900, plus $133 sales tax.
   11   M. R. Victor, the owner, invested an additional $4,800.
   12   Sold office equipment for cash at cost, $358.
   12   Collected cash from T. R. Alex, a charge customer, $55.80.
   14   Total cash sales for the week, $3,490.05, plus $244.30 sales tax.
   14   Total sales from bank credit cards for the week, $1,540, plus $107.80 sales tax.
   18   Collected cash from N. P. Tempe, a charge customer, $87.54.
   19   Borrowed $5,700 from the bank, receiving the same in cash and giving the bank a promissory note.
   21   Total cash sales for the week, $3,500, plus $245 sales tax.
   21   Total sales from bank credit cards for the week, $1,535, plus $107.45 sales tax.

Nov.	22	Collected cash from C. E. Baker, a charge customer, $235.
	24	Received cash as refund for the return of merchandise purchased, $234.
	27	Collected cash from O. Hauge, a charge customer, $150.15.
	30	Total cash sales for the week, $3,855, plus $269.85 sales tax.
	30	Total sales from bank credit cards for the week, $430.25, plus $30.12 sales tax.

Check Figure

Total Sales Credit, $18,050.30

Instructions

1. Open the following accounts in the accounts receivable ledger and record the November 1 balances as given: T. R. Alex, $193.84; C. E. Baker, $235; L. R. Case, $110; L. P. Dane, $180; O. Hauge, $150.15; N. P. Tempe, $87.54. Place a check mark in the Post. Ref. column.
2. Record a balance of $956.53 in the Accounts Receivable controlling account as of November 1.
3. Record the transactions in the cash receipts journal beginning with page 16.
4. Post daily to the accounts receivable ledger.
5. Total and rule the cash receipts journal.
6. Prove the equality of debit and credit totals.
7. Post to the Accounts Receivable controlling account in the general ledger.

P.O. 1,3

Problem 11-2B C. R. McCain Company sells candy wholesale, primarily to vending machine operators. Terms of sales on account are 2/10, n/30, FOB shipping point. The following transactions involving cash receipts and sales of merchandise took place in May of this year:

May	2	Received $784 cash from N. Rockey in payment of April 23 invoice of $800, less cash discount.
	5	Received $1,120 cash in payment of $1,000 note receivable and interest of $120.
	8	Sold merchandise on account to G. Solter, invoice no. 862, $830.
	9	Received $960.40 cash from D. Maxton in payment of April 30 invoice of $980, less cash discount.
	15	Received cash from G. Solter in payment of invoice no. 862, less cash discount.
	16	Cash sales for first half of May, $4,326.
	19	Received $296 cash from R. O. Hintz in payment of April 14 invoice, no discount.
	22	Sold merchandise on account to N. T. Johns, invoice no. 887, $753.
	25	Received $239 cash refund for return of defective equipment bought in April for cash.
	28	Sold merchandise on account to M. E. Mulder, invoice no. 910, $964.
	31	Cash sales for second half of May, $3,617.

Check Figure

Total sales on account, $2,547

Instructions

1. Journalize the transactions for May in the cash receipts journal and the sales journal.
2. Total and rule the journals.
3. Prove the equality of debit and credit totals.

P.O. 7

Problem 11-3B Jason Company uses a check register to keep track of expenditures. The following transactions occurred during February of this year.

Feb. 1 Issued Ck. No. 4311, $637, to Barnet Company for invoice no. 3113E, recorded previously for $650, less cash discount of $13.

2 Issued Ck. No. 4312 to Boxer Express Company for freight charges, $48, for merchandise purchased.

4 Issued Ck. No. 4313 to Dixie Realty for monthly rent, $560.

9 Received and paid bill for advertising in *The Nickel News*, $84, Ck. No. 4314.

10 Issued Ck. No. 4315, $990, to Dieter Company for invoice no. D642, recorded previously for $1,000, less 1 percent cash discount.

15 Paid wages recorded previously for first half of month, $1,678; Ck. No. 4316.

19 R. Jason, the owner, withdrew $900 for personal use; Ck. No. 4317.

25 Issued Ck. No. 4318 to First National Bank for payment on bank loan, $896, consisting of $800 on principal and $96 interest.

27 Issued Ck. No. 4319, $430, to Lopez Company for invoice no. 6317, recorded previously (no discount).

28 Voided Ck. No. 4320.

28 Paid wages recorded previously for second half of month, $1,648; Ck. No. 4321.

28 Received and paid telephone bill, $86; Ck. No. 4322, payable to Western Telephone Company.

Check Figure

Total First Nat'l Bank Credit, $7,957

Instructions

1. Record the transactions in the check register.
2. Total and rule the check register.
3. Prove the equality of the debit and credit totals.

P.O. 1,2,3,5,6

Problem 11-4B The following transactions were completed by Ye Restaurant Equipment during January, the first month of this fiscal year. Terms of sale are 2/10, n/30.

Jan. 2 Issued Ck. No. 6981 for monthly rent, $850.

2 L. Ye, the owner, invested an additional $4,500 in the business.

4 Bought merchandise on account from Vaughn and Company, $2,830, invoice no. A694, dated January 2; terms 2/10, n/30.

4 Received check from Vessey Appliance for $980 in payment of invoice for $1,000 less discount.

4 Sold merchandise on account to L. Parker, invoice no. 6483, $755.

6 Received check from Peterson, Inc., for $637 in payment of $650 invoice less discount.

7 Issued Ck. No. 6982, $588, to Franklin and Son, in payment of invoice no. C127 for $600 less discount.

7 Bought supplies on account from Duncan Office Supply, $93.54, invoice no. 190B; terms net 30 days. (Debit Supplies Expense— Chapter 12 explains when to use the asset account Supplies.)

7 Sold merchandise on account to English and Cole, invoice no. 6484, $1,115.

9 Issued credit memo no. 43 to L. Parker, $47, for merchandise returned.

11 Cash sales for January 1 through January 10, $4,454.87.

11 Issued Ck. No. 6983, $2,773.40, to Vaughn and Company, in payment of $2,830 invoice less discount.

Jan. 14 Sold merchandise on account to Vessey Appliance, invoice no. 6485, $2,100.

14 Received check from L. Parker, $693.84, in payment of $755 invoice, less return of $47 and less discount.

19 Bought merchandise on account from Crosby Products, $3,700, invoice no. 7281, dated January 16; terms 2/10, n/60; FOB shipping point, freight prepaid and added to invoice, $142 (total $3,842).

21 Issued Ck. No. 6984, $245, to Barclay Agency for advertising not recorded previously. (Miscellaneous Expense)

21 Cash sales for January 11 through January 20, $3,689.

23 Received credit memo no. 163, $87, from Crosby Products for merchandise returned.

29 Sold merchandise on account to Bryan Supply, invoice no. 6486, $1,697.20.

29 Issued Ck. No. 6985 to Pacific Freight, $64, for freight charges on merchandise purchased January 4.

31 Cash sales for January 21 through January 31, $3,862.

31 Issued Ck. No. 6986, $65, to M. Pierce for miscellaneous expenses not recorded previously.

31 Recorded payroll entry from the payroll register: total salaries, $5,900; employees' federal income tax withheld, $795; FICA tax withheld, $451.35.

31 Recorded the payroll taxes: FICA, $451.35; state unemployment tax, $265.50; federal unemployment tax, $47.20.

31 Issued Ck. No. 6987, $4,653.65, for salaries for the month.

31 L. Ye, the owner, withdrew $1,000 for personal use, Ck. No. 6988.

Check Figure

Trial balance totals, $63,187.61

Instructions

1. Record the transactions for January, using a sales journal, page 91; a purchases journal, page 74; a cash receipts journal, page 56; a cash payments journal, page 63; a general journal, page 119. The chart of accounts is as follows:

111	Cash	311	L. Ye, Capital
113	Accounts Receivable	312	L. Ye, Drawing
114	Merchandise Inventory		
116	Prepaid Insurance	411	Sales
121	Equipment	412	Sales Returns and Allowances
		413	Sales Discounts
212	Accounts Payable		
215	Salaries Payable	511	Purchases
216	Employees' Federal Income Tax Payable	512	Purchases Returns and Allowances
217	FICA Tax Payable	513	Purchases Discounts
218	State Unemployment Tax Payable	514	Freight In
219	Federal Unemployment Tax Payable	621	Salary Expense
		622	Payroll Tax Expense
		625	Supplies Expense
		627	Rent Expense
		631	Miscellaneous Expense

2. Post daily all entries involving customer accounts to the accounts receivable ledger.

3. Post daily all entries involving creditor accounts to the accounts payable ledger.

4. Post daily those entries involving the Other Accounts columns and the general journal to the general ledger. Write the owner's name in the Capital and Drawing accounts.
5. Add the columns of the special journals, and prove the equality of debit and credit totals on scratch paper.
6. Post the appropriate totals of the special journals to the general ledger.
7. Prepare a trial balance.
8. Prepare a schedule of accounts receivable and a schedule of accounts payable. Do the totals equal the balances of the related controlling accounts?

Instructions for General Ledger Software

1. Record the transactions in the sales journal, purchases journal, cash receipts journal, cash payments journal, and general journal.
   a. For efficiency, analyze the transactions, indicate what journal each transaction goes into, and key the entries in five groups or batches, one for each journal.
   b. Because the program uses a single-column purchases journal, add the amount of the freight to the amount of purchases.
2. Print the journals.
3. Post the amounts from the sales, purchases, cash receipts, cash payments, and general journals.
4. Print a trial balance.
5. Print a schedule of accounts receivable and compare the total with the balance of the Accounts Receivable controlling account.
6. Print a schedule of accounts payable and compare the total with the balance of the Accounts Payable controlling account.

The Computer Clinic

Cash Receipts and Cash Payments Journals

Since All About You Spa decided to streamline accounting operations by adding purchases and sales journals, Ms. Valli believes it would be logical and efficient to add two more special journals: a cash receipts journal for all increases to cash and a cash payments journal for all decreases to cash. That will leave only a few entries that will go into the general journal—for instance, returns and allowances, payroll entries (except the payment of the net payroll, which goes in the cash payments journal), adjusting and closing entries, and any other entry that does not fit the definition of what goes in a particular special journal.

As of July 31, the chart of accounts contained the following:

Chart of Accounts
All About You Spa

111	Cash	511	Purchases
113	Accounts Receivable	515	Freight In
117	Prepaid Insurance		
124	Spa Equipment	611	Wages Expense
125	Accumulated Depreciation, Spa Equipment	612	Rent Expense
		613	Office Supplies Expense
128	Office Equipment	614	Spa Supplies Expense
129	Accumulated Depreciation, Office Equipment	615	Laundry Expense
		616	Advertising Expense
		617	Utilities Expense
211	Accounts Payable	618	Insurance Expense
212	Wages Payable	619	Depreciation Expense, Spa Equipment
215	Sales Tax Payable		
		620	Depreciation Expense, Office Equipment
311	A. Valli, Capital		
312	A. Valli, Drawing	630	Miscellaneous Expense
399	Income Summary		
411	Income from Services		
412	Merchandise Sales		

Ms. Valli has provided the trial balance as of July 31, schedules of accounts receivable and payable, as well as transactions for the month of August to be recorded in one of the four special journals or the general journal.

All About You Spa
Trial Balance
July 31, 20—

ACCOUNT NAME	DEBIT	CREDIT
Cash	44 9 6 9 26	
Accounts Receivable	4 5 6 8 79	
Prepaid Insurance	8 0 0 00	
Spa Equipment	17 6 0 1 00	
Accumulated Depreciation, Spa Equipment		6 4 88
Office Equipment	1 5 7 0 00	
Accumulated Depreciation, Office Equipment		1 0 00
Accounts Payable		20 7 2 0 00
Sales Tax Payable		1 8 2 9 90
A. Valli, Capital		49 8 8 4 62
A. Valli, Drawing	2 5 0 0 00	
Income from Services		12 7 2 2 00
Merchandise Sales		10 1 5 1 65
Purchases	12 8 6 8 00	
Freight In	4 0 3 00	
Wages Expense	7 0 0 4 00	
Rent Expense	1 6 5 0 00	
Office Supplies Expense	1 1 8 00	
Spa Supplies Expense	4 9 0 00	
Laundry Expense	8 4 00	
Utilities Expense	4 7 3 00	
Miscellaneous Expense	2 8 4 00	
	95 3 8 3 05	95 3 8 3 05

All About You Spa
Schedule of Accounts Receivable
July 31, 20—

About Face Spa	$	5 2 1 59
Jill Anson		1 7 5 00
Chaco's		5 2 0 02
Holmes Condos		3 6 7 47
Tory Ligman		1 6 4 00
Los Obrigados Lodge		3 5 1 00
Mini Spa		2 2 2 48
Jack Morgan		2 8 6 00
Pleasant Spa	1	9 6 1 23
Total Accounts Receivable	$4	5 6 8 79

All About You Spa
Schedule of Accounts Payable
July 31, 20—

Giftco	$ 1 3 0 9 00
Golden Spa Supplies	4 9 0 00
Logo Products	3 7 9 6 00
Office Staples	3 0 4 00
Spa Equipment, Inc.	6 2 3 5 00
Spa Goods	5 4 4 5 00
Spa Magic	2 7 2 1 00
Superior Equipment	4 2 0 00
Total Accounts Payable	$20 7 2 0 00

Directions for August Journal Entries

1. If you are beginning the Computer Clinic problem at Chapter 11, journalize the trial balance accounts and amounts in the general journal as one big compound entry prior to recording the August journal entries. These are the July 31 balances that become the beginning balances for August.

   So that you can complete the journal entries for the month of August, Ms. Valli has also left the information you will need and directions on how to proceed.

2. Add new accounts to the chart of accounts as needed. One account that should be added is Purchases Discounts 512. Although no discounts have been taken by All About You Spa, they may be in the future. Add Sales Discounts 413 as well, since such discounts may be given to customers in the future.

3. a. Journalize in the *purchases journal* all of the August purchases of merchandise on account, which are shown in the list of invoices provided.

   b. Journalize in the *sales journal* all of the August sales of merchandise on account, which are shown in the list of merchandise sales invoices provided.

   c. Journalize the list of transactions that are to be entered in the cash receipts journal OR cash payments journal OR general journal. (*Notes:* Payroll taxes related to wages will be ignored here for purposes of simplification. All About You Spa is located in a state that levies sales tax on both merchandise and services. Some states do not tax services.)

4. After journalizing and posting all transactions to the general ledger and the subsidiary ledgers, print a trial balance dated August 31, 20—. Do not include those accounts that have a zero balance at the end of the month.

5. Print a schedule of accounts receivable dated August 31, 20—.

6. Print a schedule of accounts payable dated August 31, 20—.

Checkbook Register

Check No.	Date	Explanation	✓	Deposits	Check Amount
1044	8/1	Paid August's rent.			1,650.00
	8/1	Deposited Chaco's payment received on account, invoice no. 15.		400.00	
	8/1	Deposited Mini Spa's payment received on account, invoice no. 18 paid in full.		222.48	
1045	8/1	Paid accumulated sales tax payable to State Revenue Dept.			1,829.90
1046	8/2	Paid advertising expense for August photo ad.			455.00
1047	8/2	Paid week's wages.			1,845.50
1048	8/2	Paid Spa Magic for invoice no. 5033, dated June 2. Paid in full.			2,721.00
1049	8/3	Bought silk flower arrangement for the salon (Miscellaneous Expense).			87.90
	8/3	Deposited Tory Ligman's payment received on account, paid in full.		164.00	
1050	8/4	Bought spa supplies—5 cases of bottled water for clients (debit Spa Supplies).			45.00
	8/4	Deposited Jill Anson's payment received on account.		87.50	
1051	8/5	Bought a digital camera for confidential before-and-after pictures (debit Spa Equipment).			482.00
1052	8/5	Paid Office Staples for invoice 1417, dated July 5. Paid in full.			186.00
1053	8/5	Paid on account to Giftco, invoice no. 316, dated July 5.			709.00
	8/6	Deposited Pleasant Spa's payment received on account, invoice no. 16.		997.42	
1054	8/6	Paid Golden Spa Supplies for invoice no. 1836, dated July 1. Paid in full.			490.00
	8/7	Deposited first week's cash sales: merchandise $1,630.00; services $3,350.00; sales tax collected $398.40.		5,378.40	
	8/8	Deposited Los Obrigados Lodge's payment received on account, invoice no. 14.		200.00	
	8/9	Deposited Holmes Condo's payment received on account, invoice no. 17.		200.00	
1055	8/9	Paid week's wages.			1,850.00
	8/14	Deposited second week's cash sales: merchandise $1,330.00; services $2,340.00; sales tax collected $293.60.		3,963.60	
	8/15	Deposited About Face Spa's payment received on account, invoice no. 19.		265.00	
1056	8/16	Paid week's wages.			1,853.00

Check No.	Date	Explanation	✓	Deposits	Check Amount
1057	8/18	Paid Superior Equipment for invoice no. 3608, dated July 5. Paid in full.			420.00
	8/19	Deposited Jack Morgan's payment received on account, paid in full.		286.00	
	8/21	Deposited third week's cash sales: merchandise $2,220.00; services $2,810.00; sales tax collected $402.40.		5,432.40	
1058	8/22	Paid on account to Logo Products, invoice no. 1579, dated July 1.			2,500.00
1059	8/23	Paid on account to Spa Goods, invoice no. 312, dated July 1.			2,000.00
1060	8/23	Paid week's wages.			1,847.50
1061	8/28	Paid month's laundry bill.			95.00
1062	8/28	Owner withdrew cash for personal use.			2,500.00
1063	8/30	Paid week's wages.			1,850.00
	8/31	Deposited end of month's cash revenue: merchandise sales $2,030.00; services $4,176.00; $496.48 sales tax.		6,702.48	
1064	8/31	Paid August telephone bill.			235.00
1065	8/31	Paid on account to Spa Equipment, Inc., invoice no. 2731, dated July 3.			3,000.00
1066	8/31	Paid August power and water bill.			255.00

Purchases Invoices for Merchandise Bought on Account During August

All About You Spa will pay all freight costs associated with purchases of merchandise to the supplier.

Date of Purchase	Transaction Information	Amount
Aug. 1	Bought logo merchandise from Giftco; invoice no. 416, dated 8/1; terms 2/10, n/30.	$4,100.00 plus $180.00 freight
1	Bought bath and beauty products from Spa Magic; invoice no. 5235, dated 8/1; 2/10, n/30.	$3,562.00 plus $155.00 freight
2	Bought logo merchandise from Logo Products; invoice no. 1680, dated 8/2; terms 2/10, n/30.	$2,451.00 plus $144.00 freight
5	Bought spa accessories from Spa Goods; invoice no. 387, dated 8/5; terms 2/10, n/30.	$1,120 plus $110.00 freight

Sales Invoices for Gift Certificates Sold on Account During August

All About You Spa is responsible for collecting and paying the sales tax on merchandise that it sells. The sales tax rate where All About You Spa does business is 8 percent of each sale; for example, $650.00 \times 0.08 = \$52.00$.

Date of Sale	Transaction Information	Sales Amount (Before Tax)
Aug. 1	About Face Spa, invoice no. 20.	$ 650.00
5	Chaco's, invoice no. 21.	395.00
8	Holmes Condos, invoice no. 22.	1,294.00
9	Pleasant Spa, invoice no. 23.	1,560.00
11	Los Obrigados Lodge, invoice no. 24.	356.00
14	Mini Spa, invoice no. 25.	873.00

Note: All certificates for services were redeemed and the services were provided by the end of the month.

Other August Transactions

There were two other transactions in August. Neither involved cash.

Date	Transaction Information	Amount
Aug. 9	Issued credit memorandum no. 1 to About Face Spa, allowance for damaged goods. (New account Sales Returns and Allowances 414.)	$ 88.00
29	Received a credit memo for damaged spa accessories from Spa Magic. (New account Purchases Returns and Allowances 513.)	$123.00

Before a Test Check: Chapters 10–11

PART I: Completion

Complete each of the following statements by writing the appropriate word(s) in the spaces provided.

1. The normal balance of the Purchases Discounts account is on the _____ side.

2. Entries in the Accounts Payable Debit column of a cash payments journal are posted daily to the _____.

3. A _____ is the amount a customer may deduct for paying a bill within a specified period of time.

4. The form sent to the supplier of merchandise is called a(n) _____.

5. The _____ account is used to record the buying of merchandise only.

6. If the freight charges are FOB shipping point, the _____ pays the transportation charges.

7. The time the seller allows the buyer before full payment has to be made is the _____.

8. Increases in Sales Returns and Allowances are recorded on the _____ side.

9. The sales journal is used to record all _____.

10. The schedule of accounts receivable lists the balances of all the _____ accounts at the end of the month.

PART II: Matching

For each numbered item, choose the appropriate journal, and write the identifying letter.

____ 1. Paid freight bill on merchandise purchased.

____ 2. Bought office equipment on account.

____ 3. Received a credit memo for merchandise returned.

____ 4. Bought office equipment for cash.

____ 5. Sold merchandise on account.

S   Sales journal
P   Purchases journal (3 columns)
CR Cash receipts journal
CP Cash payments journal
J   General journal

Note: Answers to Before a Test Check begin on page A-1.

_____ 6. Journalized the closing entries.

_____ 7. Paid state sales tax to the state revenue department.

_____ 8. Bought merchandise on account.

_____ 9. Sold merchandise for cash.

_____ 10. Bought merchandise for cash.

PART III: True/False

For each question circle T if it is True or circle F if it is False.

T   F   1. The Purchases Discounts account is classified as a revenue account.

T   F   2. The normal balance of the Sales Discounts account is on the debit side.

T   F   3. Check marks in the Posting Reference column of the sales journal indicate that the amounts are not to be posted.

T   F   4. When you post directly from the purchases invoice, you eliminate the accounts payable ledger.

T   F   5. The purchases journal is used for the buying of merchandise for cash and on account.

Cash Receipts and Cash Payments: An Alternative to Special Journals

Performance Objectives

After you have completed this appendix, you will be able to do the following:

1. Record transactions pertaining to cash receipts and cash payments in a general journal.

2. Maintain an accounts receivable ledger and an accounts payable ledger.

3. Prepare schedules of accounts receivable and accounts payable.

Although most merchandising enterprises set up special journals, some businesses elect to record cash receipts and cash payments in the general journal because of personal preference or the desire to record all transactions chronologically in one place.

JOURNALIZING INCREASES TO CASH

Here are the merchandising accounts in T account form. Refer to the glossary at the end of Chapter 10 on pages 363–364 for definitions of these accounts. The same accounts are used whether transactions are journalized in special journals (as in Chapters 10 and 11) or in a general journal. The outcomes will be the same.

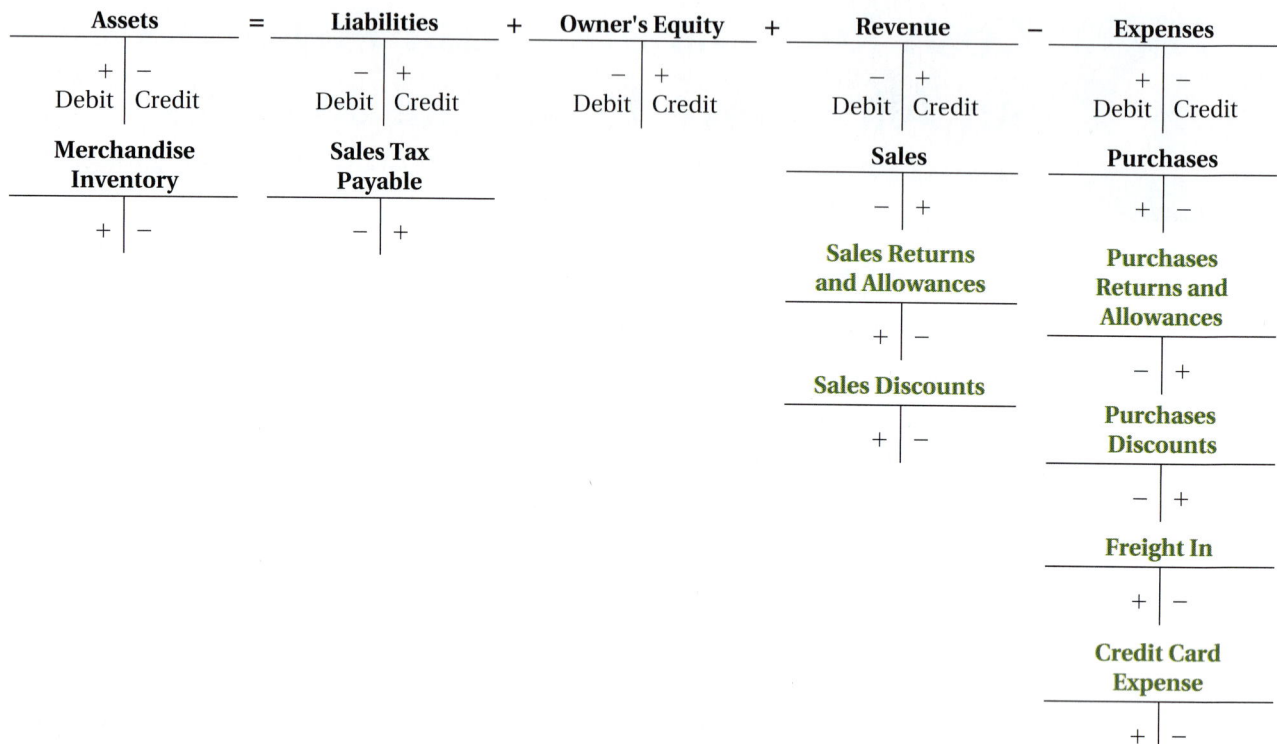

RECORDING CASH RECEIPTS (INCREASES TO CASH) IN A GENERAL JOURNAL

OBJECTIVE 1a

Record transactions pertaining to cash receipts in a general journal.

We will introduce journalizing increases (debits) to cash from a variety of sources in a general journal by looking at the following five transactions:

May 3   Sold merchandise for cash, $500, plus $40 sales tax.
4   Sold merchandise for cash. The customer charged the $500 sale on a credit card, and the cost of using the credit card was $21.60. Sales tax amounted to $40.
5   Collected cash on account from L. R. Ray, a charge customer, $416.
7   The owner, J. R. Hall, invested cash in the business, $10,000.
8   Sold computer equipment for cash at cost, $500.

GENERAL JOURNAL   PAGE _____15_____

	DATE		DESCRIPTION	POST. REF.	DEBIT	CREDIT	
1	20–						1
2	May	3	Cash		5 4 0 00		2
3			Sales			5 0 0 00	3
4			Sales Tax Payable			4 0 00	4
5			Sold merchandise for cash.				5
6							6
7		4	Cash		5 1 8 40		7
8			Credit Card Expense		2 1 60		8
9			Sales			5 0 0 00	9
10			Sales Tax Payable			4 0 00	10
11			Sold merchandise involving				11
12			a bank charge card and				12
13			sales tax.				13
14							14
15		5	Cash		4 1 6 00		15
16			Accounts Receivable, L. R. Ray			4 1 6 00	16
17			Collected cash on account.				17
18							18
19		7	Cash		10 0 0 0 00		19
20			J. R. Hall, Capital			10 0 0 0 00	20
21			Owner invested cash.				21
22							22
23		8	Cash		5 0 0 00		23
24			Computer Equipment			5 0 0 00	24
25			Sold computer equipment				25
26			at cost.				26

Posting to the General Ledger and Subsidiary Ledger

OBJECTIVE 2a

Maintain an accounts receivable ledger.

Post each entry to Cash and any other accounts involved in the general ledger. Also, post the amounts paid by customers to the subsidiary accounts receivable ledger to maintain a running balance of the amount each customer owes.

Schedule of Accounts Receivable

OBJECTIVE 3a

Prepare a schedule of accounts receivable.

At the end of the month, the accountant lists the customer names and amounts owed and totals the amounts. This listing is called the schedule of accounts receivable. The total of this schedule should equal the total of the Accounts Receivable controlling account in the general ledger. If the two amounts are different, reverse the process of adding and posting to discover and correct the error.

JOURNALIZING PURCHASES OF MERCHANDISE (FOR RESALE) ON ACCOUNT

Refer to Figures 9 (page 350), 10 (page 350), and 11 (page 351) in Chapter 10; they illustrate the forms that drive and support the merchandising transactions to be journalized.

Here are the merchandising accounts in T account form. Refer to the glossary at the end of Chapter 10 on pages 363–364 for definitions of these accounts. The same accounts are used whether transactions are journalized in special journals (as in Chapters 10 and 11) or in a general journal. The outcomes will be the same.

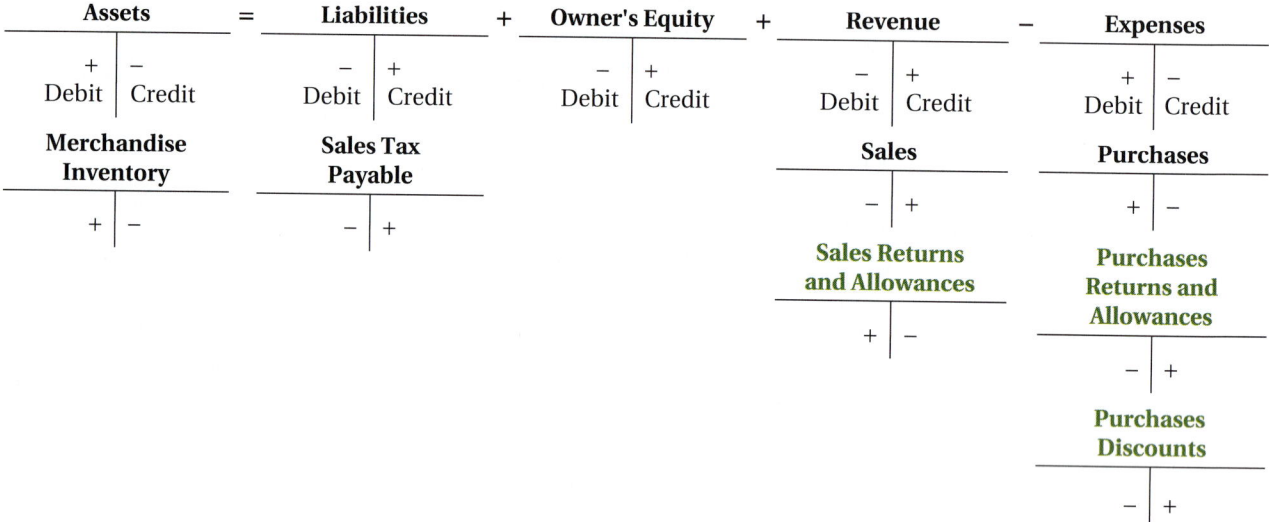

RECORDING CASH PAYMENTS (DECREASES TO CASH) IN A GENERAL JOURNAL

OBJECTIVE 1b

Record transactions pertaining to cash payments in a general journal.

We will introduce journalizing decreases (credits) to cash from a variety of sources in a general journal by looking at the following six transactions:

Aug. 8 Issued Ck. No. 2076 to Collins, Inc., in payment of invoice no. 2706, less cash discount of $34.20, $1,761.30 ($1,795.50 − $34.20). Notice that the discount applies only to the amount billed for the merchandise (2 percent of $1,710).

10 Paid wages for two-week period, Ck. No. 2077, $1,680 (previously recorded in the payroll entry).

11 Issued Ck. No. 2078 to Dana Manufacturing Company, in payment of invoice no. 10611 ($564), less return ($270); less cash discount, 2/10, n/30; $288.12 ($564 − $270 = $294; $294.00 × 0.02 = $5.88; $294.00 − $5.88 = $288.12).

12 Bought supplies for cash, Ck. No. 2079, payable to Davenport Office Supplies, $70. (Debit Supplies Expense.)

15 Issued Ck. No. 2080 to Gardner Products Company, in payment of invoice no. B643 ($1,245), less return ($315); less cash discount, 1/10, n/30; $921.60 [$1,245 − $315 = $930; freight charges totaled $90 ($930 − $90 = $840); $840.00 × 0.01 = $8.40; $930.00 − $8.40 = $921.60].

16 Bought merchandise for cash, Ck. No. 2081, payable to Jones and Son, $200.

	DATE		DESCRIPTION	POST. REF.	DEBIT		CREDIT		
1	20–								1
2	Aug.	8	Accounts Payable, Collins, Inc.		1 7 9 5 50				2
3			Cash				1 7 6 1 30		3
4			Purchases Discounts				3 4 20		4
5			Paid Collins, Inc., for invoice						5
6			no. 2706, Ck. No. 2076.						6
7									7
8		10	Wages Payable		1 6 8 0 00				8
9			Cash				1 6 8 0 00		9
10			Paid wages for two-week						10
11			period, Ck. No. 2077.						11
12									12
13		11	Accounts Payable, Dana Mfg. Co.		2 9 4 00				13
14			Cash				2 8 8 12		14
15			Purchases Discounts				5 88		15
16			Paid Dana Mfg. Co. for						16
17			invoice no. 10611,						17
18			Ck. No. 2078.						18
19									19
20		12	Supplies Expense		7 0 00				20
21			Cash				7 0 00		21
22			Bought supplies from						22
23			Davenport Office Supplies,						23
24			Ck. No. 2079.						24
25									25
26		15	Accounts Payable, Gardner		9 3 0 00				26
27			Products Co.						27
28			Cash				9 2 1 60		28
29			Purchases Discounts				8 40		29
30			Paid Gardner Products Co.						30
31			for invoice no. B643,						31
32			Ck. No. 2080.						32
33									33
34		16	Purchases		2 0 0 00				34
35			Cash				2 0 0 00		35
36			Bought merchandise from						36
37			Jones and Son, Ck. No. 2081.						37

GENERAL JOURNAL   PAGE ___27___

Posting to the General Ledger and Subsidiary Ledger

OBJECTIVE 2b

Maintain an accounts payable ledger.

Post each entry to Cash, Accounts Payable, and any other accounts involved in the general ledger. Also, post the amount owed to the vendor to the subsidiary accounts payable ledger to maintain a running balance of the amount owed to each vendor.

OBJECTIVE 3b

Prepare a schedule of accounts payable.

Schedule of Accounts Payable

At the end of the month, the accountant lists the vendor names and amounts owed and totals the amounts. This listing is called the schedule of accounts payable. The total of this schedule should equal the total of the Accounts Payable controlling account in the general ledger. If the two amounts are different, reverse the process of adding and posting to discover and correct the error.

PROBLEMS

P.O. 1, 2, 3

Check Figures

Trial Balance totals, $65,288.80; Schedule of Accounts Receivable total, $5,468; Schedule of Accounts Payable total, $4,733

P.O. 1, 2, 3

Check Figures

Trial Balance totals, $63,187.61; Schedule of Accounts Receivable total, $4,912.20; Schedule of Accounts Payable total, $3,848.54

Problem D-1A Complete Problem 11-4A on pages 420–422 *except* journalize transactions in a general journal instead of in special journals.

Problem D-1B Complete Problem 11-4B on pages 424–426 *except* journalize transactions in a general journal instead of in special journals.

internet
LINKS TO ACCOUNTING

Anyone who subscribes to a magazine has probably received subscription renewal notices enticing them to renew now and save! And the savings can seem substantial, such as save 65 percent off the newsstand price or buy one year and get one year free. Many subscribers take advantage of these offers, extending their subscriptions into future years. When subscription fees are collected more than a year in advance, they represent unearned revenue. This unearned revenue is a liability to the company because it is money received for a product or service that has not yet been provided to the customer. *TV Guide* is a weekly magazine that focuses on the scheduled television programs for the week. How do you think GEMSTAR-TV Guide International, Inc., the publisher of the magazine, records these advance sales? When does the company consider the revenue to be earned and how does it record it? Look at the company's 2005 annual report, found by going to **http://www.gemstartvguide.com**, clicking on Investors at the top of the screen, then Financial Reports in the list on the left side, and then on 2005 Annual Report. Think about the answer to this as you learn about adjusting entries for unearned revenue in this chapter.

Performance Objectives

After you have completed this chapter, you will be able to do the following:

1. Prepare an adjustment for supplies.

2. Prepare an adjustment for merchandise inventory under the periodic inventory system.

3. Prepare an adjustment for unearned revenue.

4. Record the adjustment data in a work sheet (including merchandise inventory, unearned revenue, supplies remaining, expired insurance, depreciation, and accrued wages or salaries).

5. Complete the work sheet.

6. Journalize the adjusting entries for a merchandising business under the periodic inventory system.

7. Journalize the adjusting entry for merchandise inventory under the perpetual inventory system.

e have talked about the special journals and accounts kept by a merchandising business. Now we take another step toward completing the accounting cycle by presenting the related adjustments and the work sheet. Many of the adjustments made by a service business are also made by a merchandising firm. First, let's briefly review the adjusting entries described so far. To begin, look over the following accounts. Here are the data for the adjustments, along with the related adjusting entries:

Insurance expired, $2,600. (The amount expired is the amount used.)

Prepaid Insurance				Insurance Expense		
	+	−			+	−
Bal.	3,000	Adj.	2,600	Adj.	2,600	
Bal.	400					

Additional depreciation, $2,800. (Add to both accounts.)

Depreciation Expense			Accumulated Depreciation		
	+	−		−	+
Adj.	2,800			Bal.	10,000
				Adj.	2,800
				Bal.	12,800

Accrued wages (owed but not yet paid), $3,900. (Add to both accounts.)

Wages Expense			Wages Payable		
	+	−		−	+
Bal.	26,000			Adj.	3,900
Adj.	3,900				
Bal.	29,900				

In this chapter, we introduce three more adjusting entries. One adjustment is for supplies. This adjustment can be used for merchandising and manufacturing businesses. One adjustment is for merchandise inventory, which is used exclusively for a merchandising business. Another adjustment is for unearned revenue, which could apply to either a merchandising or a service business. We also discuss how to handle the specialized accounts of a merchandising business in the work sheet. Finally, we briefly describe the perpetual inventory system and the accompanying adjustment.

ADJUSTMENT FOR SUPPLIES

OBJECTIVE 1

Prepare an adjustment for supplies.

Previously, when we were talking about the buying of supplies for a service business, we debited Supplies Expense and credited Cash or Accounts Payable.

When a merchandising business buys supplies for cash or on credit, the accounting would generally be the same as for a service business. However, if the amount of supplies held at the end of the accounting period is substantial, then an adjustment should be made to capitalize the supplies that were not consumed during the accounting period. The adjustment would be to debit Supplies (an asset account) and credit Supplies Expense. The amount is determined by a physical count of the supplies left over. For a retail business, supplies would consist of everything from paper or plastic bags to paper forms.

As an illustration, let's say that Mullene & Co. has a balance of $62,000 in the Supplies Expense account as a result of buying supplies all during the fiscal period. Now, by taking a count of the supplies on hand, it is determined that $12,000 of supplies are left.

To record the amount of the supplies used, Mullene & Co. has to make an adjusting entry. The purpose of an adjusting entry is to bring the books up to date at the end of the accounting period.

Let's look at this in T account form. We need to add to the balance sheet the supplies still on hand at the end of the accounting period (debit Supplies, an asset account) and reduce the amount of supplies expensed during the accounting period (credit Supplies Expense).

> **REMEMBER!**
>
> For the adjustment of supplies, first find the amount by determining the amount of the supplies that remain. In the adjusting entry, deduct the amount of the remaining supplies from Supplies Expense and add it to the asset account Supplies.

	Supplies				**Supplies Expense**			
		+	**–**			**+**	**–**	
Adj.	12,000			Bal.	62,000		Adj.	12,000
				Bal.	50,000			

ADJUSTMENT FOR MERCHANDISE INVENTORY USING THE PERIODIC INVENTORY SYSTEM

OBJECTIVE 2

Prepare an adjustment for merchandise inventory under the periodic inventory system.

Under the **periodic inventory system**, we do not make an entry in the Merchandise Inventory account until an actual **physical inventory** or count of the stock of goods on hand has been taken. Instead, we record the purchase of merchandise as a debit to Purchases for the amount of the cost and the sale of the merchandise as a credit to Sales for the amount of the selling price. Finally, after a physical count of merchandise has been taken, one method of adjusting inventory is to make two adjusting entries to record the dollar amount of the inventory. The first adjusting entry is to remove the beginning inventory. The second entry is to enter the ending inventory.

Consider this example. A firm has a Merchandise Inventory balance of $174,000, which represents the cost of the inventory at the beginning of the fiscal period. At the end of the fiscal period, the firm takes an actual count of the stock on hand and determines the cost of the ending inventory to be $180,000. Naturally, in any business, goods are constantly being bought, sold, and replaced. The cost of the ending inventory is larger than the cost of the beginning inventory because the firm bought more than it sold. When we adjust the Merchandise Inventory account, we place the new figure of $180,000 in the account. This method can require two steps.

Step 1 Eliminate the amount of the beginning inventory from the Merchandise Inventory account by transferring the amount into Income Summary. (Remove the beginning inventory.)

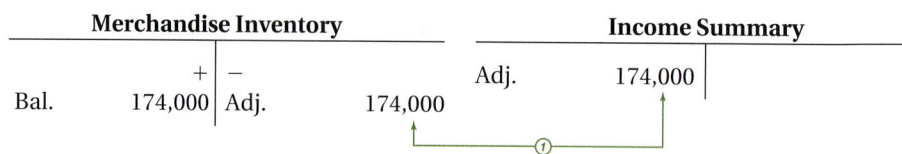

We credit Merchandise Inventory and then debit Income Summary.

Step 2 Enter the ending Merchandise Inventory, because you must record on the books the cost of the asset remaining on hand. (Enter the ending inventory.)

Let's repeat the T accounts, showing step 1 and adding step 2.

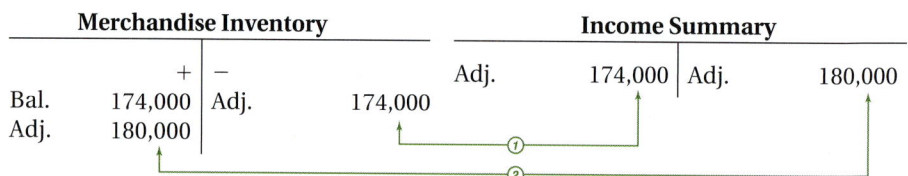

In step 2, we debit Merchandise Inventory (recording the asset on the plus side of the account) and do the opposite to Income Summary.

The reason for adjusting the Merchandise Inventory account in these two steps is that both the beginning and the ending amounts appear as distinct figures in the Income Statement columns of a work sheet, and these columns are used as the basis for preparing the income statement.

ADJUSTMENT FOR UNEARNED REVENUE

OBJECTIVE 3

Prepare an adjustment for unearned revenue.

Now let's introduce another adjusting entry, **unearned revenue,** which is cash received in advance for goods or services to be delivered or performed later. This entry could pertain to a service business as well as to a merchandising or manufacturing business. Frequently, cash is received in advance for services to be performed in the future. For example, a professional sports team sells tickets in advance, a concert association sells season tickets in advance, a magazine publisher sells subscriptions in advance, and an insurance company receives premiums in advance. If the cash amounts received by each of these organizations will be earned during the present fiscal period, the amounts should be credited to revenue accounts. On the other hand, if the amounts received will *not* be earned during the present fiscal period, the amounts should be credited to unearned revenue accounts. **An unearned revenue account is classified as a liability,** because an organization is liable for (owes) the amount received in advance until it is earned.

College students pay in advance to participate in a meal plan. Until all those meals are consumed, this money represents unearned revenue for the college or university dining hall services.

To illustrate, assume that on April 1, Bell Publishing Company receives $82,000 in cash for subscriptions covering two years and records them originally as debits to Cash and credits to Unearned Subscriptions. At the end of the year, Bell finds that $30,750 of the subscriptions have been earned. Accordingly, Bell's accountant makes an adjusting entry, debiting Unearned Subscriptions and crediting Subscriptions Income. In other words, the accountant takes the earned portion out of Unearned Subscriptions and adds it to Subscriptions Income. T accounts show the situation as follows:

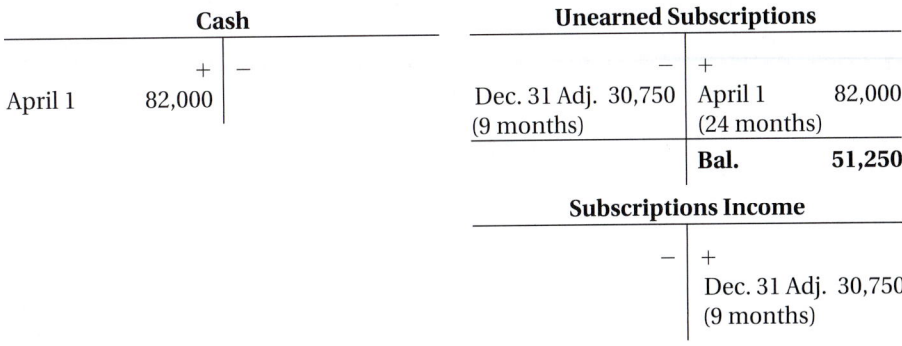

To take another example, suppose that Rainier Plumbing Supply offers a course in plumbing repairs for home owners and apartment managers. On November 1, Rainier Plumbing Supply receives $1,200 in fees for a three-month course. Because Rainier Plumbing Supply's present fiscal period ends on December 31, the three months' worth of fees received in advance will not all be earned during this fiscal period. Therefore, Rainier Plumbing Supply's accountant records the transaction as a debit to Cash of $1,200 and a credit to Unearned Course Fees of $1,200. Unearned Course Fees is a liability account, because Rainier Plumbing Supply must complete the how-to course or refund a portion of the money it collected. **Any account beginning with the word *Unearned* is always a liability.**

On December 31, because two months' worth of course fees have now been earned, Rainier Plumbing Supply's accountant makes an adjusting entry to transfer $800 (⅔ of $1,200) from Unearned Course Fees to Course Fees Income. By T accounts, the situation looks like this:

Cash				Unearned Course Fees		
	+	−			−	+
Nov. 1	1,200			Dec. 31 Adj. 800		Nov. 1 1,200
				(2 months)		(3 months)
						Bal. 400

		Course Fees Income		
			−	+
				Dec. 31 Adj. 800
				(2 months)

Rainier Plumbing Supply's chart of accounts is presented on the next page. The account number arrangement will be discussed in Chapter 13.

Assets (100–199)

111 Cash
112 Notes Receivable
113 Accounts Receivable
114 Merchandise Inventory
115 Supplies
116 Prepaid Insurance
121 Land
122 Building
123 Accumulated Depreciation, Building
124 Equipment
125 Accumulated Depreciation, Equipment

Liabilities (200–299)

211 Notes Payable
212 Accounts Payable
213 Wages Payable
217 Unearned Course Fees
221 Mortgage Payable

Owner's Equity (300–399)

311 C. F. Rainier, Capital
312 C. F. Rainier, Drawing
313 Income Summary

Revenue (400–499)

411 Sales
412 Sales Returns and Allowances
413 Sales Discounts
421 Course Fees Income
422 Interest Income

Cost of Goods Sold (500–599)

511 Purchases
512 Purchases Returns and Allowances
513 Purchases Discounts
514 Freight In

Expenses (600–699)

611 Wages Expense
622 Supplies Expense
623 Insurance Expense
624 Depreciation Expense, Building
625 Depreciation Expense, Equipment
626 Taxes Expense
634 Interest Expense

Before we demonstrate how to record adjustments, let's first look at the trial balance section of Rainier Plumbing Supply's work sheet (Figure 1).

DATA FOR THE ADJUSTMENTS

OBJECTIVE 4

Record the adjustment data in a work sheet (including merchandise inventory, unearned revenue, supplies remaining, expired insurance, depreciation, and accrued wages or salaries).

Listing the adjustment data appears to be a relatively minor task. In a business situation, however, one must take actual physical counts of the inventories and match them up with costs. One must check insurance policies to determine the amount of insurance that has expired. Finally, one must systematically write off, or depreciate, the cost of buildings and equipment.

For income tax and accounting purposes, land cannot be depreciated. Even if the building and lot were bought as one package for one price, the buyer must separate the cost of the building from the cost of the land. For real estate taxes, the county assessor appraises the building and the land separately. If there is no other qualified appraisal available, one can use the assessor's ratio or percentage as a basis for separating building cost and land cost.

Here are the adjustment data for Rainier Plumbing Supply. We will show the adjustments recorded in T accounts.

a–b. Ending merchandise inventory, $65,800. The adjustments for inventory are generally placed first.

Merchandise Inventory				
	+	−		
Bal.	67,000	**(a)** Adj.	67,000	
(b) Adj.	65,800			

Income Summary			
(a) Adj.	67,000	**(b)** Adj.	65,800

Rainier Plumbing Supply
Work Sheet
For Year Ended December 31, 20—

	ACCOUNT NAME	TRIAL BALANCE DEBIT	TRIAL BALANCE CREDIT	ADJUSTMENTS DEBIT	ADJUSTMENTS CREDIT
1	Cash	24 1 5 4 00			
2	Notes Receivable	4 0 0 0 00			
3	Accounts Receivable	29 4 4 6 00			
4	Merchandise Inventory	67 0 0 0 00			
5	Prepaid Insurance	9 6 0 00			
6	Land	120 1 0 0 00			
7	Building	130 0 0 0 00			
8	Accumulated Depreciation, Building		52 0 0 0 00		
9	Equipment	33 6 0 0 00			
10	Accumulated Depreciation, Equipment		16 4 0 0 00		
11	Notes Payable		36 4 0 0 00		
12	Accounts Payable		3 0 0 0 00		
13	Unearned Course Fees		1 2 0 0 00		
14	Mortgage Payable		8 0 0 0 00		
15	C. F. Rainier, Capital		253 6 7 4 00		
16	C. F. Rainier, Drawing	76 9 0 0 00			
17	Sales		255 1 8 0 00		
18	Sales Returns and Allowances	8 4 0 00			
19	Sales Discounts	1 8 8 0 00			
20	Interest Income		1 2 0 00		
21	Purchases	87 1 4 0 00			
22	Purchases Returns and Allowances		8 3 2 00		
23	Purchases Discounts		1 2 4 8 00		
24	Freight In	2 4 6 0 00			
25	Wages Expense	45 8 0 0 00			
26	Supplies Expense	1 4 4 0 00			
27	Taxes Expense	1 9 6 0 00			
28	Interest Expense	3 7 4 00			
29		628 0 5 4 00	628 0 5 4 00		

FIGURE 1

c. Course fees earned, $800

Unearned Course Fees				Course Fees Income	
−	+			−	+
(c) Adj. 800	Bal. 1,200				(c) Adj. 800

d. Ending supplies inventory, $412

Supplies				Supplies Expense	
+	−			+	−
(d) Adj. 412				Bal. 1,440	(d) Adj. 412

Rainier Plumbing Supply
Work Sheet
For Year Ended December 31, 20—

#	ACCOUNT NAME	TRIAL BALANCE DEBIT	TRIAL BALANCE CREDIT	ADJUSTMENTS DEBIT	ADJUSTMENTS CREDIT
1	Cash	24 1 5 4 00			
2	Notes Receivable	4 0 0 0 00			
3	Accounts Receivable	29 4 4 6 00			
4	Merchandise Inventory	67 0 0 0 00		(b) 65 8 0 0 00	(a) 67 0 0 0 00
5	Prepaid Insurance	9 6 0 00			(e) 3 2 0 00
6	Land	120 1 0 0 00			
7	Building	130 0 0 0 00			
8	Accumulated Depreciation, Building		52 0 0 0 00		(f) 4 0 0 0 00
9	Equipment	33 6 0 0 00			
10	Accumulated Depreciation, Equipment		16 4 0 0 00		(g) 4 8 0 0 00
11	Notes Payable		36 4 0 0 00		
12	Accounts Payable		3 0 0 0 00		
13	Unearned Course Fees		1 2 0 0 00	(c) 8 0 0 00	
14	Mortgage Payable		8 0 0 0 00		
15	C. F. Rainier, Capital		253 6 7 4 00		
16	C. F. Rainier, Drawing	76 9 0 0 00			
17	Sales		255 1 8 0 00		
18	Sales Returns and Allowances	8 4 0 00			
19	Sales Discounts	1 8 8 0 00			
20	Interest Income		1 2 0 00		
21	Purchases	87 1 4 0 00			
22	Purchases Returns and Allowances		8 3 2 00		
23	Purchases Discounts		1 2 4 8 00		
24	Freight In	2 4 6 0 00			
25	Wages Expense	45 8 0 0 00		(h) 1 1 2 0 00	
26	Supplies Expense	1 4 4 0 00			(d) 4 1 2 00
27	Taxes Expense	1 9 6 0 00			
28	Interest Expense	3 7 4 00			
29		628 0 5 4 00	628 0 5 4 00		
30	Income Summary			(a) 67 0 0 0 00	(b) 65 8 0 0 00
31	Course Fees Income				(c) 8 0 0 00
32	Supplies			(d) 4 1 2 00	
33	Insurance Expense			(e) 3 2 0 00	
34	Depreciation Expense, Equipment			(g) 4 8 0 0 00	
35	Depreciation Expense, Building			(f) 4 0 0 0 00	
36	Wages Payable				(h) 1 1 2 0 00
37				144 2 5 2 00	144 2 5 2 00
38					
39					
40					
41					
42					

FIGURE 2

e. Insurance expired, $320

Prepaid Insurance				Insurance Expense	
	+	−		+	−
Bal.	960	**(e)** Adj. 320	**(e)** Adj.	320	

f. Additional year's depreciation of building, $4,000

Accumulated Depreciation, Building				Depreciation Expense, Building	
−	+			+	−
	Bal.	52,000	**(f)** Adj.	4,000	
	(f) Adj.	4,000			

g. Additional year's depreciation of equipment, $4,800

Accumulated Depreciation, Equipment				Depreciation Expense, Equipment	
−	+			+	−
	Bal.	16,400	**(g)** Adj.	4,800	
	(g) Adj.	4,800			

h. Wages owed but not paid to employees at end of year, $1,120

Wages Payable				Wages Expense	
−	+			+	−
	(h) Adj.	1,120	Bal.	45,800	
			(h) Adj.	1,120	

We now record these in the Adjustments columns of the work sheet, using the same letters to identify the adjustments (see Figure 2).

COMPLETION OF THE WORK SHEET

OBJECTIVE 5
Complete the work sheet.

Previously, in introducing work sheets, we included the Adjusted Trial Balance columns as a means of verifying that the accounts were in balance after recording the adjusting entries. At this time, to reduce the number of columns in the work sheet, we will eliminate the Adjusted Trial Balance columns. The account balances after the adjusting entries will be carried directly into the Income Statement and Balance Sheet columns.

The completed work sheet looks like Figure 3 on pages 450 and 451.

Observe in particular the way we carry forward the figures for Merchandise Inventory and Income Summary. **Income Summary is the only account in which we don't combine the debit and credit figures. Instead, we carry them into the Income Statement columns in Figure 3 as two distinct figures.** The reason is that both figures appear in the income statement itself. The amount listed as Income Summary in the Income Statement Debit column is the beginning merchandise inventory. The amount listed as Income Summary in the Income Statement Credit column is the

Rainier Plumbing Supply
Work Sheet
For Year Ended December 31, 20—

	ACCOUNT NAME	TRIAL BALANCE DEBIT	TRIAL BALANCE CREDIT
1	Cash	24 1 5 4 00	
2	Notes Receivable	4 0 0 0 00	
3	Accounts Receivable	29 4 4 6 00	
4	Merchandise Inventory	67 0 0 0 00	
5	Prepaid Insurance	9 6 0 00	
6	Land	120 1 0 0 00	
7	Building	130 0 0 0 00	
8	Accumulated Depreciation, Building		52 0 0 0 00
9	Equipment	33 6 0 0 00	
10	Accumulated Depreciation, Equipment		16 4 0 0 00
11	Notes Payable		36 4 0 0 00
12	Accounts Payable		3 0 0 0 00
13	Unearned Course Fees		1 2 0 0 00
14	Mortgage Payable		8 0 0 0 00
15	C. F. Rainier, Capital		253 6 7 4 00
16	C. F. Rainier, Drawing	76 9 0 0 00	
17	Sales		255 1 8 0 00
18	Sales Returns and Allowances	8 4 0 00	
19	Sales Discounts	1 8 8 0 00	
20	Interest Income		1 2 0 00
21	Purchases	87 1 4 0 00	
22	Purchases Returns and Allowances		8 3 2 00
23	Purchases Discounts		1 2 4 8 00
24	Freight In	2 4 6 0 00	
25	Wages Expense	45 8 0 0 00	
26	Supplies Expense	1 4 4 0 00	
27	Taxes Expense	1 9 6 0 00	
28	Interest Expense	3 7 4 00	
29		628 0 5 4 00	628 0 5 4 00
30	Income Summary		
31	Course Fees Income		
32	Supplies		
33	Insurance Expense		
34	Depreciation Expense, Equipment		
35	Depreciation Expense, Building		
36	Wages Payable		
37			
38	Net Income		
39			
40			
41			
42			

FIGURE 3

	ADJUSTMENTS		INCOME STATEMENT		BALANCE SHEET		
	DEBIT	CREDIT	DEBIT	CREDIT	DEBIT	CREDIT	
					24 1 5 4 00		1
					4 0 0 0 00		2
					29 4 4 6 00		3
	(b) 65 8 0 0 00	(a) 67 0 0 0 00			65 8 0 0 00		4
		(e) 3 2 0 00			6 4 0 00		5
					120 1 0 0 00		6
					130 0 0 0 00		7
		(g) 4 0 0 0 00				56 0 0 0 00	8
					33 6 0 0 00		9
		(f) 4 8 0 0 00				21 2 0 0 00	10
						36 4 0 0 00	11
						3 0 0 0 00	12
	(c) 8 0 0 00					4 0 0 00	13
						8 0 0 0 00	14
						253 6 7 4 00	15
					76 9 0 0 00		16
				255 1 8 0 00			17
			8 4 0 00				18
			1 8 8 0 00				19
				1 2 0 00			20
			87 1 4 0 00				21
				8 3 2 00			22
				1 2 4 8 00			23
			2 4 6 0 00				24
	(h) 1 1 2 0 00		46 9 2 0 00				25
		(d) 4 1 2 00	1 0 2 8 00				26
			1 9 6 0 00				27
			3 7 4 00				28
							29
	(a) 67 0 0 0 00	(b) 65 8 0 0 00	67 0 0 0 00	65 8 0 0 00			30
		(c) 8 0 0 00		8 0 0 00			31
	(d) 4 1 2 00				4 1 2 00		32
	(e) 3 2 0 00		3 2 0 00				33
	(f) 4 8 0 0 00		4 8 0 0 00				34
	(g) 4 0 0 0 00		4 0 0 0 00				35
		(h) 1 1 2 0 00				1 1 2 0 00	36
	144 2 5 2 00	144 2 5 2 00	218 7 2 2 00	323 9 8 0 00	485 0 5 2 00	379 7 9 4 00	37
			105 2 5 8 00			105 2 5 8 00	38
			323 9 8 0 00	323 9 8 0 00	485 0 5 2 00	485 0 5 2 00	39
							40
							41
							42

ending merchandise inventory. We will talk about this topic in greater detail in Chapter 13.

Using an electronic spreadsheet, such as Excel, can be a more efficient way of preparing a work sheet. When developing the work sheet, complete one stage at a time:

1. Record the trial balance, and make sure that the total of the Debit column equals the total of the Credit column.
2. Record the adjustments in the Adjustments columns, and make sure that the totals are equal.
3. Complete the Income Statement and Balance Sheet columns by recording the adjusted balance of each account. The accounts and classifications pertaining to a merchandising business appear in these columns:

Income Statement		Balance Sheet	
Debit	**Credit**	**Debit**	**Credit**
Expenses + Sales Returns and Allowances + Sales Discounts + Purchases + Freight In + Income Summary	Revenues + Purchases Returns and Allowances + Purchases Discounts + Income Summary	Assets + Drawing	Accumulated Depreciation + Liabilities + Capital

Study the following example, noting especially the way we treat these accounts for a merchandising business:

	Location in Work Sheet			
	Income Statement		Balance Sheet	
Account Name	**Debit**	**Credit**	**Debit**	**Credit**
Merchandise Inventory			65,800.00	
Sales		255,180.00		
Sales Returns and Allowances	840.00			
Sales Discounts	1,880.00			
Purchases	87,140.00			
Purchases Returns and Allowances		832.00		
Purchases Discounts		1,248.00		
Freight In	2,460.00			
Income Summary	67,000.00	65,800.00		
Supplies Expense	1,028.00			

ADJUSTING ENTRIES UNDER THE PERIODIC INVENTORY SYSTEM

Figure 4 shows the adjusting entries as taken from the Adjustments columns of the work sheet and recorded in the general journal.

FIGURE 4

OBJECTIVE 6

Journalize the adjusting entries for a merchandising business under the periodic inventory system.

	DATE		DESCRIPTION	POST. REF.	DEBIT	CREDIT	
1	20–		**Adjusting Entries**				1
2	Dec.	31	Income Summary		67 0 0 0 00		2
3	(a)		Merchandise Inventory			67 0 0 0 00	3
4							4
5	(b)	31	Merchandise Inventory		65 8 0 0 00		5
6			Income Summary			65 8 0 0 00	6
7							7
8	(c)	31	Unearned Course Fees		8 0 0 00		8
9			Course Fees Income			8 0 0 00	9
10							10
11	(d)	31	Supplies		4 1 2 00		11
12			Supplies Expense			4 1 2 00	12
13							13
14	(e)	31	Insurance Expense		3 2 0 00		14
15			Prepaid Insurance			3 2 0 00	15
16							16
17	(f)	31	Depreciation Expense, Equipment		4 8 0 0 00		17
18			Accumulated Depreciation,				18
19			Equipment			4 8 0 0 00	19
20							20
21	(g)	31	Depreciation Expense,				21
22			Building		4 0 0 0 00		22
23			Accumulated Depreciation,				23
24			Building			4 0 0 0 00	24
25							25
26	(h)	31	Wages Expense		1 1 2 0 00		26
27			Wages Payable			1 1 2 0 00	27
28							28

GENERAL JOURNAL   PAGE __96__

ADJUSTMENT FOR MERCHANDISE INVENTORY UNDER THE PERPETUAL INVENTORY SYSTEM

OBJECTIVE 7

Journalize the adjusting entry for merchandise inventory under the perpetual inventory system.

Under the **perpetual inventory system,** a business continually maintains a record of each item in stock. **Under the perpetual inventory system, when merchandise is purchased, the Merchandise Inventory account (not the Purchases account) is debited for the cost of the merchandise and Accounts Payable or Cash is credited. When merchandise is sold, the Merchandise Inventory account is credited for the cost of the merchandise and the Cost of Goods Sold account is debited for the cost of the merchandise.**

Many firms use electronic devices to keep track of stock items. For example, when a sale is made at a supermarket checkout counter, as the bar code on each item is scanned, the price and stock number are recorded. The cash register is connected to a computer that updates the inventory record and records the cost of the item. So the business perpetually (always) knows how much inventory it should have on hand.

However, to verify the inventory record, a physical count should be taken from time to time. The amount shown by the physical count may be less than the recorded amount as a result of errors, shrinkage, or shoplifting. If this is the case, an adjusting entry must be made to record the amount of the loss. This entry is a debit to the Cost of Goods Sold account (an expense account) and a credit to the Merchandise Inventory account.

ADJUSTING ENTRY UNDER THE PERPETUAL INVENTORY SYSTEM

Here is a comparison of entries in T-account form under both the periodic and the perpetual inventory systems. Assume a beginning inventory of $80,000.

1. Bought merchandise on account, $50,000.

Periodic Inventory

Purchases			Accounts Payable		
+	−		−	+	
(1) 50,000				(1)	50,000

Perpetual Inventory

Merchandise Inventory			Accounts Payable		
+	−		−	+	
Bal. 80,000				(1)	50,000
(1) 50,000					

2. Sold merchandise for $82,000 having a cost of $61,200.

Periodic Inventory

Accounts Receivable			Sales		
+	−		−	+	
(2) 82,000				(2)	82,000

Perpetual Inventory

Accounts Receivable			Sales		
+	−		−	+	
(2) 82,000				(2)	82,000

Cost of Goods Sold			Merchandise Inventory		
+	−		+	−	
(2) 61,200			Bal. 80,000	(2)	61,200
			(1) 50,000		

> **REMEMBER!**
> The ending inventory of one period becomes the beginning inventory of the next period.

3. Adjusting entry for ending inventory by physical count, $68,400. The recorded balance of the perpetual inventory is $68,800 ($80,000 + $50,000 − $61,200).

Periodic Inventory

Income Summary			Merchandise Inventory		
+	−		+	−	
(3a) Adj. 80,000	(3b) Adj. 68,400		Bal. 80,000	(3a) Adj. 80,000	
			(3b) Adj. 68,400		

Perpetual Inventory

Cost of Goods Sold			Merchandise Inventory		
+	−		+	−	
(2) 61,200			Bal. 80,000	(2) 61,200	
(3) Adj. 400			(1) 50,000	(3) Adj. 400	

> **FYI**
> This entry would have been previously listed in the Adjustments columns of the work sheet.

The difference of $400 ($68,800 − $68,400) is the adjustment amount under the perpetual inventory system (actual physical count versus the accounting records). The adjusting entry required to record the $400 loss is shown in Figure 5.

FIGURE 5

				POST. REF.	DEBIT	CREDIT	
	DATE		DESCRIPTION				
1	20–		**Adjusting Entries**				1
2	Dec.	31	Cost of Goods Sold		4 0 0 00		2
3			Merchandise Inventory			4 0 0 00	3
4			or				4
5		31	Merchandise Inventory		5 0 0 00		5
6			Cost of Goods Sold			5 0 0 00	6

GENERAL JOURNAL   PAGE 96

Suppose, on the other hand, that the physical count of the stock of merchandise ($68,900) were more than the recorded amount ($68,400). The adjusting entry is to debit Merchandise Inventory and credit Cost of Goods Sold (account) for the difference ($68,900 − $68,400 = $500). (See Figure 5.)

Additional adjusting entries would follow, such as those for supplies remaining, insurance expired, accrued wages, and other such expenses.

In the income statement, under the perpetual inventory system, the Cost of Goods Sold account is listed under one line, rather than there being a Cost of Goods Sold section.

Here is a comparison of income statements under each of the two systems.

Periodic

Sales		$82,000
Cost of Goods Sold:		
Merchandise Inventory (beginning)	$ 80,000	
Purchases (net)	50,000	
Cost of Goods Available for Sale	$130,000	
Less Merchandise Inventory (ending)	68,400	
Cost of Goods Sold		61,600
Gross Profit		$20,400

Perpetual

Sales	$82,000
Cost of Goods Sold	61,600
Gross Profit	$20,400

<h1>CHAPTER REVIEW</h1>

Online Study Center
ACE the test!

Review of Performance Objectives

1. Prepare an adjustment for supplies.

   When supplies are bought during the year, they are recorded by debiting (increasing) Supplies Expense. At the end of the year, an inventory is taken to determine the amount of supplies on hand. If the ending inventory of supplies is significant, then an adjusting entry is made for the amount remaining, debiting Supplies (an asset account) and crediting Supplies Expense.

2. Prepare an adjustment for merchandise inventory under the periodic inventory system.

The adjustment for merchandise inventory under the periodic inventory system requires two adjusting entries. In the first adjusting entry (to remove the beginning inventory), debit Income Summary and credit Merchandise Inventory. In the second adjusting entry (to enter the ending inventory), debit Merchandise Inventory and credit Income Summary.

3. Prepare an adjustment for unearned revenue.

For revenue received in advance, an adjustment is required to separate the portion that has been earned from the portion that is unearned. We assume that the amount of cash received in advance was originally recorded as unearned revenue, which is a liability. In the adjusting entry for the amount actually earned, debit the unearned revenue account (Unearned Course Fees) and credit the revenue account (Course Fees Income).

4. Record the adjustment data in a work sheet (including merchandise inventory, unearned revenue, supplies remaining, expired insurance, depreciation, and accrued wages or salaries).

In the Adjustments columns of the work sheet, record the following adjusting entries:

For merchandise inventory: first, debit Income Summary and credit Merchandise Inventory (to remove the beginning inventory); next, debit Merchandise Inventory and credit Income Summary (to enter the ending inventory).
For unearned revenue: debit the unearned revenue account and credit the revenue account (to record revenue earned).
For supplies remaining: debit Supplies and credit Supplies Expense.
For expired insurance: debit Insurance Expense and credit Prepaid Insurance.
For depreciation: debit Depreciation Expense and credit Accumulated Depreciation.
For accrued wages or salaries: debit Wages Expense or Salaries Expense and credit Wages Payable or Salaries Payable.

5. Complete the work sheet.

Carry the Income Summary account from the Adjustments columns into the Income Statement columns as two separate figures. For merchandise inventory, record the amount of the ending inventory in the Balance Sheet Debit column. For unearned revenue, record the unearned revenue account in the Balance Sheet Credit column and the revenue account in the Income Statement Credit column.

6. Journalize the adjusting entries for a merchandising business under the periodic inventory system.

Take the adjusting entries recorded in the journal directly from the Adjustments columns of the work sheet.

7. Journalize the adjusting entry for merchandise inventory under the perpetual inventory system.

Assuming that the amount of the physical count of the stock of merchandise is less than the recorded amount, the adjusting entry is a debit to Cost of Goods Sold and a credit to Merchandise Inventory for the amount of the difference. On the other hand, if the physical count of the stock of merchandise is more than the recorded amount, the adjusting entry is to debit Merchandise Inventory and credit Cost of Goods Sold for the amount of the difference.

Glossary

Periodic inventory system The system under which the buying of merchandise during the year is recorded as a debit to Purchases and a credit to Accounts Payable or Cash. At the end of the year, a physical count of the stock of goods is taken and adjusting entries are made to record the amount of the physical count. (443)

Perpetual inventory system The system under which the buying of merchandise during the year is recorded as a debit to Merchandise Inventory and a credit to Accounts Payable or Cash. When merchandise is sold, the cost of the merchandise is recorded as a debit to Cost of Goods Sold and a credit to Merchandise Inventory. At the end of the year, a physical count of the stock of goods is taken and an adjusting entry is made to record the difference between the amount of the count and the amount previously recorded. (453)

Physical inventory An actual count of the stock of goods on hand. (443)

Unearned revenue Revenue received in advance for goods or services to be delivered later; considered to be a liability until the revenue is earned. (444)

QUESTIONS, EXERCISES, AND CASES

Discussion Questions

1. What is a physical inventory? What does the word *periodic* mean in the term *periodic inventory*?

2. On the Income Summary line of a work sheet, $126,200 appears in the Income Statement Debit column, and $124,100 appears in the Income Statement Credit column. Which figure represents the beginning inventory?

3. Using the perpetual inventory system, what account is debited when a business buys more merchandise?

4. On a work sheet, where will the amount of the ending merchandise inventory be recorded?

5. Explain what is meant by unearned revenue and why it is treated as a liability.

6. Why is it necessary to adjust the Merchandise Inventory account under a periodic inventory system?

7. A merchandising company shows $952 in the Supplies Expense account on the preadjusted trial balance. After taking inventory of the actual supplies, they still own $627.
   a. Write the adjusting entry.
   b. How much was used or expired?

8. When a college receives one semester's dormitory rent in advance, an entry is made debiting Cash and crediting Unearned Rent. At the end of the year, a large portion of the rent has been earned. What adjusting entry would you suggest?

Exercises

P.O. 2

Journalize adjustments for merchandise inventory.

Exercise 12-1 After adjusting entries are posted, the Merchandise Inventory account appears as follows. Journalize the complete entries that support these postings. The Income Summary account is numbered 313.

ACCOUNT __Merchandise Inventory__   ACCOUNT NO. __114__

	DATE		ITEM	POST. REF.	DEBIT	CREDIT	BALANCE DEBIT	BALANCE CREDIT	
1	2006								1
2	Dec.	31	Balance	✓			96 4 0 0 00		2
3	2007								3
4	Dec.	31	Adjusting	J112		96 4 0 0 00	—		4
5		31	Adjusting	J112	97 1 0 0 00		97 1 0 0 00		5
6									6
7									7
8									8

P.O. 3

Journalize the adjustment for unearned revenue.

Exercise 12-2 On October 31, the Vermillion Igloos Hockey Club received $800,000 in cash in advance for season tickets for eight home games. The transaction was recorded as a debit to Cash and a credit to Unearned Admissions. By December 31, the end of the fiscal year, the team had played three home games and received an additional $450,000 cash admissions income at the gate.

a. Journalize the adjusting entry as of December 31.
b. List the title of the account and the related balance that will appear on the income statement.
c. List the title of the account and the related balance that will appear on the balance sheet.

P.O. 3

Determine the entries in an unearned revenue account.

Exercise 12-3 For the basketball federation's Unearned Season Tickets account, list the debits and credits for each amount posted to the account and briefly describe the transaction.

ACCOUNT __Unearned Season Tickets__   ACCOUNT NO. __214__

	DATE		ITEM	POST. REF.	DEBIT	CREDIT	BALANCE DEBIT	BALANCE CREDIT	
1	20–								1
2	Jan.	1	Balance	✓				10 4 0 0 00	2
3	Oct.	15		CR42		12 6 0 0 00		23 0 0 0 00	3
4	Nov.	1		CR43		22 1 0 0 00		45 1 0 0 00	4
5	Dec.	31	Adjusting	J99	22 6 0 0 00			22 5 0 0 00	5
6									6
7									7

P.O. 1

Determine entries in the Supplies Expense account.

Exercise 12-4 For the following Supplies Expense ledger account, determine the debits and credits for each amount posted to the account and briefly describe each transaction. The entry of December 9 involved the return of defective goods. The purchases of December 17 involved the Odom Company.

ACCOUNT	Supplies Expense						ACCOUNT NO.	615	

			POST.				BALANCE		
	DATE	ITEM	REF.	DEBIT	CREDIT		DEBIT	CREDIT	
1	20–					1			1
2	Jan. 1	Balance	✓			4 2 0 00			2
3	Apr. 6		CP42	1 6 0 00		5 8 0 00			3
4	May 31		CP44	9 0 00		6 7 0 00			4
5	Nov. 21		CP53	2 2 5 00		8 9 5 00			5
6	Dec. 9		CR41		4 2 00	8 5 3 00			6
7	17		J77	1 4 1 00		9 9 4 00			7
8	31	Adjusting	J78		2 2 0 00	7 7 4 00			8
9									9

P.O. 5

Place account balances in work sheet columns.

Exercise 12-5 Indicate the work sheet columns (Income Statement Debit, Income Statement Credit, Balance Sheet Debit, Balance Sheet Credit) in which the balances of the following accounts should appear:

a. F. Dexter, Drawing
b. Advertising Expense
c. Merchandise Inventory (ending)
d. Purchases Discounts
e. Unearned Fees
f. Sales Returns and Allowances
g. Accumulated Depreciation, Building
h. Income Summary
i. Fees Income
j. Prepaid Rent

P.O. 6

Journalize adjustments for expired insurance, unearned revenue, and depreciation.

Exercise 12-6 Journalize the required adjusting entries for the year ended December 31 for Mallory Dance Studio. Begin on journal page 42.

a. On June 1 of this year, $600 was paid for a one-year insurance policy.
b. On October 1 of this year, $160 was paid for four months of advertising.
c. As of December 31, the balance of the Unearned Membership Fees account is $12,400. Of this amount, $8,200 has now been earned.
d. Equipment purchased on April 1 of this year for $3,400 is expected to have a useful life of five years, with a trade-in value of $400. All other equipment has been fully depreciated. The straight-line method is used.
e. As of December 31, two days' wages at $240 per day had accrued.

P.O. 6

Journalize adjusting entries.

Exercise 12-7 On December 31, the end of the year, the accountant for *Fidelity Magazine* was called away suddenly because of an emergency. However, before leaving, the accountant jotted down a few notes pertaining to the adjustments. Record the necessary adjusting entries.

a. Subscriptions received in advance amounting to $136,400 were recorded as Unearned Subscriptions. At year-end, $90,200 has been earned.
b. Depreciation of equipment for the year is $18,600.
c. The amount of expired insurance for the year is $916.

d. The balance of Prepaid Rent is $2,800, representing four months' rent. Three months' rent has now expired.

e. Three days' salaries will be unpaid at the end of the year; total weekly (five days') salaries are $3,600.

P.O. 7

Journalize adjustment for merchandise inventory using the perpetual inventory system.

Exercise 12-8 On December 31, Bold Company took a physical count of its merchandise inventory. It operates under the perpetual inventory system. The physical count amounted to $178,400. The Merchandise Inventory account shows a balance of $180,200. Journalize the adjusting entry.

Let's go back to the publisher of *TV Guide* again and take a look at the unearned revenues from advance magazine subscriptions and publications sales. Look at page 70 (labeled F-12) of GEMSTAR-TV Guide International, Inc.'s 2005 annual report, found by going to **http://www.gemstartvguide.com**.

1. When does GEMSTAR-TV Guide International, Inc., recognize revenue from its magazine sales?
2. Where would you find GEMSTAR-TV Guide International, Inc.'s unearned (or deferred) revenue in the financial statements, and what was the account balance as of December 31, 2005?
3. How would GEMSTAR-TV Guide International, Inc., record the receipt of cash for these advance subscription sales?
4. How would GEMSTAR-TV Guide International, Inc., record the current portion of unearned subscription revenues when it becomes earned?

CONSIDER AND COMMUNICATE

You have a friend who is a seamstress specializing in western ensembles. She receives cash well in advance of the required date, often in the fiscal period prior to the date of delivery of the ensemble, not only to enable her to purchase material, but to cover her labor. She always debits Cash and credits Ensemble Income. First, explain to her why this entry violates the matching principle. Second, identify the classification of Unearned Revenue. Third, explain when the Unearned Revenue account is used.

WHAT'S WRONG WITH THIS PICTURE?

What would happen if a business spent the cash it had received in advance for services it promised to perform at a later date?

CRITICAL THINKING

On November 1, an exterior painting company received $3,420 for a paint job that will not be finished for a few months. As of December 31, which is the end of the fiscal period, $1,200 worth of painting will have been completed. The bookkeeper completed the following entries prior to leaving on vacation:

	Cash			Painting Income				Unearned Painting Income	
11/1	3,420		12/31	2,220	11/1	3,420		12/31	2,220

The owner wants to get a bank loan by December 1. The bank requires interim financial statements to be submitted as of December 1. How will the bookkeeper's entries affect the accuracy of the interim balance sheet and income statements? What difference will the bookkeeper's methods make in the December 31 balance sheet and income statement?

A QUESTION OF ETHICS

The owner of a motorcycle shop allows his two sons to take motorcycles home to try them out on different types of ground because he believes that they need to be familiar with the products they sell. Sometimes the motorcycles are not returned to the store by the time the physical count of inventory takes place. Respond to this practice.

PROBLEM SET A

P.O. 4, 5

Problem 12-1A The trial balance of Swenson Company as of December 31, the end of its current fiscal year, is as follows:

Swenson Company
Trial Balance
December 31, 20—

		TRIAL BALANCE	
	ACCOUNT NAME	DEBIT	CREDIT
1	Cash	9 5 6 3 92	
2	Merchandise Inventory	63 5 2 2 84	
3	Prepaid Insurance	9 6 0 00	
4	Store Equipment	37 4 8 0 00	
5	Accumulated Depreciation, Store Equipment		24 3 2 0 00
6	Accounts Payable		14 5 7 8 80
7	Sales Tax Payable		2 4 3 36
8	D. N. Swenson, Capital		55 6 3 0 00
9	D. N. Swenson, Drawing	29 4 4 0 00	
10	Sales		179 0 3 6 74
11	Sales Returns and Allowances	1 4 4 3 04	
12	Purchases	76 3 6 8 46	
13	Purchases Returns and Allowances		1 8 7 8 94
14	Purchases Discounts		1 4 9 7 90
15	Freight In	4 8 7 5 00	
16	Salary Expense	36 6 5 8 80	
17	Rent Expense	14 4 0 0 00	
18	Store Supplies Expense	1 4 4 1 12	
19	Miscellaneous Expense	1 0 3 2 56	
20		277 1 8 5 74	277 1 8 5 74
21			

Here are the data for the adjustments.

a–b. Merchandise Inventory at December 31, $65,945.36.
c. Store supplies inventory, $401.50.
d. Insurance expired, $570.
e. Salaries accrued, $652.
f. Depreciation of store equipment, $3,990.

Check Figure

Net income, $43,806.62

Instructions

Complete the work sheet after entering the account names and balances onto the work sheet.

P.O. 4,5,6

Problem 12-2A The balances of the ledger accounts of Pedigo Furniture as of December 31, the end of its fiscal year, are as follows:

Cash	$ 10,592
Accounts Receivable	43,962
Merchandise Inventory	120,838
Prepaid Insurance	2,628
Store Equipment	35,924
Accumulated Depreciation, Store Equipment	29,420
Office Equipment	10,436
Accumulated Depreciation, Office Equipment	1,720
Notes Payable	5,000
Accounts Payable	29,822
Unearned Rent	3,200
P. Pedigo, Capital	120,532
P. Pedigo, Drawing	29,000
Sales	653,000
Sales Returns and Allowances	9,748
Purchases	519,374
Purchases Returns and Allowances	12,440
Purchases Discounts	8,634
Freight In	24,724
Wages Expense	54,200
Supplies Expense	1,570
Interest Expense	772

Data for the adjustments are as follows:

a–b. Merchandise Inventory at December 31, $102,765.
c. Wages accrued at December 31, $1,834.
d. Supplies inventory at December 31, $645.
e. Depreciation of store equipment, $5,782.
 f. Depreciation of office equipment, $1,791.
g. Insurance expired during the year, $845.
h. Rent earned, $2,500.

Check Figure

Net income, $38,506

Instructions

1. Complete the work sheet after entering the account names and balances onto the work sheet.
2. Journalize the adjusting entries.

P.O. 4,5,6

Problem 12-3A The accounts in the ledger of Mickey's Mountain Shop, with the balances as of December 31, the end of its fiscal year, are as follows:

Cash	$ 11,600
Accounts Receivable	3,040
Merchandise Inventory	119,600
Prepaid Insurance	3,940
Land	20,000
Building	88,000
Accumulated Depreciation, Building	37,600
Store Equipment	57,100
Accumulated Depreciation, Store Equipment	12,600
Notes Payable	11,800
Accounts Payable	18,260
Sales Tax Payable	4,940
B. Mickey, Capital	171,000
B. Mickey, Drawing	54,000
Sales	469,000
Sales Returns and Allowances	7,700
Purchases	285,850
Purchases Returns and Allowances	5,900
Purchases Discounts	5,800
Freight In	17,180
Salary Expense	53,500
Advertising Expense	5,150
Utilities Expense	6,610
Store Supplies Expense	1,620
Taxes Expense	300
Miscellaneous Expense	900
Interest Expense	810

Data for the adjustments are as follows:

a–b. Merchandise Inventory at December 31, $125,700.
c. Store supplies inventory at December 31, $440.
d. Depreciation of building, $3,200.
e. Depreciation of store equipment, $3,400.
f. Salaries accrued at December 31, $1,450.
g. Insurance expired during the year, $2,480.

Check Figure

Net income, $97,090

Instructions

1. Complete the work sheet after entering the account names and balances onto the work sheet.
2. Journalize the adjusting entries.

Instructions for General Ledger Software

1. Record the adjusting entries in the general journal.
2. Print the journal.
3. Post the general journal amounts to the general ledger.
4. Print a trial balance.
5. Print the income statement, statement of owner's equity, and balance sheet.

P.O. 4,5,6

Problem 12-4A A portion of the work sheet of Hurst Company for the year ended December 31 is as follows:

	ACCOUNT NAME	INCOME STATEMENT		BALANCE SHEET		
		DEBIT	CREDIT	DEBIT	CREDIT	
1	Cash			9 3 4 0 00		1
2	Merchandise Inventory			76 9 4 0 00		2
3	Prepaid Insurance			2 4 0 00		3
4	Store Equipment			39 2 8 0 00		4
5	Accumulated Depreciation, Store Equipment				26 2 2 0 00	5
6	Accounts Payable				14 6 0 0 00	6
7	P. R. Hurst, Capital				68 9 4 0 00	7
8	P. R. Hurst, Drawing			27 6 0 0 00		8
9	Sales		173 4 2 0 00			9
10	Sales Returns and Allowances	1 5 2 0 00				10
11	Purchases	82 3 1 2 00				11
12	Purchases Returns and Allowances		9 4 0 00			12
13	Purchases Discounts		1 6 0 0 00			13
14	Freight In	1 9 4 8 00				14
15	Salary Expense	37 5 6 0 00				15
16	Rent Expense	14 8 0 0 00				16
17	Supplies Expense	9 4 4 00				17
18						18
19	Income Summary	65 6 8 0 00	76 9 4 0 00			19
20	Depreciation Expense, Store Equipment	4 0 4 0 00				20
21	Insurance Expense	7 6 0 00				21
22	Supplies			2 5 6 00		22
23	Salaries Payable				5 6 0 00	23
24		209 5 6 4 00	252 9 0 0 00	153 6 5 6 00	110 3 2 0 00	24

Check Figure

Salaries accrued, $560

Instructions

1. Determine the entries that appeared in the Adjustments columns and present them in general journal form.
2. Determine the net income for the year.
3. What is the amount of the ending capital?

PROBLEM SET B

P.O. 4,5

Problem 12-1B The trial balance of Hakala Company as of December 31, the end of its current fiscal year, is on the next page.

Here are the data for the adjustments:

a–b. Merchandise Inventory at December 31, $65,982.90.
 c. Store supplies inventory, $510.30.
 d. Insurance expired, $853.
 e. Salaries accrued, $675.60.
 f. Depreciation of store equipment, $3,810.

Hakala Company
Trial Balance
December 31, 20—

	ACCOUNT NAME	TRIAL BALANCE		
		DEBIT	CREDIT	
1	Cash	9 1 3 6 54		
2	Merchandise Inventory	62 8 5 4 82		
3	Prepaid Insurance	1 0 2 0 00		
4	Store Equipment	37 3 4 0 00		
5	Accumulated Depreciation, Store Equipment		24 8 3 6 00	
6	Accounts Payable		14 2 8 6 96	
7	Sales Tax Payable		2 4 6 98	
8	R. P. Hakala, Capital		55 0 5 9 84	
9	R. P. Hakala, Drawing	29 0 0 0 00		
10	Sales		177 9 6 6 34	
11	Sales Returns and Allowances	1 4 9 3 84		
12	Purchases	78 8 0 0 84		
13	Purchases Returns and Allowances		1 8 5 7 82	
14	Purchases Discounts		1 5 0 3 64	
15	Freight In	2 6 3 7 00		
16	Salary Expense	36 5 6 8 86		
17	Rent Expense	14 4 0 0 00		
18	Store Supplies Expense	1 4 6 6 84		
19	Miscellaneous Expense	1 0 3 8 84		
20		275 7 5 7 58	275 7 5 7 58	

Check Figure

Net income, $43,221.36

P.O. 4,5,6

Instructions

Complete the work sheet after entering the account names and balances onto the work sheet.

Problem 12-2B The balances of the ledger accounts of Bolston Home Center as of June 30, the end of its fiscal year, are as follows:

Cash	$ 13,775
Accounts Receivable	52,300
Merchandise Inventory	71,900
Prepaid Insurance	2,080
Store Equipment	25,790
Accumulated Depreciation, Store Equipment	15,200
Office Equipment	10,600
Accumulated Depreciation, Office Equipment	5,815
Notes Payable	4,600
Accounts Payable	41,900
Unearned Rent	2,700
F. C. Bolston, Capital	95,340
F. C. Bolston, Drawing	24,000
Sales	465,500
Sales Returns and Allowances	2,210
Purchases	367,010
Purchases Returns and Allowances	6,170
Purchases Discounts	3,280

Freight In	$22,490
Salary Expense	45,250
Supplies Expense	1,470
Interest Expense	1,630

Here are the data for the adjustments:

a–b. Merchandise Inventory at June 30, $115,800.
  c. Salaries accrued at June 30, $1,560.
  d. Insurance expired during the year, $800.
  e. Supplies inventory at June 30, $385.
  f. Depreciation of store equipment, $3,240.
  g. Depreciation of office equipment, $1,870.
  h. Rent earned, $2,490.

Check Figure

Net income, $74,195

Instructions

1. Complete the work sheet after entering the account names and balances onto the work sheet.
2. Journalize the adjusting entries.

P.O. 4,5,6

Problem 12-3B Here are the accounts in the ledger of VonBehren's Jewel Box, with the balances as of December 31, the end of its fiscal year.

Cash	$ 12,280
Accounts Receivable	2,554
Merchandise Inventory	114,100
Prepaid Insurance	1,785
Land	16,000
Building	77,000
Accumulated Depreciation, Building	28,340
Store Equipment	76,490
Accumulated Depreciation, Store Equipment	18,160
Accounts Payable	13,070
Sales Tax Payable	2,784
Mortgage Payable	44,860
L. VonBehren, Capital	150,830
L. VonBehren, Drawing	46,500
Sales	380,254
Sales Returns and Allowances	3,388
Purchases	251,768
Purchases Returns and Allowances	2,760
Purchases Discounts	4,410
Freight In	11,200
Salary Expense	24,400
Advertising Expense	1,426
Store Supplies Expense	1,784
Utilities Expense	1,658
Taxes Expense	162
Miscellaneous Expense	613
Interest Expense	2,360

Here are the data for the adjustments.

a–b. Merchandise Inventory at December 31, $110,130.
c. Insurance expired during the year, $1,354.
d. Depreciation of building, $4,300.
e. Depreciation of store equipment, $7,580.
 f. Salaries accrued at December 31, $560.
g. Store supplies inventory at December 31, $439.

Check Figure

Net income, $71,340

Instructions

1. Complete the work sheet after entering the account names and balances onto the work sheet.
2. Journalize the adjusting entries.

Instructions for General Ledger Software

1. Record the adjusting entries in the general journal.
2. Print the journal.
3. Post the general journal amounts to the general ledger.
4. Print a trial balance.
5. Print the income statement, statement of owner's equity, and balance sheet.

P.O. 4,5,6

Problem 12-4B A portion of the work sheet of Susan's Flowers for the year ended December 31 appears below.

	ACCOUNT NAME	INCOME STATEMENT DEBIT	INCOME STATEMENT CREDIT	BALANCE SHEET DEBIT	BALANCE SHEET CREDIT	
1	Cash			7 7 3 6 00		1
2	Merchandise Inventory			74 2 9 8 00		2
3	Prepaid Insurance			2 5 0 00		3
4	Store Equipment			37 9 6 0 00		4
5	Accumulated Depreciation, Store Equipment				29 4 4 0 00	5
6	Accounts Payable				13 7 6 0 00	6
7	S. R. Ramirez, Capital				75 1 4 2 00	7
8	S. R. Ramirez, Drawing			30 8 0 0 00		8
9	Sales		171 8 1 6 00			9
10	Sales Returns and Allowances	1 4 3 4 00				10
11	Purchases	85 9 3 4 00				11
12	Purchases Returns and Allowances		9 6 4 00			12
13	Purchases Discounts		1 6 3 6 00			13
14	Freight In	2 6 5 8 00				14
15	Salary Expense	37 8 5 2 00				15
16	Rent Expense	14 4 0 0 00				16
17	Supplies Expense	8 8 4 00				17
18						18
19	Income Summary	68 2 2 8 00	74 2 9 8 00			19
20	Depreciation Expense, Store Equipment	4 3 6 0 00				20
21	Insurance Expense	5 5 2 00				21
22	Supplies			2 9 8 00		22
23	Salaries Payable				5 8 8 00	23
24		216 3 0 2 00	248 7 1 4 00	151 3 4 2 00	118 9 3 0 00	24

Check Figure

Salaries accrued, $588

Instructions

1. Determine the entries that appeared in the Adjustments columns and present them in general journal form.
2. Determine the net income for the year.
3. What is the amount of the ending capital?

The Computer Clinic

Work Sheet and Adjusting Entries

What additional accounts need to be adjusted?

Two months (July and August) have passed since Ms. Valli has seen the financial statements for All About You Spa. It is time to begin their preparation. Several accounts need adjusting. These include the accounts you adjusted in Chapter 4 as well as any accounts involved with merchandising.

Following is the information you will need to make adjustments that need to be journalized whether you are constructing a work sheet on paper or in Excel or you are journalizing the adjustments directly into your general ledger program.

Work Sheet and Adjusting Entry Information

Complete the work sheet using the following information. If you are using a general ledger software package, enter the adjustments directly into the general journal and post. The preadjusted trial balance for August 31 is as follows:

Check Figures

Adjustments total	$13,961.43
Income Statement Debit total	47,364.33
Income Statement Credit total	61,120.65
Balance Sheet Debit total	86,259.70
Balance Sheet Credit total	72,503.38
Net Income	13,756.32

All About You Spa
Trial Balance
August 31, 20 —

ACCOUNT NAME	DEBIT	CREDIT
Cash	4 0 3 6 1 74	
Accounts Receivable	7 1 9 6 63	
Prepaid Insurance	8 0 0 00	
Spa Equipment	1 8 0 8 3 00	
Accumulated Depreciation, Spa Equipment		6 4 88
Office Equipment	1 5 7 0 00	
Accumulated Depreciation, Office Equipment		1 0 00
Accounts Payable		2 0 3 9 3 00
Sales Tax Payable		2 0 0 1 12
A. Valli, Capital		4 9 8 8 4 62
A. Valli, Drawing	5 0 0 0 00	
Income from Services		3 0 5 2 6 00
Merchandise Sales		1 7 3 6 1 65
Sales Returns and Allowances	8 8 00	
Purchases	2 4 1 0 1 00	
Purchases Returns and Allowances		1 2 3 00
Freight In	9 9 2 00	
Wages Expense	1 6 2 5 0 00	
Rent Expense	3 3 0 0 00	
Office Supplies Expense	1 1 8 00	
Spa Supplies Expense	5 3 5 00	
Laundry Expense	1 7 9 00	
Advertising Expense	4 5 5 00	
Utilities Expense	9 6 3 00	
Miscellaneous Expense	3 7 1 90	
	12 0 3 6 4 27	12 0 3 6 4 27

Merchandise Inventory Adjustment (a) and (b)

Add a new account, Merchandise Inventory 115, to the chart of accounts. The August 31 pre-adjustment balance in that account is zero. But you know that merchandise has been purchased for resale and that you have sold merchandise. In addition, there is possible inventory shrinkage for several reasons: breakage, theft, misplacement, use as samples, etc. A physical count was taken, and the inventory was valued at $13,110.

Recall that the merchandise inventory adjustment under the periodic inventory system is a two-step adjustment.

> The inventory adjustment takes two entries.

First step (a): Get rid of the old inventory amount on the pre-adjusted trial balance (zero) by crediting Merchandise Inventory and debiting Income Summary. This may look strange on the work sheet, but it is probably the only time Merchandise Inventory would be zero. It is appropriate, but not required, to journalize and post this memo entry as a kind of placeholder so that anyone looking at the books can see exactly how it was handled.

Second step (b): Enter the latest inventory count by debiting Merchandise Inventory and crediting Income Summary.

Supplies Adjustments (c) and (d)

> Remember, you must determine the amount of supplies left and then make the adjustment.

A physical count has been taken of the two supplies accounts. The values of the remaining inventories of supplies are:

Office Supplies	$ 75.00
Spa Supplies	345.00

You will need to make two adjusting entries on the work sheet and then journalize and post them. Add two new accounts to the chart of accounts: Spa Supplies 113 and Office Supplies 114.

Prepaid Insurance Adjustment (e)

> Remember, do *not* do any calculations; the amount given *is* the amount of the adjustment.

A review of the insurance records determined that $281.67 in liability insurance coverage had been used during the last two months.

Depreciation Adjustments (f) and (g)

> There are several types of depreciation methods—all of them are an estimate of the loss of usefulness—that GAAP and the IRS allow a business to write off against its revenue.

Estimated depreciation amounts for the two equipment accounts are:

Spa Equipment	$129.76
Office Equipment	20.00

Remember to credit the accumulated depreciation account (a contra asset), *not* the equipment accounts.

Wages Expense/Wages Payable Adjustment

There is no need for a Wages Expense/Wages Payable adjustment because the end of the fiscal period did not come in the middle of a pay period. (The spa was closed on August 31.)

Completing the Adjustment Process

1. Journalize and post the adjusting entries in the general journal, page 11.
2. Print a copy of the general journal, page 11.
3. Print a copy of the general ledger.

You will prepare financial statements in Chapter 13 *before* making the closing entries. Do not close the accounts now.

Financial Statements, Closing Entries, and Reversing Entries

Barnes & Noble, acclaimed to be the world's largest bookseller and a *Fortune 500* company, operates 799 bookstores in fifty states. For the fourth year in a row, the company is the nation's top retail brand for quality, according to the EquiTrend® Brand Study. Barnes & Noble is also the Internet's largest bookstore. Through expanded Internet sales, the company ranks among the top five Web properties in the world at Barnes & Noble.com. In this chapter you will learn about two measures, working capital and current ratio, used to help determine whether a company has sufficient capital to operate and to pay its debts. You can find the figures you need to compute Barnes & Noble's working capital and current ratio in its 2005 annual report on the Web at **http://www.barnesandnoble.com.** Click on Investor Relations at the bottom of the screen and then select the link for the annual reports.

Performance Objectives

After you have completed this chapter, you will be able to do the following:

1. Prepare a classified income statement for a merchandising firm.

2. Prepare a classified balance sheet for any type of business.

3. Compute working capital and current ratio.

4. Journalize the closing entries for a merchandising firm.

5. Determine which adjusting entries can be reversed, and journalize the reversing entries.

T his chapter again demonstrates how to prepare financial statements directly from a work sheet. We also explain the functions of closing entries and reversing entries as means of completing the accounting cycle. Finally, we look at the financial statements in their entirety, and explain their various subdivisions.

FYI

Accountants sometimes number contra accounts as subaccounts. For example, Accumulated Depreciation, Building, is 122.1, Sales Returns and Allowances is 411.1, Sales Discounts is 411.2, Purchases Returns and Allowances is 511.1, and so on.

First, here is the chart of accounts for Rainier Plumbing Supply.

Assets (100–199)

111   Cash
112   Notes Receivable
113   Accounts Receivable
114   Merchandise Inventory
115   Supplies
116   Prepaid Insurance
121   Land
122   Building
123   Accumulated Depreciation, Building
124   Equipment
125   Accumulated Depreciation, Equipment

Liabilities (200–299)

211   Notes Payable
212   Accounts Payable
213   Wages Payable
217   Unearned Course Fees
221   Mortgage Payable

Owner's Equity (300–399)

311   C. F. Rainier, Capital
312   C. F. Rainier, Drawing
313   Income Summary

Revenue (400–499)

411   Sales
412   Sales Returns and Allowances
413   Sales Discounts
421   Course Fees Income
422   Interest Income

Cost of Goods Sold (500–599)

511   Purchases
512   Purchases Returns and Allowances
513   Purchases Discounts
514   Freight In

Expenses (600–699)

611   Wages Expense
622   Supplies Expense
623   Insurance Expense
624   Depreciation Expense, Building
625   Depreciation Expense, Equipment
626   Taxes Expense
634   Interest Expense

THE INCOME STATEMENT

OBJECTIVE 1

Prepare a classified income statement for a merchandising firm.

As you know, the work sheet is merely a tool used by accountants to prepare the financial statements. In Figure 1, shown on page 474, we present the part of the work sheet for Rainier Plumbing Supply that includes the Income Statement columns. Of course, **each of the amounts that appear in the Income Statement columns of the work sheet will also be used in the income statement.** Notice that the amounts for the beginning and ending merchandise inventory appear separately on the Income Summary line. Figure 2 on page 475 shows the entire income statement. Pause for a while and look it over carefully; then we will break it down into its components.

The income statement follows a logical pattern that is much the same for any type of merchandising business. The ability to interpret the income statement and extract parts from it is very useful when gathering information for decisions. To realize the full value of an income statement, however, you need to know the basic format of an income statement. Let's look at the statement section by section.

Net Sales	$252,460
− Cost of Goods Sold	88,720
Gross Profit	$163,740
− Operating Expenses	59,028
Income from Operations	$104,712

Rainier Plumbing Supply
Work Sheet
For Year Ended December 31, 20—

	ACCOUNT NAME	TRIAL BALANCE DEBIT	TRIAL BALANCE CREDIT	ADJUSTMENTS DEBIT	ADJUSTMENTS CREDIT	INCOME STATEMENT DEBIT	INCOME STATEMENT CREDIT
1	Cash	24 1 5 4 00					
2	Notes Receivable	4 0 0 0 00					
3	Accounts Receivable	29 4 4 6 00					
4	Merchandise Inventory	67 0 0 0 00		(b) 65 8 0 0 00	(a) 67 0 0 0 00		
5	Prepaid Insurance	9 6 0 00			(e) 3 2 0 00		
6	Land	120 1 0 0 00					
7	Building	130 0 0 0 00					
8	Accumulated Depr.,						
9	Building		52 0 0 0 00		(g) 4 0 0 0 00		
10	Equipment	33 6 0 0 00					
11	Accumulated Depr.,						
12	Equipment		16 4 0 0 00		(f) 4 8 0 0 00		
13	Notes Payable		36 4 0 0 00				
14	Accounts Payable		3 0 0 0 00				
15	Unearned Course Fees		1 2 0 0 00	(c) 8 0 0 00			
16	Mortgage Payable		8 0 0 0 00				
17	C. F. Rainier, Capital		253 6 7 4 00				
18	C. F. Rainier, Drawing	76 9 0 0 00					
19	Sales		255 1 8 0 00				255 1 8 0 00
20	Sales Returns and						
21	Allowances	8 4 0 00				8 4 0 00	
22	Sales Discounts	1 8 8 0 00				1 8 8 0 00	
23	Interest Income		1 2 0 00				1 2 0 00
24	Purchases	87 1 4 0 00				87 1 4 0 00	
25	Purchases Returns						
26	and Allowances		8 3 2 00				8 3 2 00
27	Purchases Discounts		1 2 4 8 00				1 2 4 8 00
28	Freight In	2 4 6 0 00				2 4 6 0 00	
29	Wages Expense	45 8 0 0 00		(h) 1 1 2 0 00		46 9 2 0 00	
30	Supplies Expense	1 4 4 0 00			(d) 4 1 2 00	1 0 2 8 00	
31	Taxes Expense	1 9 6 0 00				1 9 6 0 00	
32	Interest Expense	3 7 4 00				3 7 4 00	
33		628 0 5 4 00	628 0 5 4 00				
34	Income Summary			(a) 67 0 0 0 00	(b) 65 8 0 0 00	67 0 0 0 00	65 8 0 0 00
35	Course Fees Income				(c) 8 0 0 00		8 0 0 00
36	Supplies			(d) 4 1 2 00			
37	Insurance Expense			(e) 3 2 0 00		3 2 0 00	
38	Depreciation Expense,						
39	Equipment			(f) 4 8 0 0 00		4 8 0 0 00	
40	Depreciation Expense,						
41	Building			(g) 4 0 0 0 00		4 0 0 0 00	
42	Wages Payable				(h) 1 1 2 0 00		
43				144 2 5 2 00	144 2 5 2 00	218 7 2 2 00	323 9 8 0 00
44	Net Income					105 2 5 8 00	
45						323 9 8 0 00	323 9 8 0 00
46							

FIGURE 1

Rainier Plumbing Supply
Income Statement
For Year Ended December 31, 20—

Revenue from Sales:				
Sales		$255 1 8 0 00		
Less: Sales Returns and Allowances	$ 8 4 0 00			
Sales Discounts	1 8 8 0 00	2 7 2 0 00		
Net Sales			$252 4 6 0 00	
Cost of Goods Sold:				
Merchandise Inventory, January 1, 20—		$ 67 0 0 0 00		
Purchases	$87 1 4 0 00			
Less: Purchases Returns and				
Allowances $ 832.00				
Purchases Discounts 1,248.00	2 0 8 0 00			
Net Purchases	$85 0 6 0 00			
Add Freight In	2 4 6 0 00			
Delivered Cost of Purchases		87 5 2 0 00		
Cost of Goods Available for Sale		$154 5 2 0 00		
Less Merchandise Inventory, December 31, 20—		65 8 0 0 00		
Cost of Goods Sold			88 7 2 0 00	
Gross Profit			$163 7 4 0 00	
Operating Expenses:				
Wages Expense		$ 46 9 2 0 00		
Supplies Expense		1 0 2 8 00		
Insurance Expense		3 2 0 00		
Depreciation Expense, Equipment		4 8 0 0 00		
Depreciation Expense, Building		4 0 0 0 00		
Taxes Expense		1 9 6 0 00		
Total Operating Expenses			59 0 2 8 00	
Income from Operations			$104 7 1 2 00	
Other Income:				
Course Fees Income		$ 8 0 0 00		
Interest Income		1 2 0 00		
Total Other Income		$ 9 2 0 00		
Other Expenses:				
Interest Expense		3 7 4 00	5 4 6 00	
Net Income			$105 2 5 8 00	

FIGURE 2

To illustrate the concepts of **gross** and **net,** here is an example of a simple single-sale transaction.

Several years ago, Della Reyes bought an antique table at a second-hand store for $900. She sold the table for $1,700. She advertised it in the daily newspaper at a cost of $50. How much did she make as clear profit?

Sale of Table	$1,700
Less Cost of Table	900
Gross Profit	$ 800
Less Advertising Expense	50
Net Income or Net Profit (gain on the sale)	$ 750

Gross Profit is the profit on the sale of the table before any expenses have been deducted; in this case, it is $800. **Net Income**, or **Net Profit**, is the final or clear profit after all expenses have been deducted. In a single-sale situation such as this, we refer to the final outcome as the net profit. But for a business that has many sales and expenses, most accountants prefer the term *net income*. Regardless of which word you use, *net* refers to clear profit—after all expenses have been deducted.

Revenue from Sales

Now let's look at the Revenue from Sales section of the income statement for Rainier Plumbing Supply:

Revenue from Sales:			
Sales		$255 1 8 0 00	
Less: Sales Returns and Allowances	$ 8 4 0 00		
Sales Discounts	1 8 8 0 00	2 7 2 0 00	
Net Sales			$252 4 6 0 00

When we introduced Sales Returns and Allowances and Sales Discounts, we treated them as deductions from Sales. You can see that on the income statement, they are deducted from Sales to give us **Net Sales**. Note that we record these items in the same order in which they appear in the ledger.

REMEMBER!

Returns and Allowances (Sales or Purchases) is listed on one line, and Discounts (Sales or Purchases) is listed below.

Cost of Goods Sold

The section of the income statement that requires the greatest amount of concentration is the **Cost of Goods Sold** section, where the cost of the goods we sold is computed. Let's repeat it in its entirety:

Cost of Goods Sold:				
Merchandise Inventory, January 1, 20—			$ 67 0 0 0 00	
Purchases		$87 1 4 0 00		
Less: Purchases Returns and				
Allowances	$ 832.00			
Purchases Discounts	1,248.00	2 0 8 0 00		
Net Purchases		$85 0 6 0 00		
Add Freight In		2 4 6 0 00		
Delivered Cost of Purchases			87 5 2 0 00	
Cost of Goods Available for Sale			$154 5 2 0 00	
Less Merchandise Inventory, December 31, 20—			65 8 0 0 00	
Cost of Goods Sold				$88 7 2 0 00

First, let's look closely at the Purchases section.

Purchases					$87	1	4	0	00					
Less: Purchases Returns														
and Allowances	$ 832.00													
Purchases Discounts	1,248.00				2	0	8	0	00					
Net Purchases					$85	0	6	0	00					
Add Freight In					2	4	6	0	00					
Delivered Cost of Purchases										$87	5	2	0	00

Note the parallel to the Revenue from Sales section. To arrive at **Net Purchases**, we deduct the sum of Purchases Returns and Allowances and Purchases Discounts from Purchases. To complete the Purchases section we add Freight In to Net Purchases to get **Delivered Cost of Purchases**.

Now let's look at the full Cost of Goods Sold section. You might think of Cost of Goods Sold like this:

Amount we started with (beginning inventory)	$ 67,000
+ Net amount we purchased, including freight charges	87,520
Total amount that could have been sold (available)	$154,520
− Amount left over (ending inventory)	65,800
Cost of the goods that were actually sold	$ 88,720

Here's the Cost of Goods Sold expressed in proper wording.

Merchandise Inventory, January 1, 20—	$ 67,000
+ Delivered Cost of Purchases	87,520
Cost of Goods Available for Sale	$154,520
− Merchandise Inventory, December 31, 20—	65,800
Cost of Goods Sold	$ 88,720

Operating Expenses

Operating expenses, as the name implies, are the regular expenses of doing business. We list the accounts and their respective balances in the order in which they appear in the ledger.

Many firms use subclassifications of operating expenses, such as the following:

1. **Selling Expenses** Any expenses directly connected with the selling activity, such as

   - Sales Salary Expense
   - Sales Commissions Expense
   - Advertising Expense
   - Store Supplies Expense
   - Delivery Expense
   - Depreciation Expense, Store Equipment

2. **General Expenses** Any expenses related to the office or administration, or any expense that cannot be directly connected with a selling activity:

   - Office Salary Expense
   - Taxes Expense

- Depreciation Expense, Office Equipment
- Rent Expense
- Insurance Expense
- Office Supplies Expense

If the Cash Short and Over account has a debit balance (net shortage), the balance is added to and reported as Miscellaneous General Expense. Conversely, if the Cash Short and Over account has a credit balance (net overage), the balance is added to and reported as Miscellaneous Income, which is classified as Other Income.

Income from Operations

Now let's repeat the skeleton outline:

    Net Sales
— Cost of Goods Sold
    _____

    Gross Profit
— Operating Expenses
    _____

    Income from Operations

If Operating Expenses are the regular, recurring expenses of doing business, then Income from Operations should be the regular or recurring income from normal business operations. When you compare the results of operations over a number of years, Income from Operations is the figure to use as a basis for comparison.

Other Income and Other Expenses

The Other Income classification, as the name implies, includes any revenue account other than Revenue from Sales. What we are trying to do is to isolate Sales at the top of the income statement as the major revenue account, so that the Gross Profit figure represents the profit made on the sale of merchandise *only*. Additional accounts that may appear under the heading of Other Income are Rent Income (the firm is subletting part of its premises), Interest Income (the firm holds an interest-bearing note or contract), Gain on Disposal of Property and Equipment (the firm makes a profit on the sale of property and equipment), and Miscellaneous Income (the firm has an overage recorded in the Cash Short and Over account).

The classification Other Expenses records various nonoperating expenses, such as Interest Expense or Loss on Disposal of Property and Equipment.

THE STATEMENT OF OWNER'S EQUITY AND THE BALANCE SHEET

REMEMBER!

Net income appears on both the income statement and the statement of owner's equity.

Figure 3 is a partial work sheet for Rainier Plumbing Supply. Here again we find that **every figure in the Balance Sheet columns of the work sheet is used in either the statement of owner's equity or the balance sheet.**

Preparation of the financial statements follows the same order we presented before: first, the income statement; second, the statement of owner's equity; third, the balance sheet. The statement of owner's equity shows why the balance of the Capital account has changed from the beginning of the

Rainier Plumbing Supply
Work Sheet
For Year Ended December 31, 20—

	ACCOUNT NAME	TRIAL BALANCE DEBIT	TRIAL BALANCE CREDIT	ADJUSTMENTS DEBIT	ADJUSTMENTS CREDIT	BALANCE SHEET DEBIT	BALANCE SHEET CREDIT	
1	Cash	24 1 5 4 00				24 1 5 4 00		1
2	Notes Receivable	4 0 0 0 00				4 0 0 0 00		2
3	Accounts Receiv.	29 4 4 6 00				29 4 4 6 00		3
4	Merchandise Inven.	67 0 0 0 00		(b) 65 8 0 0 00	(a) 67 0 0 0 00	65 8 0 0 00		4
5	Prepaid Insurance	9 6 0 00			(e) 3 2 0 00	6 4 0 00		5
6	Land	120 1 0 0 00				120 1 0 0 00		6
7	Building	130 0 0 0 00				130 0 0 0 00		7
8	Accum. Depr., Build.		52 0 0 0 00		(g) 4 0 0 0 00		56 0 0 0 00	8
9	Equipment	33 6 0 0 00				33 6 0 0 00		9
10	Accum. Depr., Equip.		16 4 0 0 00		(f) 4 8 0 0 00		21 2 0 0 00	10
11	Notes Payable		36 4 0 0 00				36 4 0 0 00	11
12	Accounts Payable		3 0 0 0 00				3 0 0 0 00	12
13	Unearn. Course Fees		1 2 0 0 00	(c) 8 0 0 00			4 0 0 00	13
14	Mortgage Payable		8 0 0 0 00				8 0 0 0 00	14
15	C. F. Rainier,							15
16	Capital		253 6 7 4 00				253 6 7 4 00	16
17	C. F. Rainier, Draw.	76 9 0 0 00				76 9 0 0 00		17
18	Sales		255 1 8 0 00					18
19	Sales Returns and							19
20	Allowances	8 4 0 00						20
21	Sales Discounts	1 8 8 0 00						21
22	Interest Income		1 2 0 00					22
23	Purchases	87 1 4 0 00						23
24	Purchases Returns							24
25	and Allowances		8 3 2 00					25
26	Purchases Discounts		1 2 4 8 00					26
27	Freight In	2 4 6 0 00						27
28	Wages Expense	45 8 0 0 00		(h) 1 1 2 0 00				28
29	Supplies Expense	1 4 4 0 00			(d) 4 1 2 00			29
30	Taxes Expense	1 9 6 0 00						30
31	Interest Expense	3 7 4 00						31
32		628 0 5 4 00	628 0 5 4 00					32
33	Income Summary			(a) 67 0 0 0 00	(b) 65 8 0 0 00			33
34	Course Fees Income				(c) 8 0 0 00			34
35	Supplies			(d) 4 1 2 00		4 1 2 00		35
36	Insurance Expense			(e) 3 2 0 00				36
37	Depr. Expense,							37
38	Equipment			(f) 4 8 0 0 00				38
39	Depr. Expense,							39
40	Building			(g) 4 0 0 0 00				40
41	Wages Payable				(h) 1 1 2 0 00		1 1 2 0 00	41
42				144 2 5 2 00	144 2 5 2 00	485 0 5 2 00	379 7 9 4 00	42
43	Net Income						105 2 5 8 00	43
44						485 0 5 2 00	485 0 5 2 00	44
45								45

FIGURE 3

fiscal period to the end of it. In preparing the statement of owner's equity, always look into the ledger for the owner's Capital account to find any changes, such as additional investments, made during the year.

In Figure 4 we observe the balance of C. F. Rainier, Capital, listed on the work sheet as $253,674. We note from the ledger account a credit of $8,000 representing an additional investment. Therefore, the beginning balance of C. F. Rainier, Capital, was $245,674 ($253,674 − $8,000).

REMEMBER!

The columns *do not* represent debit or credit columns. The columns are for making computations and listing totals.

FIGURE 4

Rainier Plumbing Supply Statement of Owner's Equity For Year Ended December 31, 20—		
C. F. Rainier, Capital, January 1, 20—		$ 245 6 7 4 00
Additional Investment, August 26, 20—		8 0 0 0 00
Total Investment		$ 253 6 7 4 00
Net Income for the Year	$ 105 2 5 8 00	
Less Withdrawals for the Year	76 9 0 0 00	
Increase in Capital		28 3 5 8 00
C. F. Rainier, Capital, December 31, 20—		$ 282 0 3 2 00

BALANCE SHEET CLASSIFICATIONS

OBJECTIVE 2

Prepare a classified balance sheet for any type of business.

Balance sheet classifications are generally uniform for all types of business enterprises. You are strongly urged to take the time to learn the following definitions of the classifications and the order of accounts within them. As you read, refer to Figure 5.

Current Assets

FYI

Some companies are so successful that they accumulate cash from earnings that is not needed to pay current obligations. Rather than leaving the cash in a bank account, companies may prefer to invest it in short-term government or corporate notes or bonds. These are called marketable securities. On the balance sheet, Marketable Securities is a separate account listed just below Cash.

Current Assets consist of cash and any other assets or resources that are expected to be realized in cash or to be sold or consumed during the normal operating cycle of the business (or one year, if the normal operating cycle is less than twelve months).

Accountants list current assets in the order of their convertibility into cash—in other words, their **liquidity**. (If you've got an asset such as a car or a stereo and you sell it quickly and turn it into cash, you are said to be turning it into a *liquid* state.) If the first four accounts shown under Current Assets in Figure 5 are present, they are always recorded in the same order: (1) Cash, (2) Notes Receivable, (3) Accounts Receivable, and (4) Merchandise Inventory.

Notes Receivable (current) are short-term (one year or less) promissory notes (promise-to-pay notes) held by the firm. A note is generally received from a customer as a substitute for a charge account.

Prepaid Insurance and Supplies are considered prepaid items that will be used up or will expire within the following operating cycle or year. Generally, these prepaid items are not converted into cash and that's why they appear

Rainier Plumbing Supply
Balance Sheet
December 31, 20—

Assets																
Current Assets:																
Cash								$ 24	1	5	4	00				
Notes Receivable								4	0	0	0	00				
Accounts Receivable								29	4	4	6	00				
Merchandise Inventory								65	8	0	0	00				
Prepaid Insurance									6	4	0	00				
Supplies									4	1	2	00				
Total Current Assets													$124	4	5	2	00
Property and Equipment:																
Land								$120	1	0	0	00				
Building	$130	0	0	0	00											
Less Accumulated Depreciation	56	0	0	0	00		74	0	0	0	00					
Equipment	$ 33	6	0	0	00											
Less Accumulated Depreciation	21	2	0	0	00		12	4	0	0	00					
Total Property and Equipment													206	5	0	0	00
Total Assets													$330	9	5	2	00
Liabilities																
Current Liabilities:																
Notes Payable								$ 36	4	0	0	00				
Mortgage Payable (current portion)								2	0	0	0	00				
Accounts Payable								3	0	0	0	00				
Wages Payable								1	1	2	0	00				
Unearned Course Fees									4	0	0	00				
Total Current Liabilities													$ 42	9	2	0	00
Long-Term Liabilities:																
Mortgage Payable													6	0	0	0	00
Total Liabilities													$ 48	9	2	0	00
Owner's Equity																
C. F. Rainier, Capital													282	0	3	2	00
Total Liabilities and Owner's Equity													$330	9	5	2	00

FIGURE 5

at the bottom of the Current Assets section. There is no particular reason to list Prepaid Insurance before Supplies. Supplies could just as easily have preceded Prepaid Insurance.

Property and Equipment

Property and Equipment are relatively long-lived assets that are held for use in the production or sale of other assets or services; some accountants refer to them as *fixed assets*. The three types of accounts that usually appear in this category are Land, Building, and Equipment (refer to Figure 5). Note that

The barn, the tractor, and the land this man is working are all classified as fixed assets in the Property and Equipment section. Only the barn and tractor, however, are subject to depreciation.

the Building and Equipment accounts are followed by their respective Accumulated Depreciation accounts. We list these assets in order of their length of life, with the longest-lived asset placed first.

Current Liabilities

Current Liabilities are debts that will become due within the normal operating cycle of the business, usually within one year; they normally will be paid, when due, from current assets. List current liabilities in the order of their expected payment. Notes Payable represents the amount owed on promissory notes. Mortgage Payable is the payment one makes to reduce the principal of the mortgage in a given year. Accounts Payable are debts owed to creditors. Wages Payable and any other accrued liabilities, such as Commissions Payable and the current portion of unearned revenue accounts, usually fall at the bottom of the list of current liabilities.

Long-Term Liabilities

Long-Term Liabilities are debts that are payable over a comparatively long period, usually longer than one year. The current portion of notes, contracts, and loans (the amount of principal due within the next year) is shown as a current liability. The remaining amount is shown as a long-term liability.

Working Capital and Current Ratio

OBJECTIVE 3

Compute working capital and current ratio.

Both the management and the short-term creditors of a firm are vitally interested in two questions:

1. Does the firm have a sufficient amount of capital to operate?
2. Does the firm have the ability to pay its debts?

Two measures used to answer these questions are a firm's working capital and its current ratio; the necessary data are taken from a classified balance sheet.

Working capital is determined by subtracting current liabilities from current assets; thus,

Working Capital = Current Assets − Current Liabilities

The normal operating cycle for most firms is less than one year. Because current assets equal cash—or items that can be converted into cash or used up within one year—and current liabilities equal the total amount that the company must pay out within one year, working capital is appropriately named. It is the amount of capital the company has available to use or to work with. The working capital for Rainier Plumbing Supply is as follows:

Working Capital = $124,452 − $42,920 = $81,532

The **current ratio** is useful in revealing a firm's ability to pay its bills. It is determined by dividing current assets by current liabilities:

$$\text{Current Ratio} = \frac{\text{Current Assets (amount coming in within one year)}}{\text{Current Liabilities (amount going out within one year)}}$$

The current ratio for Rainier Plumbing Supply is calculated like this:

$$\text{Current Ratio} = \frac{\$124,452}{\$42,920}$$

$$42,920\overline{)124,452} = 2.8996$$

In the case of Rainier Plumbing Supply, $2.90 in current assets is available to pay every dollar currently due on December 31.

Chart of Accounts

When we introduced the chart of accounts and the account number arrangement, we said that the first digit represents the classification of an account. Since you are now acquainted with classified income statements and balance sheets, we can introduce the second digit. The second digit stands for the subclassification.

Assets	1– –	Revenue	4– –
Current Assets	11–	Revenue from Sales	41–
Property and Equipment	12–	Other Income	42–
Liabilities	2– –	Cost of Goods Sold	5– –
Current Liabilities	21–	Purchases	51–
Long-Term Liabilities	22–	Expenses	6– –
Owner's Equity	3– –	Selling Expenses	61–
Capital	31–	General Expenses	62–
		Other Expenses	63–

The third digit indicates the placement of the account within the subclassification. For example, account number 411 represents Sales, which is the first account listed under Revenue. Account number 512 represents Purchases Returns and Allowances, which is the second account listed under Cost of Goods Sold. Account number 312 represents Drawing, which is the second account listed under Owner's Equity.

CLOSING ENTRIES

OBJECTIVE 4

Journalize the closing entries for a merchandising firm.

Now let's look at closing entries for a merchandising business. You follow the same four steps to close or zero out the revenue, expense, and Drawing accounts as you do for a service business.

At the end of a fiscal period, you close the revenue and expense accounts so that you can start the next fiscal period with zero balances. You close the Drawing account because it, too, applies to one fiscal period. Recall that these accounts are called **temporary-equity accounts**, or *nominal accounts*.

Figure 6, shown on page 484, shows the isolated Income Statement columns. After you have looked them over, let us look at the four steps of the closing procedure.

Four Steps in the Closing Procedure

These four steps should be followed when closing:

1. Close the revenue accounts and the other accounts that appear on the income statement and have credit balances (all temporary or nominal

	ACCOUNT NAME	TRIAL BALANCE DEBIT	TRIAL BALANCE CREDIT	INCOME STATEMENT DEBIT	INCOME STATEMENT CREDIT
1	Cash	24 1 5 4 00			
2	Notes Receivable	4 0 0 0 00			
3	Accounts Receivable	29 4 4 6 00			
4	Merchandise Inventory	67 0 0 0 00			
5	Prepaid Insurance	9 6 0 00			
6	Land	120 1 0 0 00			
7	Building	130 0 0 0 00			
8	Accumulated Depreciation, Building		52 0 0 0 00		
9	Equipment	33 6 0 0 00			
10	Accumulated Depreciation, Equipment		16 4 0 0 00		
11	Notes Payable		36 4 0 0 00		
12	Accounts Payable		3 0 0 0 00		
13	Unearned Course Fees		1 2 0 0 00		
14	Mortgage Payable		8 0 0 0 00		
15	C. F. Rainier, Capital		253 6 7 4 00		
16	C. F. Rainier, Drawing	76 9 0 0 00			
17	Sales		255 1 8 0 00		255 1 8 0 00
18	Sales Returns and Allowances	8 4 0 00		8 4 0 00	
19	Sales Discounts	1 8 8 0 00		1 8 8 0 00	
20	Interest Income		1 2 0 00		1 2 0 00
21	Purchases	87 1 4 0 00		87 1 4 0 00	
22	Purchases Returns and Allowances		8 3 2 00		8 3 2 00
23	Purchases Discounts		1 2 4 8 00		1 2 4 8 00
24	Freight In	2 4 6 0 00		2 4 6 0 00	
25	Wages Expense	45 8 0 0 00		46 9 2 0 00	
26	Supplies Expense	1 4 4 0 00		1 0 2 8 00	
27	Taxes Expense	1 9 6 0 00		1 9 6 0 00	
28	Interest Expense	3 7 4 00		3 7 4 00	
29		628 0 5 4 00	628 0 5 4 00		
30	Income Summary			67 0 0 0 00	65 8 0 0 00
31	Course Fees Income				8 0 0 00
32	Supplies				
33	Insurance Expense			3 2 0 00	
34	Depreciation Expense, Equipment			4 8 0 0 00	
35	Depreciation Expense, Building			4 0 0 0 00	
36	Wages Payable				
37				218 7 2 2 00	323 9 8 0 00
38	Net Income			105 2 5 8 00	
39				323 9 8 0 00	323 9 8 0 00
40					

FIGURE 6

accounts with credit balances). **(Debit the figures that are credited in the Income Statement columns of the work sheet, except the figure on the Income Summary line.)** This entry is illustrated as follows:

GENERAL JOURNAL PAGE 97

	DATE		DESCRIPTION	POST. REF.	DEBIT	CREDIT	
1	20–		**Closing Entries**				1
2	Dec.	31	Sales		255 1 8 0 00		2
3			Interest Income		1 2 0 00		3
4			Purchases Returns and				4
5			Allowances		8 3 2 00		5
6			Purchases Discounts		1 2 4 8 00		6
7			Course Fees Income		8 0 0 00		7
8			Income Summary			258 1 8 0 00	8

2. Close the expense accounts and the other accounts appearing on the income statement that have debit balances (all temporary or nominal accounts with debit balances). **(Credit the figures that are debited in the Income Statement columns of the work sheet, except the figure on the Income Summary line.)**

   Note that you close Purchases Discounts and Purchases Returns and Allowances in step 1 along with the revenue accounts. Note also that in step 2 you close Sales Discounts and Sales Returns and Allowances along with the expense accounts.

GENERAL JOURNAL PAGE 97

	DATE		DESCRIPTION	POST. REF.	DEBIT	CREDIT	
9	Dec.	31	Income Summary		151 7 2 2 00		9
10			Sales Returns and Allowances			8 4 0 00	10
11			Sales Discounts			1 8 8 0 00	11
12			Purchases			87 1 4 0 00	12
13			Freight In			2 4 6 0 00	13
14			Wages Expense			46 9 2 0 00	14
15			Supplies Expense			1 0 2 8 00	15
16			Taxes Expense			1 9 6 0 00	16
17			Interest Expense			3 7 4 00	17
18			Insurance Expense			3 2 0 00	18
19			Depreciation Expense, Equip.			4 8 0 0 00	19
20			Depreciation Expense, Build.			4 0 0 0 00	20
21							21

3. Close the Income Summary account into C. F. Rainier, Capital. **(Debit Income Summary by the amount of the net income; credit it by the amount of a net loss.)**

			GENERAL JOURNAL							PAGE ___97___			
	DATE		DESCRIPTION	POST. REF.	DEBIT					CREDIT			
22	Dec.	31	Income Summary		105	2	5	8	00					22
23			C. F. Rainier, Capital							105	2	5	8	00	23
24														24

Here is what the T accounts look like. Note that the Income Summary account already contains adjusting entries for merchandise inventory.

Income Summary

Adjusting (Beginning Merchandise Inventory)	67,000	Adjusting (Ending Merchandise Inventory)	65,800
(Expenses and other debit balance accounts)	151,722	(Revenue and other credit balance accounts)	258,180
(Net Income)	105,258		
		Balance	———

C. F. Rainier, Capital

−	+	
	Balance	253,674
	(Net Income)	105,258

Like service businesses, merchandisers such as this CD store need to prepare closing entries to track net income.

4. Close the Drawing account into the Capital account.

	DATE		DESCRIPTION	POST. REF.	DEBIT	CREDIT	
25	Dec.	31	C. F. Rainier, Capital		76 9 0 0 00		25
26			C. F. Rainier, Drawing			76 9 0 0 00	26
27							27
28							28

GENERAL JOURNAL   PAGE __97__

Here is what the T accounts would look like:

C. F. Rainier, Drawing

	+	−	
Balance	76,900	Closing	76,900
Bal.	—		

C. F. Rainier, Capital

	−	+	
(Drawing)	76,900	Balance	253,674
		(Net Income)	105,258
		Bal.	282,032

REVERSING ENTRIES

Reversing entries are general journal entries that are the exact reverse of certain adjusting entries. A reversing entry enables the accountant to record routine transactions in the usual manner, *even though* an adjusting entry affecting one of the accounts involved in the transaction has intervened. We can understand this concept best by looking at an example.

Suppose there is an adjusting entry for accrued wages owed to employees at the end of the fiscal year. Assume that all the employees of Michaelson Company earn, altogether, $400 per day for a five-day week and that payday occurs every Friday throughout the year. When the employees get their checks at 5:00 P.M. on Friday, the checks include their wages for that day and for the preceding four days. And assume that, one year, the last day of the fiscal year happens to fall on Wednesday, December 31. A diagram of this situation would look like this:

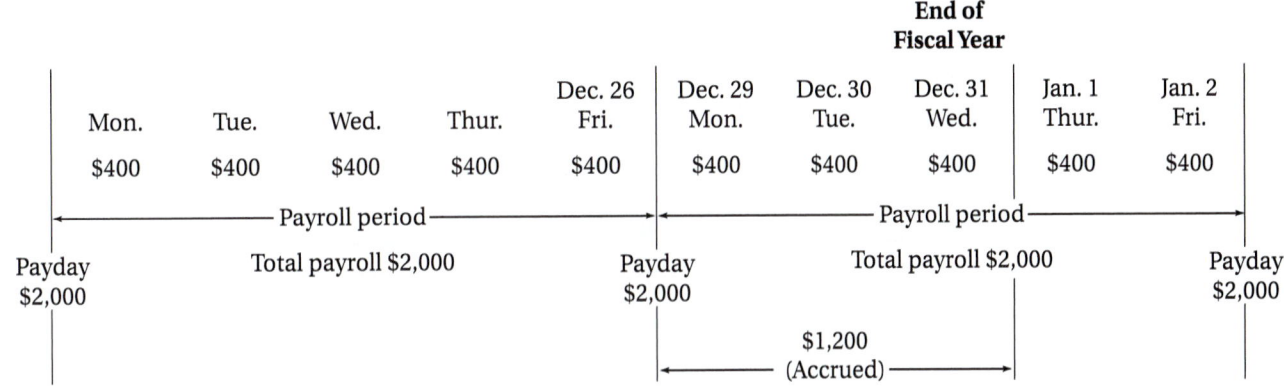

Each Friday during the year, the payroll has been debited to the Wages Expense account and credited to the Cash account. As a result, Wages Expense has a debit balance of $102,800. Here is the adjusting entry in T account form:

Wages Expense

	+	−
Bal.	102,800	
Dec. 31 Adj.	1,200	

Wages Payable

	−	+
		Dec. 31
		Adj. 1,200

Next, when all the expense accounts are closed, Wages Expense is closed by crediting it for $104,000. However, Wages Payable continues to have a credit balance of $1,200. The $2,000 payroll on January 2 must be split up by debiting Wages Payable $1,200, debiting Wages Expense $800, and crediting Cash $2,000.

The employee who records the payroll not only has to record this particular payroll differently from all other weekly payrolls for the year but also has to refer back to the adjusting entry to determine what portion of the $2,000 is debited to Wages Payable and what portion is debited to Wages Expense. In many companies, however, the employee who records the payroll does not have access to the adjusting entries.

There is a solution to this problem. The need to refer to the earlier entry and divide the debit total between the two accounts is eliminated *if a reversing entry is made on the first day of the following fiscal period.* You make an entry that is the exact reverse of the adjusting entry, as follows:

GENERAL JOURNAL   PAGE __118__

	DATE		DESCRIPTION	POST. REF.	DEBIT	CREDIT	
27							27
28	20–		**Reversing Entries**				28
29	Jan.	1	Wages Payable		1 2 0 0 00		29
30			Wages Expense			1 2 0 0 00	30
31							31

Now let's bring the T accounts up to date.

Wages Expense

	+		−	
Balance	102,800	Dec. 31 Closing	104,000
Dec. 31 Adj.	1,200		
Bal.	———	Jan. 1 Reversing	1,200

Wages Payable

	−		+	
Jan. 1 Reversing	1,200	Dec. 31 Adj.	1,200
		Bal.	———

The reversing entry has the effect of transferring the $1,200 liability from Wages Payable to the credit side of Wages Expense. Wages Expense will temporarily have a credit balance until the next payroll is recorded in the routine manner. In our example, this occurs on January 2 as shown below.

Wages Expense

	+	−	
Balance	102,800	Dec. 31 Closing	104,000
Dec. 31 Adj.	1,200		
Bal.	———		
Jan. 2	2,000	Jan. 1 Reversing	1,200
Bal.	800		

Wages Payable

	−	+	
Jan. 1 Reversing	1,200	Dec. 31 Adj.	1,200
		Bal.	———

Cash

	+	−	
		Jan. 2	2,000

There is now a *net debit balance* of $800 in Wages Expense, which is the correct amount ($400 for January 1 and $400 for January 2). To see this, look at the following ledger accounts. December 26 was the last payday of one year, and January 2 is the first payday of the next year.

GENERAL LEDGER

ACCOUNT Wages Expense   ACCOUNT NO. 611

	DATE	ITEM	POST. REF.	DEBIT	CREDIT	BALANCE DEBIT	BALANCE CREDIT
11	20–						
12	Dec. 26		CP16	2 0 0 0 00		102 8 0 0 00	
13	31	Adjusting	J116	1 2 0 0 00		104 0 0 0 00	
14	31	Closing	J117		104 0 0 0 00	——	——
15	20–						
16	Jan. 1	Reversing	J118		1 2 0 0 00		1 2 0 0 00
17	2		CP17	2 0 0 0 00		8 0 0 00	

ACCOUNT Wages Payable   ACCOUNT NO. 213

	DATE	ITEM	POST. REF.	DEBIT	CREDIT	BALANCE DEBIT	BALANCE CREDIT
1	20–						
2	Dec. 31	Adjusting	J116		1 2 0 0 00		1 2 0 0 00
3	20–						
4	Jan. 1	Reversing	J118	1 2 0 0 00		——	——

OBJECTIVE 5

Determine which adjusting entries can be reversed, and journalize the reversing entries.

The reversing entry for accrued salaries or wages applies to service as well as merchandising companies. You can see that a reversing entry simply switches around an adjusting entry. The question is: Which adjusting entries should be reversed? Here are two handy rules for reversing. **If an adjusting entry is to be reversed, it must meet both of the following qualifications:**

1. **The adjusting entry increases an asset or liability account.**
2. **The asset or liability account did not have a previous balance.**

With the exception of the first year of operations, Merchandise Inventory and contra accounts—such as Accumulated Depreciation—always have previous balances. Consequently, adjusting entries involving these accounts should never be reversed.

Let's apply these rules to the adjusting entries for Rainier Plumbing Supply.

(Do not reverse; Merchandise Inventory is an asset, but it was decreased. Also, it has a previous balance.)

Merchandise Inventory				Income Summary		
	+	−				
Balance	67,000	Adj.	67,000	Adj.	67,000	

(Do not reverse; Merchandise Inventory is an asset, but it has a previous balance.)

Merchandise Inventory				Income Summary		
	+	−				
Balance	67,000	Adj.	67,000	Adj.	67,000	Adj. 65,800
Adj.	65,800					

(Do not reverse; Unearned Course Fees is a liability, but it was decreased. Also, it has a previous balance.)

Course Fees Income				Unearned Course Fees		
	−	+			−	+
		Adj.	800	Adj.	800	Balance 1,200

(Reverse; Supplies is an asset account. It was increased, and it had no previous balance.

Supplies				Supplies Expense		
	+	−			+	−
Adj.	412			Balance	1,440	Adj. 412

(Do not reverse; Prepaid Insurance is an asset account, but it was decreased. Also, it has a previous balance.)

Insurance Expense				Prepaid Insurance		
	+	−			+	−
Adj.	320			Balance	960	Adj. 320

(Do not reverse; Accumulated Depreciation is a contra-asset, and it always has a previous balance after the first year.)

Depreciation Expense, Equipment				Accumulated Depreciation, Equipment		
	+	−			−	+
Adj.	4,800					Balance 16,400
						Adj. 4,800

(Do not reverse; Accumulated Depreciation is a contra-asset, and it always has a previous balance after the first year.)

Depreciation Expense, Building				Accumulated Depreciation, Building		
	+	−			−	+
Adj.	4,000					Balance 52,000
						Adj. 4,000

(Reverse; Wages Payable is a liability account. It was increased, and it had no previous balance.)

Wages Expense				Wages Payable		
	+	−			−	+
Balance	45,800					Adj. 1,120
Adj.	1,120					

REMEMBER!

Reversing entries are optional.

Whenever we introduce additional adjusting entries, we will make it a point to state whether they can be reversed.

CHAPTER REVIEW

Online Study Center
ACE the test!

Review of Performance Objectives

1. Prepare a classified income statement for a merchandising firm.

The outline of the income statement looks like this:

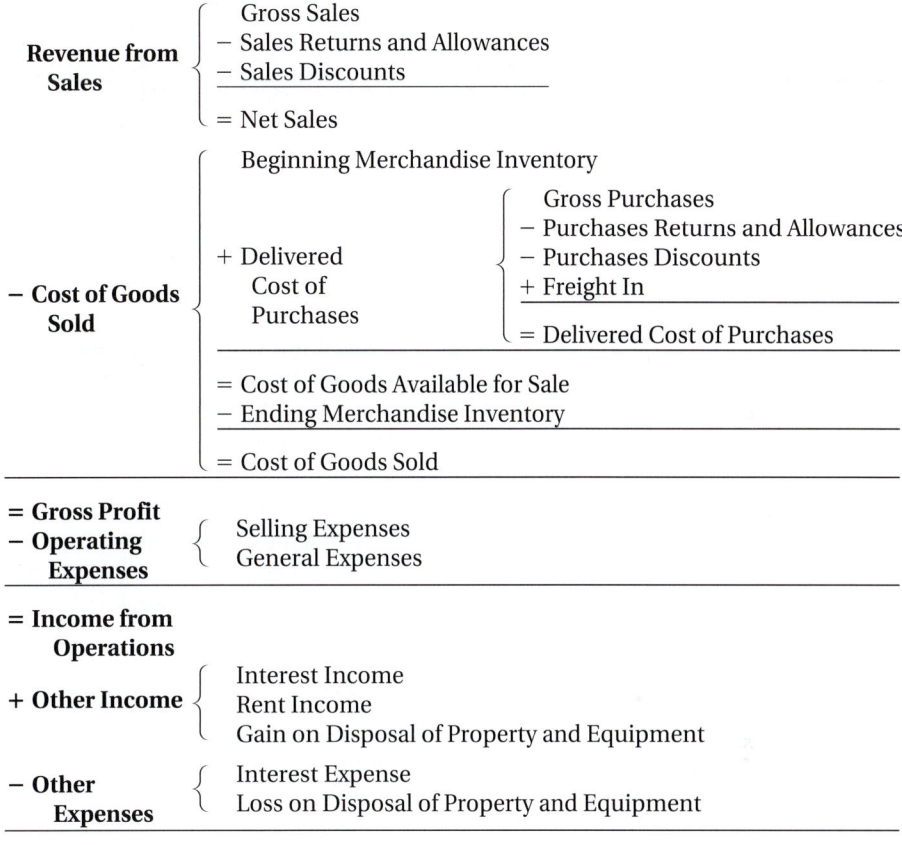

2. Prepare a classified balance sheet for any type of business.

The outline of the balance sheet looks like this:

Assets **Current Assets** (listed in the order of their convertibility into cash)

1. Cash
2. Notes Receivable
3. Accounts Receivable
4. Merchandise Inventory
5. Prepaid items (Supplies; Prepaid Insurance)

Property and Equipment (listed in the order of their length of life; the asset with the longest life is placed first)

1. Land
2. Buildings
3. Equipment

Liabilities **Current Liabilities** (listed in the order of their urgency of payment; the most pressing obligation is placed first)

1. Notes Payable
2. Mortgage Payable or Contracts Payable (current portion)
3. Accounts Payable
4. Accrued liabilities (Wages Payable; Commissions Payable)
5. Unearned Revenue

Long-Term Liabilities (Contracts Payable; Mortgage Payable)

Owner's Equity Capital balance at end of the fiscal year

3. **Compute working capital and current ratio.**

These two measures help analysts determine whether a firm has enough capital to operate and whether it can pay its debts.

Working capital = Current assets − Current liabilities

$$\text{Current ratio} = \frac{\text{Current assets}}{\text{Current liabilities}}$$

4. **Journalize the closing entries for a merchandising firm.**

There are four steps in making closing entries for a merchandising business:

Step 1. Close all revenue accounts, Purchases Returns and Allowances, and Purchases Discounts into Income Summary (any accounts listed as credits in the work sheet Income Statement columns except Income Summary).

Step 2. Close all expense accounts, Sales Returns and Allowances, and Sales Discounts into Income Summary (any accounts listed as debits in the work sheet Income Statement columns except Income Summary).

Step 3. Close Income Summary into Capital (transfer net income or net loss into the owner's Capital account). The Income Summary balance should now be zero.

Step 4. Close Drawing into Capital.

5. **Determine which adjusting entries can be reversed, and journalize the reversing entries.**

The use of reversing entries is optional. Reverse the adjusting entries that increase either asset or liability accounts that do not have previous balances. A contra-account like Accumulated Depreciation should not be reversed. Reversing entries are dated as of the first day of the next fiscal period.

Glossary

Cost of Goods Sold A section of the income statement in which the amount of the cost of the goods the business sold is calculated. Terms often used to describe the same thing are *cost of merchandise sold* and *cost of sales*.

Merchandise Inventory (beginning)
+ Delivered Cost of Purchases

Cost of Goods Available for Sale
− Merchandise Inventory (ending)

Cost of Goods Sold   (476)

Current Assets Cash and any other assets or resources that are expected to be realized in cash or to be sold or consumed during the normal operating cycle of the business (or one year, if the normal operating cycle is less than twelve months). (480)

Current Liabilities Debts that will become due within the normal operating cycle of a business, usually within one year, and that are normally paid from current assets. (482)

Current ratio A firm's current assets divided by its current liabilities. Portrays a firm's short-term debt-paying ability. (482)

Delivered Cost of Purchases Net Purchases plus Freight In:

Net Purchases
+ Freight In

Delivered Cost of Purchases   (477)

General Expenses Expenses incurred in the administration of a business, including office expenses and any expenses that are not completely classified as Selling Expenses or Other Expenses. (477)

Gross Profit Net Sales minus Cost of Goods Sold, or profit before deducting expenses:

Net Sales
− Cost of Goods Sold

Gross Profit   (476)

Liquidity The ability of an asset to be quickly turned into cash, either by selling it or by putting it up as security for a loan. (480)

Long-Term Liabilities Debts payable over a comparatively long period, usually more than one year. (482)

Net Income or **Net Profit** The final figure on an income statement after all expenses have been deducted from revenues. (476)

Net Purchases Purchases minus Purchases Returns and Allowances and minus Purchases Discounts:

Purchases
− Purchases Returns and Allowances
− Purchases Discounts

Net Purchases   (477)

Net Sales Sales minus Sales Returns and Allowances and minus Sales Discounts:

Sales
− Sales Returns and Allowances
− Sales Discounts

Net Sales   (476)

Notes Receivable (current) Written promises to pay the seller/lender the amount due in a period of less than one year. (480)

Property and Equipment Long-lived assets that are held for use in the production or sale of other assets or services; also called *fixed assets*. (481)

Reversing entries The reverse of certain adjusting entries, recorded as of the first day of the following fiscal period. The use of reversing entries is optional. (487)

Selling Expenses Expenses directly connected with the selling activity, such as salaries of sales staff, advertising expenses, and delivery expenses. (477)

Temporary-equity accounts Accounts whose balances apply to one fiscal period only, such as revenues, expenses, and the Drawing account. Temporary-equity accounts are also called *nominal accounts.* (483)

Working capital A firm's current assets less its current liabilities. The amount of capital a firm has available to use or to work with during a normal operating cycle. (482)

QUESTIONS, EXERCISES, AND CASES

Discussion Questions

1. What is the order for listing accounts in the Current Assets section of the balance sheet?

2. What is the difference between the cost of goods available for sale and the cost of goods sold?

3. What are the basic classifications found on an income statement for a merchandising business as compared to a service business?

4. On a balance sheet, what is the difference between Current Liabilities and Long-Term Liabilities? Give an example of an account in each classification.

5. On an income statement, what is the difference between income from operations and net income? Which is more useful in comparing the results of operations over a number of years?

6. Explain the calculation of net sales and net purchases.

7. In the closing procedure, what happens to (a) Purchases Discounts, (b) Sales Returns and Allowances, (c) Freight In, (d) Gain on Disposal of Property and Equipment?

8. What are the rules for recognizing whether or not an adjusting entry should be reversed?

P.O. 1

Provide missing amounts on an income statement.

Exercises

Exercise 13-1 Calculate the missing items in the following:

	Sales	Sales Returns and Allowances	Net Sales	Beginning Merchandise Inventory	Net Purchases	Cost of Goods Available for Sale	Ending Merchandise Inventory	Cost of Goods Sold	Gross Profit
a.	$248,000	$ 6,000	—	$148,000	$170,000	—	$136,000	$182,000	—
b.	304,000	—	$296,000	144,000	—	$404,000	196,000	208,000	—
c.	—	12,000	628,000	—	412,000	496,000	92,000	—	—

P.O. 1

Prepare the Cost of Goods Sold section.

Exercise 13-2 Using the following information, prepare the Cost of Goods Sold section of an income statement.

Purchases Discounts	$ 9,000
Merchandise Inventory, December 31	192,000
Purchases	480,000
Merchandise Inventory, January 1	188,000
Purchases Returns and Allowances	16,000
Freight In	27,000

P.O. 1

Classify income statement accounts.

Exercise 13-3 Identify each of the following items relating to sections of an income statement as Revenue from Sales (S), Cost of Goods Sold (CGS), Selling Expenses (SE), General Expenses (GE), Other Income (OI), or Other Expenses (OE).

a. Advertising Expense
b. Rent Expense
c. Purchases Discounts
d. Sales Returns and Allowances
e. Interest Income
f. Freight In
g. Depreciation Expense, Building
h. Interest Expense
i. Insurance Expense
j. Delivery Expense

P.O. 1

Prepare an income statement.

Exercise 13-4 The Income Statement columns of the June 30 (year-end) work sheet for Barker Company are shown here. From the information given, prepare an income statement for the company. To save time and space, the expenses have been grouped together into two categories.

	ACCOUNT NAME	INCOME STATEMENT	
		DEBIT	CREDIT
21	Income Summary	27 0 0 0 00	23 0 0 0 00
22	Sales		291 0 0 0 00
23	Sales Returns and Allowances	11 1 0 0 00	
24	Sales Discounts	4 1 0 0 00	
25	Purchases	116 0 0 0 00	
26	Purchases Returns and Allowances		1 2 0 0 00
27	Purchases Discounts		1 0 0 0 00
28	Freight In	7 5 0 0 00	
29	Selling Expenses	56 0 0 0 00	
30	General Expenses	49 0 0 0 00	
31		270 7 0 0 00	316 2 0 0 00
32	Net Income	45 5 0 0 00	
		316 2 0 0 00	316 2 0 0 00

P.O. 2

Classify balance sheet items.

Exercise 13-5 Identify each of the following items relating to sections of a balance sheet as Current Assets (CA), Property and Equipment (PE), Current Liabilities (CL), Long-Term Liabilities (LTL), or Owner's Equity (OE).

a. Accounts Receivable
b. Building
c. Wages Payable
d. Prepaid Taxes
e. Mortgage Payable (current)
f. Mortgage Payable (due in 3 years)
g. Unearned Fees
h. D. Marlor, Capital
i. Notes Payable (due in 3 months)

P.O. 3

Determine working capital and current ratio.

Exercise 13-6 On December 31, 20—, the following selected accounts and amounts appeared on the balance sheet. Determine the amount of the working capital and the current ratio.

Building	$160,000
Prepaid Insurance	600
Merchandise Inventory	72,000
Store Equipment	14,000
Unearned Fees	700
Notes Payable	7,000
Accumulated Depreciation, Building	72,000
Accounts Payable	22,000
Land	40,000
Cash	9,000
Accumulated Depreciation, Store Equipment	6,000
Notes Receivable	4,000
Mortgage Payable (current portion)	4,400
Salaries Payable	2,000
C. Rorson, Capital	101,500
Mortgage Payable (due in 4 years)	85,000

P.O. 4

Journalize closing entries.

Exercise 13-7 From the following T accounts, journalize the closing entries dated December 31:

Salary Expense		H. Beal, Drawing		Purchases Returns and Allowances	
+	−	+	−	−	+
68,000		54,000			7,600

Purchases		Miscellaneous Expense		Rent Expense	
+	−	+	−	+	−
236,800		13,200		24,000	

Sales Returns and Allowances		Freight In		Sales	
+	−	+	−	−	+
8,000		15,200			504,000

Income Summary		H. Beal, Capital		Purchases Discounts	
88,000	104,000	−	+	−	+
			336,000		5,600

P.O. 4

From T accounts, prepare a statement of owner's equity.

Exercise 13-8 From the following information, journalize the last two closing entries, and present a statement of owner's equity for Nakamura Company:

T. H. Nakamura, Capital				Income Summary			
−	+			Dec. 31 Adj.	192,000	Dec. 31 Adj.	204,000
	Jan. 1 Balance	440,000		Dec. 31 Closing	410,000	Dec. 31 Closing	490,000
	Apr. 7	16,000					

T. H. Nakamura, Drawing		
	+	−
Mar. 1	32,000	
Dec. 9	37,000	

Let's analyze Barnes & Noble's working capital and current ratio for 2005. The 2005 annual report can be found at **http://www.barnesandnoble.com**. Click on Investor Relations at the bottom of the screen and then select the link for the annual reports.

1. What was Barnes & Noble's working capital for 2005, and what does it say about the business?
2. What was Barnes & Noble's current ratio for 2005, and what does it say about the business?

CONSIDER AND COMMUNICATE

A music store sells new instruments. The store also sells used instruments for people who are willing to give the store part of the sales price. The sales of used instruments, called commissions, amount to about one-fourth of total sales. On the firm's classified income statement under the Revenue heading are both New Instrument Sales and Sales Commissions. Comment on this practice.

WHAT'S WRONG WITH THIS PICTURE?

What if the freight charges on a new desk for the owner were journalized and posted to the Freight In account? Would this affect the Cost of Goods Sold section? If so, how?

CRITICAL THINKING

You are an owner/bookkeeper in a country whose economy has been nearly destroyed. Goods are scarce; in fact, you have no goods to sell at the start of each day. You go out early each morning to purchase goods and haul them back to sell. At the end of the day, you have sold everything. Prepare a Cost of Goods Sold section for a day when you purchased $400 in goods. What conclusion can you draw?

A QUESTION OF ETHICS

Marty is an accountant. Sometimes printouts of financial statements have errors and are not usable. Marty doesn't like to waste anything, so he takes the unusable financial statements to his son's day care center to use for drawing paper. Explain why you think this is or is not unethical behavior.

PROBLEM SET A

P.O. 1,4

For additional help, see the demonstration problem at the beginning of each chapter in your Working Papers.

Problem 13-1A A partial work sheet for Preslie Music Store is presented here. The merchandise inventory at the beginning of the fiscal period was $49,584. F. L. Preslie, the owner, withdrew $35,000 during the year.

Preslie Music Store
Work Sheet
For Year Ended December 31, 20—

	ACCOUNT NAME	INCOME STATEMENT DEBIT	INCOME STATEMENT CREDIT
21	Sales		326 5 9 2 80
22	Sales Returns and Allowances	5 2 2 9 20	
23	Sales Discounts	1 9 0 8 00	
24	Interest Income		3 2 4 98
25	Purchases	195 1 9 1 00	
26	Purchases Returns and Allowances		1 6 5 6 00
27	Freight In	14 2 6 5 00	
28	Wages Expense	39 5 2 4 00	
29	Rent Expense	9 3 6 0 00	
30	Commissions Expense	9 4 4 0 00	
31	Supplies Expense	6 3 7 20	
32	Interest Expense	6 5 6 32	
33	Income Summary	49 5 8 4 00	43 9 7 2 00
34	Insurance Expense	9 3 6 00	
35	Depreciation Expense, Equipment	3 3 4 0 00	
36	Depreciation Expense, Building	4 8 0 0 00	
38		334 8 7 0 72	372 5 4 5 78
39	Net Income	37 6 7 5 06	
40		372 5 4 5 78	372 5 4 5 78
41			
42			
43			
44			
45			
46			
47			
48			
49			

Check Figure

Cost of Goods Sold, $213,412

Instructions

1. Prepare an income statement.
2. Journalize the closing entries.

P.O. 2,3

Problem 13-2A Here is the partial work sheet for Olsen Mountain Shop.

Olsen Mountain Shop
Work Sheet
For Year Ended December 31, 20—

	ACCOUNT NAME	BALANCE SHEET	
		DEBIT	CREDIT
1	Cash	9 7 2 3 00	
2	Notes Receivable	3 6 0 0 00	
3	Accounts Receivable	42 8 7 9 60	
4	Merchandise Inventory	56 6 9 7 00	
5	Prepaid Taxes	6 1 3 50	
6	Prepaid Insurance	6 3 0 00	
7	Land	8 4 0 0 00	
8	Building	63 0 0 0 00	
9	Accumulated Depreciation, Building		21 6 0 0 00
10	Computer Equipment	5 4 2 4 00	
11	Accumulated Depreciation, Computer Equipment		4 1 7 0 00
12	Store Equipment	6 5 7 0 00	
13	Accumulated Depreciation, Store Equipment		4 9 9 5 00
14	Delivery Equipment	5 5 6 5 00	
15	Accumulated Depreciation, Delivery Equipment		4 3 0 5 00
16	Notes Payable		5 4 3 0 00
17	Accounts Payable		29 5 9 1 70
18	Mortgage Payable (current portion)		2 7 0 0 00
19	Mortgage Payable		55 7 1 3 00
20	N. Olsen, Capital		65 0 5 8 90
21	N. Olsen, Drawing	25 1 9 4 00	
23	Wages Payable		1 2 7 8 00
24		228 2 9 6 10	194 8 4 1 60
25	Net Income		33 4 5 4 50
26		228 2 9 6 10	228 2 9 6 10

Check Figure

Working capital, $75,617.40

Instructions

1. Prepare a statement of owner's equity (no additional investment).
2. Prepare a balance sheet.
3. Determine the amount of the working capital.
4. Determine the current ratio (carry to two decimal places).

P.O. 4,5

Problem 13-3A The following partial work sheet covers the affairs of Komo and Company for the year ending June 30:

Komo and Company
Work Sheet
For Year Ended June 30, 20—

	ACCOUNT NAME	INCOME STATEMENT DEBIT	INCOME STATEMENT CREDIT	BALANCE SHEET DEBIT	BALANCE SHEET CREDIT	
1	Cash			33 4 1 6 34		1
2	Accounts Receivable			104 6 3 4 54		2
3	Merchandise Inventory			119 4 5 6 00		3
4	Prepaid Insurance			1 3 2 0 00		4
5	Delivery Equipment			12 9 2 0 00		5
6	Accumulated Depreciation, Delivery Equipment				6 4 8 0 00	6
7	Store Equipment			36 5 0 0 00		7
8	Accumulated Depreciation, Store Equipment				10 3 6 0 00	8
9	Accounts Payable				67 4 3 7 34	9
10	C. P. Komo, Capital				195 9 2 1 14	10
11	C. P. Komo, Drawing			37 4 4 0 00		11
12	Sales		536 3 5 2 40			12
13	Purchases	393 9 3 0 00				13
14	Purchases Returns and Allowances		7 8 2 8 00			14
15	Purchases Discounts		5 7 4 6 00			15
16	Freight In	23 3 5 0 00				16
17	Salary Expense	51 4 0 0 00				17
18	Truck Expense	9 3 4 2 00				18
19	Supplies Expense	2 5 6 4 00				19
20	Miscellaneous Expense	1 4 1 8 00				20
21						21
22	Income Summary	115 2 2 6 00	119 4 5 6 00			22
23	Salaries Payable				8 5 2 00	23
24	Insurance Expense	1 9 2 0 00				24
25	Depreciation Expense, Delivery Equipment	2 7 0 0 00				25
26	Depreciation Expense, Store Equipment	2 8 9 6 00				26
27		604 7 4 6 00	669 3 8 2 40	345 6 8 6 88	281 0 5 0 48	27
28	Net Income	64 6 3 6 40			64 6 3 6 40	28
29		669 3 8 2 40	669 3 8 2 40	345 6 8 6 88	345 6 8 6 88	29
30						30
31						31
32						32

Check Figure

Reversing entry amount, $852

Instructions

1. Journalize the seven adjusting entries.
2. Journalize the closing entries.
3. Journalize the reversing entry.

P.O. 1,2,4,5

Problem 13-4A The following accounts appear in the ledger of Shirley Company on January 31, the end of this fiscal year:

Cash	$ 6,400
Accounts Receivable	13,100
Merchandise Inventory	54,500
Prepaid Insurance	2,080
Store Equipment	26,900
Accumulated Depreciation, Store Equipment	3,700
Accounts Payable	12,800
M. R. Shirley, Capital	112,620
M. R. Shirley, Drawing	37,000
Sales	223,000
Sales Returns and Allowances	2,000
Purchases	172,000
Purchases Returns and Allowances	2,450
Purchases Discounts	3,400
Freight In	6,000
Wages Expense	23,000
Advertising Expense	4,900
Rent Expense	8,400
Store Supplies Expense	1,690

The data needed for adjustments on January 31 are as follows:

a–b. Merchandise inventory, January 31, $54,600
c. Insurance expired for the year, $1,015
d. Depreciation for the year, $5,395
e. Accrued wages on January 31, $996

Check Figure

Net income, $4,134

Instructions

1. Prepare a work sheet for the fiscal year ended January 31.
2. Prepare an income statement.
3. Prepare a statement of owner's equity. No additional investments were made during the year.
4. Prepare a balance sheet.
5. Journalize the adjusting entries.
6. Journalize the closing entries.
7. Journalize the reversing entry.

Instructions for General Ledger Software

1. Record the adjusting entries in the general journal and print a copy of the entries.
2. Post the general journal amounts to the general ledger.
3. Print an adjusted trial balance and the general ledger after adjustments.
4. Print the income statement, statement of owner's equity, and balance sheet.
5. Record the closing entries in the general journal and print a copy of the entries.
6. Post the general journal amounts to the general ledger.
7. Print a post-closing trial balance.
8. Record the reversing entry in the general journal at the beginning of the next month.

PROBLEM SET B

P.O. 1,4

For additional help, see the demonstration problem at the beginning of each chapter in your Working Papers.

Problem 13-1B A partial work sheet for The Town Shop is presented here. The merchandise inventory at the beginning of the year was $53,200. C. A. Ochs, the owner, withdrew $26,500 during the year.

The Town Shop
Work Sheet
For Year Ended December 31, 20—

	ACCOUNT NAME	INCOME STATEMENT DEBIT	INCOME STATEMENT CREDIT
21	Sales		328 0 0 0 00
22	Sales Returns and Allowances	4 4 8 0 00	
23	Sales Discounts	3 7 0 7 32	
24	Interest Income		1 8 4 0 00
25	Purchases	199 4 9 0 00	
26	Purchases Returns and Allowances		2 9 8 0 00
27	Freight In	12 7 5 0 00	
28	Wages Expense	43 2 0 0 00	
29	Rent Expense	9 6 0 0 00	
30	Commissions Expense	10 3 2 0 00	
31	Supplies Expense	8 3 2 46	
32	Interest Expense	9 6 4 22	
33	Income Summary	53 2 0 0 00	44 3 6 0 00
34	Insurance Expense	1 0 4 0 00	
35	Depreciation Expense, Equipment	3 6 0 0 00	
36	Depreciation Expense, Building	4 8 0 0 00	
38		347 9 8 4 00	377 1 8 0 00
39	Net Income	29 1 9 6 00	
40		377 1 8 0 00	377 1 8 0 00
41			
42			
43			
44			
45			
46			

Check Figure

Cost of Goods Sold, $218,100

Instructions

1. Prepare an income statement.
2. Journalize the closing entries.

P.O. 2,3

Problem 13-2B Here is the partial work sheet for Westhaven Stereo.

Westhaven Stereo
Work Sheet
For Year Ended December 31, 20—

	ACCOUNT NAME	BALANCE SHEET	
		DEBIT	CREDIT
1	Cash	12 9 1 5 00	
2	Notes Receivable	6 3 0 0 00	
3	Accounts Receivable	33 2 7 0 00	
4	Merchandise Inventory	55 3 4 4 00	
5	Prepaid Taxes	1 0 1 5 00	
6	Prepaid Insurance	5 4 0 00	
7	Land	7 8 0 0 00	
8	Building	60 0 0 0 00	
9	Accumulated Depreciation, Building		18 9 0 0 00
10	Computer Equipment	4 3 9 2 00	
11	Accumulated Depreciation, Computer Equipment		1 6 7 4 00
12	Testing Equipment	7 2 3 0 00	
13	Accumulated Depreciation, Testing Equipment		5 4 2 4 00
14	Delivery Equipment	5 4 0 0 00	
15	Accumulated Depreciation, Delivery Equipment		4 4 7 0 00
16	Notes Payable		4 2 1 5 00
17	Accounts Payable		28 1 4 0 00
18	Mortgage Payable (current portion)		1 8 0 0 00
19	Mortgage Payable		55 2 0 0 00
20	C. R. Gonzales, Capital		67 3 1 4 00
21	C. R. Gonzales, Drawing	22 4 4 0 00	
23	Wages Payable		9 8 4 00
24		216 6 8 1 00	188 1 2 1 00
25	Net Income		28 5 6 0 00
26		216 6 8 1 00	216 6 8 1 00

Check Figure

Working capital, $74,280

Instructions

1. Prepare a statement of owner's equity (no additional investment).
2. Prepare a balance sheet.
3. Determine the amount of the working capital.
4. Determine the current ratio (carry to two decimal places).

P.O. 4,5

Problem 13-3B The following partial work sheet covers the affairs of Breski and Company for the year ended June 30:

Breski and Company
Work Sheet
For Year Ended June 30, 20—

	ACCOUNT NAME	INCOME STATEMENT DEBIT	INCOME STATEMENT CREDIT	BALANCE SHEET DEBIT	BALANCE SHEET CREDIT	
1	Cash			29 0 3 4 61		1
2	Accounts Receivable			92 0 0 6 00		2
3	Merchandise Inventory			112 4 0 0 00		3
4	Prepaid Insurance			1 2 2 0 00		4
5	Delivery Equipment			12 4 0 0 00		5
6	Accumulated Depreciation, Delivery Equipment				5 8 0 0 00	6
7	Store Equipment			33 4 0 0 00		7
8	Accumulated Depreciation, Store Equipment				9 6 0 0 00	8
9	Accounts Payable				60 2 0 0 00	9
10	L. Breski, Capital				167 8 2 0 00	10
11	L. Breski, Drawing			28 0 0 0 00		11
12	Sales		520 0 0 0 00			12
13	Purchases	380 0 0 0 00				13
14	Purchases Returns and Allowances		7 6 0 0 00			14
15	Purchases Discounts		4 8 0 0 00			15
16	Freight In	24 0 0 0 00				16
17	Salary Expense	48 0 0 0 00				17
18	Truck Expense	8 6 0 0 00				18
19	Supplies Expense	2 2 0 0 48				19
20	Miscellaneous Expense	1 9 5 9 52				20
21						21
22	Income Summary	109 2 0 0 00	112 4 0 0 00			22
23	Salaries Payable				1 2 4 0 00	23
24	Insurance Expense	1 8 4 0 00				24
25	Depreciation Expense, Delivery Equipment	2 4 0 0 00				25
26	Depreciation Expense, Store Equipment	2 8 0 0 00				26
27		581 0 0 0 00	644 8 0 0 00	308 4 6 0 00	244 6 6 0 00	27
28	Net Income	63 8 0 0 00			63 8 0 0 00	28
29		644 8 0 0 00	644 8 0 0 00	308 4 6 0 00	308 4 6 0 00	29
30						30
31						31
32						32

Check Figure

Reversing entry amount, $1,240

Instructions

1. Journalize the seven adjusting entries.
2. Journalize the closing entries.
3. Journalize the reversing entry.

P.O. 1,2,4,5

Problem 13-4B The following accounts appear in the ledger of Clark and Company as of June 30, the end of this fiscal year:

Cash	$ 5,349.00
Accounts Receivable	13,910.00
Merchandise Inventory	50,480.00
Prepaid Insurance	1,085.00
Store Equipment	28,640.00
Accumulated Depreciation, Store Equipment	6,880.00
Accounts Payable	10,085.00
D. E. Clark, Capital	96,404.52
D. E. Clark, Drawing	27,260.00
Sales	201,630.00
Sales Returns and Allowances	1,640.00
Purchases	136,050.00
Purchases Returns and Allowances	3,395.00
Purchases Discounts	3,565.00
Freight In	8,260.00
Wages Expense	32,100.00
Advertising Expense	7,150.00
Rent Expense	9,200.00
Store Supplies Expense	835.52

The data needed for the adjustments on June 30 are as follows:

a–b. Merchandise inventory, June 30, $47,296
c. Insurance expired for the year, $380.80
d. Depreciation for the year, $5,290
e. Accrued wages on June 30, $572

Check Figure

Net income, $3,927.68

Instructions

1. Prepare a work sheet for the fiscal year ended June 30.
2. Prepare an income statement.
3. Prepare a statement of owner's equity. No additional investments were made during the year.
4. Prepare a balance sheet.
5. Journalize the adjusting entries.
6. Journalize the closing entries.
7. Journalize the reversing entry.

Instructions for General Ledger Software

1. Record the adjusting entries in the general journal and print a copy of the entries.
2. Post the general journal amounts to the general ledger.
3. Print an adjusted trial balance and the general ledger after adjustments.
4. Print the income statement, statement of owner's equity, and balance sheet.
5. Record the closing entries in the general journal and print a copy of the entries.
6. Post the general journal amounts to the general ledger.
7. Print a post-closing trial balance.
8. Record the reversing entry in the general journal at the beginning of the next month.

The Computer Clinic

Financial Statements, Closing Entries, and Reversing Entry

It is now August 31. You have journalized and posted the adjustments in the All About You Spa accounting records, and Ms. Valli wants to see financial statements in order to compare the results of the last two months (July and August) to those of June.

A partial copy of the August 31 work sheet after adjustments is shown on the following page.

Using the Income Statement and Balance Sheet columns of the partial work sheet, you are to do the following:

> Print all statements before entering the closing entries.

Check Figures

Net Income	$13,756.32
Aug. 31 Capital	58,640.94
Total assets	81,035.06

1. Prepare and print the following financial statements:

   a. Income statement for the two months ended August 31, 20— using the Income Statement columns of the partial work sheet.

      The following expenses have been split between selling expenses and general expenses:

Wages Expense	Selling	$12,070	General	$4,180
Utilities Expense	Selling	632	General	331

      The following are also considered general expenses: rent, office supplies, depreciation on office equipment, medical insurance, and miscellaneous. All other expenses are considered selling expenses.

   b. Statement of owner's equity for the two months ended August 31, 20— using the Income Statement and Balance Sheet (for the Capital and Drawing accounts) columns of the partial work sheet. Don't forget the two additional investments of $25,000 and $1,800.

   c. Balance sheet dated August 31, 20— using the Balance Sheet columns of the partial work sheet.

2. Journalize the four closing entries in the following order:

   a. Close the revenue accounts (every amount on the credit side of the Income Statement columns *except the Income Summary account amount*) to the Income Summary account.

   b. Close the expense accounts (every amount on the debit side of the Income Statement columns *except the Income Summary account amount*) to the Income Summary account.

   c. Close the Income Summary account to the Capital account.

      i. If the balance is a debit, it means expenses were greater than revenue and therefore you had a loss. To close the Income Summary account if there is a debit balance, credit Income Summary and debit the Capital account.

      ii. If the balance is a credit, it means revenue was greater than expenses and therefore you had a profit or net income. To close the Income Summary account if there is a credit balance, debit Income Summary and credit the Capital account.

   d. Close the Drawing account to the Capital account. Since the Drawing account will have a debit balance, credit it to achieve a zero balance and debit the Capital account.

> Why is it essential that you save and print your financial statements before zeroing out or closing the temporary owner's equity accounts?

All About You Spa
Work Sheet
August 31, 20—

	ACCOUNT NAME	INCOME STATEMENT DEBIT	INCOME STATEMENT CREDIT	BALANCE SHEET DEBIT	BALANCE SHEET CREDIT	
1	Cash			40 3 6 1 74		1
2	Accounts Receivable			7 1 9 6 63		2
3	Prepaid Insurance			5 1 8 33		3
4	Spa Equipment			18 0 8 3 00		4
5	Accumulated Depreciation, Spa Equipment				1 9 4 64	5
6	Office Equipment			1 5 7 0 00		6
7	Accumulated Depreciation, Office Equipment				3 0 00	7
8	Accounts Payable				20 3 9 3 00	8
9	Sales Tax Payable				2 0 0 1 12	9
10	A. Valli, Capital				49 8 8 4 62	10
11	A. Valli, Drawing			5 0 0 0 00		11
12	Income from Services		30 5 2 6 00			12
13	Merchandise Sales		17 3 6 1 65			13
14	Sales Returns and Allowances	8 8 00				14
15	Purchases	24 1 0 1 00				15
16	Purchases Returns and Allowances		1 2 3 00			16
17	Freight In	9 9 2 00				17
18	Wages Expense	16 2 5 0 00				18
19	Rent Expense	3 3 0 0 00				19
20	Office Supplies Expense	4 3 00				20
21	Spa Supplies Expense	1 9 0 00				21
22	Laundry Expense	1 7 9 00				22
23	Advertising Expense	4 5 5 00				23
24	Utilities Expense	9 6 3 00				24
25	Miscellaneous Expense	3 7 1 90				25
26						26
27	Income Summary	0 00	13 1 1 0 00			27
28	Merchandise Inventory			13 1 1 0 00		28
29	Office Supplies			7 5 00		29
30	Spa Supplies			3 4 5 00		30
31	Insurance Expense	2 8 1 67				31
32	Depreciation Expense, Spa Equipment	1 2 9 76				32
33	Depreciation Expense, Office Equipment	2 0 00				33
34		47 3 6 4 33	61 1 2 0 65	86 2 5 9 70	72 5 0 3 38	34
35	Net Income	13 7 5 6 32			13 7 5 6 32	35
36		61 1 2 0 65	61 1 2 0 65	86 2 5 9 70	86 2 5 9 70	36
37						37
38						38
39						39
40						40
41						41

3. Print the closing entries from the general journal, page 12.

4. Post the closing entries to the general ledger and print the general ledger.

Check Figure

Post-closing trial balance totals $79,299.70

5. Print a post-closing trial balance from the general ledger. You should only show assets, liabilities, and the owner's equity account—therefore, a relatively short trial balance. If you find any account open beyond the Capital account, you either failed to include it in the closing entries or you forgot to post it before taking this final trial balance to see if the temporary accounts are closed and only the real or permanent accounts remain open for the start of the new fiscal period.

Congratulations! You have completed your work with All About You Spa.

PART I: Completion

Complete each of the following statements by writing the appropriate word(s) in the spaces provided.

1. An actual count of a stock of goods is called a(n) _____.

2. Under the _____ system, entries to record the purchase of merchandise are recorded in the Merchandise Inventory account.

3. Unearned revenue is classified as a(n) _____.

4. Under the periodic inventory system, the first adjustment is to debit _____ for the amount of the beginning inventory.

5. Under the perpetual inventory system, after recording the sale of the goods, the accountant debits _____ and credits _____.

6. An increase in Rent Expense results in a(n) _____ to net income.

7. Gross Profit is calculated by subtracting _____ from Net Sales.

8. Current Assets minus Current Liabilities equals _____.

9. Gross Profit minus Total Operating Expenses equals _____.

10. Net Purchases plus _____ equals Delivered Cost of Purchases.

PART II: True/False

T F 1. The second adjustment for Merchandise Inventory under the periodic inventory system is to debit Cost of Goods Sold and credit Merchandise Inventory.

T F 2. Unearned Rent Income is classified as a revenue.

T F 3. The perpetual inventory system requires that each sale of goods has two entries: one to reduce inventory and affix the cost of the goods sold and one to record the sale.

T F 4. The periodic inventory system requires two adjusting entries: one to remove the old inventory amount and one to enter the latest inventory amount.

T F 5. The adjustment to unearned revenue allows the correct amount of liability and revenue to be applied to each fiscal period involved.

T F 6. Freight In is classified in the Operating Expenses section of an income statement.

T F 7. Under the perpetual inventory system, the cost of goods sold is calculated by subtracting ending inventory from the cost of goods available for sale.

T F 8. Reversing entries are optional, and only some adjusting entries are reversed.

Note: Answers to Before a Test Check begin on page A-1.

T   F   9. Delivery Expense is added to net purchases to arrive at delivered cost of purchases.

T   F   10. Purchases Returns and Allowances increases Income from Operations.

PART III: Application

1. Alphonse Company uses the periodic inventory system. Employees have just taken a physical count of its inventory. This ending inventory has been valued at $136,000. The company's accounting records show the Merchandise Inventory account with a debit balance of $132,000. Journalize the entries on December 31 to adjust the records for this situation.

2. Regletto Company uses the perpetual inventory system. Employees have just taken a physical count of its inventory. This ending inventory has been valued at $146,000. The company's accounting records show the Merchandise Inventory account with a debit balance of $148,000. Journalize the entry on December 31 to adjust the records for this situation.

3. On December 1, Wesley Company collected $20,000 for a remodeling job that will be completed on March 31 of the following year. The revenue will be earned evenly over four months. Wesley Company's fiscal period ends December 31. Make the entries to record the collection of the cash and the year-end adjustment to reflect the amount of revenue earned in December.

4. Yorkland Company has total assets of $250,000, of which noncurrent assets amount to $140,000. The company also has total liabilities of $130,000, of which $80,000 are long-term liabilities. Calculate (a) working capital and (b) current ratio.

Comprehensive Review Problem

You are to record transactions completed by Fine Fabrics during the month of February of this year. This company is located in Dallas. To gain practice in completing the steps in the accounting cycle, assume that the fiscal period consists of one month.

CHART OF ACCOUNTS

Assets

111 Cash
112 Petty Cash Fund
113 Accounts Receivable
114 Merchandise Inventory
117 Supplies
118 Prepaid Insurance
122 Equipment
123 Accumulated Depreciation, Equipment

Liabilities

221 Accounts Payable
226 Employees' Income Tax Payable
227 FICA Tax Payable
228 State Unemployment Tax Payable
229 Federal Unemployment Tax Payable
230 Salaries Payable

Owner's Equity

311 J. L. Fisher, Capital
312 J. L. Fisher, Drawing
313 Income Summary

Revenue

411 Sales
412 Sales Returns and Allowances

Cost of Goods Sold

511 Purchases
512 Purchases Returns and Allowances
513 Purchases Discounts
514 Freight In

Operating Expenses

611 Salary Expense
612 Payroll Tax Expense
613 Rent Expense
614 Utilities Expense
616 Supplies Expense
617 Insurance Expense
618 Depreciation Expense, Equipment
619 Miscellaneous Expense

JOURNALS

Sales Journal, page 56
Purchases Journal, page 62
Cash Receipts Journal, page 69
Cash Payments Journal, page 75
General Journal, pages 89–92

ACCOUNTS RECEIVABLE

Hotel Bentnor
Jerome and Woods
Wilkes Decorators

ACCOUNTS PAYABLE

Byran, Inc.
Keller Textiles
Meldon Fabrics
Taylor Manufacturing Company

TRANSACTIONS

The following transactions were completed during February of this year.

Feb.		
	1	Reversed the adjusting entry for accrued salaries, $710.
	1	Sold merchandise on account to Hotel Bentnor, $13,052.97, invoice no. 5221.
	2	Issued Ck. No. 7216, $17,271.62, to Keller Textiles, in payment of its invoice no. D1739 for $17,624.10 less 2 percent discount.
	5	Bought merchandise on account from Meldon Fabrics, $4,551.90; invoice no. RE275, dated February 2; terms 1/10, n/30; FOB Orlando; freight prepaid and added to the invoice, $147 (total, $4,698.90).
	5	Received an electric bill and paid Regional Power, Ck. No. 7217, $121.
	6	Received check from Jerome and Woods for $11,619.50 in payment of account.
	7	Issued Ck. No. 7218, $9,519.84, to Meldon Fabrics, in payment of its invoice no. RE64 for $9,616 less 1 percent discount.
	9	Cash sales for February 1 through February 9, $7,951.60.
	12	Recorded the payroll in the payroll register for regular semimonthly salaries for period ended February 12. Salaries: M. B. Corson, $2,730; K. L. Vickers, $2,240. Income tax withholdings are $382.20 for Corson and $313.60 for Vickers. Assume the following tax rates and taxable earnings limits (see the payroll register in your Working Papers for beginning cumulative earnings):

- Social Security taxable earnings, $94,200, with a rate of 6.2 percent.
- Medicare taxable earnings, all earnings, with a rate of 1.45 percent.

| | 12 | Recorded the payroll entry in the general journal, crediting Salaries Payable. |

Feb. 12 Issued Ck. No. 7219, $2,138.95, to M. B. Corson. Issued Ck. No. 7220, $1,755.04, to K. L. Vickers. Use two lines and debit Salaries Payable. (Verify these amounts.)

12 Recorded payroll taxes. Assume the following tax rates and taxable earnings:

- Federal unemployment taxable earnings, $7,000, with a rate of 0.8 percent.
- State unemployment taxable earnings, $7,000, with a rate of 5.4 percent. *Note:* Corson's taxable earnings for unemployment amount to $1,540 and Vickers's amount to $2,240.

12 Received a credit memo from Meldon Fabrics for defective merchandise, $542, credit memo no. 916.

14 Issued Ck. No. 7221, $2,912.44, to State Bank for monthly deposit of January employees' federal income tax withheld, $1,391.60, and FICA taxes, $1,520.84.

14 Sold merchandise on account to Jerome and Woods, $15,692.50, invoice no. 5222.

14 Issued Ck. No. 7222, $4,116.80, to Meldon Fabrics, in payment of its invoice no. RE275 less the credit memo for defective merchandise and less the discount ($40.10). *Note:* Debit Accounts Payable, $4,156.90, and credit Purchases Discounts, $40.10. Verify these amounts: $4,698.90, less $147 freight, less $542 return, less 1 percent cash discount (cash discounts can't be taken on freight). Remember to add $147 freight back to compute the cash credit.

18 Bought merchandise on account from Byran, Inc., $20,488.20; invoice no. 164M, dated February 14; terms 2/10, n/30; FOB Miami; freight prepaid and added to the invoice, $1,152 (total, $21,640.20).

18 Cash sales for February 10 through February 18, $7,994.14.

19 Issued Ck. No. 7223 payable to Faster Printing for invoice forms, $327 (not previously recorded). (Debit Supplies Expense.)

19 Received check from Wilkes Decorators for $4,920.14 in payment of account.

22 Issued Ck. No. 7224, $12,710, to Taylor Manufacturing Company, in payment of its invoice no. 9264D.

22 Sold merchandise on account to Wilkes Decorators, $16,721.42, invoice no. 5223.

24 Issued credit memo no. 214 to Wilkes Decorators, $156, for merchandise returned.

24 Bought merchandise on account from Keller Textiles, $16,448.01; invoice no. D1797, dated February 22; terms 2/10, n/30; FOB Dallas.

26 Recorded the payroll in the payroll register for regular semi-monthly salaries for period ended February 26. Salaries: M. B. Corson, $2,730; K. L. Vickers, $2,240. Income tax withholdings are $382.20 for Corson and $313.60 for Vickers. *Note:* See the entry of February 12 for taxable earnings limits and tax rates. See the payroll register in your Working Papers for beginning cumulative earnings.

26 Recorded the payroll entry in the general journal, crediting Salaries Payable.

26 Issued Ck. No. 7225, $2,138.95, to M. B. Corson. Issued Ck. No. 7226, $1,755.04, to K. L. Vickers. Use two lines and debit Salaries Payable.

Feb.   26   Ck. No. 7227 voided.

26   Recorded payroll taxes. *Note:* Vickers's taxable earnings for unemployment amount to $280.

27   Issued Ck. No. 7228, $994, to Greater Freight Line for transportation charge on merchandise purchased from Keller Textiles.

28   Issued Ck. No. 7229, $48.63, payable to Cash to reimburse the petty cash fund. Petty cash payments consist of Supplies Expense, $27.16, and Miscellaneous Expense, $21.47.

28   Cash sales for February 19 through February 28, $7,685.20.

28   Issued Ck. No. 7230, $650, to Grandy Realty for monthly rent.

28   J. L. Fisher (owner) withdrew $3,000 for personal use, Ck. No. 7231.

INSTRUCTIONS

1. Journalize and post the transactions completed during February.

   a. Post the amounts in the Other Accounts columns of the special journals daily.
   b. Post the general journal daily.
   c. Post the totals of the special columns of the special journals at the end of the month.

2. Prepare a schedule of accounts receivable and a schedule of accounts payable.

3. Complete the work sheet for February.
   Data for the month-end adjustments are as follows:

   a–b. Merchandise inventory at February 28, $44,262
   c. Salaries accrued at February 28, $710
   d. Insurance expired during February, $40
   e. Depreciation of equipment during February, $105

4. Journalize and post the adjusting entries.
5. Prepare an income statement.
6. Prepare a statement of owner's equity. (No additional investment was made during the month.)
7. Prepare a balance sheet.
8. Journalize and post the closing entries.
9. Prepare a post-closing trial balance.

INSTRUCTIONS FOR GENERAL LEDGER SOFTWARE

1. Journalize and post the transactions completed during February.
2. Print the journals and the general ledger.
3. Print a trial balance.
4. Print a schedule of accounts receivable and a schedule of accounts payable.

5. Journalize and post the month-end adjustments:

   a–b. Merchandise inventory at February 28, $44,262
   c. Salaries accrued at February 28, $710
   d. Insurance expired during February, $40
   e. Depreciation of equipment during February, $105

6. Print the adjusting entries, an adjusted trial balance, and the general ledger after adjustments.
7. Print the income statement, the statement of owner's equity, and the balance sheet.
8. Journalize and post the closing entries.
9. Print the closing entries.
10. Print a post-closing trial balance.

E Inventory Methods

Performance Objectives

After you have completed this appendix, you will be able to do the following:

1. Determine the amount of the ending merchandise inventory by the weighted-average-cost method.

2. Determine the amount of the ending merchandise inventory by the first-in, first-out method (FIFO).

3. Determine the amount of the ending merchandise inventory by the last-in, first-out method (LIFO).

To determine the dollar amount of the ending merchandise inventory, it is necessary to take a physical count of the various items in stock and match them up with their costs. In other words, the ending inventory consists of the number of units of each type of item on hand multiplied by the cost of each unit.

If each unit were purchased at exactly the same price, the job of determining the total cost of the inventory would be simple. For example, if there are 100 units of Product A on hand, and all 100 units were bought at $15, the total cost of the ending inventory is $1,500 (100 × $15). However, over a period of time, costs of individual purchases of units may differ. Changes in costs of individual units make the different methods of inventory valuation necessary.

We will use Carlson Appliances, a distributor of dishwashers, to illustrate the three methods of inventory valuation. Carlson's ending inventory consists of 176 Model M43 dishwashers acquired through various purchases, as follows:

Specific Purchase	Number of Units	Cost per Unit	Total Cost
Beginning inventory	34	$270	$ 9,180
First purchase	60	282	16,920
Second purchase	256	298	76,288
Third purchase	164	312	51,168
Total units available	514		$153,556

Of the 514 units available for sale, 176 units are still on hand and 338 have been sold (514 − 176).

Carlson Appliances may choose any one of the following three methods of recording the total cost of the 176 units in the ending inventory of dishwashers.

WEIGHTED-AVERAGE-COST METHOD

OBJECTIVE 1

Determine the amount of the ending merchandise inventory by the weighted-average-cost method.

$$\text{Average Cost per Unit} = \frac{\text{Total Cost}}{\text{Total Units Available}} = \frac{\$153,556}{514} = \$298.75 \text{ (rounded)}$$

$$\text{Cost of 176 units} = \$298.75 \times 176 \text{ units} = \$52,580$$

FIRST-IN, FIRST-OUT METHOD

OBJECTIVE 2

Determine the amount of the ending merchandise inventory by the first-in, first-out method (FIFO).

This method is based on the **assumption** that the first units of dishwashers purchased will be sold first. The costs of the units left will be those of the most recently purchased units. You may think of this as the way a grocery store sells milk. Because milk will sour, the oldest milk is moved to the front of the display shelf and is sold first. Consequently, the cartons of milk remaining on the shelf are the freshest milk.

Relating to our illustration of dishwashers:

Specific Purchase	Number of Units	Cost per Unit	Total Cost
Beginning inventory	34	$270	$ 9,180
First purchase	60	282	16,920
Second purchase	256	298	76,288
Third purchase	164	312	51,168
Total units available	514		$153,556

The cost of the 176 dishwashers on hand (most recently purchased) is as follows:

164 units (third purchase)	@ $312 each =	$51,168
12 units (second purchase)	@ $298 each =	3,576
176 units		$54,744

LAST-IN, FIRST-OUT METHOD

OBJECTIVE 3

Determine the amount of the ending merchandise inventory by the last-in, first-out method (LIFO).

This method is based on the **assumption** that the last units of dishwashers purchased will be sold first. The costs of the units left over will be those of the earliest purchased units. You may think of this as the way a coal yard sells coal. When the coal yard sells coal to its customers, it takes coal off the top of the pile. Consequently, the tons of coal in the ending inventory consist of those first few tons at the bottom of the pile.

Relating to our illustration of dishwashers shown above, the cost of the 176 dishwashers on hand (earliest purchased) is as follows:

34 units (beginning inventory)	@ $270 each =	$ 9,180
60 units (first purchase)	@ $282 each =	16,920
82 units (second purchase)	@ $298 each =	24,436
176 units		$50,536

<table>
<tr><th colspan="3" align="center">Comparison of Three Methods</th></tr>
<tr><th>Method</th><th>Ending Inventory
(176 units)</th><th>Cost of Goods Sold
(Goods Available for Sale
− Ending Inventory)
(338 units = 514 − 176)</th></tr>
<tr><td>Weighted-average-cost</td><td>$52,580</td><td>$100,976 ($153,556 − $52,580)</td></tr>
<tr><td>First-in, first-out</td><td>54,744</td><td>98,812 ($153,556 − $54,744)</td></tr>
<tr><td>Last-in, first-out</td><td>50,536</td><td>103,020 ($153,556 − $50,536)</td></tr>
</table>

Assume that the dishwashers were sold for $450 each.

	Weighted-Average-Cost	First-in, First-out	Last-in, First-out
Sales (338 units × $450 each)	$152,100	$152,100	$152,100
Cost of Goods Sold	100,976	98,812	103,020
Gross Profit	$ 51,124	$ 53,288	$ 49,080

As you can see, the inventory method used can have a dramatic effect on the gross profit of a business. Once an inventory method is adopted by a business, the method must be consistently used. If a company wants to change its inventory method for tax purposes, the company must request permission from the Internal Revenue Service.

PROBLEMS

P.O. 1

Check Figure

Cost of ending inventory, $399.24

Problem E-1 Bexley Nursery sells bark to its customers at retail. Bexley buys bark from a plywood mill in bulk and transports the bark in its own trucks. Information relating to the beginning inventory and purchases of bark is as follows:

Beginning inventory	1,500 cubic yards @ $0.30 per cubic yard
First purchase	2,100 cubic yards @ $0.32 per cubic yard
Second purchase	1,400 cubic yards @ $0.36 per cubic yard
Third purchase	1,000 cubic yards @ $0.37 per cubic yard

Find the cost of 1,200 cubic yards in the ending inventory by the weighted-average-cost method. Carry average cost per cubic yard to four decimals.

P.O. 2

Check Figure

Cost of ending inventory, $442

Problem E-2 Using the information presented in Problem E-1, find the cost of the ending inventory by the first-in, first-out method.

P.O. 3

Check Figure

Cost of ending inventory, $360

Problem E-3 Using the information presented in Problem E-1, find the cost of the ending inventory by the last-in, first-out method.

Financial Statement Analysis

Performance Objectives

After you have completed this appendix, you will be able to do the following:

1. Determine gross profit percentage.

2. Determine merchandise inventory turnover.

3. Determine accounts receivable turnover.

4. Determine return on investment.

An important function of accounting is to provide tools for interpreting the financial statements or the results of operations. This appendix presents a number of percentages and ratios that are frequently used to analyze financial statements.

GROSS PROFIT PERCENTAGE

OBJECTIVE 1
Determine gross profit percentage.

Southern Office Furniture will serve as our example (see the comparative income statement on the next page).

For each year, net sales is the base (100 percent). All other items on the income statement can be expressed as a percentage of net sales for the particular year involved. For example, let's look at the following percentages:

$$\text{Gross Profit \% (2008)} = \frac{\text{Gross Profit for 2008}}{\text{Net Sales for 2008}} = \frac{\$250,000}{\$528,000} = 0.473 = 47\%$$

$$\text{Gross Profit \% (2007)} = \frac{\text{Gross Profit for 2007}}{\text{Net Sales for 2007}} = \frac{\$252,000}{\$500,000} = 0.504 = 50\%$$

$$\text{Sales Salary Expense \% (2008)} = \frac{\text{Sales Salary Expense for 2008}}{\text{Net Sales for 2008}}$$

$$= \frac{\$63,600}{\$528,000} = 0.120 = 12\%$$

$$\text{Sales Salary Expense \% (2007)} = \frac{\text{Sales Salary Expense for 2007}}{\text{Net Sales for 2007}}$$

$$= \frac{\$58,000}{\$500,000} = 0.116 = 11.6\%$$

Here's how you might interpret a few of the percentages:

2008

- For every $100 in net sales, gross profit amounted to $47.
- For every $100 in net sales, sales salary expense amounted to $12.
- For every $100 in net sales, net income amounted to $22.

Southern Office Furniture
Comparative Income Statement
For Years Ended January 31, 2008, and January 31, 2007

	2008		2007	
	AMOUNT	PERCENT	AMOUNT	PERCENT
Revenue from Sales:				
Sales	$533 6 0 0 00	101	$510 0 0 0 00	102
Less Sales Returns and Allowances	5 6 0 0 00	1	10 0 0 0 00	2
Net Sales	$528 0 0 0 00	100	$500 0 0 0 00	100
Cost of Goods Sold:				
Merchandise Inventory, February 1	$ 46 0 0 0 00	9	$ 64 0 0 0 00	13
Delivered Cost of Purchases	290 0 0 0 00	55	230 0 0 0 00	46
Cost of Goods Available for Sale	$336 0 0 0 00	64	$294 0 0 0 00	59
Less Merchandise Inventory, January 31	58 0 0 0 00	11	46 0 0 0 00	9
Cost of Goods Sold	$278 0 0 0 00	53	$248 0 0 0 00	50
Gross Profit	$250 0 0 0 00	47	$252 0 0 0 00	50
Operating Expenses:				
Sales Salary Expense	$ 63 6 0 0 00	12	$ 58 0 0 0 00	12
Rent Expense	24 0 0 0 00	5	24 0 0 0 00	5
Advertising Expense	21 4 0 0 00	4	16 0 0 0 00	3
Depreciation Expense, Equipment	20 0 0 0 00	4	18 0 0 0 00	4
Insurance Expense	2 0 0 0 00	—	2 0 0 0 00	—
Store Supplies Expense	1 0 0 0 00	—	1 0 0 0 00	—
Miscellaneous Expense	1 0 0 0 00	—	1 0 0 0 00	—
Total Operating Expenses	$133 0 0 0 00	25	$120 0 0 0 00	24
Net Income	$117 0 0 0 00	22	$132 0 0 0 00	26

2007

- For every $100 in net sales, gross profit amounted to $50.
- For every $100 in net sales, sales salary expense amounted to $12.
- For every $100 in net sales, net income amounted to $26.

The gross profit percentage declined from 50% in 2007 to 47% in 2008 because the Cost of Goods Sold percentage increased from 50% in 2007 to 53% in 2008.

MERCHANDISE INVENTORY TURNOVER

OBJECTIVE 2

Determine merchandise inventory turnover.

Merchandise inventory turnover is the number of times a firm's average inventory is sold during a given year.

$$\text{Merchandise Inventory Turnover} = \frac{\text{Cost of Goods Sold}}{\text{Average Merchandise Inventory}}$$

$$\text{Average Merchandise Inventory} = \frac{\text{Beginning Merchandise Inventory} + \text{Ending Merchandise Inventory}}{2}$$

	2008	2007
Beginning Merchandise Inventory (from the Cost of Goods Sold section of the income statement)	$46,000	$ 64,000
Ending Merchandise Inventory (from the Cost of Goods Sold section of the income statement or the balance sheet)	58,000	46,000

2008

$$\text{Average Merchandise Inventory} = \frac{\$46,000 + \$58,000}{2} = \frac{\$104,000}{2} = \underline{\underline{\$52,000}}$$

$$\text{Merchandise Inventory Turnover} = \frac{\$278,000}{\$52,000} = \underline{\underline{5.35}} \text{ times per year}$$

2007

$$\text{Average Merchandise Inventory} = \frac{\$64,000 + \$46,000}{2} = \frac{\$110,000}{2} = \underline{\underline{\$55,000}}$$

$$\text{Merchandise Inventory Turnover} = \frac{\$248,000}{\$55,000} = \underline{\underline{4.51}} \text{ times per year}$$

With each turnover of merchandise, the company makes a gross profit, so the higher the turnover, the better.

The inventory turnover improved from 4.51 in 2007 to 5.35 in 2008 because the inventory was lower on average in 2008 as compared to 2007. Over the same period, net sales increased 5.6% from $500,000 in 2007 to $528,000 in 2008.

ACCOUNTS RECEIVABLE TURNOVER

OBJECTIVE 3

Determine accounts receivable turnover.

Accounts receivable turnover is the number of times charge accounts are turned over (paid off) during a given year. A turnover implies a sale on account followed by the cash collection of the amount owed.

$$\text{Accounts Receivable Turnover} = \frac{\text{Net Sales on Account}}{\text{Average Accounts Receivable}}$$

$$\text{Average Accounts Receivable} = \frac{\text{Beginning Accounts Receivable} + \text{Ending Accounts Receivable}}{2}$$

Going back to Southern Office Furniture, let's assume the following information for 2008 and 2007.

	2008	2007
Net sales on account (from the sales journal)	$330,000	$302,000
Beginning accounts receivable (from Accounts Receivable account)	39,680	37,500
Ending accounts receivable (from Accounts Receivable account)	45,840	39,680

2008

$$\text{Average Accounts Receivable} = \frac{\$39,680 + \$45,840}{2} = \frac{\$85,520}{2} = \underline{\$42,760}$$

$$\text{Accounts Receivable Turnover} = \frac{\$330,000}{\$42,760} = \underline{7.72} \text{ times per year}$$

2007

$$\text{Average Accounts Receivable} = \frac{\$37,500 + \$39,680}{2} = \frac{\$77,180}{2} = \underline{\$38,590}$$

$$\text{Accounts Receivable Turnover} = \frac{\$302,000}{\$38,590} = \underline{7.83} \text{ times per year}$$

A lower turnover rate indicates that a firm is experiencing greater difficulty in collecting charge accounts. In addition, more investment capital is tied up in accounts receivable.

The receivable turnover deteriorated slightly from 7.83 in 2007 to 7.72 in 2008, possibly because the seller granted easier credit terms or the buyers incurred cash flow problems because of a declining economy. From the end of 2007 to the end of 2008, the receivables balance increased almost 16% from $39,680 to $45,840. However, over the same period, net sales increased only 5.6%. This trend would be of concern to management and owners.

RETURN ON INVESTMENT (YIELD)

OBJECTIVE 4

Determine return on investment.

Return on investment represents the earning power of the owner's investment in the business.

$$\text{Return on Investment} = \frac{\text{Net Income for the Year}}{\text{Average Capital}}$$

$$\text{Average Capital} = \frac{\text{Beginning Capital} + \text{Ending Capital}}{2}$$

Getting back to Southern Office Furniture, let's assume the following information for 2008 and 2007:

	2008	2007
Beginning balance of owner's Capital account	$515,000	$530,000
Ending balance of owner's Capital account	530,000	510,000

2008

$$\text{Average Capital} = \frac{\$515,000 + \$530,000}{2} = \frac{\$1,045,000}{2} = \underline{\$522,500}$$

$$\text{Return on Investment} = \frac{\$117,000}{\$522,500} = 0.224 = \underline{22.4\%}$$

2007

$$\text{Average Capital} = \frac{\$530,000 + \$510,000}{2} = \frac{\$1,040,000}{2} = \underline{\underline{\$520,000}}$$

$$\text{Return on Investment} = \frac{\$132,000}{\$520,000} = 0.254 = \underline{\underline{25.4\%}}$$

As a result, we can state the following:

• In 2008, for an average investment of $100, the business earned $22.40.
• In 2007, for an average investment of $100, the business earned $25.40.

The return on investment deteriorated from 25.4% in 2007 to 22.4% in 2008 because net income declined 11% from $132,000 in 2007 to $117,000 in 2008.

PROBLEMS

P.O. 1

Problem F-1 Pena Company's abbreviated comparative income statement for years 2008 and 2007 is as follows:

Pena Company Comparative Income Statement For Years Ended December 31, 2008 and December 31, 2007	2008	2007
Net Sales	$587 2 0 0 00	$562 0 0 0 00
Cost of Goods Sold	287 4 0 0 00	277 2 0 0 00
Gross Profit	$299 8 0 0 00	$284 8 0 0 00
Total Operating Expenses	152 2 4 0 00	146 1 6 0 00
Net Income	$147 5 6 0 00	$138 6 4 0 00

Check Figure

Net income % (2007), 24.7%

Instructions

1. For the years 2008 and 2007, determine gross profit as a percentage of net sales.
2. For the years 2008 and 2007, determine net income as a percentage of net sales.

P.O. 2

Problem F-2 Pena Company's merchandise inventory figures are:

	2008	**2007**
Beginning merchandise inventory (January 1)	$188,420	$206,110
Purchases	402,190	359,510
Ending merchandise inventory (December 31)	203,210	188,420

Check Figure

Merchandise inventory turnover (2008), 2 times

Instructions

Determine the merchandise inventory turnover for the years 2008 and 2007.

P.O. 4

Problem F-3 A. L. Pena, Capital, account balances are as follows:

January 1, 2007	$475,670
January 1, 2008	593,970
December 31, 2008	626,820

Check Figure

Return on investment (2007), 25.9%

Instructions

Determine the return on investment for the years 2008 and 2007 if net income is $147,560 for 2008 and $138,640 for 2007.

G

The Statement of Cash Flows

Performance Objectives

After you have completed this appendix, you will be able to do the following:

1. Classify cash flows as Operating Activities, Investing Activities, and Financing Activities.

2. Prepare a statement of cash flows.

The fourth major financial statement is the statement of cash flows. This statement explains in detail how the balance of Cash has changed between the beginning and the end of the fiscal period. Some accountants refer to the statement as the "where got, where gone" statement of cash.

SECTIONS OF THE STATEMENT OF CASH FLOWS

OBJECTIVE 1

Classify cash flows as Operating Activities, Investing Activities, and Financing Activities.

The statement has three main sections: Operating Activities, Investing Activities, and Financing Activities. Cash flows are subdivided as cash inflows and cash outflows.

Operating Activities

This section covers cash received and used in carrying out the company's operations.

Cash Inflows

- Cash from selling of services or merchandise
- Cash from collection of miscellaneous income

Cash Outflows

- Payments for purchases of merchandise and supplies from suppliers
- Payments of salaries or wages
- Payments of rent, utilities, insurance
- Payment of interest to creditors

Investing Activities

This section covers cash used in or received from buying or selling of property and equipment assets and all other noncurrent assets, such as long-term investments.

Cash Inflows

- Cash received from the sale of noncurrent assets

Cash Outflows

- Cash payments to buy noncurrent assets

Financing Activities

This section covers cash related to changes in the owner's equity accounts and long-term liabilities accounts.

Cash Inflows

- Investment of cash by the owner
- Borrowing from creditors

Cash Outflows

- Withdrawals of cash by the owner
- Repayment of loans to creditors

Cash, for purposes of the cash flow statement, includes checking and savings accounts and also cash equivalents. A company that has idle cash temporarily during the year may prefer to invest in short-term interest-bearing notes or money market funds. These short-term funds are considered to be cash equivalents.

FINANCIAL STATEMENTS NEEDED FOR PREPARING THE STATEMENT OF CASH FLOWS

The financial statements required for preparing the statement of cash flows consist of the income statement and the statement of owner's equity for the fiscal period, the balance sheet at the end of the fiscal period, and the balance sheet at the end of the previous fiscal period. Using the two balance sheets, we can prepare a comparative balance sheet for the two fiscal periods, showing the increases and decreases in the various accounts.

ILLUSTRATION OF THE STATEMENT OF CASH FLOWS

OBJECTIVE 2

Prepare a statement of cash flows.

The financial statements for Kelley Company are shown here. Based on the comparative balance sheet, the first step is to record the increases and decreases in the accounts.

Kelley Company
Income Statement
For Year Ended December 31, 2007

Revenue from Sales:			
Net Sales	$847 0 0 0 00		
Less Cost of Goods Sold	500 0 0 0 00		
Gross Profit		$347 0 0 0 00	
Operating Expenses:			
Salary Expense	$ 70 0 0 0 00		
Rent Expense	10 0 0 0 00		
Depreciation Expense, Equipment	6 0 0 0 00		
Supplies Expense	1 0 0 0 00		
Total Operating Expenses		87 0 0 0 00	
Net Income		$260 0 0 0 00	

Kelley Company
Statement of Owner's Equity
For Year Ended December 31, 2007

B. Kelley, Capital, January 1, 2007			$120 0 0 0 00
Additional Investment, March 2, 2007			10 0 0 0 00
Total Investment			$130 0 0 0 00
Net Income for the Year	$260 0 0 0 00		
Less Withdrawals for the Year	150 0 0 0 00		
Increase in Capital			110 0 0 0 00
B. Kelley, Capital, Dec. 31, 2007			$240 0 0 0 00

Kelley Company
Comparative Balance Sheet
December 31, 2007, and December 31, 2006

	2007	2006	INCREASE (DECREASE)
Assets			
Cash	$ 12 0 0 0 00	$ 7 0 0 0 00	$ 5 0 0 0 00
Accounts Receivable	70 0 0 0 00	66 0 0 0 00	4 0 0 0 00
Merchandise Inventory	220 0 0 0 00	113 0 0 0 00	107 0 0 0 00
Supplies	3 0 0 0 00	4 0 0 0 00	(1 0 0 0 00)
Equipment	$72 0 0 0 00	$60 0 0 0 00	12 0 0 0 00
Less Accumulated Deprec.	(62 0 0 0 00) 10 0 0 0 00	(56 0 0 0 00) 4 0 0 0 00	(6 0 0 0 00)
Total Assets	$315 0 0 0 00	$194 0 0 0 00	$121 0 0 0 00
Liabilities			
Accounts Payable	$71 0 0 0 00	$69 0 0 0 00	$ 2 0 0 0 00
Salaries Payable	4 0 0 0 00	5 0 0 0 00	(1 0 0 0 00)
Total Liabilities	$ 75 0 0 0 00	$ 74 0 0 0 00	$ 1 0 0 0 00
Owner's Equity			
B. Kelley, Capital	240 0 0 0 00	120 0 0 0 00	120 0 0 0 00
Total Liabilities and			
Owner's Equity	$315 0 0 0 00	$194 0 0 0 00	$121 0 0 0 00

Note the $5,000 increase in Cash. First let's see how this increase comes about.

- Cash flows related to operating activities involve changes in current asset and current liability accounts.
- Cash flows related to investing activities involve changes in property and equipment (long-term asset) accounts (with the exception of Accumulated Depreciation).
- Cash flows related to financing activities involve changes in owner's equity accounts and long-term liabilities accounts.

Now let's present the statement of cash flows.

Kelley Company
Statement of Cash Flows
For Year Ended December 31, 2007

Cash Flows from (Used by) Operating Activities											
Net Income	$260	0	0	0	00						
Add (Deduct) Items to Convert Net Income from Accrual Basis to Cash Basis											
Depreciation Expense	6	0	0	0	00						
Increase in Accounts Receivable	(4	0	0	0	00)						
Increase in Merchandise Inventory	(107	0	0	0	00)						
Decrease in Supplies	1	0	0	0	00						
Increase in Accounts Payable	2	0	0	0	00						
Decrease in Salaries Payable	(1	0	0	0	00)						
Net Cash Flows from Operating Activities						$157	0	0	0	00	
Cash Flows from (Used by) Investing Activities											
Purchase of Equipment	$ (12	0	0	0	00)						
Net Cash Flows Used by Investing Activities						(12	0	0	0	00)	
Cash Flows from (Used by) Financing Activities											
Cash Investment by Owner	$ 10	0	0	0	00						
Cash Withdrawals by Owner	(150	0	0	0	00)						
Net Cash Flows Used by Financing Activities						(140	0	0	0	00)	
Net Increase (Decrease) in Cash						$ 5	0	0	0	00	

EXPLANATION OF ITEMS IN THE STATEMENT OF CASH FLOWS

Cash Flows from Operating Activities

- Net income of $260,000, from the income statement, included such items as sale of services or merchandise, miscellaneous income, and payment of expenses such as salaries or wages, utilities, and interest.
- Depreciation of $6,000 was included as an expense on the income statement, but it did not result in the payment of cash to anyone. Since depreciation expense was deducted on the income statement, we now add $6,000 back in. Depreciation expense is always an addition under Cash Flows from Operating Activities.
- Accounts Receivable increased by $4,000. Of the amount shown as Sales on the income statement, $4,000 was in the form of additional charge account balances and therefore were not cash inflows. So we deduct $4,000 from Cash Flows from Operating Activities.
- Merchandise Inventory increased by $107,000. Because the inventory increased by $107,000 during the year (more merchandise was bought than was sold), we can assume that the change resulted in a $107,000 decrease in Cash Flows from Operating Activities.
- Decrease in Supplies of $1,000 means that the company used up supplies bought in a previous fiscal period and included the entire amount of supplies used as Supplies Expense on the income statement. In other words, the $1,000 of Supplies Expense shown on the income statement did not result in a payment of cash in the current period. For this appendix, Supplies is considered a significant asset of the business, so the ending inventory is recorded as an asset.

- Increase in Accounts Payable of $2,000 in this case means that $2,000 of the amount listed as Purchases on the income statement (not shown because we included Purchases in Cost of Goods Sold) did not result in the payment of cash. So we add $2,000 to Cash Flows from Operating Activities.
- Decrease in Salaries Payable of $1,000 means that the amount listed as Salary Expense on the income statement is $1,000 less than the amount of cash spent by the company. So we deduct $1,000 from Cash Flows from Operating Activities.

Cash Flows from Investing Activities

Equipment increased by $12,000. We would have to look at the journal entry to determine how much cash was involved. In this case, we assume that the purchase of equipment resulted in a payment of $12,000 cash. So we deduct $12,000 from Cash Flows from Investing Activities.

Cash Flows from Financing Activities

- The owner's Capital account increased by $10,000 as a result of an additional investment. We would have to look at the journal entry to determine how much cash was involved. In this case, we assume that the investment was in the form of cash. So we add $10,000 to Cash Flows from Financing Activities.
- The owner's Drawing account increased by $150,000. We would have to look at the journal entries to determine how much cash was involved. In this case, we assume that the withdrawals were in the form of cash. So we deduct $150,000 from Cash Flows from Financing Activities.

Here are some handy guidelines for preparing a statement of cash flows.

Add to Net Income	Why?
If Current Assets decrease	If an account like Accounts Receivable decreases, this means that we received more cash than the amount listed as Net Sales.
If Current Liabilities increase	If an account like Accounts Payable increases, this means that we bought more merchandise or supplies than we paid for in cash.
Deduct from Net Income	**Why?**
If Current Assets increase	If an account like Prepaid Insurance increases, this means that we paid more cash for insurance than the amount listed as Insurance Expense on the income statement.
If Current Liabilities decrease	If an account like Notes Payable decreases, this means that we paid out cash to pay off the note.

The statement of cash flows can be used as a source in the preparation of a cash budget. The cash budget is an important management tool that focuses on understanding and managing the cash flow of a business.

PROBLEMS

P.O. 1,2

Problem G-1 Monroe Company has the following financial statements for 2006 and 2007. Assume that the withdrawals were in the form of cash.

Check Figure

Net cash flows from operating activities, $44,500

Instructions

Prepare a statement of cash flows for the year ended December 31, 2007.

Monroe Company
Income Statement
For Year Ended December 31, 2007

Revenue:		
Income from Services		$134 000 00
Expenses:		
Wages Expense	$77 000 00	
Rent Expense	8 000 00	
Depreciation Expense, Equipment	5 000 00	
Supplies Expense	2 000 00	
Total Expenses		92 000 00
Net Income		$ 42 000 00

Monroe Company
Statement of Owner's Equity
For Year Ended December 31, 2007

B. N. Monroe, Capital, January 1, 2007		$94 000 00
Net Income for the Year	$42 000 00	
Less Withdrawals for the Year	40 000 00	
Increase in Capital		2 000 00
B. N. Monroe, Capital, December 31, 2007		$96 000 00

Monroe Company
Comparative Balance Sheet
December 31, 2007, and December 31, 2006

	2007		2006		INCREASE (DECREASE)
Assets					
Cash		$ 9 0 0 0 00		$ 6 5 0 0 00	$2 5 0 0 00
Supplies		5 0 0 0 00		2 5 0 0 00	2 5 0 0 00
Equipment	$100 0 0 0 00		$98 0 0 0 00		2 0 0 0 00
Less Accumulated Depreciation	(18 0 0 0 00)	82 0 0 0 00	(13 0 0 0 00)	85 0 0 0 00	(5 0 0 0 00)
Total Assets		$96 0 0 0 00		$94 0 0 0 00	$2 0 0 0 00
Owner's Equity					
B. N. Monroe, Capital		$96 0 0 0 00		$94 0 0 0 00	$2 0 0 0 00
Total Liabilities and					
Owner's Equity		$96 0 0 0 00		$94 0 0 0 00	$2 0 0 0 00

P.O. 1,2

Problem G-2 The financial statements for Rhyne and Company follow. Assume that the additional investment and the withdrawals were in the form of cash.

Check Figure

Net cash flows from operating activities, $77,000

Instructions

Prepare a statement of cash flows for the year ended December 31, 2007.

Rhyne and Company
Income Statement
For Year Ended December 31, 2007

Revenue:		
Income from Services		$270 0 0 0 00
Expenses:		
Wages Expense	$161 0 0 0 00	
Rent Expense	18 0 0 0 00	
Depreciation Expense, Equipment	12 0 0 0 00	
Supplies Expense	4 0 0 0 00	
Insurance Expense	1 0 0 0 00	
Total Expenses		196 0 0 0 00
Net Income		$ 74 0 0 0 00

Rhyne and Company
Statement of Owner's Equity
For Year Ended December 31, 2007

S. T. Rhyne, Capital, January 1, 2007						$150	0	0	0	00
Additional Investment, April 1, 2007						2	0	0	0	00
Total Investment						$152	0	0	0	00
Net Income for the Year	$74	0	0	0	00					
Less Withdrawals for the Year	70	0	0	0	00					
Increase in Capital						4	0	0	0	00
S. T. Rhyne, Capital, December 31, 2007						$156	0	0	0	00

Rhyne and Company
Comparative Balance Sheet
December 31, 2007 and December 31, 2006

	2007					2006					INCREASE (DECREASE)				
Assets															
Cash			$ 11	8	0	0	00			$ 2	8	0	0	00	$ 9	0	0	0	00
Accounts Receivable			32	0	0	0	00			26	0	0	0	00	6	0	0	0	00
Supplies			10	0	0	0	00			9	4	0	0	00	6	0	0	00
Prepaid Insurance			3	2	0	0	00			6	0	0	00	2	6	0	0	00
Equipment	$145	4	0	0	00				$145	4	0	0	00			—		
Less Accumulated Depreciation	(36	0	0	0	00)	109	4	0	0	00	(24	0	0	0	00)	121	4	0	0	00	(12	0	0	0	00)
Total Assets			$166	4	0	0	00			$160	2	0	0	00	$ 6	2	0	0	00
Liabilities															
Accounts Payable			$ 10	4	0	0	00			$ 10	2	0	0	00	$	2	0	0	00
Owner's Equity															
S. T. Rhyne, Capital			156	0	0	0	00			150	0	0	0	00	6	0	0	0	00
Total Liabilities and															
Owner's Equity			$166	4	0	0	00			$160	2	0	0	00	$ 6	2	0	0	00

P.O. 1,2

Problem G-3 The financial statements for Salinas Company follow. Assume that the withdrawals were in the form of cash.

Check Figure

Net cash flows used by financing activities, ($70,000)

Instructions

Prepare a statement of cash flows for the year ended December 31, 2007.

Salinas Company
Income Statement
For Year Ended December 31, 2007

Net Sales	$942 0 0 0 00		
Less Cost of Goods Sold	753 6 0 0 00		
Gross Profit		$188 4 0 0 00	
Operating Expenses:			
Salary Expense	$ 86 9 0 0 00		
Rent Expense	18 0 0 0 00		
Depreciation Expense, Equipment	10 0 0 0 00		
Supplies Expense	4 7 0 0 00		
Insurance Expense	2 8 0 0 00		
Total Operating Expenses		122 4 0 0 00	
Net Income		$ 66 0 0 0 00	

Salinas Company
Statement of Owner's Equity
For Year Ended December 31, 2007

C. L. Salinas, Capital, January 1, 2007		$196 0 0 0 00
Net Income for the Year	$66 0 0 0 00	
Less Withdrawals for the Year	70 0 0 0 00	
Decrease in Capital		(4 0 0 0 00)
C. L. Salinas, Capital, December 31, 2007		$192 0 0 0 00

Salinas Company
Comparative Balance Sheet
December 31, 2007 and December 31, 2006

	2007	2006	INCREASE (DECREASE)
Assets			
Cash	$ 9 4 0 0 00	$ 10 9 0 0 00	$ (1 5 0 0 00)
Accounts Receivable	56 0 0 0 00	48 6 0 0 00	7 4 0 0 00
Merchandise Inventory	104 6 0 0 00	104 4 0 0 00	2 0 0 00
Supplies	8 2 0 0 00	6 0 0 0 00	2 2 0 0 00
Prepaid Insurance	1 6 0 0 00	1 8 0 0 00	(2 0 0 00)
Equipment	$156 0 0 0 00	$156 0 0 0 00	————
Less Accumulated Depreciation	(76 4 0 0 00) 79 6 0 0 00	(66 4 0 0 00) 89 6 0 0 00	(10 0 0 0 00)
Total Assets	$259 4 0 0 00	$261 3 0 0 00	$ (1 9 0 0 00)
Liabilities			
Accounts Payable	$ 62 7 0 0 00	$ 60 4 0 0 00	$ 2 3 0 0 00
Salaries Payable	4 7 0 0 00	4 9 0 0 00	(2 0 0 00)
Total Liabilities	$ 67 4 0 0 00	$ 65 3 0 0 00	$ 2 1 0 0 00
Owner's Equity			
C. L. Salinas, Capital	192 0 0 0 00	196 0 0 0 00	(4 0 0 0 00)
Total Liabilities and			
Owner's Equity	$259 4 0 0 00	$261 3 0 0 00	$ (1 9 0 0 00)

Before a Test Check Solutions

CHAPTERS 1–3

Part I: 1. d; 2. e; 3. d; 4. b; 5. e; 6. a

Part II: 1.

	DATE		DESCRIPTION	POST. REF.	DEBIT	CREDIT	
1	20–						1
2	Dec.	1	Cash	111	9 5 0 0 00		2
3			Service Income	411		9 5 0 0 00	3
4			Sold services for cash.				4
5							5
6		4	Rent Expense	513	1 0 0 0 00		6
7			Cash	111		1 0 0 0 00	7
8			Ck. No. 2331.				8
9							9
10		11	Cash	111	1 7 5 0 00		10
11			Accounts Receivable	113		1 7 5 0 00	11
12			Cash on account from				12
13			customers, Cash Receipt				13
14			Nos. 1430-1438.				14
15							15
16		19	Accounts Receivable	113	2 0 7 5 00		16
17			Service Income	411		2 0 7 5 00	17
18			Sales Inv. No. 2591.				18
19							19
20		22	Utilities Expense	512	2 5 5 00		20
21			Cash	111		2 5 5 00	21
22			Ck. No. 2332.				22
23							23
24		23	Supplies Expense	514	2 9 2 00		24
25			Accounts Payable	221		2 9 2 00	25
26			Office Works, Inv. No. 2606.				26
27							27
28		31	Wages Expense	511	1 7 7 5 00		28
29			Cash	111		1 7 7 5 00	29
30			Paid month's wages, Ck. No.				30
31			2333.				31
32							32
33		31	J. Dunn, Drawing	312	1 5 0 0 00		33
34			Cash	111		1 5 0 0 00	34
35			Ck. No. 2334.				35

GENERAL JOURNAL   PAGE   31

2, 3, 4.

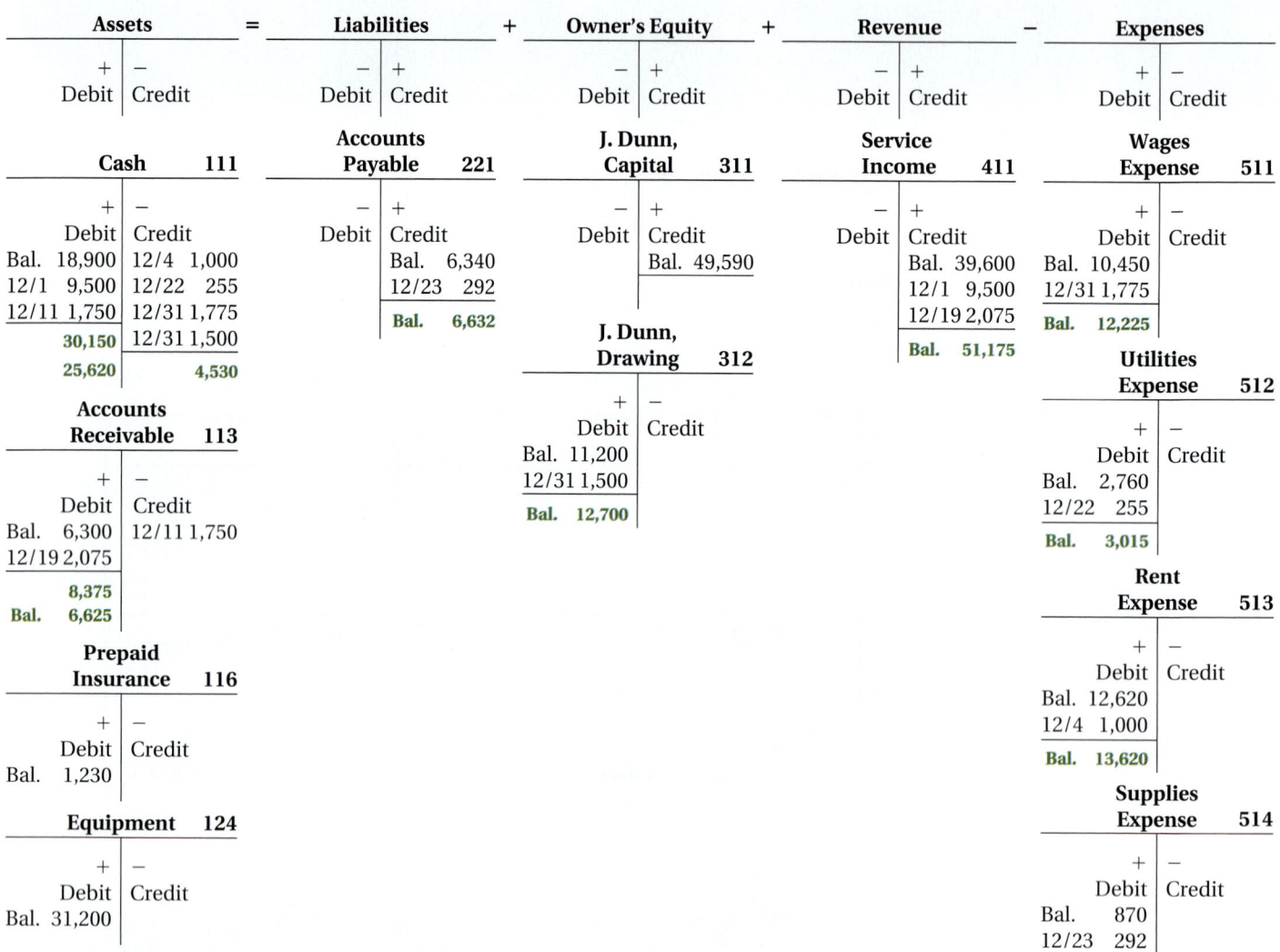

Assets	=	Liabilities	+	Owner's Equity	+	Revenue	−	Expenses
+ | −		− | +		− | +		− | +		+ | −
Debit | Credit		Debit | Credit		Debit | Credit		Debit | Credit		Debit | Credit

Cash   111

+	−
Debit	Credit
Bal. 18,900	12/4 1,000
12/1 9,500	12/22 255
12/11 1,750	12/31 1,775
30,150	12/31 1,500
25,620	4,530

Accounts Receivable   113

+	−
Debit	Credit
Bal. 6,300	12/11 1,750
12/19 2,075	
8,375	
Bal. 6,625	

Prepaid Insurance   116

+	−
Debit	Credit
Bal. 1,230	

Equipment   124

+	−
Debit	Credit
Bal. 31,200	

Accounts Payable   221

−	+
Debit	Credit
	Bal. 6,340
	12/23 292
	Bal. 6,632

J. Dunn, Capital   311

−	+
Debit	Credit
	Bal. 49,590

J. Dunn, Drawing   312

+	−
Debit	Credit
Bal. 11,200	
12/31 1,500	
Bal. 12,700	

Service Income   411

−	+
Debit	Credit
	Bal. 39,600
	12/1 9,500
	12/19 2,075
	Bal. 51,175

Wages Expense   511

+	−
Debit	Credit
Bal. 10,450	
12/31 1,775	
Bal. 12,225	

Utilities Expense   512

+	−
Debit	Credit
Bal. 2,760	
12/22 255	
Bal. 3,015	

Rent Expense   513

+	−
Debit	Credit
Bal. 12,620	
12/4 1,000	
Bal. 13,620	

Supplies Expense   514

+	−
Debit	Credit
Bal. 870	
12/23 292	
Bal. 1,162	

5.

Antec Services
Trial Balance
December 31, 20—

ACCOUNT NAME	DEBIT	CREDIT
Cash	25 6 2 0 00	
Accounts Receivable	6 6 2 5 00	
Prepaid Insurance	1 2 3 0 00	
Equipment	31 2 0 0 00	
Accounts Payable		6 6 3 2 00
J. Dunn, Capital		49 5 9 0 00
J. Dunn, Drawing	12 7 0 0 00	
Service Income		51 1 7 5 00
Wages Expense	12 2 2 5 00	
Utilities Expense	3 0 1 5 00	
Rent Expense	13 6 2 0 00	
Supplies Expense	1 1 6 2 00	
	107 3 9 7 00	107 3 9 7 00

6.

Antec Services
Income Statement
For Year Ended December 31, 20—

Revenue:		
Service Income		$51 1 7 5 00
Expenses:		
Wages Expense	$12 2 2 5 00	
Utilities Expense	3 0 1 5 00	
Rent Expense	13 6 2 0 00	
Supplies Expense	1 1 6 2 00	
Total Expenses		30 0 2 2 00
Net Income		$21 1 5 3 00

7.

Antec Services Statement of Owner's Equity For Year Ended December 31, 20—										
J. Dunn, Capital, January 1, 20—						$49	5	9	0	00
Net Income for Year	$21	1	5	3	00					
Less Withdrawals for Year	12	7	0	0	00					
Increase in Capital						8	4	5	3	00
J. Dunn, Capital, December 31, 20—						$58	0	4	3	00

8.

Antec Services Balance Sheet December 31, 20—										
Assets										
Cash	$25	6	2	0	00					
Accounts Receivable	6	6	2	5	00					
Prepaid Insurance	1	2	3	0	00					
Equipment	31	2	0	0	00					
Total Assets						$64	6	7	5	00
Liabilities										
Accounts Payable						$ 6	6	3	2	00
Owner's Equity										
J. Dunn, Capital						58	0	4	3	00
Total Liabilities and Owner's Equity						$64	6	7	5	00

CHAPTERS 4–5

Part I

1. b;   2. d;   3. d;   4. a;   5. a;   6. b;   7. c;   8. c

Part II

	DATE		DESCRIPTION	POST. REF.	DEBIT	CREDIT	
1	20–		**Closing Entries**				1
2	Dec.	31	Income from Services		35 9 0 0 00		2
3			Income Summary			35 9 0 0 00	3
4							4
5		31	Income Summary		20 4 0 0 00		5
6			Wages Expense			11 5 0 0 00	6
7			Rent Expense			2 4 0 0 00	7
8			Utilities Expense			1 0 0 0 00	8
9			Depreciation Expense,				9
10			Equipment			5 0 0 00	10
11			Supplies Expense			4 1 0 0 00	11
12			Miscellaneous Expense			9 0 0 00	12
13							13
14		31	Income Summary		15 5 0 0 00		14
15			K. Payton, Capital			15 5 0 0 00	15
16							16
17		31	K. Payton, Capital		16 4 0 0 00		17
18			K. Payton, Drawing			16 4 0 0 00	18

GENERAL JOURNAL   PAGE ___4___

Part III

1. b;   2. h;   3. m;   4. q;   5. d;   6. k;   7. u;   8. w;   9. o;   10. s;   11. e;
12. f;   13. i;   14. n;   15. a;   16. t;   17. x;   18. p;   19. y;   20. v;   21. j;   22. c;
23. r;   24. l;   25. g

CHAPTERS 7–9

Part I

1. canceled; 2. deposit in transit or late deposit; 3. endorsement; 4. payee; 5. petty cash fund.

Part II

1. $1,775 per month × 12 months = $21,300 per year
   $21,300 per year ÷ 52 weeks = $409.62 per week
   $409.62 per week ÷ 40 hours = $10.24 per regular hour
   $10.24 per regular hour × 1.5 = $15.36 per overtime hour

Earnings for 45 hours:

Forty hours at straight time = 40 × $10.24 = $409.60
Five hours overtime = 5 × $15.36 =   76.80

Total gross pay $486.40

2.

		GENERAL JOURNAL				PAGE _____		
	DATE	DESCRIPTION	POST. REF.	DEBIT		CREDIT		
1	20–							1
2	June 30	Cleaning Salary Expense		9 0 0 0 00				2
3		Office Salary Expense		3 0 0 0 00				3
4		Employees' Federal Income Tax Payable				1 5 0 0 00		4
5		FICA Tax Payable ($12,000 × 0.062) + ($12,000 × 0.0145)				9 1 8 00		5
6		Savings Bonds Payable				5 0 0 00		6
7		Medical Insurance Payable				9 6 2 00		7
8		Salaries Payable				8 1 2 0 00		8

3.

		GENERAL JOURNAL				PAGE _____		
	DATE	DESCRIPTION	POST. REF.	DEBIT		CREDIT		
1	20–							1
2	Dec. 31	Payroll Tax Expense		12 4 7 7 50				2
3		FICA Tax Payable ($143,000 × 0.062) + ($155,000 × 0.0145)				11 1 1 3 50		3
4		State Unemployment Tax Payable ($22,000 × 0.054)				1 1 8 8 00		4
5		Federal Unemployment Tax Payable ($22,000 × 0.008)				1 7 6 00		5

Part III

1. T; 2. F; 3. F; 4. T; 5. F

CHAPTERS 10–11
Part I

1. credit; 2. accounts payable ledger; 3. cash discount; 4. purchase order; 5. Purchases; 6. buyer; 7. credit period; 8. debit; 9. sales of merchandise on account; 10. charge customers.

Part II

1. CP; 2. J; 3. J; 4. CP; 5. S; 6. J; 7. CP; 8. P; 9. CR; 10. CP

Part III

1. F; 2. T; 3. F; 4. F; 5. F

CHAPTERS 12–13
Part I

1. physical inventory; 2. perpetual inventory; 3. current liability; 4. Income Summary; 5. Cost of Goods Sold, Merchandise Inventory; 6. decrease; 7. Cost of Goods Sold; 8. working capital; 9. Income from Operations; 10. Freight In.

Part II

1. F; 2. F; 3. T; 4. T; 5. T; 6. F; 7. F; 8. T; 9. F; 10. T

Part III

1.

	DATE		DESCRIPTION	POST. REF.	DEBIT	CREDIT	
1	20–		**Adjusting Entries**				1
2	Dec.	31	**Income Summary**		132 0 0 0 00		2
3			**Merchandise Inventory**			132 0 0 0 00	3
4							4
5		31	**Merchandise Inventory**		136 0 0 0 00		5
6			**Income Summary**			136 0 0 0 00	6

GENERAL JOURNAL — PAGE _____

2.

	DATE		DESCRIPTION	POST. REF.	DEBIT	CREDIT	
1	20–		**Adjusting Entries**				1
2	Dec.	31	**Cost of Goods Sold**		2 0 0 0 00		2
3			**Merchandise Inventory**			2 0 0 0 00	3

GENERAL JOURNAL — PAGE _____

3.

		GENERAL JOURNAL			PAGE _____	
	DATE	**DESCRIPTION**	**POST. REF.**	**DEBIT**	**CREDIT**	
1	20–					1
2	Dec. 1	Cash		20 0 0 0 00		2
3		Unearned Revenue			20 0 0 0 00	3
4		To record collection of cash				4
5		for a four-month job.				5
6						6
7		Adjusting Entry				7
8	31	Unearned Revenue		5 0 0 0 00		8
9		Remodeling Revenue			5 0 0 0 00	9
10		To record one month's				10
11		revenue earned.				11

4. a. $250,000 total assets − $140,000 noncurrent assets = $110,000 current assets
$130,000 total liabilities − $80,000 long-term liabilities = $50,000 current liabilities
$110,000 current assets − $50,000 current liabilities = $60,000 working capital

b. $\dfrac{\$110{,}000 \text{ current assets}}{\$50{,}000 \text{ current liabilities}} = 2.2$ current ratio

Photo Credits

Introduction

p. 2, Tony Freeman/PhotoEdit, Inc.; p. 4, Michael Newman/PhotoEdit, Inc.; p. 5, © Syracuse Newspaper/Gary Walts/The Image Works.

Chapter 1

p. 8, AP Photo/Paul Vathis; p. 10, Tony Freeman/PhotoEdit, Inc; p. 16, Bob Daemmrich/Stock, Boston.

Chapter 2

p. 39, Digital Vision/Getty Images; p. 49, Terry Huseby/Getty Images; p. 52, Myrleen Ferguson Cate/PhotoEdit, Inc.

Chapter 3

p. 76, John Elk/Stock Boston; p. 92, Chris Fredrikson/Alamy.

Chapter 4

p. 126, Rudi Von Vriel/PhotoEdit, Inc.

Chapter 5

p. 157, Jeff Greenberg/PhotoEdit, Inc; p. 164, David Young Wolff/PhotoEdit, Inc.

Chapter 6

p. 200, R. P. Kingston/Index Stock; p. 202, Richard Pasley/Stock Boston; p. 204, Brian Hainer/PhotoEdit, Inc.

Chapter 7

p. 232, Courtesy, JP Morgan Chase Corporation; p. 242, Tony Freeman/PhotoEdit, Inc; p. 246, Chris Salvo/Taxi/Getty Images.

Chapter 8

p. 270, Bruce Forester/Getty Images; p. 271 (left), C. Greenlar/The Image Works; p. 271 (right), Bilderbox/INSADCO Photography/Alamay; p. 278, Courtesy of United Way.

Chapter 9

p. 296, Stephen Perry/Getty Images; p. 302, B. Roland/The Image Works; p. 313, Alan Thornton/Getty Images; p. 315, Gregg Mancuso/Stock Boston.

Chapter 10

p. 358, Check Pefley/Alamy.

Chapter 11

p. 392, AFP/Getty Images; p. 397, Bill Aaron/PhotoEdit, Inc.

Chapter 12

p. 444, Bob Mahoney.

Chapter 13

p. 482, Joe Sohm/Stock Boston; p. 486, Bob Daemmrich/Stock Boston.

Index

Note: Boldface type indicates key terms and the pages on which they are defined.